Dissertation Research Me

Dissertation Research Methods: A Step-by-Step Guide to Writing Up Your Research in the Social Sciences focuses specifically on the methodology for planning, writing and submitting your dissertation thesis. Written by two methodology experts in the social sciences, the book provides a step-by-step guide through each stage of the dissertation process.

It covers all aspects of the methodological considerations needed, from choosing a topic or research question, developing a literature review, identifying research gaps, accessing potential study participants, utilizing the right sampling strategies, analyzing data and writing up findings. Readers are introduced to the main research methods normally used in dissertations and their characteristics, and they are guided to choose an appropriate research method for their study, provide a substantial description of the selected method and articulate strong arguments in support of it. The book is filled with templates, exemplars and tools to help students write about methodology in their thesis and to equip readers to successfully troubleshoot any methodology challenges they may face.

This compact book will be of use to all graduate students and their supervisors in the Social Sciences and Education and Behavioral Sciences who are looking for a guide to working with robust and defensible methodological principles in their dissertation research and theses.

Philip Adu is a methodology expert and founder of the Center for Research Methods Consulting. He has provided research methodology services to clients for over ten years. He is also a contributing faculty at Walden University. Dr. Adu is the author of *A Step-by-Step Guide to Qualitative Data Coding* (2019). He is also a co-author of *The Theoretical Framework in Phenomenological Research* (2022).

D. Anthony Miles is CEO and founder of Miles Development Industries Corporation®, a consulting practice and venture capital acquisition firm. He also has extensive experience with dissertations and assisting doctoral students. Dr. Miles has served as a dissertation chair, methodologist and statistician. He has over ten years' experience with dissertations and has worked with over 100 doctoral students. In 2009, he was awarded the *USASBE Doctoral Consortium* fellowship for his doctoral research.

Dissertation Research Methods

A Step-by-Step Guide to Writing Up Your Research in the Social Sciences

Philip Adu and D. Anthony Miles

Routledge
Taylor & Francis Group
LONDON AND NEW YORK

Cover image: Getty Images/kevinjeon00

First published 2024
by Routledge
4 Park Square, Milton Park, Abingdon, Oxon OX14 4RN

and by Routledge
605 Third Avenue, New York, NY 10158

Routledge is an imprint of the Taylor & Francis Group, an informa business

British Library Cataloguing-in-Publication Data
A catalogue record for this book is available from the British Library

Library of Congress Cataloging-in-Publication Data
Names: Adu, Philip, editor. | Miles, D. Anthony, editor.
Title: Dissertation research methods : a step-by-step guide to writing up your research in the social sciences / Philip Adu and D. Anthony Miles, [editors].
Description: Abingdon, Oxon ; New York, NY : Routledge, 2023. |
Includes bibliographical references and index. |
Identifiers: LCCN 2023014791 (print) | LCCN 2023014792 (ebook) |
ISBN 9781032213859 (paperback) | ISBN 9781032213835 (hardback) |
ISBN 9781003268154 (ebook)
Subjects: LCSH: Social sciences–Research. | Social sciences–Study and teaching. |
Dissertations, Academic.
Classification: LCC H62 .D577 2023 (print) | LCC H62 (ebook) |
DDC 300.72–dc23/eng/20230425
LC record available at https://lccn.loc.gov/2023014791
LC ebook record available at https://lccn.loc.gov/2023014792

ISBN: 9781032213835 (hbk)
ISBN: 9781032213859 (pbk)
ISBN: 9781003268154 (ebk)

DOI: 10.4324/9781003268154

Typeset in Baskerville
by Newgen Publishing UK

I (Philip Adu) dedicate this book to my lovely and supportive wife, Monique, and my wonderful children, Miriam, Olivia and Evan.

I (D. Anthony Miles) want to dedicate this book to many people. There are so many people I want to thank for the publication of this book. First, I want to dedicate this book to my family for supporting me in writing it. Second, I want to dedicate this book to all the doctoral students I have taught and worked with. I want to thank you for not only inspiring us to write this book but also inspiring us to be better scholars of our prospective fields of study. Lastly, I want to dedicate this book to all my colleagues at the universities where I have worked and to the colleagues I have worked with on research I have presented at various conferences around the country. This book was a true labor of love.

Contents

22 Writing Your Dissertation: The Standard Format – Chapter 4 (Data Analysis and Findings)

23 Writing Your Dissertation: The Standard Format – Chapter 5 (Discussion and Conclusions)

Figures

Tables

Acknowledgments

I (Philip Adu) want to acknowledge all my colleagues at Walden University, especially Drs. Belinda McFeeters and Jamie Patterson. I really appreciate your incredible support. Thank you to my LinkedIn, Facebook, Twitter and YouTube family, followers and subscribers for being so supportive of my content. And to my wife, thank you for your unwavering support throughout the manuscript-writing process.

I (D. Anthony Miles) wish to acknowledge several great individuals and organizations that have supported me in this endeavor. First, very special thanks to members of the Miles family and other extended family members for their undying support, love and faith. Next, I want to acknowledge and thank all my friends, colleagues and co-researchers for their support. I want to acknowledge and thank all my doctoral students. I want to acknowledge and thank all my clients for their relentless support and encouragement. I want to acknowledge and thank all the universities that have taken part in my development as a scholar: the University of the Incarnate Word; Our Lady of the Lake University; and the University of Texas at San Antonio.

1 Planning Your Dissertation

Objectives

- Readers will be able to:
  1. Describe the dissertation process
  2. Recognize the stage they are at in the dissertation journey
  3. Choose an appropriate dissertation topic

Dissertation Process

Conducting a dissertation is part of doctoral students' research task, which they need to complete before being conferred a doctorate degree. It is part of the induction process – preparing you to join the community of researchers or practitioner-researchers who have expertise in a specific area in your field (Adu, 2011; Petersen, 2007). Completing a dissertation gives you the unique skills of navigating the role of an independent researcher while working within research guidelines and boundaries. The role of your dissertation supervisor (advisor) is to make sure your research actions and decisions are in line with the set guidelines and boundaries. The hope is that, at the end of the induction process, you would be skilled in critically consuming and independently conducting research, with the goal of contributing to the field and/or addressing practical problems (Useem, 1997).

The dissertation process varies depending on the country you are studying in, your field of study and the program or department you are in. However, the following dissertation stages reflect most of the doctoral programs, irrespective of the country and field. The stages include preparing, planning, performing and presenting.

Preparing

Preparation for the dissertation project starts at the moment one begins their doctoral education. However, for some institutions or doctoral programs, it starts at the time prospective students are asked to share their research interest as a part of their application requirements. The first action you need to take (especially after you have been accepted to a doctoral program) is to learn more about the program/department in terms of the kind of courses you will be taking and the

DOI: 10.4324/9781003268154-1

experience and research interest of the main faculty members. It would be great if you could learn as much as you can about the organizational culture and structure of the program, trying to address the following questions: Who is the head of the department? What are their roles and responsibilities? How do faculty members relate to students? What kind of support do students receive when working on their dissertations? What kinds of topics have students researched when working on their dissertations? What specific research methods courses should students take as part of the dissertation preparation? What kinds of research areas are the faculty members working on? Is there potential funding for dissertation work? Who should you contact if you have issues with choosing a research topic and methodology (Useem, 1997)?

Addressing some of the above questions will help you to understand what is expected of you by the faculty members and the department/program as a whole. This is also a good time to strategize ways of successfully completing your dissertation.

The coursework taken before the start of the dissertation is very crucial in preparing you for the project. It is very important to take the research methods courses seriously, focusing on not only getting good grades in the research method classes but also ensuring that you are gaining skills in consuming research reports and doing research (Useem, 1997). At this point, take the opportunity to learn different research methods, including their strengths and weaknesses and how they are used in studies. It is just like filling your toolbox with good and efficient tools so that when the right time comes, you can select the right tool for your study. Avoiding familiarizing yourself with different kinds of research methods limits what you plan to research and how you want to do it.

Another issue you should pay attention to is the assignments and projects done in the classes you take. This is a great opportunity to explore the topics of interest so that, by the time coursework is completed, you already know the topic you want to explore for your dissertation. However, if by the end of the coursework you haven't chosen a topic, it is not too late. At the early stage of the dissertation process, you may still have the chance to change the topic as you review literature and/or have conversations with your dissertation supervisor.

Having conservation with your fellow dissertation students about their experience, challenges and strategies for conducting their studies can also help you to be better prepared for this journey. It is important to get an idea about how a dissertation defense is organized (in terms of the structure and duration), including the expectations of the dissertation students and the kinds of questions dissertation committee members ask. Lastly, attending such sessions can be a source of inspiration – knowing that a dissertation project can be successfully done and defended.

Planning

Some institutions or doctoral programs allow their students to choose their supervisors and even determine who they want to be a part of their dissertation committee. However, other programs assign supervisors to students. Irrespective of what dissertation supervisory structure your program has put in place, you are more likely to successfully complete your dissertation if the roles, responsibilities and expectations of you and your supervisor are clearly laid out and followed. Therefore, there is a need to discuss your role and your supervisor's role, responsibilities and expectations – making sure everyone is on the same page.

The supervisors' main role is to guide and support students as they embark on their independent research journey. However, the kind of guidance and level of support differ from one supervisor to another. How can you know the way your supervisor guides and supports students working on their dissertation? You could address this question by engaging in informal inquiry – having a discussion with them and talking to current and previous advisees. Gathering this rich information to help address the above questions would assist in strategizing ways to leverage the expected guidance and support you will receive in accomplishing your dissertation goals.

However, not all supervisors will give you the guidance and support you need. After figuring out what your advisor will provide, you need to reflect on what your needs are and how you plan to meet them, considering the kind of support and guidance you will be receiving. Be flexible, in the sense that, in the course of your journey, there may be times where you feel supported by your supervisor, and at other times you may feel like you are alone in the journey. Learning to figure things out on your own is an effective strategy. For instance, if you are not familiar with a specific research approach you plan to use, and your supervisor is also not totally familiar with it, spend time and learn more about it, and if you are not clear about what is expected in each chapter of the dissertation, review other dissertation document examples. All these experiences improve your problem-solving and research skills and equip you to be an independent researcher.

One of the main strategies you could use to complete your dissertation journey is to act and think like an independent researcher – seeing your supervisor as a coach, but not a co-researcher. Having this mindset will help you to make informed decisions, and take actions with strong reasons behind them, while preparing you to defend those actions. Whenever you fail to convincingly defend your actions and decisions, you open doors of suggestion for potentially unfavorable changes of your topic, purpose and/or methodology. For instance, let's assume that you want to conduct a qualitative study using a phenomenological approach and you don't have good justification for using this approach. Someone may suggest a different approach for you which may not be the best. This doesn't mean that you shouldn't accept suggestions. However, having a reasonable defense behind your decision will help invite valuable suggestions, with good reasons for incorporating those suggestions.

Planning also involves deciding on your topic, determining the specific problem you want to address in the study, constructing the purpose of the study, deciding the right research method and data collection strategy and selecting an appropriate data analysis strategy. We'll discuss each of these areas later in this book. However, at this point, the take-home message is that, when planning, you should consider the norms and expectations in the program. You need to make sure your actions and decisions are not only in line with how research should be done but also consistent with your research goals (Emelin et al., 2021). Also, thinking about the consequence of your proposed actions, and devising ways of defending them, is one of the keys to successful dissertation completion.

Performing

At this stage, it is expected that structures have been put in place and the needed resources have been made available to conduct the study. After Institutional Review Board (IRB) approval, you use the specified and approved sampling strategy and recruitment channel to access potential participants. Interested participants should then complete a screening questionnaire, which contains questions that help the researcher to determine whether one qualifies to be a part of the study or not. Upon meeting the research recruitment requirements, they are ushered into the research participation phase. But before initiating their participation, participants are presented with a consent form educating them about the purpose of the study, their rights and responsibilities and any potential risks involved.

After agreeing to participate, they provide responses to questions/statements, generating the data needed to address the research questions/hypotheses. Alternatively, or additionally, existing data or documents may be gathered to help address research questions. After data collection, the next step is to analyze the data. It starts with conducting data cleaning – removing any identifiable information and making it ready for statistical analysis, qualitative analysis or both. All the analyses are mainly driven by the research questions or hypotheses.

Presenting

The presentation stage is not only about communicating your findings but also presenting your entire study. Thinking about who will be reading your dissertation document helps in effectively communicating your study. It starts with presenting the background and general information about the topic – preparing a way to make known the research problem of the study. Traditionally, research problems are informed by a gap you have identified in existing literature. Alternatively, the research problem can be informed by the problem generated as a result of a critical review and synthesis of literature. It is important to note that, when conducting action research, you could even just present a practical problem that is related to an issue within your profession or currently happening.

After presenting the problem statement, you state the purpose of the study and research questions/hypotheses. You then write about your theoretical or conceptual framework, which consists of the specific theories or concepts that inform what you are studying. It is important to provide a strong argument in support of your study, reasoning why it is important to conduct your study.

All the components described above are a part of the introduction of your study. Besides the introduction, you are to share the literature you have reviewed and the research methodology, as well as describe and display your results, discussion and conclusion. We will be discussing these components further in other chapters/ sections of this book.

Engaging in Writing

One component of the dissertation process that you will be doing often is writing. Writing is the art of putting your observations, ideas and/or thoughts on paper or electronically, using any writing or typing device. We see the mind as a sophisticated natural machine capable of creating new ideas. The main obstacle preventing us from fully utilizing it to accomplish our writing goal is fear. When the mind is pre-occupied with negative thoughts, it leaves few cognitive resources available for creative activity, including writing (O'Connor, 2017). Some of our thoughts may include: "I don't know how to perfectly write," "I don't know what to write," and "I won't be able to finish writing my dissertation." Having negative thoughts impedes our flow of ideas and inhibits creative writing. As Chintamani (2014) indicates, anticipation of failure dissipates creativity: "[Reluctance to write] … is most often initiated by conflicted feelings and an attempt to have a perfect draft (perfect draft syndrome) at the very outset" (Chintamani, 2014, p. 3).

During the initial writing process, it helps to focus less on writing perfect ideas and more on documenting your seemingly imperfect ideas. After putting your initial ideas on paper, you can go back to perfect the draft. Finding a quiet place to write, with or without playing calming music, mentally creates a conducive environment that could switch on your creative writing mood.

Using First Person

Writing in the first-person point of view (i.e., I, we, us and our) has been an acceptable way of engaging in academic writing (APA, 2019). However, to engage in scholarly writing, one of the writing practices you should rarely use is the first person when you are describing your thoughts, feelings and personal views (OASIS: Writing Center, 2023). Ideally, the first-person point of view is appropriate when describing your research actions and decisions (OASIS: Writing Center, 2023; Purdue Online Writing Lab, 2023). Also, a consistently active voice is more appropriate to help in knowing the subject who is performing the action (Purdue Online Writing Lab, 2023). Here are examples of sentences with both active voice and first-person point of view:

- I developed the survey questionnaire.
- We interviewed each participant in the morning.
- We conducted an independent t test to determine whether there is a statistically significant difference in job satisfaction between full-time and part-time employees.

However, your institution, department, field or supervisor may require that you write in the third person. So, we advise that you check with your supervisor about an acceptable writing style before you start working on your dissertation. Alternatively, you could review completed dissertations from your department or program to see how they were written. Lastly, if you have a writing center in your institution, you could contact the center for clarification about the required writing style.

Please note that we have intentionally written some of the example dissertation chapters in the third person for you to see how they are written in case you are required to use this type of writing style (see Chapters 19–23).

Choosing a Topic

The word "interest" comes in mind when thinking about a topic you may want to do a study on. This word sometimes makes its presence known when having a conversation with colleagues and faculty members about what you plan to do in your dissertation. Therefore, one's level of interest in a topic could be the main determinant for the focus of a dissertation project. However, there are other factors that should be considered when deciding on a topic. But before we come to what these contributing factors are, let's address the question: What is a topic? A topic is a core idea that has the potentiality to be studied. In other words, it is the main issue that a researcher wants to research. Topics differ based on the level of abstraction, connection to practical issues and relatedness to a research area within your field.

A topic with a high level of abstraction (with no connection to practical issues and no relation to the area of research in your field) becomes challenging to explore. Let's say you want to study "artificial intelligence capabilities" in the field of education. This topic could be seen as too high in the level of abstraction, since it doesn't represent a specific issue in education. With this topic, your supervisor may say that it is too broad and ask you about how it is connected to issues in education or educational practices. Thinking about what area, situation and/or event this proposed topic is related to would help in reducing the level of abstraction. For instance, you could revise it to "the role of machine learning on students' learning." As you can see, the "artificial intelligence" has been replaced by its sub-area, which is "machine learning," and "role" has been further added to reduce the abstraction level. In addition, including the phrase "students' learning" helped to relate the topic to an area in the education field.

We want to emphasize that coming up with a topic is not always linear as discussed above. It may emerge when taking a course, talking to someone, reading an article, doing a course assignment or reflecting on a problem you have encountered. The most important thing is to make sure it meets the criteria of a good topic, which are as follows: It should be less abstract in nature; it should have a connection with practical issues in a field; and it should be related to the research within a field (see Table 1.1). In addition, you may address the following questions: How important is the topic to you? How important is the topic to your field of study? How important is the topic to your future endeavors? Responding to these questions will help you to make informed decisions about what to focus on (Useem, 1997).

Table 1.1 Criteria for deciding on an appropriate topic

Criteria	Meaning	Rating
Level of abstraction	How distant a topic is from an actual and specific happening, situation, behavior, etc.	The level of abstraction of my topic is: • Very high • High • Moderate • Low • Very low
Connection to practical issues	How close the topic is to what is happening in our day-to-day lives.	How connected is the topic to practical issues? • Very highly • Highly • Moderately • Loosely • Very loosely
Relatedness to research area within your field	How much connection the topic shares with a research area in the field of your study.	How related is your topic to a research area within your field? • Very highly • Highly • Moderately • Loosely • Very loosely
Degree of interest in the topic	How much delight and curiosity you have towards the topic.	How interested would you be in the topic? • Very • Somewhat • Unsure • Not very • Not at all
Degree of relevance to your experience	How important the topic is to you, considering what you have experienced.	How relevant is the topic to you, considering what you have experienced? • Very relevant • Relevant • Unsure • Irrelevant • Very irrelevant
Degree of relevance to your field of study	How important the topic is to your field of study.	How relevant is the topic to your field of study? • Very relevant • Relevant • Unsure • Irrelevant • Very irrelevant
Degree of relevance to your future endeavors	How important the topic is to your career ambitions and future research focus.	How relevant is the topic to your future endeavors? • Very relevant • Relevant • Unsure • Irrelevant • Very irrelevant

Summary

The dissertation process can be grouped under four stages: preparing for your research journey, planning to carry out your research, performing by implementing the study, and presenting by writing and showing that you conducted your study and what you found, including demonstrating their relevance, interpretation, applications and implications. Throughout the dissertation process, you engage in academic writing. Writing your dissertation is a challenging endeavor, but with adequate support from your institution and dissertation committee it can be done. Besides, with an unwavering determination to complete your research journey, you are more likely to reach your dissertation destination. We encourage you to start thinking about potential topics you could choose from to begin your journey. We did it, and we know you can do it too.

References

Adu, P. K. (2011). *Conceptualizing doctoral advising from professors' and doctoral students' perspectives using concept mapping* (Order No. 3531922) [Doctoral dissertation, West Virginia University]. ProQuest Dissertations and Theses, 210. Retrieved from http://search.proquest.com/docview/1221263677?accountid=34120 (1221263677).

APA. (2019). *Publication manual of the American Psychological Association* (7th ed.). American Psychological Association.

Chintamani. (2014). "Challenges in writing" – The writer's block?. *The Indian Journal of Surgery*, *76*(1), 3–4. https://doi.org/10.1007/s12262-014-1058-x

Emelin, D., Le Bras, R., Hwang, J. D., Forbes, M., & Choi, Y. (2021). Moral stories: Situated reasoning about norms, intents, actions, and their consequences. In *Proceedings of the 2021 Conference on Empirical Methods in Natural Language Processing* (pp. 698–718). Association for Computational Linguistics.

OASIS: Writing Center. (2023, February 6). *Scholarly voice: First-person point of view*. Walden University: Writing Center. Retrieved February 6, 2023, from https://academicguides.waldenu.edu/writingcenter/scholarlyvoice/first

O'Connor, J. (2017). Inhibition in the dissertation writing process: Barrier, block, and impasse. Psychoanalytic Psychology, *34*(4), 516–523. https://doi.org/10.1037/pap0000132

Petersen, E. B. (2007). Negotiating academicity: Postgraduate research supervision as category boundary work. *Studies in Higher Education*, *32*(4), 475–487.

Purdue Online Writing Lab. (2023, February 16). *APA stylistics: Basics*. Pursue University: Purdue Online Writing Lab. Retrieved February 16, 2023, from https://owl.purdue.edu/owl/research_and_citation/apa6_style/apa_formatting_and_style_guide/apa_stylistics_basics.html

Useem, B. (1997). Choosing a dissertation topic. *PS: Political Science & Politics*, *30*(2), 213–216. https://doi.org/10.2307/420498

2 Conducting a Literature Review and Developing a Theoretical/ Conceptual Framework

Objectives

- Readers will be able to:
  1. Conduct a literature search
  2. Choose relevant literature
  3. Write about their selected literature
  4. Select appropriate theories or concepts
  5. Develop a theoretical/conceptual framework

Conducting a Literature Review

Conducting a literature review is not an easy endeavor. It can be time consuming and labor intensive. However, a literature review is worth the investment, due to the huge benefits it accrues when done right. Before we move further to outline the rationale, process and importance of conducting a review of existing literature, let's first define the literature review. A literature review is a process of searching for and selecting relevant literature, with the purpose of critically analyzing them and presenting the outcome.

Conducting a literature review is a great opportunity to solidify what you want to study. Exploring empirical research articles, conceptual/theoretical papers, books, position papers, government agency reports, evaluation reports and the like helps you to better understand your topic or the problem of interest.

One may ask, "Why should I review literature? I have already identified a topic I'm passionate about, and I think this is unique and I believe no one has done it before. I'll be the first person to explore this idea. I'll one day be an expert in this emerging area."

One of the core features of conducting research is to contribute to the existing body of knowledge. The question is how can one best contribute without knowing how, where and when to contribute, and even why there may be a need to add to what is existing? The advancement of scientific knowledge always depends on the research community's dedication to familiarizing themselves with existing knowledge and engaging in inquiry to build on it. Similarly, knowing what has been done

DOI: 10.4324/9781003268154-2

- Structuring
- Chronologically
- Conceptually
- Methodologically
- Thematically

- Consuming
- Critiquing
- Communicating

Contributing to knowledge

Perfecting your skills

Building argument

Building your knowledge

- Building a strong argument

- Exploring trends
- Comparing discoveries

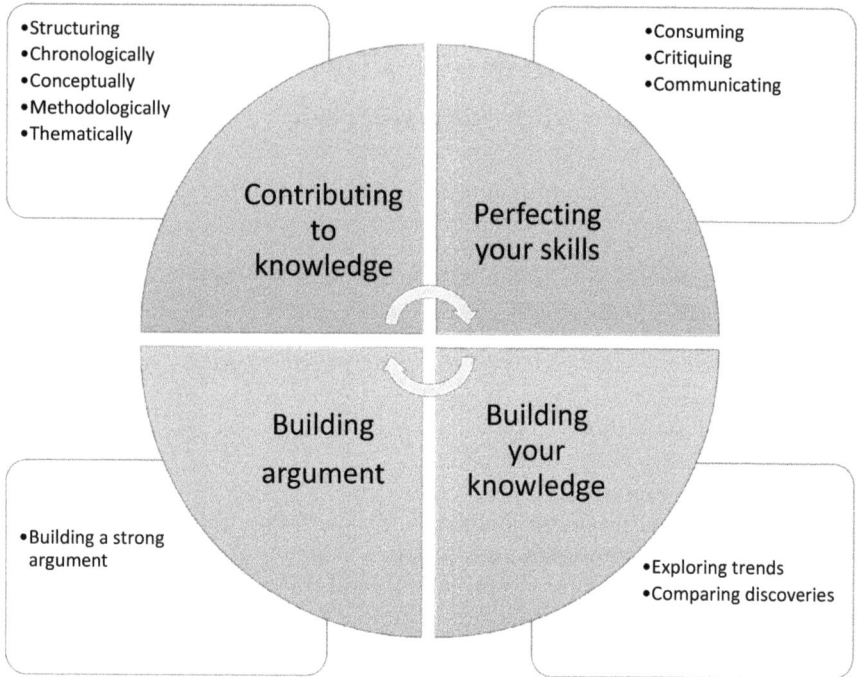

Figure 2.1 The essence of engaging in a review of literature.

helps in discovering gaps in the literature and determining which one you would want to fill.

Even if you are conducting an action research study in which your main intent is not to contribute to the body of knowledge but to address the problem of practice, a literature review is still relevant. You could learn about existing concepts, theories and best practices, and it could inform your action research.

Have you thought about what you are doing a literature review for, regarding your dissertation project? You may give a general, well-known reason such as knowing what has been done, identifying a gap and demonstrating that you have well researched the topic (Callahan, 2014). Thinking deeply about why you are doing a literature review as a part of your dissertation, you may notice that there are four main goals you are expected to achieve (see Figure 2.1). The essence of you engaging in this learning experience of conducting a literature review is to:

- Perfect your skills in consuming, critiquing and communicating academic research, concepts and theories
- Build your knowledge about the topic through exploring research trends and comparing research discoveries
- Generate an argument(s) in support of your study

- Contribute to existing knowledge through structuring the review based on a sequence of ideas, sub-topics, methods and/or population

Perfecting Your Research Skills

It is important to note that, separate from general information in books and articles about why we conduct a literature review, there are other relevant reasons why students doing their dissertation should review literature. One reason is that doing a literature review helps students to perfect their skills in consuming, critiquing and communicating research projects. After the end of their literature review experience, they should be able to recognize differences among empirical research articles, positional papers, conceptual/theoretical articles, editorial pieces, evaluation reports or government white papers. Being able to differentiate between these documents is the gateway to selecting the right literature for your review. After reading and gaining an understanding of the literature, you can then critically examine the literature – exploring the quality of all the components of the literature. Successfully examining the literature should lead to the following questions:

- What kind of literature should I consume?
- How should I consume them?
- What is the purpose of reviewing the literature?
- What is the consistency among the components of the literature?
- What claims does it make?
- How does the evidence support the claims?
- What is the purpose-driven outcomes of the literature review?
- Who are the literature review outcomes communicated to?
- How should the literature review be presented?

Being an Active Research Consumer

As a doctoral student working on your dissertation project, one of the rationales for conducting a literature review is to equip you to become an active research consumer. As you are thinking and searching for the right kinds of literature related to your topic, you are being exposed to a variety of articles, papers, reports and editorial pieces. This experience helps you to recognize and distinguish among literature and facilitates the selection of the right literature for review.

There are two main types of literature: black and white literature and grey literature. Any literature published by a commercial publishing company (or an organization whose main mission is to publish literature) is considered black and white literature (Western University, 2012). Some of the publishing companies that publish academic literature are Routledge, SAGE, Springer, Elsevier, Oxford University Press, Harvard University Press and University of Chicago Press, just to mention a few. Peer-reviewed articles, including empirical, conceptual, theoretical and the like, are some of the literature published by these companies besides producing academic books.

Since you are doing research on a chosen topic, the first set of literature you should look for to review is peer-reviewed articles that are authors' reports of the study they did. You could also look into conceptual and theoretical articles, including positional papers relevant to your topic. In addition, grey literature would be a great source of information, especially when there is limited black and white literature. So, what is grey literature? It is literature published by organizations or entities that do not engage in publishing as their sole focus (Western University, 2012). Examples of grey literature are reports from government agencies, corporations and non-publishing businesses, dissertations, white papers, blog posts and the like (McKenzie, 2022).

Besides being able to determine different kinds of literature, as an active research consumer you are able to select the literature not only relevant to your topic but also acceptable as appropriate literature for review. The first-tier literature (such as empirical research articles) you need to access for review is peer-reviewed literature. This is because this kind of literature has been vetted by the author's peers in the research community, making sure the articles are of good quality and meet the research standards and publication criteria ascribed in the publication guidelines of the publishing journals.

You could supplement selected empirical research articles with positional, conceptual and theoretical papers, including grey literature, especially when conducting a literature review and having limited research articles. In a nutshell, doing a literature review helps in gaining skills to become an active consumer of research. As an active consumer of research, you should be able to distinguish between the literature types and select the ones that are relevant and related to your topic.

Being a Good Critic of Research

Conducting a literature review at the dissertation stage helps you to be a good critic of literature. As a critic of research literature, you have to know what is required in each component of the articles you are reviewing. The review starts with having a general sense of the literature in terms of who the authors are, what the document is about and what they hope to achieve in writing the article. Having a general sense starts with reading the document to understand what they want to communicate to the audience (i.e., research/academic community). At this point, you could document the main points/ideas in the literature, such as:

- The problem the author(s) wanted to address or the main issue that warranted engaging in that inquiry
- The purpose of the empirical study or non-empirical inquiry
- The research questions or issues that needed to be addressed
- The research methods or strategy used to address the issues
- The data collection procedure
- The data analysis process
- The findings
- The interpretation of the findings

This will aid in conducting a critical examination of the literature. As you are extracting ideas from the literature, you could also document what you see. Keeping notes of your thoughts can be called memoing. Some of the questions that could facilitate your reflection practice are as follows: What do I think about what the author is presenting/saying? How are the main areas/ideas identified in the literature related to my topic? What is interesting about the literature? Is there any surprising information I want to take note of? How consistent are the components of the literature? Answers to these questions will be helpful when you start your critical evaluation of the literature. Your goal here is to assess the literature and compare its components to a set standard in terms of research quality, transparency and consistency. This implies that you need to know what good literature looks like before you can adequately and critically evaluate articles, reports and research documents.

Let's limit our discussion to empirical and conceptual research articles (see Table 2.1). What conditions should a research or conceptual article meet to determine it is a good one? As researchers reviewing a peer-reviewed article, should we focus on assessing its quality or do we not have to, since we could assume that the article has passed through a rigorous review process before its publication? Even if it is so, we think it is still beneficial to review for quality. In acting as a second eye to the reviewer – curiously looking for best practices and potential flaws – you are familiarizing yourself with what the characteristics of good research looks like and gaining skills in extensively evaluating research articles.

Conceptual Article: Component

The articles should clearly state the phenomenon the authors want to explain, the problem they plan to address, concepts, models and/or theory selection procedures and their roles (Jaakkola, 2020). The authors explain each model or theory, describing what they represent and what their properties are, including associated assumptions. Besides this, conceptual articles highlight and/or establish relationships among the concepts, providing evidence in support of the relationships. According to Jaakkola (2020), there are three elements a conceptual paper should have: claim, grounds and warrant. A claim could be an assertion, conclusion or inference one makes.

Table 2.1 Kinds of academic articles and their respective features and examples

Literature	Feature	Example
Empirical research article	A report of a primary study that involves data collection and analysis (Jaakkola, 2020)	Burkard et al. (2014)
Conceptual paper	An article that contains a summary, review, synthesis and/or discussion of concepts, models and/or theories (Jaakkola, 2020).	MacInnis & de Mello (2005)

Grounds are evidence that support the claim. The conditions that need to exist for the claim and grounds to be valid is warrant (or assumption) (Jaakkola, 2020).

Empirical Research Article: Components

The article should have a problem that has been addressed in the study, a review of the literature, purpose of the study, research method, procedure, data analysis, results and discussion. The article should narrate the issue that necessitated the need to conduct the study, using the literature to layout where the study was in relation to research done about the topic and what contribution the study has made. There should be a statement of what the research hoped to achieve and questions the researcher(s) addressed in the study. It should have information about the research method used and related data collection and analysis procedures. The outcome addressing the research question(s) should be provided, including the interpretation and implications of the findings. In conclusion, here are the five issues you should be looking for when reviewing an empirical research article:

1. Focus of the study
2. Goal of the study
3. How data was accessed and assessed
4. Findings of the study
5. Conclusions made based on the findings

Being a Communicator of Research

Conducting a literature review improves your skills in communicating research studies in a way that is meaningful and meets the needs of the audience. See yourself as a commentator or analyst of a specific game (let's use soccer as an example). Before the match, the commentator/analyst provides a preview of the performance-related history of the two teams, helping the audience to put the soccer match into proper perspective, exciting the crowd about what they should expect and helping them to properly connect what may happen during the match to the previous happenings. In addition, the pre-match commentary/analysis helps the spectators to make sense of the outcome of the match. Similarly, your role at the literature review stage is to provide a preview of what has been done. The preview should be intentional and well thought through – knowing what is expected of you and the needs of your audience. When writing about the literature you have reviewed, you need to be transparent, sharing how relevant literature was accessed and sampled for the review. This will contribute to making your literature review process repeatable and the outcome of the review credible. You also need to craft the review in such a way that it meets the goal of the review. You need to make sure readers can easily follow your flow of thoughts and you are presenting a narration of the literature about your topic in a historical or topical manner. As a communicator of research, your role is to extensively digest relevant literature and present the literature review outcome in such a way that readers understand what you are

Synthesized Studies

Your Study

Previous Studies

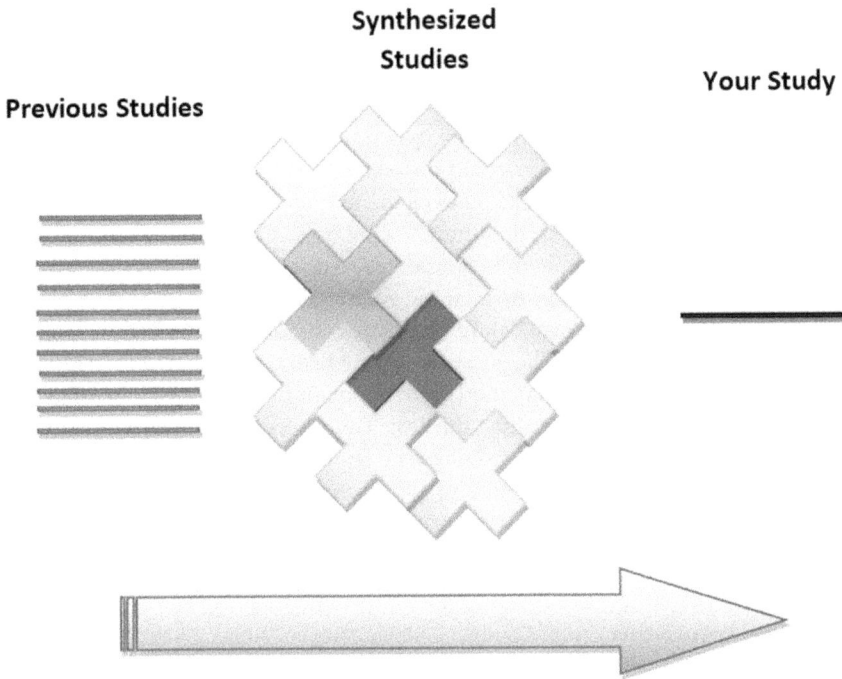

Figure 2.2 Literature review process.

presenting and can make sense of where you are in relation to studies done and where you are going, connecting it to what you want to do (see Figure 2.2).

Building Your Knowledge

Before doing research, you need to be knowledgeable in the area you are researching. One of the main ways is by familiarizing yourself with the research done or issues scholarly discussed about your topic. Reviewing literature is the beginning of your journey to becoming an expert in the area you are studying. You gain skills in exploring trends and comparing discoveries.

Exploring Trends in the Literature

As you keenly review the elements of literature, especially empirical or conceptual research articles, you may notice patterns that need further exploration. For empirical studies, you are interested in examining the focus of the study, the method used, results after the data analysis and the conclusions made based on the findings. For conceptual papers, you are looking into the phenomenon being examined, claims made, evidence provided and assumptions presented (Jaakkola, 2020). Exploring patterns in the literature helps in determining where to appropriately situate your study.

Comparing Discoveries in the Literature

As you keenly go through the literature, you may see interesting information that needs further examination. You could do a cross-section analysis, which involves comparing and contrasting ideas and elements identified in the literature (for example, a research article). For instance, checking consistency across purpose, research questions and findings is considered one of the cross-section analysis tecniques. We also have cross-case analysis, where you compare and contrast ideas and elements across literature. Before comparing literature, you need to establish the basis of the comparison. The question is, what brings together the literature you are comparing? Is it the topic, method used, population, procedure or findings (just to mention a few)? After establishing the basic commonalities among the literature, you then explore the similarities and differences among them with respect to a specific issue, such as the demographics of participants. You can consider exploring studies with the same topic and methodology but different results or conceptual literature with the same focus but a different theoretical perspective.

Building Arguments

Engaging in a literature review assists in gaining the skill to make strong augments in support of your study. One of the purposes of conducting a literature review is to help provide a rationale for your study. The questions that readers of your research documents want you to address are how relevant is your study, considering what has been done, and why is your study important, considering previous studies done? This is where you provide strong arguments justifying the need to conduct your study and properly situating your study among studies related to your topic.

An argument should have four main elements, namely, claim, evidence, assumptions (which could be implicit or explicit) and conclusion (Jaakkola, 2020). When writing a review of the literature, you are expected to present your observations or conclusions drawn from an extensive examination of studies done and information written in relation to your topic. For example, you may observe that there are limited studies done on a topic using qualitative approaches. What evidence do you have to support this claim? Can we assume that you have extensively searched enough studies done on your topic before making this claim?

Contributing to Knowledge

Conducting a literature review helps in gaining the skills to contribute to the existing knowledge of a field. By conducting a review, you are helping readers to be abreast with the trend and with discoveries in the field in relation to the topic of interest. As you gather and synthesize relevant literature and others also do similar reviews, the

Table 2.2 Literature review presentation format and examples

Literature review presentation	Example	
	Article title	*Authors*
Chronological presentation of a literature review	"The History and Future of Genetically Modified Crops: Frankenfoods, Superweeds, and the Developing World."	Glass-O'Shea (2021)
Thematic presentation of a literature review	"An Organizational Intervention to Reduce Physician Burnout."	Gregory et al. (2018)
Conceptual presentation of a literature review	"Burnout in Nursing: A Theoretical Review."	Dall'Ora et al. (2020)
Methodological presentation of a literature review	"Mixed Methods Research Designs in Counseling Psychology."	Hanson et al. (2005)

body of knowledge in the field of study continues to increase. You are also setting the stage for current and future researchers to build on what you have created. The outcome of the review (i.e., knowledge) could be presented chronologically, thematically, conceptually and/or methodologically (see Table 2.2).

Chronological Presentation of a Literature Review

If your goal of reviewing literature is to show the studies done and their related purpose, method, findings and conclusions across time, presenting the review in a chronological manner would be great. If as part of the literature review you plan to explore how a theory, model or phenomenon has been studied over a period of time, then you could do a chronological presentation of the literature. In other words, when writing a review chronologically, you are presenting a synthesis of literature about a topic spread out across a set period of time.

Thematic Presentation of a Literature Review

This is quite similar to presenting qualitative findings, where themes with supporting evidence are generally presented. With this approach, you first determine the themes/concepts you want to explore and write a review on. You then organize components of the literature under their respective themes before presenting a synthesized review under their respective themes related to the topic of interest.

Conceptual Presentation of a Literature Review

This is about presenting a synthesis of the literature based on a theory and/or model selected for the study. With this kind of presentation, you discuss the literature in terms of researchers' development, confirmation, refinement and explanatory characteristics of theories and/or models. One strategy of writing a literature review in a conceptually structured way is to present each relevant theory or model and discuss studies done or papers written about it, exploring its capacity to explain the phenomenon of study.

Methodological Presentation of a Literature Review

This is where you present a review based on the research methods used. This type of presentation is more appropriate when you want to justify why you have selected a particular research method. It is also a way of comparing research findings and conclusions across qualitative, quantitative and mixed methods studies. It can also be used to show whether studies with diverse methods arrived at similar findings and/or conclusions.

Searching for Relevant Literature

Searching for relevant literature starts with addressing the following questions: What kinds of literature are you looking for? Where are the potential sources of literature relevant to your topic? How do you search for the literature? To put it differently, when conducting a literature review, you need to know the kinds of literature you are looking for, potential sources of the literature and the search strategies you plan to use. The literature search process should be thoughtful, thorough, systematic, transparent and documented. When writing about the outcome of the literature you reviewed, you need to demonstrate that you have done a comprehensive search of the literature related to your topic. This could contribute to the credibility of your literature review outcome.

Deciding on the Kinds of Literature to Review

Deciding comes after familiarizing yourself with the features of objects or phenomena you are deciding on. In this case, it is important to be knowledgeable about the kinds of literature that researchers in your field normally use to conduct their review. As mentioned above, generally we have two kinds of literature: black and white literature and grey literature. As already suggested, focusing more on peer-reviewed articles would be great. However, if there are limited peer-reviewed articles related to your topic, we suggest you consider looking into other articles, including relevant grey literature.

Deciding on Where to Find Relevant Literature

There are a lot of databases you can choose from. You could start with the ones that are related to your discipline. Some of the more popular databases include ECOhost, MEDLine and the like. Other publishers such as Routledge, SAGE and the like have databases of articles and books that can be explored. There are also open-source databases such as the Directory of Open Access Journals,

ScienceOpen and OpenDOAR that may have literature relevant to your topic. The Google Scholar search engine can easily display potential academic literature and where you can access them if they are not readily available. Lastly, ResearchGate, which is a site where researchers share mainly research articles and ideas, could be another source of getting access to relevant literature.

Determining Literature Search Strategies

Similar to Google Search, when searching for literature related to your topic, you are retrieving literature that has a specific word or group of words and/or a word or group of words related to a specific word or phrase. Before you determine appropriate literature search techniques to use, you need to familiarize yourself with the signs used for searching: AND, OR, ( ), " " (CityU, 2022). It is important to note that search strategies my differ depending on the kind of database you are using. However, Table 2.3 has the ones most commonly used. Also, these search command symbols do not apply to non-traditional academic databases and other academic social media platforms such as Google Scholar and ResearchGate.

Apart from searching electronic databases (as described above), there are two other strategies you could use to search for relevant literature: backward searching and forward searching (Xiao & Watson, 2019). Backward searching involves looking at the reference list of a relevant literature to see whether there is potential literature of interest. However, with forward searching, you look for literature that has cited a relevant literature. Google Scholar is a useful tool for the forward searching strategy (Xiao & Watson, 2019). When you use Google Scholar to search for a particular article or book, it will show a list of literature that has cited that literature.

Table 2.3 Search command symbols, their meaning and examples

Search command symbol	Meaning	Example
OR	Searching for literature that contains Concept A or Concept B	Burnout OR Fatigue
AND	Searching for literature that has both Concept A and Concept B	Burnout AND Fatigue
NOT	Searching for literature that does not have Concept A	Burnout NOT Fatigue
*	Searching for words that have the same stem word	Prevent*
( )	Grouping search commands	(Burnout NOT Fatigue) OR (exhaustion)
?	Searching for literature with a word and its variations based on changes in a character or group of characters in that word	Organi?ation

Determining Literature Extraction Criteria

The next action you need to take is to determine the parameters of your search in terms of year of publication, the discipline within which the literature was published, the kind of literature and other related extraction criteria (Adu, 2021). At this stage, you have to be flexible. Your initial extraction criteria may not yield the desired response. You should be ready to adjust them and explore other databases until you arrive at the desired outcome. You should be ready to either narrow or broaden the search. Here are some of the questions you could think about if your initial search did not yield a satisfactory outcome:

- Should I adjust the search terms?
- Should I use another database?
- Should I change the publication date range?
- Should I include other kinds of literature, including grey literature?
- Should I explore Google Scholar?

Searching for Relevant Literature

By now, you know the search strategies and extraction criteria you should use. The next step is to do the actual searching. At this point, you need to be flexible because your initial search may not yield the desired outcome. You could have a lot of literature, resulting in the need to adjust the filtering options. Conversely, your search may produce very little literature. You could address this by making adjustments to your search strategies and extraction criteria, exploring another database and/or using the forward or backward search strategy.

One may say, "I can't find literature related to my topic." If there is limited research done about your topic in your field or discipline, you can explore other fields to see whether similar topics have been treated (see Table 2.4). If there is limited research done related to the kind of population or research location you want to study, explore studies done about your topic with similar participants/population or research location. For instance, if there are limited studies done about the people of Ghana, you could look into studies done on any of the African counties that are related to your topic. If there are limited studies done about the concept you are studying, you can look at studies done on other related concepts. For example, if you are doing research on burnout, you could also explore studies on physical and mental exhaustion.

Managing your Search Outcomes

Managing your search outcomes is simply retrieving relevant literature you have searched for and finding a place to store it for easy access and review. Traditionally, this is done by downloading (if they are in an electronic format) and storing them on your computer or printing them to have hard copies. Alternatively, you could use a literature management application to easily store the literature, including

Table 2.4 Strategies for searching for literature after an unsuccessful initial search

Area	Similar	Narrow	Broad
Theory	Exploring studies done on similar theories	Searching for studies done on a narrower theory	Searching for studies done on a broader theory
Concept/phenomenon of study	Exploring studies done on similar concepts/phenomena	Looking into studies done on concepts/phenomena narrower than your initial focus	Searching for studies done on concepts/phenomena broader than your initial focus
Population of focus	Searching for studies on a topic of interest done with a similar population	Exploring studies on a topic of interest done with a smaller population	Exploring studies on a topic of interest done with a larger population
Discipline	Searching for studies on a topic of interest done with a similar field	Exploring studies on a topic of interest done with a sub-discipline	Exploring studies on a topic of interest done with a larger discipline

reviewing and making notes. Some of the more popular ones are RefWorks, Mendeley, Zotero and Endnote. Due to continuous technological advancement, there may be new and improved literature management software with high functionality and user-friendliness. Therefore, before you select a literature management application, list a specific task you want it to be used for and review existing software to see which one can help you meet your literature review goals. You could also check with the librarian in your institution to see whether the institution has a particular application available to students.

Selecting Relevant Literature

Let's use fishing as an analogy. Now that you have finished fishing, it is time to review what you have in your net. Sometimes, not everything you caught in the net is what you wanted. You may need to review what you have and dispose of what you didn't like or expect. Similarly, after extracting literature, you need to do a quick review to determine which literature is truly relevant and eliminate literature that is irrelevant to your topic. It is always a good strategy to have a specific criterion for selecting the right literature for review. It makes the selection of articles for review more systematic and transparent and less biased in terms of choosing what you like for the review (Machi & McEvoy, 2012).

So, the question is, "What conditions should literature meet for it to be part of the literature you plan to review?" It would be great if you listed specific criteria the literature should meet. You could use the following questions to help you generate literature selection criteria:

- What information do you want to see in the title, abstract, introduction or body of the literature for the literature to be selected?
- What type of literature will you select for the review?
- If the literature is about research, what kind of research are you looking for?
  - Are you looking for:
    - Traditional research, action research and/or program evaluation studies?
    - Qualitative, quantitative and/or mixed methods studies?
- Will scoping review and/or systematic review studies be part of the selected literature for review?
- Should the qualifying literature be from a specific country?
- What research location and/or population should the research literature focus on for it to be selected?

Selecting relevant literature and reviewing it can be done sequentially or concurrently. With the sequential strategy, you start with skimming through literature to determine whether it meets the set criteria. After skimming all the available literature, you review the selected literature. With the concurrent approach, when you skim literature and it meets the criteria, you review it before moving on to skim other literature.

When selecting literature, with the criteria in mind, you could first look at the title, abstract, summary and/or conclusion to help you decide which is appropriate (Subramanyam, 2013). Sometimes, you can determine the right literature by just looking at the titles. If you are not sure about selecting literature by reviewing the title, you could look at the abstract, summary or conclusion (Subramanyam, 2013).

Extracting Relevant Information

Now that you have selected the literature to review, the next step is to extract information that will be helpful for you to write the review. You may ask, "How can I determine which information is relevant for my review?" Firstly, the information should have some connection to your topic. Secondly, it should help you meet the purpose of the review. Lastly, it could be used to support the claims you will make when writing the review. You could use one of the three main strategies to extract relevant information from the selected literature. These are developing:

1. An annotated bibliography
2. A literature characteristics matrix
3. A literature matrix based on themes

Developing an Annotated Bibliography

This involves reviewing literature, generating pertinent pieces of information and writing a summary that reflects the ideas gathered and connects to the topic of interest. Besides having a summary, an annotated bibliography should have a responding reference. To put it differently, an annotated bibliography contains references and their respective summaries. For empirical literature, the summary could be based on the problem of the study, research purpose, research question, participants, data collection and analysis, findings and their interpretation and conclusions. For non-empirical literature, you could investigate the claims and their associated assumptions, evidence in support of the claim and concluding statements to help you generate summaries (Jaakkola, 2020).

Creating a Literature Characteristics Matrix

This strategy involves creating a matrix with all the literature selected and their features, including a summary of their main components. The characteristics may include author(s), year of publication, title and type of article/literature. Also, the matrix could include the problem of the study or the problem the article has addressed, the purpose of the study or the non-empirical literature, research questions, method used, participants' characteristics, data collection and analysis strategies, findings and their interpretation and conclusions. When completing the matrix, we recommend you provide (in your own words) brief information about each component under each piece of literature. It is important to note that creating the matrix is not the end of the literature review but a means to writing a strong, insightful and comprehensive synthesis of the literature.

Creating a Literature Matrix Based on Themes

This strategy involves creating a matrix or table that shows information extracted from the literature and their corresponding themes and literature. One of the strategies for developing themes is description-focused coding (Adu, 2019). With this coding strategy, you go through each piece of literature, extract information that is relevant and generate a phrase (i.e., a theme) that best describes the excerpt. The theme will then be connected to subsequent excerpts selected from the literature.

When extracting and organizing information from the literature, you could use existing themes (i.e., the content analysis technique) or generate them as you go through the literature (i.e., the thematic analysis technique). With the content analysis technique, you could develop themes based on the conceptual/theoretical framework, a theory or a group of theories that informs your study or sub-topics associated with the focus of your study.

Other Innovative Strategies

When it comes to reviewing literature and extracting what you need to help you write about what has been done and talked about with respect to your topic, there are many innovative ways of going about it. Some just take notes, writing about what they have observed in the literature, then examine the notes to highlight patterns discovered and write about those discoveries. Other researchers document what they see in the literature alongside their thoughts, leading to the presentation of an analytical synthesis of what they have learned. We suggest that you review best practices of conducting a literature review and select strategies that you can efficiently and effectively use to provide a well-written and informative review.

Writing About Your Selected Literature

You start the writing process by describing how you searched for and selected your literature. This also involves showing the sources of the selected literature and the selection criteria you used. All this information contributes to promoting transparency in the literature search and extraction process. It also helps in highlighting the best practices and educating researchers in effective ways of conducting a literature review. Lastly, providing your literature review process promotes credibility of your outcome of the review.

You then need to decide whether you want to present the review "chronologically, thematically, conceptually, methodologically or a combination" (Frederiksen & Phelps, 2018, p. 93). These types of review have been discussed earlier, but irrespective of the type you plan to use, you need to synthesize what you found in a meaningful way.

A synthesized review portrays a well-constructed combination of ideas, concepts and assertions from the literature that are seamlessly presented in a logical manner. To simplify, each of the main paragraphs should have a claim (which could also be called a topic sentence), definition or explanation of the claim, supporting statements or evidence and a concluding statement. Alternatively, you could creatively present these elements in a variety of sequences, but the most important thing is that the paragraph contains the components listed above.

Understanding the Conceptual/Theoretical Framework

A conceptual/theoretical framework is a group of statements that discusses theories and/or concepts related to your focus of study (Adu, 2020). Visual representation could be used to reflect selected theories and/or concepts and connections between them. You may ask, "Why should I have a conceptual or theoretical framework when conducting research?" In order to effectively contribute to the field or to best practices in your profession, you need to identify and use already-developed theories and/or concepts related to what you are studying.

Exploring the Goal of Conducting Research

Looking at the three main types of research, the main goal of conducting traditional research, action research and program evaluation is to fill a research gap, address a practical problem and access a program to develop, discontinue or improve, respectively. To understand how you can effectively meet the goal of a study, you need to first make sense of how researchers and research practitioners build knowledge and improve research best practices.

We do research to study behaviors, situations, phenomena and/or events. When conducting a qualitative study, we end up generating concepts and ideas. Based

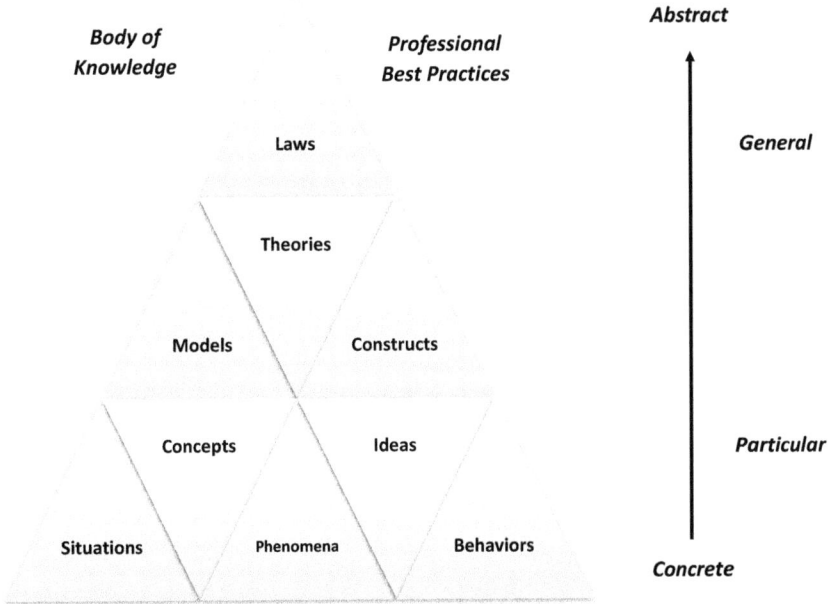

Figure 2.3 How a body of knowledge and professional best practices are built.
Source: Adapted from Adu (2020).

on the aim of the study and the research questions and research method used, we could further explore relationships among the concepts and ideas to generate constructs, models and/or theories.

With these constructs, models and/or theories, we could conduct quantitative research, generating hypotheses and testing them. As we continue to do quantitative, qualitative and mixed methods research, ideas, concepts, constructs, theories and laws are built, confirmed, refined and/or rejected. As we do research, we continue to contribute to the development of the body of knowledge and best practices in the field we are affiliated with (see Figure 2.3).

When conducting research, you could select concepts, constructs, models and/or theories, creating a framework to help inform your study (see Table 2.5). So, a conceptual/theoretical framework is like a bridge connecting your study to existing models, theories and the like. In other words, creating such a framework helps in connecting the concrete focus of the study to an abstract body of knowledge or general best practices (see Figure 2.3).

Developing and Writing a Conceptual/Theoretical Framework

Developing and writing your conceptual/theoretical framework can be a challenging task. You are expected to look for the right model or theory that best relates to

Table 2.5 Research-related terms, their meanings and examples

Term	Meaning	Example	Reference
Concept	A term "representing a particular behavior, situation or idea" (Adu, 2020, slide 7)	• Blended learning • Flipped classroom • Gamification • Instructional effectiveness • Learning outcome	Adu (2019); Green (2014)
Construct	"Comprises of concepts and the connections among them" (Adu, 2020, slide 8)	• Classroom management • Cultural intelligence • Emotional intelligence • Personality trait • Quality of life	Jabareen (2009)
Theory	• "Contains concepts/ construct, [and] relationships among them" • "Explains and/or predicts [a] situation, phenomenon [or] behavior" • Can be "refuted, confirmed, [or] adjusted" (Adu, 2020, slide 9)	• Behaviorism • Cognitivism	Abend (2008); Wallis and Wright (2020)

what you are studying, which can sometimes make you feel as if you are looking for a needle in a haystack. After selecting the right model or theory, you are expected to explore what it stands for and the assumptions associated with it. You then demonstrate how it is related to your study and describe the role it will play in the study. The final step is to write about your framework and develop an illustration (if possible) to represent it. A book by Larsen and Adu (2021), *The Theoretical Framework in Phenomenological Research: Development and Application*, details the conceptual/theoretical framework development and writing process.

Identify Theories or Models Related to Your Topic

During this stage, you look at literature to locate specific models and/or theories that are related to what you plan to study. For example, if your study is about how burnout is experienced, you could identify theories or models that explain burnout, such as equity theory, Maslach theory and job demands-resources theory (Larsen & Adu, 2021). In terms of a specific strategy to access potential models and/or theories, you could use a scoping review. Scoping reviews are a type of literature review that focuses on "searching for information about a phenomenon of interest, organizing and analyzing what the researcher found, and providing a summary of the outcome of the review" (Larsen & Adu, 2021, p. 145).

Table 2.6 Questions to ask to select the right model or theory

Question to ask	Yes	No
Is the model or theory identified related to the focus of your study?	Then move on to assess how much the model/ theory covers, explains or addresses what you are studying	Then review other models or theories to see whether they have any connection with what you are studying
Does the model or theory have the potential to fully explain the phenomenon of study?	Then use it to build your conceptual/theoretical framework	Then explore other models or theories that can better explain or complement the initial model or theories in explaining the phenomenon of study

Alternatively, another strategy you could use is to take note of models and theories when reviewing literature. This will save you a lot of time, since you are simultaneously working on reviewing literature and keeping your eyes on potential models and theories for the development of a conceptual/theoretical framework.

You may ask, "How do researchers determine the best model or theory for the development of their framework?" According to Dix (2008), there are two things you should take into consideration when selecting a model or theory for your study: the degree of relatedness and the degree of completeness (Dix, 2008). Assessing whether the potential model or theory relate to what is being studied and how much it covers or explains the focus of the study will help you to determine the right model or theory for your study (Dix, 2008; Larsen & Adu, 2021) (see Table 2.6).

Also, you may ask, "What if I did not get the right model or theory?" We suggest you explore whether more than one model or theory could help explain the phenomenon of study. You could also consider incorporating concepts into the building of your framework.

Examine the Characteristics of the Selected Model or Theory

This is the stage where you learn a lot about the selected model, theory or concepts by addressing the following questions:

- What is the description of the model or theory?
- What is the model or theory explaining?
- How was it created?
- What are the assumptions, limitations and delimitations associated with the model or theory?
- What are the components or concepts associated with the model or theory?
- How is the model or theory related to what you plan to study?
- How much does it explain the phenomenon of study?

Asking yourself these questions will help you to better understand how the selected concepts, model or theory relate or explain the focus of your study. In terms of examining the assumptions related to the selected model or theory, your goal is to find out what needs to exist or be true in order for the model or theory to be valid (Adu, 2023; Epstein, 1984). Concerning the limitations, you need to look for what the model or theory fails to explain or cover because of covering a specific aspect of a phenomenon. Lastly, the deliminations of the model or theory are about what the limits or boundaries of the model or theory are in terms of what kinds of concepts are involved and aspects of the phenomenon of study that can be explained (Adu, 2023).

Determine the Use of the Selected Model or Theory

After selecting the right model or theory, the next step is to determine how you plan to use it in the study. It could be used to explain, represent, justify, inform or view the study (see Table 2.7) (Larsen & Adu, 2021).

- ***Using the model or theory as an explanatory tool:*** You may have identified a problem you plan to study but have limited understanding of areas such as the emergence, frequency, causes and emergence of the problem. A model or theory could be used to help provide a potential explanation of the problem and get a better understanding before the implementation of the study (Larsen & Adu, 2021). It can also be used to explain a topic, facilitating the determination of the focus of the study. In addition, by using it as an explanatory tool, you also assess the model's or theory's strengths and weaknesses in terms of explaining the phenomenon or problem of study.
- ***Using the model or theory as a labeling tool:*** The selected model or theory could be used to help transform practical or lay terms into concepts used within a particular field of study or professional practice (Larsen & Adu, 2021). For instance, concepts associated with a particular model or theory can

Table 2.7 The use of concepts, models and theories and their goals

Use	Goal
Explaining the study	To make meaning of the topic or problem of study
Representing the study	To label relevant ideas in the study
Justifying the study	To establish the reason why it is important to conduct the study
Informing the study	To guide the conceptualization of the problem of study, the development of the research purpose and questions, the determination of a research approach, data collection techniques and data analysis strategies and/or the interpretation of findings
Viewing the study	To carry out a research inquiry from a particular perspective

Source: Adopted from Larsen and Adu (2021, p. 135).

be used to inform the variables you want to measure when conducting a quantitative study. They could also help with the operationalization of the concepts of interest and choosing the right instrument to measure them. In a qualitative study, when conducting content analysis, themes and codes could be generated from the selected model or themes. You can then use these themes and codes (i.e., code frame) to connect to relevant information extracted from the data (Larsen & Adu, 2021).

- *Using the model or theory as a justification tool:* The selected model or theory could be used to justify the decisions and actions taken in your study (Larsen & Adu, 2021). You could use it to support why:
  - It is important to focus on a specific phenomenon and/or address a problem
  - You are focusing on specific concepts or variables
  - You are using a qualitative, quantitative or mixed methods design
  - You are choosing a specific data collection and/or analysis strategy
- *Using the model or theory to inform the study:* The model or theory can be used as a guide, informing how you conceptualize the problem of study, determine and present the focus of the study, construct the research questions, state your hypothesis, determine the research method for the study, collect and analyze the data and present and interpret the findings (Larsen & Adu, 2021).
- *Using the model or theory as a lens:* As a researcher, you could take a certain perspective with the help of the selected model or theory and use the standpoint to conduct the study (Larsen & Adu, 2021).

Writing About the Conceptual/Theoretical Framework

After selecting the right model or theory, learning more about it and determining the role it will play in the study, the next step is to write about your framework. Your goal is to inform your readers about the model or theory, including its characteristics, associated assumptions and components or concepts. In addition, you are also expected to write about how the framework will be used in the study. In case you only have concepts for the development of your conceptual/theoretical framework, you could discuss them and their relationships and how they are going to be utilized in the study.

According to Adu (2020), there are five elements that a good conceptual/theoretical framework should have:

1. The meaning of the concept, model or theory being used to form the framework
2. The kind of phenomenon it represents, including its assumptions, strengths, limitations and delimitations (if any)
3. The connection between the concept, model or theory and what you are studying
4. Utilization of the framework
5. How the concept, model or theory will be used to help implement the framework

There are many ways of writing a conceptual/theoretical framework. The most important thing is to make sure you include all the elements as you creatively write about your framework. Also, at the initial stage of your study, see your conceptual/theoretical framework as a work in progress, continuously perfecting it as the need arises.

Develop an Illustration

Creating a visual representation of your conceptual/theoretical framework is not required but recommended. Design an illustration of your framework, translating the written information about your conceptual/theoretical framework into a visual representation. Having an illustration will help your readers to get a better understanding of the components (concepts) within the framework and the relationship between them. It will also help your readers to make a quick review of the structure of the framework.

There are a lot of concept or mind map tools/software available to create an illustration of your framework. You could even use the SmartArt function in Microsoft Word to create an illustration. Alternatively, you could use Cmap software to create your conceptual/theoretical framework illustration (see: https://cmap.ihmc.us/).

So, what should an illustration of a conceptual/theoretical framework look like? It should reflect what you have written about your framework. We see an illustration as a creative but simplified form of the text description of your framework.

Summary

One of the main ultimate goals of conducting research is to contribute to the body of knowledge in your field. However, you cannot adequately contribute if you are not aware of what has been related to your topic. The best way of having an in-depth knowledge of the current research, discoveries and conversations about your phenomenon of study is to conduct a literature review. The literature review process should be systematic, searching and selecting relevant literature, making meaning of them and writing a synthesis of what you found. Besides conducting a literature review, you are expected to create and/or write about your conceptual/theoretical framework. A framework can be seen as a bridge that connects your study to the existing body of knowledge (Larsen & Adu, 2021). It can also be seen as the foundation on which your study is built (Adu, 2020). As you work on your research proposal, it is important to search for potential theories, models and concepts that are related to your topic and determine the right one to help build your framework. Following the suggestions and strategies discussed above will help you to do an extensive literature review and create a relevant conceptual/theoretical framework.

References

Abend, G. (2008). The meaning of "theory." *Sociological Theory, 26*(2), 173–199. www.jstor. org/stable/20453103

Adu, P. (2019). *A step-by-step guide to qualitative data coding.* Routledge.

Adu, P. (2020, July 12). *Differentiating theoretical and conceptual frameworks* [Video]. YouTube. https://www.youtube.com/watch?v=HZnjOcY9_O0

Adu, P. (2021, January 16). *Doing a systematic literature review* [Video]. YouTube. https://www.youtube.com/watch?v=mf4hQNf34rY

Adu, P. (2023, April 26). *Writing the methodology chapter of your dissertation* [Video]. YouTube. https://youtu.be/NFLzd267UOg

Burkard, A. W., Knox, S., DeWalt, T., Fuller, S., Hill, C., & Schlosser, L. Z. (2014). Dissertation experiences of doctoral graduates from professional psychology programs. *Counselling Psychology Quarterly, 27*(1), 19–54. https://doi.org/10.1080/09515070.2013.821596

Callahan, J. L. (2014). Writing literature reviews: A reprise and update. *Human Resource Development Review, 13*(3), 271–275. https://doi.org/10.1177/1534484314536705

CityU. (2022, December 22). *Literature review – Finding the resources.* https://libguides.library.cityu.edu.hk/litreview/evaluating-sources

Dall'Ora, C., Ball, J., Reinius, M., & Griffiths, P. (2020). Burnout in nursing: A theoretical review. *Human Resources for Health, 18*(1), 41. https://doi.org/10.1186/s12960-020-00469-9

Dix, A. (2008). Theoretical analysis and theory creation. In P. Cairns & A. L. Cox (Eds.), *Research Methods in Human-Computer Interaction* (pp. 175–195). Cambridge University Press.

Epstein, R. (1984). The principle of parsimony and some applications in psychology. *Journal of Mind and Behavior, 5*(2), 119–130.

Frederiksen, L., & Phelps, S. F. (2018). *Literature reviews for education and nursing graduate students.* Rebus Community Press.

Glass-O'Shea, B. (2021). The history and future of genetically modified crops: Frankenfoods, superweeds, and the developing world. *Journal of Food Law & Policy, 7*(1). https://scholarworks.uark.edu/jflp/vol7/iss1/3

Green, H. E. (2014). Use of theoretical and conceptual frameworks in qualitative research. *Nurse Researcher, 21*(6), 34–38. http://doi.org/10.7748/nr.21.6.34.e1252

Gregory, S. T., Menser, T., & Gregory, B. T. (2018). An organizational intervention to reduce physician burnout. *Journal of Healthcare Management / American College of Healthcare Executives, 63*(5), 338–352. https://doi.org/10.1097/JHM-D-16-00037

Hanson, W. E., Creswell, J. W., Clark, V. L. P., Petska, K. S., & Creswell, J. D. (2005). Mixed methods research designs in counseling psychology. *Journal of Counseling Psychology, 52*(2), 224–235. https://doi.org/10.1037/0022-0167.52.2.224

Jaakkola, E. (2020). Designing conceptual articles: Four approaches. *AMS Review, 10*, 18–26.

Jabareen, Y. (2009). Building a conceptual framework: Philosophy, definitions, and procedure. *International Journal of Qualitative Methods, 8*(4), 49–62. https://doi.org/10.1177/160940690900800406

Larsen, H. G. & Adu, P. (2021). *The theoretical framework in phenomenological research: Development and application.* Routledge.

Machi, L. A., & McEvoy, B. T. (2012). *The literature review: Six steps to success.* Corwin Press.

MacInnis, D. J., & de Mello, G. E. (2005). The concept of hope and its relevance to product evaluation and choice. *Journal of Marketing, 69*(1), 1–14. https://doi.org/10.1509/jmkg.69.1.1.55513

McKenzie, J. (2022, June 7). *Grey literature: What it is & how to find it.* Simon Fraser University. www.lib.sfu.ca/help/research-assistance/format-type/grey-literature

Subramanyam, R. (2013). Art of reading a journal article: Methodically and effectively. *Journal of Oral and Maxillofacial Pathology: JOMFP, 17*(1), 65–70. https://doi.org/10.4103/0973-029X.110733

Wallis, E. S., & Wright, B. (2020, June 28). *Basics of theory: A brief, plain language, introduction.* MethodSpace.   www.methodspace.com/blog/basics-of-theory-a-brief-plain-language-introduction

Western University. (2012, September 4). *Grey literature tutorial* [Video]. YouTube. www.youtube.com/watch?v=m9-0ZYnCmAI&list=PLBC826C3769B18E1F

Xiao, Y., & Watson, M. (2019). Guidance on conducting a systematic literature review. *Journal of Planning Education and Research, 39*(1), 93–112. https://doi.org/10.1177/0739456X17723971

3 Understanding the Types of Dissertation Research

Objectives

- Readers will be able to:
  1. Differentiate between traditional research, action research, and program evaluation
  2. Select the type of research they plan to do
  3. Describe the characteristics of each of the types of research

About Dissertation Research

Dissertation research is like any other research. The only difference is that it involves mainly engaging in independent research lead by you but supervised and evaluated by your dissertation committee in fulfillment of your doctoral degree requirements. Research inquiry includes deciding on what kind and scope of problem you plan to study, determining the purpose of the study and the questions that need to be addressed, deciding on an appropriate research method, thinking about and choosing the right data collection and analysis strategies and deciding how the findings should be presented to show how they are addressing the research questions and, in the end, solving the problem identified. Irrespective of the type of research you want to conduct, it should have the above elements.

Types of Dissertation Research

There are three main types of dissertation research: traditional research, action research and program evaluation.

Traditional Research

The main goal of conducting traditional research is to contribute to the body of knowledge in a field. This type of research involves going through the literature, reviewing what has been done and determining what is lacking, which is normally called a research gap. Alternatively, you could critically examine a model, theory, treatment or procedure, identifying a flaw through the process called

DOI: 10.4324/9781003268154-3

problematization. Based on the gap identified, you conduct research to fill it or to contribute to the body of knowledge in your field. What would the five chapters under traditional research look like?

Chapter One

You start chapter one by providing background information on the topic of interest. The "background of the study" section in this chapter focuses on introducing your topic by starting with general information that will draw your readers' attention and prepare the way so that your topic will be well introduced to your readers. You can also describe your research problem, which is the limitation or gap you have identified in the literature. In this section, you tell your readers about what is lacking in the literature that you plan to address. You present to them the purpose of the study, stating what you plan to do in the study. We suggest you make sure there is a consistency between what you plan to do and the problem you want to solve.

After describing the purpose of the study, you present the questions you plan to address. If you plan to conduct a qualitative study, your research question should be open-ended in nature, starting with words such as what, how and why. However, your research questions should be closed-ended in nature if you plan to conduct a quantitative study. For example, "Is there a relationship between job satisfaction and productivity?" If you are not conducting a descriptive quantitative study, you may need to state your hypotheses. For instance, the alternative hypothesis for the above research question would be: " H_a : There is a statistically significant relationship between job satisfaction and productivity."

Next, you present the conceptual or theoretical framework, describing the features of the concepts, model or theory related to the focus of your study, including the role they will play in your study. You could complete the presentation of the framework with a visual representation. You then end the chapter with the "significance of the study" section. This is where you explain why your study is important and what contributions it will make.

Chapter Two

This is the literature review chapter. It contains a description of studies done, including the assertations and conclusions researchers have made in relation to your topic. This kind of content is presented in a synthesized format, with the goal of educating readers about what has been done and discussed in relation to the topic of interest, situating your study amid the body of knowledge in your field and making a case in support of conducting your study. You start this chapter with an overview describing what the chapter is about and what readers should expect.

Next, you describe in detail the process, strategies and outcome of searching for and selecting literature. Describing how you searched for and found the literature helps to improve the credibility of your review and assists future researchers to learn from your literature review procedure. It should include which databases you used, examples of the key words used to extract literature, the criteria you used to select relevant materials and how much literature you selected for the review.

You then move to the main body of the chapter, which contains a commentary about what you found, structured under topics and sub-topics and/or presented in a chronological format. You end this chapter by writing a concluding statement summarizing what has been presented in the chapter.

Chapter Three

This chapter mainly consists of a description of your research methodology for how you plan to carry out your study (if you are writing a proposal) or how you conducted the research (if you are writing a report after completing the study). Assuming you are writing the methodology portion of your proposal, you start this chapter with an overview. This section contains brief information on the problem you plan to address and the purpose of the study, reminding readers about what the research gap is and what you want to find out in the study. In addition, you could state your research questions and/or hypotheses and provide reasons why there is a need to address them. You end the overview section with a description of what readers should expect in the chapter.

The next section would be your research design. In this section, you are expected to state the specific research method you plan to use and describe what it entails. In order words, this section is about explaining what your research approach is, what it is used for and why it is the best approach. In this chapter, there is also a section called "Population and Sample," which houses the description of your data source and what population they will be drawn from. It also contains the selection criteria, sampling technique and number of units/participants for your proposed study. Lastly, you can describe how you plan to recruit participants and where you plan to recruit them from.

In the "Procedure" section, you provide detailed information on how you plan to collect data from participants, including describing the data collection strategy and how it will be used to access and gather information for the data source(s). You then move on to describe the instruments (such as questionnaire, interview questions and observation protocol) you plan to use to collect data under the "Instrumentation" section. You end this chapter with the following sections: validity and reliability, data analysis, limitations, ethical issues and conclusion. Note that the final dissertation should be written in the past tense.

Chapter Four

This chapter mainly focuses on describing how you analyzed your data and presenting the results. It starts with an "Overview" section, which provides a brief description of the problem and the purpose of the study and states what readers should expect in this chapter. This is followed by an optional section called "Research Setting." This will be a good section in which to write about your experience of collecting data, especially the unexpected challenges you faced and how you addressed them.

This section is not a repetition of the "Procedure" section in chapter three but an additional data collection-related experience at the research location (whether physical or virtual). This information could help future researchers to learn from your experience and put your findings in the right perspective, especially if you did a qualitative study.

The next section in chapter four is "Participants' Demographics'." Here is where you describe the number of participants you collected data from and those whose data was included in the main data analysis that led to the generation of results to address your research questions or test your hypotheses. When reporting the demographics of a quantitative study, you are expected to present them in a collective manner, showing mean and standard deviation values for the continuous variables (such as age and work experience) and counts and percentages for categorical data (such as gender and ethnicity). You could provide a collective description of participants' demographics for a qualitative study, but in addition you could consider describing them in an individual format (see Adu, 2016).

"Data Analysis Strategy and Process" is the next section in chapter four. In this section, you provide a detailed description of the data analysis strategies used and how the data was analyzed. This section is followed by the "Results" section. For a quantitative study with hypotheses to test, you could present the findings based on the hypotheses you are testing and state whether they are supported or rejected based on what you have found. For a qualitative study, you normally present the themes based on the research questions you are addressing (Adu, 2016). You end this chapter with a summary touching on the main issues you have described in the chapter.

Five

This chapter contains a chapter overview and a presentation of the main results, an interpretation of the findings and how they relate to the existing study or literature, application and implication of the findings, weaknesses of the study and recommendations for not only future researchers but also practitioners, policy makers and stakeholders (if applicable).

Action Research

Action research involves conducting research about a practical problem with the goal of using the findings to develop an action plan to help address the problem. This type of research is normally conducted by practitioners who plan to conduct research to address an issue they have identified or encountered. Sometimes, researchers with a transformative philosophical paradigm tend to do research with elements of action research, focusing on involving participants in identifying or understanding their problem or developing solutions to address the problem.

You could conduct action research if your goal is to do a study to solve an issue that is happening or has happened such as the impact of COVID-19 on people's livelihood, the increase in petroleum prices and its impact on family living expenses, and the user experience of Web3. Based on Adu's (2017) presentation action research, here are how the chapters will look.

Chapter One

This chapter starts with a background of the problem you plan to address. The goal of this background section is to provide a depiction of what the problem is, how it happened, what the causes and consequences of the problem are, the people who are affected by the problem, what is being done to address it and how stakeholders view the problem. At this point you may not get relevant information to address these areas, but your aim is to present what is known about the problem. Next, you state the problem you want to focus on in the study. We call it a "practical research problem." In this section, you could focus on at least one of the following areas:

- Limited knowledge or understanding of the problem
- Unexplored potential solutions
- Lack of assessment of the current solution
- Lack of an effective solution

You then state what you want to do in the study in the "Purpose of the Study" section. You could use words such as describe, determine, demonstrate, examine, explore, understand, explain, compare and conceptualize to portray what you intend to do in the study. Someone may ask, "What is the 'thing' that you plan to do or conduct?" This is where you state the phenomenon, issue, concepts or variables you plan to study. Also, if you have information about the research location and population (or data sources), you can add this to the purpose statement. Here are examples of a purpose statement:

> *The purpose of this phenomenological study is to understand the college graduates' experience of waiting for a job offer in a Fortune 500 tech company.*
>
> *The purpose of this quasi-experimental study is to determine the effect of personalized learning on students' performance in their statistics course.*

Like traditional research, you write the following sections in addition to the ones described above (see Adu, 2017, slide 7):

- **Research Questions:** Stating the questions you want to address in your study
- **Definition of Key Words:** Stating what the key terms you plan to use in your study mean and represent
- **Conceptual/Theoretical Framework:** Describing, explaining and critiquing the theory, model or concepts you plan to use to inform your study
- **Significance of the Study:** Describing the benefits and contributions your study will make

- **Delimitations:** Describing what your study will and will not cover in terms of the focus of the problem and study, the research location, the population/participants, the number of participants and/or the solution to the problem
- **Limitations:** Describing the shortcomings as a result of the choices made, research tools and strategies you plan to use and actions you plan to take

Chapter Two

This chapter is about reviewing literature to help inform your action research study. By reviewing literature, you can learn more about the problem, best practices related to addressing the problem and theories and models that inform the understanding of the problem and development of a solution. Similar to the literature review chapter for traditional research, you provide an "Overview" section that briefly describes the problem and purpose of the study and what readers should expect in this chapter. You can have a "Literature Search" section, where you describe how you searched for and selected relevant literature and where you accessed it. You then present the review based on the topics and/or a specified sequence, synthesizing what you found.

Chapter Three

The content of the methodology chapter of an action research study is the same as that of a traditional research study. You will have an overview of the chapter, research questions and their justification, research design, population and sample, data collection process, instrumentation, quality assurance (i.e., validity and reliability of the study), data analysis process and ethical issues.

Because of the closeness of the connection between you and what you are studying, it is important to discuss your background, experience, expectations, biases and beliefs with respect to the topic and how you plan to manage these influences. This issue should especially be addressed when using a qualitative approach (Adu, 2017). Therefore, having a section such as "Researcher's Beliefs, Background and Biases" would be great.

Chapter Four

This chapter is mainly about describing how you analyzed your data and presenting the results. It has five main sections: overview, participants' demographics, data analysis process, findings and summary.

Chapter Five

This chapter focuses on discussing the findings, making sense of the results and exploring their practical implication and application. Besides this, you can include research limitations and recommendations for future research practitioners and stakeholders. One distinct feature of this chapter is the action plan. An action plan denotes the road map for how the findings will be used to help address the problem.

Program Evaluation

Program evaluation is the process of assessing the need for a yet-to-be-developed intervention, examining whether there are enough appropriate resources for the implementation of a program, exploring how activities in the program are meeting the expected targets and/or finding out the impact of the program. The outcome of the program assessment can help with the stakeholders' decision to develop, improve or discontinue a program. Program evaluation can be grouped into six types: developmental, formative, implementation, economic, summative and attribution (impact) evaluation.

Let's briefly go through them to help you better understand the main features of each type of evaluation (see Table 3.1).

- *Developmental Evaluation:* This type of evaluation is done before the implementation of the evaluation and focuses on assessing the needs of the potential beneficiaries of the problem, the expectations, roles and views of the stakeholders and the program resources, activities and expected outcomes (Patton, 2012). The results of the developmental evaluation are used to help create a program.
- *Formative Evaluation:* This type of evaluation can also be called a process evaluation. It involves assessing the program resources and activities to see whether they meet the desired expectations (Alkin & Vo, 2018; Patton, 2012). With a formative evaluation, you address questions such as are the program resources enough to carry out the program activities and are the program activities going on as expected? It is conducted during the implementation of the program and the results help to improve the program resources and activities.
- *Implementation Evaluation:* This type of evaluation can also be labeled as an investigative, demonstrative or explanatory evaluation. An implementation evaluation is normally done at the end of the program to examine what happened in the program and to explain what lead to the success or failure of a program or how the program resources and activities led to set goals (Patton, 2012). It is normally used to make a decision on continuing with the program, creating a new program or expanding the intervention (Adu, 2020).
- *Economic Evaluation:* An economic evaluation revolves around cost assessment. The focus is to find out whether a program is worth the financial cost (Office of the Associate Director for Policy and Strategy, 2021). There are three main types of analysis in an economic evaluation:
  - *Program cost analysis:* This is used to determine how much a program will cost (Adu, 2020).
  - *Cost-effectiveness analysis:* This type of analysis is appropriate if you plan to compare the cost of program resources and activities with that of its outcome (Adu, 2020).

Table 3.1 Evaluation purposes and their corresponding evaluation types

Evaluation Purpose	Evaluation Type					
	Developmental Evaluation	Formative Evaluation	Implementation Evaluation	Summative Evaluation	Attribution (Impact) Evaluation	Economic Evaluation
• Explore the conditions that led to the development of a program	Yes					
• Examine a problem of practice that is yet to be addressed	Yes					
• Review changes in the program's input, activity, output and/or outcome	Yes					
• Examine ongoing program implementation		Yes				
• Address concerns about whether the program's inputs, activities and/or outputs are meeting expectations		Yes				
• Create awareness (among program staff or policy implementers) about the state of the inputs, activities and/or outputs		Yes				
• Examine how a program occurred or a policy was executed			Yes			
• Deconstruct the pathway to realizing a program's success or failure			Yes			
• Explain the factors that contributed to a program's success or failure			Yes			
• Examine the outcomes of a program				Yes		
• Assess the benefits of a program for its beneficiaries				Yes		
• Explore the unintended consequences of a program				Yes		
• Determine the causal connection between the program's implementation and outcome(s)					Yes	

Establish if changes in the program participants' behavior, attitudes and/or emotions can be attributed to the program's activities	Yes
Rule out explanations for the attainment of the program's outcomes other than its activities	Yes
Determine the cost of the program's/policy's implementation	Yes
Compare the cost of the program's inputs and outcomes	Yes
Compare the program's cost and the benefits (in monetary terms) of the program	Yes

Source: Adopted from Adu (2020, slides 11–12).

- ***Cost-benefit analysis:*** This involves comparing how much the program cost with the financial benefit of the program (Adu, 2020).

An economic evaluation can be conducted at any stage of the program, whether it is the pre-implementation, implementation or post-implementation stage (Office of the Associate Director for Policy and Strategy, 2021).

- ***Summative evaluation:*** A summative evaluation is conducted at the end of the program, with the goal of assessing its outcomes (Bamberger et al., 2012). If you plan to find out whether a program met a specified target and benefited its participants or to examine the implications of the program, then a summative evaluation will be appropriate.
- ***Attribution (impact) evaluation:*** This type of evaluation focuses on determining the effect of a program (Alkin & Vo, 2018; Patton, 2012). Similar to conducting an experimental or quasi-experimental study, the goal of an impact evaluation is to find out the causal relationship between the program and the observed outcome. An impact evaluation is done at the end of the program, with the aim of utilizing the results to assess whether the program effect was worth the resources invested and activities organized (Adu, 2020).

So, what kind of information is needed in each of the five chapters of a program evaluation dissertation?

Chapter One

In this introductory chapter, you are to provide information about the program, the problem it addresses and its background. You can also describe the stakeholders of the program, including the beneficiaries. In addition, you could present the current state of the program, describing whether it is in its development, implementation or completion stage. Next, you address the following question: What specific problem do you want to solve by conducting an evaluation? This is asking about your evaluation problem. An evaluation problem could be limited information about the needs of the beneficiaries of the program, limited information about resources needed to implement the program, not knowing whether the program is going according to plan and/or a lack of informal assessment of the outcome of the program.

Based on the evaluation problem, you then develop the purpose of the evaluation. Before stating your evaluation purpose, you need to know the type of evaluation you are conducting. For instance, if you plan to conduct a developmental evaluation, you could state the purpose as follows: "*The purpose of this developmental evaluation is to examine the needs of potential beneficiaries of the program and the resources needed to implement the stress reduction program. The findings will be used to design the yet-to-be-developed program.*" Table 3.1 can help you to determine and state the purpose of the study.

After describing the purpose of the evaluation, you then think about specific questions you want to address. Make sure the purpose statement informs the evaluation questions, maintaining consistency between them. There are three main types of evaluation questions: qualitative, quantitative and mixed methods (Adu, 2020). Qualitative evaluation questions are mainly exploratory and open-ended in nature and usually start with *what, how* or *why* (Larsen & Adu, 2021). However, quantitative evaluation questions are normally confirmatory and closed-ended in nature (Adu, 2020). For example, "*Is there a relationship between happiness and job satisfaction?*" Sometimes, you can have a quantitative open-ended question, especially when conducting a descriptive quantitative evaluation study with the purpose of measuring and describing variables using numbers. For example, "*What is the level of job satisfaction among health care workers?*" Lastly, mixed methods evaluation questions are made up of both qualitative and quantitative questions in an evaluation study.

The rest of the sections in chapter one of a program evaluation dissertation are the same as with traditional research and action research. However, the section that is uniquely different is "Conceptual/Theoretical Framework." In this section, you could discuss a theory or group of theories that inform the program and its components, an aspect of the program, the problem being addressed and/or the strategy or perspective you plan to use to conduct the evaluation. The common approach to developing a framework is to use a theory or model to help understand the program and the relationship between them.

A logic model is one of the program models used to help understand the program and its component (Alkin & Vo, 2018; Kettner et al., 2017; Patton, 2012). Under this model, the program can be categorized into five components: inputs, activities, outputs, outcomes and impact.

- Inputs are the resources (including personnel) needed to implement the program (Kettner et al., 2017).
- Activities involve utilizing the program resources to help accomplish the set goals (Kettner et al., 2017).
- Outputs are immediate effects as the results of the program activities carried out (Kettner et al., 2017).
- Outcomes are the benefits of the program on the conditions of the program's beneficiaries (Kettner et al., 2017).
- Impact is about the effect as the results of the implementation of the program (Kettner et al., 2017).

A logic model can be used to build your conceptual/theoretical framework by reviewing the program and categorizing its features into the five components, helping both you (the evaluator) and the stakeholders know what the resources are as well as the specific program activities and their outputs, the results of the program and the impact. Also, it helps you to easily determine which aspect of the program needs to be evaluated.

Chapter Two

There is some flexibility in terms of what you want to present in chapter two, which is the literature review chapter. The most important thing is to have a specific goal in mind in terms of what you plan to achieve by writing a literature review for a program evaluation dissertation. Do you want to educate your readers about the problem being addressed by the program? Do you want to share research done or literature written about the program? Do you want to present theories and models in support of the implementation of the program? Do you want to reach best practices in relation to evaluating a program? Do you want to review literature to justify the selected type of evaluation and/or strategies you plan to use to conduct the evaluation? Do you want to use literature to support the focus of your evaluation and/or the role you plan to play? Having a goal enables you to present a well-structured review of the literature and aids readers in easily following the assertions you made based on what you found in the literature.

Chapter Three

Like the methodology chapter for traditional research, you are expected to provide the following sections: chapter overview, research questions and their justification, research design, population and sample, procedure, instrumentation, research validity and reliability (i.e., quality assurance), data processing, limitations, assumptions, ethical assurance and chapter summary (Adu, 2023). An additional section you could include would be about your roles, background and biases. In this section, you could describe your roles in this evaluation research. Do you see yourself as an internal or external evaluator? What are your responsibilities as an internal or external evaluator? What do you want to share to help your readers know who will be conducting the evaluation? What biases do you have and how do you plan to address them? You could write this section after the research design section.

Chapter Four

This chapter is all about describing how you analyzed your evaluation data and presenting what you found. You start the chapter with the "Chapter Overview" section, where you state the purpose of the evaluation and what readers should expect. You could also have an "Evaluation Setting," which explains what when on during the data collection phase. This helps readers to get a sense of what happened (in terms of the data collection experience, challenges and lesson learned), the context of which data was collected and best practices. The next section is "Participants' Demographics," which focuses on presenting the characteristics of the participants. This section could also be called "Data Source Characteristics," especially when the data includes documents, artifacts and the like. As with traditional research, you then present the following sections: data analysis process, results and summary.

Chapter Five

This discussion chapter contains a summary of the findings, their interpretation and their connection to the literature reviewed. It also has a translation of what was found into practical application, making it easy for readers to determine how the results could be utilized. Here are the sections in chapter five:

- **Overview:** This section provides what readers should expect in chapter five. However, it starts by reminding readers about the problem and purpose of the study.
- **Results Summary:** In this section, you are to provide the main aspects of the findings, especially the areas where your interpretation is based.
- **Results Interpretation:** This section includes providing your understanding of the findings, presenting your views, patterns seen, projections, assertions and/ or evaluations (Bloomberg & Volpe, 2008). Who will be reading this report or document should always be kept in mind when communicating the meanings being derived. You could also connect to the best practices or literature you reviewed in chapter two.
- **Results Utilization:** Here is where you describe how the results will be used and who should use them.
- **Limitations of the Study:** In this section, you write about any shortcomings as the result of the decision and action you took in the evaluation study.
- **Recommendations:** In this section, you share your suggestions, looking at the entire evaluation process and outcomes. What should be done to the program? What should future evaluators do? What should stakeholders learn from the evaluation? These are some of the questions you could address in this section.
- **Conclusion:** You then provide a concluding statement summarizing and briefly synthesizing what you have written in the sections above. One strategy is to write a sentence or two to represent each of the above sections.

Summary

Not all dissertations are the same in terms of how the chapters and their sections should be structured. Knowing what type of dissertation you are doing will help you to properly structure your study to reflect the characteristics of the selected type of research. In this chapter, we discussed the three types of research, namely, traditional research, action research and program evaluation. To recap, if you plan to address a practical problem by doing a study to understand the problem and general solutions and/or implement a solution to see its impact, then action research will be best. However, if your focus is on doing research to address a gap identified in the literature or a problem generated from a theory or model, then traditional research will be appropriate. The final type of research is program evaluation, which involves doing research to help develop a program, assess on ongoing program or review the outcome or impact of a completed program. Knowing your dissertation type will influence the way you conduct and write about the study.

References

Adu, P. (2016, August 25). *Conducting qualitative analysis using NVivo 11 (Part3) by Philip Adu, Ph.D.* [Video]. YouTube. www.youtube.com/watch?v=xEyGGFtVQFw

Adu, P. (2017, September 6). *Action research dissertation: What to think about (Philip Adu, PhD)* [Video]. YouTube. www.youtube.com/watch?v=S4sWHYMG5cQ

Adu, P. (2020, April 21). *Program evaluation questions with Philip Adu* [Video]. YouTube. www.youtube.com/watch?v=YJA--ZfGE7s

Adu, P. (2023, April 26). *Writing the methodology chapter of your dissertation* [Video]. YouTube. https://youtu.be/NFLzd267UOg

Alkin, M. C., & Vo, A. T. (2018). *Evaluation essentials from A to Z.* Guilford Press.

Bamberger, M., Rugh, J., & Mabry, L. (2012). *RealWorld evaluation: Working under budget, time, data, and political constraints.* SAGE.

Bloomberg, L. D., & Volpe, M. (2008). *Completing your qualitative dissertation: A roadmap from beginning to end.* SAGE Publications, Inc. https://dx.doi.org/10.4135/9781452226613

Kettner, P. M., Moroney, R. M., & Martin, L. L. (2017). *Designing and managing programs: An effectiveness-based approach.* SAGE.

Larsen, H. G. & Adu, P. (2021). *The theoretical framework in phenomenological research: Development and application.* Routledge.

Office of the Associate Director for Policy and Strategy. (2021, March 3). *Economic evaluation overview.* Centers for Disease Control and Prevention. www.cdc.gov/policy/polaris/economics/index.html

Patton, M. Q. (2012). *Essentials of utilization-focused evaluation.* SAGE.

4   Choosing an Appropriate Research Methodology

Objectives

- Readers will be able to:
  1. Distinguish between the three main research approaches
  2. Decide on an appropriate research method
  3. Write about the selected research method

About Research Methodology

The research method can be regarded as the research inquiry tool used to complete the research task stated in the purpose statement and framed in the research question(s) or hypotheses. This implies that, typically, you must know what you want to find out in the study, including the questions you want to address or hypotheses you want to test, before thinking about the appropriate method for your study. However, besides this linear strategy of coming up with the best research approach, there is a possibility that a researcher could first consider the research tool they are familiar with and structure the purpose and questions to align with the chosen method. Whether you want to take the linear or non-linear route, the most important thing is to ensure that there is consistency between the purpose of the study, the research questions or hypotheses and the selected research method. There are three main types of research methods: quantitative, qualitative and mixed methods (Creswell & Creswell, 2018).

Exploring Quantitative Research Methods

What comes to mind when we hear of a quantitative method is a research tool used to help measure variables or quantify observations. It also assists in collecting and analyzing data in numerical form, aiding in addressing research questions or testing hypotheses. Examples of studies that warrant the use of a quantitative approach include:

- Determining the quality of life among a group of people
- Examining the relationship between job satisfaction and work performance
- Finding the impact of substance abuse on quality of life

DOI: 10.4324/9781003268154-4

Aliaga and Gunderson (2002) define quantitative research methods as explaining phenomena by collecting numerical data that are analyzed using mathematically based methods (in particular statistics). Muijs (2004) defines quantitative research as collecting numerical data. This is closely connected to the final part of the definition: analysis using mathematically based methods. He also states that, in order to be able to use mathematically based methods, our data have to be in numerical form. He also refers to the use of mathematically based methods, in particular statistics, to analyze the data.

Creswell (2003) asserts that quantitative research originated in the physical sciences, particularly in chemistry and physics. The researcher uses mathematical models as the methodology of data analysis. Three historical trends pertaining to quantitative research include research design, test and measurement procedures and statistical analysis. Quantitative research also involves data collection that is typically numeric, and the researcher tends to use mathematical models as the methodology of data analysis. Additionally, the researcher uses inquiry methods to ensure alignment with the statistical data collection methodology.

In addition, according to Cohen and Manion (1980), quantitative research is defined as social research that employs empirical methods and empirical statements. He further states that an empirical statement is defined as a descriptive statement about what "is" the case in the "real world" rather than what "ought" to be the case. Typically, empirical statements are expressed in numerical terms. Another factor in quantitative research is that empirical evaluations are applied. Empirical evaluations are defined as a form that seeks to determine the degree to which a specific program or policy empirically fulfills or does not fulfill a particular standard or norm (Sukamolson, 2007). Furthermore, a quantitative research method deals with quantifying and analyzing variables in order to get results. It involves the utilization and analysis of numerical data using specific statistical techniques to answer questions such as *who, how much, what, where, when, how many* and *how* (Leedy & Ormrod, 2010).

When Do We Use Quantitative Methods?

Muijs (2004) defines five main advantages of quantitative research:

1. "Quantitative research is good at providing information in breadth from a large number of units, but when we want to explore a problem or concept in depth quantitative methods are too shallow. To really get under the skin of a phenomenon, we will need to go for ethnographic methods, interviews, in-depth case studies and other qualitative techniques" (p. 7).
2. "Quantitative research is well suited for the testing of theories and hypotheses. What quantitative methods cannot do very well is develop hypotheses and theories. The hypotheses to be tested may come from a review of the literature or theory, but can also be developed using exploratory qualitative research" (p. 8).
3. Quantitative research is well suited for when we often want to explain phenomena. What factors predict the recruitment of mathematics teachers? What

factors are related to changes in student achievement over time? As we will see later in this book, these kinds of questions can also be studied successfully using quantitative methods, and many statistical techniques have been developed that allow us to predict scores on one factor or variable (e.g., teacher recruitment) from scores on one or more other factors or variables (e.g., unemployment rates, pay, conditions).

4. Quantitative research is well suited for testing hypotheses. We might want to explain something, for example whether there is a relationship between a pupil's achievement and their self-esteem and social background. We could look at the theory and come up with the hypothesis that a lower social class background leads to low self-esteem, which would in turn be related to low achievement. Using quantitative research, we can try and test this kind of model.

5. Quantitative research is well suited "for looking at cause and effect (causality, as it is known), qualitative methods are more suited to looking at the meaning of particular events or circumstances" (p. 8).

Many students look at quantitative research as an avenue for conducting statistical based research. As we have shown, quantitative research has advantages over qualitative research methods. Muijs (2004) argues that quantitative research is often placed in opposition to qualitative research. This belief is often turned into a "paradigm war," which is seen to result from the apparently incompatible worldviews underlying the methods. However, when looking at researchers' actual beliefs, it appears that the so-called subjectivist (qualitative) versus realist (quantitative) divide is not that clear-cut.

Types of Quantitative Methods

There are different types and varieties of quantitative methods. In this book, we focus on the most commonly used quantitative methods. There are five core quantitative research designs that are commonly used with dissertation studies:

- Descriptive method
- Correlational method
- Causal-comparative method
- Experimental method
- Quasi-experimental method

Leedy and Ormrod (2010) assert that there are three broad classifications of quantitative research: descriptive, experimental and causal-comparative. The descriptive research approach is a basic research method that examines the situation as it exists in its current state. There are three types of exploratory approaches: pre-experimental, true-experimental and quasi-experimental (Leedy and Ormrod, 2010). The pre-experimental design involves an independent variable that does not vary or a control group that is not randomly selected. The true experimental design results in a systemic approach to quantitative data collection involving mathematical models in the analyses. However, the quasi-experimental design involves a nonrandom selection of study participants. Therefore, control is limited and true experimentation is not possible. Since the variable cannot be controlled, validity may be sacrificed.

Descriptive research involves the identification of attributes of a particular phenomenon based on an observational basis, or the exploration of a correlation between two or more phenomena (Williams, 2007). In causal-comparative research, the researcher examines how the independent variables are affected by the dependent variables and looks at the cause-and-effect relationships between the variables. The factorial design focuses on two or more categories with independent variables as compared to dependent variables (Vogt, 1999). The causal-comparative research design provides the researcher with the opportunity to examine the interaction between independent variables and their influence on dependent variables (Vogt, 1999).

Descriptive Method

This quantitative method is used when you plan to measure a variable or a group of variables and conduct descriptive statistics to help address your research question. For example, let's say you plan to explore parents' perceptions about homeschooling and your research question is, "*What are the perceptions of parents about homeschooling?*" The appropriate qualitative research approach is the descriptive method, since you plan to use an instrument to measure the parents' perceptions and report what you have found. You could report the mean score with the standard deviation of their perception.

In many cases, descriptive study designs are useful for simply describing the desired characteristics of the sample that is being studied, e.g., an abnormal presentation of a disease in a case report or a case series that includes a collection of cases with the same disease/condition. A descriptive study may also try to generalize the findings from a representative sample to a larger target population as in a cross-sectional survey. The common aspect between the descriptive study designs is that there is only one single sample without any comparison group (Omair, 2015).

Furthermore, descriptive research involves collecting data in order to answer questions or test hypotheses concerning the current status of the situation under study (Long et al., 1985). In the behavioral sciences, descriptive research can be classified as survey research or observational research (Long et al., 1985). For example, survey research typically employs questionnaires or in some cases interviews to determine people's opinions, attitudes and perceptions about a situation being studied. Typically, survey research ordinarily uses quantitative methods (Long et al., 1985).

With the descriptions approach, your focus is on measuring something about your participants in order to learn about them. The descriptive approach does not allow for determining relationships between variables. However, your goal is to use numbers to describe the variable of interest.

Alternatively, you could see the descriptive research method as a quantitative research tool used to learn about the sample you have drawn from a population. It can also be viewed as a tool used to learn about an instrument in terms of its validity and reliability. For instance, you could conduct a descriptive quantitative study with the purpose of validating an instrument, determining whether it is measuring what is supposed to measure (e.g., validity) and if it is providing a consistent measure (e.g., reliability) (see Williams et al., 2010).

Common Statistical Tests used with Descriptive Research Designs

The common statistical tests for a descriptive research design are used for focusing on minimal inferential analyses. Again, descriptive research provides an account of the characteristics of individuals, groups or situations. The objective in using descriptive research designs is that, by using descriptive statistics, the researcher reports on the frequency and percentages of the data sample.

When conducting statistical tests for a descriptive research design, there are three commonly used tests: (a) descriptive statistics; (b) frequency distribution; and (c) crosstab analysis. Descriptive statistics is used to describe the characteristics in the data such as the range, which is the mean, mode and median. Next, the frequency distribution is used to describe the frequency and percentages of the data's variables (e.g., the distribution of students in college is by year, listing the number or percentage of students at each of the four years).

Lastly, crosstab analysis is used to quantitatively analyze the relationship between multiple variables. Cross tabulations are also commonly referred to as *contingency tables*. Crosstab analysis groups variables together and enables researchers to understand the correlation between the different variables.

These are the best approaches for using statistical tests with descriptive statistics designs.

Correlational Method

This method is used if you plan to determine the relationship between variables. For instance, you could use the correlational method for a study that focuses on determining whether there is a relationship between exercise and quality of life. In this case, you would identify your population, recruit the right number of participants and ask them to complete a survey measuring the frequency of exercise and degree of their quality of life. You then run a correlation analysis to find out whether the relationship between the two variables is statistically significant. If there is a correlation between them, you could also review the direction (i.e., there is a positive or negative relationship) and the strength (i.e., there is a small, medium or strong relationship).

Correlational research involves collecting data to determine the existence of a relationship between two or more variables and to estimate the relationship's magnitude. This relationship is usually described by a statistic called the Pearson Product-Moment Correlation Coefficient, Pearson's *r* or the correlation coefficient. This number, which is between −1.00 and 1.00, describes the extent of a linear relationship between two variables; that is, how closely the points represented by ordered pairs of individuals' scores on each variable approximate a straight line when graphed in a coordinate system. The values of −1.00 and 1.00 indicate a perfect linear relationship (inverse and direct respectively), while a value of .00 indicates no linear relationship. Values approaching +1.00 indicate a strong positive correlation, values nearing −1.00 mean that a strong negative correlation exists, and values closer to zero indicate a weak or lack of correlation. In this case, the r value is −.975, meaning that a strong negative correlation does exist, just as we expected. Generally, the strength of the linear relationship is measured by squaring the correlation coefficient (Long et al., 1985; Terrell, 2017).

Furthermore, correlational research studies are usually classified as relationship studies. Relationship studies examine the association between measures of different variables obtained at approximately the same time. In addition to investigating relationships between variables of interest, these studies often try to obtain a better understanding of factors that make up a complex construct such as intelligence, self-concept or school ability. Relationship studies are also often done as a preliminary to causal-comparative and experimental studies in order to identify important variables that the researcher may want to include in the design of later studies. In addition, correlational research studies normally employ quantitative methods, so a dissertation involving correlational research would use the aforementioned format (Terrell, 2017). In correlational research, the investigator deliberately seeks to examine links (or relationships) between variables without introducing an intervention (Williams, 2007).

Rule #1: Correlation is Not Prediction; Prediction is Not Correlation. When you are conducting correlation research (or relationship research), you must understand that measuring a relationship between two variables (usually two dependent variables) is not prediction or measuring a causal relationship. A considerable number of doctoral students get this wrong. They fail to understand the relationship differences between the dependent variables and independent variables and the independent variables and dependent variables. That is the key difference. Again, correlational research studies are usually classified as relationship studies. The point is that relationship studies examine the association between measures of different variables obtained at approximately the same time. In addition to investigating relationships between variables of interest, these studies often try to obtain a better understanding of factors that make up a complex construct (Williams, 2007). Correlation is not the same as prediction. Furthermore, prediction is not correlation.

Rule #2: You Cannot Correlate Independent Variables with Dependent Variables. When you are conducting prediction research (or causal research), you must understand that measuring a causal relationship between two variables or predictions is measuring a causal relationship. You are measuring the relationship between the independent variables and the dependent variables. Again, a considerable number of doctoral students get this wrong.

Again, the casual relationship measurement between the independent variable and the dependent variable is not a correlational relationship. You cannot measure and correlate independent variables with dependent variables. That is a statistical no-no. Most likely you will not find a correlative relationship between the independent variables and dependent variables for two key reasons: (1) because of issues with *unidimentionality* between the independent variables and dependent variables; each of the scales between the independent variables and dependent variables are different in scale variables content and do not align; and (2) because you cannot correlate independent variables with dependent variables. It will create a false positive or false negative correlation coefficient and cannot be relied on for the results. That is wrong (Miles, 2021).

Common Statistical Tests Used with Correlation Research Designs

The common statistical tests used for correlation research designs are used for measuring relationships. Again, correlational research attempts to determine the extent of a relationship between two or more variables using statistical data. The objective in using correlational research is for the researcher to examine links (or relationships) between variables without introducing an intervention.

When conducting statistical tests for a correlational research design, there are two commonly used tests: Pearson's *r* and Spearman's *r* (see Table 4.1). Pearson's *r* is

Table 4.1 Quantitative research designs and their respective purposes and statistical analyses

Quantitative Research Design	Purpose	Statistical Test Used for Analysis
Descriptive method	The purpose of the descriptive research methodology is to provide an account of the characteristics of individuals, groups or situations. The aim of the descriptive method is to "discover new meaning," describe what exists, determine the frequency with which something occurs and categorize information.	• Descriptive statistics • Frequency distribution • Crosstab analysis
Correlational method	The purpose of the correlational methodology is to determine the extent of a relationship between two or more variables. Variables are not manipulated; they are only identified and are studied as they occur in a natural setting.	• Pearson's *r* • Spearman's *r** • Chi square test of independence*

(Continued)

Table 4.1 (Continued)

Quantitative Research Design	Purpose	Statistical Test Used for Analysis
Causal-comparative method	The purpose of the causal-comparative methodology is to examine cause-and-effect relationships between nonrandom variables. Subjects are not randomly assigned groups and must use ones that are naturally formed or pre-existing groups.	• Paired sample t-test • Independent t-test • Simple linear regression • Multiple linear regression • Logistic regression • Wilcoxon Rank-Sum test* • Wilcoxon Signed-rank test*
Experimental method	The purpose of the experimental methodology is to investigate cause-and-effect relationships between the random independent variable and dependent variable in an experiment. Subjects are randomly assigned to experimental treatments rather than identified in naturally occurring groups. Also pre-test and post-test designs are used to investigate the effect of a treatment in an experiment.	• Paired sample t-test • Independent t-test • Simple linear regression • Multiple linear regression • Logistic regression • Time series analysis • Wilcoxon rank-sum test* • Wilcoxon signed-rank test*
Quasi-experimental method	The purpose of the quasi-experimental methodology is to compare and contrast groups. The researcher examines groups. The *non-equivalent groups* approach is commonly used for this methodology. This methodology examines the *post facto* effects of an intervention on groups and examines the group differences. At the heart of experimental research is the ability to randomly assign membership to a group, as well as treatment to a specific group.	• Paired sample t-test • Independent t-test • ANOVA • MANOVA • ANCOVA • MANCOVA • Discriminant analysis • Time series analysis • Kruskal–Wallis *H** • ANOSIM* • Wilcoxon rank-sum test* • Wilcoxon signed-rank test*

Note: *Asterisk denotes non-parametric statistical test.

used to describe the Pearson's correlation coefficient, which is the test statistics that measures the statistical relationship, or association, between two variables. It is the best method for calculating the number between -1.00 and 1.00 that measures the strength and direction of the relationship between two variables.

Lastly, Spearman's *r* is the nonparametric counterpart to Pearson's *r* that measures rank correlation (statistical dependence between the rankings of two variables). It is used to assess how well you have two ranked variables and when you want to see whether the two variables covary. Again, Spearman's *r* is a nonparametric correlation analysis. It is best used and is more appropriate for measurements taken from ordinal scales. Spearman's rank correlation measures the strength and direction of association between two ranked variables.

Causal-Comparative Method

The causal-comparative method of research design was formerly another name for the quasi-experimental research design. This type of method is used if you plan to determine a causal relationship between variables. A causal-comparative method of research attempts to measure cause-and-effect relationships between two variables. Most often, a researcher seeks to provide evidence for cause-and-effect relationships by examining the effect of one or more variables (independent) on another variable (dependent), without being able to manipulate any of the variables. Thus, this type of research is called causal-comparative. Causal-comparative research occurs frequently in the behavioral sciences because the manipulation of many variables, such as personality traits, race, handicaps, ability, smoking, diseases and home experiences, is impossible, impractical or unethical (Long et al., 1985).

Casual-comparative studies are also called *prediction studies*. Prediction studies involve the establishment of an equation that is used to predict future performance on some variable, called the dependent variable or criterion, using information obtained from other variables, called the independent variables or predictors. In addition to predicting performance on criterion, researchers often seek to identify which predictors are most important in explaining changes in the criterion. Prediction studies are used to aid in the selection or placement of individuals, to identify individuals to perform certain tasks or receive special services, to determine the criterion-related or predictive validity of measuring instruments and to test hypotheses concerning variables believed to be predictors of a given criterion (Long et al., 1985).

In causal-comparative research, the researcher examines how the independent variables are affected by the dependent variables and looks at cause-and-effect relationships between the variables. The factorial design focuses on two or more categories with the independent variables as compared to the dependent variables (Vogt, 1999). The causal-comparative research design provides the researcher with the opportunity to examine the interaction between independent variables and their influence on dependent variables (Williams, 2007).

Rule #3: Independent Variable = "Cause" and Dependent Variable = "Effect." Two rules that doctoral students should remember regarding the distinction between the two variables: (1) independent variables equal "cause"; and (2) dependent variables equal "effect." These two rules are what drives the causal-comparative or predictive research. If the novice researcher can remember these

two rules, it will save them a lot of confusion and misunderstanding concerning the role of the variables in their study.

The following example is typical of causal-comparative research. In attempting to explain differences in the reading performance of first graders, a researcher might hypothesize that parents reading to the child at home for 30 minutes or more each day is the major contributing factor. To test this hypothesis, the researcher could select a group of first graders whose parents read to them every day for 30 minutes or more and a group whose parents don't do this. If the group whose parents do read to them every day for at least 30 minutes has a higher reading performance, then the researcher's hypothesis would apparently be supported. Alternatively, the researcher could select a group of better readers and a group of poorer readers and determine the number of children in each group whose parents read to them for at least 30 minutes each day. If this number is higher in the better readers' group, then once again the researcher's hypothesis would apparently be supported (Long et al., 1985).

An association between variables is not sufficient evidence of causality. Furthermore, a researcher cannot determine simply by examining the association between two variables (Long et al., 1985).

Ordinarily, the methods used to analyze data from a causal-comparative study are the same as those used to analyze data from an experimental research study. Some additional examples of causal-comparative studies are an investigation into whether smoking is a factor in the development of lung cancer, an examination of factors contributing to different dropout rates among black and white urban secondary school students, and a comparison of the language development of hearing-impaired students with hearing parents and hearing-impaired students with hearing-impaired parents (Long et al., 1985).

Common Statistical Tests Used with Causal-Comparative Research Designs

The common statistical tests for a causal-comparative research design are used for focusing on minimal inferential analyses. Again, the objective of the causal-comparative research design is to examine cause-and-effect relationships between nonrandom variables. Subjects are not randomly assigned groups and must use ones that are naturally formed or pre-existing groups in the data.

When conducting statistical tests for a descriptive research design, there are five commonly used tests: (a) paired sample t-test; (b) independent t-test; (c) simple linear regression; (d) multiple linear regression; and (e) logistic regression.

First is the *paired sample t-test*, which is used to determine whether the mean difference between two sets of observations is zero. In a paired sample t-test, each subject or entity is measured twice, resulting in pairs of observations.

Second is the *independent t-test*, which is used to assesses whether the means of two groups, or conditions, are statistically different from one other. They are reasonably powerful tests used on data that is parametric and normally distributed.

Third is the *simple linear regression*, which is used to estimate the relationship between one independent variable and one dependent variable using a straight line. In addition, the simple linear regression is a statistical method that allows the researcher to summarize and study relationships between two continuous variables.

Fourth is the *multiple linear regression*, which uses several explanatory variables to predict the outcome of a response variable. The key objective of multiple linear regression analysis is to use the independent variables whose values are known to predict the value of the single dependent value. The multiple linear regression is an extension of the simple linear regression that uses just one explanatory variable. Furthermore, as a predictive analytic, the multiple linear regression is also used to explain the relationship between one continuous dependent variable and two or more independent variables.

Lastly, the *logistic regression* is used when the dependent variable is dichotomous (binary). Like the other types of regression analyses, the logistic regression is a predictive analytic. Researchers use a logistic regression to predict a dependent data variable by analyzing the relationship between one or more existing independent variables.

The logistic regression estimates the probability of an event occurring, such as if a voter voted or didn't vote, based on a given dataset of independent variables. These five statistical tests are the best approaches for using statistical tests with a causal-comparative research design.

Experimental Method

Experimental research is regarded by many as the optimum quantitative methodology for obtaining reliable information about the treatment or intervention effect (Walker, 2005). The basis of the experimental method is the experiment, which can be defined as a test under controlled conditions that is made to demonstrate a known truth or examine the validity of a hypothesis (Muijs, 2004). A key element of experimental research is control, and this is where it differs from non-experimental quantitative research. The issue is that, when doing an experiment, the researcher wants to control the environment as much as possible and only concentrate on those variables that they want to study. Therefore, this is why most experiments traditionally take place in such places as laboratories, environments where all extraneous influences can be controlled. Furthermore, in non-experimental research, the researcher will not be able to control out extraneous influences (Muijs, 2004).

The purpose of an experiment is to determine the degree to which outcomes of interest are caused by the treatment (intervention) as opposed to extraneous factors. The true or randomized experiment is generally considered best equipped to provide such evidence due to its control over possible sampling bias (Spector et al., 2008). The basis of experimental research involves an examination of the effects of at least one independent variable on one or more dependent variables while the other relevant variables are controlled. Direct manipulation of at least one independent variable is the main characteristic that differentiates experimental research from other methods. Experimental studies provide the strongest evidence for cause-and-effect relationships (Long et al., 1985). Kerlinger (1986) asserts that experimental research fulfills the ideal of science by addressing research questions less ambiguously than other methods of research. Random sampling, manipulation and control are the characteristics of "true" experimental research.

A good research design maximizes both the internal and external validity of an experiment. *Internal validity* is the extent to which changes in the dependent variable can be attributed to changes in an independent variable. However, external validity refers to the generalizability or representativeness of the findings (Long et al., 1985). Campbell et al. (1966) provide an extensive treatment of threats to the internal and external validity of experiments and suggest designs that control for these threats.

One common way to control for extraneous variables is through randomization. Randomization primarily refers to the random assignment of individuals to experimental conditions. Ideally, random assignment should follow the random selection of the sample from the population. Random assignment is the primary way of reducing the initial differences between groups. Experimental designs in which random assignment to groups is not possible are called *quasi-experimental* (Long et al., 1985).

Extraneous variables can also be controlled for by introducing them directly into the design and including them as sources of variation in the statistical model used to analyze the data. For example, the use of blocking variables in the analysis of variance, covariates in the analysis of covariance and predictors entered prior to other independent variables in regression provides statistical control for the variables involved. Experimental research studies are normally considered to be quantitative because of the frequent use of descriptive and inferential statistics in the analysis of data from studies (Long et al., 1985).

Pre-Experimental Designs

Typically, when a researcher is conducting a pre-experimental study, it means that the researcher is conducting a study with only one group. Unlike in a quasi-experimental study, the researcher does manipulate any variables and is able to randomly assign subjects to groups formed by combinations of these variables (Long et al., 1985).

Pre-test/Post-test Experimental Designs

The traditional experimental design is also known as the pre-test/post-test control group design. It works as follows: participants (often known as "subjects" in experimental research) are placed into two groups, the experimental group and the control group. The experimental group will receive the "treatment" (e.g., watching a violent music video). However, the control group will not. Both groups will receive a pre-test on whatever instrument is used to assess the effect of the experiment (e.g., a test) before the treatment is given and a post-test, usually on the same instrument, after the treatment has been given (Muijs, 2004; Terrell, 2017).

The Static Group Comparison Design

The last of the pre-experimental designs, the static group comparison is very similar to the one-shot case study, which is when you are comparing the post-test performance of two groups, with no pre-test information available (Long et al., 1985).

Common Statistical Tests Used with Experimental Research Designs

The common statistical tests for an experimental research design are used for focusing on minimal inferential analyses. Again, the objective of the experimental research design is to examine cause-and-effect relationships between nonrandom variables. Subjects are not randomly assigned groups and must use ones that are naturally formed or pre-existing groups in the data. When conducting statistical tests for a descriptive research design, there are six commonly used tests: (a) paired sample t-test; (b) independent t-test; (c) simple linear regression; (d) multiple linear regression; (e) logistic regression; and (f) time series analysis.

First, again, when doing a statistical test using the paired sample t-test, it is primarily used to determine whether the mean difference between two sets of observations is zero. Furthermore, with the paired sample t-test, each subject or entity is measured twice, resulting in pairs of observations.

Second, the independent t-test is used to assesses whether the means of two groups, or conditions, are statistically different from one other. In addition, they are reasonably powerful tests used on data that is parametric and normally distributed.

Third, the simple linear regression is used to estimate the relationship between one independent variable and one dependent variable using a straight line. It is a statistical method that allows the researcher to summarize and study relationships between two continuous variables.

Fourth, the multiple linear regression is used for several explanatory variables to predict the outcome of a response variable. One key objective of using the multiple linear regression analysis is to use the independent variables' values that are known to predict the value of the single dependent value. The multiple linear regression is also used to explain the relationship between one continuous dependent variable and two or more independent variables. That is what makes it a powerful tool in experimental research designs.

Fifth is the logistic regression, which is used when the dependent variable is dichotomous (binary). Again, the logistic regression is a predictive analytic. The researcher uses a logistic regression to predict a dependent data variable by analyzing the relationship between one or more existing independent variables. That is what makes it another powerful tool in experimental research designs.

Lastly, the time series analysis is used to analyze a sequence of data points collected over an interval of time. The objective of using a time series analysis is to record data points at consistent intervals over a set period of time rather than just recording data points intermittently or randomly. What makes the time series analysis a powerful tool in experimental designs is that the analysis can show how variables change over time. Time series analysis has the advantage of showing how the data adjusts over the course of the data points as well as the final results. Its other advantage is that it provides an additional source of information and a set order of dependencies between the data. These six statistical tests are the best approaches to use in experimental research designs.

Quasi-Experimental Method

Quasi-experimental research is also referred to as *ex post facto* research, since both the effect and the alleged cause have already occurred and are studied by the researcher "after the fact." Typically, a researcher observes groups that differ in some variable (the alleged effect) and attempts to identify factors that have led to this difference. Unlike the experimental researcher, the quasi-experimental researcher does not manipulate any variables and is not able to randomly assign subjects to groups formed by combinations of these variables (Long et al., 1985; Pedhazur, 1982).

A quasi-experimental design differs from an experimental design, in that, in the former, the treatment is consciously manipulated by the researcher, but the units are not randomly assigned to treatment and control groups. Thus, this design offers less of a basis for assuming the initial equivalence of treatment and control groups and requires researchers to consider how third, extraneous variables might confound efforts at ascertaining causal effects and to be explicit about alternative hypotheses (Munck & Verkuilen, 2005). Lastly, an important component of the quasi-experimental study is the use of the pre-testing or analysis of prior achievement to establish group equivalence (Spector et al., 2008).

At the heart of experimental research is the ability to randomly assign membership to a group, as well as treatment to a specific group. Unfortunately, sometimes this is not possible. For example, if the researcher is interested in comparison and cannot assign membership to a city, a class or an organization, the researcher has to work with the groups they have. With that in mind, the researcher has to control for threats to validity rising from these types of studies. Furthermore, the researcher, for reasons beyond his control, is using pre-existing groups with a treatment randomly assigned to one of the groups (Terrell, 2017).

Researchers need to recognize two important limitations of quasi-experimental research that may make the interpretation of such studies very difficult. First, since the independent variables cannot be manipulated, the researcher must be content with analyzing the differences between variable groups (Long et al., 1985). Second, since subjects cannot be randomly assigned to groups, control over other relevant variables is seriously restricted. Groups that have already been established may differ on other important variables that contribute to differences in the variables of interest. The issue here, basically, is proper model specification. In our example, only differences in parent practices were considered as contributing to differences in reading achievement (Long et al., 1985).

Common Quasi-Experimental Method: Non-Equivalent Control Group Design.

The most common type of quasi-experimental research is the *non-equivalent control group design*. It is primarily used for measuring differences between groups in the study. A non-equivalent control group design is a quasi-experimental design in which the responses of a treatment group and a control group are compared on measures collected at the beginning and end of the research (Cook & Campbell, 1979; Shadish et al., 2001; Reichardt, 2019).

The most commonly used quasi-experimental designs are nonequivalent group pre-test/post-test group design, control-group interrupted time series design, single group interrupted time-series design and counterbalanced design (Sousa et al., 2007).

The non-equivalent pre-test/post-test control group design is identical in many ways to the pre-test/post-test control group design, except that subjects are not randomly (NR) assigned to groups. Both groups are pre-tested (O) and post-tested (O). However, only the experimental group is exposed to a treatment (X) (Sousa et al., 2007).

In psychology and other social sciences, these designs often involve self-selection, in which the members of the treatment group are those who volunteer or otherwise seek the treatment, whereas the comparison group members do not. Since participants are not assigned to conditions at random, the two groups are likely to exhibit pre-existing differences on both measured and unmeasured factors that must be taken into account during statistical analyses (VandenBos, 2015).

Common Statistical Tests Used with Quasi-Experimental Research Designs

When using a quasi-experimental research design, in contrast to an experimental design, the participants are not randomly assigned to treatments. Furthermore, with the quasi-experimental design the participants are not randomly assigned to any controlled treatments or environments. Considering that quasi-experiments use pre-existing groups or convenience samples that are not randomly composed, this makes the research more attainable in terms of achieving results (Spector et al., 2008).

There is an important component to the quasi-experimental research design. Quasi-experimental study is the use of the pre-testing or analysis of prior achievement to establish group equivalence. In the true experiment, randomization makes it improbable that one group will be significantly superior in ability to another, but systematic bias can easily be introduced in the quasi-experiment; for example, although the first- and third-period algebra classes may have the same teacher and identical lessons, it may be the case that honors English is offered in the third period only, thus restricting those honors students to taking first-period algebra (Spector et al., 2008).

When conducting statistical tests under a quasi-experimental research design, there are three commonly used tests: (a) t-Test; (b) Analysis of Variance (ANOVA);

and (c) Multiple Analysis of Variance (MANOVA). t-Tests are used to compare two groups (e.g., males and females, pre-test and post-test). ANOVA is used to compare more than two groups (e.g., age groups or categorical groups). Lastly, a MANOVA is also used to compare more than two groups (e.g., many categorical groups).

In many cases with quasi-experimental research, an ANOVA was used to compare the post-test scores of the two groups, and a MANOVA was used to analyze group differences between social and cognitive interaction behaviors (Spector et al., 2008). If your instrument has constructs or categories, in many cases you will use a factorial approach. This means you will conduct your statistical tests in categories based on the constructs in the instrument. This is the best approach for organizing your analyses. Assessments include a post-test, attitude survey and group interaction behaviors.

Exploring Qualitative Research Methods

Qualitative methods are used when you plan to study a phenomenon of interest, collecting and analyzing non-numeric data to help address mainly exploratory research questions. Qualitative data could be in the form of words, visuals including illustrations, photos and videos, artifacts and audios. There are five main qualitative methods, which we will call traditional qualitative methods (Creswell, 2013). They are:

- Case study approach
- Ethnographic approach
- Grounded theory approach
- Narrative approach
- Phenomenological approach

Case Study Approach

The case study approach is used to describe or learn about a case with the goal of highlighting, understanding or explaining a case (Baxter & Jack, 2008). So then, what is a case? A case is anything that has distinctive characteristics that separate it from other units, entities, phenomena, events or situations. A case could be a group of people, organizations, places or issues. The most important thing is that they are well-defined, with well-drawn boundaries based on specified characteristics such as time, location and the like. Here are examples of a case:

- Financial organizations located in New York City with not less than 40 employees that have laid off 30% of their staff over the last three years
- African American women working in the healthcare industry for at least two years who have experienced micro-aggression in the workplace
- People suffering from long-term symptoms of COVID-19 after contracting it

The purpose of utilizing the case study approach is to highlight the characteristics of the case, help people to understand the case, compare and contrast cases or explain the unique features of a case. Users of a case study approach tend to collect data from multiple sources such as interviews, focus groups, document collection and observation. The essence of this best practice is to make sure a rich variety of information is collected about the case to ensure that the research question is adequately addressed, thus improving the credibility of the study. We want to note that there are various types of case study approaches to choose from if you want to be more specific about the case study approach you plan to use, including single, multiple, collective, intrinsic, exploratory and explanatory (see Baxter & Jack, 2008).

Ethnographic Approach

An ethnographic approach is used when you plan to engage with a person or group of people in their natural setting, collecting rich data to help meet the purpose of the study. Engagement with participants could include conducting observations, participating in what they do, collecting artifacts, interviewing them and conducting focus groups. The unique aspect of an ethnographic approach is the need to spend considerable time with the source(s) data and the taking of field notes to help generate relevant data for the study (Adu, 2019).

Grounded Theory Approach

A grounded theory approach is used when you plan to use collected data to develop a theory that explains a process, an event, a phenomenon, a behavior or a situation (Adu, 2019). Here are some unique features of this approach:

- Collecting data from a larger number of participants compared to a phenomenological and narrative approach
- Simultaneously collecting and analyzing data
- Conducting follow-up interviews based on an initial analysis of the data
- Comparing an initially developed theory to a new set of data
- Refining or confirming an initial theory based on the new data

Narrative Approach

A narrative approach is used when you collect, analyze and report participants' stories (Bell, 2003). For instance, based on the purpose of your study, participants can share stories about working from home, taking paternity leave, dealing with depression, the experience of going to college and the like. As a qualitative researcher utilizing this approach, your role is to create a conducive environment for participants to share their stories. You then retell their stories after systematically reviewing them, extracting relevant components to help present a narrative that best represents what they have shared.

Phenomenological Approach

A phenomenological approach is used to describe, explore, understand or examine the experience of participants. There are two main types of phenomenological approach: transcendental (i.e. a phenomenological approach informed by transcendental phenomenology) and interpretative (i.e., a phenomenological approach informed by interpretative phenomenology) (Larsen & Adu, 2021).

Transcendental Phenomenological Approach

Edmund Husserl (1859–1938), who was a proponent of transcendental phenomenology, believed that you experience a phenomenon when you become conscious of it. In other words, an experience occurs when one becomes conscious of the object (phenomenon) of experience. For example, if you take a look at a house and you become aware of what you are viewing, then an experience has occurred. The transcendental phenomenological approach focuses on giving participants the chance to describe what they have become conscious of. After collecting the data, you extract features of each participant's experience and gather all the common features, thus generating the essence of their experience.

Interpretative Phenomenological Approach

Martin Heidegger (1889–1976), who was a proponent of interpretative phenomenology, asserted that an experience occurs when a subject interacts with the things of the world. As a researcher, your role is to help participants to narrate their experience, which includes how they make sense of it. You then make meaning of it and use the outcome to address your research question. In the end, your goal is to interpret participants' expressions, views and narratives of their experience.

Innovative Qualitative Approaches

Besides the common qualitative approach we have described above, there are other innovative methods you could use to effectively conduct your qualitative research. One of the ways of coming up with a qualitative methodology is to combine two approaches, such as combining a phenomenological approach with a narrative approach (see Larsen & Adu, 2021) or linking a case study to a grounded theory (see Alzaanin, 2020). As indicated, it is possible to effectively combine and utilize two qualitative approaches in a study. The most important thing is to make sure their roles in the study are well-defined by addressing the following questions: "*What roles are the methods going to play in the study?*"; and "*At what stage in the study are the methods going to be utilized?*"

Other innovative qualitative methods you could explore are the arts-based research method (see van der Vaart et al., 2018), autoethnography (see Ellis et al., 2010), the content analysis method (see Bengtsson, 2016), netnography (see Costello et al., 2017) and the photovoice method (see Nykiforuk at al., 2011).

Exploring Mixed Methods Designs

A mixed methods design is a type of research method that has quantitative and qualitative components, and both methods are utilized in a signal study. It is simply collecting and analyzing quantitative and qualitative data in a study to help address the purpose of the study (Creswell & Creswell, 2018). There are two main types of mixed methods design: sequential and concurrent (Hanson et al., 2005).

Sequential Mixed Methods Design

This type of design involves implanting one approach and completing data collection and analysis before carrying out the second approach. For instance, you could start with a qualitative approach and implement a quantitative approach based on the findings of the initial approach. There are three main kinds of sequential mixed methods design.

Sequential Exploratory Mixed Methods Design

With this approach, you start with a qualitative phase and use the findings to inform a quantitative phase. Since it starts with a qualitative phase, the qualitative approach plays a dominate role in the study. In addition, because more priority is given to qualitative data, the researcher's philosophical paradigm should be openly described and made known to your audience (Hanson et al., 2005). The mixing of the two methodologies can take place in the data analysis and findings interpretation stage. There are situations that warrant the need to use sequential exploratory mixed methods design.

- ***Developing an instrument:*** If you plan to develop an instrument based on the concepts (i.e., themes) generated from the qualitative phase of the study
- ***Expanding findings to the larger sample size:*** If you want to see how the qualitative findings apply to the larger sample
- ***Confirming qualitative findings:*** If you want to determine whether the quantitative findings correspond with the qualitative results

Sequential Explanatory Mixed Methods Design

This kind of sequential mixed methods design entails starting with a quantitative phase and using its findings to inform the qualitative phase (Creswell & Plano Clark, 2018; Hanson et al., 2005). With this design, the quantitative method plays a dominant role, and the researcher doesn't have to openly describe their philosophical paradigm (Creswell et al., 2003). The integration can happen at both the data analysis stage and the findings interpretation stage. So, in what situation is sequential explanatory mixed methods design recommended?

- ***Seeking a deeper understanding of the quantitative findings:*** The quantitative phase helps us to measure variables and determine whether relationships between variables exist. What it is less able to do is to assist us in finding out the reasons behind the quantitative outcomes. This is where the qualitative phase comes in, which is used to address some of the questions that may arise based on the quantitative findings.
- ***Determining the areas of focus for the qualitative phase of the study:*** It is sometimes difficult for researchers to determine which aspects of the phenomenon of study they should explore. So, quantitative findings can help them to determine the direction of the qualitative phase. In some cases, researchers can use the results of the quantitative phase to recruit participants for the qualitative phase.

Sequential Transformative Mixed Methods Design

This kind of mixed methods design has features of both the sequential exploratory and explanatory design. The only difference is that the sequential transformative mixed methods design has an advocacy role feature. This means that the researcher's main goal of conducting a mixed methods study is to use the findings to improve the lives of participants.

Concurrent Mixed Methods Design

With this type of mixed methods design, the quantitative and qualitative phases are carried out simultaneously (Creswell et al, 2003; Hanson et al., 2005). This means that you collect and analyze both quantitative and qualitative data at the same time. In other words, you don't collect one type of data and analyze it before collecting another type of data. There are three kinds of concurrent mixed methods design: concurrent triangulation, concurrent nested and concurrent transformative.

- ***Concurrent triangulation mixed methods design:*** This design comprises of collecting and analyzing both quantitative and qualitative data at the same time. Also, both have equal priority, meaning they play an equal role in studying the same phenomenon. It is about studying an issue from two different methodology perspectives and seeing whether they arrive at similar findings.
- ***Concurrent nested mixed methods design:*** With this design, one of the methods (either quantitative or qualitative) plays a less dominant role in the study by focusing on relatively small aspect(s) of the phenomenon of study. For example, let's assume that you plan to explore factors that contribute to burnout, and you plan to use a concurrent nested mixed methods design. The qualitative approach could play a major role, since you plan to look at all potential contributing factors to burnout. However, the quantitative approach will play a less dominant role if you plan to determine whether job dissatisfaction is a significant predictor of burnout. As you can see in this case, the quantitative approach

is not considered to be playing the dominant role because it is only used to address an aspect of the phenomenon.

- ***Concurrent transformative mixed methods design:*** This approach has features related to a concurrent triangulation or nested mixed methods design. However, a unique feature of the concurrent transformative mixed methods design is the advocacy component, thus making it possible to use the research to improve the lives of people who have been marginalized.

Mixed Methods Design Characteristics

Most of the mixed methods designs have characteristics that are related to the following five areas: timing, theoretical lens, integration, priority and purpose. You could use the acronym TTIPP to represent the areas related to the mixed methods features (see Adu, 2015).

Timing

The timing feature refers to the sequence in which the quantitative and qualitative phases will be conducted (Creswell & Plano Clark, 2018; Hanson et al., 2005). If your mixed methods design has a *sequential feature*, it means you start with one methodology phase and analyze data before continuing the study with the second methodology phase. It is important to note that your mixed methods design is considered sequential if and only if the findings of the first phase inform aspects of the implementation of the second phase. For example, if your quantitative findings help to determine who you should recruit to participate in the qualitative phase of the study, it is considered a sequential mixed methods design.

However, a mixed methods design with a *concurrent feature* focuses on implementing both the quantitative and qualitative phases simultaneously. In other words, at the data collection stage you collect the quantitative and qualitative data at the same time. Similarly, at the data analysis stage you analyze both data at the same time.

Theoretical Lens

Your theoretical lens is the philosophical paradigm that informs the research process. Some of the theoretical lenses are positivism, post-positivism, constructivism, social-constructivism, pragmatism and transformative perspective (Creswell & Plano Clark, 2018; Hanson et al., 2005). If a qualitative approach plays a dominant role in your study or collecting qualitative data is your top priority, then you need to communicate your theoretical lens when writing about your research methodology. This helps readers to know your perspective and to better understand how you conducted your study, what you found and how you interpreted these findings. However, if a quantitative approach plays a dominant role, you do not have to make known your theoretical lens. This is because, when using a quantitative approach, it is assumed to attain objectivity, as the researchers tend to distance themselves from what they are studying. As a result, they do not have to share their philosophical paradigm, since it may have no influence on the data being collected and analyzed. Lastly, if the quantitative and qualitative methods play an equal role in your study, you do not need to share your theoretical lens.

Integration

Integration refers to where the mixing takes place and how it is done. It can happen at the data analysis stage or the interpretation of findings stage (Hanson et al., 2005). In terms of how the mixing is done, the quantitative and qualitative phase could be *connected*, especially when using any of the sequential mixed methods designs. With these kinds of mixed methods designs, the findings of one methodological phase is connected to the implementation of the other methodological phase. Another way of mixing is *merging*. This could involve transforming, qualifying quantitative data or quantifying qualitative data to be consistent in their features with the other data set (i.e., qualitative or quantitative data) and mixing them. It could also involve mixing without transforming one of the types of data or findings.

Purpose

One of the questions you may be asked if you want to conduct a mixed methods study is "Why are you combining two different methodologies in your study?" Providing a justification for utilizing your mixed methods design is needed when writing about the research design for your study. This kind of justification is referred to as the *purpose* of your mixed methods design. There are five main purposes you could choose from to support why you are combining quantitative and qualitative methods: complementarity, development, expansion, triangulation and initiation (see Hanson et al., 2005).

- **Complementarity:** This rationale is used when you want to argue that the weakness of one approach is offset by the strength of another approach. It is also used to defend a mixed methods design where each of the methods address parts of the phenomenon of study.
- **Development:** This rationale is used when you want to argue that one method informs the implementation of another method.
- **Expansion:** This rational focuses on arguing that one of the methods is expanding the inquiry to a large sample (i.e., emphasizing the breadth) or exploring to get a deep description, understanding or explanation of the phenomenon of study (i.e., emphasizing the depth).
- **Triangulation:** This rationale involves arguing that you are using two methods to study the same phenomenon with the goal of determining whether both methods arrive at similar findings.
- **Initiation:** If you plan to conduct a mixed methods study with the goal of exploring uniqueness and contradictions between the findings of the two methods, you could use the initiation rationale.

The priority feature refers to the role that each of the methods play in the study. A method can be used to play one of the following roles: dominant, minor or equal (Creswell & Plano Clark, 2018; Hanson et al., 2005). If a method is used to help explore, examine or inquire a large portion of the phenomenon of study, then it is considered to be playing a dominant role. However, if it is used to address a comparatively small aspect of the phenomenon of study, then the method is playing a less dominant role. Also, the quantitative and qualitative method can play an equal role in a study, especially when using a concurrent triangulation mixed methods design (see Table 4.2).

Determining the Right Research Method

There are many ways of determining the right research method for your study. The common strategy is arriving at an appropriate method in a linear manner, with more emphasis on achieving consistence across the purpose of the study, research question(s) and research method. This process starts by examining the kind of terms you used to describe what you want to do in the study and the phenomenon you want to study. For instance, if the purpose statement has words such as explore, examine, narrate or describe, then you are more likely to conduct a qualitative study. However, if it has words such as determine, find out or report, then you are more likely to conduct a quantitative study.

The next step is to look at potential methods for your study and their functions in terms of what they are used for. Compare the functions of the method to the purpose of the study and choose the one that will help you to conduct the study. For example, if the purpose of your study is to examine participants' experience of near-death events, you could use a phenomenological (specifically, an interpretative phenomenological) approach. This is because the phenomenological approach is used to describe participants' experience or examine their understanding of what they have experienced (Larsen & Adu, 2021).

If you are still not sure about the right research approach for your study, you could further examine your research questions. Ask yourself: "What research tool will help me to address this question?"; "What kind of information will I arrive at if I use this tool?"; and "Will the information have the potential to address the research question(s) I have?" Once you have identified the best approach for your study, the next step is to learn more about when, how and where it is used, including its strengths and limitations. You can review textbooks to gain more information about your selected approach. Research articles can also be rich sources for learning about how the approach is used in studies. Familiarizing yourself with your approach will help you to better describe, utilize and defend it.

Table 4.2 Mixed methods designs and their characteristics as suggested by Cresswell et al. (2003)

Mixed Methods Design	Theoretical Lens (Philosophical Paradigm)	Timing	Integration	Methodological Rationale	Priority
Sequential explanatory design	Implicit (post-positivist lens)	Sequential, beginning with quantitative phase	Data Analysis stage (connected) and interpretation stage (merged)	Complementarity	Quantitative data/method
Sequential exploratory design	Explicit (constructivist lens)	Sequential, beginning with qualitative phase	Data Analysis stage (connected) and interpretation stage (merged)	Development, complementarity and/or expansion	Qualitative data/method
Sequential transformative design	Explicit (advocacy lens)	Sequential, beginning with either quantitative or qualitative phase	Data Analysis stage (connected) and interpretation stage (merged)	Complementarity; development and/or expansion	Equal or unequal weight
Concurrent triangulation design	Implicit	Concurrent	Data analysis stage (separated) and interpretation stage (merged)	Triangulation	Equal weight
Concurrent nested design	Implicit or explicit	Concurrent	Data analysis stage (data transformed and/or merged) and interpretation stage (merged)	Complementarity; initiation and/or expansion	Unequal weight
Concurrent transformative design	Explicit (advocacy lens)	Concurrent	Data analysis stage (separated) and interpretation stage (merged)	Complementarity; initiation and/or expansion	Equal or unequal weight

Source: Adopted from Adu (2015, slide 29).

Writing About Your Selected Research Method

After you have selected the right method for your study, your next step is to introduce the tool to your readers or research/practitioner community. When writing about the method, you first state what it is. Here is an example: "*The research approach I will be using to conduct this study is a causal-comparative design.*" You then describe what it is used for, which is about stating the functions and circumstances that warrants the use of the approach. This is followed by a justification supporting the selection of the method. You could also add the philosophical paradigm or theoretical foundations that informed your decision to use the approach. By providing a justification, you are also demonstrating the consistency between the purpose of the study, the research questions and the method chosen. In other words, your role is to show how the method of your choice will help you to meet what you want to achieve in your study. Lastly, you could briefly discuss the role that the method will play in your study, sharing how it will be used in the study.

Summary

As discussed above, research methods can be categorized into three main types: quantitative, qualitative and mixed methods. Each encompasses a variety of research approaches. As you familiarize yourself with them, including knowing their strengths and weaknesses, you will be able to choose the right research method for your study. After selecting the appropriate method, you then write about it, sharing its characteristics and providing reasons why it is appropriate considering the purpose of the study and the research questions you want to address or the hypotheses you plan to test.

References

Adu, P. (2015, April 8). *Planning a mixed methods research by Philip Adu, Ph.D.* [Video]. YouTube. www.youtube.com/watch?v=iqCFIivhHE0

Adu, P. (2019). *A step-by-step guide to qualitative data coding.* Routledge.

Aliaga, M., & Gunderson, B. (2002). *Interactive statistics.* Sage.

Alzaanin, E. I. (2020). Combining case study design and constructivist grounded theory to theorize language teacher cognition. *The Qualitative Report, 25*(5), 1361–1376. https://doi.org/10.46743/2160-3715/2020.4047

Baxter, P., & Jack, S. (2008). Qualitative case study methodology: Study design and implementation for novice researchers. *The Qualitative Report, 13*(4), 544–559. https://doi.org/10.46743/2160-3715/2008.1573

Bell, A. C. (2003). A narrative approach to research. *Canadian Journal of Environmental Education, 8, 95–110.*

Bengtsson, M. (2016). *How to plan and perform a qualitative study using content analysis. NursingPlus Open, 2, 8–14.*

Campbell, D. T., Stanley, J. C., & Gage, N. L. (1966). *Experimental and quasi-experimental designs for research.* Rand McNally.

Cohen, L. & Manion, L, (1980) *Research methods in education.* Groom Helm Ltd.

Cook, T. & Campbell, D. (1979). *Quasi-experimentation: Design & analysis issues for field settings.* Houghton Mifflin Company.

Costello, L., McDermott, M.-L., & Wallace, R. (2017). Netnography: Range of practices, misperceptions, and missed opportunities. *International Journal of Qualitative Methods, 16*(1). https://doi.org/10.1177/1609406917700647

Creswell, J. (2003). *Research design: Qualitative, quantitative, and mixed methods approaches.* Sage Publications.

Creswell, J. W. (2013). *Qualitative inquiry and research design: Choosing among five approaches* (3rd ed.). Sage.

Creswell, J. W., & Creswell, J. D. (2018). *Research design: Qualitative, quantitative, and mixed methods approaches.* SAGE Publications, Inc.

Creswell, J. W., & Plano Clark, V. L. (2018). *Designing and conducting mixed methods research* (3rd ed.). Sage Publications, Inc.

Creswell, J. W., Plano Clark, V. L., Gutmann, M. L., & Hanson, W. E. (2003). *Advanced mixed methods research designs.* In A. Tashakkori & C. Teddlie (Eds.), *Handbook of mixed methods in social and behavioral research* (pp. 209–240). Sage.

Ellis, C., Adams, T. E., & Bochner, A. P. (2010). Autoethnography: An overview. *Forum Qualitative Sozialforschung / Forum: Qualitative Social Research, 12*(1). https://doi.org/10.17169/fqs-12.1.1589

Hanson, W. E., Creswell, J. W., Plano Clark, V. L., Petska, K. S., & Creswell, J. D. (2005). Mixed methods research designs in counseling psychology. *Journal of Counseling Psychology, 52*(2), 224–235. https://doi.org/10.1037/0022-0167.52.2.224

Kerlinger, F. (1986). *Foundations of behavioral research* (3rd ed.). Harcourt Brace & Company Publishing.

Larsen, H. G. & Adu, P. (2021). *The theoretical framework in phenomenological research: Development and application.* Routledge

Leedy P. D., & Ormrod J. E. (2010). *Practical research: Planning and design* (9th ed.). Pearson Educational International.

Long, T., Convey, J., & Chwalek, A. (1985). *Completing dissertations in the behavioral sciences and education.* Jossey-Bass Publishers.

Miles, D. A. (2021, October 7). *Descriptive Statistics 3: Correlation* [Class Workshop: EDUC 607 Quantitative Research Methods and Design in Education I: Quantitative Research Methods for SJ]. University of San Diego.

Muijs, D. (2004). *Doing quantitative research in education with SPSS.* Sage Publications Ltd.

Munck, G., & Verkuilen, J. (2005). Research designs. *Encyclopedia of Social Measurement, 1*(3).

Nykiforuk, C. I., Vallianatos, H., & Nieuwendyk, L. M. (2011). Photovoice as a method for revealing community perceptions of the built and social environment. *International Journal of Qualitative Methods, 10*(2), 103–124. https://doi.org/10.1177/160940691101000201

Omair, A. (2015). Selecting the appropriate study design for your research: Descriptive study designs. *Journal of Health Specialties, 3*(3).

Pedhazur, E. J. (1982). *Multiple regression in behavioral research: Explanation and prediction.* Holt, Rinehart & Winston.

Reichardt, C. (2019). *Quasi-experimentation: A guide to design and analysis.* The Guilford Press.

Shadish, W., Cook, T., & Campbell, D. (2001). *Experimental and quasi-experimental: Designs for generalized causal inference.* Houghton Mifflin Company.

Sousa V. D., Driessnack M., & Mendes I. C. (2007). An overview of research designs relevant to nursing: Part 1: Quantitative research designs. *Rev. Latino-Am. Enfermagem, 15*(3), 502–507.

Spector, J., Merrill, M., van Merriënboer, J. & Driscoll, M. (2008). *Handbook of research on educational communications and technology* (3rd ed.). Lawrence Erlbaum Associates–Taylor & Francis Group.

Sukamolson, S. (2007). Fundamentals of quantitative research. *Language Institute Chulalongkorn University, 1*(1), 1–20.

Terrell, S. (2017). *Writing a proposal for your dissertation: Guidelines and examples.* The Guilford Press.

Vaart, G. van der, Hoven, B. van, & Huigen, P. P. (2018). Creative and arts-based research methods in academic research. Lessons from a participatory research project in the Netherlands. *Forum Qualitative Sozialforschung / Forum: Qualitative Social Research, 19*(2). https://doi.org/10.17169/fqs-19.2.2961

VandenBos, G. (2015). *APA dictionary of psychology* (2nd ed.). American Psychological Association Publishers.

Vogt, W. (1999). *Dictionary of statistics and methodology: A nontechnical guide for the social sciences* (2nd ed.). Sage Publications.

Walker, W. (2005). The strengths and weaknesses of research designs involving quantitative measures. *Journal of Research in Nursing, 10*(5), 571–582.

Williams, B., Brown, T., & Onsman, A. (2010). Exploratory factor analysis: A five-step guide for novices. *Australasian Journal of Paramedicine, 8*(3). Retrieved from http://ro.ecu.edu.au/jephc/vol8/iss3/1

Williams, C. (2007). Research methods. *Journal of Business & Economic Research, 5*(3), 65–72.

5 Understanding the Seven Types of Research Gaps

Objectives

- Readers will be able to:
  1. Recognize common research gap types
  2. Identify research gaps
  3. Write about research gaps

Introduction

One of the most prevailing issues in the craft of research is developing a research agenda and building the research on the development of the *research gap*. Most research of any endeavor is chiefly attributed to the development of the research gap. This is a primary basis for the investigation of any problem, phenomenon or scientific question. Given this accepted tenet of engagement in research, it is surprising in the research fraternity that we do not train researchers on how to systematically identify research gaps as a basis for their investigation. This continues to be a common problem with novice researchers. Little theory and research has been developed on identifying research gaps as a basis for a line of inquiry.

When working with doctoral students, this concept of addressing a gap in prior research seems to be foreign to them. The idea of finding gaps in the research has been troubling for most researchers, most particularly doctoral students. For a considerable period of time, there were no formal or established frameworks for identifying or characterizing research gaps. It appears that identifying research gaps is in the eye of the beholder. One researcher's gap may be another researcher's non-gap. Most of this conflict with research gaps tends to touch on perception. Many researchers may argue that a gap is one thing or it is not. It is still a struggle for most researchers, especially doctoral researchers, to identify and define gaps in their studies. This chapter will introduce the *seven types of research gap* (see Figure 5.1).

Theoretical Foundation and Development

This theoretical model was developed from two important articles by two researchers who did an outstanding job of building a taxonomy of research gaps.

DOI: 10.4324/9781003268154-5

The first known article that developed a framework for defining research gaps was by Robinson et al. (2011). In their model, they identified and described five types of research gap: (a) population, (b) intervention, (c) comparison, (d) outcomes, and (e) setting.

Müller-Bloch and Kranz (2014) developed a research gap model that itself was developed from Robinson et al.'s (2011) framework. Their theoretical framework was developed after exhaustive research on the conducting of literature reviews and was based on Jacob's (2011) theory on research problems. Jacobs (2011) identified six kinds of research problem. These problems parallel research gaps as discussed by Müller-Bloch and Kranz (2014). While research problems are not necessarily research gaps, they might be synonymous with research gaps. Their framework consists of six types of research gap: (a) contradictory evidence; (b) knowledge void; (c) action-knowledge conflict; (d) methodological; (e) evaluation void; and (f) theory application void (Müller-Bloch & Kranz, 2014).

We found the frameworks proposed by Müller-Bloch and Kranz (2014) and Robinson et al. (2011) to be significant theoretical developments on research gaps. Building on the foundation of these two theories, we developed a theoretical framework that is an amalgamation of the two theories and did two things. First, the new framework is a mixture of the two frameworks but only uses one construct from Robinson et al.'s (2011) model. Second, we reconceptualized the model developed from Müller-Bloch and Kranz (2014) by simplifying the names of the constructs in their proposed framework. Miles (2017) proposed a new model built on the two previous models that consists of seven core research gaps, renamed and ranked from the most common to the least common: (a) population; (b) empirical; (c) methodological; (d) knowledge; (e) theoretical; (f) evidence; and (g) practical-knowledge (see Figure 5.1).

The Seven Research Gaps from Most Common to Least Common

Another prevailing issue with research gaps is being aware of the most common to the least common. Many doctoral students are not aware that some gaps are more common than others. To help the readers of this book, we have strategically ranked the most common research gaps to the least common (see Figure 5.1).

Population Gap

This gap concerns a focus on a population that is under-researched or not adequately represented in prior research (e.g., gender, race/ethnicity, age, etc). A *population gap* is the most common gap recognized by researchers.

Characteristics

- **Very common gap**. A population gap is the most common gap recognized by researchers.

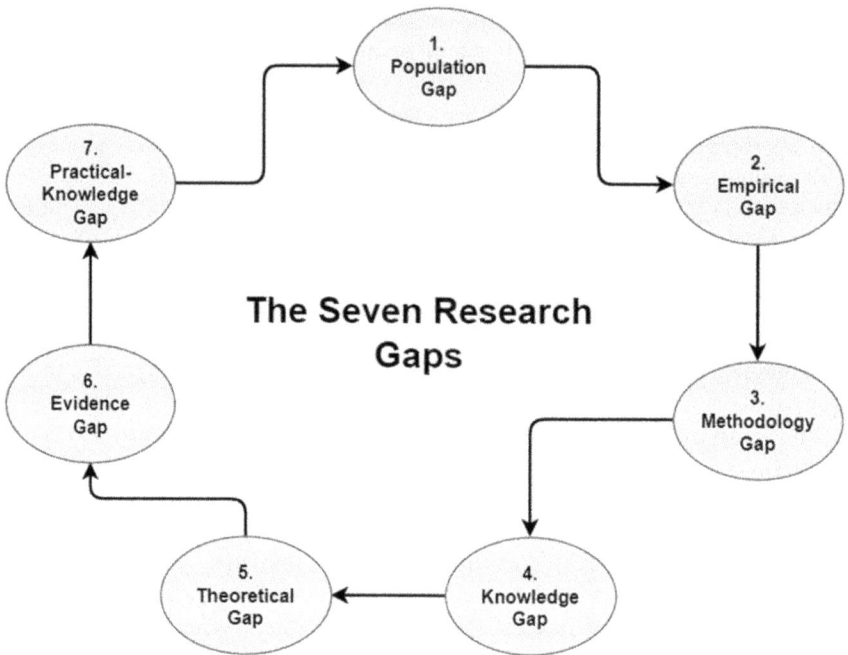

Figure 5.1 The seven types of research gap, from the most common to the least common.

- **Underserved population.** There are always underserved populations that have been under-researched. This gap addresses a population that is under-researched or not adequately represented in the evidence base or prior research (Miles, 2021; Robinson et al., 2011).

Empirical Gap

This gap is concerned with research findings in prior research that lack empirical research or a subject matter that needs to be evaluated or empirically verified. An *empirical gap* deals with gaps in prior research. This conflict deals with the research findings or propositions that need to be evaluated or empirically verified.

Characteristics

- **Common gap.** An empirical gap is the second most common gap recognized by researchers.
- **Conflict with prior findings.** This gap deals with the research findings or propositions that need to be evaluated or empirically verified.
- **Lack of an empirical line of inquiry.** For example, the empirical gap often addresses conflicts that no study to date has directly attempted to evaluate a

subject or topic using an empirical approach (Miles, 2017, 2021; Jacobs, 2011; Müller-Bloch & Kranz, 2014).

Methodological Gap

This gap is the type of gap that deals with the lack of variation in research methods in prior research that could use a different line of inquiry (Jacobs, 2011; Müller-Bloch & Kranz, 2014; Miles, 2017). A *methodological gap* is the type of gap that deals with the conflict that occurs due to the influence of methodology on research results.

Characteristics

- **Common gap.** A methodological gap is the third most common gap recognized by researchers.
- **Conflict with prior research methods.** This gap addresses the conflicts with research methods in prior studies and offers a new line of research that is divergent from those research methods.
- **Variation.** A variation in research methods is necessary to generate new insights or to avoid distorted findings.
- **New line of inquiry.** For the researcher, it might be useful to vary research methods, especially if certain research topics have been mainly explored using a singular or common research methodology (Miles, 2021).

Knowledge Gap

This gap is concerned with the lack of research on a particular subject. Thus, the desired research findings do not exist (Jacobs, 2011; Müller-Bloch & Kranz, 2014; Miles, 2017). The *knowledge gap* is a common gap in prior research. There are two situations where a knowledge gap (knowledge void) might occur.

Characteristics

- **Common gap.** The knowledge gap is the fourth most common gap in prior research.
- **Two conditions.** There are two settings where a knowledge gap (knowledge void) might occur:
  - *Knowledge may not exist.* Knowledge may not exist in the actual field compared to theories and prior literature from related research domains.
  - *Differing results.* It might be the case that the results of a study differ from what was expected (Miles, 2021).

Theoretical Gap

This gap is concerned with a lack of theory on or conceptual/theoretical models for a particular subject matter in prior research. Because there is a lack of theory, a gap exists (Jacobs, 2011; Müller-Bloch & Kranz, 2014; Miles, 2017). The *theoretical gap* deals with gaps in the theory in prior research.

Characteristics

- **Common gap.** The theoretical gap is the fifth most common gap in prior research.
- **Lack of theory.** For example, if one phenomenon is being explained through various theoretical models, then, similar to a methodological conflict, there might be a theoretical conflict.
- **Examine the theory.** Researchers and scholars could examine whether one of the theories is superior in terms of the gap in prior research.
- **Common occurrence.** Theoretical gaps are a common occurrence when examining prior research on a phenomenon (Miles, 2021).

Evidence Gap

This gap is concerned with contradictions in the findings of prior research. There are conflicts in prior studies that have contradictory results and conclusions (Jacobs, 2011; Müller-Bloch & Kranz, 2014; Miles, 2017).

Characteristics

- **Somewhat common gap.** An evidence gap is somewhat common compared to its counterparts. However, it is recognized by researchers and does exist in prior research.
- **Evidence conflict.** An evidence gap occurs when a provocative exception arises, when new research finding contradicts widely accepted conclusions.
- **Contradiction.** This occurs if results from studies allow for conclusions in their own right but these results are contradictory when examined from a more abstract point of view.
- **Analyze the research stream.** The identification of contradictory evidence starts with analyzing each research stream.
- **Analyze the results.** The results from these analyses need to be synthesized in order to reveal contradictory evidence (Miles, 2021).

Practical-Knowledge Gap

This gap is concerned with professional behavior or practices that deviate from research findings or are not covered by research (Jacobs, 2011; Müller-Bloch & Kranz, 2014; Miles, 2017).

Characteristics

- **Uncommon gap.** A practical-knowledge gap is not a common gap compared to its counterparts. However, it is recognized by researchers and does exist in prior research.

Table 5.1　The seven research gaps from most common to least common

Research Gap Type	Definition
Population gap *(also known as the "under-researched sub-groups gap")*	Research regarding the population that is under-represented or not adequately represented in the evidence base or prior research (e.g., gender, race/ethnicity, age, etc.). (Robinson et al., 2011).
Empirical gap *(also known as the "evaluation void gap")*	Research findings or propositions that need to be evaluated or empirically verified (Jacobs, 2011; Müller-Bloch & Kranz, 2014; Miles, 2017).
Methodological gap *(also known as the "methodology void gap")*	A variation of research methods is necessary to generate new insights or to avoid distorted findings (Jacobs, 2011; Müller-Bloch & Kranz, 2014; Miles, 2017).
Knowledge gap *(also known as the "knowledge void gap")*	The desired research findings do not exist (Jacobs, 2011; Müller-Bloch & Kranz, 2014; Miles, 2017).
Theoretical gap *(also known as the "theory application void gap")*	Theory should be applied to certain research issues to generate new insights. There is a lack of theory, thus a gap exists (Müller-Bloch & Kranz, 2014; Jacobs, 2011; Müller-Bloch & Kranz, 2014; Miles, 2017).
Evidence gap *(also known as the "contradictory evidence gap")*	Results from studies allow for conclusions in their own right but these are *contradictory* when examined from a more abstract point of view (Jacobs, 2011; Müller-Bloch & Kranz, 2014; Miles, 2017).
Practical-knowledge gap *(also known as the "action-knowledge conflict gap")*	Professional behavior or practices deviate from the research findings or are not covered by the research (Jacobs, 2011; Müller-Bloch & Kranz, 2014; Miles, 2017).

Source: Robinson et al. (2011); Müller-Bloch & Kranz (2014); Miles (2017).

- **Discrepancy**. This kind of gap tends to be a discrepancy that can motivate new research in this direction.
- **Conflict with practices vs. advocated behavior.** A practical-knowledge (action-knowledge) conflict arises when the actual behavior of professionals is different from their advocated behavior.
- **Determine the scope of conflict.** In this case, research could seek to determine the scope of the conflict and to uncover the reasons for its existence (see Table 5.1).

Writing Up the Research Gaps in a Research Proposal

To discuss the gaps in prior research, you must first highlight some of the prior research in the literature that does not address the particular focus of the research. The contributions noted should relate back to the gaps, inconsistencies and controversies noted earlier (see Figure 5.2).

Example 1: (Identify the *research gap*) Previous research has addressed several aspects of
_____: (1) _____ (cite two to three relevant articles), (2)
_____ (cite two to three relevant articles), and (3) _____ (cite two to three
relevant articles) [Summers, 2001].

Figure 5.2 Example 1 of how to write up a research gap (general).

Example 2: (Identify the *research gap*) However, in addition, _____
encompasses several unexplored dimensions that lately have attracted research attention in
other disciplines (cite two to three relevant articles) [Summers, 2001].

Example 3: (Identify the *research gap*) Some of these unexplored_____ appear to be
important and worthy of investigation in the context of _____. An
investigation of these issues is important because _____.
Furthermore, previous empirical research has focused primarily on _____.
Very little research has been done on _____ [Summers, 2001].

Figure 5.3 Examples 2 and 3 of how to write up a research gap (general).

Then, researchers need to identify important gaps, inconsistencies and/or controversies in the literature. This serves to establish the need for additional research in the topic area of interest. This task, like those that precede it, can be achieved in a concise manner (see Figure 5.3).

Finally, and most importantly, the researcher must provide a concise statement about the manuscript's purposes and the contributions made by the manuscript to the literature. This statement should follow logically from the text that identifies the gaps, inconsistencies and/or controversies in the literature (see Figure 5.4 and Table 5.2).

Summary

This chapter proposed a theoretical model based on the two preceding models concerning research gaps. This chapter examined the different types of research gap and the characteristics that afflict researchers, and it offers a theoretical framework that simplifies the concept of research gaps. This research contributes to the practice of research by providing a taxonomy for novice and experienced researchers, and it highlights the importance of understanding the different constructs of research gaps and their functionality. The chapter discusses a proposed seven-point theoretical framework that encompasses the most common gaps a researcher will encounter in a review of the prior research and literature. The foundation of this research is based on asking questions and finding a new line of inquiry based on gaps in prior research. This is a driving force in the inquiry of new knowledge. We

Example 4: In this study we seek to extend _____ by addressing the gaps in_____. The study investigates the impact of four _____ (1) _____, (2) _____, (3) _____, and (4) _____. In addition, interrelationships among _____ are examined [Summers, 2001].

Example 5: The researcher identified four major gaps in the prior research and literature. First, the researcher identified an apparent theoretical gap in the prior research concerning _____. The previous research has addressed several aspects of _____: (1) _____ (cite two to three relevant articles), (2) _____ (cite two to three relevant articles), and (3) _____ (cite two to three relevant articles).

Second, based on the review of the prior research, there is a population gap. There is gap with_____. This population segment has been under researched in the prior literature. In addition, _____ encompasses several unexplored dimensions that lately have attracted research attention in other disciplines (cite two to three relevant articles).

Third, the researcher identified an apparent knowledge gap in the prior research concerning _____. In addition, the prior research there is a conflict and contradiction in the findings of the prior studies that did not address the subject of _____. Some of these unexplored _____ contradictions in the prior research appear to be important and worthy of investigation in the context of _____. An investigation of these issues is important because _____.

Lastly, the researcher identified an empirical gap in the prior research. There is a lack of rigorous research in the prior literature. The previous research has focused primarily on _____. Very little research has been done on _____ to properly evaluation the problem. In this study we seek to provide a new inquiry on management practices with the federal government by addressing the gaps in _____. The study investigates the impact of four: (1) _____, (2) _____, (3) _____, and (4) _____ [Summers, 2001].

Figure 5.4 Examples 4 and 5 of how to write up a research gap (general).

hope that the proposed framework will provide researchers with a template and a foundation for conducting a systematic and thorough literature review.

Summary of Key Points in the Chapter

Four key points and the following topics were discussed in the chapter:

- The background and history of research gaps. If you develop a taxonomy of research gaps, there are seven primary research gaps. The research gaps model proposed by Miles combines two previous models from Robinson et al. (2011) and Müller-Bloch and Kranz (2014). Forensic science has grown and spread into many specialized fields. Forensics began in the medical field but has since grown and integrated into the field of criminology as a science.
- Some research gaps are more common than others. Most interestingly, the population gap is the most common gap found in research. The second most

Table 5.2 Performing a gap audit: The research gap audit tool

Research Gap Type	Audit for Research Gaps
Population gap (also known as the "under-researched sub-groups gap")	• Are there any underserved populations in the prior research that have not been investigated? Yes___ No ___ • Are there any subpopulations or sub-groups underserved in the prior research that have not been researched? Yes___ No ___ • Are there any subpopulations or sub-groups that present any opportunities for further research that have not been investigated? Yes___ No ___
Empirical gap (also known as the "evaluation void gap")	• Does the majority of the prior research use only one type of research methodology or design (non-empirical)? Yes___ No ___ • Does the majority of the prior research use only a qualitative research methodology and design (case studies, narrative and so on)? Yes___ No ___ • Does the majority of the prior research use a non-empirical or non-evaluation type of research methodology and design? Yes___ No ___
Methodological gap (also known as the "methodology void gap")	• Does the majority of the prior research use only one type of research methodology or design (empirical)? Yes___ No ___ • Does the majority of the prior research use an empirical type of research methodology? Yes___ No ___ • Is the majority of the prior research empirical or evaluative? Yes___ No ___
Knowledge gap (also known as the "knowledge void gap")	• Has the topic as the basis of the research been discussed in prior research? Yes___ No ___ • Has the majority of the prior research ever discussed the topic in depth? Yes___ No ___ • Has the majority of the prior research ever discussed the topic extensively? Yes___ No ___
Theoretical gap (also known as the "theory application void gap")	• Has a theory or conceptual model ever been developed on the topic as the basis of research in prior research? Yes___ No ___ • Has the majority of the prior research ever discussed the topic as a theory or conceptual model? Yes___ No ___ • Has the majority of the prior research ever developed a theoretical framework or structural construct concerning this topic? Yes___ No ___

Table 5.2 (Continued)

Research Gap Type	Audit for Research Gaps
Evidence gap (also known as the "contradictory evidence gap")	• Is the majority of the prior research consistent in its findings on the topic of interest? Yes_____ No _____ • Is the majority of the prior research in agreement in its findings on the topic of interest? Yes_____ No _____ • Does the majority of the prior research contradict itself in its findings on the topic of interest? Yes_____ No _____
Practical-knowledge gap (also known as the "action-knowledge conflict gap")	• Does the majority of the prior research overwhelmingly agree with the practices of professionals in the field concerning the topic of interest? Yes_____ No _____ • Does the majority of the prior research moderately agree with the practices of professionals in the field concerning the topic of interest? Yes_____ No _____ • Does the majority of the prior research overwhelmingly disagree with the practices of professionals in the field concerning the topic of interest? Yes_____ No _____

popular research gap is the empirical gap. One of the least common research gaps is the practical-knowledge gap, which is rarely encountered.

- The chapter discusses writing up the research gaps in a research proposal and the different methods for doing so, providing three examples.
- The last section of the chapter discusses how to perform a "research gap audit." The audit provides the researcher with a tool to help them find the most appropriate research gap in prior research. This section of the chapter discusses the research gap audit based on the seven primary research gaps.

References

Barrios, L. O., (2016). *The only academic phrasebook you'll ever need: 600 examples of academic language*. CreateSpace Independent Publishing Platform.

Jacobs, R. L. (2011). Developing a research problem and purpose statement. In T. S. Rocco & T. Hatcher (Eds.), *The handbook of scholarly writing and publishing* (pp. 125–141). Jossey-Bass.

Miles, D. A. (2017). *A taxonomy of research gaps: Identifying and defining the seven research gaps* [Doctoral student workshop]. Finding Research Gaps – Research Methods and Strategies, Dallas, Texas.

Miles, D. A. (2021). *Understanding, defining and ranking the seven research gaps* [Doctoral student workshop]. Finding Research Gaps – Research Methods and Strategies, Dallas, Texas.

Müller-Bloch, C., & Kranz, J. (2014). A framework for rigorously identifying research gaps in qualitative literature reviews. In *The Thirty Sixth International Conference on Information Systems* (pp. 1–19). Fort Worth.

Peterson, S. L. (1998), *The research writer's phrase book: A guide to proposal writing and research phraseology*. International Scholars Publications.

Robinson, K., Saldanha, I., & McKoy, N. A. (2011). Development of a framework for to identify research gaps systematic reviews. *Journal of Epidemiology, 64*(1), 1325–1330.

Summers, J. (2001). Guidelines for conducting research and publishing in marketing: From conceptualization through the review process. *Journal of the Academy of Marketing Science, 29*(4), 405–415.

6 Developing the Research Problem

Objective

- Readers will be able to:
  1. Write a problem statement

Introduction

Many researchers and doctoral students in particular are not properly taught how to write a clear problem statement. Let's face it, some of the universities do a poor job of teaching students how to write a problem statement. Many are confused and do not know how to frame a research problem and a rationale for their investigation.

So, this is the reason why many doctoral students and researchers have considerable trouble writing the problem statement for their study. The reason stems from a poor research agenda leading to a poor problem statement. The research problem is one of the most important tasks of a research proposal or dissertation because it provides a focus and direction for the study. This chapter illustrates how to develop and write a problem statement with key words and syntax and is based on a conference workshop we conducted in Atlanta, GA, for doctoral students. Perhaps unsurprisingly, our workshop had a surprising large turnout.

Problem Statement: Definition and Meaning

A well-written problem statement defines the problem and helps identify the variables investigated in the study. The problem statement (a) provides the rationale for the study and (b) uses data and research to confirm the need to address the problem in the study (Miles & Scott, 2017). Hernon and Schwartz's (2007) definition of a problem statement includes many key points: (1) *clarity and precision* (a well-written statement does not make sweeping generalizations and irresponsible statements); (2) the *identification of what will be studied* while avoiding the use of value-laden words and terms; (3) the *identification of an overarching question and key factors or variables*; (4) the *identification of key concepts and terms*, the *articulation of the study's boundaries or parameters, some generalizability*, a *conveyance of the study's importance*, benefits and justification (regardless of the type of research, it is important to address the "so

DOI: 10.4324/9781003268154-6

what" question and to demonstrate that the research is not trivial); (5) *no use of unnecessary jargon*; and (6) a *conveyance of more than the mere gathering of descriptive data providing a snapshot.* This pretty much lays down the foundation of what a problem statement is.

Newton and Rudestam (2007) argue that a problem statement is important and timely. It should include a timely and relevant literature review, problem statement with corresponding hypotheses and method of data collection and analyses. They referenced the research wheel of iterative processes. Jacobs (2011) asserts that, in general, problem statements describe a gap in sets of information, which results in a call for action or resolution. There are usually three major functions of a problem statement. First, problem statements establish the existence of two or more factors, which by their interactions produce a perplexing or troublesome state that yield an undesirable consequence (Jacobs, 2011).

Furthermore, a problem might be defined as the issue that exists in the literature, theory or practice that leads to a need for the study (Mauch & Birch, 1998; Thomas & Brubaker, 2000; Creswell, 2009). Lastly, Creswell (2013) describes the problem statement in terms of steps that need to be taken to conduct the research: (a) establishing the problem leading to the study; (b) reviewing the literature about the problem; (c) identifying deficiencies in the literature about the problem; and (d) targeting an audience and noting the significance of the problem for this research.

Trouble with the Problem Statement: Ask Two Questions

Many times, when I work with doctoral students trying to pick a topic and research a problem, they fail to ask *two questions*: (1) *Why does this topic warrant an investigation?* and (2) *What drives the investigation?* Below are some of the reasons for a poorly written problem statement by doctoral students and researchers:

- *No compelling reason.* Lack of a compelling reason for the research. Many students lack a compelling reason for investigating the problem (research).
- *Lack of persuasion.* Not persuasive enough in identifying the problem as a basis for the study. They don't sell it.
- *Clarity.* Lack of clarity about the problem. As a result, this lack of clarity pervades the dissertation. Thus, there is failure to identify gaps in prior research as a basis for the investigation.
- *Topic choice.* Poor topic choice for researching a problem is an issue. For example, you do not want to pick a problem related to something like "basket weaving" if there is no basis for the problem and investigation.
- *Problem nexus.* There is a nexus issue with the problem under investigation and the research. Many doctoral students do not make the connection between the problem and the basis for the study. Thus, a poor problem statement is written.
- *Failure to develop a clear problem statement.* This is the fault of the academic community. There is always a clear purpose statement, but there is never a clear problem statement (Miles, 2016; Miles & Scott, 2017).

You must consider these points when you are developing a problem for investigation or as a basis for research. When you have identified a problem as the basis for your study, the task is easier to address.

When developing your problem statement, consider two points:

- *Uniformity.* You should always write each of your subproblem statements in the same way for the dissertation.
- *Completeness.* Your problem statement should list all the variables that are under focus in the study. This is important to the structure and will minimize confusion (Miles & Scott, 2017).

Writing Up the Problem Statement

There is a tool that I use when helping doctoral students to develop their problem statement called the *Statement Grid*. The *Statement Grid* is a helpful tool that aids students and shows their problem and problem statement visually. It guides them through the problem and develops the problem statement with supporting statements. I use this to help doctoral students who are having trouble coming up with their problem statement. It helps them with their thought process and describes three possible subproblems as a basis for their research, which helps with the *rule of three* (supporting your argument and position with three points) (see Table 6.1).

Webster (1998a, 1998b) provides a very good template for constructing the problem statement. Here is an example: The central problem to be researched in the proposed study is the identification of salient motivating influences characteristic of college-bound high-achieving African American high school graduates of low socio-economic backgrounds. These influences are likely to include parental values and influences, peer influences, significant others and many other unknown variables.

Directions

Using this template, we set up the foundation for building the problem statement. **First:** Write the overall problem statement template. **Second:** Divide the

Table 6.1 Introducing the Statement Grid for problem statement development

Problem Statement:

Issue (subproblem) 1:	**Issue (subproblem) 2:**	**Issue (subproblem) 3:**

Table 6.2 Example: The Statement Grid for problem statement development

Problem Statement:
Write and describe the overall problem as identified by the researcher. Then write,
"The central problem to be researched by the proposed study is…" Last write, *"As a basis for this study, the researcher identified the problem to be* [number of issues]." Or write, *"The researcher identified three major problems as a basis for this study"* (Webster, 1998a).

Issue (subproblem) 1:	**Issue (subproblem) 2:**	**Issue (subproblem) 3:**
First, …	Second, …	Last, …

Table 6.3 Example: The Statement Grid for problem statement development

Problem Statement:
The central problem to be researched by the proposed study is the shortage in the nursing field. This has a lot to do with the current nursing shortage and the need for more nurses in the field. There is a huge problem with this shortage and the availability of nurses. As a basis for this study, the researcher identified the problem to be threefold.

Issue (subproblem) 1:	**Issue (subproblem) 2:**	**Issue (subproblem) 3:**
First, the prevailing issue is that the education of new nurses is the responsibility of institutions of higher education, but the national shortage of nursing faculty (McSherry et al., 2012; Rosseter, 2015) is limiting the enrollment, education and graduation of new nurses from institutions of higher learning.	*Second, the prevailing issue in the United States is that 75% of nursing faculty will reach retirement age in 2017 (Brett et al., 2014). This is alongside the existing problem that 6.9% of nursing faculty positions remain unfilled due to a lack of qualified nursing educators (Rosseter, 2015).*	*Last, the prevailing issue is that the current nursing faculty express low job satisfaction (Bittner & O'Connor, 2012) due to complexities in the nursing educator role making the retention and recruitment of qualified faulty difficult (Byme & Martine, 2014). The current problems include a shortage of qualified nursing faculty to educate new nurses, the complexity of nursing education and current faculty complaints of poor job satisfaction (Cook, 2017).*

problem to be investigated into two or three parts (or subproblems) that are compelling (see Table 6.2). Please note, use the word *issue* when writing the subproblem so that it is not misinterpreted as four separate problem statements (see Table 6.3).

The Example in Paragraph Form

The central problem to be researched by the proposed study is the shortage in the nursing field. This has a lot to do with the current nursing shortage and the need for more nurses in the field. There is a huge problem with this shortage and the availability of nurses. As a basis for this study, the researcher identified the problem to be threefold.

(FIRST) The first prevailing issue is that the education of new nurses is the responsibility of institutions of higher education, but a national shortage of nursing faculty (McSherry et al., 2012, Rosseter, 2015) is limiting the enrollment, education and graduation of new nurses from institutions of higher learning.

(SECOND) The second prevailing issue is that, in the United States, 75% of the nursing faculty will reach retirement age in 2017 (Brett et al., 2014). This is alongside the existing problem that 6.9% of nursing faculty positions remain unfilled because of a lack of qualified nursing educators (Rosseter, 2015).

(THIRD) Last, the prevailing issue is that the current nursing faculty express low job satisfaction (Bittner & O'Connor, 2012) because of complexities in the nursing educator role making the retention and recruitment of qualified faculty difficult (Byme & Martine, 2014).

The current problems include a shortage of qualified nursing faculty to educate new nurses, the complexity of nursing education and current faculty complaints of poor job satisfaction (Cook, 2017). See the examples of problem statements from real studies.

Advantages of Using the Statement Grid

A key advantage to using the *Statement Grid* to develop your problem statement is that it also provides alignment with the development of your purpose statement and research questions (see Examples 6.1 to 6.4). We will discuss this further in Chapter 9 on research alignment for dissertations and research projects.

Example 6.1

The central problem to be researched in the proposed study is the lack of intercultural competence within peer mentoring between international students and domestic students' relationships and the lack of a personal account of students' experience in a peer-mentoring program. As a basis for the study, the researcher identified the problem to be twofold.

The first prevailing issue identified by the researcher is the lack of research on intercultural competence and the peer-mentoring skills of domestic students. Universities admit international students to drive globalization but fail to bridge the gap between domestic and international students to help create intercultural competency. Past researchers conducted different studies within formal classroom settings and extracurricular settings (Kohnova, 2007; Maeda, 2017; Washburn & Hargis, 2017). The researcher for the present study will reference Kohnova's research to determine ways to sustain effective intercultural interaction by investigating how the attitudes, skills and knowledge of both domestic and international student peer mentors affect external and internal outcomes (Deardorff, 2011).

Last, the prevailing issue identified by the researcher is the lack of personal accounts from students about their experiences with a peer-mentoring program. International students will share their experiences to increase understanding of the impact of peer mentoring from a domestic student mentor on their intercultural competence and vice versa. Giving students a voice to share these experiences might contribute greatly to the effectiveness of such a peer-mentoring program. Once these personal accounts are known, it might shed light on the experiences of both domestic and international students and how they relate to each other (Akanwa, 2015; Bartlett, et al., 2016; Gartman, 2016, Kwapong, 2019).

[Note: In-text citations included for illustrative purposes only]

Example 6.2

The central problem to be researched in the proposed study is the extent to which the completion of Teen Leadership, a character education class, impacts the academic achievement of high school students in Texas. As a basis for the study, the researcher identified the overall problem to be threefold.

First, there is an issue concerning a variance in the scores for the Texas Assessment of Knowledge and Skills (TAKS) that was present in schools throughout the state for the overall reporting category. For this study, student discipline and a lack of successful interaction skills were considered influencing factors in that disparity. The prevailing issue identified by the researcher was whether there is a difference between the group that took the character education program and the group that did not. The issue is whether a character education program influences passing rates on the TAKS for the overall part of the assessment.

Second, there is an issue concerning a variance in the scores for the TAKS that was present in schools throughout the state for the Math reporting category. Patterns in the variance could not be attributed to the geographical location, size or demographic makeup of the campus. Personal accountability, attendance and social intelligence are determined to be factors. The issue identified by the researcher was whether there is a difference between the group that took the character education program and the group that did not. The issue is whether a character education program influences passing rates on the TAKS for the Math part of the assessment.

Last, there is an issue concerning a variance in the scores for the TAKS that was present in schools throughout the state for the ELA category. Again, patterns in the variance could not be attributed to the geographical location, size or demographic makeup of the campus. It is believed that the variances were influenced by factors that include student discipline and time distracted from work, attendance and accountability toward academic responsibilities. The issue identified by the researcher was whether there is a difference between the group that took the character education program and the group that did not. The issue is whether a character education program influences passing rates on the TAKS for the ELA part of the assessment (Zeig, 2019).

Example 6.3

The central problem to be researched in the proposed study is that the achievement gap between minority students and non-minority students has barely narrowed over the last half century. Academic gains have been produced among minorities, but these gains are insignificant, resulting in the gap persisting and minority students continuing to be left behind (Williams, 2013). As a basis for the study, the researcher identified the problem to be threefold.

The first issue identified as a basis for this study is the question of achievement gaps between minorities and non-minorities in public schools located in southwest Virginia. Generally, the "achievement gap" refers to assessment performances that are compared between minority students and their non-minority peers. The National Education Association posits that achievement gaps are complex and interconnected and vary from school to school and district to district. The differences between the achievement scores of minorities and non-minorities are apparent on large-scale standardized assessments.

The second issue identified as the basis for this research study is the comparative achievement gaps between additional subgroups such as students with disabilities and English language learners. Achievement gaps are not specific to just minority and non-minority students. Gaps in achievement may exist between groups of students from different backgrounds on state-administered assessments that include gender, disability and income.

Last, the third issue identified is the factors that contribute to these achievement gaps. There are factors that are within a school's or district's control that directly impact student performance such as class sizes, highly qualified teachers and school safety. Other factors that are outside a school's control may include safety in the community, after-school programs and the socioeconomic status of families.

[Note: In-text citations included for illustrative purposes only]

Example 6.4

The central problem to be researched by the proposed study is the issue of organizational performance, leadership and employee empowerment. As a basis for this study, the researcher identified three key problems that demanded this investigation. The first major issue identified as a basis for this study regards customer and market focus and operational performance in air transportation organizations. Market orientation strategies in these organizations have been shown to have a positive relationship to organizational performance and profitability (Balas et al., 2014). Market-oriented strategies improve operational effectiveness (Mokhtar et al., 2014).

Pekovic et al. (2016) stated that customer-orientation strategies permit the organization to identify and respond to customers while creating value for them. Chu et al. (2016) stated that organizations achieve competitive advantages and better performance when they oriented themselves to customers. In a study about shift work schedules in the nursing sector, Faraz et al. (2014) mentioned evidence that reflects working beyond 50 hours per week is harmful to workers' health. Stefanovska-Petkovska et al. (2015) stated that employee satisfaction has been demonstrated to promote organizational performance. They mentioned that, when their employees' job satisfaction increases, companies create a comparative advantage for themselves. The intention of this investigation is to study customer- and market-focus issues within air transportation organizations.

The second major issue as a basis for this study is the concerns with employee empowerment and organization performance in air transportation organizations. Malik et al. (2013), in their study of the telecommunication sector in Pakistan, mentioned that future researchers might target other cities to conduct research about employee empowerment. Verhulst and Boks (2014), in their study related to employee empowerment in various Benelux firms, mentioned that a larger study could look at firms in different countries and companies that integrate sustainability into the entire company. Abbasi et al.'s (2011) study about employee empowerment in Pakistani banks might stimulate further research in other parts of the world, especially in other developing countries.

The last major issue identified as a foundation for this study concerns leaders' openness to new business strategies and organizational performance in air transportation organizations. Organizational performance statistically measures how the organization is addressing their leaders-employees work relation and employee empowerment towards the goals of the company. The problem identified in this study, based on prior research, is that corporations and organizations in related industries have a limited knowledge of the variables that strive for excellent organizational performance. Miller (2014) stated that many organizations need to strive for operational excellence, not for perfection, using a comprehensive approach focusing on people and effecting change by engaging customers, always innovating, continuously improving operations and moving at optimal speed (Morales, 2017).

[Note: In-text citations included for illustrative purposes only]

Summary

This chapter discussed the issue with problem statement development for novice and burgeoning researchers and proposed a conceptual model based on the research methods. The chapter provided conceptual models and tools for helping doctoral students and researchers to develop their problem statement. It contributes to the research method literature by demonstrating the importance of problem statement development and the factors that are vital. It also makes a key contribution by providing a conceptual contribution. The chapter provides a conceptual model and some theory with regard to problem statement development. The foundation of the research is based on providing a template for problem statement development.

The development of the problem statement can be challenging, but it is an integral part of the research endeavor. Possible future studies in research methods and strategies could provide further development for problem statement development in research. Also, future work on research methods could focus on other aspects of research development such as purpose, research questions and other items of interests. We hope that our proposed framework will provide researchers with a template and a foundation for developing a solid and clear problem statement in their research projects and dissertations.

References

Bittner, N. P., & O'Connor, M. (2012). Focus on retention: Identifying barriers to nurse faculty satisfaction. *Nursing Education Perspectives, 33*(4), 251–254.

Brett, A. L., Branstetter, J. E., & Wagner, P. D. (2014). Nurse educators' perceptions of caring attributes in current and ideal work environments. *Nursing Education Perspectives, 35*(6), 360–366. https://doi.org/10.5480/13-1113.1

Byme, D. M., & Martine, B. N. (2014). A solution to the shortage of nursing faculty. Awareness and understanding of the leadership style of the nursing department head. *Nurse Educator, 39*(3). https://doi.org/10.1097/NNE.0000000000000031

Cook, L. (2017). *The current issues affecting job satisfaction by nursing faculty as a lived experience* [Unpublished dissertation]. ProQuest Dissertations and Theses.

Creswell, J. W. (2009). *Research design: Qualitative, quantitative, and mixed methods approaches.* Sage Publishers.

Creswell, J. W. (2013). *Qualitative inquiry and research design: Choosing among five approaches* (3rd ed.). Sage Publishers.

Hernon, P., & Schwartz, C. (2007). What is a problem statement? *Library & Information Science Research, 29*(3), 307–309. https://doi.org/10.1016/j.lisr.2007.06.001

Jacobs, R. L. (2011). Developing a research problem and purpose statement. In T. S. Rocco & T. Hatcher (Eds.), *The handbook of scholarly writing and publishing* (pp. 125–141). Jossey-Bass.

Kwapong, S. (2019). *Investigating the experiences of international and domestic students in a peer mentoring program and its effects on intercultural competence at a university: A qualitative study.* ProQuest Dissertations and Theses.

Mauch, J., & Birch, Jack (1998). *Guide to the successful theses and dissertation: A handbook for students and faculty* (4th ed.) Marcel Dekker, Inc. Publishers.

McSherry, R., Pearce, P., Grimwood, K., & McSherry, W., (2012). The pivotal role of nurse managers, leaders, and educators in enabling excellence in nursing care. *Journal of Nursing Management, 20*(1), 7–19. https://doi.org/10.1111/j.1365-2834.2011.01349.x

Miles, D. A., & Scott, L. (2017, October 26–29). *Confessions of a dissertation chair, Part 1: The six mistakes doctoral students make with the dissertation* [Workshop]. 5th Annual 2017 Black Doctoral Network Conference, Atlanta, GA.

Miles, D. A. (2016). *The one-page dissertation proposal matrix: A guide for developing the dissertation proposal.*

Morales, L. (2017). *A Baldrige assessment of an organization: An empirical study of Baldrige criteria and organizational performance in air transportation organizations* [unpublished dissertation]. ProQuest Dissertations and Theses.

Newton, R., & Rudestam, K. (2007). *Surviving your dissertation: A comprehensive guide to content and process* (3rd ed.). Sage Publishers.

Rosseter, R. (2015). *Nursing faculty shortage fact sheet.* American Association of Colleges of Nursing. Retrieved September 17, 2015, from www.aacn.nche.edu/media-relations/FacultyShortageFS.pdf

Thomas, R. M., & Brubaker, D. (2000). *Theses and dissertations: A guide to planning, research, and writing.* Bergin and Garvey.

Webster, W. (1998a). *Developing and writing your thesis, dissertation or project.* Academic Scholarwrite.

Webster, W. (1998b). *21 models for developing and writing your theses, dissertations or projects.* Academic Scholarwrite.

Zeig, M. (2019). *Effects of a character education course on standardized testing in Texas high schools.* ProQuest Dissertations and Theses.

7 Developing the Purpose Statement

Objective

- Readers will be able to:
  1. Develop a purpose statement

Introduction

The purpose statement is a key component in the development of your study. The craft of developing your purpose statement follows the development of the problem statement. The purpose statement is a type of go-between for the problem statement and the research statement with research questions. In my experience of working with doctoral students, they sometimes do not make the connection between these aforementioned items. This causes them to have trouble connecting the dots, which affects the alignment of their study. This is a common issue for novice researchers and doctoral students.

Researchers must think of the purpose statement as a continuation of the problem statement. The purpose statement acts as a support for the problem statement. If novice researchers can view the purpose statement this way, it will save a considerable amount of time when developing it. The purpose statement is a key component of the study and must be developed carefully. Again, the craft of research has some foundation of making them align and connect. Therefore, this chapter focuses on the importance of developing the problem statement.

Purpose Statement: Definition and Meaning

The *purpose statement* is defined as a declarative statement that describes the goal and objective of the study. The purpose statement has two key questions: (1) What is the overall objective of the study?; and (2) What are the specific objectives of the study (Miles & Scott, 2017)? Again, many doctoral students have considerable trouble writing the purpose statement. The reasons stem from a poor research objective leading to a poor significance statement. The research purpose is a statement of "why" the study is being conducted, or the goal of the study. Also, the purpose statement follows the description and analysis of the problem. The purpose

DOI: 10.4324/9781003268154-7

statement identifies the variables, population and setting for a study. Every study has an explicit or implicit purpose statement. The research purpose statement should be stated objectively or in a way that does not reflect particular biases or values of the researcher (Long et al., 1985; Jacobs, 2011; Abbas, 2020).

A well-written purpose statement defines the purpose and helps identify the variables investigated in the study. The purpose statement (a) provides the rationale for the study and (b) uses data and research to confirm the need to address the purpose in the study (Long et al., 1985).

Based on goals to alleviate or reduce the problem, you can create your purpose statement (Weintraub, 2016). For example, it would be written something like this: "The purpose of this study is to discover what tools are needed to better prepare high school students for the AP Spanish exam and to measure the level of efficacy of those tools" (Weintraub, 2016).

Another way to look at the purpose statement is to view it as a restatement. For example, the purpose of the study can be described as a succinct restatement of the problem statement. The purpose of the study offers a precise summation of the study's overall purpose. There are some cases where the purpose statement may include several subcategories: research questions, hypotheses, limitations, delimitations and definitions of the key terms. The researcher must state the purpose and provide a rationale that supports this purpose. Thus, it acts as a precursor to the questions. The purpose of the study also includes the variables studied and the primary unit of analysis (Calabrese, 2006, 2009).

Another approach to developing the purpose statement is to begin with a declarative statement. This would be an economical way of grounding the study in a context. An example would be: *This study will analyze or study or explore or be about …* . A paragraph or two is sufficient. A researcher wants to keep the purpose statement short, direct and to the point (Bryant, 2003).

The research purpose is a statement of "why" the investigation is being conducted or the objective of the examination. The objective of the research may be to distinguish or depict an idea or to elucidate or foresee a circumstance or answer for a circumstance that shows the kind of concentration to be directed (Singh, 2020). The research purpose is generally classified into three research methods: descriptive, exploratory and explanatory. As the research question can be both explanatory and descriptive, the research project may have more than one reason (Singh, 2020).

Purpose Statements Based on the Research Methodology

Development of the Purpose Statement for Quantitative Studies

Another approach to developing the purpose statement is to base it on the methodology. The purpose statement tends to tell the reader the overarching focus or goal of the study, with the methodology (quantitative and qualitative) included. For example, the quantitative purpose statement includes variables, participants and sometimes the specific location of the problem being investigated (Terrell, 2015). In

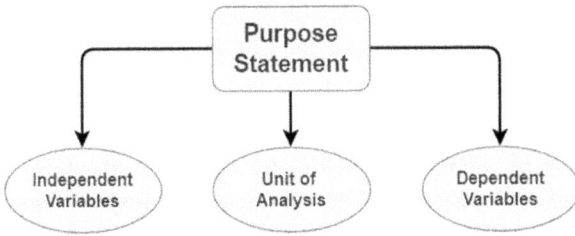

Figure 7.1 The quantitative purpose statement components.

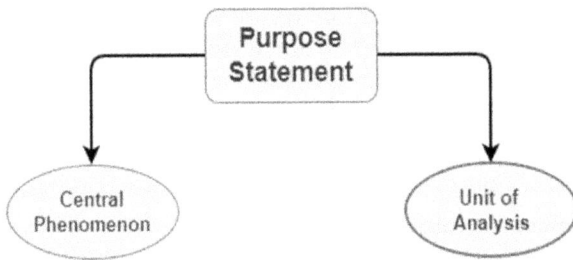

Figure 7.2 The qualitative purpose statement components.

addition, the purpose statement identifies the unit of analysis, which is the who or what the researcher is studying. Lastly, the purpose statement allows the researcher the opportunity to identify the independent variables and dependent variables. More specifically, the independent variable is the "cause" and the dependent variable is the "effect" in the study (Terrell, 2015) (see Figure 7.1).

Development of the Purpose Statement for Qualitative Studies

For qualitative studies, there is a different approach to developing the purpose statement. For example, when developing the purpose statement for qualitative studies, you include the participants and location of the study. However, rather than focus on the variables and unit of analysis, the researcher focuses on the central phenomenon of the study. The central phenomenon for the qualitative purpose of the study is clear (Terrell, 2015) (see Figure 7.2).

In a qualitative study, these two components are very important in developing the purpose statement. This is a completely different approach compared to the quantitative study.

So, when a researcher chooses a particular methodology, understanding the different characteristics of the two methodologies will be a tremendous help in developing the purpose statement. In a qualitative study, the purpose statement is developed from both the phenomenon and unit of analysis.

The Most Powerful Purpose Statement Verbs

One of the key problems that novice researchers face is not only how to develop the purpose statement but also what verbs to use. Not knowing the most powerful verbs to use is one of the biggest issues when it comes to the development of the problem statement. Remember, the purpose statement is a declarative statement that defines the goal and objective of the study. Using the right verbs and terminology is key to developing a good purpose statement. I like to help novice researchers with this particular area. Table 7.1 shows the most powerful purpose statement verbs. I really do like the proactive trait of these purpose statement verbs.

I like to advise students to use verbs such as *analyze, compare, define, examine, investigate* and *interpret*. When the researcher uses these types of verbs, it makes them sound like a researcher. However, one word that I do not recommend novice researchers use is *understand*. In my opinion, the word *understand* is a weak purpose statement verb. So, if the researcher uses some of the verbs in Table 7.1, this will help them develop their purpose statement.

Writing Up the Purpose Statement

When developing the purpose statement, we will use the *Statement Grid*. Again, the Statement Grid is a helpful tool that aids students visually with the purpose statement. This tool helps doctoral students when they have trouble coming up with their purpose statement. It helps them with their thought process and describes three possible subproblems as a basis for their research (see Table 7.2).

Directions

First, write the overall purpose statement. **Second,** divide the purpose to be investigated into two or three objectives (or subpurposes) that align with the issues (subproblems) of the problem statement (see Table 7.2). Please note, use

Table 7.1 A list of the 40 most powerful purpose statement verbs

analyze	compare	define	examine	interpret
apply	conceptualize	demonstrate	explain	investigate
appraise	consolidate	design	evaluate	justify
argue	construct	describe	formulate	propose
calculate	contrast	develop	identify	recommend
categorize	criticize	differentiate	illustrate	relate
challenge	debate	dissolve	indicate	review
clarify	deduce	establish	integrate	suggest

Source: Miles and Scott (2017).

Table 7.2 The Statement Grid for purpose statement development

The Purpose Statement:

Objective 1:	Objective 2:	Objective 3:

Table 7.3 Example: The Statement Grid for purpose statement development

The Purpose Statement:

The purpose of this study is to investigate the issues affecting the job satisfaction of nursing faculty members in metropolitan New York. Interviewing and questioning nursing faculty living in metropolitan New York provides insight into their personal experiences of job satisfaction while working in the nurse educator role. The researcher has identified three primary objectives as a basis for this study.

Objective 1:	Objective 2:	Objective 3:
First, ...	Second, ...	Last, ...

Table 7.4 Example: The Statement Grid for purpose statement development

The Purpose Statement:

The purpose of this study is to investigate the issues affecting the job satisfaction of nursing faculty members in metropolitan New York. Interviewing and questioning nursing faculty living in metropolitan New York provides insight into their personal experiences of job satisfaction while working in the nurse educator role. The researcher has identified three primary objectives as a basis for this study.

Objective 1:	Objective 2:	Objective 3:
First, the objective of this study is to examine the issue of job satisfaction among the nursing faculty.	Second, the objective of this study is to investigate the impact of low wages on the nursing faculty.	Lastly, the objective of this study is to examine the complexities of the nursing faculty role (Cook, 2017).

the word *objective* when writing the subpurpose. It is done this way to prevent mis-interpretation of the objectives as four separate purpose statements (Tables 7.3 and 7.4).

Here is another example using the Statement Grid for purpose statement development (see Table 7.5). Also provided are examples in paragraph form from actual dissertations .

Table 7.5 Example: The Statement Grid for purpose statement development

The Purpose Statement:

The purpose of this study is to examine the relationship between leadership self-perceptions of communal or agentic attributes and follower perceptions of authentic leadership in different industry sectors. The researcher has identified three primary objectives as a basis for this quantitative study.

Objective 1:	**Objective 2:**	**Objective 3:**
First, the objective of this study is to measure leader self-perceptions of communal or agentic attributes.	Second, the objective of this study is to measure follower perceptions of leader identity.	Last, the objective of this study is to perform a study focusing on the relationship between leadership self-perceptions of communal (or agentic) attributes and follower perceptions of authentic leadership, since the previous study used transformational leadership theory (Hemmi, 2020).

Example 7.1

The purpose of this study is to examine if there is a statistically significant difference among K–12 performing arts and non-performing arts teachers' opinions on the necessity of music education in the Southern part of the US. The researcher has identified two primary objectives as a basis for this study.

The first objective of this study is to examine if there is a statistically significant difference among K–12 performing arts and non-performing arts teachers' opinions on the necessity of music education in school. Analyzing performing art teachers' opinions versus non-performing arts teachers' opinions will be interesting for the study. Performing arts teachers have a direct relationship with the music education curriculum because of the courses they teach (Daykin & Stickley, 2015). Non-performing arts teachers can consist of core, physical education and vocational teachers that are not governed by the music education curriculum.

The second objective of this study is to determine if there is a statistically significant difference among K–12 elementary, middle and high school teachers' opinions on the necessity of music education in school. Teachers who teach at different grade levels will probably contain different opinions. Elementary teachers begin the molding process of their students and can be over-protective because the students cannot cognitively depend on themselves. Middle school teachers are teaching the students to use their minds more and become more self-sufficient. High school teachers are pushing students to be more mature and to think critically. The different focuses and approaches that these teachers are using can directly impact their opinion towards music education (Jefferson, 2022).

Example 7.2

The purpose of this study is to investigate how veterans describe the challenges, if any, of limited transferability and second-career preparedness in making the transition from active duty to the teaching profession in the Southeast. The researcher identified two phenomena of the study, which are the challenges that active-duty military veterans encounter with their limited transferability and preparedness. The researcher has identified two primary objectives for this study.

The first objective of the study is to investigate how active-duty veterans describe the challenges they encounter with the limited transferability of their Military Occupation Specialty (MOS) and skills. Service-members that perform combat occupations or military occupational specialties possess skills that are less transferable to civilian careers than those in non-combat MOSs (MacLean & Parsons, 2010; Mangum & Ball, 1987). The transferability of military veterans' MOSs and skills demonstrates the importance that these have transferred to the success of civilian occupational programs (Mangum & Ball, 1989). One such civilian occupational program that can benefit from this transferability is the teaching career field, which is not a career choice for military service members (Jones, 2017). Skills transfer is still a work in progress, and military veterans continue to encounter barriers to teaching and require additional training to earn state teacher certification (Doe & Doe, 2013; Moorhouse, 2014; Robertson & Brott, 2014).

The second objective of the study is to investigate how active-duty veterans describe the challenges they encounter with second-career preparedness as they transition from the military to the teaching profession. Military transition programs provide planning and logistical assistance for transitioning veterans; however, studies have shown that, emotionally, veterans feel they are unprepared to manage the transition to the civilian workforce (Wolpert, 2000; Baruch & Quick, 2009; Robertson & Brott, 2014). Research has also found that pre-retirement planning and preparation for retirement is essential to military personnel being better prepared for the successful transition into the civilian workplace (Shultz et al., 2003; Spiegel & Shultz, 2003; Vigoda-Gadot et al.,

2010). Despite documented improvements in the military's transition program in recent years, the military's Transition Assistance Program (TAP) remains the only preparation that service members receive prior to leaving the military (Zogas, 2017). The effectiveness of the program is hindered by its brevity, and by service members only being able to complete the training weeks before retirement (Zogas, 2017; Martinez, 2021).

[Note: In-text citations included for illustrative purposes only]

Example 7.3

The purpose of this study is to investigate the lived experiences of parental involvement and how it contributes to the lives of their disabled children in special education classrooms in a Title 1 school in Brooklyn, New York. This is a qualitative research study using a phenomenological approach that will utilize semi-structured interviews with open-ended questions to investigate participants' lived experiences of parental involvement in the lives of disabled students. The sample is derived from a population of parents of disabled children studying in Title 1 schools that offer special education in Brooklyn, New York. The study employs a sample size of 15 parents committed or involved with the educational activities of their disabled children. The participants' share their lived experiences through interviews that will focus on questions centered specifically on the six categories outlined by Joyce Epstein. Thus, the purpose of this study is to illustrate how the lived experiences of parental involvement contribute to the academic achievement of disabled children in special education classrooms in Brooklyn, New York. As a basis for the study, the researchers identified two primary objectives of the study.

The first objective is to examine the parents' lived experiences with disabled children in special education classrooms. Based on this objective, the researcher seeks to know how the parents' experiences influence the academic performance of their disabled children. Moreover, the objective is derived from categories of the Epstein Parental Involvement Model, whereby various involvement approaches are proposed and proven to influence the academic achievement of disabled children (Epstein, 1987).

The second objective is to investigate the lived experiences of parental involvement and its importance in developing the child. The development of children is determined by parental care and overall involvement in every other aspect of a child's life. This objective seeks to know how using the six categories of the Epstein Parental Involvement Model impacts on the overall development of children (Epstein, 1987; Hussain, 2020).

[Note: In-text citations included for illustrative purposes only]

Summary

The development of the purpose statement is an integral part of the research endeavor. The foundation of research is based on providing a template for the purpose statement development. The development of the purpose statement can be a challenging endeavor. This chapter discussed the writing of the purpose statement for novice and burgeoning researchers. It also provided a conceptual model for developing the purpose statement as well as a conceptual model and tool for helping doctoral students and researchers to develop their purpose statement.

In this chapter, we covered four things. First, we discussed the definition of the purpose statement. Second, we illustrated how to develop and write the purpose statement. Third, we provided a model and a framework for developing the purpose statement. Fourth, we provided examples of how a purpose statement is written.

We hope that our proposed model and framework provided students and researchers with a template for developing a solid and clear purpose statement in their research projects and dissertations.

References

Abbas, W. (2020). *The research purpose.* PDF4PRO. Retrieved from https://pdf4pro.com/view/the-research-purpose-3-dr-wafa-a-k-abbas-definition-6307e5.html

Bryant, M. T. (2003). *The portable dissertation advisor.* Corwin Press, Inc.

Calabrese, R. (2006). *The elements of an effective dissertation and thesis: A step-by-step guide to getting it right the first time.* Rowman & Littlefield Education, Inc.

Calabrese, R. (2009). *The dissertation desk reference: The doctoral student's manual to writing the dissertation.* Rowman & Littlefield Education, Inc.

Cook, L. (2017). *The current issues affecting job satisfaction by nursing faculty as a lived experience* [Unpublished dissertation]. ProQuest Dissertations and Theses.

Daykin, N. & Stickley, N. (2015). The role of qualitative research in arts and health. In S. Clift & P. M. Camic (Eds.), *Oxford textbook of creative arts, health, and wellbeing: International perspectives on practice, policy and research* (pp. 73–82). Oxford University Press. https://doi.org/10.1093/med/9780199688074.003.0010

Hemmi, J. (2020). *Leader self-perception of gender identity: Its influence upon follower perceptions of authentic leadership* [Unpublished dissertation]. ProQuest Dissertations and Theses.

Hussain, E. (2020). *Contributions of involvement of parents in the lives of their disabled children* [Unpublished dissertation, Grand Canyon University]. ProQuest Dissertations and Theses.

Jacobs, R. L. (2011). Developing a research purpose and purpose statement. In T. S. Rocco & T. Hatcher (Eds.), *The handbook of scholarly writing and publishing* (pp. 125–141). Jossey-Bass.

Jefferson, R. (2022). *A quantitative study on the opinions of K–12 administrators towards music education* [Unpublished dissertation].

Long, T., Convey, J., & Chwalek, A. (1985). *Completing dissertations in the behavioral sciences and education: A systematic guide for graduate students.* Jossey-Bass.

Martinez, O. (2021). *A qualitative descriptive study examining the experiences of active-duty veterans that have transitioned from the military to the teaching profession* [Published dissertation]. ProQuest Dissertations and Theses.

Miles, D. A., & Scott, L. (2017, October 26–29). *Confessions of a dissertation chair, Part 1: The six mistakes doctoral students make with the dissertation* [Workshop]. 5th Annual 2017 Black Doctoral Network Conference, Atlanta, GA.

Singh, S. (2020). Purpose and process of research. In R. N. Subudhi & S. Mishra (Eds.), *Methodological issues in management research: Advances, challenges and the way ahead* (pp. 27–36). Emerald Publishing Limited.

Terrell, S. (2015). *Writing a proposal for your dissertation: Guidelines and examples* (3rd ed.). The Guilford Press.

Weintraub, D. (2016). *The problem and purpose statement.* NSU/FCE Summer Institute 2016, Nova Southeastern University. https://education.nova.edu/summer/2016-presentati ons/The%20Problem%20and%20Purpose%20Statement.pdf

8 Developing the Research Statement and Research Questions

Objective

- Readers will be able to:
  1. Develop a research statement and research questions

Introduction

The craft of conducting research is one of the most exciting endeavors for professors and students. Conducting research provides us with many fascinating subjects of inquiry. To conduct research, we must develop research questions. Research questions are the driving force behind many studies.

Some researchers and doctoral students in particular are not properly taught how to develop research questions. This is a common issue with researchers. They mix quantitative research questions with qualitative research questions. This presents a challenge that we want to underscore with this problem.

Research Questions: Definition and Meaning

How do we define what a research question is? There are many definitions, so we will try to keep this simple. A research question is defined as a specific inquiry that the research seeks to provide a response to. The research question resides at the core of systematic investigation, and it helps you to clearly define a path for the research process (Formplus Blog, n.d; White, 2017).

The research question is usually the first step in any research project. The research question is the primary interrogation point of your research, and it sets the pace for your work (Formplus Blog, n.d.). Most commonly, the research question focuses on the research, determines the methodology and hypothesis and guides all stages of inquiry, analysis and reporting. For the researcher, with the right research questions, you will be able to gather useful information for your investigation (Formplus Blog, n.d.).

For doctoral students, developing research questions is one of the hardest parts of starting a dissertation. It is important to make sure that the research questions address these characteristics: (a) your questions must be precise; (b) your questions

DOI: 10.4324/9781003268154-8

must cover the problem you want to address; and (c) your questions must indicate how you will create the answer (Creswell, 2009, 2013; Newton & Rudestam, 2007).

Developing Research Questions for a Quantitative Study

In quantitative studies, investigators use research questions and hypotheses to shape and focus on the purpose of the study. These research questions tend to be inter-rogative questions that the researcher seeks to answer.

Creswell (2009) asserts that there are two usual types of quantitative questions: (a) *descriptive questions*, based on descriptive statistics; and (b) *inferential questions*, based on inferential statistics. Here are some examples.

Descriptive Research Questions

- What is the students rate on critical thinking skills (a descriptive question focused on the independent variable)?
- What are the students' achievement levels (or grades) in science classes (a descriptive question focused on the dependent variable)?

Inferential Research Questions

- Does critical thinking ability relate to student achievement (an inferential question relating the independent variable and the dependent variable)?
- Does critical thinking ability relate to student achievement, controlling for the effects at prior grades in science and the educational attainment of the eighth graders' parents (an inferential question relating the independent and the dependent variables) (Creswell, 2009)?

These two question types are one approach to developing quantitative research questions. Another approach to developing research questions for a quantitative study is to use a typical template. The typical research question for a quantitative study uses about four to five phrases, such as *"To what degree …," "How much …," "Is there a relationship between …," "What is the relationship between …,"* and *"What is the difference… ."*

The researcher will be measuring the relationship between the independent variables and dependent variables (Creswell, 2009). Table 8.1 shows typical examples of quantitative questions that will drive the investigation.

Using the Theoretical Constructs in the Instrument as a Basis for Developing Quantitative Research Questions

Using a Researcher-Designed Instrument and Developing Research Questions

When developing research questions, the researcher usually develops them based on the problem statement. Sometimes the researcher can do this and sometimes

Table 8.1 Example of common research questions for a quantitative study

Question Type	Question Example
Type 1a	1a: To what degree do first-year department managers subscribe to Theory X management beliefs as measured by the Myers-Brigg Scale?
Type 2a	2a: Does a rise in bad management behavior lead to employee turnover in an organization as measured by the Myers-Brigg Scale?
Type 3a	3a: Do first-year department managers report adhering to an authoritative leadership style as measured by the Myers-Brigg Scale?
Type 4a	4a: Is there a relationship between autocratic management style and the narcissistic behaviors of first-year department managers as measured by the Myers-Brigg Scale?
Type 5a	5a: What is the relationship between autocratic management style and the narcissistic behaviors of first-year department managers as measured by the Myers-Brigg Scale?
Type 6a	6a: How much time do first-year department managers spend mentoring and coaching during their first year as measured by the Myers-Brigg Scale?
Type 7a	7a: What is the difference between autocratic management style and the narcissistic behaviors of first-year department managers as measured by the Myers-Brigg Scale? (Miles & Scott, 2017)

they can't. Take that into consideration when using an instrument. Many times, when doctoral students are using an established instrument for their dissertation research, they should use the theoretical constructs in the instrument as a basis for the research questions. However, that does not work if the researcher creates their own instrument. This is because the instrument is neither established nor has it been proven to have both reliability and validity. So, the rule for developing research questions with a researcher-developed instrument is that the researcher can develop the research questions from a descriptive or inferential point of view. The researcher can develop general descriptive or inferential types of research questions. Again, because the researcher-developed instrument generally does not have constructs or a theoretical framework, the researcher would have to develop general research questions.

Using an Established Instrument and Developing Research Questions

Nevertheless, when the researcher uses an established instrument, it is best to use the theoretical constructs in the instrument as a basis for developing the research questions. You must align the research questions with the theoretical constructs or subscales within the instrument used for the study. For statistical analyses, most likely the researcher will align their data analyses with the theoretical constructs of the instrument. For example, if the instrument has three theoretical constructs or

Table 8.2 Example of aligning quantitative research questions with instrument/scale constructs for a dissertation study

Theoretical Constructs and Subscales in the Baldrige Instrument	Quantitative Research Questions
CONSTRUCT 1: Category 1: Leadership	R1: Is there a relationship between *leadership* behaviors and management style as measured by the Baldrige Instrument?
CONSTRUCT 2: Category 2: Strategic Planning	R2: Is there a relationship between *strategic planning* behaviors and management style as measured by the Baldrige Instrument?
CONSTRUCT 3: Category 3: Customer and Market Focus	R3: Is there a relationship between *customer and market focus* behaviors and management style as measured by the Baldrige Instrument? (Morales, 2017)

subscales, there must be three different research questions to align with those theoretical constructs (Table 8.2).

Another rule for developing research questions using an established instrument is always use the name of the instrument in the research question. For example, if you are using an instrument in the research question, it should be written like this:

- **RQ1:** Is there a relationship between autocratic management style and the narcissistic behaviors of first-year department managers as measured by the Myers-Brigg Scale?
- **RQ2:** Is there a relationship between autocratic management style and the followship behaviors of first-year department managers as measured by the Myers-Brigg Scale?

Once more, the researcher should always use the name of the established instrument in the research question. The researcher must align the research questions with the theoretical constructs or subscales within the instrument used for the study. This is usually not taught by dissertation chairs and committee members, but it is a much-needed practice that needs to be shared with doctoral students (Bryant, 2003; Jacobs, 2011; Madsen, 1990; Mauch & Birch, 1998; Thomas & Brubaker, 2000; Webster, 1998a, 1998b).

Writing Up the Research Statement and Research Questions

When developing the research statement, we will use the *Statement Grid*. Again, the Statement Grid is a useful tool that helps doctoral students visually when they are

Table 8.3 The Statement Grid for research statement development

The Research Statement:

Research Question 1:	**Research Question 2:**	**Research Question 3:**

Table 8.4 Example: The Statement Grid for research statement development

The Research Statement:
The central problem to be researched is … . There are three research questions that will guide this research.

Research Question 1:	**Research Question 2:**	**Research Question 3:**
RQ1: …	RQ2: …	RQ3: …

having trouble coming up with their research statement. It helps them with their thought process by describing three possible research question that will guide the study (see Table 8.3).

Directions

First, write the research statement. **Second,** divide the research questions to be investigated into two or three questions that align with the issues (subproblems) of the problem statement and the purpose statement objectives (see Table 8.4).

Here is another example using the Statement Grid for research statement development and research questions (see Table 8.5)

Here is another example using the Statement Grid for research statement development and research questions (Table 8.6). Also provided are examples in paragraph form from actual dissertations.

Table 8.5 Example: The Statement Grid for research statement development

The Research Statement:
The central problem to be researched involves how principals manage job stress. There are three research questions that will guide this research.

Research Question 1:	**Research Question 2:**	**Research Question 3:**
RQ1: How do K–12 principals and administrators describe their experiences of job stress in an urban Central Texas school district environment?	RQ2: How do K–12 principals and administrators describe their experiences of using coping skills for job stress in an urban Central Texas school district environment?	RQ3: How do K–12 principals and administrators describe their experiences of coping with work-life balance and job stress in an urban Central Texas school district environment (Beltran, 2020)?

Table 8.6 Example: The Statement Grid for research statement development

The Research Statement:
The central problem identified by the researcher is the issue of organizational performance, leadership and employee empowerment. There are three research questions that will guide this research.

Research Question 1:	**Research Question 2:**	**Research Question 3:**
RQ1: To what extent does a relationship exist between customer and market focus and organizational performance?	RQ2: To what extent does a relationship exist between employee empowerment and organizational performance?	RQ3: To what extent does a relationship exist between leaders' openness to new business strategies and organizational performance (Morales, 2017)?

Example 8.1: Quantitative Research Questions Based on the Theoretical Framework and Constructs in the Instrument (with Hypotheses)

The research questions and hypotheses included in this study are for addressing if and to what extent statistically significant differences in levels of technostress exist among employee groups in US higher education (faculty administrative, staff and contractors). Five objectives delineate the purpose of this study for analyzing differences in technostress levels (techno-overload, techno-invasion, techno-complexity, techno-insecurity and techno-uncertainty) based on employee groups (faculty, administrative, staff and contractors) in the stated population. The following five research questions and hypotheses guide this quantitative study:

- **RQ1**: Is there a statistically significant difference in levels of techno-overload among employee groups (faculty, administrative, staff and contractors) in US higher education as measured by the Technostress Productivity Instrument?
- **RQ2:** Is there a statistically significant difference in levels of techno-invasion among employee groups (faculty, administrative, staff and contractors) in US higher education as measured by the Technostress Productivity Instrument?
- **RQ3:** Is there a statistically significant difference in levels of techno-complexity among employee groups (faculty, administrative, staff and contractors) in US higher education as measured by the Technostress Productivity Instrument?
- **RQ4:** Is there a statistically significant difference in levels of techno-insecurity among employee groups (faculty, administrative, staff and contractors) in US higher education as measured by the Technostress Productivity Instrument?
- **RQ5:** Is there a statistically significant difference in levels of techno-uncertainty among employee groups (faculty, administrative, staff and contractors) in US higher education as measured by the Technostress Productivity Instrument? (Cornish, 2022).

Example 8.2: Quantitative Research Questions Based on the Theoretical Framework and Constructs in the Instrument (with Hypotheses)

A correlational analysis will be conducted to determine if there is a relationship between the following variables: leadership; strategic planning; customer and market focus; measurements, analysis, and knowledge management; human resources focus; process management; and business results. Six questions guided this study:

RQ1:   Is there a statistically significant relationship between leadership and strategic planning as measured by the National Baldrige Quality Survey Instrument?

Ho1:   There is no statistically significant relationship between leadership and strategic planning as measured by the National Baldrige Quality Survey Instrument.

Ha1:   There is a statistically significant relationship between leadership and strategic planning as measured by the National Baldrige Quality Survey Instrument.

RQ2:   Is there a statistically significant relationship between strategic planning and customer and market focus as measured by the National Baldrige Quality Survey Instrument?

Ho2:   There is no statistically significant relationship between strategic planning and customer and market focus as measured by the National Baldrige Quality Survey Instrument.

Ha2:   There is a statistically significant relationship between strategic planning and customer and market focus as measured by the National Baldrige Quality Survey Instrument.

RQ3:   Is there a statistically significant relationship between customer and market focus and measurements, analysis and knowledge management as measured by the National Baldrige Quality Survey Instrument?

Ho3:   There is no statistically significant relationship between customer and market focus and measurements, analysis and knowledge management as measured by the National Baldrige Quality Survey Instrument.

Ha3:   There is a statistically significant relationship between customer and market focus and measurements, analysis and knowledge management as measured by the National Baldrige Quality Survey Instrument.

RQ4:   Is there a statistically significant relationship between measurements, analysis and knowledge management and human resources focus as measured by the National Baldrige Quality Survey Instrument?

Ho4:   There is no statistically significant relationship between measurements, analysis and knowledge management and human resources focus as measured by the National Baldrige Quality Survey Instrument.

Ha4:   There is a statistically significant relationship between measurements, analysis and knowledge management and human resources focus as measured by the National Baldrige Quality Survey Instrument.

RQ5:   Is there a statistically significant relationship between human resource focus and process management as measured by the National Baldrige Quality Survey Instrument?

Ho5:   There is no statistically significant relationship between human resource focus and process management as measured by the National Baldrige Quality Survey Instrument.

Ha5:   There is a statistically significant relationship between human resource focus and process management as measured by the National Baldrige Quality Survey Instrument.

RQ6:   Is there a statistically significant relationship between process management and business results as measured by the National Baldrige Quality Survey Instrument?

Ho6:   There is no statistically significant relationship between process management and business results as measured by the National Baldrige Quality Survey Instrument.

Ha6: There is a statistically significant relationship between process management and business results as measured by the National Baldrige
Quality Survey Instrument.

These research questions, in conjunction with the Baldrige Quality Criteria
survey, have the purpose to demonstrate Theory X and Theory Y of Douglas
McGregor. These theories have been studied in different organizations, but there
is a lack of studies based on these theories in air transportation organizations. The
Baldrige Quality Criteria instrument is developed in a way that demonstrates,
based on empirical data, if the employees surveyed have work responsibilities
on their own (Theory Y) or need incentive (Theory X) to perform their duties
at work.

(Morales, 2017)

**Example 8.3: Quantitative Research Questions Based on the
Theoretical Framework and Constructs in the Instrument
(with Hypotheses)**

The purpose of this quantitative, correlational study is to determine if or to what
extent OCBs predict job stress among middle grade-level teachers in one district located in the southwestern United States. OCBs, categorized as OCB-I
and OCB-O, are the predictor variables for this study as measured by Somech's
(2016) OCBs (OCB-I and OCB-O) Scale. OCB-I are geared towards the individual, and the OCB-I tasks are those that employees perform with intentions
that the tasks will aid individuals to include students, fellow workers or colleagues.
OCB-O are geared towards the organization, and the OCB-O tasks are those
that employees perform with the intentions that the tasks will benefit the whole
organization. "Job stress" is the criterion variable as measured by Yozgat's et al.
(2013) Job Stress Scale. The criterion variable "job stress" is described as an emo-
tional condition experienced by individuals when they encounter circumstances,
demands and restrictions that have important and undetermined outcomes
(Yozgat et al., 2013).

This study will use the the OCB (OCB-I and OCB-O) Scale (Somech,
2016) and the Job Stress Scale (Yozgat et al., 2013) quantitative surveys to
collect data on OCBs and job stress among middle grade-level teachers. The
OCB (OCB-I and OCB-O) Scale will be used to measure the predictor variable
"OCBs". The OCB Scale contains 13 questions for measuring the degree of
OCBs. The Job Stress Scale will be used to measure the criterion variable "job
stress." The Job Stress Scale contains 13 statements used to measure the degree of

stress experienced by middle grade-level teachers. The OCBs and the job stress are scaled at the interval level. The research questions and hypotheses are framed from the theoretical concept observation of resources theory (Halbesleben, et al., 2014) and the role theory (Biddle, 2013). The research questions and hypotheses may be answered using a quantitative methodology. The sample will include a minimum of 68 public middle grade-level teachers. The following research questions and hypotheses will be used to guide this study.

RQ1:   If or to what extent do organizational citizenship behaviors *individualized* (OCB-I) have a relationship with job stress behaviors among middle grade-level teachers?

Ho1:   Organizational citizenship behaviors in the *individualized* (OCB-I) do not have a significant relationship with job stress behaviors among middle grade-level teachers.

Ha1:   Organizational citizenship behaviors *individualized* (OCB-I) do have a significant relationship with job stress behaviors among middle grade-level teachers.

RQ2:   If or to what extent do organizational citizenship behaviors *organization* (OCB-O) have a relationship with job stress behaviors among middle grade-level teachers?

Ho2:   Organizational citizenship behaviors *organization* (OCB-O) do not have a significant relationship with job stress behaviors among middle grade-level teachers.

Ha2:   Organizational citizenship behaviors *organization* (OCB-O) do have a significant relationship with job stress behaviors among middle grade-level teachers (Kinsey, 2021).

[Note: In-text citations included for illustrative purposes only]

Developing Research Questions for a Qualitative Study

Because qualitative research is exploratory in nature, your qualitative research questions should be open-ended and start with words such as *what, why, where* and *how.* Qualitative researchers normally generate research questions from the purpose of the study in order to maintain consistency among the main components of the study. For example, if your plan is to explore the way Generation Z (i.e., people born between 1997 and 2021) use social media to create worth (Dimock, 2019), your research question could be, "How does Generation Z use social media to create worth?" As shown here, you can see that the research question is open-ended and aligned with the purpose statement.

Qualitative research questions can be grouped into descriptive, exploratory, process-focused, comparative and explanatory (see Table 8.7). Note that some

Table 8.7 Types of research questions and their characteristics

Type of Research Question	When To Use	First Word Normally Used	Example
Descriptive	When you plan to use data collected to describe the phenomenon of interest	What	What is the experience of mothers homeschooling their children?
Exploratory	When you want to engage in inquiry to find out what is going on	What, How	What makes physicians quit their jobs?
Process-focused	When you want to demonstrate how a phenomenon occurs	How	How do people labeled as Generation Z become financially independent?
Comparative	When you plan to compare entities or phenomena or processes	How	How is working from home different from working in the office?
Explanatory	When you plan to explain a phenomenon or process	Why, How	Why are some CEOs concerned about allowing employees to work from home?

questions can be associated with more than one type of research question. For instance, an exploratory research question could also be considered a process-focused question.

You may ask, "How many research questions do I need?" You can have as many questions as you want, but make sure they are consistent with your purpose statement. Also, it is important to note that the more questions you have, the more data you need to help you address the questions. So, we advise that you focus on not more than three questions. You could even have one research question if it covers everything you plan to find out as depicted in the purpose statement.

Concerning whether you need to have a sub-research question, you do not need to have one unless it would assist you to adequately address the main research question. Some research questions may have some layers/components that warrant the need to be broken down into simple questions. These questions generated from the main questions become sub-research questions.

Let's look at this example, "How does experience of mindfulness contribute to doctoral students' quality of life?" With this main research question, there are two main concepts in the question: (1) experience of mindfulness; and (2) quality of life. Based on these components, these are the suggested sub-research questions:

1. What is the experience of mindfulness among doctoral students?
2. What is the experience of quality of life among doctoral students?

Table 8.8 Example of research questions for a qualitative study

Question Type	Question Example
Type 1b	1b: How do freshmen students describe the experiences of living in a residence hall learning environment?
Type 2b	2b: How does a 9/11 tragedy survivor describe their lived experiences and health issues in the US?
Type 3b	3b: What is the experience of nursing staff during an interrogation following Chief Nursing Officer separation turnover?
Type 4b	4b: Why does domestic violence often occur with victims who are financially dependent on the perpetrators for shelter (Miles & Scott, 2017)?

With this format, addressing these two sub-questions will help in answering the main questions. Alternatively, you could add a question to the main research question to get two main questions, such as:

1. What is the experience of mindfulness among doctoral students?
2. How does the experience of mindfulness contribute to doctoral students' quality of life?

As you can see, you can create any number of qualitative main questions and sub-questions. The most important thing is to make sure they align with the purpose of the study, and you have the rich data to adequately address them.

Qualitative research questions assume two forms: (a) *central questions*; and (b) *associated sub-questions*. The format of the qualitative research questions usually relates back to the strategy of inquiry (Bryant, 2003).

The typical research question for a qualitative study uses a few different phrases, such as "*How do …,*" "*How does …,*" "*What is the experience of …*" and "*Why does …*" (see Table 8.8). In the practice of conducting qualitative research, the researcher will be investigating a phenomenon.

Qualitative research questions typically use *exploratory verbs* and convey the research design. Common verbs used in qualitative research questions include (a) *discover* (e.g., grounded theory); (b) *seek to understand* (e.g., ethnography); (c) *explore a process* (e.g., case study); (d) *describe the experiences* (e.g., phenomenology); and (e) *report the stories* (e.g., narrative research) (Bryant, 2003). Table 8.8 shows some typical examples of qualitative questions that drive the investigation.

Using the Theoretical Framework as a Basis for Developing Qualitative Research Questions

Previously, we stated that, with developing quantitative research questions, you most likely will be using an established instrument for your dissertation research.

You will use the theoretical model or theoretical constructs based on the research instrument as a basis for the research questions.

However, this does not necessarily work with qualitative research and methodology. With qualitative research, you can use a theoretical framework as a basis for your research questions, or you can develop your research questions based on the problem to be investigated as a basis for the study. Because qualitative research is primarily exploratory in nature, it does not follow the theoretical framework or theoretical constructs in an instrument compared to quantitative research. It can be very confusing for doctoral students to understand this difference when using a qualitative approach to research.

In essence, the qualitative researcher creates their own instrument; this is the interview questions. However, with the qualitative researcher, the interview must align with the research questions. The researcher usually develops the research questions for the study first then the interview questions. Here are some examples from actual dissertation studies.

Example 8.4: Qualitative Research Questions (without a Theoretical Framework)

Research questions are the basis of a study, since they determine the methods or research designs, data collection techniques, analysis procedures and reporting of the results. The present study seeks to explain how the internal and external daily experiences of African American women college presidents determine a successful presidency role. The study employs Collins' (2021) five dimensions derived from the model of *Black Feminist Thought*, leading to the following research questions:

RQ1: How do African American women college presidents describe their experiences in terms of success and achievements in their leadership role in the higher education environment?

RQ2: How do African American women college presidents describe their experiences with external/internal daily activities and leadership role in the higher education environment?

This framework explored five specific dimensions that identify how African American women link their voice to the reality of lived experiences based on several factors of life that involve race, gender and class. These dimensions include: (a) core themes of a Black woman's standpoint, (b) a variation in the responses to core themes, (c) the interdependence of experience and consciousness, (d) consciousness and the struggle for a self-defined standpoint, and (e) the interdependence of thought and action (Collins, 2021). Thus, the first research question proposed to know how African American women college presidents defined success utilizing Collins' five dimensions listed above. The second research question proposed to identify how African American women college presidents described the experience of internal and external daily activities in their leadership role at an institution of higher education (Ray, 2020).

Example 8.5: Qualitative Research Questions (with Theoretical Framework)

The overarching research question that guided this qualitative descriptive study was intended to address the following problem statement: it is not known how African American women small business owners in the services industry describe challenges with professional social networks, challenges with professional mentoring and challenges with access to resources in their businesses. Networking is defined in research as a tool for career development (Gibson, 2014), and networking could provide access to social resources embedded in the network (Murwatingsih et al., 2019). Dodd (2019) determined in research the influence professionals have in providing intangible resources for organizations and the significance managers play in the social capital for their organizations. In the context of small businesses, networking aids business owners in identifying needed resources to sustain their firms (Mohamad & Chin, 2019). The theoretical framework derives from the social networking theory and the Social Entrepreneurship model that guide this proposed study. The research questions were developed based on the synthesis and on this theory and model.

According to Ritchie et al. (2013), a sample size of under 50 participants is appropriate for single studies. The research questions that guide this study are:

RQ1: How do African American women small business owners in the services industry describe their experiences with the challenges of professional social networks in the context of the success of their businesses?

RQ2: How do African American women small business owners in the services industry describe their experiences with the challenges of professional mentoring in the context of the success of their businesses?

RQ3: How do African American women small business owners in the services industry describe their experiences with the challenges of access to resources in the context of the success of their businesses?

The research questions mentioned in this section will address the gap determined by literature on African American women small business owners in the services industry and their descriptions of the challenges with professional social networks, challenges with professional mentoring and challenges with access to resources. The research questions provided a guideline for developing interview protocols in this proposed study. They were intended to provide specific data to develop perspectives on challenges with professional social networks, challenges with professional mentoring and challenges with access to resources in the context of the business success of African American women small business owners in the services industry. Aamir (2015) noted in research that it is the way the research question is structured that will determine the most appropriate study design (Dwight, 2022).

[Note: In-text citations included for illustrative purposes only]

Summary

The craft of developing a research statement and research questions is based on the methodology of the research. The craft of developing quantitative research questions is quite different compared with qualitative research questions. Understanding the differences between the two research question types is the first step to getting them done correctly.

First, this chapter discussed approaches to developing the research statement and research questions for a quantitative study. We also discussed using the theoretical constructs in the instrument as a basis for developing quantitative research questions.

Second, this chapter discussed approaches to developing research questions for a qualitative study. We also discussed using the theoretical constructs in the instrument as a basis for developing qualitative research questions.

Third, this chapter discussed approaches to examples of quantitative research questions. We also provided examples of qualitative research questions.

Lastly, this chapter discussed different types of research questions and their characteristics. A potential shortcoming of developing research questions is that it can be confusing if the research methodology for the study is not established first. This will provide a strong foundation.

References

Beltran, V. (2020). *Descriptive study of southwest urban school principals' experience of job stress.* ProQuest Dissertations and Theses.

Bryant, M. T. (2003). *The portable dissertation advisor.* Corwin Press, Inc.

Collins, P. H. (2021). *Black feminist thought, 30th anniversary edition. Knowledge, consciousness, and the politics of empowerment.* Taylor & Francis Group.

Cornish, D. (2022). *An empirical study of technostress within U.S. higher education employees.* ProQuest Dissertations and Theses.

Creswell, J. W. (2009). *Research design: Qualitative, quantitative, and mixed methods approaches.* Sage Publishers.

Creswell, J. W. (2013). *Qualitative inquiry and research design: Choosing among five approaches* (3rd ed.). Sage Publishers.

Dimock, M. (2019, January 17). Defining generations: Where Millennials end and Generation Z begins. Pew Research Center. https://pewrsr.ch/2szqtJz

Dwight, C. (2022). *African American women small business owners: Networking and success – A descriptive study* [UMI document]. ProQuest Dissertations and Theses.

Formplus Blog. (n.d.). Research questions: Definitions, types + (examples). Retrieved November 14, 2022, from www.formpl.us/blog/research-question

Jacobs, R. L. (2011). Developing a research purpose and purpose statement. In T. S. Rocco & T. Hatcher (Eds.), *The handbook of scholarly writing and publishing* (pp. 125–141). Jossey-Bass.

Kinsey, T. (2021). *The impact of organizational behavior on job stress among K–12 grade teachers: A correlational study* [Unpublished dissertation].

Madsen, D. (1990). *Successful dissertations and theses: A guide to graduate student research from proposal to completion*. Jossey-Bass Publishers.

Mauch, J., & Birch, J. (1998). *Guide to the successful thesis and dissertation: A handbook for students and faculty* (4th ed.). Marcel Dekker, Inc. Publishers.

Miles, D. A., & Scott, L. (2017, October 26–29). *Confessions of a dissertation chair, Part 1: The six mistakes doctoral students make with the dissertation* [Workshop]. 5th Annual 2017 Black Doctoral Network Conference. Atlanta, GA.

Morales, L. (2017). *A Baldrige assessment of an organization: An empirical study of baldrige criteria and organizational performance in air transportation organizations* [Unpublished dissertation proposal].

Newton, R., & Rudestam, K. (2007). *Surviving your dissertation: A comprehensive guide to content and process* (3rd ed.). Sage Publishers.

Ray, P. (2020). *Success profile: A case study of the african-american women in the president's office* [UMI Document]. ProQuest Dissertations and Theses.

Thomas, R. M., & Brubaker, D. (2000). *Theses and dissertations: A guide to planning, research, and writing*. Bergin and Garvey.

Webster, W. (1998a). *Developing and writing your thesis, dissertation or project*. Academic Scholarwrite.

Webster, W. (1998b). *21 models for developing and writing your theses, dissertations or projects*. Academic Scholarwrite.

White, P. (2017). *Developing research questions* (2nd ed.). Palgrave-Macmillian/ Red Globe Press.

9 Research Alignment

Achieving Research Alignment in the Study

Objective

- Readers will be able to:
  1. Attain research alignment in their studies

Introduction

Many doctoral students and novice researchers have considerable trouble with the concept of alignment. They have trouble getting their study in alignment. The reasons stem from not having the knowledge of aligning the problem statements, purpose statement and research questions. Based on my experience of working with doctoral students, most of their dissertations or research projects are misaligned.

Alignment is a rather new development with dissertations, emerging probably within the last five years. So, a considerable number of professors that work with doctoral students are not familiar with it. If they are not familiar with it, they cannot possibly assist doctoral students with it. We hope to address this and enlighten doctoral students (and chairs, if possible). This chapter illustrates how to achieve research alignment with the research study and dissertation. It is based on a workshop we conducted at a conference in Atlanta, GA, for doctoral students in 2017.

Research Alignment: Definition and Meaning

Alignment refers to the logical progression of ideas between the structural elements of your dissertation proposal (Booton, 2014). One of the most important factors to keep in mind is that alignment between your problem statement, purpose statement and research questions is critical. The researcher must actively create a nexus between the problem, purpose and methodology through the process of the research. Many times, when your chair or dissertation committee talks about your proposal's lack of "alignment," they are referring to the logical progression from the introduction to the problem statement, then to the purpose statement, the research questions and hypotheses (if applicable), and finally the methodology.

DOI: 10.4324/9781003268154-9

Alignment is key to a good dissertation (Weintraub, 2017; Booton, 2020; *Alignment of problem*, 2020).

Alignment has gained increasing popularity in research and implementation studies. Although alignment is frequently suggested as important for successful implementation, it has rarely been the centerpiece of studies. Our study systematically collected evidence related to alignment from implementation studies in different healthcare settings (Lundmark et al., 2021). The practice of alignment also helps us be sure we are collecting the right data to answer our research questions (Fan et al., 2017).

The Importance of Alignment

Good alignment across the components in your study is critical for several reasons:

- A well-aligned study will have methodological rigor. Your research will be of higher scholarly quality, and the knowledge to be generated will be of more value to your discipline.
- A well-designed study will reflect that you have a solid understanding of the nature of the proposed research and the application of a given research method and research design to your topic.
- A well-aligned study will support implementing the research plan with fidelity to the research design, helping you to achieve your research objectives and answer your research questions.
- A well-aligned letter of intent, prospectus, concept paper or proposal is much more likely to be approved by your chair, committee or research review board, allowing you to move forward with your dissertation research ("Aligning the problem," n.d.).

In contrast, poor alignment across a study's components is problematic. Here are the key issues with a poorly aligned study:

- A poorly aligned study will lack methodological rigor and reflect a lack of understanding of the nature of your research and of the application of a given research method and research design to your topic.
- A poorly aligned study will not generate valuable information to achieve your research objectives or answer your research questions.
- A poorly aligned letter of intent, prospectus, concept paper or proposal will not be approved by your chair, committee and/or research review board, leading to delays in moving forward with your dissertation research.

The merits of having alignment in a study is critical. The researcher must consider the various components of the study (general problem, specific problem, knowledge gap, research objective, research question, hypotheses, research method and research design). In addition, the researcher must make sure these components align well. The researcher must be aware of incongruence and inconsistencies throughout the descriptions ("Aligning the problem," n.d.).

Another perspective on alignment, in terms of quantitative methodology and validity, is by Hoadley (2004). Hoadley asserts the notion that alignment is essential to our understanding of research validity. Usually, when people discuss validity, they are referring to *measurement validity*, or the ability to ensure that our measurements accurately reflect the constructs that we are trying to measure. However, validity has a larger sense: The validity of a study is the likelihood that our interpretation of the results accurately reflects the truth of the theory and hypotheses under examination. In this sense, we need to be concerned with two other kinds of validity in research. We need to ensure that we have *treatment validity* – that is, that the treatments we create accurately align with the theories they are representing – and we need *systemic validity* – that is, the whole research endeavor must not only create a fair test of the theories, but those theories must be communicated in a way that is true to the inferences used to prove them (Hoadley, 2004).

In broader terms of alignment in a study, the research task consists of alignment between all elements of the process: literature review, theories, research paradigms, research questions, research methods, data analysis and findings. Furthermore, there should be alignment between the research paradigm and the theory selected. There should be a strong relationship between the theory and research questions; these two aspects should align (McCuaig et al., 2022).

The differences between quantitative and qualitative research methodology is striking. Quantitative research is applied to describe current conditions, investigate relationships and study cause-effect phenomena. Qualitative research, in contrast, is suited to promoting a deep understanding of a social setting or activity as viewed from the perspective of the research participants (Bloomberg, 2019; Bloomberg & Volpe, 2019).

The Rules of Alignment in a Study

Many times when working with doctoral students, I was surprised to find that they are completely unaware of research alignment. Below are three basic rules for achieving alignment:

- ***Rule #1:*** If you have three problem statement issues as a basis for the study, you must have three purpose statement objectives and three research questions. This is the first step in achieving alignment. This is important.
- ***Rule #2:*** You cannot achieve alignment if the elements are misaligned with an incompatible number of problem statement issues, purpose statement objectives and research statement questions (e.g., three issues, two objectives or four research questions). This is important.
- ***Rule #3:*** You must have an equal number of statements. This means you must have an equal number of problem statement issues, purpose statement objectives and research statement questions to properly achieve alignment (Miles, 2020).

Table 9.1 The research alignment model

Problem Statement:		
Issue (subproblem) 1:	**Issue (subproblem) 2:**	**Issue (subproblem) 3:**
Purpose Statement:		
Objective 1:	**Objective 2:**	**Objective 3:**
Research Statement:		
Research Question 1:	**Research Question 2:**	**Research Question 3:**

Lack of alignment between the dissertation elements is one of the most common reasons why a dissertation proposal does not get approval from the committee. The researcher must consider these three points when developing the problem statement, purpose statement and research questions. Research alignment is necessary to manage the dissertation. To achieve alignment, you must align the problem statement, purpose statement and research questions. It is imperative that these three components align properly. This chapter provides an alignment model and template for developing research alignment in a study (see Table 9.1).

Developing Alignment in a Research Study

The basis of the researcher's problem is the foundation for the research: the problem statement, purpose statement and research statement. Once the researcher has identified the problem as a basis for the study, the researcher is ready to develop the

Table 9.2 Example: The Statement Grid for problem statement development

Problem Statement:		
Issue (subproblem) 1:	**Issue (subproblem) 2:**	**Issue (subproblem) 3:**

purpose statement and the research statement (and questions). All three components are important.

These are the three core components that form the foundation of your study. The problem statement provides the background and context of the research problem as a basis for the study. The purpose statement provides the objective of the study. It is also an extension of the research problem. Lastly, the research statement (and research questions) is an extension of the purpose of the study. These three core components must align.

Phase 1: Writing up the Problem Statement

First, before you can achieve alignment, you have to develop the problem statement. The tool that I use when working with doctoral students is the **Statement Grid** (Miles & Scott, 2017). This helps doctoral students develop the problem statement with supporting statements. I use this to help doctoral students when they have trouble coming up with their problem statement. It helps them with their thought process, describing three possible subproblems as a basis for the research. It also helps with the **rule of three** (three plausible reasons to support your argument and position with three points) (Miles & Scott, 2017) (see Table 9.2).

First, write the overall problem statement. **Second,** divide the problem to be investigated into two or three parts (or subproblems or issues) that are compelling. Please note, use the word *issue* when writing the subproblem. This is so it does not cause readers to misinterpret the issues as four separate problem statements (Table 9.3).

Phase 2: Writing up the Purpose Statement

In the next step, you must complete the purpose statement. **First,** write the overall purpose statement. **Second,** divide the purpose to be investigated into two or three parts (or objectives) that are compelling. Please note, use the word *objectives* when writing the purpose. This is so it does not cause readers to misinterpret them as four separate purpose statements (see Table 9.4).

Table 9.3 Example: The Statement Grid for problem statement development

Problem Statement:

The central problem to be researched by the proposed study is the shortage in the nursing field. This has a lot to do with the current nursing shortage and the need for more nurses in the field. There is a huge problem with this shortage and the availability of nurses. As a basis for this study, the researcher identified the problem to be threefold.

Issue (subproblem) 1:	Issue (subproblem) 2:	Issue (subproblem) 3:
The first issue is that the education of new nurses is the responsibility of institutions of higher education, but there is a national shortage of nursing faculty (McSherry et al., 2012, Rosseter, 2015), which is limiting the enrollment, education and graduation of new nurses from institutions of higher learning.	The second issue is that, in the United States, 75% of the nursing faculty will reach retirement age in 2017 (Brett et al., 2014). This is alongside the existing problem that 6.9% of nursing faculty positions remain unfilled due to a lack of qualified nursing educators (Rosseter, 2015).	Last, the issue is that the current nursing faculty express low job satisfaction (Bittner & O'Connor, 2012) due to complexities of the nursing educator role making the retention and recruitment of qualified faculty difficult (Byme & Martine, 2014). The current problems include a shortage of qualified nursing faculty to educate new nurses, the complexity of nursing education and current faculty complaints of poor job satisfaction (Cook, 2017).

Note: In-text citations included for illustrative purposes only.

Table 9.4 Example: The Statement Grid for purpose statement development

Purpose Statement:

The purpose of this study is to investigate the issues affecting job satisfaction by nursing faculty members in metropolitan New York. Interviewing and questioning nursing faculty living in metropolitan New York provides insight into their personal experiences of job satisfaction while working in the nurse educator role. The researcher has identified three primary objectives as a basis for this study.

Objective 1:	Objective 2:	Objective 3:
First, the objective of this study is to examine the issue of job satisfaction among nursing faculty.	Second, the objective of this study is to investigate the impact of low wages on the nursing faculty.	Lastly, the objective of this study is to examine the complexities of the nursing faculty role (Cook, 2017).

Table 9.5 Example: The Statement Grid for research statement development

---

Research Statement:
The central problem to be researched is the shortage in the nursing field. As a basis for this study, three research questions will guide this research.

Research Question 1:	**Research Question 2:**	**Research Question 3:**
RQ1: How do nurses describe their experiences with job satisfaction on the nursing faculty?	RQ2: How do nurses describe their experiences with the impact of low wages on nursing faculty?	RQ3: How do nurses describe their experiences with the complexities of the faculty role (Cook, 2017)?

Phase 3: Writing up the Research Statement

In the last step, you must complete the research questions. **First,** rewrite the problem statement as the overall research statement. **Second,** divide the research questions into separate parts. This will help align your research questions with (a) the problem statement and issues, and (b) the purpose statement and objectives (see Table 9.5).

Introducing the Alignment Matrix: Achieving Alignment in the Dissertation

First, before you achieve research alignment, you must develop the problem statement. The tool that I use when working with doctoral students is the **Alignment Matrix** (Miles, 2020). The *Alignment Matrix* helps doctoral students align the problem statement, purpose statement and research questions. This is a tremendous help with providing structure for the dissertation and study (see Tables 9.6 and 9.7).

See the following formula:

RESEARCH ALIGNMENT = Problem + Purpose + Research Questions

First and foremost, you must observe the key words in the problem statements, purpose statements and research statement and questions (see the key word examples in italics). This is the key to achieving alignment between the three statements. Once you coordinate this, you have achieved research alignment (see Table 9.7).

Table 9.6 The Alignment Matrix for research alignment

Problem Statement	Purpose Statement	Research Statement
Issues (subproblems)	Objectives (subpurposes)	Research Questions
Issue 1:	**Objective 1:**	**Research Question 1:**
Issue 2:	**Objective 2:**	**Research Question 2:**
Issue 3:	**Objective 3:**	**Research Question 3:**

Table 9.7 Example: The Alignment Matrix

Problem Statement	Purpose Statement	Research Statement
The central problem to be researched by the proposed study is the shortage in the nursing field. As a basis for this study, the researcher identified the problem to be threefold.	The purpose of this study is to investigate the issues affecting job satisfaction by nursing faculty members in metropolitan New York. The researcher has identified three primary objectives as a basis for this study.	The central problem to be researched is the shortage in the nursing field. There are three research questions that will guide this research.
Problem (Issues)	Purpose (Objectives)	Research Questions
Issue 1: The first issue identified as a basis for this study is the question of *job satisfaction* as experienced by nursing faculty.	**Objective 1:** First, the objective of this study is to examine the issue of *job satisfaction* among nursing faculty.	**Research Question 1:** RQ1: How do nurses describe their experiences with *job satisfaction* on the nursing faculty?

Table 9.7 (Continued)

Problem Statement	Purpose Statement	Research Statement
Issue 2: The second issue identified as the basis for this research study is the *impact of low wages* on the lived experiences of job satisfaction by current nursing faculty.	**Objective 2:** Second, the objective of this study is to investigate the *impact of low wages* on the nursing faculty	**Research Question 2:** RQ2: How do nurses describe their experiences with the *impact of low wages* on nursing faculty?
Issue 3: Lastly, the third issue identified affecting the job satisfaction of the nursing faculty is the *complexities of the faculty role.*	**Objective 3:** Lastly, the objective of this study is to examine the *complexities of the nursing faculty role.*	**Research Question 3:** RQ3: How do nurses describe their experiences with the *complexities of the faculty role* (Cook, 2017)?

Example 9.1

Problem Statement	Purpose Statement	Research Statement
The central problem identified in this study involves how principals manage job stress. The issue of how principals manage stress is threefold.	The purpose of this study is to investigate the experiences of 20 urban Central Texas school district K–12 principals in encountering job stress, coping with this stress and achieving work-life balance. The researcher has identified three primary objectives for this qualitative descriptive study.	The central problem to be researched involves how principals manage job stress. There are three research questions that will guide this research.

Issues (subproblems)	*Objectives (subpurposes)*	*Research Questions*
Issue 1: First, there is the prevailing issue concerning the effect of principals' job stress level. Stressed workers are more likely to be unhealthy, less productive, unmotivated and not safe at work.	**Objective 1:** First, the objective of this study is to investigate the effect of principals' job stress level on their subordinates and staff.	**Research Question 1:** RQ1: How do K–12 principals and administrators describe their experiences of job stress in an urban Central Texas school district environment?
Issue 2: Second, there is the prevailing issue concerning the lack of research on how the job stress level can affect the principals' ability to use coping skills. Many authors have investigated how principals cope with stress.	**Objective 2:** The second objective is to investigate how job stress affects principals' ability to use coping skills.	**Research Question 2:** RQ2: How do K–12 principals and administrators describe their experiences of using coping skills for job stress in an urban Central Texas school district environment?
Issue 3: Lastly, there is a prevailing issue concerning the impact that job stress can have on how principals balance their work and home life.	**Objective 3:** Lastly, the final purpose of the qualitative study is to investigate the impact that job stress can have on how principals balance their work and home life.	**Research Question 3:** RQ3: How do K–12 principals and administrators describe their experiences of coping with work-life balance and job stress in an urban Central Texas school district environment (Beltran, 2020)?

Example 9.2

Problem Statement	Purpose Statement	Research Statement
The central problem to be researched in the proposed study is the lack of intercultural competence within peer mentoring between international students and domestic students' relationships and the lack of personal accounts of students' experience in a peer-mentoring program. As a basis for this study, the researcher identified the problem to be threefold.	The purpose of this study is to investigate how international and domestic students perceive the effectiveness, if any, of peer mentoring on intercultural competence at a Western, private, Christian university in southern California. This study has three primary objectives.	The central problem to be researched is the lack of intercultural competence within peer mentoring between international students and domestic students' relationships and the lack of personal accounts of students' experience in a peer-mentoring program There are three research questions that will guide this research.

Issues (subproblems)	Objectives (subpurposes)	Research Questions
Issue 1: First, there is a lack of data regarding the cultural challenges with international students' experience at a Christian university in southern New York.	**Objective 1:** The first objective of this study is to identify whether there are cultural challenges that students face on a Christian university campus and what these challenges entail. This study will include 30 students.	**Research Question 1:** RQ1: What are the cultural challenges faced by students in Christian higher education?

Problem Statement	Purpose Statement	Research Statement
Issue 2: The second issue is the lack of research on the intercultural competence and peer mentoring skills of domestic students.	**Objective 2:** The second objective of this study is to examine and interpret peer-mentoring interactions between international and domestic undergraduate students and their influence on intercultural competence.	**Research Question 2:** RQ2: Does peer mentoring influence the intercultural competence of undergraduate, international and domestic students in a private Christian university and, if so, how?
Issue 3: Lastly, the researcher identified a lack of personal accounts from students about their experiences with a peer-mentoring program.	**Objective 3:** Lastly, the third objective of the study is to examine the actual lived experiences of international students through their own words on the effectiveness of the American International Mentoring program.	**Research Question 3:** RQ3: What are students' experiences during the American International Mentoring program (Kwapong, 2021)?

Example 9.3

Problem Statement	Purpose Statement	Research Statement
The central problem identified by the researcher is the issue of organizational performance, leadership and employee empowerment. As a basis for this study, the researcher identified three key problems demanding this investigation.	The purpose of this study is to determine whether a relationship exists between customer and market focus, employee empowerment, leaders' openness to new business strategies and organizational performance in transportation companies located on the west side of Puerto Rico. The researcher has identified three primary objectives as a basis for this study.	The central problem identified by the researcher is the issue of organizational performance, leadership and employee empowerment. There are three research questions that will guide this research.

Issues (subproblems)	Objectives (subpurposes)	Research Questions
Issue 1: The first major problem identified as a basis for this study is the issue regarding customer and market focus and operational performance in air transportation organizations.	**Objective 1:** The first objective of this study is to determine if there is a relationship between customer and market focus and organizational performance in air transportation organizations.	**Research Question 1:** RQ1: To what extent does a relationship exist between customer and market focus and organizational performance?

Problem Statement	Purpose Statement	Research Statement
Issue 2: The second major problem as a basis for this study is the concerns with employee empowerment and organizational performance in air transportation organizations.	**Objective 2:** The second objective of this study is to determine if there is a relationship between employee empowerment and organizational performance in air transportation organizations.	**Research Question 2:** RQ2: To what extent does a relationship exist between employee empowerment and organizational performance?
Issue 3: The last major problem identified as a basis for this study is the issue relating to leaders' openness to new business strategies and organizational performance in air transportation organizations.	**Objective 3:** The last objective of this study is to determine if there is a relationship between leaders' openness to new business strategies and organizational performance in air transportation organizations.	**Research Question 3:** RQ3: To what extent does a relationship exist between leaders' openness to new business strategies and organizational performance (Morales, 2017)?

Summary

The concept of alignment is relatively new in the research community. The goal of achieving research alignment is important when it comes to research. This chapter discussed the concept of alignment. Research alignment is a necessary task to manage the dissertation. To achieve research alignment, it is imperative that it be taught to both novice and experienced researchers. The purpose of this chapter is to illustrate and discuss how to achieve research alignment in studies. This chapter provided a model and template for developing research alignment in a study.

The chapter discussed four key components. First, the chapter discussed the meaning and definition of alignment. Second, the chapter discussed the basic rules for alignment. Third, the chapter introduced two tools: the *Statement Grid*, for developing problem statements and purpose statements, and the *Alignment Matrix*, a tool used for aligning the problem statement, purpose statement and research questions. Last, the chapter provided examples of alignment with all three. It is our expectation that our proposed conceptual models and frameworks will provide researchers with a template and a foundation for alignment in research projects and dissertations.

References

Aligning the problem, research objectives, research questions, and research design. (n.d.). Retrieved from http://wpc.6fdc.edgecastcdn.net/006FDC//UOR_Curriculum/ canvas/courseFiles/RES/RES8920/08CH_Heitner_Dissertation.pdf

Alignment of problem, purpose, and research questions [Presentation]. (2020). Center for Teaching and Learning, Northcentral University.

Beltran, V. (2020). *A descriptive study of central Texas urban school principals' experience of influences contributing to job stress.* ProQuest Dissertations and Theses.

Bloomberg, L. (2019). Achieving alignment in your qualitative dissertation [Webinar]. Northcentral University/Center for Teaching and Learning. Retrieved from https://libr ary.ncu.edu/c.php?g=1069271&p=7782825

Bloomberg, L. D., & Volpe, M. (2019). *Completing your qualitative dissertation: A road map from beginning to end* (4th ed.). Sage Publications.

Booton, C. (2014). Using rich pictures to verify, contradict, or enhance verbal data. *The Qualitative Report 2018, 23*(11), 2835–2849.

Booton, C. (2020). *How to align the elements of your dissertation proposal.* Love Your Dissertation. Retrieved from https://loveyourdissertation.com/alignment/

Cook, L. (2017). *The current issues affecting job satisfaction by nursing faculty as a lived experience* [Unpublished dissertation]. ProQuest Dissertations and Theses.

Fan, M., Antle, A. N., Hoskyn, M., Neustaedter, C., & Cramer, E. (2017). Why tangibility matters: A design case study of at-risk children learning to read and spell. In *Proceedings of the 2017 Conference on Human Factors in Computing Systems* (pp. 1805–1816).

Hoadley, C. (2004). Methodological alignment in design-based research, *Educational Psychologist, 39* (4), 203–212. https://doi.org/10.1207/s15326985ep3904_2

Kwapong, S. (2021). *Investigating the experiences of international and domestic students in a peer mentoring program and its effects on intercultural competence at a university: A qualitative study.* ProQuest Dissertations and Theses.

Lundmark, R., Hasson, H., Richter A., Khachatryan, E., Åkesson, A., & Eriksson, L. (2021). Alignment in implementation of evidence-based interventions: A scoping review. *Implementation Sci, 16*(93). https://doi.org/10.1186/s13012-021-01160-w

McCuaig, L., Dyson, B., Sutherland, S., & Hiromi, M. (2022). *Research paradigms & research questions: Alignment, alignment, alignment* [Presentation]. College of Biology and Education, Ohio State University.

Miles, D. A. (2020). *Achieving alignment: How to achieve research alignment in a study.* Doctoral Student Workshop (no publication), pp. 1–12.

Miles, D. A. & Scott, L. (2017, October 26–29). *Confessions of a dissertation chair, Part 1: The six mistakes doctoral students make with the dissertation* [Workshop]. 5th Annual 2017 Black Doctoral Network Conference, Atlanta, GA.

Morales, L. (2017). *A Baldrige assessment of an organization: An empirical study of Baldrige criteria and organizational performance in air transportation organizations* [Unpublished dissertation]. ProQuest Dissertations and Theses.

Weintraub, D. (2017). *Alignment: The key to a strong dissertation* [Presentation]. NSU/FCE Summer Institute 2017, Nova Southeastern University.

10 Understanding Limitations and Delimitations

Objective

- Readers will be able to:
  1. Write about the limitations and delimitations of their studies

Introduction

In my many years working with doctoral students, I have found that there is still a prevailing confusion between the terms *limitations* and *delimitations*. I have seen this to be the case with both experienced and novice researchers. There is a dearth in the research methods class that is required for doctoral students. After all my years of working with and editing the work of doctoral students, there still seems to be a prevailing problem.

The problem is that most of them do not know the difference between the two terms *limitations* and *delimitations*. They either have never learned the differences between the two terms or have learned alternate definitions that further confuse them. However, I think I have found a useful definition and examples to help students and researchers understand the differences between the two terms. The outline of the chapter will provide information on the differences between the two terms. First, the chapter will provide clear definitions of a limitation and a delimitation. Second, the chapter will provide some examples of how to use them in a sentence and paragraph. Last, the chapter will provide examples of them from journal chapters and studies.

Definition of Limitations

Limitations are defined as constraints on your study based on the *research methodology and design*. Primarily, limitations deal with the constraints on the research method (Miles & Scott, 2017). Limitations are constraints you cannot control in your study (Simon & Goes, 2013). This is why limitations are often defined as being out of the control of the researcher.

DOI: 10.4324/9781003268154-10

However, many students do not know the reason for this definition. A recurring problem with doctoral students is that they are completely misinformed regarding the true meaning of a limitation. This is confusing to them because of the generic definition of a limitation: The characteristics of a study in which the researcher cannot control delimitations. Many dissertation committee chairs are just as confused. This generic definition leaves both the dissertation committee and the doctoral student confused. There is a reason why a researcher has no control over the characteristics of a study. It is because you cannot control inherent flaws in your researcher methodology and design. *This is the reason why this is out of the researchers' control.*

With limitations, your research method and design remain constant. For example, 30 years from now, a researcher who wishes to replicate your study can do so by using the same research method. A future researcher using the same research method will face the same limitations you faced. These have to do with the means you have chosen for gathering and analyzing data. Limitations are those restrictions created by your research methodology. Limitations are the built-in limits of the method you use to explore your question. If you are thoughtful and analytical about your chosen method, you should have no trouble identifying the design factors that might produce inaccurate or misleading data and possibly lead to mistaken conclusions (Bryant, 2004).

Another definition of a limitation is that it is a design flaw. Limitations identify potential weaknesses in the study's research design and methodology. Limitations tend to act as an anticipator of the study's flaws (Calabrese, 2006). Limitations are restrictions in the study over which you have no control. For example, your study may be limited to a narrow segment of the population. You want to study them but may be limited in the research method you choose to use (Newton & Rudestam, 2007). Further, limitations are constraints outside of the researcher's control and are inherent in the study, which could affect the generalizability of the results (Terrell, 2016).

A limitation is a factor that may or will affect the study but is not under the control of the researcher. In such studies that use questionnaires, a common limitation is the willingness of the individuals to respond at all, to respond in a timely fashion and to respond accurately. Limitations are important for the possible effects they may have on the outcomes of the study, and they are not controlled by the researcher. Limitations typically surface as variables that cannot be controlled by the researcher but may limit or affect the outcome of the study. Limitations can become a problem for students if they are not specified (Mauch & Park, 2003).

When a researcher discusses limitations, they are discussing the possible and real weaknesses of their research design. Limitations described by the researcher are those that may or did affect the study's validity or findings. The limitations tend to address the researcher's awareness of the shortcomings in their research design and methodological approach to the study, thus adding to the researcher's credibility (Calabrese, 2009) (see Tables 10.1 and 10.2; Figure 10.1).

Table 10.1 Examples of limitations

Common Quantitative Limitations	Common Qualitative Limitations
• Research methodology • Research design (type) • Use of self-reported data (survey) • Time constraints (time to collect data) • Length of survey instrument • Design of survey instrument • Sampling design (random, stratified or clustering, systematic, convenience); probability sampling-based • Sampling bias • Target population constraints • Data collection modality type • Survey question types (closed-ended) • Survey bias • Researcher misinterpretation of participant data from surveys	• Research methodology • Research design (type) • Use of self-reported data (interviews) • Time constraints (time to interview subjects) • Length of study interview time with participants • Design of interview questions • Sampling design (purposive, quota and snowball); non-probability sampling-based • Target population constraints • Data collection modality type • Interview question types (open-ended) • Researcher bias • Researcher misinterpretation of participant data from interviews

Table 10.2 The Statement Grid for limitations

Overall Statement:
The study was limited by certain conditions that were identified for this research inquiry. The researcher identified three major limitations as a basis for this study.

Limitation 1:	**Limitation 2:**	**Limitation 3:**
First, a key limitation was the use of self-reported data. Data reflected the owner's perception of domestic violence, which may have been distorted or incomplete. Some of the participants may not have properly comprehended the subject matter.	Second, another key limitation was time constraints. The window of opportunity to collect the data was very limited (less than a month). It would have been more beneficial to take more time to collect additional surveys.	Last, another key limitation was the length of the survey instrument. The instrument was too long, and participants refused to complete the survey. There were a number of incomplete surveys, which was attributed to the length and amount of time needed to fill out the survey (Miles, 2019).

Limitations = Constraints to the Study Based on Research Methodology and Design

---

Figure 10.1 Formula for limitations.

Example 10.1

Limitations. Limitations are comprised of the restrictions implemented by the researcher's choice of methodology. These are factors in a study that cannot be controlled by the researcher. As a basis for this study, the limitations were threefold:

1. The first limitation in this study is the instrumentation. This study used an instrument that was closed and did not have open-ended questions.
2. The second limitation is the data collection. This study used aggregated data that was collected from the state in a publicly accessible medium. This is limited in descriptive statistics.
3. The last limitation is the course. Teen Leadership is one of several different character education opportunities offered throughout the state. Further investigation into other programs may offer different insights (Zeig, 2019).

Example 10.2

Limitations. Limitations are potential weaknesses that are out of a researcher's control. Limitations are inherent limits in the research methodology and research design. These areas make the study a scientifically rigorous investigation. As a basis for this study, the researcher identified three limitations:

1. First, this study was limited to personal interviews with the participants. This limits the length of data collected and thus has a time constraint as to how much data can be collected during a period of time.
2. The second limitation is the lack of closed-ended questions, which result in data that is not empirically quantifiable.
3. The last limitation is the method of data collection. All responses are self-reported, and the researcher assumes all answers are truthful (Kwapong, 2021).

Example 10.3

Limitations. Limitations commonly focus on the internal and external validity of the study. Internal validity addresses the rigorous conduct of the study, while external validity focuses on the applicability of the findings to larger populations (generalization). Limitations are inherent limits in the research methodology and research design. These areas make the study a scientifically rigorous investigation. The following limitations are present in this study:

1. The first limitation is the methodology. This study uses a survey design as a basis for research. This is a limitation because the survey questions may not collect all the necessary data. To minimize the limitation of the methodology, the researcher will collect as much data as possible to have an excellent representation of the population.
2. The second limitation is one of time constraint. Employees may not understand the survey questions because of time constraints, as the survey has too many questions. To minimize the time constrain, the researcher will provide the necessary time to collect the data.
3. The third limitation is that the study will be held only during the day shift and night shift. To minimize the shift limitation, the researcher will obtain data from the most population possible during shifts.
4. The last limitation is the instrumentation to be used to conduct the research. The instrument to be used is the questionnaire of the Baldrige National Quality Program survey, with demographics questions added. To minimize the instrumentation limitation, reliability data will be present showing that the instrument is reliable to conduct the proposed study (Morales, 2017).

Definition of Delimitations

Delimitations are constraints on your study based on *population scope* (Miles & Scott, 2017). Think of delimitations as the boundaries of your study. Delimitations are defined as chiefly concerned with the *scope of the study*. Delimitations describe the scope of the study or establish parameters. Delimitations also prevent you from stating that your findings are generalizable to the whole population.

Another recurring problem that doctoral students have is with misunderstanding the true meaning of a delimitation. This is confusing to them because of the generic definition of a delimitation: The characteristics of a study in which the researcher can control delimitations. Okay, why is that? The primary reason why they have problems writing delimitations is because that definition is only surface level and does not give further rationale as to why it is. There is no context behind the definition. So, again, doctoral students often do their delimitations wrong! This generic definition of a delimitation does not help students understand why they often write them wrong in a study. As mentioned earlier, they confuse delimitations and limitations as though they are interchangeable. This has been a recurring problem with doctoral students.

One of the prevailing issues on delimitations is that there is no consensus on what they actually are. Many authors profess different definitions of delimitations. So, we have a conflict in terms of what delimitations actually mean. Many authors state the conventional definition of delimitations – that they are within the control of the researcher (Madsen, 1990; Mauch & Birch, 1998). Again, the key meaning of delimitations is defined as factors that prevent you from claiming that your findings are true for all people in all times and places (Thomas & Brubaker, 2000; Jacobs, 2011).

Another interesting aspect of delimitations is that they imply limitations on the populations to which the results of the study can be generalized. For example, you may decide to only study males, either because the theory on which your hypotheses are based has not been studied in females or because you have a readily accessible population of males but not females (Newton & Rudestam, 2007). Think of delimitations as self-imposed boundaries that you use to delimit the scope of your study (Calabrese, 2006). The fact is that delimitations also act as denotations, meaning as a boundary of the study and ways in which the findings may lack generalizability. In considering this, you should examine such concerns as the nature and size of the sample, the uniqueness of the setting, the time period during which the study was conducted and the limitations of the particular methods selected (Glatthorn, 1998).

Delimitations are the factors that prevent you from claiming that your findings are true for all people in all times and places. For a quantitative study, these are the factors that limit generalization. For a qualitative study, these are the factors that limit the relevancy of your study to other populations or individuals. For example, if you study nurses in Oregon, you will not be able to extend your results to nurses in Arkansas. The point is that many quantitative studies gather data at a moment in time. For example, if a researcher 30 years from now would seek to replicate your study, then they would have to decide what factors would get in the way. Delimitations would be those factors (Bryant, 2004).

When a researcher uses the term *delimitation*, it means they will point to how he or she narrowed the study to focus on specific aspects. The researcher will indicate how they will narrow the specific focus of the study by identifying a precise type of research methodology, participant characteristic, context or research site or phenomenon studied during the research (Calabrese, 2009). Furthermore, delimitations are further limitations actively put in place by a researcher in order to control for factors that might affect the results or to focus more specifically on a problem (Terrell, 2016).

One strong consideration of a researcher is that delimitations are controlled by the researcher. In some studies, it is common to have a delimitation regarding the size or nature of the group questioned. The size might be limited to those working in a region. Size may also be limited by percentage in a field or sector. Delimitations help everyone involved think through the design of the study. Delimitations are integral parts of the design because they set boundaries. They tell the readers what will be included, what will be left out and why (Mauch & Park, 2003).

Delimitations detail all the aspects of a study that will not be included. This process is exactly one of "walling out" those segments that are beyond the scope and purpose of the study. Delimitations inform readers in a given subject area to hold certain basic expectations. Readers may want to know (a) about the criteria for determining the scope of the study; (b) what sources will be used to determine the salient background of the target population; (c) whether gender differences are important; and (d) how you define "significant others," to list just a few. However, while delimitations will inform readers what not to expect, you should note that you cannot use the section arbitrarily. Furthermore, you cannot exclude those aspects that are somehow difficult to research. You cannot narrow the breadth of the study for your convenience. You cannot use delimitations to exclude logical and credible expectations (Webster, 1998a).

You should use delimitations carefully and conservatively. The following are delimitations typical of many research studies: (a) exclusions related to gender differences; (b) exclusions related to socioeconomic backgrounds; (c) absence of concern for the size of cities, organizations, utility districts or school districts studied; and (d) exclusions related to years' training or experience (Webster, 1998b).

When I work with doctoral students, I usually have them list four categories of delimitations that set the parameters of the study. If the study is being conducted externally, with data being collected outside of an organization, these are the most common delimitations: (a) *the unit of analysis of the study* for which the data is being collected from the participants; (b) *the metropolitan area or city* in which the data is being collected from the participants; (c) *the surrounding counties and/or municipalities* (or parishes) of the area in which the data is being collected from the participants; and lastly (d) the *state* in which the data is being collected from the participants. Think of it as a funnel. Now, if a study is being conducted internally within an organization, then you may have fewer categories for the delimitations (see Figure 10.2).

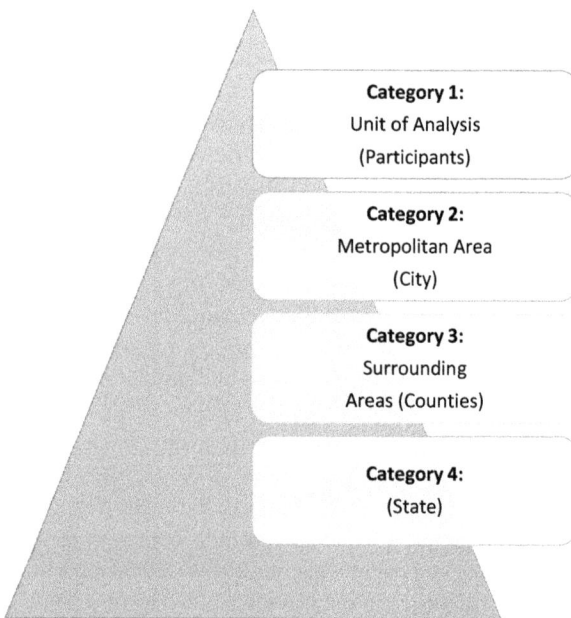

Category 1:
Unit of Analysis
(Participants)

Category 2:
Metropolitan Area
(City)

Category 3:
Surrounding
Areas (Counties)

Category 4:
(State)

Figure 10.2 Delimitations categories in a study.

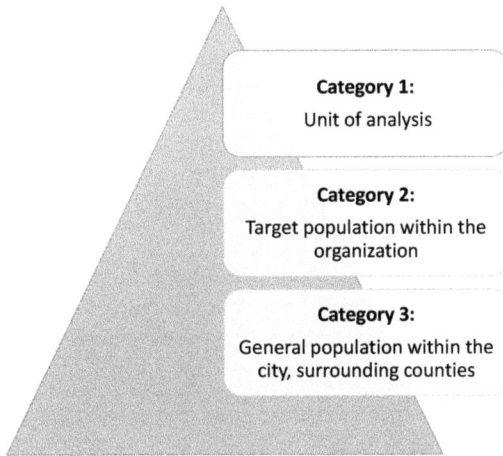

Figure 10.3 Delimitations categories in a study within an organization.

If a study is being conducted internally within an organization mainly by collecting data, these are the most common delimitations: (a) *the unit of analysis of the study within the organization* (or department) from which the data is being collected from the participants; (b) *the target population or type of group within the organization* from which the data is being collected from the participants; and lastly (c) *the general population within the city, surrounding counties* and state from which the data is being collected from the participants. Sometimes if a study is being conducted internally within an organization, you may have fewer categories for the delimitations (see Figure 10.3 and Examples 10.4 to 10.6).

When you write your delimitations, the proper sentence should always be written as: *This study was delimited to … .* You have to set the parameters of your study so that you cannot say your results are generalizable to other areas of the country or other studies with dissimilar results. You want to start off with four categories, from the unit of analysis to the state of the data collection (see Table 10.3, Figure 10.4 and Examples 10.4 to 10.6).

Example 10.4

Delimitations. The delimitations of a study are those characteristics that arise from limitations in the scope of the study (defining boundaries) and from the conscious exclusionary and inclusionary decisions made during the development of the study plan (Simon & Goes, 2013). The delimitations are those characteristics that limit the scope and define the boundaries of your study (Simon & Goes, 2013). The following delimitations will be present at the time this study will be conducted:

1. The study is delimited to air transportation organizations' employees and will not assess other types of organizations in the geographical location of Puerto Rico. To mitigate the delimitation of the organizations where the study will be conducted, the researcher will collect data from the most possible air transportation companies.
2. The study is delimited to organizations in Puerto Rico. To minimize the delimitation of the employees, the study will collect data from employees in all positions within the organization.
3. The study is delimited to floor employees, office employees and managers at the air transportation organization site. No employees at the higher leadership level (CEO, vice presidents of operations, etc.) will be assessed in this study (Morales, 2017).

Table 10.3 The Statement Grid for delimitations

Overall Statement:

This study had some delimitations that restricted the study. The researcher identified four delimitations concerning the scope of this study. The study was delimited by certain conditions that were identified for this research inquiry.

Delimitation 1:	**Delimitation 2:**	**Delimitation 3:**	**Delimitation 4:**
First, the study was delimited to domestic violence victims (DVV). [unit of analysis]	Second, the study was delimited to the metropolitan city of Los Angeles. [metropolitan city]	Third, the study was delimited to the surrounding counties of the Los Angeles area. [surrounding counties and non-city areas]	Lastly, the study was delimited to the state of California. [state]

**Delimitations = Constraints to the Study
Based on Population Scope**

Figure 10.4 Formula for delimitations.

Example 10.5

Delimitations. Delimitations are weaknesses associated with the scope of the study (Simon & Goes, 2013). While limitations are not under the researcher's control, delimitations are factors that can be controlled. The researcher noted three delimitations that will affect this study:

- The study is delimited to private Christian institutions in Southern California.
- The study is delimited to students participating in the AIM peer-mentoring program.
- The study is delimited to the population sample of ten international students and ten domestic students (Kwapong, 2021).

Example 10.6

Delimitations. Delimitations are things over which the researcher has control, such as the location of the study. The following delimitations will be present in the current study.

1. The survey of parents is delimited to Southern New Jersey's public schools. A lack of funding prevents the study being conducted over a larger, more widespread region. This limits the geographic range of the sample and in turn impacts the generalizability of the findings. Expanding the range could produce results that are more widely generalizable and applicable to other regions.

2. The study will be delimited to a sample study of 20–25 parents of students who attend New Jersey public schools in the South New Jersey region and are in kindergarten through eighth grade. Although this limits the applicability of this study to the parents of high school students, the intent of the study is to focus on the phenomenon of parent involvement as it exists in lower grades as a foundation to helping students establish sound academic achievement (Forbes, 2017).

Summary

This chapter discussed the confusion around the terms *limitations* and *delimitations*. It addressed three key points to understanding and differentiating between the two terms.

This chapter highlighted the main definitions of limitations and their characteristics. Also, the chapter discussed the definition of delimitations and their characteristics. First, the chapter defined and discussed the meanings of the two terms. Second, the chapter gave some examples and characteristics of the two terms. Last, the chapter discussed the differences between the two terms based on research questions and data collection methods.

We hope this chapter will act as a guide for helping researchers learn and understand the distinct differences between the terms *limitations* and *delimitations*. We hope to build a foundation for enlightening both experienced and novice researchers on the two terms and lessen the confusion.

References

Bryant, M. T. (2004). *The portable dissertation advisor*. Corwin Press, Inc.

Calabrese, R. (2006). *The elements of an effective dissertation and thesis: A step-by-step guide to getting it right the first time*. Rowman & Littlefield Education, Inc.

Calabrese, R. (2009). *The dissertation desk reference: The doctoral student's manual to writing the dissertation*. Rowman & Littlefield Education, Inc.

Forbes, S. (2017). *Parental involvement in education: The lived experience* [Unpublished dissertation]. ProQuest Dissertations and Theses.

Glatthorn, A. (1998). *Writing the winning dissertation: A step-by-step guide* (1st ed.). Corwin Press, Inc.

Jacobs, R. L. (2011). Developing a research problem and purpose statement. In T. S. Rocco & T. Hatcher (Eds.), *The handbook of scholarly writing and publishing* (pp. 125–141). Jossey-Bass.

Kwapong, S. (2021). *Investigating the experiences of international and domestic students in a peer mentoring program and its effects on intercultural competence at a university: A qualitative study* [UMI No. 77854669]. ProQuest Dissertations and Theses.

Madsen, D. (1990). *Successful dissertations and theses: A guide to graduate student research from proposal to completion*. Jossey-Bass Publishers.

Mauch, J., & Birch, J. (1998). *Guide to the successful theses and dissertation: A handbook for students and faculty* (4th ed.). Marcel Dekker, Inc. Publishers.

Mauch, J. E., & Park, N. (2003). *Guide to the successful thesis and dissertation: A handbook for students and faculty*. M. Dekker.

Miles, D. A. (2019). Research methods and strategies: Let's stop the madness Part 2: Understanding the difference between limitations vs. delimitations. ResearchGate. www.researchgate.net/publication/334279571_ARTICLE_Research_Methods_and_Str ategies_Let%27s_Stop_the_Madness_Part_2_Understanding_the_Difference_Between_ Limitations_vs_Delimitations

Miles, D. A., & Scott, L. (2017, October 26–29). *Confessions of a dissertation chair, Part 1: The six mistakes doctoral students make with the dissertation* [Workshop]. 5th Annual 2017 Black Doctoral Network Conference, Atlanta, GA.

Morales, L. (2017). *A Baldrige assessment of an organization: An empirical study of Baldrige criteria and organizational performance in air transportation organizations* [Unpublished dissertation]. ProQuest Dissertations and Theses.

Newton, R., & Rudestam, K. (2007). *Surviving your dissertation: A comprehensive guide to content and process* (3rd ed.). Sage.

Simon, M., & Goes, J. (2013). *Dissertation and scholarly research: Recipes for success*. Dissertation Success, LLC.

Terrell, S. (2016). *Writing a proposal for your dissertation: Guidelines and examples*. The Guilford Press.

Thomas, R. M., & Brubaker, D. (2000). *Theses and dissertations: A guide to planning, research, and writing*. Bergin and Garvey.

Webster, W. (1998a). *21 models for developing and writing your theses, dissertations or projects*. Academic Scholarwrite.

Webster, W. (1998b). *Developing and writing your thesis, dissertation or project*. Academic Scholarwrite.

Zeig, M. (2019). *Effects of a character education course on standardized testing in Texas high schools* [UMI No. 5458799]. ProQuest Dissertations and Theses.

11 Understanding Assumptions and How to Write Them in a Study

Objective

- Readers will be able to:
  1. Write about the assumptions of their studies

Introduction

In our years of working with many doctoral students, we have found that there is still a prevailing confusion with the term *assumptions* when developing dissertations. In fact, in discussions with even many experienced researchers and doctoral mentors, this confusion exists. There is a dearth of research methods classes for doctoral students. As we reflect on our own doctoral journey, an in-depth discussion on the implications of assumptions on the research development process is vital to doctoral students. At best, doctoral students gained a background in philosophical assumptions centered on the values and belief systems of individuals, such as those related to (a) *epistemological assumptions,* or what counts as knowledge and justified (Creswell & Poth, 2018), (b) *ontological assumptions,* or questioning whether there are universal or multiple realities, and (c) *axiological assumptions,* or the extent to which the researcher's own values and biases are known and enter the study.

We believe that having a more robust presentation of information on the topic of assumptions, as well as providing examples from journal articles and studies, will help doctoral students and even experienced researchers and doctoral mentors to become more astute as they investigate, examine or explore problems requiring research and comprehensive findings that improve decision-making among researchers and other stakeholders. Therefore, the purpose of this chapter is to provide a framework for the presentation of information that defines or clarifies (a) what is meant by the term *assumption* when developing research proposals or reports, (b) making and justifying assumptions, (c) assumptions in qualitative research, (d) the general types of assumptions, (e) the Statement Grid for assumptions, and (f) the significance of participant bias on assumptions.

DOI: 10.4324/9781003268154-11

Definition of Assumptions

Assumptions can be defined as things that are somewhat out of your control, but if they disappeared your study would become irrelevant (Hubbard, 1973; Simon, 2011; Simon & Goes, 2013). For example, if you are doing a study on the middle school music curriculum, there is an underlying assumption that music will continue to be important in the middle school program. If you are conducting a survey, you need to assume that people will answer *truthfully*. If you are choosing a sample, you need to assume that this sample is *representative* of the population you wish to make inferences to (Hubbard, 1973; Simon, 2011; Simon & Goes, 2013). Another definition of an assumption is an unexamined belief that the researcher brings to the study and that is accepted as being valid (Bryant, 2004; Webster, 1998a, 1998b).

Assumptions are statements that are taken for granted or considered true, even though they have not been scientifically tested. Think of assumptions as principles that are accepted as being true based on logic or reasons but without proof or verification. Assumptions provide a basis for the development of theories and research instruments and therefore influence the development and implementation of the research process (Happen, 2008; Patidar, 2010; Sampson, 2010). Also, assumptions must clarify aspects of the study that are believed but cannot be proven to be true. Furthermore, only include assumptions critical to the meaningfulness of the study. The researcher must describe the reasons why the assumptions were necessary in the context of the study (Terrell, 2016; Lani, 2018).

During the research synthesis process, Wolgemuth et al. (2017) argued that focused attention on the constructs of methodology and research design can be viewed with more objectivity when there is an examination of assumptions that could affect the decisions related to the research inquiry processes. When considering writing the assumptions, researchers need to give them some careful thought. The "basic assumption" that drives design-based research should not be plucked out of thin air (e.g., "iPods will make students more motivated"), nor should it only be derived from the literature (e.g., "learning communities enhance learning") (Herrington et al., 2007). As an alternative, the assumptions that direct study are derived from the definition of the research problem in close collaboration with practitioners and finetuned through literature that serves to (a) help flesh out what is already known about the problem; and (b) guide the development of potential solutions. In such instances, the inquiry that forms the basis of the study helps the researcher to understand the underpinning processes and variables and how they impact the learning and learning outcomes (Herrington et al., 2007).

Making Assumptions in the Study

In many cases, we make assumptions about how research subjects will behave. Will they tell the truth as they see it? Will they be forthright with us? Will they intentionally deceive us? We make assumptions about our own behavior. Will we ask the right questions? Will we gather the right kind of information in sufficient data and amount? Will we, as the products of our own experiences, examine our data and information impartially (Bryant, 2004)?

In many other cases, we make assumptions about the tools we use to gather and analyze data. That is, our chosen research method is predicated on epistemological assumptions about what constitutes legitimate knowledge and what constitutes legitimate ways of acquiring that knowledge. If we do survey research, we make assumptions about the validity of our individual questions and how these questions will be understood by our subjects. When considering doing a case study, we make assumptions about whether the case chosen really contains the information being sought. In this case, if we do statistical analyses, assumptions are made about the normal distribution of the data. In doing qualitative research sampling, for example, a scholar will be gathering data from a limited number of subjects, usually at a single point in time (Bryant, 2004).

In order to generalize one's findings from this sample to a larger population, one must make assumptions about both the representativeness of the sample and the stability of findings gathered at one point in time. Many factors can impact the stability of one's findings (Bryant, 2004).

Lastly, in short, all of our research projects spring from assumptions. These are not the theories that we might be exploring. Rather, they are the beliefs we bring to the study and will accept as valid. The identification of these beliefs helps bring legitimacy to your role as a scholar. In this section, it is appropriate to attempt to identify some of the major assumptions that you bring to your study (Bryant, 2004).

Researchers Must Justify Their Assumptions

Researchers need to try and expose their assumptions and justify them. Let's expand on this further. Considering their hypothesis, researchers need to write about the assumptions underlying their measures in order to tighten them into a form where they can be debated with others (Evans et al., 2011). Furthermore, assumptions must be included in chapter one. Underlying assumptions are present in every research study, allowing them to only be implicit (Newman et al., 1997).

It may be that the measures themselves are something you have assumed and not made explicit; it is critical that you directly ask yourself how the outcomes will be assessed and what the measures are so that these decisions are made clear to the examiner (Newman et al., 1997). Nevertheless, a final but significant note on this point is that, ultimately, the argument and your assumptions are subjective. Your final line of defense in your choice of assumptions, method and so on is that they are reasonable and consistent (Repp & Glaviano, 1987; Evans et al., 2011).

Assumptions Are the Starting Point for the Investigation

For the researcher, the assumptions should be viewed as the starting point for an investigation. A basic assumption, or postulate, is a proposition that is not testable but is accepted as true in the light of the best available evidence. This act of faith is important because, without basic assumptions, each investigation would have to begin at the very earliest stage of knowledge (Hubbard, 1973). A third underlying assumption is that anything which exists must exist in some measurable quantity. These unstated and often unrecognized assumptions are, in essence, unprovable value judgments so basic and so universally accepted that we proceed with our research without giving them a second thought. These are the assumptions underlying research methodology (Hubbard, 1973; Ostler, 1996; Pemberton, 2012). The third class of assumptions that must be made are those specific to the study at hand. Such assumptions must be clearly stated or explicitly implied. They may relate to the total field of inquiry on which a study rests or may pertain to a single aspect of the study. An investigator studying the effects of an exercise routine on physical fitness must assume, for example, that physical fitness is a real, identifiable entity subject to definition and measurement (Hubbard, 1973; Thompson, 1994a; Velez, 2008).

Assumptions are statements taken to be true without the presentation of data to support them. They must be consistent with present information and readily acceptable, i.e., statements that would not be disputed. They involve conditions that underlie the research conditions upon which the research is built in contrast to the hypothesis, which is tested by the study. If the assumptions are false, the whole research study will be inadequate. Just as there are assumptions upon which certain statistical procedures are based, there may be assumptions upon which the research study itself is based. If any of the formulae that assume a normal distribution are used with skewed data, the results may be incorrect; in the same way, a research study built upon a wrong assumption may lead to false conclusions. Again, the assumptions prevent a researcher from making a scientific choice and narrowing their list of alternative approaches (Ostler, 1996; Thompson, 1994b).

Assumptions Clarify Aspects of the Study

When thinking of assumptions, researchers must think of them as clarity in the study, clarifying aspects of the study that are believed but cannot be proven to be true. Only include assumptions critical to the meaningfulness of the study. Describe the reasons why the assumptions were necessary for the context of the study (Lani, 2018).

In the dissertation, assumptions are usually stated in this section of chapter one. They also usually address limitations that the researcher is aware of that may affect the study, but which the researcher will not attempt to control (Happen, 2008; Baron, 2010). Assumptions may also be used to state whether or not limiting factors are likely or unlikely to affect the outcome of the study. Generally, conditions that have already been stated as limitations or delimitations should not be addressed in this section. (For example, if respondents' honesty has been listed as a possible limitation, there should not also be an assumption that respondents will answer honestly.) Examples of assumptions might include the following: (1) It is assumed that during this study, participants' gender will not significantly affect their perceptions; and (2) It is assumed that all respondents will answer all survey questions honestly and to the best of their abilities (Happen, 2008; Talab, 2008; Sampson, 2010).

Assumptions in Qualitative Research

Many characteristics make up the collective term of qualitative research, methods used to specify a certain framework in which researchers operate (Walters, 2001). Considering working from this framework, there are two major assumptions that take precedence. Inductive reasoning and topic specificity are the two characteristics that define qualitative research, and inductive reasoning is the epitome of qualitative research design (Repp & Glaviano, 1987; Walters, 2001; Calabrese, 2006). Often, researchers seek information from the data that is gathered; they do not proceed to a project looking for specific findings. According to Maxwell (2013), qualitative research allows researchers to examine explanations and data, not to prove a self-fulfilling prophecy. Inductive reasoning looks for meaning from within the subjects (Repp & Glaviano, 1987; Happen, 2008; Sampson, 2010).

General Types of Assumptions

When considering the assumptions, again, the researcher should list the major assumptions underlying the study. Here are some general types of assumptions:

- Behavior is characterized by some degree of consistency
- The behavior of interest is observable and properly measured
- All individuals in a group benefit equally from a group treatment
- Subjects have the ability to report their perceptions accurately
- The time allotted for the treatment is adequate to produce the desired effects
- All the important variables influencing the dependent variable have been controlled or explicitly included in the design
- Student achievement is a function of both in-school and out-of-school factors (Long et al., 1985).

Based on my experience working with doctoral students, typically, they are confused when it comes to listing assumptions for their study. They usually write them, and they are completely wrong. As a chair, this is where you come in and provide the student with proper guidance.

For more exhaustive types of assumptions, there are many other classifications. There are generally thirteen types of assumptions that researchers can make about their study: (1) participant behavior in terms of truthfulness and ethical behavior; (2) participant qualifications for the study; (3) participant cognitive abilities in terms of their understanding of the questions being asked; (4) the tools and instruments used to collect data; (5) the researchers' beliefs they bring to the study; (6) selected statistical analyses for the study; (7) the normal distribution of the data; (8) the chosen research methodology and design, and the information we seek; (9) the validity and reliability of the survey questions; (10) the time constraints of collecting data in the study; (11) the representativeness of the sample; (12) the stability of the findings gathered from the study; and (13) the sampling, or the gathering of

Table 11.1 Examples of assumptions

Common Quantitative Assumptions	Common Qualitative Assumptions
• **Truthfulness and Honesty**. Assumptions concerning the truthfulness and honesty of the participants in the study.	• **Truthfulness and Honesty**. Assumptions concerning the truthfulness of the participants in the study.
• **Qualifications**. Assumptions concerning the participants' qualifications for the study (knowledge).	• **Qualification**. Assumptions concerning the participants' qualifications for the study (knowledge).
• **Mental Capabilities**. Assumptions concerning the participants' mental capabilities and cognitive abilities for participating in the study.	• **Mental Capabilities**. Assumptions concerning the participants mental capabilities and cognitive abilities for participating in the study.
• **Research Methodology**. Assumptions concerning the research methodology appropriateness.	• **Research Methodology**. Assumptions concerning the research methodology appropriateness.
• **Research Design**. Assumptions concerning the research design (type) appropriateness.	• **Research Design**. Assumptions concerning the research design appropriateness.
• **Self-Reported Data**. Assumptions concerning the use of self-reported data (surveys) from the participants.	• **Self-Reported Data**. Assumptions concerning the use of self-reported data (interviews) from the participants.
• **Time Constraints**. Assumptions concerning time constraints (time to collect data).	• **Time Constraints**. Assumptions concerning the use of time constraints (time to interview subjects and collect data).
• **Instrument**. Assumptions concerning the length of survey instrument appropriateness.	• **Instrument**. Assumptions concerning the length of study interview time with participants.
• **Instrument Design**. Assumptions concerning the design of the survey instrument.	• **Instrument Design**. Assumptions concerning the design of the interview questions.
• **Sampling Design**. Assumptions concerning the sampling design type (random, stratified or clustering, systematic, convenience, probability sampling-based).	• **Sampling Design**. Assumptions concerning the sampling design type (purposive, quota and snowball, non-probability sampling-based).
• **Sample Representation**. Assumptions concerning the sampling representativeness of the study.	• **Sample Representation**. Assumptions concerning the sampling representativeness of the study.
• **Population Appropriateness**. Assumptions concerning the appropriateness of the study's population.	• **Population Appropriateness**. Assumptions concerning the appropriateness of the study's population.
• **Data Collection Type**. Assumptions concerning the data collection modality type for the study.	• **Data Collection Type**. Assumptions concerning the data collection modality type for the study.
• **Survey Question Types**. Assumptions concerning the survey question types (closed-ended).	• **Interview Question Types**. Assumptions concerning the interview question types (open-ended).
• **Researcher Data Interpretation**. Assumptions concerning the researcher's interpretation of participant responses from the data from surveys.	• **Researcher Data Interpretation**. Assumptions concerning the researcher's interpretation of participant data from interviews (Miles, 2016a, 2016b; Miles & Scott, 2017).

data from the targeted population (Bryant, 2004; Miles, 2016a, 2016b; Miles & Scott, 2017).

When the researcher discusses the assumptions, they are discussing the possible and real influences on the study. Think of assumptions as described by the researcher as those things that usually address limitations that the researcher is aware may affect the study, but which the researcher will not attempt to control (Baron, 2010). Assumptions may also be used to state whether or not limiting factors are likely or unlikely to affect the outcome of the study. Assumptions may or may not affect the study's validity or findings. The assumptions tend to address the researcher's awareness and shortcomings of their research design and methodological approach to the study, thus adding to the researcher's credibility. For example, in order to generalize one's findings from this sample to a larger population, one must make assumptions about both the representativeness of the sample and the stability of findings gathered at one point in time. Many factors can impact the stability of one's findings (Bryant, 2004; Newton & Rudestam, 2007; Calabrese, 2009) (see Table 11.1).

An assumption is a factor that may or will affect the study but is not under the control of the researcher. In such studies that use questionnaires, a common assumption is the willingness of the individuals to respond at all, to respond in a timely fashion and to respond accurately. Assumptions are important to the possible effects on the outcomes of the study, and they are not controlled by the researcher. Assumptions typically surface as variables that cannot be controlled by the researcher but may limit or affect the outcome of the study. Assumptions can become a problem for students if they are not specified (Mauch & Birch, 1998).

When the researcher discusses the assumptions, they are discussing the possible and real weaknesses of their research design. Assumptions described by the researcher are those that may or did affect the study's validity or findings. The assumptions tend to address the researcher's awareness of the shortcomings in their research design and methodological approach to the study, thus adding to the researcher's credibility (Calabrese, 2009) (see Table 11.2 and Examples 11.1 to 11.3).

Example 11.1 Assumptions

The school district that is the foundation of this study has a variety of races, which is represented in the teaching pool. Though there are more non-performing arts teachers than performing arts teachers in the school district, there should be a good representation as far as the data is concerned. The following assumptions are present in this study:

1.   It is assumed that participants in this study will answer the survey as honestly as possible.

2. It is assumed that participants will be mentally capable of answering and completing the survey.
3. It is assumed that participants have the background and experience to answer and complete the survey.
4. It is assumed that participants are employed as teachers in the K–12 school system in the area where the study is being conducted (Jefferson, 2022).

Table 11.2 Introducing the Statement Grid for assumptions

Overall Statement:
This research has some assumptions regarding the participants that were a part of the study. An assumption is an unexamined belief that the researcher brings to the study and that is accepted as being valid (Bryant, 2004). The researcher identified four assumptions for this study.

Assumption 1:	Assumption 2:	Assumption 3:	Assumption 4:
The researcher assumes the participants will be truthful and honest.	The researcher assumes the participants will answer the interview questions to the best of their knowledge.	The researcher assumes the participants will be mentally capable and have the cognitive ability to answer the interview questions.	Lastly, the researcher assumes the participants have the experience and background knowledge as an educator to answer the interview questions with credibility (Martinez, 2021).

Example 11.2 Assumptions

This qualitative descriptive study was concerned with the perceptions of ethical leadership styles based on the lived experiences of twenty FBHCO employees. The researcher determined that the best approach for obtaining data was to conduct and record face-to-face interviews. This research has some assumptions regarding the participants in the study. An assumption is an unexamined belief that the researcher brings to the study and that is accepted as being valid (Bryant, 2004).

The researcher identified four significant assumptions for this study:

1. It is assumed that the participants will have knowledge and experience of the healthcare field and aid the researcher with understanding the problem.
2. It is assumed that the participants responded truthfully to the interview questions asked by the researcher during the interviewing process.

3. It is assumed that the responses to the questions are accurate, as the researcher relies on the voice of the participants (Creswell, 1994).
4. It is assumed that the data collected will represent a purposeful sample from the target population. Purposeful sampling will be performed in this research because it allows the researcher to acquire a sample that best represents a larger population (Yin, 2017). Patton (2002, p. 230) revealed that purposeful sampling gives an in-depth understanding rather than empirical generalizations (McCain, 2022).

Example 11.3 Assumptions

This study has some assumptions. Assumptions are defined as something the researcher accepts as true without any concrete proof (Ellis & Levy, 2009). The researcher has some assumptions about the participants in the study. The following assumptions are present in this study:

1. It is assumed that the participants (higher education employees) across the sector use some form of ICT in the scope of their job functions.
2. It is assumed that the participants are susceptible to technostress based on the higher education industry's use of new and changing technology for teaching students and managing university operations (Jang et al., 2017; Raspopovic et al., 2016; Sweet et al., 2013).
3. It is assumed that the participants respond truthfully and are forthright regarding the nature of their internal attitudes when using new and changing technologies in the workplace.
4. It is assumed that the participants are mentally capable of understanding the questions in the survey and answering them (Cornish, 2022).

[Note: In-text citations included for illustrative purposes only]

Participant Bias and Assumptions

As can be seen in Examples 11.1, 11.2 and 11.3, one assumption that appears in many research studies is the participants being honest in providing information during data collection. In fact, the assumption that a participant is being honest might, in fact, be a normalized belief without considering that the participants come to the data collection process with biases. In many dissertations, the notation of participant honesty is oftentimes not challenged and mistakenly taken as a norm in the writing of assumptions. However, this is an underlying construct that has implications for the outcome of any study. Farnsworth (2019) noted that participants, depending on the environment or purpose of the study, might change their answers or behaviors; therefore, this bias could produce errors that might affect the research findings. In fact, understanding the significance of participant bias or assumptions could present the possibility of reconsidering or reframing the problem (Wolgemuth et al., 2017).

Summary

This chapter discussed the use of assumptions in the dissertation. The chapter discussed assumptions as statements that are taken for granted or considered true, even though they have not been scientifically tested.

The chapter discussed a framework that presents information that defines or clarifies: (a) what is meant by the term assumption when developing research proposals or reports; (b) making and justifying assumptions; (c) assumptions in qualitative research; (d) the general types of assumptions; (e) the Statement Grid for assumptions; and (f) the significance of participant bias on assumptions.

Overall, we wanted to build a foundation for enlightening both experienced and novice researchers on the nature of assumptions and their underlying implications in relation to the research development and implementation processes. We hope this chapter will act as a guide to help novice and experienced researchers learn and understand the use of assumptions.

References

Baron, M. (2010). *Guidelines for writing research proposals and dissertations*. Division of Educational Administration, University of South Dakota.

Bryant, M. T. (2004). *The portable dissertation advisor*. Corwin Press, Inc.

Calabrese, R. (2006). *The Elements of an Effective Dissertation and Thesis: A Step-by-Step Guide to Getting it Right the First Time*. Lanham, MD: Rowman & Littlefield *Education, Inc.*

Calabrese, R. (2009). *The dissertation desk reference: The doctoral student's manual to writing the dissertation*. Rowman & Littlefield Education, Inc.

Cornish, D. (2022). *An empirical study of technostress within U.S. higher education employees* [UMI document]. ProQuest Dissertations and Theses.

Creswell, J. (1994). *Research design*. SAGE Publications.

Creswell, J., & Poth, C. (2018). *Qualitative inquiry and research design: Choosing among five approaches*. Sage.

Evans, D., Gruba, P., & Zobel, J. (2011). *How to write a better thesis* (3rd ed.). Springer.

Farnsworth, B. (2019). *What is participant bias? (And how to defeat it)*. iMotions. https://imotions. com/blog/participant-bias/

Happen, B. (2008) Writing for publication: A practical guide. *Nursing Standard, 22*(28), 35–40.

Herrington, J., McKenney, S., Reeves, T., & Oliver, R. (2007). *Design-based research and doctoral students: Guidelines for preparing a dissertation proposal*. Retrieved from https://ro.ecu.edu.au/ecuworks/1612

Hubbard, A. (1973). *Research methods in health, physical education and recreation*. American Association for Health, Physical Education, and Recreation.

Jefferson, R. (2022). *A quantitative study on the opinions of K–12 administrators towards music education* [UMI document]. ProQuest Dissertations and Theses.

Lani, J. (2018). *The essential dissertation resource.* Statistics Solutions: Advancement Through Clarity. www.statisticssolutions.com/

Long, T., Convey, J., & Chwalek, A. (1985). *Completing dissertations in the behavioral sciences and education: A systematic guide for graduate students.* Jossey-Bass, Inc.

Martinez, O. (2021). *A qualitative descriptive study examining the experiences of active duty veterans that have transitioned from the military to the teaching profession* [UMI document]. ProQuest Dissertations and Theses.

Mauch, J., & Birch, J. (1998). *Guide to the successful theses and dissertation: A handbook for students and faculty* (4th ed.). Marcel Dekker, Inc.

Maxwell, J. A. (2013). *Qualitative research design: An interactive approach* (3rd ed.). Sage Publications.

McCain, M. (2022). *A descriptive study: How leadership behaviors and ethical practices are described in faith-based healthcare organizations* [UMI document]. ProQuest Dissertations and Theses.

Miles, D. A. (2016a). *The one-page dissertation proposal matrix: A guide for developing the dissertation proposal* [Unpublished document].

Miles, D. A. (2016b). *The one-page literature review matrix: A guide for developing the literature review for the dissertation* [Unpublished document].

Miles, D. A., & Scott, L. (2017, October 26–29). *Confessions of a dissertation chair, Part 1: The six mistakes doctoral students make with the dissertation* [Workshop]. 5th Annual 2017 Black Doctoral Network Conference, Atlanta, GA.

Newman, I., Benz, C. R., Weis, D., & McNeil, K. (1997). *Theses and dissertations: A guide to writing in the social and physical sciences.* University Press of America, Inc.

Newton, R. & Rudestam, K. (2007). *Surviving your dissertation: A comprehensive guide to content and process* (3rd ed.). Sage.

Ostler, E. (1996). *Guidelines for writing research proposals, reports, theses, and dissertations.* Retrieved from https://files.eric.ed.gov/fulltext/ED396284.pdf

Patidar, J. (2010). *Research assumptions.* Retrieved from www.drjayeshpatidar.blogspot.com/

Patton, M. Q. (2002). *Qualitative research & evaluation methods.* SAGE Publications.

Pemberton, C. (2012). A how to guide for the education thesis/dissertation process. *Kappa Delta Pi Record, 48,* 82–86. https://doi.org/10.1080/00228958.2012.680378

Repp, J., & Glaviano, C. (1987) Dissertations: A study of the scholar's approach. *College & Research Libraries, 48*(2), 148–159.

Sampson, J. (2010). A guide to quantitative and qualitative dissertation research [Paper 1]. Educational Psychology and Learning Systems Faculty Publications. http://diginole.lib.fsu.edu/edpsy_faculty_publications/1

Simon, M. K. (2011). Dissertation and *scholarly research: Recipes for success.* Dissertation Success, LLC.

Simon, M. K., & Goes, J. (2013). *Dissertation and scholarly research: Recipes for success.* Dissertation Success, LLC.

Talab, R. (2008). *Guidelines For writing dissertation proposals and dissertations.* Retrieved from http://coe.k-state.edu/annex/ecdol/Dissertation_Guide.pdf

Terrell, S. (2016). *Writing a proposal for your dissertation: Guidelines and examples.* The Guilford Press.

Thompson, B. (1994a, April 4–6). *Common methodology mistakes in dissertations, revisited.* Annual Meeting of the American Educational Research Association, New Orleans, LA. Retrieved from https://files.eric.ed.gov/fulltext/ED368771.pdf

Thompson, B. (1994b). Essential elements in a qualitative dissertation proposal. *Journal of Nursing Education, 35*(4), 188–190. https://doi.org/10.3928/0148-4834-19960401-15

Velez, A. M. (2008). *Evaluating research methods: Assumptions, strengths, and weaknesses of three educational research paradigms.* Retrieved from www.unco.edu/AE-Extra/2008/9/velez.html

Walters, C. H. (2001). Assumptions of qualitative research methods. *Perspectives in Learning, 2*(1). Retrieved from http://csuepress.columbusstate.edu/pil/vol2/iss1/14

Webster, W. (1998a). *21 models for developing and writing your theses, dissertations or projects.* Academic Scholarwrite.

Webster, W. (1998b). *Developing and writing your thesis, dissertation or project.* Academic Scholarwrite.

Wolgemuth, J., Hicks, T., & Agosto, V. (2017). Unpacking assumptions in research synthesis: A Critical construct synthesis. *Educational Researcher, 46*(3), 131–139. https://journals.sagepub.com/doi/full/10.3102/0013189X17703946

Yin, R. K. (2017). *Case study research and applications.* SAGE Publications.

12 Understanding the Differences Between Contributions and the Significance of a Study

Objective

- Readers will be able to:
  1. Understand the differences between the contributions and significance of a study

Introduction

In my many years of working with doctoral students, I have found that there is still a prevailing confusion among them. There is substantial confusion around the terms *contributions of a study* and *significance of a study*. This is so common that I have seen it to be the case with both experienced and novice researchers, but it is most common with doctoral students. Again, as professors we need to do a better job at helping our students to understand the differences between these two terms.

One of the prevailing issues is that they did not properly understand these concepts in their research methods courses. They either have never learned the differences between the two terms or they assume they are the same. This shows when they write their dissertations. However, help is on the way. I think we have found a useful definition and examples to help doctoral students and novice researchers understand the differences between the two terms.

The outline of this chapter will provide information on the differences between the two terms. First, this chapter will provide clear definitions of the contributions of a study and significance of a study. This chapter discusses the differences between and definitions of the two terms *the contributions of a study* and *the significance of a study*. Second, this chapter will provide some examples of how to use them in a sentence and paragraph. It discusses the three types of study significance. Last, the chapter discusses the three types of research significance. The chapter will provide examples of these from journal articles and studies.

Contributions: What Are They and Why Are They Important?

The contributions of a study describe how the study will contribute to the body of knowledge. There are three types of study contribution: (a) *conceptual/theoretical*,

DOI: 10.4324/9781003268154-12

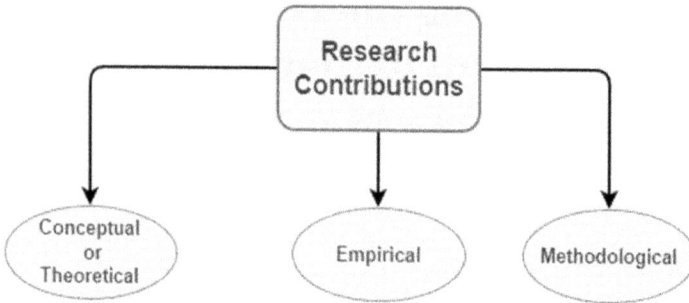

Figure 12.1 The three types of research contribution.

(b) *empirical,* and (c) *methodological.* These three types of contribution define most research contributions in a study (see Figure 12.1).

Conceptual/Theoretical Contributions

The conceptual (theoretical) contribution of a study involves contributions such as (a) improved conceptual definitions of the original constructs; (b) the identification and conceptual definition of additional constructs to be added to the conceptual framework (e.g., additional dependent, independent, mediating and/or moderator variables); (c) the development of additional theoretical linkages (e.g., research hypotheses) with their accompanying rationale; and (d) the development of improved theoretical rationale for existing linkages (Summers, 2001; Asgari, 2015; Miles, 2018; Miles, 2019).

Empirical Contributions

The empirical contribution of a study involves contributions such as (a) testing a theoretical linkage between two constructs that has not previously been tested; (b) examining the effects of a potential moderator variable on the nature of the relationship between two constructs; (c) determining the degree to which a variable mediates the relationship between two constructs; and (d) investigating the psychometric properties of an important scale (Summers, 2001; Asgari, 2015; Miles, 2018; Miles, 2019).

Methodological Contributions

The methodological contribution of a study involves contributions such as (a) reducing the potential problems with shared method variance through the insightful use of multiple methods of measurement; (b) increasing the generalizability of the research through more appropriate sampling procedures; (c) allowing the investigation of the plausibility of "third-variable explanations" for the results of past

Table 12.1 Introducing the Statement Grid for the contributions of a study

Overall Statement:
The researcher identified a key contribution of this study. This study makes two important
_____ *contributions.*

Contribution 1: First, this study makes a contribution by offering a _____ _____ that is lacking in the prior research that primarily focused on _____

Contribution 2: Second, this study offers a _____ line of inquiry that was not addressed in the prior research. This study attempts to address the potential problems in the prior studies with a _____ through the insightful use of _____.

studies; and (d) enhancing the construct validity of key measures through the use of refined multiple-item measures and/or the use of measurement approaches that do not rely on self-reports (Summers, 2001; Asgari, 2015; Miles, 2018; Miles, 2019).

Other Research Contributions

These are rare contributions and rarely used except for special situations. The *applied contribution* refers to when a theoretical model applies in a different industry that hasn't been empirically tested earlier. *Survey contributions* are attempts to review and synthesize work done in a research field with the goal of exposing trends, themes and gaps in the literature (Asgari, 2015). See the *Statement Grid* (Tables 12.1 to 12.3) for examples of how to write the contributions of a study.

See, also, Examples 12.1 to 12.3, which provide some actual examples of how the contributions of a study are written.

Example 12.1

The researcher identified two contributions of this study. First, this study will make a conceptual contribution to the field of leadership and management studies. This study hopes to contribute to the theory of leadership and body of knowledge. Many researchers have explored the impact of leaders' behavior on their employees. Many of these studies deal with leadership styles and how employees respond to their managers' actions. The results of such studies indicated that "employees would respond to the manager's actions with attitudes reflecting their perception of a supervisor's leadership style" (Mulki et al., 2015, p. 6). Kim (2014) suggested that leaders set the tone and atmosphere in the organization, therefore defining the organization's culture. This study will contribute to the development of additional theoretical linkages (e.g., research hypotheses) with their accompanying rationale.

The second contribution will be methodological. This study makes a contribution by providing a divergent research method variance through the insightful use of multiple methods of measurement. A qualitative line of inquiry is lacking in the prior research. Some of these unexplored research methods appear to be important and worthy of investigation in the context of management and job performance. Yoonk and Poister (2014) also asserted that, by engaging employees in the building of a team work environment, this could be a leading factor towards increasing organizational performance and sustainability. An investigation of these issues is important because there is a dearth in prior research that approaches this topic from a qualitative line of inquiry. Furthermore, the previous empirical research has focused primarily on quantitative methodology and assessment. Very little research has contributed from a qualitative line of inquiry (Platt, 2019).

Table 12.2 The Statement Grid – Contributions of a study

Overall Statement:
The researcher identified a key contribution of this study. This study makes a methodological contribution. *This study makes two key methodological contributions.*

Contribution 1: First, this study makes a contribution by offering a qualitative inquiry that is lacking in the prior research that primarily focused on empirical research.

Contribution 2: Second, this study offers a divergent line of inquiry that was not addressed in the prior research. This study attempts to address the potential problems in the prior studies with shared method variance through the insightful use of multiple methods of inquiry.

Table 12.3 The Statement Grid – Contributions of a study

Overall Statement:
The researcher identified a key contribution of this study. This study makes an empirical contribution. *This study makes two key empirical contributions.*

Contribution 1: First, this study makes an empirical contribution by offering an empirical line of inquiry that is lacking in the prior research. The primary line of inquiry in the prior research tended to focus on a non-empirical approach to studying this topic.

Contribution 2: Second, this study offers an evaluative line of inquiry that was not addressed in the prior research. The majority of the prior research tended to focus on a non-evaluative approach to the research. This study attempts to address the potential problems in the prior studies with shared method variance through the insightful use of evaluative methods of inquiry.

Example 12.2

The researcher identified a major contribution of this study. First, this study will offer a much-needed empirical contribution. This study makes two important empirical contributions. First, the research uses archival data maintained by the state for public access to make connections. This information is stored specifically for research purposes as shown in Appendix F. This facilitates the use of larger amounts of data and greater populations.

Second, this study will contribute to the empirical evidence for the requirement of a student's socio-intellectual development in the high school setting. This research may be appropriate for understanding the impact that precise character and behavioral skills have on student interactions with peers, adults and their studies. Additionally, the need for a specific, codified character education curriculum may be indicated from the results of the study. Further evidence may be provided that character education may positively impact student success outside the classroom (Zeig, 2019).

Example 12.3

The researcher identified a key contribution of this study. This study makes a methodological contribution. This study makes two key methodological contributions. First, this study makes a contribution by offering a qualitative inquiry that is lacking in the prior research that primarily focused on empirical research. Second, this study offers a divergent line of inquiry that was not addressed in the prior research. This study attempts to address the potential problems in the prior studies with shared method variance through the insightful use of multiple methods of inquiry.

In addition, this study encompasses several unexplored dimensions that lately have attracted research attention and calls for another research method. Some of these unexplored research methods appear to be important and worthy of investigation in the context of technostress and job performance. An investigation of these issues is important because there is a dearth in prior research that approaches this topic from a qualitative line of inquiry. Furthermore, the previous empirical research has focused primarily on quantitative methodology and assessment. Very little research has made a contribution from a qualitative line of inquiry (Beltran, 2019).

Significance: What Is It and Why Is It Important?

A second problem that doctoral students have is with the meaning of significance. Many doctoral students have considerable trouble writing and supporting the significance statement in their dissertation proposal. The reasons stem from a poor research objective. The significance statement gives plausible rationale as to why the study matters.

This is a very important section of the proposal. The significance is an explanation of why the proposed study is important, why it represents a potential contribution to the field. Its emphasis should be on why the study is worthwhile (Webster, 1998). The significance of a study is your argument that the study makes a significant and original contribution to the profession, the scholarly literature and your discipline. The significance of the study answers questions related to why the topic is worth studying (Calabrese, 2006). You offer reasons and arguments pertaining to why your study is important. The reasons may be confined to the possibility that your study will add new knowledge to existing information about your area of interest. These reasons relate to how practitioners behave in carrying out their work (Bryant, 2004).

With significance, the researcher describes how the study (a) contributes to existing research, (b) benefits participants, (c) contributes to practice, and (d) generates new theory. If the significance of the study is presented in the dissertation proposal, then the researcher is speculative, theorizing his or her contributions in these four areas (Calabrese, 2009)

It provides answers as to why your study is important and how it will add something to the body of knowledge. There are three key points to a significance statement: (a) Why is this research important; (b) How does this research contribute to the body of knowledge; and (c) How does this research contribute to the practice and field.

The significance of a study describes why the study is important. There are three types of study significance: (a) *theoretical*, (b) *practical*, and (c) *research*. These three types of significance define most research significance in a study (see Figure 12.2).

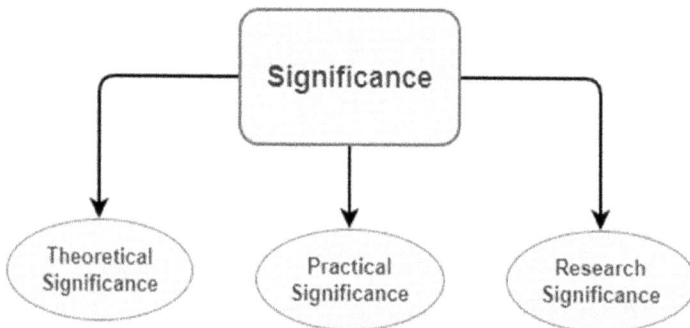

Figure 12.2 The three types of study significance.

Table 12.4 The Statement Grid – Significance of a study

Overall Statement:
As a basis for this study, the researcher identified one major reason why this study is significant (two examples).

Example 1: First, this study is important because it provides *theoretical significance*. This study breaks some new ground in management and human resources theory. This study makes a strong theoretical contribution in terms of offering a theory that goes beyond the prior models from Masterson's (2008) own management task.

Example 2: Second, this study is important because it provides *theoretical significance* by making a strong contribution to the body of knowledge by developing a new conceptual model. This study makes a strong contribution to the theory in the field of marketing.

Theoretical Significance

The idea of saying why a study is important can be challenging. This is why there is a term called *significance*. Furthermore, we have *theoretical significance*. Theoretical significance is defined as theoretical contributions, which include contributions you expect to make to the establishment or verification of theories or models or to an existing body of research. The researcher provides arguments for theoretical contributions that should be developed from the literature (Long et al., 1985). Thus, the study is important because it provides a theoretical contribution to the body of knowledge.

This type of significance is important because it focuses on adding new knowledge or theory to the body of knowledge in the field. Novice researchers and doctoral students find theoretical importance confusing. They still do not understand the basics of writing up the significance of a study. The basis of the significance of a study is your argument that your study makes a significant and original contribution to the scholarly literature and your discipline (Calabrese, 2009; Miles, 2018; Miles, 2019; Webster, 1998) (see Table 12.4).

Practical Significance

The second significance type is called *practical significance*. Practical significance is defined as a focus on the impact of your results on the profession or on the solution of practical problems (Long et al., 1985). This is the opposite of its predecessor, theoretical significance. The researcher provides arguments for theoretical contributions that should be developed from the literature (Long et al., 1985). Thus, the study is important because it provides a practical contribution to the profession, industry and practitioners as a body of knowledge.

This type of significance is important because it focuses on the impact of your results on the profession or on the solution of practical problems (Madsen, 1990). These reasons relate to how practitioners behave in carrying out their work (Bryant,

Table 12.5 The Statement Grid – Significance of a study

Overall Statement:
As a basis for this study, the researcher identified one major reason why this study is significant (two examples).

| **Example 1:** This study is important because it also provides practical significance. This research attempts to provide insight into new practicing teachers considering a transition to a career role in the teaching profession. This study is important because it illuminates the experiences of new teachers in their new job. | **Example 2:** This study is vital because it provides *practical significance*. This research attempts to provide a template for policy makers in the engineering industry and field. Second, this study also makes a contribution to establishing new policy for the engineers in the field. Lastly, this study provides insight into new practicing engineers. |

2004). The significance of a study is your argument that the study makes a significant contribution to the profession. The key factor here is how your research contributes in terms of practice (Calabrese, 2009) (see Table 12.5).

Research Significance

The last type of significance is called *research significance*. Research significance is defined as a focus on the research importance of your study and its contribution to the body of knowledge in terms of research (Miles & Scott, 2017). This type of significance is important because it focuses on the importance of your study and how it is important from a research perspective. Research significance is usually one of three types: (a) *continuation*; (b) *extension*; and (c) *new inquiry* (Miles & Scott, 2017).

(a) **Continuation**. A continuation is the type of research significance that continues the prior research with the same or similar population. This would also be called a *replication study* (Miles, 2018; Miles, 2019).

(b) **Extension**. An extension is the type of significance that is used when you are extending the prior research or theory to a new, underserved or underresearched population. Normally you are applying prior established theory or conceptual framework or research methodology to a new population (Miles, 2018; Miles, 2019).

(c) **New Inquiry**. A new inquiry is the type of significance that is used when you are conducting a new study (brand new) with a new theory and/or new population or a new research method and design. You are doing something new (Miles, 2018; Miles, 2019).

Table 12.6 The Statement Grid – Significance of a study

Overall Statement:
As a basis for this study, the researcher identified three major reasons why this study is significant.

Example 1: This study is important because it also provides *research significance*. This study is important because it is a replication study or a continuation. This study is a continuation of the prior research on the nursing shortage. This study will replicate a prior study by Malvey and Slovensky (2017). This study will provide additional insight into the shortage and inform the nursing professoriate of the current lived experiences of job satisfaction by the nursing faculty teaching classroom and clinical education of baccalaureate nursing students (Cook, 2017). [continuation/replication]	**Example 2:** This study is important because it also provides *research significance*. This study is important because it extends the prior research on the theory of marketing strategy (Kenner, 2015). Second, this study is important because it is an extension of the concept of marketing strategy (Kenner, 2015). This study is an extension of the prior research on marketing strategy tactics. [extension]	**Example 3:** This study is important because it also provides *research significance*. This study is important because it is a new inquiry on the prior research on techniques for teaching mathematics to gifted and talented students in K–12 schools. Second, this study is important because it breaks new ground and proposes a new inquiry into teaching mathematics with a new population of teachers for the gifted and talented students. Lastly, this study provides a new frontier in the area of teaching and learning with gifted and talented students in K–12. [new inquiry]

We need to think of significance as a ship that explores uncharted waters. As a novice researcher, you must provide the importance of your study, what your study tackles in terms of unexplored areas. Throughout this research endeavor, you as a researcher must try and convince the readers of your work that your study offers something valuable. Whether it is a continuation (replication), an extension or a new inquiry. As a researcher, you must convince your readers that you are studying something new and worthy, possibly adding some value to your field or practice. Think of significance as the selling point of why your study is necessary and why it is important. As a researcher, you should craft your significance carefully and conservatively. See the *Statement Grid* (Tables 12.6 and Table 12.7) for examples of how to write your significance (Miles, 2018; Miles, 2019).

See, also, Examples 12.4 to 12.6, which provide some actual examples of how the significance of a study is written.

Table 12.7 The Statement Grid – Significance of a study

Overall Statement:
As a basis for this study, the researcher identified three major reasons why this study is significant.

Significance 1: First,	**Significance 2:**	**Significance 3:**
this study is important because it provides *theoretical significance*. This study breaks some new ground in management and human resources theory. Many nursing program deans and administrators will gain insight into how nursing faculty experience job satisfaction in order to facilitate a workplace conducive of job satisfaction. [theoretical significance]	Second, this study is important because it also provides *practical significance*. This research attempts to provide insight into practicing nurses considering a transition to a role in nursing education by elucidating experiences of job satisfaction by nursing faculty. [practical significance]	Last, this study is important because it also provides *research significance*. This study is important because it is a replication study or a continuation. This study is a continuation of the prior research on the nursing shortage. This study will replicate a prior study by Morgan and Somera (2014). This study will provide additional insight into the shortage and inform the nursing professoriate of the current lived experiences of job satisfaction by nursing faculty teaching classroom and clinical education of baccalaureate nursing students (Cook, 2017). [research significance]

Example 12.4

Based on the literature, there are two main reasons why this study is significant: research and practical. First, this study provides research significance. This study is an extension of the prior research on technostress among academics working in universities in India (Jena & Mahanti, 2014). This study is extending the prior research to a new population (U.S. higher education employees). This study is important because the study's results will show differences in the extent of technostress experienced based on the technology awareness, demographic factors and job characteristics of higher education workers.

In addition, the proposed study is an extension of the prior research on demographic differences in technostress conducted by Jena and Mahanti (2014). The researchers utilized the technostress-demographic model for investigating the effects of technology awareness, gender, age, tenure and marital status on the technostress of academics working in universities in India (Jena & Mahanti,

2014). Jena and Mahanti (2014) called for future research to include a more diverse sample within higher education, as well as investigate relationships between technostress and additional demographic factors. This study, therefore, includes both academic and non-academic roles for investigation and extends the technostress-demographic model by including additional demographic factors and job characteristics.

In prior technostress research, technostress has been found to negatively affect job satisfaction and job performance (Kumar et al., 2017). This study, therefore, may achieve research significance because it can provide new information germane to some factors potentially affecting or contributing to technostress in this population and, based on past technostress research, can be used as justification for developing programs for mitigating the effects of technostress among U.S. higher education workers. Conducting this study may also open up new inquiries into further technostress research within the higher education realm, such as how technostress affects technology acceptance and organizational effectiveness among this population.

Second, this study provides practical significance. This study is essential because if results reveal statistically significant differences in the extent of technostress based on technology awareness, demographic factors and job characteristics, then these results can become helpful for designing programs for lessening the effects or preventing technostress in U.S. higher education employees. In other populations, technostress has been linked to absenteeism, lower productivity and job satisfaction and costly mistakes (Chiappetta, 2017). This study offers practical significance to those in the field who may experience technology-related stress to the extent that it negatively affects work-related progress. These examples demonstrate how addressing the problem of the extent to which technology-related stress differs based on technology awareness, demographic factors, employment status and department in the U.S. higher education population can add value to this population by making their institutions more aware of the problem, potentially prompting the creation of better-coping programs and reducing the costs associated with lost revenue due to technostress (Galluch et al., 2015; Cornish, 2022).

Example 12.5

The researcher found two major reasons why this study is significant. First, this study offers a theoretical significance. This study breaks new ground by introducing the parental perception of parental involvement with schools into the existing framework of the phenomenon. This study is important because through identification of the parental perspective on their involvement in school to support the education of their children, school systems may be able to use the information to address the issue of parental involvement more effectively.

Lastly, the study offers research significance by extending research to the under-researched parent population through an investigation into their perceptions of parental involvement in school. This study is an extension of the prior research on the topic. The study is significant because it will extend the prior research to the new and under-researched population of parents (Forbes, 2019).

Example 12.6

As a foundation for this investigation, there are three major reasons why this study is significant. First, this study provides theoretical significance. The contribution of this study will add to the field of management in theory and practice. This study will test the linkage between two constructs: the air transportation organization and the geographical location of Puerto Rico, which has not previously been tested. The foundation theories in this study are the Douglas McGregor's Theory X and Theory Y. Miner (2002) stated that this theory has a lack of investigation and needs to be tested. Douglas McGregor's Theory X and Theory Y of management remain virtually untested (Schein, 2011). Due to the lack of published studies related to the theories, a study testing McGregor's Theory X and Y with field data would be an important theoretical contribution to the body of knowledge (Sahin, 2012). This study will allow the researcher to examine and compare the results of the data from air transportation organizations in Puerto Rico.

Second, this study also offers practical significance. It is significant to the field of management practices and relations with employees. This study will identify if there is a relationship between leaders' openness to new business strategies, customer and market focus and employee's empowerment, on the one hand, and the organizational performance of air transportation companies located in Puerto Rico, on the other. There are studies that demonstrate the relationship of the variables; however, none of these studies are related to air transportation companies located in the geographical area of Puerto Rico. Although there are studies in other industry sectors such as health care (Chen et al., 2014) and the bank industry (Abbasi et al., 2018), it cannot be assumed that the behavior of the variables will be the same in the air transportation sector located in Puerto Rico.

Last, this study also offers research significance because it is an extension of the prior research. This study will extend prior research to a new population and new industry sector. This study will contribute to the field of knowledge by extending and enhancing research related to the air transportation organizations' performance. The new population on which this study will be conducted is employees in Puerto Rico. The new industry sector to which this study will extend is air transportation organizations. This study will fill the gaps presented by conducting research in air transportation organizations by conducting research in the geo-graphical location of Puerto Rico, extending current studies about the correl-ation between customer and market focus, employee empowerment, leaders' openness to new business strategies and organizational performance. The investi-gation will demonstrate the behavior of the variables in the study regarding cor-relation with similar studies in previous research in other geographical locations (Morales, 2019).

[Note: In-text citations included for illustrative purposes only]

Summary

This chapter discussed the differences between and characteristics and definitions of the terms *the contributions of a study* and *the significance of a study*. This chapter addressed the two key differences between the contributions of a study and the significance of a study. First, this chapter addressed the three key study contributions: (a) *conceptual/ theoretical*, (b) *empirical*, and (c) *methodological*. Definitions and examples of the three types of contribution were provided.

Last, this chapter addressed three types of study significance: (a) *theoretical*, (b) *practical*, and (c) *research*. Definitions and examples of the three types of signifi-cance were provided. In addition, the chapter discussed the three types of research significance: (a) *continuation*, (b) *extension*, and (c) *new inquiry*. We hope this chapter will act as a guide to help novice and experienced researchers learn and understand the distinct differences between the contributions of a study and the significance of a study. We hope to build a strong foundation for enlightening both experienced and novice researchers on the two terms and lessen the confusion.

References

Abbasi, F. K., Ali, A., & Bibi, N. (2018). Analysis of skill gap for business graduates: Managerial perspective from banking industry. *Education + Training, 60*(4), 354–367. https://doi.org/ 10.1108/et-08-2017-0120

Asgari, A. (2015). *Types of the contributions in a research paper*. LinkedIn. www.linkedin.com/ pulse/types-contributions-research-paper-ali-asgari

Beltran, V. (2019). *A phenomenological study of central Texas urban school principals' experience of influences contributing to job stress*. ProQuest Dissertations and Theses.

Bryant, M. T. (2004). *The portable dissertation advisor* (1st ed.). Corwin Press.

Calabrese, R. (2006). *The elements of an effective dissertation & thesis: A step-by-step guide to getting it right the first time* (1st ed.). Rowman & Littlefield Education.

Calabrese, R. (2009). *The dissertation desk reference: The doctoral student's manual to writing the disser-tation* (1st ed.). Rowman & Littlefield Education.

Chen, S.-C., Lai, Y.-H., Liao, C.-T., Huang, B.-S., Lin, C.-Y., Fan, K.-H., & Chang, J. T.-C. (2014). Unmet supportive care needs and characteristics of family caregivers of patients with oral cancer after surgery. *Psycho-Oncology, 23*(5), 569–577. https://doi.org/10.1002/ pon.3458

Chiappetta, M. (2017). The technostress: Definition, symptoms and risk prevention. *Senses and Sciences, 4*(1), 358–361. https://doi.org/10.14616/sands-2017-1-358361

Cook, L. (2017). *The current issues affecting job satisfaction by nursing faculty as a lived experience* [Unpublished dissertation]. ProQuest Dissertations and Theses.

Cornish, D. (2022). *An empirical study of technostress within the US higher education sector.* ProQuest Dissertations and Theses.

Forbes, S. (2019). *Parental involvement in education: The lived experience* [Unpublished dissertation]. ProQuest Dissertations and Theses.

Galluch, P. S., Grover, V., & Thatcher, J. B. (2015). Interrupting the workplace: Examining stressors in an information technology context. *Journal of the Association for Information Systems, 16*(1), 1–47. https://doi.org/10.17705/1jais.00387

Jena, R. K., & Mahanti, P. K. (2014). An empirical study of technostress among Indian academicians. *International Journal of Education and Learning, 3*(2), 1–10. https://doi.org/10.14257/ijel.2014.3.2.01

Kenner, C. (2015). Neonatal nursing workforce: A global challenge and opportunity. *Newborn and Infant Nursing Reviews, 15*(4), 165–166. https://doi.org/10.1053/j.nainr.2015.09.006

Kim, T. (2014). The role of leaders in intra-alliance bargaining. *Asian Security, 10*(1), 47–69. https://doi.org/10.1080/14799855.2013.874338

Kumar, P., Singh, P. P., & Bhuchar, V. (2017). A study of techno stress in relation to job satisfaction, job performance and mental health among IT professionals. *International Journal of Education & Management, 7*(3), 403–407. Retrieved from www.proquest.com/publication/publications_2032132?accountid=7374

Long, T., Convey, J., & Chwalek, A. (1985). *Completing dissertations in the behavioral sciences and education: A systematic guide for graduate students* (1st ed.). Josey-Base Publishers.

Madsen, D. (1990). *Successful dissertations and theses: A guide to graduate student research from proposal to completion.* Jossey-Bass Publishers.

Malvey, D. M., & Slovensky, D. J. (2017). Global mHealth policy arena: status check and future directions. *MHealth, 3,* 41. https://doi.org/10.21037/mhealth.2017.09.03

Masterson, J. (2008). Employer perspective of the new Irish public works contract. *Proceedings of the Institution of Civil Engineers – Management, Procurement and Law, 161*(3), 99–105. https://doi.org/10.1680/mpal.2008.161.3.99

Miles, D. (2018). *Doctoral student workshop: The three types of research significance.* ResearchGate. www.researchgate.net/publication/323151037_NEW_ARTICLE_RESEARCH_METHODS_The_Three_Types_of_Research_Significance

Miles, D. (2019). *Let's stop the madness Part 3: Understanding the difference between contributions of the study vs. significance of the study.* ResearchGate. www.researchgate.net/publication/338163051_ARTICLE_Let%27s_Stop_the_Madness_Part_3_Understanding_the_Difference_Between_Contributions_of_the_Study_vs_Significance_of_the_Study

Miles, D. A., & Scott, L. (2017, October 26–29). *Confessions of a dissertation chair, Part 1: The six mistakes doctoral students make with the dissertation* [Workshop]. 5th Annual 2017 Black Doctoral Network Conference, Atlanta, GA.

Morgan, D., & Somera, P. (2014). The future shortage of doctoral prepared nurses and the impact on the nursing shortage. *Nursing Administration Quarterly, 38*(1), 22–26. https://doi.org/10.1097/naq.0000000000000001

Morales, L. (2019). *A Baldrige assessment of an organization: An empirical study of Baldrige criteria and organizational performance in air transportation organizations* [Unpublished dissertation]. ProQuest Dissertations and Theses.

Mulki, J., Caemmerer, B., & Heggde, G. (2015). Leadership style, salesperson's work effort and job performance: The influence of power distance. *Journal of Personal Selling & Sales Management, 35*(1), 3–22. https://doi.org/10.1080/08853134.2014.958157

Platt, P. (2019). *An investigation of leadership styles and managerial practices within the federal government: A qualitative study of the transportation security administration (TSA)* [Unpublished dissertation]. ProQuest Dissertations and Theses.

Summers, J. (2001). Guidelines for conducting research and publishing in marketing: From conceptualization through the review process. *Journal of the Academy of Marketing Science, 29*(4), 405–415.

Webster, W. (1998). *21 models for developing and writing theses, dissertations and projects: A manual of sound advice about conceptualizing, organizing, developing and finalizing your terminal graduate research.* Academic Scholarwrite.

Yoonk, J., & Poister, T. H. (2014). Managerial practices, trust in leadership, and performance. *Public Personnel Management, 43*(2), 179–196. https://doi.org/10.1177/0091026014523136

Zeig, M. (2019). *Effects of a character education course on standardized testing in Texas high schools* [UMI No. 6584585]. ProQuest Dissertations and Theses.

13 Deciding on the Source of Data

Objectives

- Readers will be able to:
    1. Choose an appropriate data source(s) for their study
    2. Determine a sampling strategy for their study
    3. Determine the number of participants for their study
    4. Recognize ethical issues associated with accessing the data source

About Data

As you engage in your research journey, one of the crucial moments is deciding on the appropriate data to collect, analyze and use to address your research questions or test your hypotheses. Because of this, it is important to get a good understanding of the features, sources and purpose of data. Before we go further, we want to note that the word "data" will be used in this text as both singular and plural. So, what is a data? In a research context, a data is any information that has the potential of being collected and analyzed, generating findings to meet the purpose of the study.

When it comes to kinds of data, they are grouped based on the type of research approach you are using to conduct your study (see Table 13.1). We have quantitative data and qualitative data for a quantitative and qualitative method, respectively. Also, data can be categorized into numeric data and non-numeric data, which are collected when we conduct a quantitative and qualitative study, respectively. However, irrespective of the kind of study you are conducting, your data could be primary or secondary. Primary data are information generated in a study with the purpose of analyzing them to address research questions or test hypotheses. They could be data collected in a study when conducting an interview, focus group or survey. With regards to secondary data, they comprise of any data that were not generated within your current study, but you plan to retrieve and use them in your study. They could be archival data, data generated in a previous study, research literature, documents and artifacts. Lastly, based on its volume, data can be considered small, such as a survey, or big, such as data generated based on consumers' online interactions with a product (see Kitchin & McArdle, 2016).

DOI: 10.4324/9781003268154-13

Table 13.1 Kinds of data and their respective examples and sources

Kinds of Data	Example	Source
Quantitative data	Likert scale survey data	Bhattacherjee (2012)
Qualitative data	Interview data	Patton (2002)
Numeric data	Math score data	Salkind (2014)
Non-numeric data	Open-ended survey data	Craig (2009)
Primary data	Data on leadership styles	Sethuraman and Suresh (2014)
Secondary data	Existing interview data from genetic modification specialists	Cook and Robbins (2005)
Small data	Level of depression data	Shanthi et al. (2007)
Big data	Posts and reactions of a Facebook group	Kitchin and McArdle (2016)

Table 13.2 Data sources, their respective examples and sources

Data Source	Example	Source
People	Staff in an organization	The Pell Institute and Pathways to College Network (2022)
Document	Newsletter	The Pell Institute and Pathways to College Network (2022)
Observation	Parents and teachers' association meeting	The Pell Institute and Pathways to College Network (2022)
Primary source	Fieldwork	Benedictine University Library (2022)
Secondary source	Census database	Benedictine University Library (2022)

Data Sources

A data source is where the data originated from. It could also mean where you got your data from. Sources of data can be categorized into people, documents or observations (The Pell Institute and Pathways to College Network, 2022). Alternatively, data sources can be categorized based on the kind of data they produce. Secondary sources house data, literature or information generated independent of and adopted for the current study (Benedictine University Library, 2022) (see Table 13.2). For example, let us assume that your focus is to examine a leader-subordinate relationship in an organization, and you plan to analyze its meeting minutes to help you address your research questions. In this case, the organization's meeting minutes are the secondary source of data. However, the primary source category denotes a data source where you extract data generated for the purpose of addressing your research questions or testing your hypotheses (Benedictine University Library, 2022). Let's say you plan to determine the relations between employees' sense of belongingness and job satisfaction.

Determining an Appropriate Data and Its Source

Determining the right data sources for your study starts with examining what you want to find out (i.e., purpose of the study), the questions you plan to address (i.e., research questions) and the method you will use to conduct the study. For a qualitative study, you brainstorm, thinking and listing potential data and its source while addressing the following questions:

- What kind of data do I need to address my research questions?
- Who or where is the source of the data I'm interested in?

After making a list of potential sources and their respective data, you could rank the data sources based on their accessibility and the data based on the richness of the information. Degree of accessibility in this context denotes the perceived level of ease with which the researcher can obtain approval or permission to extract data from the potential data sources. It could also include the willingness of potential participants to be part of the study. The degree of richness of the data focuses on a researcher's perceived level of ease with respect to transforming the data in order to address the research questions. In other words, it is about how far the raw data is from being transformed into answers that can adequately address the research questions. We know that all these criteria are based on a researcher's perception, but utilizing this guide will help you to get closer to choosing the best data sources and, in effect, to collect the data you need to complete your research journey.

You then select the top four data sources and, with their respective kind of data, categorize them into (1) high accessibility and high richness, (2) high accessibility and low richness, (3) low accessibility and high richness, and (4) low accessibility and low richness (see Figure 13.1). Hopefully, after completing this activity, you will know the data and its source that belongs to the first quadrant, which is labeled the "extremely suitable" option (see Figure 13.1). However, in a situation where nothing was found in the first option, you could consider the second option, which is considered to be "moderately suitable." With this option, you have easy access to the data source, but the information you extract is not as rich as that of the first option. This means you will need to spend a considerable amount of time and resources making sense of the data. Conversely, with the third option, you are more likely to spend time and resources accessing the source, but you will end up getting rich data if you successfully gain access to it.

Let's now focus on strategies you could use to determine the kind of data and its sources you need to conduct a quantitative study. You begin this process by addressing these questions:

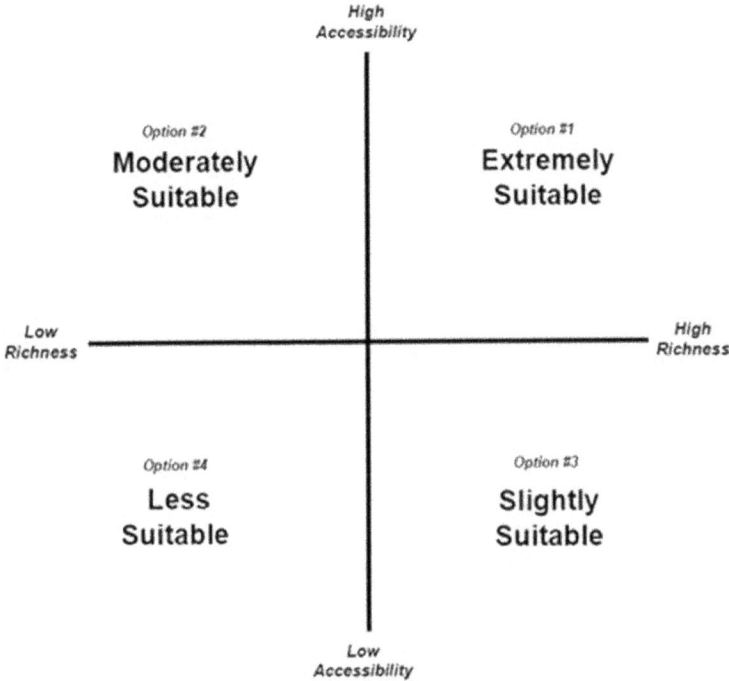

Figure 13.1 Data source categorization chart for a qualitative study.

- Who are being studied?
- What are the variables of focus?

You will be able to address the above questions by reviewing your purpose statement and research questions or hypotheses. What you need to do is to describe the population and information (related to the variable of interest) you plan to extract from them. You can then think about where and how you plan to access potential participants (i.e., accessibility) and the possibility of being able to appropriately measure the variables of interest (i.e., feasibility). The goal of this activity is to decide on a data source that is highly accessible and variables that are highly feasible in terms of being measured (see Figure 13.2).

All the above steps are a guide to help you choose the right primary data source. At this point, you need to be flexible because you may need to make adjustments to your initial purpose statement, research questions (hypotheses) and sometimes the problem statement to get a highly accessible data source and feasible process for measuring your variables. In terms of feasibility criterion, you could reflect on the following questions:

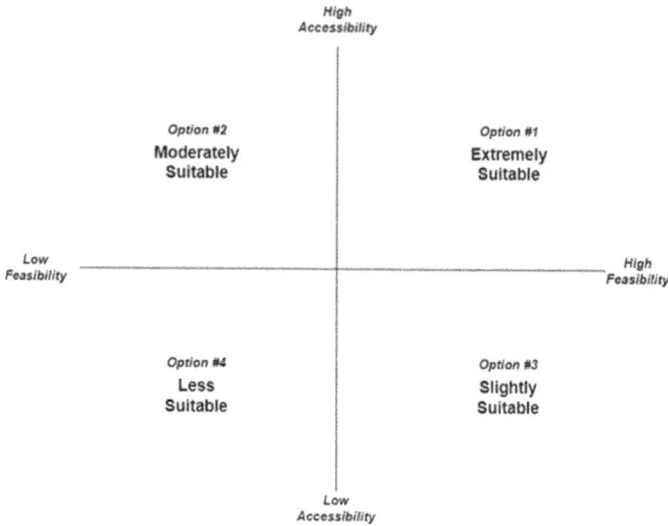

```
                          High
                       Accessibility
                            |
                            |
        Option #2           |           Option #1
        Moderately          |           Extremely
        Suitable            |           Suitable
                            |
   Low                      |                      High
Feasibility ----------------+---------------- Feasibility
                            |
                            |
        Option #4           |           Option #3
        Less                |           Slightly
        Suitable            |           Suitable
                            |
                          Low
                       Accessibility
```

Figure 13.2 Data source categorization chart for a quantitative study.

- Can the variables be operationalized?
- Are there existing validated instrument(s) that can be used to measure the variables?

If there is no validated instrument, then you may need to create your own and use the data you collect to determine whether the instrument was measuring what it was supposed to measure (i.e., reliability) and producing a consistent response (i.e., reliability) (see Williams et al., 2010). Alternatively, you could adjust the variables of interest to align with an existing instrument with a good validity and reliability score.

Determining Your Sample Size

Samples are drawn from a population that could be labeled as a data source. Since most dissertations use humans as their data sources, let us limit our discussion to recruiting human subjects for research. Generally speaking, when conducting qualitative research, you need a small sample size compared to doing quantitative research (Crouch & McKenzie, 2006). This is because the goal of conducting a qualitative study and its philosophical assumptions are fundamentally different from those of a quantitative study.

Determining an Appropriate Sample Size for Your Qualitative Study

The focus of qualitative researchers is to describe, explore or explain a phenomenon of interest using non-numeric information. Because they mainly work with video, audio, text and artifacts, with the purpose of qualitatively making sense of them, they are not interested in generalizing what they have found. Their role is to collect rich qualitative data, analyzing it to generate themes with which to address their research questions. What they are concerned about is making sure the data collected reflects the features or covers all aspects of what they are studying. For example, let's say that the focus of your study is to examine the experience of burnout among corporate executives. When recruiting participants, your focus is to select corporate executives who have experienced burnout, but not only those who have effectively dealt with this condition. Also, to capture variations in the experience of burnout, you could draw a sample that reflects demographic variation based on age, work experience and/or highest educational level. This technique is based on a concept in phenomenology called imaginative variation (see Larsen & Adu, 2021).

Now that we know you need a small sample size when conducting a qualitative study, how many participants are needed? We do not have a specific strategy for determining an appropriate number of participants, but the following factors could be considered when deciding on the right sample size for your qualitative study (see Adu, 2019; Larsen & Adu, 2021; Baker & Edwards, 2012).

- **Attainment of saturation:** When deciding on the number of participants for your qualitative study, a question you could ask is, *"How many participants do I need to reach the level of saturation?"* Saturation occurs when researchers reach a stage where they are receiving no new information from participants during interviews (Adu, 2023). In a qualitative study, saturation can be reached between the 12th and 15th participant, but it could depend on the selected research method, variation of participants' background, perspectives and experience and complexity of the phenomenon being studied. We recommend you look into previous studies that used your chosen research approach to get an idea of the sample size they used.
- **Accessibility of participants:** You may have an idea about the appropriate sample size for your study, but how you access the potential participants could influence the desired number of participants (Adu, 2023; Baker & Edwards, 2012). For instance, you may not be able to get your anticipated sample size due to difficulties in accessing potential participants. This could affect getting the number you need to adequately collect rich data from them. You could address this challenge by spending more time with each participant, making sure that all your questions are addressed and conducting follow-up interviews when needed (Larsen & Adu, 2021).
- **Type of research approach chosen:** Sample size could vary, depending on the type of research approach you select. For example, you are more likely to go for between 5 and 25 or between 20 and 30 participants if you plan to use a phenomenological or grounded theory approach, respectively (Creswell, 2013). Before you determine your sample size, we suggest you read more about your selected approach, including whether it has been used in studies and its corresponding number of participants. Lastly, you could have an idea of the

number by looking at the suggestions of qualitative researchers and the rationale behind their recommendations (see Baker & Edwards, 2012).

Determining an Appropriate Sample Size for Your Quantitative Study

Before you decide on the sample size for your quantitative study, you need to have at least basic statistics and take on the role of a quantitative researcher. The role of quantitative researchers is to study a population (Adu, 2022). However, due to limited resources and time, they focus on sampling a faction of the population to study, measuring the variables of interest. Consequently, data collected are then used to conduct statistical analysis. After determining the purpose of the study and the research questions they want to address, they could conduct descriptive statistics, inferential statistics or both (see Figure 13.3). Descriptive statistical analysis focuses on quantitatively reducing the data to mean, median and mode (I.e., measure of central tendency), frequencies and percentages, and range, variance and standard deviation (i.e., measure of variability). However, inferential statistical analysis involves conducting parametric tests (such as Pearson's *r* correlation, t-test, regression, ANOVA and MANOVA) and/or non-parametric tests (such as Chi-square, Mann-Whitney and Wilcoxon signed-ranks test).

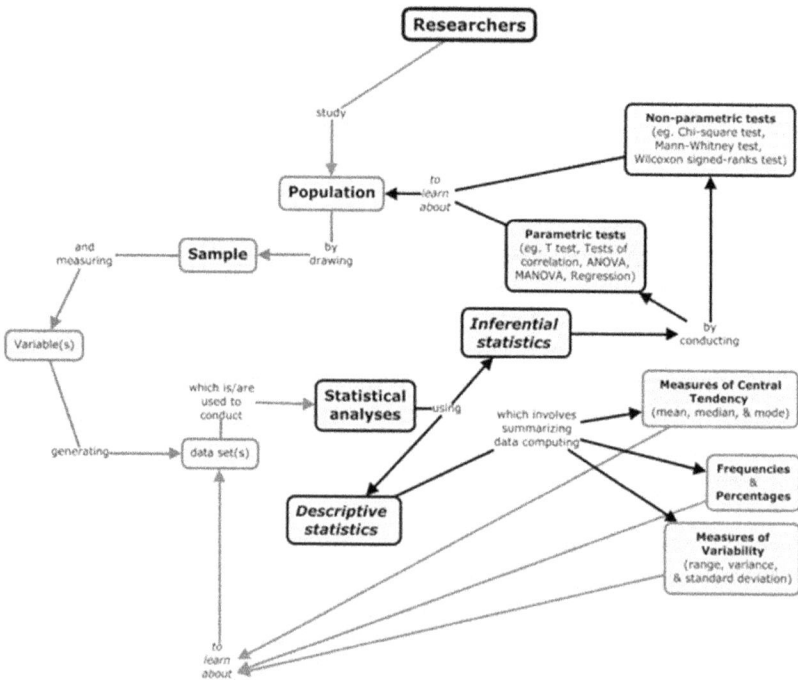

Figure 13.3 About quantitative data collection and statistics (see Adu, 2022).

In terms of determining your sample size, there are several strategies you could use to determine the appropriate sample size for your quantitative study (see Israel, n.d.; Serdar et al., 2021). You could determine your sample size based on the type of quantitative research design you are using, known population size and the type of inferential statistics chosen.

If you are using a descriptive design with the purpose of measuring variables of interest and conducting descriptive statistics, "then nearly any sample size will suffice" (Israel, n.d., p. 4). This is because, for a descriptive study, your plan is not to make an inference to the population but to describe (using means, standard deviations, percentages and frequencies) and learn about the sample (Israel, n.d). Although there is not a set required sample size for a descriptive study, recruiting a sample of 50 or more participants for a dissertation would be great, in that the more participants you have, the less likely the influence of extreme scores will have on the outcome of the test of central tendency and variability.

Alternatively, you could determine the right sample size if you know the size of the population you are studying. Israel (n.d, p. 4) noted that you could use the following formula if you know your population size:

$$n = \frac{N}{1 + N(e)^2}$$

Where:

- n represents sample size
- N represents total population
- e represents statistical significance level (which could be 0.01, 0.05 or 0.10)

Imagining your population of interest is 8,000, then, based on the above formula, your sample size will be 381 at the significance level of 0.05 (see Israel, n.d., Table 1).

$$n = \frac{N}{1 + N(e)^2} \quad N = 8,000; e = 0.05$$

$$n = \frac{8000}{1 + 8000(0.05)^2}$$

$$n = \frac{8000}{1 + 8000(0.0025)}$$

$$n = \frac{8000}{1 + 20}$$

$$n = \frac{8000}{21}$$

$n = \mathbf{381}$

What if you don't know the size of your population? What would you do? You could use software to determine your sample size. For some software, you need to know and provide (enter) the kind of inferential statistical analysis you plan to conduct before the software can generate an appropriate sample size. For example, you could use G*Power software to help determine the minimum number of participants needed to prevent you from conducting a Type II error (Faul et al., 2007). A Type II error is wrongly rejecting the alternative hypothesis when it is true (see Serdar et al., 2021).

Let's do an example. Imagine you plan to conduct a quantitative study to find out whether there is a statistically significant difference of burnout between healthcare workers who work during the day and those who work during the night. With this purpose statement, you can see that you have one dependent variable, which is "burnout," and one independent variable, which is "type of work shift," with two groups, which are (1) day shift workers and (2) night shift works. Therefore, an independent t-test will be appropriate for this study. Now that you know the right statistical analysis for your study, the next step is to use the G*Power software to determine the sample size. You can download this software for free by going to www.psychologie.hhu.de/arbeitsgruppen/allgemeine-psychologie-und-arbeitspsychologie/gpower

*Demonstration on How to Use G*Power Software*

Now you know that an independent t-test is appropriate for the study (based on the above example), you open the G*Power software. Here are the steps you could take to arrive at the sample size (see Figure 13.4):

1. Under "Test family," select "*t*-tests"
2. Under "Statistical test," select "Means: Difference between two independent means (two groups)"
   a. *This type of test is also known as an independent t-test*
3. Under "Type of power analysis," select "A priori: Compute required sample size–given α, power, and effect size"
4. Select "Two" under "Tail(s)"
   a. *Based on the purpose statement, the alternative hypothesis will be, "There is a statistically significant difference of burnout between healthcare workers who work during the day and those who work during the night." This hypothesis is considered to be two-tailed (or non-directional) because it did not show that one group will have a higher burnout than the other.*
5. Select "0.5" (i.e., medium effect size) for the "Effect size *d*"
   a. *The higher the effect size, the bigger the sample size. In other words, you will need more participants if you select a large sample size.*

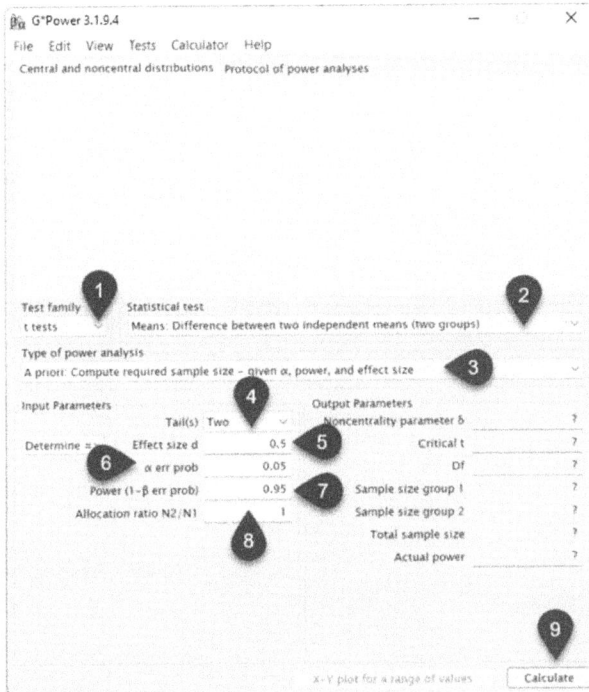

Figure 13.4 Steps on using G*Power.

6. You indicate "0.05" under the "α err prob" (which is also called the significance level)
7. You indicate "0.95" under "Power (1-β err prob)" (which is also called statistical power)
   a. *You could indicate the statistical power as .80 as suggested by social science researchers.*
8. The "Allocation ratio *N2/N1*" will be "1" by default
9. You then click on "Calculate" (see Figure 13.4)

As shown in Figure 13.5, the total number of participants needed is 210.

Ethical Issues

Conducting research on what we are curious about, what interests us and what could immensely contribute to the body of knowledge is a good approach. However, we need to think about the wellbeing of the people who will be providing us with the information to help us accomplish our research goals. Hence the need to have a guide to govern our decisions and actions in relation to participants' participation in our study. A well-known ethical guide that has provisions to regulate how we should conduct research is called the Belmont report (see OHRP, 2016). This

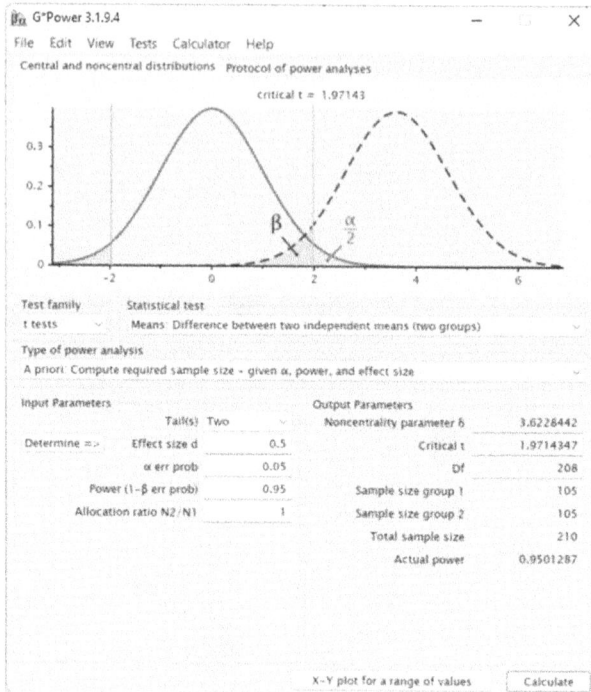

Figure 13.5 Display of the sample size after using G*Power.

ethical guide was put together in 1978 to regulate research activities and prevent researchers from putting participants at risk, undermining their rights and violating their privacy (Barrow et al., 2021). The Belmont report explains three ethical principles: respect for persons, beneficence and justice.

Respect for Persons

This ethical principle relates to respecting the rights of participants. They have the right to participate in a study without being forced to do so, and they can choose to withdraw from the study at any time (Barrow et al., 2021). They also have the right to know the purpose of the study and what is expected of them in the study, including potential risks and benefits (Barrow et al., 2021). In addition, researchers have an obligation to protect participants' rights, including protecting their privacy and ensuring their anonymity. Lastly, researchers should make sure that extra protections are given to those whose freedom has been limited, such as prisoners and people who need guidance to decide to participate (such as children and people with a disability).

Beneficence

This kind of ethical principle focuses on the risks and benefits of the research. There are always risks and benefits associated with conducting a study. As a researcher, you are responsible for identifying and assessing any potential harm that the study could cause to participants and comparing them with what participants and/or stakeholders, including the research community, could gain (Barrow et al., 2021; Löfman et al., 2004). Similarly, the research board/committee in your institution (i.e., the Institutional Review Board) are responsible for reviewing your proposed study to make sure all your actions and decisions in the study meet the ethical standard enshrined in the Belmont report. In other words, they ensure that the risk of participating in the study does not outweigh the benefit. According to Barrow et al. (2021), "The beneficence principle includes two specific research aspects: (1) participants' right to freedom from harm and discomfort, and (2) participants' rights to protection from exploitation" (para. 4, under "Issues of Concern").

Justice

This ethical principle pertains to the application of fairness in your study (Barrow et al., 2021). This also implies that a person should not be punished, discriminated against or unfairly treated if they decide not to participate in a study. For example, if a teacher plans to do action research to determine how a new teaching strategy could improve students' academic performance and a student decides not to participate in the study, they should not be deprived of receiving and learning content that they have the right to have.

Summary

Accessing the right source of data for your study is important for the successful completion of your dissertation. In this chapter, we have explored different kinds of data and factors to consider when accessing them from their data sources. We also provided strategies you could use to determine the right sample size for your study. As you consider your data sources and the kind of data you plan to collect, it is important to think about the ethical principles associated with doing research. You should make sure your decisions and actions are in line with the ethical principles of research, which relate to the need to respect the rights of participants (i.e., respect for persons), do research where the benefits outweigh the risks (i.e., beneficence) and promote fairness (i.e., justice).

References

Adu, P. (2019). *A step-by-step guide to qualitative data coding*. Routledge.

Adu, P. (2022, December 27). What is statistics? [Video]. YouTube. www.youtube.com/watch?v=tMN3MfC12WQ

Adu, P. (2023, April 26). Writing the methodology chapter of your dissertation [Video]. YouTube. www.youtube.com/watch?v=NFLzd267UOg

Baker, S. E., & Edwards, R. (2012). How many qualitative interviews is enough? National Center for Research Methods.

Barrow, J. M., Brannan, G. D., & Khandhar, P. B. (2021). *Research ethics.* StatPearls Publishing.

Benedictine University Library (2022, September 3). *Public health research guide: Primary data sources.* https://researchguides.ben.edu/c.php?g=282050&p=7037027

Bhattacherjee, A. (2012). *Social science research: Principles, methods, and practices.* Open University Press. https://digitalcommons.usf.edu/oa_textbooks/3/

Cook, G., & Robbins, P. T. (2005). *Presentation of genetically modified (gm) crop research to non-specialists, 1997–2002: A case study* [Data collection]. UK Data Service. https://doi.org/10.5255/UKDA-SN-5069-1

Craig, D. V. (2009). *Action research essentials.* Jossey-Bass.

Creswell, J. W. (2013). *Qualitative inquiry and research design: Choosing among five approaches* (3rd ed.). Sage Publications.

Crouch, M., & McKenzie, H. (2006). The logic of small samples in interview-based qualitative research. *Social Science Information, 45*(4), 483–499. https://doi.org/10.1177/0539018406069584

Faul, F., Erdfelder, E., Lang, A. G., & Buchner, A. (2007). G*Power 3: A flexible statistical power analysis program for the social, behavioral, and biomedical sciences. *Behavior research methods, 39*(2), 175–191. https://doi.org/10.3758/bf03193146

Israel, G. D. (n.d). *Determining sample size.* University of Florida. https://web.tarleton.edu/academicassessment/wp-content/uploads/sites/119/2022/05/Samplesize.pdf

Kitchin, R., & McArdle, G. (2016). What makes big data, big data? Exploring the ontological characteristics of 26 datasets. *Big Data & Society, 3*(1). https://doi.org/10.1177/2053951716631130

Larsen, H. G., & Adu, P. (2021). *The theoretical framework in phenomenological research: Development and application.* Routledge.

Löfman, P., Pelkonen, M., & Pietilä, A. M. (2004). Ethical issues in participatory action research. *Scandinavian Journal of Caring Sciences, 18*(3), 333–340. https://doi.org/10.1111/j.1471-6712.2004.00277.x

OHRP. (2016, March 15). *The Belmont report.* Office for Human Research Protections. www.hhs.gov/ohrp/regulations-and-policy/belmont-report/index.html

Patton. M. Q. (2002). *Qualitative research and evaluation methods* (3rd ed.). Sage Publications.

The Pell Institute and Pathways to College Network. (2022, September 1). *Identify types & sources.* Evaluation Toolkit. http://toolkit.pellinstitute.org/evaluation-guide/collect-data/identify-types-sources/

Salkind, N. J. (2014). *Statistics for people who (think they) hate statistics.* SAGE.

Serdar, C. C., Cihan, M., Yücel, D., & Serdar, M. A. (2021). Sample size, power and effect size revisited: simplified and practical approaches in pre-clinical, clinical and laboratory studies. *Biochemia Medica, 31*(1), 010502. https://doi.org/10.11613/BM.2021.010502

Sethuraman, K., & Suresh, J. (2014). Effective leadership styles. *International Business Research, 7*(9), 165.

Shanthi, A. G., Damodharan, J., & Priya, G. (2007). Depression and coping: A study on HIV positive men and women. *Sri Ramachandra Journal of Medicine, 2*(1), 15–19.

Williams, B., Brown, T., & Onsman, A. (2010). Exploratory factor analysis: A five-step guide for novices. *Australasian Journal of Paramedicine, 8*(3). Retrieved from http://ro.ecu.edu.au/jephc/vol8/iss3/1

14 Understanding the Different Kinds of Data Collection Strategies

Objectives

- Readers will be able to:
    1. Differentiate between the kinds of data collection strategies
    2. Recognize the strengths and limitations of conducting surveys, interviews, document collection and focus groups
    3. Choose an appropriate data collection strategy

Introduction

Your selected data source(s) may have information in terms of variety, uniqueness and volume. However, your role is not to collect any kind of data they can provide but to extract the type of data you need to meet the purpose of your study and address the research questions you have. This is where you must think about a tool that could be used to effectively and efficiently generate the information you need for your study. There are a lot of innovative data collection strategies you could use. However, let's limit our discussion to the most commonly used ones: testing, survey, interview, focus group, document collection and observation (see PHINEO, 2021).

Testing Method

The testing method is a kind of data collection method that encompasses the assessment of participants' ability, knowledge, skills and capability. It normally involves completing a task such as a memory test, where participants are asked to recall the words they were shown a few moments before. It could also involve answering a series of questions to test their knowledge level, such as the Implicit Bias Test (see ABA, 2022).

If you plan to conduct a test, make sure the instrument is validated. A validated instrument is a measure that has been used to test a population similar to the one you are focusing on. In addition, the tool should have acceptable validity and reliability outcomes. If there is no available instrument to help measure what you plan to measure, then you could consider developing your own tool and, if possible, use your study to validate it (see Borsa et al., 2012; Braghetta et al., 2021).

DOI: 10.4324/9781003268154-14

You may ask, "What are the channels through which a test can be administered?" You could give participants a hard copy of the instrument for them to complete or ask them to complete it online. It is always advisable to review studies done using a similar instrument to learn about the best practices and their implications. This would help you to make informed choices, making you less likely to repeat the mistakes of previous researchers.

Methods of Data Collection

The task of data collection is a very technical process. Data collection methods are a key part of the research practice. Data collection methods are an integral part of research design. There are many types of data collection methods. For our chapter, we want to separate the quantitative data collection methods from the qualitative data collection methods. There are several data collection methods, and each one has its advantages and disadvantages. Using the appropriate methods to research problems greatly enhances the value of the research. There are two primary data collection methods: quantitative and qualitative.

Quantitative Data Collection Methods

Quantitative data collection is a method of data collection that focuses on measurement. When researchers choose quantitative data collection, they are contemplating the implementation of numerical research analysis. Quantitative research methods are concerned with collecting and analyzing data that is structured and can be represented numerically. Quantitative data collection is based on the concept of building accurate and reliable measurements that allow for statistical analysis. The objective is to focus on quantifiable measurements. Quantitative research is defined as research that addresses research objectives through empirical assessments that involve numerical measurement and analysis approaches (Babin & Zikmund, 2008).

Surveys and Questionnaires

The survey is a data collection strategy used to capture or measure people's opinions, thoughts and/or experience of a phenomenon. In a quantitative study, a survey is used to measure a specific variable or a group of variables. It normally consists of closed-ended questions accompanied with answers to choose from. For example, a researcher could ask, "*Do you consider yourself to be an entrepreneur?*" and provide the following options: (a) Yes, (b) No, (c) Not sure. Besides this, a survey could contain statements with Likert scale responses. For example, a statement such as "I feel nervous when I'm about to speak to a group" could have Likert scale options such as (a) Strongly Disagree, (b) Disagree, (c) Unsure, (d) Agree, (e) Strongly Agree (see Joshi et al., 2015).

We also have a survey containing open-ended questions. This data collection tool is usually used when conducting a qualitative study. Qualitative researchers opt for administering an open-ended survey when working with limited resources and time and/or targeting a large sample of participants who are not willing to be interviewed (Huer & Saenz, 2003). Here are a few examples of open-ended survey questions:

- What do you do when you feel burnout?
- How do you feel about working on your dissertation?
- What do you do when your subordinate is reluctant to work?

Because you will not be there to ask follow-up questions, it is important to make sure you create simple questions and ask one question at a time. Also, some participants may skip the questions, and this is one of the reasons why you should have a larger sample size compared to when conducting interviews. By so doing, you will get substantial data even if not all the participants addressed all the questions.

Surveys are one of the key methods in terms of quantitative data collection (Alessi & Martin, 2010). A survey is a system for collecting information on a range of topics, including health, education, psychology, law, etc., of which the main characteristics are that data are collected from a number of individuals using a systematic and standardized approach (e.g., questionnaire/structured interview schedule/scales or tests) and that these individuals are a representative sample of the population under study (Meadows, 2003).

There are three fundamental types of survey that are popular with social investigators: *factual, attitude* and *explanatory.* The *factual survey* is used to collect descriptive information about a population of people. The national population census of any country falls within this category of survey. The factual survey can be used to investigate the sociological problems of a specific population of people (Ahmad, 2018).

The *attitude survey* is designed to investigate the subjective stance of individuals on events, issues and trends. A typical example of an attitude survey is opinion polling on political issues and events such as elections, voting patterns and the government's policies and activities. Market research that is conducted to know consumers' attitudes towards products also belongs to this category of survey (Ahmad, 2018).

Lastly, the *explanatory survey* is the most sophisticated and most comprehensive, in that it takes an inquiry beyond description. It is a survey that involves theory development through hypotheses testing. It is also the survey type that is used to test the validity of existing theories and to generate new hypotheses from such theories in order to examine patterns of statistical correlation among variables. A typical example of an explanatory survey is a study conducted purposively to know why a section of a community prefers to vote for a particular candidate in an election (Ahmad, 2018).

Quantitative Observations

A quantitative data collection method that focuses on observational assessment is a *direct observation* (see Table 14.1). A direct observation is an observational assessment

Table 14.1 Quantitative data collection methods

Research Method	Characteristics	Example
Surveys and questionnaires	The survey is a data collection strategy used to capture or measure people's opinions, thoughts and/or experiences of a phenomenon. In a quantitative study, the survey is used to measure a specific variable or a group of variables. It normally consists of closed-ended questions.	The national population census of any country falls within this category of survey. The factual survey can be used to investigate the sociological problems of a specific population of people (Ahmad, 2018).
Quantitative observations	A direct observation is an observation assessment that produces detailed records of what people actually do during an event. The researcher is responsible for recording the behavior of the subjects, with observational assessment as a measurement approach.	An example of this method is counting the number of customers entering a retail store and observing their behavior. In a structured observation, the researchers, rather than observing everything, focus only on very specific behaviors of interest. It allows them to quantify the behaviors they are observing.
Quantitative interviews	Quantitative interviews involve question and response categories that are determined in advance. Responses are fixed, and respondents choose from among these fixed responses.	An example of this method is recording data from interviews with participants while administering a survey. The survey questions are closed-ended, as are the participants' responses.
Quantitative focus groups	This quantitative data collection method takes a quantitative approach. Rather than using qualitative methods, this method administers surveys and questionnaires to focus groups. This method uses quantitative (survey) research to guide the design of appropriate research protocols.	An example of this is administering newly developed or previously validated surveys to a group of people who are representative of a population. Quantitative focus groups only focus on collecting data from the focus group with a survey or questionnaire. Rather than using qualitative methods, this method administers surveys and questionnaires to focus groups. Thus, the results of the quantitative focus group are analyzed.

that produces detailed records of what people actually do during an event. The researcher is responsible for recording the behavior of the subjects, with observational assessment as a measurement approach. The researcher plays a passive role, making no attempt to control or manipulate a situation, instead merely recording what occurs. The researcher assesses the subjects in the observation, then records and scores the assessment. Every effort is made for the researcher not to insert himself or herself into the situation (Babin & Zikmund, 2008). In this method, researchers collect quantitative data through systematic observations by using techniques such as counting the number of people present at a specific event at a particular time and a particular venue or the number of people attending an event in a designated place. More often, for quantitative data collection, researchers have a naturalistic observation approach that needs keen observation skills and senses for getting the numerical data about the "what" and not the "why" and "how" (Calderon et al., 2000).

Structured observation is an example of this. In this type of observation method, the researcher has to make careful observations of one or more specific behaviors in a more comprehensive or structured setting compared to naturalistic or participant observation. In a structured observation, the researchers, rather than observing everything, focus only on very specific behaviors of interest. It allows them to quantify the behaviors they are observing. When the observations require a judgment on the part of the observers, it is often described as coding, which needs a clearly defined set of target behaviors (QuestionPro, 2019).

Another example of an observation assessment is recording traffic counts and traffic flows within a supermarket to help managers to design store layouts that maximize a typical customer's exposure to the merchandise offered while also facilitating search efforts. Such an observation assessment will also ensure that a manufacturer can then better determine shelf locations, the arrangement of departments and merchandise within those departments, the location of checkout facilities and other characteristics that improve the shopping value that consumers obtain from visiting a store (QuestionPro, 2019). In this example, data can be more accurately gathered simply by observing consumers' movements in a store rather than by asking them about their movements.

Quantitative Interviews

The *quantitative interview* is a quantitative data collection method that focuses on interviews. Quantitative interviews involve question and response categories that are determined in advance. Responses are fixed, and the respondents choose from among these fixed responses. With quantitative interviews, the data analysis is simple. Lastly, the responses can be directly compared and easily aggregated; many short questions can be asked in a short amount of time (Cohen et al., 2007). An example of this is recording the data from interviews with participants while administering a survey. The survey questions are closed-ended, as are the participants' responses. Another example of an observation assessment is when data can be more accurately gathered simply by interviewing consumers with a survey and recording their closed-ended responses.

Quantitative Focus Groups

Quantitative focus groups are a divergent research data collection method. Focus groups can be used to collect a shared understanding from several individuals as well as to get views from specific people (George, 2013). They are also useful when the time to collect information is limited and individuals are hesitant to provide information (some individuals may be reluctant to provide information in any type of interview) (Creswell, 2012). However, quantitative focus groups take a completely different data collection approach. This quantitative data collection method takes a quantitative approach. Rather than using qualitative methods, this method administers surveys and questionnaires to focus groups. It uses quantitative (survey) research to guide the design of appropriate research protocols. An example of this is administering newly developed or previously validated surveys to a group of people who are representative of a population. When a survey is going to be used on a larger scale and focus groups will subsequently be conducted with the same group based on these surveys, this approach allows the researcher to obtain information that ensures the survey's cultural appropriateness, readability and comprehensibility (Calderon et al., 2000).

Qualitative Data Collection Methods

Qualitative data collection is a method of data collection that focuses on a phenomenon.

In the practice of qualitative research, the intent is not to generalize to a population but to develop an in-depth exploration of a central phenomenon. Thus, to best understand a phenomenon, the qualitative researcher purposefully or intentionally selects individuals and sites (Creswell, 2012).

The craft of qualitative research explores attitudes, behavior and experiences through such methods as interviews and focus groups. It attempts to get an in-depth opinion from participants. As it is concerned with attitudes, behavior and experiences, qualitative research often concentrates on conversational and similar exchanges between people in interviews, the media, counselling and so forth. It is rarely, if ever, concerned with analysis at the level of individual words, phrases or even sentences. It analyzes broader units of text, though what the minimum unit of analysis is depends on the theoretical orientation of the qualitative analysis (Howitt & Cramer, 2011).

Lastly, with qualitative research, you select people or sites that can best help you understand the central phenomenon. You have to remember that this understanding emerges through a detailed understanding of the people or site. This line of inquiry can lead to information that allows researchers to learn about the phenomenon. There is no focus on random sampling like what is used in quantitative research.

There are primarily five types of qualitative research collection methods, and we will illustrate and discuss them here.

Interviews

The interview is considered to be one of the most used data collection strategies in a qualitative study (Jowett et al., 2011; Turner, 2010). Why is conducting interviews so prominent in a qualitative study? When used properly, you can generate rich and relevant information from participants, especially when you spend time building trust with them and creating a conducive space for them to freely express what they think, feel and have experienced (Gray et al., 2020). Also, asking the right questions could help to extract rich data from participants. Your interview questions should be consistent with the research questions. Your research questions help you to know what you are looking for, while your interview questions for your participants are to assist you get what you are seeking.

There are two main types of interviews: structured and semi-structured. With a structured interview, the researcher strictly follows a set of predetermined questions, including their order, when interviewing participants. The essence of having structured questions is to standardize the interview process, making sure that each participant is asked the same questions, including in the same order. This is appropriate if you plan to cover a large number of participants with more than one interviewer. One of the main advantages is that it saves time for the researcher when generating questions and interviewing participants, for the research assistants when training to collect data from participants, and for the participants when being asked only predetermined questions. However, one main disadvantage is that it inhibits the free flow of conversation and participants' ability to freely express themselves. Also, participants may feel that the researcher is not listening to what they are saying if they ask questions that participants feel they have already addressed.

A semi-structured interview involves interviewing participants with guided questions. This means that you don't have to strictly follow the questions prepared for the interview, but they are there to guide your conversation with participants. In other words, the questions help draw the parameters of the topics or areas that the interview will cover. With this kind of interview, you don't have to follow a certain order when asking the pre-prepared questions; you ask questions based on the participants' initial responses, thus enhancing the flow of the conversation. You have the liberty to provide prompts and ask follow-up questions for elaboration and clarification. The semi-structured interview strategy is more effective if you want to give participants a chance to freely tell their stories with less interruption to their flow of thought. One of the disadvantages is that participants may veer off the issue they need to share, and, if not checked, this may lead to the collection of data that are less relevant to the research questions being addressed. To tackle this issue, the researcher should be prepared to gently guide participants back to the topic being discussed.

CREATING INTERVIEW QUESTIONS

First, you need to review the research questions to determine the kind of information you need to address. You then embark on a brainstorming phase to come up with a list of potential questions you could ask participants (see Table 14.2). During the brainstorming process, you do not need to focus on the quality and clarity of the potential interview questions. You can go back to review each of the questions

Table 14.2 Research questions, their respective topics and potential interview questions

Research Questions	Kinds of Topics	Potential Interview Questions
How do people with a mental health condition experience mental health stigma?	• Feelings and emotions experienced in relation to their mental health • Incidences that portray or trigger their experience of mental health stigma • Perspectives, reactions and understanding of the negative attitudes that people have towards mental health conditions • Where their stigma originates from	• Can you share with me the mental health condition you face? • How does the experience of a mental health condition make you feel? • What are people's reactions when they learn you have a mental health condition? • Can you share any situations where you experienced negative feeling towards your mental health condition? • How does that negative attitude make you feel? • What was your reaction to their negative attitude? • Can you share instances where you were treated badly because you have a mental health condition? • What was your reaction to this bad treatment? • How does discriminatory treatment make you feel?
How do people with a mental health condition deal with mental health stigma?	• The kind of mental health-related stigma they experience • How they cope with the stigma	• How do you handle an experience of discrimination due to your mental health condition? • How do you react to an experience of rejection due to your mental health condition? • Can you share with me a time when you felt reluctant to disclose your mental health condition due to a fear of the negative attitude you may receive? • How did you cope with that feeling? • What strategies do you use to deal with the stigma associated with the mental health condition you have?

afterwards, accessing their appropriateness and clarity, including their alignment with the research questions.

Focus Group Discussions

The focus group discussion is considered a qualitative data collection strategy. It involves gathering a group of people with the goal of collecting relevant information from them to help address the research questions (Leung & Savithiri, 2009). You may ask, "In what situation is the focus group appropriate as a data collection strategy?" It is most suitable when you want to gather participants' views about a situation, event, phenomena or experience that is considered as non-sensitive. Gathering a group of people together to have a conversation that generates converging as well as diverging views is the hallmark of a focus group.

Your role in a focus group session is to facilitate the conversation, making sure everyone is given the chance to speak. As the facilitator, you start the session by letting them know the purpose of the study and their role as participants. You make sure that they have consented to be a part of the study and are aware of their rights and expectations. After that, you can ask them the open-ended questions you have prepared. Similar to conducting interviews, you can make your questions semi-structured and be ready to ask follow-up questions when needed. Also, be ready to politely guide participants back to the focus of the discussion if they move beyond the topic.

Using the focus group technique could dramatically cut the data collection time, compared to conducting interviews that involve talking to each individual participant. Also, we see the data collected during a focus group session as a consolidation of the views and opinions shared in the group. Because of this, researchers are generally more likely to spend less time analyzing focus group data compared to interview data.

Besides the above strengths of the focus group discussed above, there are weaknesses that researchers should be aware of. Focus groups may not be appropriate when researching sensitive issues. Sensitive issues are experiences, events and conditions that participants may feel uncomfortable sharing in a group setting. They could also be issues considered forbidden to share in a public setting. Lastly, a sensitive issue could be any issue that is capable of traumatizing or retraumatizing participants when discussed in a group.

Another limitation is that, as the facilitator, you have limited control over participants' decision to disclose what was discussed in the group. To minimize this risk, you should explain to the group the potential breach of confidentiality and anonymity and encourage participants not to share with the outside world what is discussed during the session.

Document Collection

Written words can be a useful source of data when conducting a qualitative study. Also, an artifact which is also considered a document in qualitative research can be collected and analyzed to address the research questions you have. Therefore, anything that is created by an individual or a group of people before or during a research study can be considered a document. Some examples of documents include the minutes of a meeting in an organization, students' written assignments completed in a class, photos of a cultural event, a daily journal created by participants, an organization's yearly reports, research articles and artwork produced by members of a community.

If you plan to collect documents, the question you may ask is, "How do I determine the right documents to collect?" You first need to think about the research question(s) you plan to address and note the kind of document(s) (and their potential features) you plan to collect. Similar to determining selection criteria when sampling participants from their population, you come up with the conditions a document should meet to be part of the data you would analyze. You could create criteria based on when and how the document was created, who created it and why it was created.

Another question you should address before embarking on collecting a document is, "How can the document be accessed?" Knowing the process for accessing the document you are interested in helps reduce the challenges you may face during the actual data collection stage. Are the documents publicly available? Is an approval needed to access the document? How long will it take to be given an approval to access the documents? What are the conditions associated with using and storing the document? Addressing these questions will help you to make informed decision in terms of collecting documents.

One of the advantages of document collection is that it saves the researchers' time and resources compared to interview and focus group discussions. This is because, with document collection, the main data collection action you need to take is collecting existing data. With this data collection strategy, you are not concerned about recruiting participants and scheduling time with them to collect data. Another advantage is that it complements well with other qualitative data collection strategies. For instance, imagine you are interested in studying events that occurred after Elon Musk bought Twitter in October 2022. In addition to interviewing current and former employees of Twitter, you could gather documents such as social media posts, documented expert opinions and press releases in relation to the aftermath of Elon Musk's purchase of Twitter.

One limitation is that data analysis can be time consuming, the reason being that, most of the time, the documents were not produced for the purpose of the study. So, you have to gather and understand the background information to the documents before making sense of their content. Also, when developing codes and themes, you need to consider their history, such as who wrote/created them, under what circumstances and for what purpose? Knowing more about the documents' background will help you to better understand what was written/created.

Observation

This type of data collection method can be used in either a quantitative or qualitative study. In a quantitative study, you could quantify what you observe in terms of existence, intensity, magnitude and/or occurrence. However, the content of this section will be limited to conducting an observation in a qualitative study. In qualitative research, observation involves viewing an object, event, practice, situation, process or behavior and documenting it for a qualitative analysis. Let's discuss observation by addressing questions related to who, what, how, where, when and why.

- ***Who does the observation?*** As a researcher you could do the observation yourself. The most important thing is to make sure you know your role as a researcher-observer. As a qualitative researcher, you are considered to be an instrument, especially at the data collection and analysis stage. During the observation period, your role is to document what you consider to be relevant to your focus of the study and helpful to addressing your research question. As you capture and take notes of what is happening, you also need to be conscious of the potential influence you may have on what you are observing (i.e., the observed). For instance, your presence could influence the behavior of the people you are observing if they notice you.

  The question is, can you manage the influence and at the same time collect rich data for your study? Deciding how to effectively manage your influence will be the start to properly planning the observation process. You can choose to observe and being noticed (i.e., obtrusive observation), observe without being noticed and participating in a situation, activity or event, (i.e., unobtrusive observation) or observe and participate in what is going on (i.e., participant observation). Each has their strengths and weaknesses. We suggest you examine them and select which one could yield the kind of data you want.

- ***What do you plan to observe?*** During the period of observation, there may be a lot of things happening, and if you do not plan ahead of time, you may not capture areas relevant to your study. Design an observation protocol that will be appropriate to help guide what you need to observe. You can start designing an observation protocol (with the research question in mind) by listing the kinds of data you plan to collect. You then review the list of expected data and determine what needs to be observed to generate such data.

  For example, let's say you plan to explore how corporate leaders relate to their employees and address the research question, "How do corporate leaders relate to their employees in the financial sector?" With this question, you could focus on extracting data related to leaders' interactions with their employees. Now you know the kind of data you want to gather, you can then decide on what you want to observe. You could attend leaders' meetings with their employees to observe and document their interactions. You could also attend an event held by the organization you are studying to observe their interactions.

- ***How do you plan to observe?*** Planning is key to a successful observation. At the end of the planning process, you should have a protocol that contains information about who, where, what, when and how you plan to observe. You also need to have instruments that will help you to conduct the observation. Examples of the tools you may need are a computer, notebook, audio recorder and video recording device. If you plan to employ a research assistant to help you do the observation, you should ensure that they are well prepared for the task. As you plan for the observation, it is important to consult a gatekeeper to help understand the culture and norms of the people or event you plan to observe, including what instruments are allowed to be used at the data collection site. A gatekeeper is a person who introduces you to the place and people you plan to collect data from. They are considered a liaison between you and your potential participants.

During the observation, if it is allowed, you could use a video recording device to record what you are observing. Sometimes, you may not be allowed to video record the observed. In some cases, video recording may be allowed, but doing so could adversely impact the way participants normally behave, affecting the richness of the data being collected. Alternatively, you could audio record or take notes on the observed. In case you want to take field notes, there are two main things you need to document. First, you need to write about what you see, and second, you should document your thoughts on what you are observing. It is important to separate the actual data (which is the former) from the memo you write about the data (which is the latter). When analyzing the actual data, your memo could help you to better make sense of the data.

- ***Where will the observation take place?*** This is about determining the location(s) you plan to observe in. To make sure the selected locations are appropriate for conducting the observation, it is important to have a conversation with your gatekeeper. Talking to the gatekeeper will help you to understand the culture and norms of the research location(s) and what is expected of you. As a researcher going to an unfamiliar location to conduct a study, you should be ready to learn, listening more and checking with your gatekeeper when in doubt. You always need to be sensitive and respectful to the culture and beliefs of the observed.
- ***Why should the observed be observed?*** To ensure that what you will be watching and documenting is relevant, you need to address why you plan to observe the event, situation, behavior or process of interest. We need to always remind ourselves that the purpose of doing the observation is to gather useful information and analyze it to address our research question.
- ***When do you plan to observe?*** It is a good practice to work with the gatekeeper to determine the potential dates and times that observations can take place. To get comprehensive information during the data collection stage, it is advisable to observe the same phenomenon at different times or occurrences of events when the need arises. The essence is to capture variations of the features of the observed access times (see Table 14.3).

How to Choose an Appropriate Data Collection Strategy

Choosing an appropriate data collection strategy starts with knowing the kind of data you need to address your research question(s). Also, the data collection tool should go well with the selected research method. For instance, if you plan

Table 14.3 Qualitative data collection methods

Research Method	Characteristics	Example
Interviews	When used properly, you can generate rich and relevant information from participants, especially when you spend time building trust with them and creating a conducive space for them to freely express what they think, feel and have experienced. Also, asking the right questions could help to extract rich data from participants.	An example of this is the semi-structured interview, which involves interviewing participants with guided questions. This means that you don't have to strictly follow the questions prepared for the interview, but they are there to guide your conversation with participants. In other words, the questions help draw the parameters of the topics or areas that the interview will cover.
Focus groups	Focus groups involve gathering a group of people together with the goal of collecting relevant information from them to help address the research questions (Leung & Savithiri, 2009).	An example of this is conducting a focus group with salespeople. The researcher takes on the facilitator role and manages the focus group session to facilitate the conversation. They continue making sure everyone is given the chance to speak. As a facilitator, you start the session by letting them know the purpose of the study and their role as participants.
Observation	Observation involves viewing an object, event, practice, situation, process or behavior and documenting it for a qualitative analysis. You should have a protocol that contains information about who, where, what, when and how you plan to observe.	An example of this type of method is conducting an observation of female nurses at a hospital. The researcher wants to examine their behavior in their natural environment and observe their actions, behavior and other items of interest to the researcher.
Document collection	This is when written words can be a useful source of data when conducting a qualitative study. Anything that is created by an individual or a group of people before or during a research study can be considered a document.	An example of this type of method is the minutes of a meeting in an organization, students' written assignments completed in a class, photos of a cultural event, a daily journal created by participants, an organization's yearly reports, research articles and artwork produced by members of a community.

to examine participants' understanding of their experience and you plan to use a phenomenological approach, an appropriate data collection strategy would be interviews. Conducting interviews gives you the chance to ask participants relevant questions and receive responses that would be useful at the data analysis phase. In addition, a focus group could help you to generate relevant data to meet the purpose of the study.

Alternatively, relying on best practices when it comes to choosing the right data collection strategy would be a good approach. When you decide on the research method for your study, you could look into studies done to see the data collecting tool used by the researchers and their implications. This would help you to make an informed decision when selecting your data collection strategy.

Summary

The tasks of data collection and data sampling are the most fundamental part of the research process. The foundation of all research is based on the task of data collection. This chapter discussed the essentials of quantitative data collection and qualitative data collection for novice and burgeoning researchers. The chapter provided a conceptual model and tool for helping novice researchers and doctoral students understand the rudiments of quantitative data collection and qualitative data collection.

In this chapter, we discussed three things: the different sources of data; the different methods of data collection, such as quantitative data collection and qualitative data collection; and the different examples of data collection, such as qualitative data collection. By the end of this chapter, the reader should be able to understand the different data collection methods and how to apply them to conducting research. We hope that our chapter provided a foundation for novice researchers and doctoral students to understand both quantitative and qualitative data collection methods.

References

ABA. (2022, September). *Implicit bias test.* American Bar Association. www.americanbar.org/groups/litigation/initiatives/task-force-implicit-bias/implicit-bias-test/

Ahmad, M. (2018). Quantitative data collection methods. In V. Ayedun-Aluma, O. Ajibade, & B. Folayan (Eds.), *Research methods in communication & media studies* (pp. 188–213). Franklin International Publishers.

Alessi, E. J., & Martin, J. I. (2010). Conducting an internet-based survey: Benefits, pitfalls, and lessons learned. *Social Work Research, 34*(2), 122–128.

Babin, B. J., & Zikmund, W. G. (2008). *Essentials of marketing research* (4th ed.). Cengage Learning.

Borsa, J. C., Damásio, B. F., & Bandeira, D. R. (2012). Cross-cultural adaptation and validation of psychological instruments: Some considerations. *Paidéia (Ribeirão Preto), 22*(53), 423–432. https://doi.org/10.1590/S0103-863X2012000300014

Braghetta, C. C., Gorenstein, C., Wang, Y. P., Martins, C. B., Leão, F. C., Peres, M., Lucchetti, G., & Vallada, H. (2021). Development of an instrument to assess spirituality: Reliability and validation of the attitudes related to spirituality scale (ARES). *Frontiers in Psychology, 12,* 764132. https://doi.org/10.3389/fpsyg.2021.764132

Calderon, J., Baker, R., & Wolf, K. (2000). Focus groups: A qualitative method complementing quantitative research for studying culturally diverse groups. *Education for Health, 13*(1), 91–95. Retrieved from https://lopes.idm.oclc.org/login?url=https://www.proquest.com/scholarly-journals/focus-groups-qualitative-method-complementing/docview/2258170762/se-2

Cohen, L., Manion, L., & Morrison, K. (2007). *Research methods in education* (6th ed.). Routledge.

Creswell, J. W. (2012). *Educational research: Planning, conducting, and evaluating quantitative and qualitative research.* Pearson Education International.

George, M. (2013). Teaching focus group interviewing: Benefits and challenges. *Teaching Sociology, 41*(3), 257–270. https://doi.org/10.1177/0092055X12465295

Gray, L. M., Wong-Wylie, G., Rempel, G. R., & Cook, K. (2020). Expanding qualitative research interviewing strategies: Zoom Video Communications. *The Qualitative Report, 25*(5), 1292–1301. Retrieved from https://nsuworks.nova.edu/tqr/vol25/iss5/9

Howitt, D., & Cramer, D. (2011). *Introduction to research methods in psychology* (3rd ed.). Prentice Hall.

Huer, M. B., & Saenz, T. I. (2003). Challenges and strategies for conducting survey and focus group research with culturally diverse groups. *American Journal of Speech-Language Pathology, 12*(2), 209–220. https://doi.org/10.1044/1058-0360(2003/067)

Joshi, A., Kale, S., Chandel, S., & Pal, D. K. (2015). Likert scale: Explored and explained. *British Journal of Applied Science & Technology, 7*(4), 396.

Jowett, A., Peel, E., & Shaw, R. (2011). Online interviewing in psychology: Reflections on the process. *Qualitative Research in Psychology, 8*(4), 354–369. https://doi.org/10.1080/14780887.2010.500352

Leung, F. H., & Savithiri, R. (2009). Spotlight on focus groups. *Canadian Family Physician / Medecin de famille canadien, 55*(2), 218–219.

Meadows, K. (2003). So you want to do research? 4: An introduction to quantitative methods. *British Journal of Community Nursing, 8*(11), 519–526. https://doi.org/10.12968/bjcn.2003.8.11.11823

PHINEO. (2021). An overview of data-collection methods. Social Impact Navigator. www.social-impact-navigator.org/impact-analysis/data/methods-overview/

QuestionPro. (2019, July 3). Five methods used for quantitative data collection. www.questionpro.com/blog/quantitative-data-collection-methods/

Turner, D. W. (2010). Qualitative interview design: A practical guide for novice investigators. *The Qualitative Report, 15*(3), 754–760. https://doi.org/10.46743/2160-3715/2010.1178

15 Planning and Implementing the Data Collection Process

Objectives

- Readers will be able to:
    1. Prepare a consent form
    2. Uphold ethical issues
    3. Decide on a data collection location or platform
    4. Draw responses from participants
    5. Protect participants' data
    6. Develop a survey
    7. Develop an observation protocol
    8. Develop an interview protocol
    9. Collect data
    10. Write about the data collection process

Introduction

One of the most important aspects of the research project is planning. Planning the research project involves careful thought, implementation and execution. An appreciation for planning and implementing your research project is understated. The planning of the research project takes place on many levels. The researcher has to plan all the activities involving in the research, from collecting data and planning interviews. An important aspect of planning the research project is that it makes the researcher stick to a procedure.

The planning of the research project entails many aspects that are very important. When the researcher must complete interviews, observations, surveys, questionnaires or whatever their chosen technique, planning the research project is imperative. As part of the process of planning and managing the project, the researcher must approach the key individuals or gatekeepers involved in the administration of the project. Another important aspect of planning the research project is that the researcher must carefully weigh the pitfalls of the project. The pitfalls can be uncooperative institutions and organizations.

The progress of a research project is attributed to its successful planning. The planning of a project is further attributed to how the researcher executes the project

DOI: 10.4324/9781003268154-15

and their ability to manage the many aspects of it. The planning of the research project also involves collecting the kind of data needed and the cooperation of the organizations involved. The research project's success is critically dependent on the cooperation of organizations and institutions. The planning of the research has to also consider the management of participants, sampling, data preparation and data analysis.

In this chapter, we provide an introduction to many elements associated with the planning of a research project, including information on defining the research problem and the research objective. The chapter then discusses the many aspects of planning the research project. It also provides much-needed information on the practice of planning a research project for novice researchers and doctoral students.

Developing the Plan for Research

When planning a research project, the project should be divided into subparts. This is key to ensuring that every aspect of the project and its elements are addressed. Again, the progress of a research project is attributed to its successful planning. The planning of a research project also involves data collection management and the cooperation of the organizations involved. The planning of a research project has to consider the management of participants, sampling, data preparation and data analysis. The research plan is a document that sets forth a clear objective and precisely what the researcher must do to address the research problem. Finn (2005) asserts that there are five significant phases associated with the successful management and execution of a research project:

- *Initiation.* This includes important activities such as a student's selection and application for a project, liaison with a potential supervisor and registration at a university.
- *Planning.* This typically involves a considerable amount of project definition, during which the scope and objectives of the project are clarified. Once the objectives of the project and the research are clear, the researcher can identify the tasks that must be conducted to achieve these objectives.
- *Execution of tasks.* This requires the majority of the time and effort of the project and is where the traditional research activities are accomplished. However, other project activities also need to be addressed, such as attending training courses, participating in workshops and interacting with other researchers.
- *Monitoring of project progress.* This ensures that the timing, cost and quality of the tasks proceed as planned. In addition to your own monitoring and controlling practices, your supervisor should provide important guidance. Formal arrangements may also contribute to the monitoring of progress (e.g., formal project meetings, meetings of your thesis committee, end-of-year meetings).
- *Completion of the project.* This involves such activities as production of a final report (the thesis), the PhD examination, dissemination of the research

findings (publications and presentations) and acknowledging the contribution of others (Finn, 2005).

It is important that the researcher is familiar with these five phases. The researcher must consider the many prevailing issues of the research project and make sure they align with the objective of the research problem. The most important aspect of the project is to *align* with the objectives. The research project can conflict with the objectives in addressing the research problem. It is important for the researcher to prioritize and rank the importance of activities when managing the planning of the research project. In Figure 15.1, we provide a template for developing a plan for the research project.

Define the Research Problem

The first phase in the data planning process is to define the research problem. The driving impetus for doing any research is articulating the research problem. Researchers build the impetus for the research with the research problem. The research problem statement (a) provides the rationale for the study, and (b) uses data and research to confirm the need to address the problem in the study (Miles, 2016). The reason for the investigation of a problem is the foundation of all research.

The central idea in gathering information on a phenomenon (instead of merely dealing with the manifest symptoms) is that these might often reveal the root of the real problem. A critical step in doing research is to try and pin down the issue or question (which refers to the research problem) that the researcher will use as a basis for the study (Leedy & Ormrod, 2019). This is the foundation for doing the research. Remember, the ultimate goal of the research is to specifically identify, in a complete sentence, the question the researcher will try to answer. When a researcher describes their research objective in clear, concrete terms, they will have a good idea of what is needed to accomplish it and can direct their research efforts accordingly (Leedy & Ormrod, 2019).

The research problem is also based on the topic of interest, the research endeavor is based on the research problem, and the problem is based on the selection of the topic. If the researcher is undertaking the research project as part of a line of inquiry, the most important attribute will be that it meets the examining body's requirements and, in particular, that it is at the correct level. This means that the researcher must choose the topic with care (Saunders et al., 2009).

When investigating the problem, the researcher needs to consider the resources involved. The resources that the researcher will have available is a consideration when it comes to *investigating* the problem. For example, if the researcher has colleagues or friends willing to help them with the research, then this will clearly allow them to do more than if they were on their own. Thus, they must make sure they are aware of any regulations or restrictions relating to this. When most researchers undertake small-scale research projects, however, they will probably be working largely on their own. The researchers will have to leverage their contacts to access those resources to assist them (Blaxter et al., 2010).

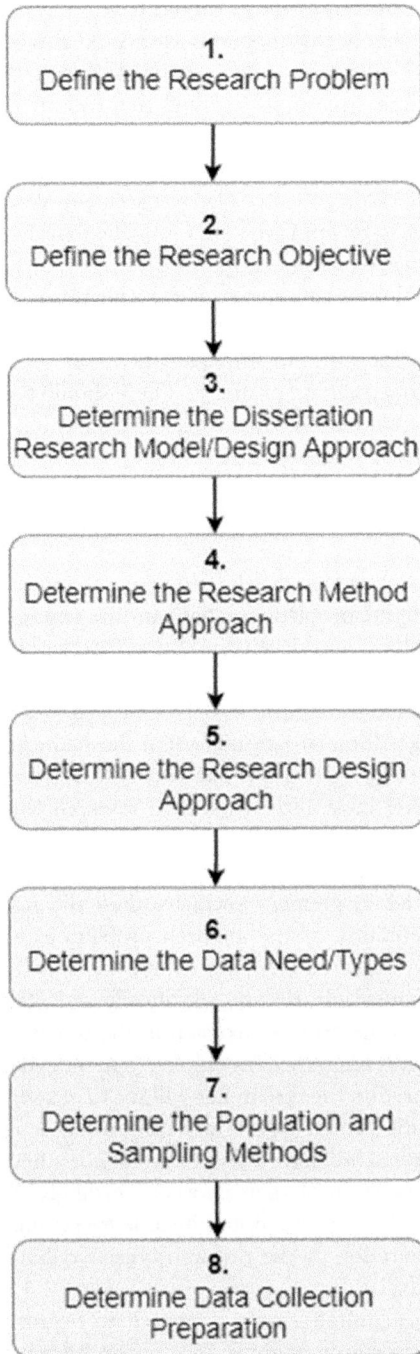

Figure 15.1 Developing the plan for research.

We will discuss this in the later chapters on the literature review and investigation of the research problem. The research problem should have what is in the literature review to determine the problem of investigation. This could also be used to uncover any research gaps that have relevance to the research problem. The literature review should have revealed some questions or issues that call for further investigation in the research problem.

If possible, the research problem to be tackled in the research should emerge naturally and inexorably from the literature review. The research problem may arise as a result of past work that needs to be improved on. It may be that there is a crucial test that will help to decide between competing theories (Leedy et al., 2021). The researcher may do the following in terms of researching the problem: (a) propose a novel theoretical or methodological slant on a topic; (b) create an interesting intellectual friction by bringing together hitherto unrelated fields or topics; or (c) develop a new area of application for a method or theory. There should be some sense that the problem that has been identified is worthwhile (Blaxter et al., 2010; Saunders et al., 2009; Bell, 2010; Leedy & Ormrod, 2019).

Define the Research Objective

The next phase in the data planning process is to develop the research objective or the purpose of the study. After defining the problem as a basis for the research, the researcher should have a doable transition into developing the research objective. The researcher must have an objective to embark on the research project. The basis for the objective of a research project is to distinguish or depict an idea or to elucidate or foresee a circumstance or answer for a circumstance that shows the kind of concentration to be directed (Singh, 2020). As every research problem is the basis for the research endeavor, the researcher must also have a clear research objective for the study.

Leedy & Ormrod (2019) asserts that the researcher must contend that research objectives are sometimes likely to lead to greater specificity than the research problem. This is based on a clear definition of the research problem as a basis for the study. The development of the research objective cannot be understated. In terms of planning, the researcher must clearly and specifically articulate the objective of the research endeavor. It is the critical next step in the research project: The research must be set forth in a grammatically complete sentence that specifically and precisely identifies the question the researcher will try to answer. The researcher puts themself in a solid position when the research objective is described in clear, concrete terms, and the researcher will have a good idea of what they need to accomplish and can optimize the direction of their efforts accordingly. All too often, novice researchers and doctoral students attempt to include everything they have learned, without a strong consideration of the research objective (Saunders et al., 2009; Bell, 2010; Leedy et al., 2021).

Finn (2005) recommended a project management approach to defining the research objective. He asserts that a project management approach can help provide "the guiding lines of discipline" and "analysis" that direct and channel the creative effort necessary to support the intellectual demands of research of a doctoral standard. He further states that project management is a research tool that helps translate the researcher's creativity into an effective approach in two ways: (a) it helps the researcher develop clarity on the strategic objectives of their project; and (b) it assists the researcher's achievement of the strategic objectives (Finn, 2005).

The task of planning typically involves a considerable amount of project definition, during which the scope and objectives of the project are clarified. When the objectives of the project and the research are clear, one can identify the tasks that must be conducted to achieve these objectives. Finn (2005) further states that, in the project plan or research proposal, the researcher then defines the variety of tasks and schedules their timing and duration. He asserts, as an effective project manager, that the researcher needs to continuously plan to cope with change and deviations from their original plan.

He recommends that, when planning the research, especially a quantitative study, and working towards achieving clarity in their objectives, the researcher should use the concept of SMART objectives, which are defined individually: (a) *Specific* – the objective is well defined and unambiguous; (b) *Measurable* – there is a quantitative method for determining if progress toward the objective is being achieved or not; (c) *Attainable* – are the objectives agreed upon (with all supervisors, for example); (d) *Realistic* – the objective is achievable within the limitations of resources, knowledge and time; and (e) *Time-bound* – the time required to conduct the tasks has been considered and there is a stated deadline for the achievement of the objective (Finn, 2005). In terms of specifically describing the scope of the research objective, the researcher must review this at an early stage. Thus, they will make much quicker progress and save a lot of time and effort that might have been wasted on irrelevant actions (Finn, 2005; Saunders et al., 2009; Bell, 2010; Leedy et al., 2021).

Determine the Dissertation Research Model/Design Approach

Considering some of the research projects that I (the second author) have conducted in the past, I must say that I wished I had been taught the value and practice of developing the research model first. In many cases of working with novice researchers and doctoral students, I am still bewildered that they are not being taught the practice of developing the research model. We as professionals have to stop this dreadful practice and do better to help our novice researchers and doctoral students. Essentially, we must establish a proper foundation for research projects for our novice researchers and doctoral students. So, what is a research model? It a structural depiction of a research enquiry process, including its research components and their respective relationship and associated philosophical assumptions. Looking from the research methodology standpoint, there are three main dissertation research models: quantitative, qualitative and mixed methods.

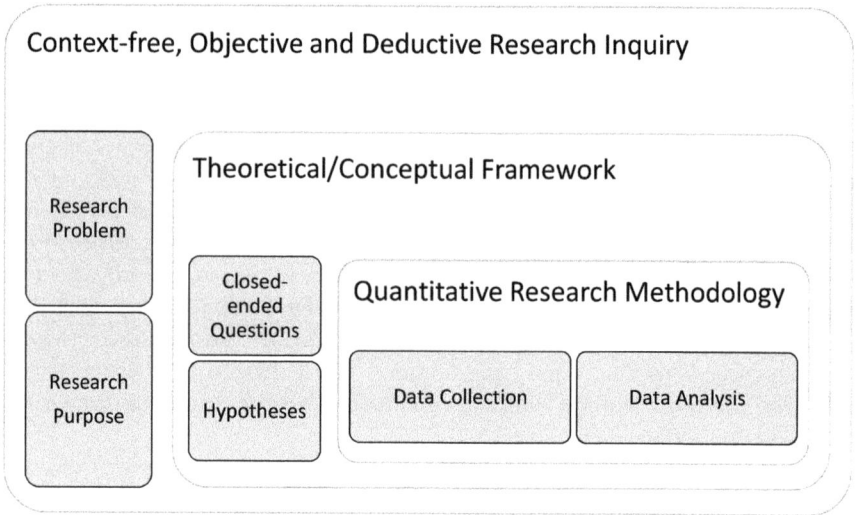

Figure 15.2 Quantitative research model.

Quantitative Research Model

Quantitative research is generally based on deductive reasoning. After a research problem has been identified, researchers determine the objectives and/or purpose of the study. Based on the purpose and informed by the theoretical or conceptual framework, they develop mainly closed-ended research questions and their corresponding hypotheses. They access the right data sources and collect and analyze data to address the questions and test the hypotheses. In sum, with a quantitative research study, your role is to collect data to test hypotheses drawn from a theory, model or group of constructs fulfilling the deductive aspects of this research model (see Figure 15.2).

Another aspect of the quantitative research model is the goal of attaining objective findings. What does it mean to maintain objectivity when conducting a quantitative study? It means recruiting participants in an ethical and systematic way using either a probability or non-probability sampling technique that is free from sampling bias, using a reliable and validated instrument to measure the variables of interest and conducting appropriate statistical analyses, including assessing whether all the assumptions associated with selected statistical tests are met. The quantitative research model also includes the concept of arriving at context-free results. With a quantitative study, the findings can be generalized to the population you sampled from, providing you randomly sampled participants for the population.

When would you select the quantitative research model for your study? You are more likely to choose the quantitative research model if you plan to:

• Collect numeric data
• Measure specific variables and/or determine relationships between variables

- Address closed-ended research questions and/or test hypotheses
- Recruit a large sample for your study

Qualitative Research Model

Qualitative research is generally based on inductive reasoning. This is because qualitative research involves collecting and analyzing data, leading to the development of a description, explanation, themes, model or theory for the phenomenon of study. Like the quantitative research model, a research inquiry under the qualitative research model starts with having a research problem and objectives and/or a purpose statement that are consistent with the problem identified. However, due to the exploratory nature of qualitative research, the research questions are normally open-ended in nature, starting with words such as what, how and why (see Figure 15.3). Also, the theoretical or conceptual framework can be used to inform how the phenomenon of interest should be studied, the development of the research questions, areas for interview questions to focus on and how data should be analyzed.

Subjectivity encompasses the notion that the researcher is an instrument, developing the questions that participants will be asked, interviewing participants to extract relevant information from them, making sense of data through systematic data analysis and presenting the findings in a way that best represents the relevant data collected and addresses the research questions. Subjectivity in qualitative research is a product of philosophical assumptions associated with doing qualitative research (Creswell, 2013). Ontologically, a qualitative researcher conducts research with the belief that there is more than one truth, and their goal is to capture those

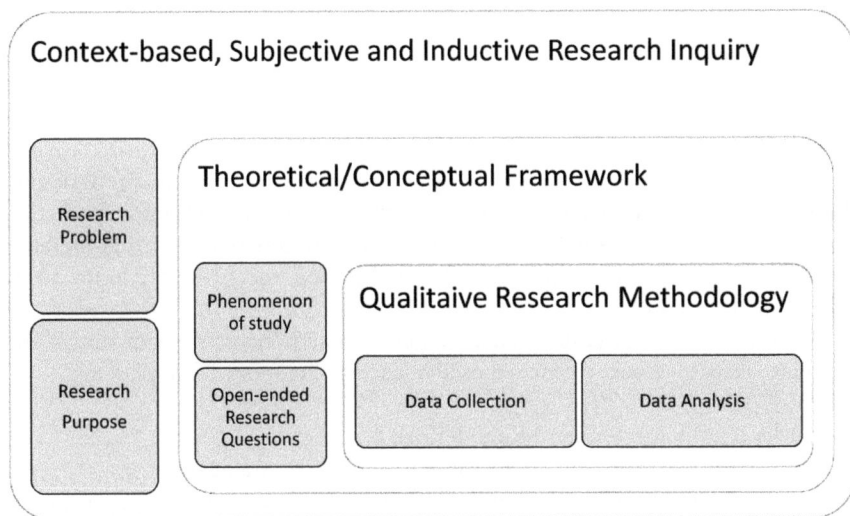

Figure 15.3 Qualitative research model.

multiple perspectives of the phenomenon of study. Epistemologically, to capture the richness of data, a qualitative researcher tends to get closer to both what and who they are studying. However, this kind of closeness could lead to the researcher having an influence on both the phenomenon of study and the source(s) of data. You could overcome this challenge by engaging in bracketing, which is taking note of your preconceptions, biases and background and preventing them from influencing the study.

Axiologically, every knowledge is generated from a particular source. The source, whether it is a group of participants, an organization or a community, has its identity, values, beliefs, experience and preconceptions. This background information influences the data extracted from them. In other words, the context is part of the data, helping researchers to make sense of the data as they generate codes, themes and/or theories. Similarly, the context is connected to the qualitative findings. Although generalization is not possible, transferability of the findings is appropriate. Transferability is one of the quality assurances of qualitative research, where qualitative researchers provide rich context so that findings can be transferred to a similar context.

When would you select the qualitative research model for your study? You are more likely to choose the qualitative research model if you plan to:

- Collect non-numeric data
- Describe, highlight, explore, understand or explain a phenomenon of study
- Address open-ended research questions
- Recruit a small sample for your study

Mixed Methods Research Model

The mixed methods research model is generally based on both deductive and inductive reasoning. It has both quantitative and qualitative research characteristics that focus on collecting and analyzing both quantitative and qualitative data to help meet the purpose of the study and address the research questions. As described in Chapter 4, when you decide on using the mixed methods research model, you need to then decide on the appropriate type of mixed methods design, the theoretical lens that informs your design, the sequence of implementation of the quantitative and qualitative phase, when and how both research methods components will be mixed and the weight of the role they will play in the study (Hanson et al., 2005).

When would you select the mixed methods research model for your study? You are more likely to choose the mixed methods research model if you plan to:

- Collect both numeric and non-numeric data
- Use both quantitative and qualitative data collection strategies
- Recruit a large and small sample for the quantitative and qualitative phase, respectively

Determine the Research Method Approach

The next phase in the data planning process is to determine the research method approach. After determining the research model as the basis for the research, the researcher should have a clear idea of the research method to be used. The objective here is to have a solid research method to build the foundation for the research project. In the most basic terms, the research methods are concerned with collecting and analyzing data. For example, one of the key goals is to build a foundation for the research design. Again, as every research problem is the basis for the research endeavor, the researcher must also have a clear research methodology for the study (Goertzen, 2017).

To determine the research method, the researcher needs to decide between two types of methodologies: quantitative and qualitative. However, they can choose both quantitative and qualitative methods if they plan to conduct a mixed methods study (Terrell, 2012). The researcher must also decide what the optimal and strongest research methodology model is for the study, as well as understand the advantages of both research methods and the optimal choice for their study. Keep in mind that the objective of the research methodology is to maintain the evaluation's feasibility and usefulness by selecting the method that will give the most accurate information without overburdening the researcher's resources and capacities (Strategic Prevention Solutions, n.d.).

Quantitative Research vs. Qualitative Research

Let's explore the differences between quantitative research and qualitative research in determining the research method approach. The task of quantitative research involves experiments and surveys, where data collection uses standardized methods such as questionnaires and structured interviews. With this method, data are in the form of numbers, from which statistical generalizations can be made. A key characteristic of quantitative research is that much of it is pre-specified in terms of what and how it is going to be done (Meadows, 2003; Barrett, 2008; Yilmaz, 2013; Babones, 2015; Goertzen, 2017). Lastly, quantitative research chiefly uses a probability sampling method that consists of four key types: simple random sampling, stratified random sampling, systematic random sampling and cluster random sampling. In essence, quantitative research generally focuses on measuring social reality due to the fact that quantitative research has a tendency to search for quantities in phenomena and establish research mathematically. This is one of the nuances of quantitative research: It allows researchers to view the world as a reality that can be objectively determined, so rigid guides in the process of data collection and analysis are very important (Sukamolson, n.d.).

In contrast, the aim of qualitative research is to help us understand, describe or explain social phenomena in a natural, as opposed to an experimental, setting, with emphasis on the meanings, experiences, attitudes and views of the participants and the focus on determining "why?" rather than "how many?"

(Turner et al., 1998; Dauter, 1999; Sukamolson, n.d.; Bourenkov & Popov, 2005; Dana & Yendol-Hoppey, 2009). Moreover, qualitative researchers collect non-numeric data utilizing a data collection strategy such as interviews, focus group discussions, observations or document collection. Lastly, qualitative research chiefly uses a non-probability sampling method that consists of four key types: convenience sampling, purposive sampling, snowball sampling and quota sampling.

The practice of quantitative research involves looking at amounts, or quantities, of one or more variables of interest. In contrast, the practice of qualitative research involves looking at characteristics, or qualities, that cannot be entirely reduced to numerical values. When the researcher can see their differences, they can understand why they measure different aspects of social phenomenon (Finn, 2005; Bell, 2010; Leedy & Ormrod, 2019).

Choosing Between Quantitative and Qualitative Research Approaches

For the researcher that wants to use a quantitative research approach, it is based on: (a) *Causality* – seeking the facts and related causes of the social phenomena; (b) *Measurement* – a careful and explicit definition of the tools (scales or questionnaires) or devices (instruments) used to measure phenomena; (c) *Replicability* – ensuring that the results obtained can be repeated in replication studies by other investigators; (d) *Generalizability* – how applicable the findings are to other situations, settings and people (in other words, the "generalizability" of the study); (e) *Validity* – the confidence that you are measuring what you think you are, the accuracy of your results; (f) *Probability* – a sampling where every sampling unit has an equal chance of being selected from the target population; (g) *Objectivity* – seeking to eliminate any biases in the way data are collected and interpreted so that conclusions reflect the true facts about a phenomenon; and (h) *Statistical significance* – looking for statistical significance in the data collected in the study (Meadows, 2003; Bourenkov & Popov, 2005; Botti & Endacott, 2008; Blaxter et al., 2010).

For the researcher that wants to use a qualitative research approach, it is based on: (a) *Exploration* – gaining initial insights into what has previously been a little-studied topic or phenomenon; (b) *Multifaceted description* – to revealing the complex, possibly multilayered nature of certain situations, settings, processes, relationships, systems or people; (c) *Verification* – allowing you to test the validity of certain assumptions, claims, theories or generalizations within real-world contexts; (d) *Theory development* – enabling you to develop new concepts or theoretical perspectives related to a phenomenon; (e) *Problem identification* – helping you to uncover key problems, obstacles or enigmas that exist within the phenomenon; and (f) *Evaluation* – providing a means by which you can judge the effectiveness of particular policies, practices or innovations (Leedy et al., 2021).

Some may see qualitative research as lacking rigor and not being scientific. As a researcher in the field of marketing, the field of marketing uses both research methodologies. I (the second author) like to think that both research approaches tend to complement each other. This is because they measure different things, and we as researchers need to appreciate the strengths of both research methods. It is really unfair to label qualitative research as unscientific and lacking research rigor. It is a disservice to qualitative researchers, who are masters at their craft. As a researcher, choose the optimal research method for your study and choose wisely.

Determine the Research Design Approach: Quantitative Designs

The next phase in the data planning process is to determine the dissertation research design approach. After determining the research method approach as a basis for the research, the researcher will be able to determine the research design. The researcher now has an idea of the research designs and which design they would prefer to use as a basis for the study. Since we have illustrated two different research methods (quantitative and qualitative) we must look at the research designs for them both. Now we have the research method, we can narrow down which research design we will choose. We will begin with the five core research designs under the quantitative research approach (see Figure 15.4).

We want to introduce and define these five research designs in order to familiarize novice researchers and doctoral students with each type and their utilization in the task of research.

Descriptive Design

This research design is defined as research that encompasses a variety of methodologies that are best suited to examining and trying to make sense of a situation. Its objective is simply to describe characteristics of the domain or state of affairs as it exists at present. A quantitative descriptive study involves measuring

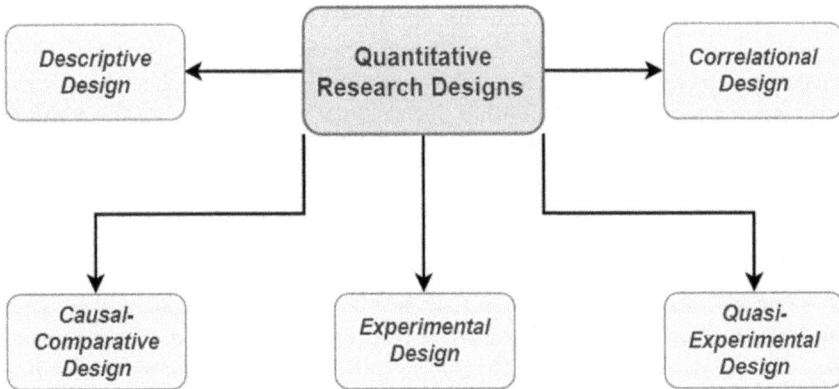

Figure 15.4 Qualitative research designs.

one or more variables in some way. The task of descriptive research is to produce an accurate profile of persons, events or situations in the investigation. Descriptive research studies address complex variables such as people's or animals' day-to-day behaviors, or perhaps people's opinions and attitudes toward a particular topic. It is descriptive of a population under investigation. Nevertheless, descriptive research does not involve changing or modifying the situation under investigation, nor does it involve determining cause-and-effect relationships. Descriptive research primarily uses surveys to gather information about people, groups, organizations and so forth (Kothari, 2004; Swanson & Holton, 2005; Jackson, 2009; Saunders et al., 2009; McNiff & Whitehead, 2010; Leedy & Ormrod, 2019).

Correlation Design

This research design is defined as a statistical investigation of the relationship between two or more variables. Correlational research examines common relationships but does not examine casual relationships between variables. The objective of correlational research is to seek and determine relationships between two or more variables without necessarily inferring causality. Both causal-comparative and correlational research generally begin with hypotheses generated from a theory or theoretical framework. Again, we reiterate that correlations do not tell us anything about causation, which is a mistake that novice researchers frequently make when interpreting them. There are several methods for determining a relationship between variables; furthermore, no method can tell us for certain that a correlation is indicative of a causal relationship.

If a correlation exists, then when one variable increases, another variable either increases or decreases in a somewhat related fashion. In statistics, this is represented by a correlation coefficient. Statistically, a correlation coefficient enables you to quantify the strength of the linear relationship between two ranked or numerical variables. Furthermore, this coefficient (usually represented by the letter r) can take on any value between $+1$ and -1. Notwithstanding, a value of $+1$ represents a perfect positive correlation. This means that the two variables are precisely related; as the values of one variable increase, the values of the other variable will also increase. Conversely, a value of -1 represents a perfect negative correlation, which is called an *inverse relationship*. There are issues with correlation, such as *illusory correlation*, the perception of a relationship that does not exist (Kothari, 2004; Swanson & Holton, 2005; Jackson, 2009; Saunders et al., 2009; McNiff & Whitehead, 2010; Leedy et al., 2021).

Causal-Comparative Design

This research design is defined as a statistical investigation that attempts to determine a cause-and-effect relationship between variables. This, in essence, means the influence of the independent variable on the dependent variable. Please note that independent variables equal *cause*, and dependent variables equal *effect* (Miles & Scott, 2017). To establish causal relationships, the independent variable is manipulated. In some cases, it is not always *possible* to control all the covariates while manipulating the independent variable in organizational settings where events flow or occur naturally and normally.

Typically, causal-comparative studies in organizational research include a number of variables (Sekaran, 2003). Interestingly, causal-comparative research is similar to an experiment, except that the researcher does not manipulate the variables under examination. The causal comparative research design measures the predictive relationship between the independent variables in relation to dependent variables. There is another name for causal relationships: *explanatory research*. The emphasis here is on studying a problem in order to explain the relationships between variables (Saunders et al., 2009). Causal comparative research is also called *ex post facto designs* (the term *ex post facto* literally means "after the fact"), which provide an alternative means by which a researcher can investigate the extent to which specific independent variables, perhaps involving a virus, lack of schooling, a history of family violence or a personality trait, may possibly affect the dependent variable(s) of interest (Sekaran, 2003; Swanson & Holton, 2005; Kothari, 2004; Saunders et al., 2009).

Experimental Design

This research design is defined as a statistical investigation in which participants are randomly assigned to groups that undergo various researcher-imposed treatments or interventions, followed by systematic assessments of the treatments' effects (Leedy et al., 2021). The purpose of an experiment is to study causal links, also whether a change in one independent variable produces a change in another dependent variable (Saunders et al., 2009; Leedy et al., 2021). Kothari (2004) and Jackson (2009) both use a research method that allows a researcher to establish a cause-and-effect relationship through the manipulation of a variable and control of the situation. There are two categories of experimental design: experiments done in an artificial or contrived environment, known as *lab experiments*; and experiments done in a natural environment in which activities regularly take place, known as *field experiments* (Sekaran, 2003).

An example of an experimental research design is a marketing researcher who wants to study how humor in television commercials affects sales in North America. To do so, the researcher studies the effectiveness of two commercials that have been developed for a new soft drink (Swanson & Holton, 2005; Jackson, 2009; Leedy et al., 2021). For a researcher to better control extraneous variables when performing an experimental design, they frequently include a *control group*, which is a group that receives no intervention so as to have little or no effect on the dependent variable. The next step for the researcher is to compare the performance of this group to an *experimental group* (also known as a *treatment group*), which is the group that participates in an intervention. You do not see too many of these types of studies with dissertations, as they take more time and more resources (Kothari, 2004; Leedy et al., 2021; Leedy & Ormrod, 2019; Saunders et al., 2009; McNiff & Whitehead, 2010; Malhotra, 2015).

Quasi-Experimental Design. This research design is defined as a statistical investigation in which an independent variable is manipulated in order to determine its possible effect on another (dependent) variable, but without total control over additional variables that might have an impact on the dependent variable. Sometimes, however, randomness is either impossible or impractical. In such situations, researchers often use quasi-experimental designs (Leedy & Ormrod, 2019; Kothari, 2004). The quasi-experimental design is also referred to as an *ex post facto design*. Quasi-experimental is a method similar to experimental research, but without random assignment to groups. The objective of the quasi-experimental design is to conduct the study without the restrictions of using randomness. This is to minimize the restrictions of the randomness of the experimental design. The focus is on the selection of group members in a multiple-group study or on the presentation of various treatments in a single-group study (Leedy & Ormrod, 2019; Kothari, 2004).

There are three main types of quasi-experimental research design. The first type is *non-equivalent groups*. This is a between-subjects design in which participants have not been randomly assigned to conditions, so the resulting groups are likely to be dissimilar in some ways. This is a common research method for dissertations. The second type is the *regression discontinuity design*. This design involves the use of pre-tests and post-tests, with the assignment of groups based on a cut point. Such a design does control for many issues related to internal validity, such as history, maturation, testing and mortality (Swanson & Holton, 2005). The last type is a *time series analysis*. This design is used to determine the influence of a variable or treatment on a single sample group. It measures the change in behavior after the treatment. The time series analysis provides a longitudinal analysis over a period of time (Sekaran, 2003; Swanson & Holton, 2005; Jackson, 2009; Saunders et al., 2009; McNiff & Whitehead, 2010). These designs are the most common quantitative research designs used in quantitative methodology for dissertation research and general research.

Determine the Research Design Approach: Qualitative Designs

Again, as stated previously, the next phase in the data planning process is to determine the dissertation research design approach. After determining the research method approach as a basis for the research, the researcher will be able to determine the research design. We already discussed and illustrated the quantitative research designs. Now we will discuss and illustrate the qualitative research designs. We will begin with the six core research designs under the qualitative research approach (see Figure 15.5).

We want to introduce and define these different qualitative research designs in order to familiarize novice researchers and doctoral students with each type and their utilization in the task of research.

Phenomenological Research Design

This approach is a qualitative research tool used to describe or understand an experience shared by participants. There are two main levels of phenomenological

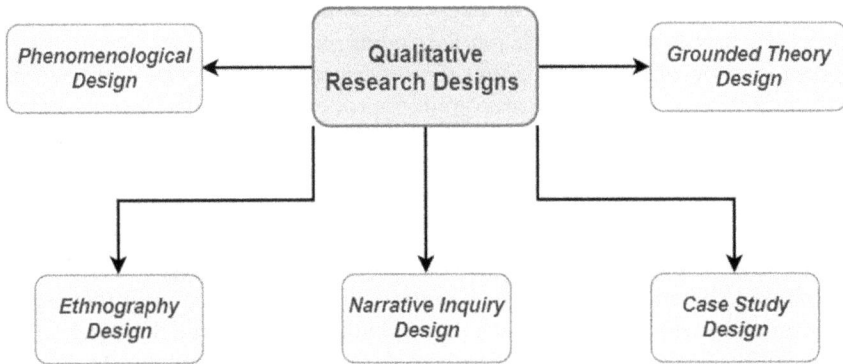

Figure 15.5 Quantitative research designs.

research: descriptive and interpretative. With the descriptive level, researchers' role is to give the participants the space to share what they have experienced. They then gather a relevant description of participants' narratives of their experience, analyzing them to extract the core features of the experience (Larsen & Adu, 2021). These core features are collectively called the essence of the experience (Eddles-Hirsch, 2015). This type of phenomenology is informed by transcendental phenomenology.

With the interpretative level, researchers focus on letting participants reflect on their experience and provide how they make sense of it. It also involves collecting views, perspectives and understandings of a phenomenon that participants have direct or indirect experience of. With this kind of phenomenological approach, the role of researchers is to give participants the chance to express their views about a phenomenon or an understanding of what they have experienced. They then examine participants' statements with their background to better understand what they commented. They extract meanings from their selected statements and develop codes and themes to address their research questions. This kind of phenomenological approach is influenced by interpretative phenomenology (Larsen & Adu, 2021).

Grounded Theory Research Design

This qualitative research approach is used to generate a data-driven model or theory to explain a phenomenon, process, situation or behavior (Adu, 2019; Charmaz, 2014). The model or theory developed comprises of a group of concepts and their relationship, reflecting data collected and explaining a phenomenon of study (Charmaz, 2014). There are a couple of features associated with the grounded theory approach that sets it apart from other qualitative approaches. First, data analysis starts normally with the data collection stage. After getting access to your initial data, you can start analyzing it. The outcome of the initial data analysis could lead to a refinement of the interview questions, helping to collect relevant data from participants. Second, you use coding strategies such as initial or open coding, focused or axial coding and theoretical coding (Charmaz, 2014). Initial coding involves going through data (transcripts), extracting relevant information and assigning codes to them. Codes generated are then categorized using focused or axial coding, leading to the development of themes. The themes are examined to determine the relationships between them using theoretical coding. Third, you use theoretical sampling to sample participants and ask them questions that came up when analyzing data. Fourth, you then use the constant comparative method to compare the initial theory generated to the new sets of data, with the goal of confirming or refining the proposed theory. Fifth, you repeat the third and fourth steps until you reach saturation. Saturation within the data analysis phase is the stage at which new data confirms the proposed theory and no new sets of data are needed to conduct a constant comparison analysis.

Ethnography Research Design

This type of research method involves describing, exploring or examining a phenomenon of study by being in the space where your potential research participants are located and gathering data as you directly or indirectly interact with them and/ or participate in what they do (Adu, 2019; Murtagh, 2007). To put it in simple terms, your goal is to study a group of people, a situation or an event in their natural setting. Researchers using the ethnographic approach normally spend considerable amounts of time at the research site making observations, interviewing participants, participating in an event/activity and/or facilitating in focus group discussions. Another unique aspect of this research method is taking field notes, which includes documenting not only those being observed but also your reflections. Moreover, the effectiveness of this approach is partly dependent on proper preparation, which includes having a clear plan of what kinds of data you plan to collect, how you intend to collect them and the data collection strategies you want to use. Also, having a gatekeeper is key to a successful data collection experience. The gatekeeper can help you to understand the norms and culture of the people you plan to study, connect to the organization or community you want to study and build trust with them.

Narrative Inquiry Research Design

Narrative inquiry research design is a type of qualitative approach that focuses on collecting participants' stories and analyzing them, leading to the generation of an overarching story reflecting what participants shared. Collecting participants' stories is one of the ways that researchers (using the narrative approach) can generate data. Other options are open-ended surveys, document collection, observations and focus groups (Bell, 2003). Arriving at a rich narrative starts with gathering relevant data from selected data sources and having an in-depth understanding of the data collected. According to Bell (2003), when analyzing your data, you could group relevant information extracted from the data into six "literary concepts": "setting, storyline, perspective, diction, motif and theme" (p. 105). Think about the setting as the context, which could be geographical, historical, situational and/or cultural. Also, see the storyline as a series of happenings in a story that lead to corresponding responses from participants. Further, perspectives are emotions that inform the participants' actions and decisions. "The 'diction' categories included key metaphors used by participants to refer to the type of work in which they were engaged (e.g., habitat restoration; naturalization). I used 'motif' to bring together those coding categories which identified elements of knowledge gained by participants through their involvement (e.g., names and lives of plants and animals; what plants need and how to do it)" (Bell, 2003, p. 106). Lastly, the theme concept constitutes the expressions of participants that reflect the main ideas in their story.

Alternatively, Richmond (2002) suggested that, when conducting narrative analysis, you could group relevant information extracted from the data into four categories: orientation, abstract, complicating action and resolution. According to Richmond (2002), *orientation* is about descriptions of the "setting and character," *abstract* is about descriptions of "the events or incidents of the story," *complicated* action encompasses description of "events, conflicts and themes" and resolution focuses on describing "the outcomes of the story or conflict" (pp. 5–6).

Case Study Research Design

This approach is used when you plan to describe, explore, examine or compare with the purpose of highlighting, understanding, explaining or showing the distinctive characteristics of a case (Baxter & Jack, 2008). A case can be a person, a group of people, an organization or a group of organizations. It can be a community or a country. It can even be an event or a phenomenon. The most important thing is that a case should be well-defined in terms of what it covers, who are part of it, where the case is and/or when the case happened. For example, a case could be "the experience of ChatGPT (AI powered information/knowledge generator) among content creators between 18–35 years living in the US." One of the unique features of a case study is collecting data from multiple sources and/or using more than one data collecting strategy (Baxter & Jack, 2008). Another unique aspect of the case study approach is the flexibility to adopt data analysis techniques from other qualitative approaches. You could conduct content or thematic analysis or use coding strategies for grounded theory, such as open coding, focused coding and theoretical coding.

These designs are the most common qualitative research designs used in qualitative methodology for dissertation research and general research.

Determine the Data Need / Type

The next phase in the data planning process is to determine the data need and data type. This will involve illustrating and discussing the various types of data. To help the researchers further understand the distinctions of data, we must illustrate and explain the different types of data that researchers will encounter while determining the data need and type. The acquisition of data is an important process and task for the research project. Every aspect of the data and data types are vital to managing the research project. As a basis for the research project, the researcher must also have a clear understanding of the different data types under the appropriate research methodology.

Types of Data

There are two types of data: *primary* and *secondary*. Researchers must have a clear understanding of the differences in the data types. When researchers begin to acquire data, they really do not understand these two types of data or their differences. In the case of a supplementary analysis that is sometimes used with collected primary data, there is a tendency for the novice researcher to get confused about how to use the data. Furthermore, it can be a problem for many novice researchers who collect primary data and have some understanding on the uses of secondary data, especially if they are not aware of the differences between the two. Historical research, one of the more interesting sources of data, can be classified into two main groups: *primary sources*, which are the lifeblood of historical research, and secondary sources, which may be used in the absence of, or to supplement, primary data (Cohen et al., 2018).

PRIMARY DATA

Primary data is defined as information that is collected for the specific purpose of a study either by the researcher or by someone else. The key definition of primary data is originated by the researcher for the specific purpose of investigating the research problem. Primary data can be both qualitative and quantitative. The most common method of generating primary data is through a survey. There are several methods of collecting primary data, particularly surveys and descriptive research. Important ones are (a) the observation method, (b) the interview method, (c) through questionnaires, and (d) through schedules (Malhotra & Birks, 2007; Kothari, 2004; Leedy et al., 2021). There are also other methods such as (a) warranty cards, (b) distributor audits, (c) pantry audits, (d) consumer panels, (e) using mechanical devices, (f) through projective techniques, (g) in-depth interviews, and (h) content analysis (Malhotra & Birks, 2007; Kothari, 2004; Leedy et al., 2021). One of the important things about primary data is that it is individually tailored for the decision-makers of organizations that pay for well-focused and exclusive support. Also, compared with secondary data, it is readily available data from a variety of sources (Sekaran, 2003; Malhotra & Birks, 2007; Kothari, 2004; Sreejesh et al., 2014; Malhotra, 2015).

According to the literature, there are many types of primary data. However, there are four fundamental types of primary data, which are distinguished by the way they are compiled: (a) *Measurement* is the collection of numbers indicating amounts, (e.g., voting polls, exam results, car mileages, oven temperatures, etc.); (b) *Observation* is the recording of events, situations or things experienced with your own senses and perhaps with the help of an instrument (e.g., camera, tape recorder, microscope, etc.); (c) *Interrogation* is data gained by asking and probing (e.g., information about people's convictions, likes and dislikes, etc.); and (d) *Participation* is data gained by experiences of doing things (e.g., the experience of learning to ride a bike tells you different things about balance, dealing with traffic, etc.) rather than just observing (Walliman, 2011; Kothari, 2004).

SECONDARY DATA

Secondary data is defined as data collected for a purpose other than the problem at hand, and secondary analysis is usually undertaken by researchers who did not conduct the primary data collection. For this reason, they have a more distant relationship to the data and may not, therefore, fully appreciate the processes by which the data were constructed (Malhotra & Birks, 2007; Alasuutari et al., 2002; Kothari, 2004; Walliman, 2011; Sreejesh et al., 2014; Malhotra, 2015; Leedy & Ormrod, 2019). Secondary data tends to enable the researcher to (1) diagnose the research problem; (2) develop an approach to the problem; (3) develop a sampling plan; (4) formulate an appropriate research design; (5) answer certain research questions and test some hypotheses; (6) interpret primary data with more insight; and (7) validate qualitative research findings (Malhotra & Birks, 2007).

Secondary data, like primary data, includes both quantitative and qualitative data. Secondary data is principally used in both descriptive and explanatory research. With secondary data, the researcher can use *raw data*, where there has been little if any processing, or *compiled data*, which have received some form of selection or summarizing (Sekaran, 2003; Saunders et al., 2009).

Interestingly, secondary data has some significant advantages over primary data. The first key primary advantage of secondary data is its availability. It is always faster and less expensive than acquiring primary data. Second, the use of secondary data eliminates many of the activities normally associated with primary data collection, such as sampling and data processing. Third, secondary data is more feasible when data cannot be obtained using primary data collection procedures. Fourth, secondary data cuts out the need for time-consuming fieldwork because it has been produced by teams of expert researchers, often with large budgets and extensive resources way beyond the means of a single student. Lastly, secondary data can also be used to compare with primary data you may have collected in order to triangulate the findings and put your data into a larger context (Sekaran, 2003; Malhotra & Birks, 2007; Kothari, 2004; Zikmund & Babin, 2010).

Quantitative Data Types in Research

Quantitative data is a numerical-based data. Quantitative data can be measured more or less accurately because it contains some form of magnitude, usually expressed in numbers. Quantitative data primarily uses four levels of measurement in the collection of the data: (a) *nominal*, (b) *ordinal*, (c) *interval*, and (d) *ratio* (Walliman, 2011). Below is a definition of each of these quantitative data types:

- **Nominal data.** This is a type of data for which numbers are used only to identify different categories of people, objects or other entities; this data doesn't reflect a particular quantity or degree of something.
- **Ordinal data.** This is a type of data for which the assigned numbers reflect an order or sequence. Ordinal data indicate the degree to which people, objects or other entities have a certain quality or characteristic (a variable) of interest.
- **Interval data.** This is a type of data that reflects equal units of measurement. Interval data is defined as numbers reflecting differences in degree or amount. This type of data tells us the differences between the numbers and how much difference exists in the characteristic being measured.
- **Ratio data.** This is a type of data that reflects equal intervals between values for the characteristic being measured. However, they also have a true zero point: a value of 0 tells us that there's a complete absence of the characteristic (Leedy et al., 2021; McNiff & Whitehead, 2010).

Furthermore, quantitative data represent phenomena by assigning numbers in an ordered and meaningful way. The primary purposes of quantitative analysis are to measure, make comparisons, examine relationships, make forecasts, test hypotheses, construct concepts and theories, explore, control and explain (Saunders et al., 2009; Zikmund & Babin, 2010). Also, quantitative data can be divided into two distinct groups: *categorical* and *numerical*. Categorical data refers to data whose values cannot be measured numerically but can be either classified into sets (categories) according to the characteristics that identify or describe the variable or placed in rank order (Saunders et al., 2009).

There are two types of categorial data: *descriptive* and *ranked*. Descriptive data (or nominal data) as an approach is impossible to define numerically or to rank. Rather, these data simply count the number of occurrences in each category of a variable. Ranked (or ordinal) data are a more precise form of categorical data. In such instances, you know the relative position of each case within your data set, although the actual numerical measures (such as scores) on which the position is based are not recorded (Saunders et al., 2009).

There are two types of numerical data: *continuous* and *discrete*. Continuous data refers to data whose values can theoretically take any value (sometimes within a restricted range), provided they can be measured with sufficient accuracy. Discrete data refers to data whose values are measured in discrete units and therefore can take only one of a finite number of values from a scale that measures changes in this way (Saunders et al., 2009).

There is also *dichotomous data*, which is when the variable is divided into two categories, such as the variable gender being divided into female and male. Rating or scale questions, such as where a respondent is asked to rate how strongly she or he agrees with a statement, collect ranked (ordinal) data. *Numerical data*, which are sometimes termed "quantifiable," are those whose values are measured or counted numerically as quantities (Kothari, 2004; Little, 2014; Blaxter et al., 2010; Saunders et al., 2009; Zikmund & Babin, 2010; Leedy et al., 2021).

Qualitative Data Types in Research

Qualitative data has many unique characteristics that are quite different from quantitative data. Qualitative research can be quite different from quantitative research in another important way as well. In qualitative research, however, the methodology often involves an iterative and recursive process in which the researcher moves back and forth between data collection and data analysis. In another distinguishing characteristic, qualitative data cannot be accurately measured and counted and are generally expressed in words rather than numbers – essentially, human activities and attributes such as ideas, customs, mores and beliefs. However, quantitative data that are investigated in the study of human beings and their societies and cultures cannot be pinned down and measured in any exact way (Walliman, 2011). Qualitative data has three key characteristics: (a) it is based on meanings expressed through words; (b) its collection results in non-standardized data requiring classification into categories; and (c) its analysis is conducted through the use of conceptualization (Saunders et al., 2009).

Qualitative analysis generally involves one or more of the following: summarizing data, categorizing data and structuring data using narrative to recognize relationships, developing and testing propositions and producing well-grounded conclusions. It can lead to reanalyzing categories developed from qualitative data quantitatively (Saunders et al., 2009). One interesting aspect of qualitative data is that it has two key characteristics: (a) it deals with meaning, and those meanings are mediated primarily through language and action; and (b) it is data in the form of words that are derived from observations, interviews or documents (Swanson & Holton, 2005). Qualitative data analysis is a process that entails (1) sensing themes, (2) constant comparison, (3) recursiveness, (4) inductive and deductive thinking, and (5) interpretation to generate meaning (Swanson & Holton, 2005).

Again, qualitative researchers don't usually measure things in terms of the numerical sense of the word. Conversely, qualitative research is based on trustworthiness, that data are collected ethically and accurately and the findings are credible, plausible and well-substantiated. Many qualitative researchers reject the terms validity and reliability, viewing them as inappropriate concepts for evaluating the rigor of qualitative research studies. They instead embrace notions such as credibility and transferability as criteria for judging whether the results from a study are plausible and believable from participants' perspectives and if the findings can be applied to other settings (Saunders et al., 2009; Walliman, 2011; Leedy et al., 2021).

Qualitative data is a non-numerical type of data. Qualitative data can be generally expressed in words rather than numbers; essentially, it is expressed in human activities and attributes. Qualitative data primarily uses five levels of data in the collection of data: (a) *interview data*, (b) *observation data*, (c) *focus group data*, (d) *content data*, and (e) *documentary secondary data*. Below is a definition of each of these qualitative data types:

- **Interview data.** The most common qualitative data are interviews. This is the most common way to collect qualitative data. The researcher uses predefined questions and conducts either structured, semi-structured or unstructured interviews.
- **Observation data.** This is also a common type of qualitative data and is collected from an outsider's perspective. This data is collected by close observation. The researcher uses field notes for data analysis. In observation data, it is sometimes necessary for the researcher to become part of the group that is being studied. This will help the researcher to acquire this type of data and be a part of the lived experience.
- **Focus group data.** This is another common type of qualitative data. This type of data is collected from focus groups, members of a small group who are asked a series of guided questions. This type of data is about their perceptions, beliefs or attitudes toward an event, products, concepts and so on.
- **Content data.** This is also a common type of qualitative data. This type of data is collected from existing published sources such as documents, journal articles, newspaper articles, reports, organizational documents and the like. Artifacts are also a part of this type of qualitative data. This type of data is primarily a secondary type of data. Also, another example of this data type is organizations' databases, both internal and external.
- **Documentary secondary data.** Documentary secondary data are often used in research projects that also use primary data collection methods. Documentary secondary data include non-written materials (such as voice and video recordings, pictures, drawings, films and television programs). This type of data also includes digital documents and digital recordings such as DVDs and CD-ROMs (Saunders et al., 2009; Terrell, 2016; Leedy et al., 2021).

The use of qualitative data is quite comprehensive compared to its quantitative data counterpart. There are two tasks involved in using content data. First, there is the task of *data conversion* (also called *data transformation*), which is the process of changing the original form of the data to a format more suitable for achieving a stated research objective. Second, there is the task of *cross-checks*. This is a comparison of data from one source with data from another. When the data are not consistent, researchers should attempt data conversion (Zikmund & Babin, 2010).

Determining the Population and Sampling Methods in Quantitative Research

Step 1. Defining and Choosing the Population

Before a sample is taken, the researcher must define the population from which they want to collect the data. Choosing the population of interest is a key first step in conducting research. Choosing the population of interest is very important. Our experience from working with novice researchers and doctoral students is that they have difficulty doing and understanding this. The population could be a city, county, state or region, the population in an organization, a subgroup of the population in the United States, college students at a university or voters in a district.

We want to make the point here that a sample can be extracted from any population of interest to the researcher. Also, the population is one that the researcher wants to generalize, thus the population the researcher is interested in. The key is generalizability. Generalizability refers to the capacity of the case to be informative about a general phenomenon, to be broadly applicable beyond the specific site, population, time and circumstances studied (Alasuutari et al., 2002). A researcher must understand that populations that can be sampled from good organizational lists include elementary schools, high schools, university students and faculties; church members; factory workers; fraternity or sorority members; members of social, service or political clubs; and members of professional associations (Babbie, 2008). That is how a researcher chooses the population for a quantitative research project.

Step 2. Drawing the Sample from the Population

After completing a list of population members, the researcher must choose a sampling method. Because this is in the area of quantitative research, the sampling method has to be a probability sampling method. One thing a researcher must remember is that the chosen sampling method is very important and needs to be justified and replicable (Bell, 2010).

With quantitative research, probability sampling is the main type of sampling method. One of the most widely understood probability sampling approaches is random sampling, where every individual or object in the group or population of interest (e.g., MPs, dog owners, course members, pages, archival texts) has an equal chance of being chosen for study (Blaxter et al., 2010). Figure 15.6 illustrates the different probability sampling methods a researcher can choose in quantitative research.

Sample size formulas provide the means for calculating the size of your sample based on several factors. There are two formulas used to calculate sample size: (a) *sampling error formula* for surveys; and (b) a *power analysis formula* (or G-Power analysis) for experiments. Using these formulas can take the conjecture out of determining the number of participants for a study and provides a precise estimate of

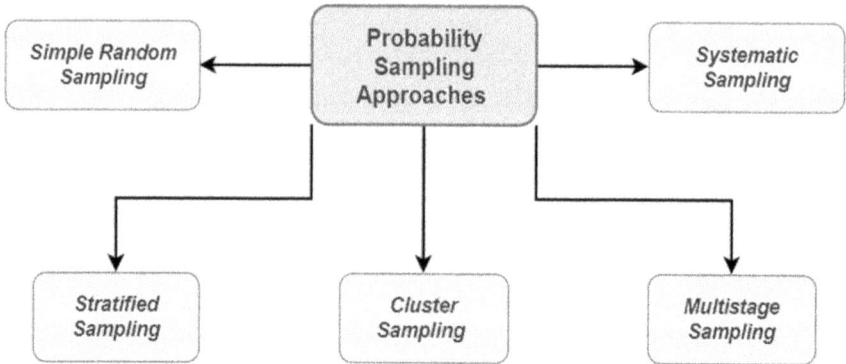

Figure 15.6 Probability sampling approaches.

your sample size. The formulas take into consideration several factors important to determining sample size, such as confidence intervals in the statistical test and sampling error (Creswell, 2012).

Determining the Population and Sampling Methods in Qualitative Research

Step 1. Defining and Choosing the Population

Again, before a sample is taken, the researcher must define the population from which they want to collect the data. The researcher must choose the population. This is a key first step in conducting research. In my experience of working with novice researchers and doctoral students, they have difficulty doing and understanding the non-probability approach to this as well. In the area of qualitative research that involves choosing the population of interest, the researcher has some considerations. First, find the population of interest that is the most convenient, cost-prohibitive and easily accessible. Second, choose a population of interest in which any particular member of the population being chosen is unknown.

It is essential for the researcher to choose a population of interest that meets these considerations. However, it is not as rigorous as the quantitative approach. In qualitative research, with the population investigation, the researcher selects participants on the basis of their expertise in the subject matter under investigation. When targeting the population, the most easily accessible members are chosen as subjects. Also, when targeting the population, the subjects are conveniently chosen from targeted groups or according to some predetermined number or quota of participants (Sekaran, 2003; Miller & Yang, 2007; Zikmund & Babin, 2010; Price et al., 2017). That is how a researcher chooses the population for a qualitative research project.

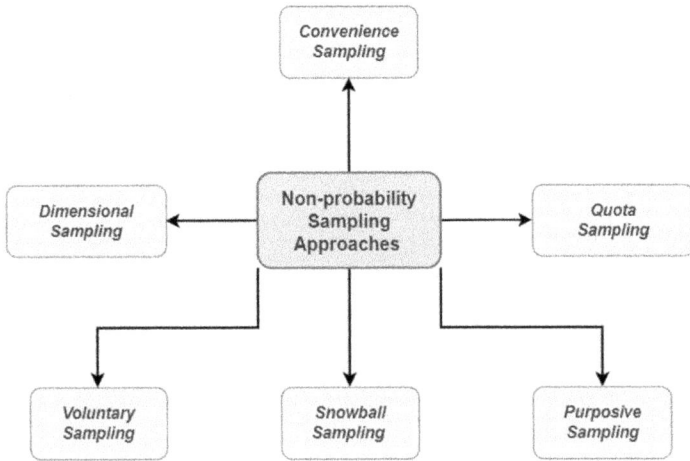

Figure 15.7 Non-probability sampling approaches.

Step 2. Drawing the Sample from the Population

After completing a list of population members, the researcher must choose a sampling method. For qualitative research, the researcher uses a non-probability sampling method, a sampling technique in which units of the sample are selected on the basis of personal judgment or convenience and the probability of any particular member of the population being chosen is unknown (Zikmund & Babin, 2010).

Because this is in the area of qualitative research, the sampling method has to be a non-probability sampling method. With qualitative research, non-probability sampling is the main type of sampling method. One of the most widely used non-probability sampling approaches is *convenience sampling*. This type of non-probability sampling approach is where every individual or object in the group or population is of interest. With the non-probability sampling approach, it is sufficient to choose participants as a convenience sample. This is a group of individuals who meet the general requirements of the study and are recruited in a variety of nonrandom ways. Quite often, they are from the "subject pool" –general psychology students being asked to participate in a study or two (Goodwin & Goodwin, 2013). Figure 15.7 illustrates the different non-probability sampling methods a researcher can choose in qualitative research.

Data Saturation. In addressing this issue, many of the research methods textbooks simply recommend continuing to collect qualitative data, such as by conducting additional interviews, until data saturation is reached: in other words, until the additional data collected provides few, if any, new insights (Bell, 2010; Blaxter et al., 2010; McNiff & Whitehead, 2010).

For qualitative research, sample size is not the focus. With the non-probability sampling technique, in which units of the sample are selected on the basis of *personal judgment* or *convenience*, the probability of any particular member of the population being chosen is unknown (Alasuutari et al., 2002; Goodwin & Goodwin, 2013; Blaxter et al., 2010; Leedy et al., 2021; Sekaran, 2003; Price et al., 2017).

Data Collection Preparation

Data collection preparation starts by considering where you plan to collect data, who you want to collect data from and the instrument or tools you will use to collect data. You also need to think about the time and resources available for you to successfully collect data. In addition, you need to make sure you have the skills to apply selected data collection strategies such as interviews, online surveys, focus groups and observations to generate the kind of data you want for your study. To use your selected data collection strategy effectively, you need to know how, learning about the best practices related to its use and its strengths and weakness (Sreejesh et al., 2014).

Data Collection Preparation under a Quantitative Study

At this point, you may have decided where you will be accessing your participants and the potential number of participants you need to complete the questionnaire for the study. You also have the questionnaire you plan to give to participants to complete. The next task is to choose the channel through which potential participants can complete the questionnaire. One option is to administer a paper version of the questionnaire. It could also be in the form of an in-person or mail survey (Deutskens et al., 2004). Alternatively, you can build it on an online survey planform such as Google Forms, SurveyMonkey or Qualtrics. It is important to choose a channel that potential participants can easily access to complete the questionnaire. You also need to consider which one would be less challenging to gather, store and clean participants' responses, preparing them to be analyzed.

It is also important to think about the cost involved in collecting data, which could include the cost of using a survey platform, accessing potential participants and analyzing data (Sreejesh et al., 2014). If it is within your research budget, you could provide incentives to improve your survey response rate, which is normally between 10% and 30%, but make sure your research ethics board that approves research is aware of the incentive you plan to give to participants. Sending reminders to potential participants to complete the survey is another strategy for increasing the response rate.

Data Collection Preparation under a Qualitative Study

At this point, you should have determined or secured the place you will be looking for data, determined how you plan to access participants, decided whether you want to meet them physically or virtually to interview them and developed an interview guide or protocol (Creswell, 2012). Alternatively, if you plan to collect documents, you should know where and how to access them and whether approval is needed. Whatever qualitative data collection strategy you select, you need to have a guide that will inform your decisions and actions when collecting data.

Because you are an instrument, engaging in self-reflection is an integral part of the data collection preparation. This self-reflection process involves thinking about who you are, your connection to the phenomenon of study and participants, your preconceptions, your experience and the role you will be playing in the data collection process. When collecting the data, you then set them aside so that they do not influence how you collect data from participants. Also, as an instrument, you need to be knowledgeable about the selected data collection strategy, including exploring its best practices, strengths and weakness. If it is your first time using the selected data collection strategy, such as interviews, focus groups and observations, we recommend you practice it with a group of people (preferably colleagues) to help gain skills and confidence in utilizing the chosen strategy.

It is important to learn as much as you can about the research location and the people you will be collecting data from (Creswell, 2012). The best person to help you learn about the research location and potential participants and build trust with them is a gatekeeper. Having conservations with someone who has connections with the society or community you plan to study at the data collection preparation stage is a great opportunity to learn and build trust. You will also get ideas about the best way to access participants and the estimated number of participants willing to be a part of the study.

Lastly, you need to make sure you have all the instruments needed to collect and securely store the data. You may need a recording device, computer, notepad and related equipment. If you plan to do your interview virtually using any of the available virtual communication platforms, then make sure your potential participants are familiar with the one you plan to use. Such planning does not always go as intended, but you are guaranteed of having less unexpected events to deal with.

Preparing the Consent Form

Before collecting data from participants, they need to first agree to be a part of the study. The document provided to potential participants that contains information about the purpose of the study, what they will be doing in the study, their rights and the risks and benefits of the study is called a *consent form*. A consent form should be clearly written and free from jargon and should have space for both you and the participants to sign. When preparing the consent form, you need to think about who will be reading and signing it and address the question, "How can I write the consent form in such a way that potential participants will understand it?" Concerning the content of the consent form, you are expected to describe the purpose of the study, state who qualifies to be a part of the study, which participants will be asked to do, the amount of time the data collection will take, the specific risks involved in participating in the study, the specific benefits of participating in the study, the rights they have as participants, including their right to withdraw from the study at any time, and how their confidentiality and privacy will be protected.

Consent forms are only given to potential participants who are considered adults (normally 18 years old and over) and cognitively and physically capable of participating in the study. As Goodwin and Goodwin (2013) put it, "Not all research participants are capable of giving consent, due to such factors as age or disability, and some persons might experience undue coercion to volunteer for research (e.g., prisoners)" (p. 52). For example, if you are focusing on children, you will need to obtain consent from a parent or guardian. In other words, their parent or guardian needs to agree and sign the consent form before they are allowed to participate. In addition, assent is required from the children before they are allowed to participate (Goodwin & Goodwin, 2013). This means that they can choose not to participate in the study even if their parents or guardians have approved their participation.

Besides a written consent form, there is also electronic and oral consent. A consent form can be sent to potential participants in electronic form through a channel such as email, a document signing system or survey platform. The researcher needs to make sure that the selected channel for the delivery and completion of the consent form is secure (Price et al., 2017). Also, the consent form should be separate from the data collected and stored in a secure place where only the researcher has access to it (Price et al., 2017).

There are certain circumstances where a written consent form (either in print or electronic form) will not be feasible. In such situations, the researcher may opt for oral consent. For example, oral consent could be an option when working with potential participants who cannot read or write. Another situation is when the researcher plans to collect sensitive information from participants and using a consent form could adversely affect their confidentiality and/or anonymity. When in doubt regarding which type of informed consent is appropriate for your study, we advise you have a discussion with your dissertation supervisor or a representative of the ethical board of your institution.

Ethical Issues Related to Data Collection

During the data collection stage, you should make sure you are following all the instructions you have been given by the ethical board of your institution and the one at the research location (if any). To put it differently, you are expected to do what you have told the ethical board you will be doing. Also, you are expected to notify the board if you plan to go beyond the specified ethical parameters given to you. For example, if you plan to change the source of your data, you need to let the board know. Moreover, if you realize that you have gone beyond what the ethical board has approved, you need to notify them immediately for direction.

In terms of the sequence of the data collection process when conducting an online survey, participants can be asked to verify their eligibility by completing a screening questionnaire. After that, they read the informed consent and click on

"Agree" if they want to be a part of the study. It is a best practice to state the estimated amount of time it will take for participants to complete the survey. It is important to be honest and state the appropriate amount of time. This is because, if they realize that they are spending way more time than was stated in the consent form, they could stop completing the survey, which would affect the completion rate.

After consenting to participate in the study, they can then complete the survey. At the end of the survey, there should be a "Thank you" note and any other information that will be helpful to participants, including a debriefing, if needed (Price et al., 2017). Lastly, make sure that participants' data, including any identifiable information, are well protected. It is important to review the survey platform's privacy policy in relation to participants' data so that you make informed decisions about the ways to protect participants' data.

In the same way, a qualitative researcher should be proactive in upholding the ethical principles when collecting qualitative data. Because in qualitative research you normally focus on a small sample size, you need to be careful when collecting demographic information. In some cases, participants can easily be identified if you collect and share their demographic information. In other words, demographic information is very useful in understanding participants' experiences, perspectives and/or stories, and it can positively add to the richness of your findings. However, you need to ensure that sharing participants' background does not adversely affect their privacy and confidentiality.

Another ethical practice in qualitative research is to choose a secure location to conduct interviews with participants. If you have limited control about the choice of the interview location, you should guide participants to select a place where they feel comfortable and no one will be listening to the conversation between you and the participants. Also, throughout the interview, if you notice any discomfort, pause the interview and ask how they are doing and if they would like to take a break. As a qualitative researcher collecting data from participants, one of your roles is to protect participants and make resources available in case they need help as a result of participating in the study.

Implementing Data Collection

Implementation of the data collection starts by recruiting people who qualify to be part of the study. Similarly, if you are focusing on documents as your data, you start the data collection process by getting access to the source of the data. After recruiting potential participants, the next stage is to invite them to be a part of the study if they meet the eligibility criteria. Those who qualify are asked to review and complete the consent form. If they consent to be a part of the study, they then do what is expected of them as participants, such as completing a survey or participating in an interview or a focus group discussion. The final step in the data collection process is to store the data collected, making it ready for analysis.

Participants' Recruitment

There are many strategies used to recruit potential participants for a study. One option is to go to the research location and verbally invite potential participants to be a part of your study. When interacting with them, you should share what the research is about, who qualifies to be a participant, what they will be doing, how long participation in the study will be and who to contact if they want to take part in the study or have questions. Another option is to send a recruitment letter through an email list. This would be an email list of an organization or association. If the list is not publicly available, you may need to contact the authorities of the institution where the potential participants are and ask whether they can send the recruitment letter to them on your behalf. Alternatively, you can request an online survey platform such as SurveyMonkey or Qualtrics to send your survey to people who may qualify for your study. We suggest you check with your dissertation supervisor if letting an online survey platform send your survey to potential participants is appropriate. You can also check with the ethical board of your institution to see whether they would approve of this participant recruitment strategy.

You could also use social media to access potential participants. For example, you could create a flyer or poster and post it on your LinkedIn page, inviting qualified participants to complete your survey or take part in an interview. When doing a qualitative study, you can ask a gatekeeper to help you recruit potential participants to be interviewed. Gatekeepers can give you an idea of many people you can get for your study. They can give you suggestions about where and how to search for participants. As you can see, there are many participant recruitment strategies you can choose from. The most important thing is to choose the most appropriate and feasible avenue to access qualified participants for your study.

Ensuring the Eligibility of Potential Participants

When potential participants show an interest in completing your survey, the first step is to ask them to complete a screening questionnaire. This kind of questionnaire contains a few closed-ended questions that are consistent with the eligibility criteria for your study. Here are some examples of questions that researchers ask: Are you 18 years old or older? Do you have at least three years of work experience? Have you experienced bullying at your workplace before? The screening questions should be structured in such a way that respondents have an option to indicate "Yes" or "No," thus helping you to decide whether they qualify or not. Screening potential participants to make sure they qualify can be done verbally, especially when conducting interviews. In this case, they are asked the screening questions, and if they meet the selection criteria, you then move on to talk about informed consent.

Completing Informed Consent

For a survey study, qualified participants read the consent form and indicate that they agree to participate in the study before they proceed to complete the survey.

As mentioned above, a consent form should be written in such a way that, after reading it, participants should know the purpose of the study, who qualifies to be a part of the study, when it needs to be completed, what they will be asked to do in the study, the rights they have, the risks and benefits involved in participating in the study, the amount of time it will take, how the data will be stored to ensure participants' privacy and confidentiality and contact information about the research. When conducting interviews, you can provide a written consent form for participants to read, and you can ask for clarification if needed. Both you and the participants can sign it. You give a copy to the participants and keep one in a safe place. It is important to note that signing the consent form does not prevent them from withdrawing from the study if they want to. As it is required to state in the consent form that their participation is voluntary, they can withdraw at any time without any repercussions.

Participating in the Study

After completing the informed consent, the next stage is to engage in the main data collection activities leading to the generation of data for analysis. For a quantitative study, participants will be asked to complete a test or questionnaire with the goal of measuring variables of interest, collecting the numbers needed to describe a variable or group of variables and/or test hypotheses. In most quantitative studies utilizing a survey instrument, participants are asked to first finish the demographic questions and then complete the main questionnaire (measuring the variables of interest). After that, participants are provided with "Thank you" information, which shows appreciation of their time spent completing the survey.

Similarly, in a qualitative study using interview as a data collection strategy, you can start by asking demographic-related questions. These simple questions could be a great opportunity to get to know participants and build rapport. In case you are using focus groups, asking each participant to introduce themselves is a way of building trust with participants. The next phase is to ask participants questions that will help generate the responses needed to address your research questions. Also, be ready to clarify questions and ask follow-up questions when needed. Lastly, make sure the interview does not go beyond the agreed length of time stated in the consent form. Before you finish the interview, ask whether they want to share any last thoughts, giving them a sense of closure and making them feel their voice was heard.

Storing Collected Data

As researchers, we are responsible for protecting participants' data, making sure they are stored in a secure location and used purposely for what they were intended to be used. "It is also important that data are seen as a valuable commodity that needs to be treated with respect. This means that they should be stored securely and, when a project is finished, disposed of securely" (Dale et al., 2012, p. 530). Their data should be stored in such a way that you are the only person who has access to them (Cohen et al., 2018). Participants should be informed if the data is used for something other than what was in the informed consent. Moreover, they can request their data and ask that their information not be used in the study. We suggest you follow the directives provided by the ethical board of your institution with regard to how you should use, store and destroy data after use.

Writing about the Data Collection Process

Writing about your data collection process involves giving a detailed description of how you gather data from your source. You are expected to describe the data collection process in such a way that future researchers can repeat what you did by following your data collection steps. Note that if you are writing your dissertation proposal, you should write about your process in the future tense. However, after completing your study, you can write this section in the past tense. Readers can easily follow the narration of your data collection process if you present your actions in a chronological manner. The main components that you could share in relation to your data collection process are recruiting potential participants, screening interested participants, completing informed consent, generating data and storing data. Below are questions to address to help you write about the data collection process (see Adu, 2016).

- *Recruiting potential participants*
  - Where will you find potential participants?
  - How do you plan to recruit participants?
  - Will you be using a flyer, poster, email and/or word of mouth?
  - How do you plan to implement your selected recruitment strategy?
- *Screening interested participants*
  - What do you plan to do to ensure that potential participants qualify to be a part of your study?
  - If you plan to use a screening questionnaire, where, when and how will you be administering it?
- *Completing informed consent*
  - How and where will the consent form or informed consent procedure be completed?
- *Generating data*
  - What will be the next step after the informed consent process has been completed?
  - What data collection strategy will you be using? Will it be interviews, online surveys, focus groups or observation (just to mention a few)?
  - If it is a survey, where will the participants be taking it?
  - If it is an interview, focus group or observation, where will it take place?
  - What will the participants be doing or completing to help generate data?
  - On average, how long will it take for the participants to complete the survey, interview and the like?

- How long is the data collection period?
- What tools will you be using to gather the data?
- What will you be doing at the data gathering stage?
- Will you be giving participants a token (or compensation) for being a part of the study? If yes, what will you give to them and how are they going to receive it?
- **Storing data**
    - How, where and when do you plan to store the data?

We recommend you address the above questions, arrange your responses in a chronological manner and write the data collection process with detail and clarity, promoting the reliability of your study and the credibility of your findings.

Summary

The task of data collection and data sampling are the most fundamental part of the research process. The foundation of all research is based on the task of data collection. This chapter discussed the essentials of quantitative data collection and qualitative data collection for novice and burgeoning researchers. The chapter provided a conceptual model and tool to help novice researchers and doctoral students understand the rudiments of quantitative data collection and qualitative data collection.

In this chapter we went through the procedure of planning your research. We discussed numerous items in terms of planning the research endeavor: defining the research problem; defining the research objective; determining the dissertation research model/design approach; determining the research method approach; determining the research design approach; determining the data need/type; determining the data need/type; preparing the consent form; ethical issues related to data collection; and, lastly, writing about the data collection process. By the end of this chapter, the reader should be able to understand how to plan and implement the data collection process.

We hope that this chapter has provided a foundation for novice researchers and doctoral students to understand quantitative data collection methods and qualitative data collection methods.

References

Adu, P. (2016, March 6). Writing the methodology chapter of a qualitative study by Philip Adu , Ph.D. [Video]. YouTube. www.youtube.com/watch?v=KRHvxY3N708

Adu, P. (2019). A step-by-step guide to qualitative data coding. Routledge.

Alasuutari, P., Bickman, L., & Brannen, L. (2002). The SAGE handbook of social media research methods. Sage Reference.

Babbie, E. (2008). *The basics of social research*. Wadsworth Publishing Company.

Babones, S. (2015). Interpretive quantitative methods for the social sciences. *Sociology, 50*(3), 453–469. https://doi.org/10.1177/0038038515583637

Barrett, M. (2008). Practical and ethical issues in planning research. In G. M. Breakwell, S. Hammond, & C. Fife-Schaw (Eds.), *Research methods in psychology* (pp. 24–48). John Wiley & Sons, Inc.

Baxter, P., & Jack, S. (2008). Qualitative case study methodology: Study design and implementation for novice researchers. *The Qualitative Report, 13*(4), 544–559. https://doi.org/10.46743/2160-3715/2008.1573

Bell, A (2003). A narrative approach to research. *Canadian Journal of Environmental Education, 8*, 95–110.

Bell, J. (2010). *Doing your research project: A guide for first-time researchers* (5th ed.). McGraw-Hill–Open University Press.

Blaxter, L., Hughes, C., & Tight, M. (2010). *How to research* (4th ed.). Open University Press-McGraw-Hill Education.

Botti, M., & Endacott, R. (2008). Clinical research 5: Quantitative data collection and analysis. *International Emergency Nursing, 16*(2), 132–137. https://doi.org/10.1016/j.aaen.2006.12.004

Bourenkov, G. P., & Popov, A. N. (2005). A quantitative approach to data-collection strategies. *Acta Crystallographica Section D Biological Crystallography, 62*(1), 58–64. https://doi.org/10.1107/s0907444905033998

Charmaz, K. (2014). Constructing grounded theory. SAGE Publications.

Cohen, L., Manion, L., & Morrison, K. (2018). *Research methods in education* (8th ed.). Routledge.

Creswell, J. W. (2012). *Educational research: Planning, conducting, and evaluating quantitative and qualitative research* (4th ed.). Pearson Education International.

Creswell, J. W. (2013). *Qualitative inquiry and research design: Choosing among five approaches* (3rd ed.). Sage.

Dale, A., Wathan, J., and Higgins, V. (2012). Secondary analysis of quantitative data sources. In P. Alasuutari, L. Bickman, & J. Brannen (Eds.), *The Sage handbook of social research methods* (pp. 520–535). SAGE Publications.

Dana, N. F., & Yendol-Hoppey, D. (2009). *The reflective educator's guide to classroom research: Learning to teach and teaching to learn through practitioner inquiry.* Corwin.

Dauter, Z. (1999). Data-collection strategies. *Acta Crystallographica Section D Biological Crystallography, 55*, 1703–1717.

Deutskens, E., de Ruyter, K., Wetzels, M., & Oosterveld, P. (2004). Response rate and response quality of internet-based surveys: An experimental study. *Marketing Letters, 15*, 21–36.

Eddles-Hirsch, K. (2015). Phenomenology and educational research. *International Journal of Advanced Research, 3*(8), 251–260.

Finn, J. A. (2005). *Getting a PhD: An action plan to help manage your research, your supervisor and your project.* Routledge Publishers.

Goertzen, M. J. (2017). *Applying quantitative methods to e-book collections.* Ala Techsource.

Goodwin, C. J., & Goodwin, K. A. (2013). *Research in psychology: Methods and design* (7th ed.). Wiley.

Hanson, W. E., Creswell, J. W., Plano Clark, V. L., Petska, K. S., & Creswell, J. D. (2005). Mixed methods research designs in counseling psychology. *Journal of Counseling Psychology, 52*(2), 224–235. Accessed from https://digitalcommons.unl.edu/psychfacpub/373

Jackson, S. L. (2009). *Research methods and statistics: A critical thinking approach.* Wadsworth.

Kothari, C. R. (2004). *Research methodology: Methods & techniques* (2nd ed.). New Age International.

Larsen, H. G., & Adu, P. (2021). The theoretical framework in phenomenological research: Development and application. Routledge

Leedy, P. E., & Ormrod, J. E. (2019). *Practical research: Planning and design* (12th ed.). Pearson.

Leedy, P. E., Ormrod, J. E., & Johnson, L. R. (2021). *Practical research: Planning and design.* Pearson.

Little, T. D. (2014). *The Oxford handbook of quantitative methods in psychology. Volume 2: Statistical analysis.* Oxford University Press.

Malhotra, N. K. (2015). *Essentials of marketing research: A hands-on approach.* Pearson.

Malhotra, N. K., & Birks, D. F. (2007). *Marketing research: An applied approach* (3rd ed.). Pearson.

McNiff, J., & Whitehead, J. (2010). *You and your action research project.* Routledge.

Meadows, K. (2003). So you want to do research? 4: An introduction to quantitative methods. *British Journal of Community Nursing, 8*(11), 519–526. https://doi.org/10.12968/bjcn.2003.8.11.11823

Miles, D. A. (2016). *The one-page dissertation proposal matrix: A guide for developing the dissertation proposal* [Unpublished document].

Miles, D. A., & Scott, L. (2017, October 26–29). *Confessions of a dissertation chair, Part 1: The six mistakes doctoral students make with the dissertation* [Workshop]. 5th Annual 2017 Black Doctoral Network Conference, Atlanta, GA.

Miller, G. J., & Yang, K. (2007). *Handbook of research methods in public administration.* CRC Press.

Murtagh, L. (2007). Implementing a critically quasi-ethnographic approach. *The Qualitative Report, 12*(2), 193–215. https://doi.org/10.46743/2160-3715/2007.1634

Price, P., Jhangiani, R., Chiang, I. C., Leighton, D., & Cuttler, C. (2017). *Research methods in psychology* (3rd ed.). Creative Commons Attribution-NonCommercial-ShareAlike.

Richmond, H. J. (2002). Learners' lives: A narrative analysis. *The Qualitative Report, 7*(3), 1–14. Retrieved from http://nsuworks.nova.edu/tqr/vol7/iss3/4

Saunders, M., Lewis, P., & Thornhill, A. (2009). *Research methods for business students* (5th ed.). Pearson Education Limited.

Sekaran, U. (2003). *Research methods for business: A skill-building approach.* Wiley Corporation.

Singh, S. (2020). *Methodological issues in management research: Advances, challenges and the way ahead.* Emerald Publishing Limited.

Sreejesh, S., Mohapatra, S., & Anusree, M. R. (2014). *Business research methods: An applied orientation.* Springer.

Strategic Prevention Solutions. (n.d.) *Example data collection methods.* www.strategicpreventionsolutions.com/

Sukamolson, S. (n.d.). *Fundamentals of quantitative research.* Maejo University. www.researchgate.net/publication/242772176_Fundamentals_of_quantitative_research

Swanson, R. A., & Holton, E. F. (2005). *Research in organizations: Foundations and methods of inquiry.* Berrett-Koehler Publishers.

Terrell, S. R. (2012). Mixed-methods research methodologies. *The Qualitative Report, 17*(1), 254–280. https://doi.org/10.46743/2160-3715/2012.1819

Terrell, S. R. (2016). *Writing a proposal for your dissertation: Guidelines and examples.* The Guilford Press.

Turner, S. M., Eisele, W. L., Benz, R. J., & Holdener, D. J. (1998). *Travel time data collection handbook.* Office of Highway Information Management, Federal Highway Administration, U.S. Dept. of Transportation.

Walliman, N. (2011). *Research methods: The basics* (2nd ed.). Oxon Routledge.

Yilmaz, K. (2013). Comparison of quantitative and qualitative research traditions: Epistemological, theoretical, and methodological differences. *European Journal of Education, 48*(2), 311–325.

Zikmund, W. G. & Babin, B. J. (2010). *Essentials of marketing research* (4th ed.). Thomson.

16 Understanding Populations and Sampling

Objectives

- Readers will be able to:
  1. Determine the population for their study
  2. Know the different types of sampling techniques
  3. Determine an appropriate sampling strategy for their study

Introduction

The practice of sampling is one of the most important parts of the study. Another very important aspect of conducting research is that the researcher needs to decide how to conduct a sample of a population. When the researcher has to conduct sampling, there are many types and categories of sampling that need to be considered. Based on your research methodology, different sampling methods need to be used. Consider that qualitative research typically focuses on a different form of sampling compared to a quantitative method. The researcher has to consider different sampling methods depending on the particular methodology. For example, you would not consider using purposeful sampling with a quantitative study or using random sampling with a qualitative study. Sampling has rules that need to be understood by the researcher.

Sampling is frequently employed to estimate the sizes of populations, groups and other types of populations. The practice of sampling has so many more uses for research. When researchers gather information obtained from properly selected populations, it can give rise to an interesting sample. The researcher must remember that the sample is selected from the sampling frame, which is a list of all the units from a population to be surveyed. Consider that the sampling frame will contain all the units of the population under consideration, which includes the target population. For example, many qualitative methods texts offer valuable types of sampling methods. Consider the theoretical sampling method. This aspect of theoretical sampling refers to data gathering directed by emerging concepts. With theoretical sampling, the researcher follows the process of the trailing of concepts, looking for sites, persons or events that will enable further comparisons of data.

DOI: 10.4324/9781003268154-16

In this chapter, we provide an introduction to many elements associated with sampling methods and define the basic terminology and underlying principles of sampling. The chapter goes on to explain sampling strategies and approaches to both quantitative and qualitative methodologies. The chapter also provides an introduction to sampling techniques to identify the differences between groups and populations.

Population, Sampling and Definitions

There are different terms that need to be introduced before we get into the finer points of sampling. There are some terms and definitions that need to be underscored.

A *population* is defined as an aggregate of units such as people, households, cities, districts, countries, states or provinces. It is also an entire group of people, events or things of interest that the researcher wishes to investigate (Rao, 2000; Upton & Cook, 2008; Sekaran & Bougie, 2013; Yaremko et al., 2013). A population under investigation depends on the nature of the investigation. A population may be homogenous or heterogeneous. A population can be homogenous when its every element is similar to each other in all aspects and when its elements are not similar to each other in all aspects. The variables that make a population heterogeneous can vary greatly from research to research. Common variables that make a population heterogeneous are gender, age, ethnicity, socioeconomic status and so on (Zedeck, 1986; Alvi, 2016).

A *target population* is defined as a collection of elements or objects that possess the information sought by the researcher and about which inferences are to be made. An *element* is a single entity of any given population which is not decomposable further. An element may be an individual, a household, a factory, a marketplace, a school, etc. What an element is going to be depends on the nature of the population. An element is also defined as a single member of the population. Think of a census as a count of all the elements in the human population (Malhotra et al., 2013; Alvi, 2016; Sekaran & Bougie, 2013). A *census* involves a complete enumeration of the elements of a population or study objects.

A *sample* can be defined as a subgroup of the elements of the population selected for participation in the study. Sampling is also defined as the selection of some part of an aggregate or totality on the basis of which a judgment or inference about the aggregate or totality is made (Upton & Cook, 2008; Yaremko et al., 2013; Haque, n.d.). A sample is a relatively small group of people selected from a population for investigation purposes. The members of the sample are called *participants*. A *sample* is measured to make generalizations about populations. In order words, a sample is a subset of a population. It is comprised of members selected from the population. Some but not all of the elements of a population form the sample (Sekaran & Bougie, 2013). A *sampling unit* is an element or set of elements that is available for selection at some stage of the sampling process. Some examples of sampling units in a multistage sample are city blocks, households and individuals within those households. A *subject* is considered a single member of the sample, just as an element is a single member of the population (Alvi, 2016; Malhotra et al., 2013; Sekaran & Bougie, 2013).

A *sampling frame* is a list that identifies the individual elements of the population. A sampling frame should contain all the elements of the population. It is from a frame, which is a list of all the units of the population to be surveyed, that a sample is selected. The frame should contain all the units of the population under consideration (Pedhazur & Pedhazur Schmelkin, 1991; Kerlinger & Lee, 1999; Rao, 2000; Thomas & Brubaker, 2000). A *sampling design* is a mathematical function that gives you the probability of any given sample being drawn. Considering that sampling is the foundation of nearly every research project, the study of sampling design is a crucial part of statistics. Sampling design involves not only learning how to derive the probability functions that describe a given sampling method but also understanding how to design a best-fit sampling method for a real-life situation (Glen, 2020).

A *sampling error* is a statistical error that occurs when a sample used in a study does not represent the entire population. Also, a sampling error is a measure of the departure of all the possible estimates of a probability sampling procedure from the population quantity being estimated. An important feature of probability sampling is that, in addition to providing an estimate of the unknown population quantity, it enables the assessment of the sampling error of the estimate, the standard error. These errors often occur in the process of sampling, which is analyzing a selected number of observations from a larger population. Furthermore, a sampling error is the value of difference between the sampled value versus the true or total population value (Rao, 2000; Calabrese, 2009; Beins & McCarthy, 2012; Lepcha, 2022).

Sampling bias is defined as bias that happens when the data sample in a systematic investigation does not accurately represent what is obtainable in the research environment. The samples of a stochastic variable that are collected to determine its distribution are selected incorrectly and do not represent the true distribution because of non-random reasons. Furthermore, when you collect data in such a way that some members of the intended population have a lower or higher sampling probability than others, often the result is sampling bias (Panzeri et al., 2008; FormPlus Blog, n.d.; Tao, 2022; Terrell, 2015). To reduce sampling bias, the two most important steps when designing a study or an experiment are (a) to avoid judgment or convenience sampling; and (b) to ensure that the target population is properly defined and that the sample frame matches it as closely as possible. When finite resources or efficiency reasons limit the possibility to sample the entire population, care should be taken to ensure that the excluded populations do not differ from the overall one in terms of the statistics to be measured. In the social sciences, population representative surveys most commonly are not simple random samples but follow more complex sample designs (Cochran, 1977).

Confirmation bias is defined as a tendency to seek information and sources that support our already held opinions. We tend to avoid sampling websites, opinion articles and news sources that contradict or challenge our values and views (Nardi, 2016).

A *unit of analysis* is defined as the basic entity or object about which generalizations are based in an analysis and for which data has been collected. The unit of analysis is determined by an interest in exploring or explaining a specific phenomenon. The unit of analysis is shaped by three attributes: (a) *social phenomena*; (b) *time*; and (c) *space*. An example would be observations of a single social entity, such as a person or an institution (Humphrey, 2001; Miles, 2019).

A *unit of observation* is defined as the who or what about which data is collected in a survey or the who or what being studied in an analysis. In a data set, this is represented by a row. The unit of observation refers to the category, type or classification to which each who or what belongs rather than to the specific people or objects included. It is also defined as the entity in primary research that is observed and about which information is systematically collected. The unit of observation is determined by the method by which observations are selected. An example would be observations of multiple entities with a defined relationship, such as family, employer-employee, etc. In order words, think of the unit of analysis as *singular* and the unit of observation as *plural*. For example, in the United States, the country is the unit of observation (plural), but each individual state is the unit of analysis (singular) (Miles, 2019).

Reasons for Sampling

Based on the definitions, sampling is used to take a piece of the population under investigation. Samples are selected, usually by some random process, so that they represent the population of interest. Sometimes, in the practice of research, populations are frequently best defined in terms of samples rather than vice versa; the population is the group from which you were able to randomly sample. We have to keep in mind that the sampling objective here is to ensure that all subjects come from the same population before you treat them differently. Normally, you take elaborate precautions to ensure that you have achieved a representative sample of that population; you define your population and then do your best to randomly sample from it.

The advantage of random sampling consists of randomly assigning subjects to treatment groups (levels of the independent variable) to ensure that, before differential treatment, all subsamples come from the same population. Statistical tests provide evidence as to whether, after treatment, all samples still come from the same population. Furthermore, generalizations about treatment effectiveness are made to the type of subjects who participated in the experiment (Tabachnick & Fidell, 2013). An interesting note is that only random sampling allows for findings of significance. How the sample was taken will determine whether the researcher can make scientific statements about the significance of their findings (Garson, 2002).

The following steps should be followed for good sampling: (1) describing the study population; (2) listing the members of the population; (3) identifying the sampling type; (4) determining the sample size; (5) selecting the sample; and (6) testing the representation power of the sample. The reliability of research is closely related to its repeatability. When writing up, the researcher should pay special attention to presenting information about the characteristics of the sample, including details on sampling strategies, that would enable others to repeat the research (Delice, 2010).

Advantages and Benefits of Sampling

There are many advantages of the practice of sampling in research. Most people view sampling as a compromise to be avoided whenever possible. It is much more feasible to examine a sample rather than a population. There are key primary advantages of sampling. First, it is feasible and economical. Studying a population of interest is not a viable option. The total coverage needed to study a population may be financially cost prohibitive. There is also the issue of the inefficient use of human resources. Sampling is mandatory in situations where the elements are destroyed or rendered useless in the process of obtaining the information sought. Another advantage is that it is more economical to collect a sample from a population rather than study the whole population (Pedhazur & Pedhazur Schmelkin, 1991).

A second benefit of sampling is the potential for increased accuracy. A sample may produce more accurate results than the kind of complete enumerations that can be taken. If accurate information is required for many subdivisions of the population, the size of the sample needed to do the job is sometimes so large that a complete enumeration offers the best solution (Cochran, 1977).

Sampling errors are a very common problem. Not surprisingly, the larger the data set is, the larger the percentage of nonsampling errors will be. In general, limiting the investigation to a sample affords improved management and control in such areas as the training and supervision of interviewers and testers, obtaining responses from participants and amassing and analyzing the data (Cochran, 1977; Pedhazur & Pedhazur Schmelkin, 1991).

A third advantage of sampling is speed. Data can be collected and summarized more quickly with a sample than with a complete count. Another advantage of sampling is scope. A complete census is not practical. The choice lies between obtaining the information by sampling or not at all. Thus, surveys that rely on sampling have more scope and flexibility regarding the types of information required for many subdivisions of the population (Pedhazur & Pedhazur Schmelkin, 1991; Tabachnick & Fidell, 2013).

A *state* is an ongoing duration of meaningful behavior. An *event* is a momentary behavior that happens so rapidly that it is normally recorded only as an occurrence and not a duration.

Events are often changes in states, such as a hen flying (state), landing on the ground (event), and then walking (state). All the sampling methods discussed above will be effective in recording the occurrence of states, but only continuous recording sampling methods (All Occurrences, Sequence and Sociometric Matrix) will effectively sample events (Christensen et al., 2003; Cokley & Awad, 2013; Lehner, 1992).

There are two other main advantages of sampling. One, it offers faster data collection and a lower cost. Second, each observation measures one or more properties of observable subjects distinguished as independent individuals.

Lastly, most commonly used in business research, medical research and agriculture research, sampling is widely used for gathering information about a population (Nanjundeswaraswamy & Divakar, 2021). There are three major sources of error in a survey: (1) *sampling variability*, generally called *sampling error*, which depends on the sample size and design; (2) *sample biases*, which are a function of how well the study design is executed; and (3) *response effects*, which are the differences between the reported and true measures of behavior, characteristics or attitudes (Sudman, 1976).

The Sampling Process

The objective of sampling is to select a specific number of people in a population. The practice of sampling is a process that is important to conducting research. Thus, there is a need to select a sample. Again, the objective of sampling is for the researcher to draw from a population. Figure 16.1 illustrates the major steps in the sampling process.

Before choosing a specific type of sampling technique, a broad sampling technique needs to be decided on. One of the difficult aspects of research is launching an experience-sampling study. It can provide a challenge to even the most seasoned researcher (Christensen et al., 2003). When a researcher decides to begin the research process, they must go through the sampling process first. The first stage in the sampling process is to clearly define the problem. Defining the problem is the basis for all research. This also relates to determining the sampling frame. The sampling frame must be representative of the population of interest. This is vital to the research.

The next step is to determine the sample design. Establishing the sample design is very important to the researcher. The next step is to determine the appropriate sample size for the study. We have to remember that the population is commonly related to the number of people living in a particular area of the country. Lastly, the researcher has to execute the sampling process. Again, sampling can be used to make inferences about a population.

Types of Sampling

The practice of sampling can be used to make an inference about a population or to make a generalization in relation to an existing theory. This is based on the choice of sampling technique.

The practice of evaluating the characteristics of an entire population through a representative sample can be an arduous endeavor. As with many research studies, the best strategy to investigate a problem in an entire population is through the use of sampling. How, it is not always possible to conduct a study on an entire population. So, we use the practice of sampling. Thus, the researcher studies a sample of the population, which is a suitable representation of the entire population. We must think of a sample as a subset of the population; thus it is selected to be representative of the population. Again, one of the advantages of sampling is that it can be less costly and more efficient. Being able to use a sample to generalize the results to

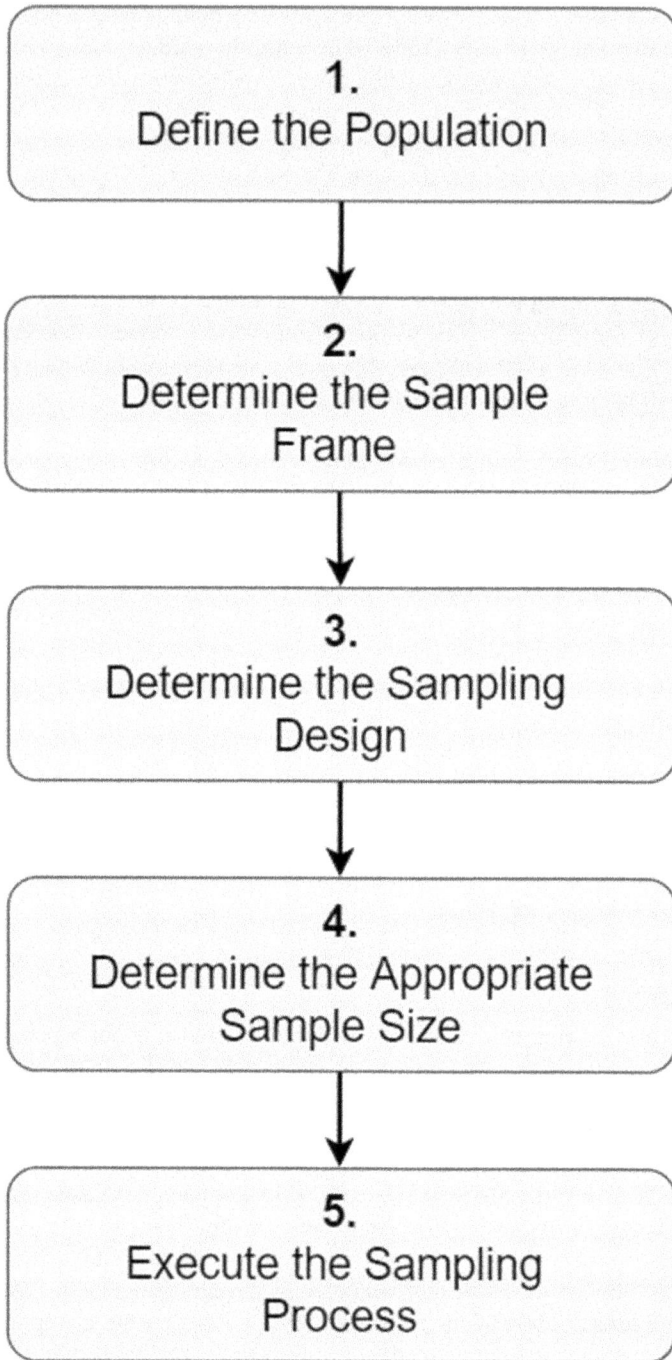

Figure 16.1 The sampling process.

Source: Adopted from Sekaran and Bougie (2013).

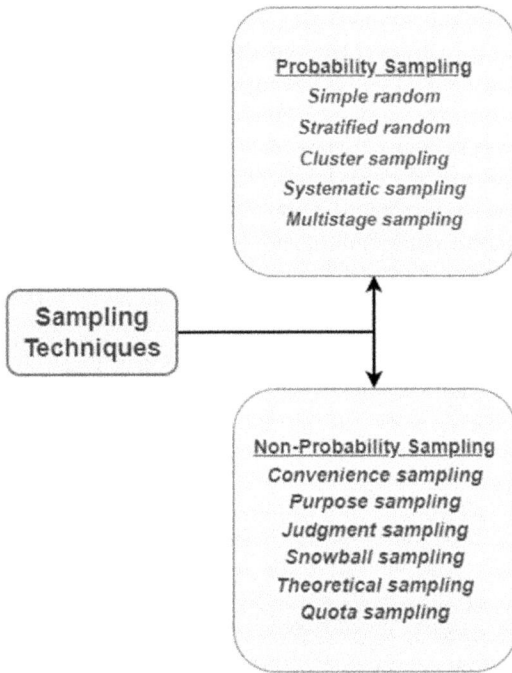

Figure 16.2 Types of sampling techniques.

a whole population requires the use of one of the statistical sampling methods for evaluation. Taking a subset from a chosen sampling frame or entire population is the basic practice of sampling.

There are many types of sampling techniques. However, there are two basic types: (a) *probability* or *random sampling*; and (b) *non-probability sampling*. Before choosing a specific type of sampling technique, a broad sampling technique needs to be decided on. Figure 16.2 shows the various types of sampling techniques (Acharya et al., 2013; Taherdoost, 2016).

Probability Sampling

The definition of *probability sampling* is that every item in the population has an equal chance of being included in the sample. The key is, if all participants are equally likely to be selected in the study, *equiprobability sampling* is being used. The odds of being selected by the research team may be expressed by the formula: $P=1/N$, where P equals the probability of taking part in the study and N corresponds to the size of the target population (Martínez-Mesa et al., 2016).

An interesting aspect of probability sampling methods is that they share three properties. First, the sampling units' selection process is random. Second, each potential sampling unit has a known probability of being selected for the sample, which is different from zero. Lastly, it is possible to identify all potential samples of a given size that can be drawn from the population before the actual selection process starts (Sarstedt et al., 2017). In the context of probability sampling, all units of the target population have a nonzero probability of taking part in the study. Probability sampling is the most favored form of sampling by the research community. In this method, there are five primary sampling designs that are preferred for accurate, unbiased sampling (Nanjundeswaraswamy & Divakar, 2021).

One way to undertake random sampling is for the researcher to construct a sampling frame first and then use a random number generation computer program to pick a sample from the sampling frame (Lancaster & Keller-McNulty, 1998; Zikmund, 2003; Westfall, 2009). The major advantage of probability sampling is that it has the greatest freedom from bias but may represent the costliest sample in terms of time and energy for a given level of sampling error (Taherdoost, 2016).

ADVANTAGES OF PROBABILITY SAMPLING

There are three key advantages of probability sampling. First, the probability sampling technique reduces the chance of systematic errors. Second, the probability methods minimize the chance of sampling biases. Lastly, probability sampling provides a better representative sample, and inferences drawn from the sample are generalizable to the whole population (Alvi, 2016).

DISADVANTAGES OF PROBABILITY SAMPLING

The disadvantages are minimal. There are three key disadvantages of probability sampling. First, probability sampling requires a considerable amount of effort. Second, it requires a lot of time. Lastly, probability sampling is costly. It tends to be more expensive and not cost prohibitive (Alvi, 2016).

Quantitative Sampling Methodology

In the practice of quantitative research, the primary goal of quantitative sampling is to get a representative sample from a much larger population. To accomplish this task, researchers may resort to probabilistic sampling (i.e., each member of the population has the same probability of being included in the sample). In quantitative research, the intent of sampling is to choose individuals who are representative of a population so that results can be generalized to it (external validity) (Gelo et al., 2008).

With quantitative sampling, the researcher can study the smaller group and produce accurate generalizations about the larger group. An interesting aspect of quantitative sampling is that researchers focus on the specific techniques that will yield highly representative samples (i.e., samples that are like the population). Lastly, quantitative researchers tend to use a type of sampling based on theories of probability from mathematics, which is called probability sampling (Tao, 2022; Hancock & Mueller, 2010).

The practice of probability sampling is based on a sampling technique in which each unit in a population has a specifiable chance of being selected. The rationale behind using probability sampling is to generate a sample that is representative of the population from which it was drawn. With probability and random sampling, it does not guarantee that every random sample perfectly represents the population. Instead, what it means is that the sample will be close to the population most of the time, and that one can calculate the probability of a particular sample being accurate (Alvi, 2016; Tong, 2006; Gelo et al., 2008; Singh & Masuku, 2013; Sarstedt et al., 2017).

Quantitative Sampling Designs for Research

Simple Random Sampling

Simple random sampling is a method in which any two groups of equal size in the population are equally likely to be selected. Mathematically, simple random sampling selects n units out of a population of size N. So that every sample of size n has an equal chance of being drawn in this case, we have a full list of sample units or participants (sample basis), and we randomly select individuals using a table of random numbers. This sampling technique provides an unbiased and better estimate of the parameters if the population is homogeneous (Brown, 1947; Sudman, 1976; Lomax, 2001; Acharya et al., 2013; Singh & Masuku, 2013; Taherdoost, 2016; Fricker, 2020; Rai & Thapa, 2015).

In situations where the population is heterogeneous regarding the measures of interest, simple random sampling easily leads to estimates with unacceptably high variance, especially when the sample size is restricted. Interestingly, in survey research, much time and effort are spent in following a method of simple random sampling until an individual is actually identified and enrolled in the sample. However, this is called *cluster sampling*. Given that there is usually a tendency for individuals found within a cluster to share characteristics, however, the use of cluster sampling can be expected to decrease the precision of the sample result (Lasswell, 1949; Henderson & Sundaresan, 1982; Scheaffer et al., 2006; Sarstedt et al., 2017).

Systematic Random Sampling

Systematic random sampling is when participants are selected from fixed intervals previously defined from a ranked list of participants. Systematic sampling is when every nth case after a random start is selected. With systematic sampling, the selection of the first subject is done randomly, and then the subsequent subjects are selected by a periodic process. A systematic random sample is one in which every kth item is selected; k is determined by dividing the number of items in the sampling frame by the desired sample size. An initial starting point is selected by a random process, and then every kth number on the list is selected.

This type of sampling provides a better estimate of the parameters in a study compared to purposive sampling. This is because every single individual in the sampling frame has a known and non-zero chance of being selected into the sample. For this reason, it is the ideal and recognized single stage random sampling. The advantage of this sampling is that it has moderate usage and moderate cost, internal and external validity is high, and it is simple to draw and easy to verify. The disadvantage is that, technically, only the selection of the first subject is a probability selection, since for subsequent selections there will be subjects with zero chance of selection (Scheaffer et al., 2006; Tabachnick & Fidell, 2013; Acharya et al., 2013; Singh & Masuku, 2013; Taherdoost, 2016; Rao, 2000; Martino et al., 2018).

Stratified Sampling

Stratified sampling is most suitable when the population consists of heterogeneous subpopulation groups. Stratified sampling is used when the population is divided into strata (or subgroups) and a random sample is taken from each subgroup. A subgroup is a natural set of items. Subgroups might be based on company size, gender or occupation (to name but a few). Stratified sampling is often used where there is a great deal of variation within a population. In this type of sampling, the target population is first divided into separate strata. Then, samples are selected within each stratum, either through simple or systematic sampling. The total number of individuals to be selected in each stratum can be fixed or proportional to the size of each stratum. Each individual may be equally likely to be selected to participate in the study. However, the fixed method usually involves the use of sampling weights in the statistical analysis (inverse of the probability of selection or $1/P$). With stratified sampling, the sampling error depends on the population variance within the stratum but not between the strata (Sudman, 1976; Lomax, 2001; Scheaffer et al., 2006; Tong 2006; Acharya et al., 2013; Singh & Masuku, 2013; Taherdoost, 2016; Nanjundeswaraswamy & Divakar, 2021). There are two types of stratified sampling approaches:

- ***Proportionate stratified sampling***. In proportionate stratified sampling, variables are selected for the sample based on their original distribution in the population of interest. This shows that the relative size of a stratum in the population of interest determines the likelihood of selecting a variable from that stratum for the sample.
- ***Disproportionate stratified sampling***. It is common for social science researchers to employ this method when they do not select a sample representing the entire population they wish to research. The idea is that people from various groups will not have the same possibilities of being included in the research sample (Rahman et al., 2022).

Cluster Sampling

Cluster sampling is also known as *area sampling*. Cluster sampling is used when the whole population is divided into clusters or groups. Subsequently, a random sample is taken from these clusters, all of which are used in the final sample. In cluster sampling, the total population is divided into a number of relatively small subdivisions or groups, which are themselves clusters. However, some of these clusters are then randomly selected for inclusion in the sample. Cluster sampling is advantageous for those researchers whose subjects are fragmented over large geographical areas, as it saves time and money. Another advantage of using cluster sampling is economical, but in reducing the cost by concentrating on the selected clusters, it gives less precision than the simple random sampling (Etikan & Bala, 2017).

A cluster random sample is a two-step process in which the entire population is divided into clusters or groups, usually geographic areas or districts such as villages, schools, wards, blocks, etc. It is more commonly used in epidemiologic research than in clinical research. It is most practical to be used in large national surveys. The clusters are chosen randomly. All individuals in the cluster are taken in the sample. Usually, it requires a larger sample size. Cluster sampling is very useful when the population is widely scattered and it is impractical to sample and select a representative sample of all the elements (Sudman, 1976; Lomax, 2001; Scheaffer et al., 2006; Acharya et al., 2013; Taherdoost, 2016; Haque, n.d.; Nanjundeswaraswamy & Divakar, 2021).

Multi-Stage Sampling

Multi-stage sampling is an additional progression of the belief that cluster sampling has. Normally, the multi-stage sampling design is applicable to big inquiries of a geographical area, e.g., an entire country. For example, multi-stage sampling in combination with the various methods of probability sampling is the most effective and efficient approach (Etikan & Bala, 2017). Multi-stage sampling is a process of moving from a broad to a narrow sample using a step-by-step process. This is a complex form of cluster sampling because it involves two or more levels of units that are embedded one in the other. It involves the repetition of two basic steps, i.e., listing and sampling. Typically, at each stage the cluster gets smaller in size, and in the end subject sampling is done.

So, the population is organized into groups; subsequently, groups are randomly selected and then the members are randomly selected in these groups (an equal number selected per group). This method of sampling is mostly carried out to increase precision and reduce and non-response (Scheaffer et al., 2006; Acharya et al., 2013; Martínez-Mesa et al., 2016; Taherdoost, 2016).

How to Avoid Sampling Bias

Sampling bias is said to occur when the selected sample does not truly reflect the characteristics of the population. The best way to avoid sampling bias is to stick to *probability-based sampling methods*. These include simple random sampling, systematic sampling, cluster sampling and stratified sampling. In these methodologies, respondents are only chosen through processes of random selection, even if they are sometimes sorted into demographic groups along the way.

The opposite form of sampling is called *non-probability sampling*, and it injects forms of bias into data collection. This bias can come down to convenience, as is the case in convenience sampling, or it can involve predetermined ideas about a population of interest, as is the case in quota sampling. Non-probability sampling does play a role in data collection and analysis. Among other things, it's typically more affordable than true random sampling, but its downside is its vulnerability to bias (Alvi, 2016; Tao, 2022). Tao (2022) outlines the six types of sampling bias:

1. **Self-selection bias**. Also known as non-response bias, this source of bias plagues studies that rely on voluntary responses. When samples show self-selection bias, they over-represent the subset of the population that feels some sort of inclination to weigh in on an issue. For example, in presidential election polls, self-selection bias has been shown to over-represent people who trust institutions (such as polling firms) and closely follow the news.
2. **Observer bias**. This type of sampling bias often pops up when researchers weave their own opinions into questionnaires, which can impede people from answering neutrally. Surveys weighed down by loaded questions often surface in the partisan polling industry.
3. **Survivorship bias**. Survivorship bias overweighs respondents who have "survived" the selection criteria but don't necessarily represent an overall population. For instance, surveying high school graduates about the efficacy of public schools may cut out the needed perspective of dropouts who did not earn a diploma.
4. **Undercoverage bias**. Also called exclusion bias, this occurs when a population of interest is under-surveyed by researchers. This can sometimes trace back to the practice of convenience sampling, where researchers and field workers only survey individuals who are easy to reach.
5. **Healthy user bias**. This type of bias is most commonly found in health studies, which can oversample healthy members of a population.
6. **Berkson's fallacy**. The opposite of a healthy user bias, Berkson's fallacy occurs when surveyors only study those who are very ill, such as hospital patients. In this situation, healthy people end up under-represented (Tao, 2022).

A summary of probability sampling designs is illustrated in Table 16.1.

Non-probability Sampling

The practice of sampling has a non-probability, non-statistical based counterpart. This is called *non-probability sampling*. The practice of non-probability sampling is most often associated with qualitative research methodology and design. With non-probability sampling, a sample of participants does not need to be representative of the population or random, but a clear rationale is needed for the inclusion of some individuals rather than others. Non-probability sampling means one cannot generalize beyond the sample. The practice of non-probability sampling allows for selection bias to occur based on the type of person that would opt in to complete a survey online (Lamm & Lamm, 2019).

Table 16.1 Probability sampling research designs

Sampling Design	Characteristics	Pros	Cons
Simple random sampling	Each person in the population has an equal chance of being selected.	The process is easy to follow and viewed as fair, as each person can be selected.	A complete and up-to-date list is needed for all persons in the population. This information is often not available.
Systematic sampling	Selection is based on a systematic algorithm such as every 5th or 10th person.	Easier to conduct than simple random sampling and tends to select more evenly across the population.	The selection process can miss an important characteristic of the population based on the use of the systematic algorithm.
Stratified random sampling	Sampling involves dividing the population into smaller groups called strata, which are formed based on shared and/or unique characteristics.	A stratified sample should be more representative of the population, as it considers shared and/or unique characteristics during selection. This approach should increase the external validity and generalizability of the study.	Stratified sampling is not useful when the population cannot be exhaustively divided into shared or unique characteristics. Another problem exists when the strata cannot be divided into appropriate proportional sizes.
Cluster sampling	Naturally occurring groups are selected as sampling clusters. For example, specific schools in a district may be selected rather than all schools in the district.	Cluster sampling is highly economical and feasible when dealing with large populations. In addition, cluster sampling usually avoids reduced variation.	If the naturally occurring group selected as a cluster has a bias, then the population might be assumed to also have that bias. Use of selection rather than random probabilities can increase error.
Multistage sampling	A complex form of cluster sampling in which two or more levels of units are embedded one in the other. It involves the repetition of two basic steps, e.g, listing and sampling. Typically, at each stage the cluster gets smaller in size, and in the end subject sampling is done.	It is cost prohibitive. Multi-stage sampling is a cheaper alternative to random sampling. It is extremely useful, as it involves multiple stages of randomization. The costs are thereby reduced as compared to traditional cluster sampling (Acharya et al., 2013; Taherdoost, 2016).	It is not as robust as true random sampling but probably helps to resolve the limitations inherent in random sampling. Multi-stage sampling is used frequently when a complete list of all the members of the population does not exist and/or is inappropriate. Also, multi-stage sampling does not cover all survey participants, and study outcomes cannot be 100% accurate (Rahman et al., 2022).

Source: Berndt, 2020; Gill, 2020; Acharya et al., 2013; Scheaffer et al., 2006; Taherdoost, 2016; Rahman et al., 2022.

One of the interesting aspects of non-probability sampling is that there are no principles embraced by all non-probability sampling methods. Each method embraces different principles and fulfils different criteria, depending on the objectives and aims of the research. Therefore, it is not surprising that the term non-probability sampling covers a broad range of sampling methods that considerably vary in their qualities and features (Yang & Banamah, 2014). Quantitative sampling techniques, therefore, are designed to accommodate these goals of minimizing bias and maximizing generalizability. On the other hand, qualitative sampling focuses on minimizing bias, but maximizing generalizability is not a primary goal of qualitative research. Nevertheless, rather than aiming to generalize about large populations, the purpose of qualitative studies is to offer a "window-like" or "mirror-like" view on the specific situation or phenomenon in the investigation (Koerber & McMichael, 2008).

Researchers must remember that quantitative methods are used to describe the investigated phenomena and expand on a macro-level and to guide qualitative sampling. On the other hand, qualitative research provides the information necessary for fully fledged explanatory arguments, which can be further examined by subsequent quantitative research. The purpose of qualitative research is to gain a deeper understanding of a phenomenon rather than to generalizing the findings (Kelle, 2008; Naderifar et al., 2017). With regards to the qualitative research methodology, non-probability sampling tends to focus on small samples and is intended to examine a real-life phenomenon. However, it is not intended to make statistical inferences in relation to the wider population (Yin, 2003; Acharya et al., 2013; Taherdoost, 2016). Non-probability samples are those in which the probability that a subject is selected is unknown and results in selection bias in the study. They include the most commonly used types of sampling, including convenience sampling, purposive sampling, quota sampling, snowball sampling and so on.

Qualitative Sampling Methodology

In the practice of qualitative research, the primary goal of qualitative sampling is to comprehend, i.e., aspire to reconstruct the personal perspectives, experiences and understandings of the individual actors. Qualitative studies aim to provide illumination and understanding of complex psychosocial issues and are most useful for answering humanistic "why?" and "how?" questions. Qualitative research has always been the preferred method to explore new theories and provide support to different phenomena (Altmann, 1974; Gelo et al., 2008; Shaheen et al., 2019).

In qualitative research, the intent of sampling is to focus in depth on small samples, even a single sampling unit ($n = 1$), selected purposefully for the study. A qualitative sampling technique is one in which each unit in a population does not have a specifiable probability of being selected. In other words, in the practice of non-probability sampling, the researcher does not select their units from the population in a random way. Consequently, because non-probability sampling takes a nonrandom approach, it typically produces samples that are not representative of the population. This means the ability to generalize from the population is highly limited (Altmann, 1974; Marshall, 1996; Alvi, 2016; Gelo et al., 2008; Shaheen et al., 2019).

Qualitative inquiry has no stringent rules regarding the sample size. It depends on the purpose of the research, research question(s), research method and what is the line of research that can be undertaken within the timeframe and use the resources at hand. So, an appropriate sample size for a qualitative study is one that adequately answers the research question. Furthermore, with the practice of qualitative research, it is considered meaningful if the sample selected is information-rich and the analytical capabilities of the researcher are high (Marshall, 1996; Shaheen et al., 2019). Relying on recommendations by qualitative researchers and best practices (in terms of the sample sized used to attain rich data and/or arrive at saturation in a study that uses a particular research method) would help in getting an estimate of an adequate sample size for one's qualitative study.

Qualitative approaches make use almost exclusively of purposive sampling strategies. Shaheen et al. (2019) argues that these allow "information-rich cases to be studied in depth" (p. 154). These sampling strategies include, among others: convenience sampling, homogeneous case sampling (i.e., picking elements from a subgroup to study in depth), snowball sampling (e.g., using informants to identify cases that would be useful to include in the study), extreme/deviant and typical case sampling (which involve seeking out, respectively, the most outstanding cases in order to learn as much as possible about the outliers – or the most average cases from a subpopulation) (Shaheen et al., 2019; Marshall, 1996). The credibility and transferability of the findings of qualitative research rely heavily on the information provided by the participants of the sample. In terms of data collection in qualitative research, data has to be collected in order to allow an in-depth understanding of the participants' perspective (Shaheen et al., 2019).

Qualitative Sampling Designs for Research

Convenience Sampling

Convenience sampling is a non-probability sampling technique that attempts to obtain a sample of convenient elements. The selection of sampling units is primarily left to the discretion of the interviewer. Convenience sampling (also known as *haphazard sampling* or *accidental sampling*) is also a type of non-probability or nonrandom sampling, where members of the target population that meet certain practical criteria, such as easy accessibility, geographical proximity, availability at a given time or the willingness to participate, are included for the purpose of the study (Malhotra et al., 2013; Etikan et al., 2016). The main objective of convenience sampling is to collect information from participants who are easily accessible to the researcher, such as recruiting providers attending a staff meeting for study participation (Etikan et al., 2016). So, the convenience sampling method includes members of the population who are available to the researcher at the time of the research. For example, a researcher asking questions from passers-by on the street is another example of this method of sampling. This method is also called *accidental sampling* (Naderifar et al., 2017).

This is the most commonly used sampling method. The sample is chosen on the basis of the convenience of the investigator. Often the respondents are selected because they are in the right place at the right time. Convenience sampling is most commonly used in clinical research, where patients who meet the inclusion criteria are recruited in the study. The advantages are that they are most commonly used, less expensive and there is no need for a list of all the population elements. However, they are not without limitations, the foremost being that variability and bias cannot be measured or controlled. Secondly, results from the data cannot be generalized beyond the sample (Acharya et al., 2013). It is not a mutually exclusive category of the sampling technique; rather, many other non-probability techniques are purposive in nature. Thus, all the other types of sampling techniques are described under the heading of purposive sampling. In purposive sampling the sample is approached with a prior purpose in mind. The criteria of the elements to be included in the study is predefined (Taherdoost, 2016; Alvi, 2016).

Convenience sampling is selecting participants because they are often readily and easily available. Typically, convenience sampling tends to be a favored sampling technique among students as it is inexpensive and an easy option compared to other sampling techniques (Ackoff, 1953; Taherdoost 2016). However, convenience sampling has some serious limitations. It has the potential to be prone to selection bias. Convenience sampling is also not representative of a population. This type of sampling is not appropriate for research involving population inferences. Lastly, convenience sampling is not appropriate for descriptive research or causal research. However, it can be used for pre-test studies or pilot studies (Malhotra et al., 2013). Convenience sampling often helps to overcome many of the limitations associated with research.

Convenience sampling has the reputation of being the least rigorous technique and involving the selection of the most accessible subjects. Conversely, it is the least costly to the researcher in terms of time, effort and money. There is an element of convenience sampling in many qualitative studies, but a more thoughtful approach to the selection of a sample is usually justified. The obvious disadvantage of convenience sampling is that it is likely to be biased. It is advised that researchers must understand convenience sampling should not be taken to be representative of the population (Marshall, 1996; Szolnoki & Hoffmann, 2013; Wilson, 2014; Etikan et al., 2016).

Purposive Sampling

Purposive sampling is the most common non-probability sampling technique. This is a sampling strategy in which particular settings, persons or events are selected deliberately in order to provide important information that cannot be obtained from other choices (Maxwell, 1996; Taherdoost, 2016). The purposive sampling technique is the deliberate choice of a participant due to the qualities the participant possesses. It is a nonrandom technique that does not need underlying theories or a set number of participants. It is where the researcher includes cases or participants in the sample because they believe that they warrant inclusion and would help in generating rich data.

The main objective of purposive sampling is to focus on characteristics of a population that are of interest and that will best enable you to answer your research questions. The sample being studied is not representative of the population, but for researchers pursuing qualitative or mixed methods research designs this is not considered to be a weakness (Rai &Thapa, 2015). The goal of purposive sampling is to produce a sample that can be considered "representative" of the population. The selection of a purposive sample is often accomplished by using expert knowledge of the population to select, in a nonrandom manner, a sample of elements that represents a cross-section of the population (Etikan et al., 2016). An example of purposive sampling is the selection of a sample of jails from which prisoner participants will be sampled. This is referred to as two-stage sampling, but the first-stage units are not selected using probability sampling techniques (Desai & Potter, 2006; "Non-probability Sampling," n.d.).

Judgment Sampling

Judgment sampling is one type of purposeful sampling. "Judgement sampling is a form of non-probability sampling which the population elements are selected based on the judgement of the researcher" (Marshall, 1996, p. 277). Furthermore, with this sampling approach, the researcher makes a decision on who to recruit based on, but not limited to, the knowledge they have about the phenomenon of study, their opinion of who will be the great source of information they are looking for, and knowledge gained from gatekeepers about the potential research site. The advantages of judgmental sampling are that it is inexpensive, convenient and quick, but it cannot be used as a representative of the population (Marshall, 1996; Malhotra, et al., 2013). This sampling technique is similar to convenience sampling. The main difference is that, with the practice of convenience sampling, the researcher actively selects the most accessible and available sample to answer the research question.

If potential participants are known to the researcher, they may be stratified according to known public attitudes or beliefs. Judgmental sampling may be advantageous when studying a broad range of subjects (maximum variation sample), outliers (deviant sample), subjects who have specific experiences (critical case sample) or subjects with special expertise (key informant sample) (Marshall, 1996; Yang & Banamah, 2014; Naderifar et al., 2017; Sarstedt et al., 2017). This sampling technique is useful when using a phenomenological approach influenced by transcendental phenomenology. With this research approach, the researcher needs to apply *imaginative variation*, which starts with recruiting participants with a diversity of specified characteristics so that variance of the experience is well captured during the data collection stage (see Larsen & Adu, 2021). For instance, by utilizing judgmental sampling, you could sample participants across gender, specified age groups, departments (if you are recruiting from an organization) and/or levels of organizational leadership.

Quota Sampling

Quota sampling is another type of purposeful sampling. This is a non-probability sampling technique where the sample of individuals obtained matches the proportions of individuals for the entire population of interest (Moser & Stuart, 1953). This is so that the total sample will have the same distribution of characteristics as the wider population (Davis, 2005; Taherdoost, 2016). Furthermore, quota sampling is especially important if you have a very specific, targeted group of individuals for your research study and do not necessarily know their demographic breakdown in advance (Lamm & Lamm, 2019). It is the sampling procedure that ensures that a certain characteristic of a population sample will be represented to the exact extent that the investigator desires. Stratified sampling and quota sampling are similar in that, in both, population is divided into categories/strata and subjects are selected from each category. The purpose is to select a representative sample and/or to allow subgroup analyses (Acharya et al., 2013).

However, there are certain differences between *stratification* and *quota* sampling. In the former, the selection of subjects is by simple random sampling once the categories have been created. The basic idea of quota sampling is to set a target number of completed interviews with specific subgroups of the population of interest. Ideally, the target size of the subgroups is based on known information about the target population (such as census data). "A sampling frame is required for stratified sampling but not for quota sampling. More importantly, stratified sampling" (Daniel, 2012, p. 141) uses probability sampling, thus permitting an estimation of sampling error, which is not possible with quota samples (Acharya et al., 2013; "Non-probability Sampling," n.d.).

Often, quota sampling is comparable to stratified sampling. The fundamental difference between quota sampling and probability sampling lies in the last stage. If the participants in quota sampling are assigned equal probability of being included in the sample, then quota sampling will be equivalent to stratified sampling, which is a probability sampling method, and the results of both methods should be the same or very close (Yang & Banamah, 2014). Nevertheless, because the method for choosing the participants in quota sampling is left to the discretion of the interviewers, the samples drawn with the two methods agree only in the quota controls and may vary in other characteristics. In the practice of quota sampling, the entire population is divided into relevant strata, such as gender, age, class, etc. These strata are called "quota controls," and they are chosen according to their relevancy to the topic of interest. One of the "well-known users of quota sampling including many well-established polling agencies such as Gallop in the USA and Mori in the UK would argue that these characteristics – and therefore the potential biases – are irrelevant to the topic of concern and that the efficiency and low cost of quota sampling will outweigh the potential bias" (Yang & Banamah, 2014, p. 6).

Snowball Sampling

In this sampling procedure, the initial respondents are chosen by probability or non-probability methods, then additional respondents are obtained by information provided by the initial respondents (Acharya et al., 2013). Snowball sampling is a variation of the convenience sampling method. The snowball sampling method, which is also known as the "chain method," is an efficient and cost effective way of accessing people who would otherwise be very difficult to find. Snowball sampling is a nonrandom sampling method that uses a few cases to help encourage other cases to take part in the study, thereby increasing sample size (Naderifar et al., 2017).

This approach is most applicable in small populations that are difficult to access due to their closed nature, e.g., secret societies and inaccessible professions (Breweton & Millward, 2001; Taherdoost, 2016). One clear advantage of snowball sampling is that the method is applied when it is difficult to access subjects with the target characteristics. In this non-probability method, the existing study subjects recruit future subjects among their acquaintances. Sampling continues until data saturation. Also in this method, the researcher asks the first few samples, who are usually selected via convenience sampling, if they know anyone with similar views or situations to take part in the research (Naderifar et al., 2017). The snowball method not only takes little time but also provides the researcher with the opportunity to communicate better with the participants, as they are acquaintances of the first participant or group of participants, and the first sample is linked to the researcher. One of the greatest advantages of the snowball method is that this type of networking is particularly useful for finding people who are unwilling to reveal their identities (e.g., people who are addicted to illegal substances) (Naderifar et al., 2017). A summary of non-probability sampling designs is illustrated in Table 16.2.

Theoretical Sampling

Theoretical sampling is defined as a sampling strategy "that involves the purposive sampling of further data while a theoretical framework is still under construction." Furthermore, "to gain a deeper understanding of the constructs involved, the researcher samples new research sites, cases, incidents, time periods, or data sources to compare with those that have already been studied. In this way, they seek to build a theory from the emerging data while continuing to select new samples to examine and elaborate on the theory" (American Psychological Association, n.d.). Another definition of theoretical sampling is *analysis-driven purposeful sampling* or *analysis-governed purposeful sampling*. In some situations, the practice of purposeful sampling could be confused with theoretical sampling. These two sampling techniques certainly resemble each other insofar as both involve a more clearly defined purpose than that involved in selecting a convenience sample. In purposeful sampling, however, the sampling criteria are developed in advance of the study, and the sample does not change throughout the study (Koerber & McMichael, 2008).

In the practice of theoretical sampling, by contrast, the criteria for sampling emerge along with the study itself. Furthermore, theoretical sampling differs from purposeful sampling in that theoretical sampling is a basic tenet of grounded theory and thus should always be understood in that context (Koerber & McMichael, 2008; Robbins, 2017). An important note about the pitfall of theoretical sampling would be a researcher using this technique without having an adequate understanding of

Table 16.2 Non-probability sampling research designs

Sampling Design	Characteristics	Pros	Cons
Convenience sampling	This is the most commonly used sampling method. The sample is chosen on the basis of the convenience of the investigator. Often the respondents are selected because they are in the right place at the right time. Convenience sampling is most commonly used in clinical research, where patients who meet the inclusion criteria are recruited in the study.	It is the most commonly used sampling method. The sample is chosen on the basis of the convenience of the investigator. Often the respondents are selected because they are in the right place at the right time. Convenience sampling is most commonly used in clinical research, where patients who meet the inclusion criteria are recruited in the study.	The foremost con is that variability and bias cannot be measured or controlled. Secondly, results from the data cannot be generalized beyond the sample.
Purposive sampling	Uses sampling techniques that rely on the researcher's judgment for selecting persons. These techniques include maximum variation sampling, expert sampling and typical case sampling. There are two types of purposive sampling: (a) judgment sampling; and (b) quota sampling.	Purposive sampling can help researchers justify selections based on analytical, logical or theoretical grounds. Purposive sampling is not used. Quota sampling can be useful in qualitative research that has multiple phases and/or aims.	Purposive sampling can be prone to researcher bias, particularly if rules or criteria for judgment are poorly documented or explained. In addition, purposive sampling can make it difficult to defend the representativeness of the population.
Quota sampling	Based on identifying strata with shared or unique characteristics of the population and selecting persons proportionate to the population.	Quota sampling is quicker and easier to conduct than stratified sampling because random sampling is not used. Quota sampling makes it easier to explore distinctions in subgroups.	As random sampling is not used, sampling error cannot be calculated. Further, sampling bias is a possibility. Finally, it can be difficult to draw conclusions about the population.
Snowball sampling	Strategy in which existing participants recruit future participants from others they know. Strategy is often used for hard-to-recruit populations.	Very useful strategy when persons in the population are difficult to identify and hard to recruit.	As random selection is not used, sampling error cannot be calculated and the degree of confidence in the interpretation cannot be determined.

| *Theoretical sampling* | The researcher samples to generate theory. Developed by Glaser and Strauss and the foundation of grounded theory (GT). | The first advantage is the possibility to strengthen the rigor of the study if the study attempts to generate a theory in the research area. The second is that the application of the theoretical sampling method can provide a certain structure to data collection and data analysis processes. Lastly, the advantage is that this type of sampling usually integrates both inductive and deductive characteristics, thus increasing the depth of studies (Dudovskiy, 2008). | The first disadvantage is that the application of the theoretical sampling method may require more resources such as time and money compared to many other sampling methods. The second is that there are no clear processes or guidance related to the application of theoretical sampling in practice. Lastly, the method of theoretical sampling is more complicated than other sampling methods (Rahman et al., 2022). |

Source: Berndt, 2020; Gill, 2020; Acharya et al., 2013; Dudovskiy, 2008.

grounded theory or failing to document the sampling strategy as it unfolds (Koerber & McMichael, 2008; Somekh & Lewin, 2005).

Determining Sampling Size in Non-probability Research

The task of determining the sample size in a study has been a paradox to novice researchers. In many situations, novice researchers mix the sampling requirements for both probability sampling and non-probability sampling. The primary objective of qualitative sampling is to recruit enough participants and/or observations to provide enough rich, in-depth data to understand the phenomenon studied. Qualitative researchers could pre-determine the sample size for their study to satisfy human objects' review of communities. Generalizability is not important or the goal in qualitative research. Therefore, sample sizes are much smaller than those needed in quantitative designs.

Quantitative researchers typically use large samples, determined by a power analysis, while qualitative samples are smaller in order to examine a phenomenon in depth. Sample size in qualitative research may refer to the number of persons but also to the number of interviews and observations conducted, the number of events sampled or the number of artifacts gathered. Furthermore, sample size must be sufficient to generate quality data that provides a rich understanding of the experience. Concerning the issue of data saturation, it is linked to sampling strategies and sample size. In the realm of non-probability research, sufficient samples are necessary for quality data. Data saturation occurs when no new information is obtained from interviews and/or observations (Gill, 2020).

An appropriate sample size for a qualitative study is one that adequately answers the research question. For simple questions or very detailed studies, this might be in single figures; for complex questions, large samples and a variety of sampling techniques might be necessary Furthermore, even if everyone could agree on a magically correct sample size in qualitative research, researchers might not be able to actually achieve that sample size; time and funding constraints, as well as considerations such as study attrition, affect the sample size in quantitative research just as they do in qualitative research (Alvi, 2016; Koerber & McMichael, 2008; Yang & Banamah, 2014; Naderifar et al., 2017).

Summary

Researchers must understand the process of sampling. Sampling is an art form in the realm of research in the social sciences. The craft of sampling has many aspects. With sampling in both quantitative and qualitative research, there are vast differences between the two research methods. It is vital that the researcher understands the differences behind the rationale and foundation concerning different types of sampling methods. This chapter attempts to explain and address this practice of sampling and determining sample size.

First, this chapter discussed population, sampling and definitions. Second, the chapter also discussed the reasons for sampling. Third, the chapter discussed the sampling process. Fourth, the chapter discussed the different types of sampling. Fifth, the chapter discussed probability sampling and non-probability sampling. Sixth, the chapter discussed different sampling designs and how to determine sampling size. And lastly, the chapter discussed sampling methods in quantitative research and sampling methods in qualitative research. This chapter primarily discussed the characteristics of sampling for a research study.

References

Acharya, A. S., Prakash, A., Saxena, P., & Nigam, A. (2013). Sampling: Why and how of it? *Indian Journal of Medical Specialities*, *4*(2), 330–333. www.researchgate.net/profile/Anita-Acharya-2/publication/256446902_Sampling_Why_and_How_of_it_Anita_S_Acharya_Anupam_Prakash_Pikee_Saxena_Aruna_Nigam/links/0c960527c82d44978 8000000/Sampling-Why-and-How-of-it-Anita-S-Acharya-Anupam-Prakash-Pikee-Saxena-Aruna-Nigam.pdf

Ackoff, R. (1953). *Design of social research*. University of Chicago Press.

Altmann, J. (1974). Observational study of behavior: Sampling methods. *Behaviour*, *49*(3), 227–266. https://doi.org/10.1163/156853974x00534

Alvi, M. (2016). *A manual for selecting sampling techniques in research*. Munich Personal RePEc Archive.

American Psychological Association. (n.d.). Theoretical sampling. In *APA dictionary of psychology*. Retrieved December 1, 2022, from https://dictionary.apa.org/theoretical-sampling

Beins, B., & McCarthy, M. (2012). *Research methods and statistics*. Pearson Education Inc.

Berndt, A. E. (2020). Sampling methods. *Journal of Human Lactation*, *36*(2), 224–226. https://doi.org/10.1177/0890334420906850

Breweton, P. M., & Millward, L. (2001). *Organizational research methods*. SAGE.

Brown, G. H. (1947). A comparison of sampling methods. *Journal of Marketing*, *11*(4), 331. https://doi.org/10.2307/1246272

Calabrese, R. (2009). *The dissertation desk reference: The doctoral student's manual to writing the dissertation*. Rowman & Littlefield Education, Inc.

Christensen, T. C., Barrett, L. F., Bliss-Moreau, E., Lebo, K., & Kaschub, C. (2003). A practical guide to experience-sampling procedures. *Journal of Happiness Studies*, *4*(1), 53–78. https://doi.org/10.1023/a:1023609306024

Cochran, W. G. (1977). *Sampling techniques* (3rd ed.). John Wiley & Sons.

Cokley, K., & Awad, G. H. (2013). In defense of quantitative methods: Using the "master's tools" to promote social justice. *Journal for Social Action in Counseling & Psychology*, *5*(2), 26–41. https://doi.org/10.33043/jsacp.5.2.26-41

Daniel, J. (2012). *Sampling essentials: Practical guidelines for making sampling choices*. Sage Publishers.

Davis, D. (2005). *Business research for decision making*. Thomson South-Western.

Delice, A. (2010). The sampling issues in quantitative research. *Educational Sciences: Theory & Practice*, *10*(4), 2001–2018.

Desai, V., & Potter, R. (2006). *Doing development research*. SAGE Publications.

Dudovskiy, J. (2008). *Theoretical sampling*. Research-Methodology. https://research-methodology.net/sampling-in-primary-data-collection/theoretical-sampling/

Etikan, I., & Bala, K. (2017). Sampling and sampling methods. *Biometrics & Biostatistics International Journal*, *5*(6), 215–217. https://doi.org/10.15406/bbij.2017.05.00149

Etikan, I., Musa, S. A., & Alkassim, R. S. (2016). Comparison of convenience sampling and purposive sampling. *American Journal of Theoretical and Applied Statistics*, *5*(1), 1–4.

Formplus Blog. (n.d.). Sampling bias: Definition, types + (examples). www.formpl.us/blog/sampling-bias

Fricker, R. (2020). Sampling methods for online surveys. In N. G. Fielding, R. M. Lee & G. Blank (Eds.), *The SAGE handbook of online research methods* (pp. 162–183). Sage.

Garson, G. D. (2002). *Guide to writing empirical papers, theses, and dissertations*. Marcel Dekker Publisher.

Gelo, O., Braakmann, D., & Benetka, G. (2008). Quantitative and qualitative research: Beyond the debate. *Integrative Psychological and Behavioral Science, 43*(4), 406–407. https://doi.org/10.1007/s12124-009-9107-x

Gill, S. L. (2020). Qualitative sampling methods. *Journal of Human Lactation, 36*(4), 579–581. https://doi.org/10.1177/0890334420949218

Glen. S. (2020). *Sampling design: Definition, examples*. Statistics How To: Statistics for the rest of us! Retrieved from www.statisticshowto.com/sampling-design/

Hancock, G. R., & Mueller, R. O. (2010). *The reviewer's guide to quantitative methods in the social sciences*. Routledge.

Haque, M. (n.d.). Sampling methods in social research. http://grmgrlaranya.org/Journals/SAMPLING%20METHODS%20IN%20SOCIAL%20RESEARCH.pdf

Henderson, R., & Sundaresan, T. (1982). Cluster sampling to assess immunization coverage: A review of experience with a simplified sampling method. *Bulletin of the World Health Organization, 60*(2), 253–260.

Humphrey, C. (2001). *Units of analysis: The basics* [PowerPoint slides]. SlidePlayer. Retrieved May 8, 2023, from https://slideplayer.com/slide/14887441/

Kelle, U. (2008). Combining qualitative and quantitative research methods to support psychosocial and mental health programmes in complex emergencies. *Intervention, 6*(3), 348. https://doi.org/10.1097/wtf.0b013e32831e12d4

Kerlinger, F., & Lee, H. (1999). *Foundations of behavioral research*. Wadsworth Publishing.

Koerber, A., & McMichael, L. (2008). Qualitative sampling methods. *Journal of Business and Technical Communication, 22*(4), 454–473. https://doi.org/10.1177/1050651908320362

Lamm, A., & Lamm, K. (2019). Using non-probability sampling methods in agricultural and extension education research. *Journal of International Agricultural and Extension Education, 26*(1), 52–59. https://doi.org/10.5191/iaee.2019.26105

Lancaster, V. A., & Keller-McNulty, S. (1998). A review of composite sampling methods. *Journal of the American Statistical Association, 93*(443), 1216–1230. https://doi.org/10.1080/01621459.1998.10473781

Larsen, H. G., & Adu, P. (2021). *The theoretical framework in phenomenological research: Development and application*. Routledge.

Lasswell, H. (1949). Why be quantitative? In H. D. Lasswell & N. Leites (Eds.), *Language of politics: Studies in quantitative semantics* (pp. 40–52). The MIT Press. https://uk.sagepub.com/sites/default/files/upm-binaries/19018_Franzosi_V1_Ch01.pdf

Lehner, P. N. (1992). Sampling methods in behavior research. *Poultry Science, 71*(4), 643–649.

Lepcha, M. (2022). What is a sampling error? Capital.com. Retrieved from https://capital.com/sampling-error-definition

Lomax, R. G. (2001). *An introduction to statistical concepts for education and behavioral sciences*. Lawrence Erlbaum Associates.

Malhotra, N., Birks, D., & Wills, P. (2013). *Essentials of marketing research*. Pearson.

Marshall, M. (1996). Sampling for qualitative research. *Family Practice, 13*(6), 522–525.

Martínez-Mesa, J., González-Chica, D. A., Duquia, R. P., Bonamigo, R. R., & Bastos, J. L. (2016). *Sampling: How to select participants in my research study?* Anais Brasileiros de Dermatologia, *91*(3), 326–330. https://doi.org/10.1590/abd1806-4841.20165254

Martino, L., Luengo, D., & Míguez, J. (2018). *Independent random sampling methods*. Springer International Publishing.

Maxwell, J. A. (1996). *Qualitative research design: An interactive approach*. Sage.

Miles, D. (2019). Research methods and strategies: Let's the stop the madness. Part 1: Understanding the difference between unit of analysis vs. unit of observation. Retrieved from www.researchgate.net/publication/331315067_ARTICLE_Research_Methods_and_Strategies_Let's_the_Stop_the_Madness_Part_1_Understanding_the_Difference_Between_Unit_of_Analysis_vs_Unit_of_Observation

Moser, C. A., & Stuart, A. (1953). An Experimental Study of Quota Sampling. *Journal of the Royal Statistical Society. Series A (General)*, *116*(4), 349–405. https://doi.org/10.2307/2343021

Naderifar, M., Goli, H., & Ghaljaie, F. (2017). Snowball sampling: A purposeful method of sampling in qualitative research. *Strides In Development of Medical Education*, *14*(3). https://doi.org/10.5812/sdme.67670

Nanjundeswaraswamy, T. S., & Divakar, S. (2021). Determination of sample size and sampling methods in applied research. *Proceedings on Engineering Sciences*, *3*(1), 25–32. https://doi.org/10.24874/pes03.01.003

Nardi, P. M. (2016). *Doing survey research: A guide to quantitative methods*. Routledge.

Non-probability sampling. (n.d.). *Encyclopedia of survey research methods*. https://doi.org/10.4135/9781412963947.n337

Panzeri, S., Magri, C., & Carraro, L. (2008). Sampling bias. *Scholarpedia*, *3*(9), 4258. https://doi.org/10.4249/scholarpedia.4258

Pedhazur, E. J. & Pedhazur Schmelkin, L. P. (1991). *Measurement, design, and analysis: An integrated approach*. Lawrence Erlbaum Associates, Publishers.

Rahman, Md. M., Tabash, M. I., Salamzadeh, A., Abduli, S., & Rahaman, Md. S. (2022). Sampling techniques (probability) for quantitative social science researchers: A conceptual guidelines with examples. *SEEU Review*, *17*(1), 42–51. https://doi.org/10.2478/seeur-2022-0023

Rai, N., & Thapa, B. (2015). *A study on purposive sampling method in research*. Kathmandu School of Law.

Rao, P. S. R. (2000). *Sampling methodologies with applications*. Chapman & Hall/CRC Publishers.

Robbins, M. L. (2017). Practical suggestions for legal and ethical concerns with social environment sampling methods. *Social Psychological and Personality Science*, *8*(5), 573–580. https://doi.org/10.1177/1948550617699253

Sarstedt, M., Bengart, P., Shaltoni, A. M., & Lehmann, S. (2017). The use of sampling methods in advertising research: A gap between theory and practice. *International Journal of Advertising*, *37*(4), 650–663. https://doi.org/10.1080/02650487.2017.1348329

Scheaffer, R. L., Mendenhall, W., & Ott, L. (2006). *Elementary survey sampling*. Thomson Brooks/Cole.

Sekaran, U., & Bougie, R. (2013). *Research methods for business: A skill-building approach* (6th ed.). John Wiley and Sons Ltd.

Shaheen, M., Pradhan, S., & Ranajee, R. (2019). Sampling in qualitative research. In M. Gupta, M. Shaheen, & K. Reddy (Eds.), *Qualitative techniques for workplace data analysis* (pp. 25–51). IGI Global. https://doi.org/10.4018/978-1-5225-5366-3.ch002

Singh, A., & Masuku, M. (2013). Fundamentals of applied research and sampling techniques. *International Journal of Medical and Applied Sciences*, *2*(4), 124–132.

Somekh. B., & Lewin, C. (2005). *Research methods in the social sciences*. SAGE Publications.

Sudman, S. (1976). *Applied sampling*. Academic Press.

Szolnoki, G., & Hoffmann, D. (2013). Online, face-to-face and telephone surveys – Comparing different sampling methods in wine consumer research. *Wine Economics and Policy, 2*(2), 57–66. https://doi.org/10.1016/j.wep.2013.10.001

Tabachnick, B. G., & Fidell, L. S. (2013). *Using multivariate statistics.* Allyn And Bacon.

Taherdoost, H. (2016). Sampling methods in research methodology: How to choose a sampling technique for research. *SSRN Electronic Journal, 5*(2), 18–27.

Tao, T. (2022, February 24). *6 types of sampling bias: How to avoid sampling bias.* MasterClass. www.masterclass.com/articles/sampling-bias

Terrell, S. (2015). *Writing a proposal for your dissertation: Guidelines and examples* (3rd ed.). The Guilford Press.

Thomas, R. M., & Brubaker, D. L. (2000). *Theses and dissertations: A guide to planning, research, and writing.* Bergin & Garvey Publishing.

Tong, C. (2006). Refinement strategies for stratified sampling methods. *Reliability Engineering & System Safety, 91*(10–11), 1257–1265. https://doi.org/10.1016/j.ress.2005.11.027

Upton, G. & Cook, I. (2008). *Oxford dictionary of statistics.* Oxford University Press.

Westfall, L. (2009). Sampling methods. In *The Certified Software Quality Engineer Handbook.* ASQ Quality Press.

Wilson, V. (2014). Research methods: Sampling. *Evidence Based Library and Information Practice, 9*(2), 45. https://doi.org/10.18438/b8s30x

Yang, K., & Banamah, A. (2014). Quota sampling as an alternative to probability sampling? An experimental study. *Sociological Research Online, 19*(1), 1–11. https://doi.org/10.5153/sro.3199

Yaremko, R. M., Harari, H., Harrison, R., & Lynn, E. (2013). *Handbook of research and quantitative methods in psychology: For students and professionals.* Lawrence Erlbaum Associates.

Yin, R. K. (2003). *Case study research: Design and methods.* Sage.

Zedeck, S. (1986). *APA dictionary of statistics and research methods.* American Psychological Association.

Zikmund, W. G., (2003). *Exploring marketing research* (8th ed.). South-Western Cengage Learning.

17 Planning and Implementing the Data Analysis Process

Objectives

- Readers will be able to:
  1. Determine the appropriate data analysis strategy
  2. Analyze data
  3. Write data analysis process

Introduction

Data analysis can be a challenging task of many proportions. To take collected data and analyze it can be a daunting process. There are many steps in the process of measuring and analyzing data. The practice of data analysis involves the preparation of the data, its analysis, the reporting of the results, and a discussion of the findings.

The first step is to prepare the data for analysis. This involves determining the optimal data analysis technique that aligns with the research methodology and the research design. The second step begins the actual data analysis. The third step is to report the results of the data analysis, which is expressed using tables, figures and other graphics. The fourth step is reviewing the key results. The researcher attempts to interpret the results from the key results and discuss the findings. This step consists of summarizing the findings, comparing the findings with past literature and theories and advancing the limitations of the study. Then the research ends with some suggestions for future research.

By the end of this chapter, the reader should be able to: (a) understand and identify the steps in the process of analyzing and interpreting data; (b) understand and describe the process of preparing their data for data analysis; (c) understand and identify the process and procedures involved in analyzing data; (d) understand and learn how to describe and report the results of the data analysis; and, lastly, (e) understand and learn how to interpret the results and write up the findings from the data analysis.

DOI: 10.4324/9781003268154-17

Quantitative Data Analysis

The use of quantitative data to conduct research is usually the primary choice among researchers. When researchers use quantitative research, the major focus is to understand a problem and use a measurement with numbers to further understand it. The focus of quantitative research is to make sense of a problem through measurement and numbers. To the quantitative researcher, the numbers represent some hint of what the problem is. In the realm of social science research, the quantitative researcher takes social data and converts it to numerical form for statistical analyses. When using this approach, the researcher can interpret and summarize these numbers by utilizing statistical analyses to measure the phenomena. When analyzing quantitative data, there are a number of variations of data types for options with statistical tests. Each has its own unique focus and use in statistical analyses. Quantitative analysis may be descriptive or explanatory; it can involve several variables. Consequently, with quantitative data analyses, the focus is on manipulating data to attain conclusions.

Determining an Appropriate Data Analysis Technique in Quantitative Research

The task of choosing the appropriate data analysis technique should not be a challenge for the quantitative researcher. Often, determining the statistical test is based on the research methodology and research design. This is where the researcher wants to start first. It would be quite helpful if the reader is well versed in statistics and familiar with various statistical tests. This would be very advisable because if the reader is not, then there will be repercussions and questions about the validity and reliability of their statistical test results (see Figure 17.1).

Once the researcher goes through this process, they can determine the appropriate data analysis for the study. This allows the researcher to think logically about how to conduct the data analysis. Given that there are so many statistical tests and techniques, this is quite helpful. Each statistical test is suitable for a different purpose and can answer different questions based on a particular set of data.

Once the researcher has determined the appropriate data analysis process, they must go through the data preparation process. After the data has been collected

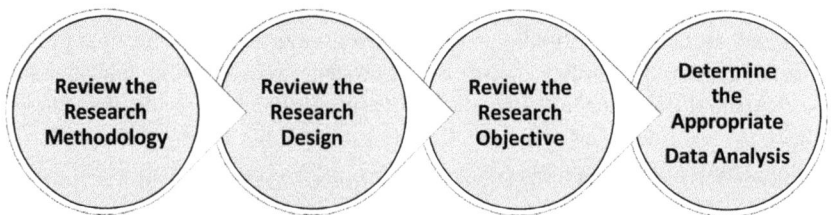

Figure 17.1 Determining the appropriate data analysis process.

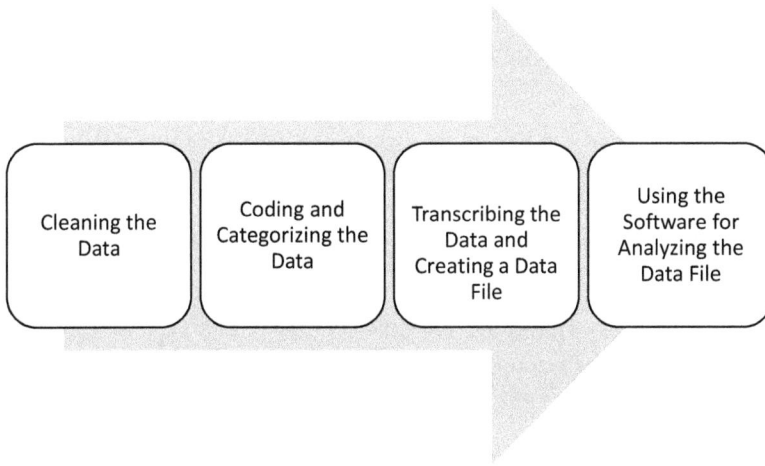

Figure 17.2 Flow diagram of the data preparation process.

from the surveys or questionnaires, it needs to be cleaned up. When editing the data, there will be incomplete surveys with blank responses. The researcher must decide whether to discard the incomplete surveys or recode the blank responses with selected code. The next step with the data is to put the data file into a statistical software program. After this, the researcher will analyze the data with the software program. Figure 17.2 illustrates the stages of data preparation, which are discussed below.

Cleaning the Data

First, the data must be cleaned. This is especially the case when the data includes surveys or questionnaires with missing responses. Participants sometimes skip questions or just quit completing questions on surveys. The research must be either discarded or coded with a variable, which we will discuss further. Failure to do this will result in bad data and will also later result in bad statistical analysis of the data. It is recommended that such data cleaning should be done preferably on the same day the data is collected in case any further information is needed.

When the researcher detects missing values in the data, there are two remedies: (a) delete the missing values; or (b) substitute a missing value.

Treatment of Missing Responses

Most importantly, the missing responses in a survey instrument represent values of a variable that are unknown either because respondents provided ambiguous answers or they skipped or refused to answer the questions. Missing responses cause numerous problems in the data analysis, so the researcher can delete the responses and keep the data clean. Missing responses pose problems with the data and particularly if the proportion of missing responses is more than 10% (Malhotra & Birks, 2007).

Substitute a Neutral Value

Another option when the researcher detects missing values in the data is to substitute a neutral value. The researcher will code the missing values as a neutral value. A neutral value, typically the mean response to the variable, is substituted for the missing responses. If the variable response is a five-point Likert scale, then the researcher will code it a "3," a middle variable, or a "4" with a seven-point Likert scale. This causes the mean of the variable to remain unchanged, and other statistics such as correlations are not affected much. The logic of substituting a mean value (say 4) for respondents who, if they had answered, might have used either high ratings (6 or 7) or low ratings (1 or 2) is questionable.

Coding and Categorizing the Data

The next step is to code the data from the survey responses. When coding the data, the researcher should use a codebook. A *codebook* is defined as a book that contains instructions and the necessary information about the questions and potential answers in an instrument or survey. The researcher codes each question and the variable responses. The purpose of the codebook is to guide the coders in their work and help the researcher identify and align the questions in the instrument properly. A codebook contains the following information: (1) column number; (2) record number; (3) variable number; (4) variable name; (5) question number; and (6) instructions for coding (Malhotra & Birks, 2007; Malhotra, 2015).

Coding can be done using the instrument that was used for collecting the data for the study. Many times, the instrument has different categories, which help manage the coding for the variables in the data. This will be easier for input into statistical software. It is recommended that the researcher use individual coding sheets for each of the categories in the instrument. It is advisable to use a coding sheet first to transcribe the data from the questionnaire and then key in the data.

When having to code a Likert scale, the researcher should code the response properly. With a 7-point Likert scale, the highest response in the scale ("Highly Likely") should be coded a 7, denoting the highest agreement. The lowest response on the scale ("Highly Unlikely") should be coded a 1, denoting the lowest agreement. An advantage of coding the data in this way is that it also makes it possible to calculate cumulative scores in the instrument. There are many other advantages of coding the data responses using this method (Sekaran, 2006; Malhotra & Birks, 2007; Malhotra, 2015).

Transcribing the Data and Creating a Data File

Next in the process is to transcribe the data and create a data file. Transcribing is defined as keying the coded data from the collected questionnaires into computer software or from coding sheets onto disks or directly into computers by keypunching and developing a data file. However, if the data was collected through the Internet, CATI or CAPI, then this step is unnecessary because the data are entered directly into the computer as they are collected (Malhotra & Birks, 2007; Malhotra, 2015).

Developing a Transcribed Data File

After transcribing the data, the researcher then inputs the data into a statistics software program. My preference for statistics software is SPSS. So, we will use the SPSS software to illustrate and discuss data transcription. However, there are other compatible statistical software packages. The questionnaire data can be directly entered into the computer as a data file; the raw data will have to be manually keyed into the SPSS software on the computer. For example, the SPSS Data Editor, which looks like a spreadsheet, can be used to enter, edit and view the contents of the data file. The raw data will be entered through the SPSS software program. For example, each column represents a variable, and each row represents a participant case.

The researcher will want to use Microsoft Excel and SPSS to manage the data set. Transcribed data can be entered into a spreadsheet program such as Excel. Many of the statistics analysis programs will allow the researcher to import data from a spreadsheet. As illustrated in Figure 17.3, the data for each respondent for each field is a cell. Now, each row of the spreadsheet contains the data of one respondent or case (Malhotra & Birks, 2007; Malhotra, 2015).

As illustrated in Figure 17.3, "Variable View" shows 47 items from the survey instruments for the study. The columns contain the variables, with one column for each variable or response. This table gives the data from a pre-test sample of 20 respondents on their preferences for department stores. Each respondent was asked to rate their preference when answering the survey instrument questions (1 = Strongly Disagree, 7 = Strongly Agree).

In SPSS, the researcher has the ability to add, change or delete values easily after the data have been entered. It is also easy to compute the new variables that have been categorized earlier using the "Compute" dialog box, which opens when the "Transform" icon is chosen. In SPSS, the researcher should start in "Variable View" to input and code the data in the file. Lastly, the researcher should go to "Data View" to see the variables in the dataset (see Figure 17.3). Once the missing values, the recodes and the coding of the new variables are addressed, the data is ready for analysis (Malhotra & Birks, 2007; Malhotra, 2015).

After this, the researcher wants to make sure the data is okay and aligned with the survey instrument. This is really important. The researcher wants to view the data as a way to come up with an idea for the selection of a data analysis strategy. This will allow the researcher to get an idea of which approach to take with the data analysis. The preliminary plan for the preparation of data analysis is to conduct a rigorous analysis. As part of the research design, the data analysis should be used as a foundation for the analysis. The next step is to create the data file.

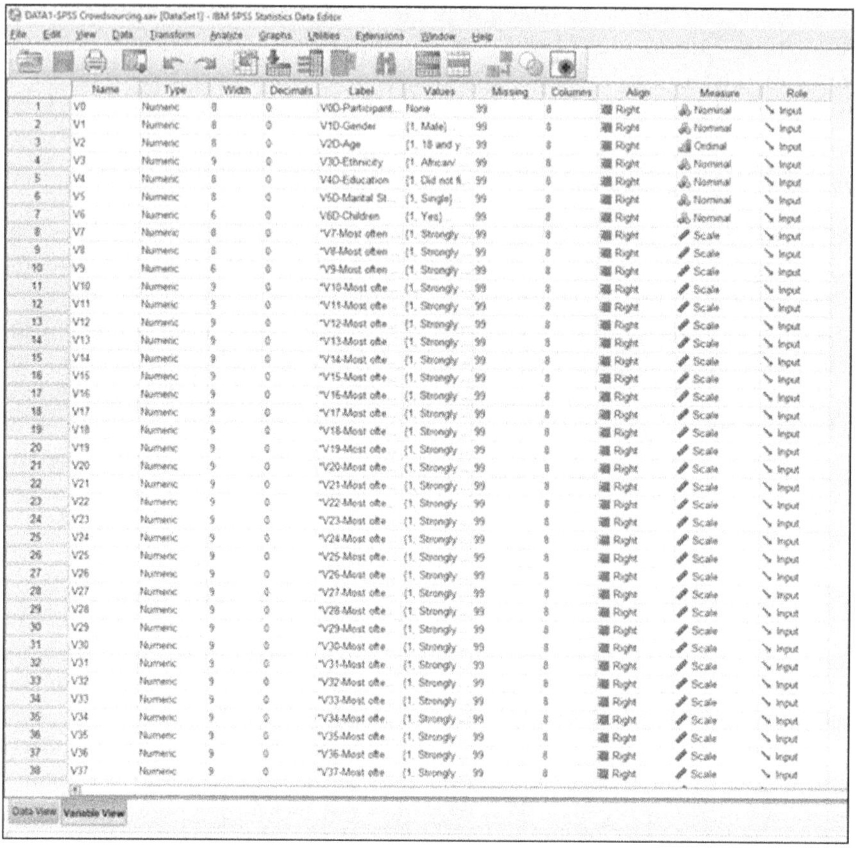

	Name	Type	Width	Decimals	Label	Values	Missing	Columns	Align	Measure	Role
1	V0	Numeric	8	0	V0-Participant	None	99	8	Right	Nominal	Input
2	V1	Numeric	8	0	V1-Gender	{1. Male}	99	8	Right	Nominal	Input
3	V2	Numeric	8	0	V2-Age	{1. 18 and y	99	8	Right	Ordinal	Input
4	V3	Numeric	9	0	V3-Ethnicity	{1. African	99	8	Right	Nominal	Input
5	V4	Numeric	8	0	V4-Education	{1. Did not fi	99	8	Right	Nominal	Input
6	V5	Numeric	8	0	V5-Marital St	{1. Single}	99	8	Right	Nominal	Input
7	V6	Numeric	6	0	V6-Children	{1. Yes}	99	8	Right	Nominal	Input
8	V7	Numeric	8	0	*V7-Most often	{1. Strongly	99	8	Right	Scale	Input
9	V8	Numeric	8	0	*V8-Most often	{1. Strongly	99	8	Right	Scale	Input
10	V9	Numeric	6	0	*V9-Most often	{1. Strongly	99	8	Right	Scale	Input
11	V10	Numeric	9	0	*V10-Most ofte	{1. Strongly	99	8	Right	Scale	Input
12	V11	Numeric	9	0	*V11-Most ofte	{1. Strongly	99	8	Right	Scale	Input
13	V12	Numeric	9	0	*V12-Most ofte	{1. Strongly	99	8	Right	Scale	Input
14	V13	Numeric	9	0	*V13-Most ofte	{1. Strongly	99	8	Right	Scale	Input
15	V14	Numeric	9	0	*V14-Most ofte	{1. Strongly	99	8	Right	Scale	Input
16	V15	Numeric	9	0	*V15-Most ofte	{1. Strongly	99	8	Right	Scale	Input
17	V16	Numeric	9	0	*V16-Most ofte	{1. Strongly	99	8	Right	Scale	Input
18	V17	Numeric	9	0	*V17-Most ofte	{1. Strongly	99	8	Right	Scale	Input
19	V18	Numeric	9	0	*V18-Most ofte	{1. Strongly	99	8	Right	Scale	Input
20	V19	Numeric	9	0	*V19-Most ofte	{1. Strongly	99	8	Right	Scale	Input
21	V20	Numeric	9	0	*V20-Most ofte	{1. Strongly	99	8	Right	Scale	Input
22	V21	Numeric	9	0	*V21-Most ofte	{1. Strongly	99	8	Right	Scale	Input
23	V22	Numeric	9	0	*V22-Most ofte	{1. Strongly	99	8	Right	Scale	Input
24	V23	Numeric	9	0	*V23-Most ofte	{1. Strongly	99	8	Right	Scale	Input
25	V24	Numeric	9	0	*V24-Most ofte	{1. Strongly	99	8	Right	Scale	Input
26	V25	Numeric	9	0	*V25-Most ofte	{1. Strongly	99	8	Right	Scale	Input
27	V26	Numeric	9	0	*V26-Most ofte	{1. Strongly	99	8	Right	Scale	Input
28	V27	Numeric	9	0	*V27-Most ofte	{1. Strongly	99	8	Right	Scale	Input
29	V28	Numeric	9	0	*V28-Most ofte	{1. Strongly	99	8	Right	Scale	Input
30	V29	Numeric	9	0	*V29-Most ofte	{1. Strongly	99	8	Right	Scale	Input
31	V30	Numeric	9	0	*V30-Most ofte	{1. Strongly	99	8	Right	Scale	Input
32	V31	Numeric	9	0	*V31-Most ofte	{1. Strongly	99	8	Right	Scale	Input
33	V32	Numeric	9	0	*V32-Most ofte	{1. Strongly	99	8	Right	Scale	Input
34	V33	Numeric	9	0	*V33-Most ofte	{1. Strongly	99	8	Right	Scale	Input
35	V34	Numeric	9	0	*V34-Most ofte	{1. Strongly	99	8	Right	Scale	Input
36	V35	Numeric	9	0	*V35-Most ofte	{1. Strongly	99	8	Right	Scale	Input
37	V36	Numeric	9	0	*V36-Most ofte	{1. Strongly	99	8	Right	Scale	Input
38	V37	Numeric	9	0	*V37-Most ofte	{1. Strongly	99	8	Right	Scale	Input

Data View Variable View

Figure 17.3 SPSS variable view of the data file.

Using the Software to Analyze the Data File

The next step in the process is to conduct the statistical tests, choosing the software for analyzing the data or the data file. Logically, the research design will favor certain statistical techniques. For example, a correlational research design is well suited to analyzing relationships with variables, which favors using a Pearson correlation statistical test. The task of conducting the data analysis from the data preparation is an important step in the research process. This can be valuable for selecting the appropriate statistical design. The purpose of data analysis is to produce information that will address the research problem, and the plan of data analysis is to properly extract information from the data to tell the story of the data (see Figure 17.4).

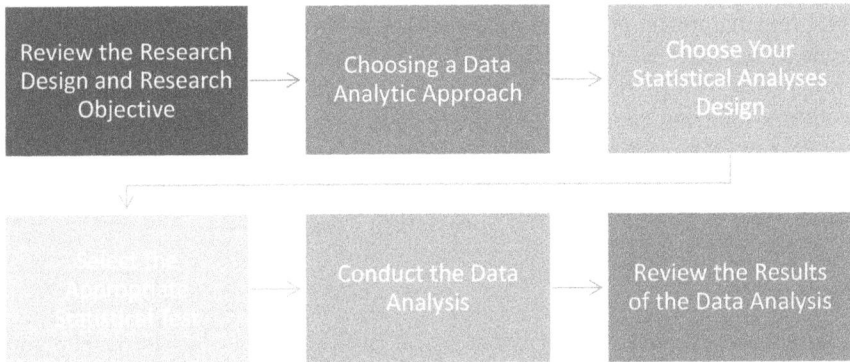

Figure 17.4 Selecting the statistical data analysis strategy process.

Choosing a Data Analytic Approach

The next step is to select a data analytic approach and strategy. The data analysis strategy is based on the establishment of the research design. As presented in Chapter 12, choosing an analytic approach is based on the five quantitative research designs: (a) *descriptive design*; (b) *correlational design*; (c) *causal-comparative design*; (d) *experimental design*; and (e) *quasi-experimental design*. The types of analytic approach can be properly performed depending on the research design chosen for the study. Consequently, it is imperative that the techniques of analysis be selected prior to data collection (Smith & Albaum, 2010).

Descriptive Design

This research design is defined as research that encompasses a variety of methodologies that are best suited to examining and trying to make sense of a situation. The objective of descriptive design research is to describe the characteristics of the domain or state of affairs as it exists at present. A quantitative descriptive study involves measuring one or more variables in some way. For a statistical test, a frequency and crosstab analysis of the variables with the variables in the data are primarily used (Saunders et al., 2012; McNiff & Whitehead, 2010; Leedy et al., 2019).

Correlational Design

This research design is defined as a statistical investigation of the relationship between two or more variables. The objective of correlational research is to seek and determine relationships between two or more variables without necessarily inferring causality. For a statistical test, a Pearson's correlation is primarily used for the data analysis (Kothari, 2004; Swanson & Holton, 2005; Jackson, 2009).

Causal-Comparative Design

This research design is defined as a statistical investigation that attempts to determine a cause-and-effect relationship between variables. The objective of causal-comparative design research is to determine a predictive relationship between variables inferring causality. This, in essence, means the influence of the independent variable on the dependent variable. For a statistical test, a linear or logistical regression with the data is primarily used (Kothari, 2004; Swanson & Holton, 2005; Miles & Scott, 2017; Leedy et al., 2019).

Experimental Design

This research design is defined as a statistical investigation in which participants are randomly assigned to groups that undergo various researcher-imposed treatments or interventions, followed by systematic assessments of the treatments' effects. The objective of experimental design research is to investigate causal links and whether a change in one independent variable produces a change in another dependent variable. For a statistical test, a t-test, an ANOVA or a time series analysis is primarily used with the data (Kothari, 2004; Saunders et al, 2012; Leedy et al., 2019; Swanson & Holton, 2005).

Quasi-Experimental Design

This research design is defined as a statistical investigation in which an independent variable is manipulated in order to determine its possible effect on another (dependent) variable, but without total control of additional variables that might have an impact on the dependent variable. The objective of the quasi-experimental design is to conduct the study without the restrictions of using randomness. This is to minimize the restrictions of randomness of the experimental design. The focus is on the selection of group members in a multiple-group study or the presentation of various treatments in a single-group study. For a statistical test, a t-test or ANOVA is primarily used with the data (Saunders et al., 2012; Jackson, 2009; Swanson & Holton, 2005).

Choose Your Statistical Analyses Design

The next step in the process is to choose your statistical analyses design strategy. The data analysis strategy is based on the establishment of the research design. There are generally two statistical analysis designs used: (a) *descriptive analysis*; and (b) *inferential analysis*. These types of statistical analysis can be properly performed and are based on the research design chosen for the study (Burns & Bush, 2003) (see Figure 17.5).

Statistics have two principal functions: (a) *descriptive*; and (b) *inferential*. First, the purpose of descriptive statistics is to describe what the data look like, where their center or midpoint is, how broadly they are spread, how closely two or more

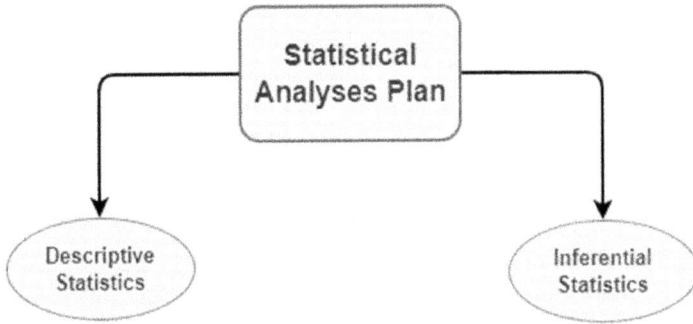

Figure 17.5 The statistical analysis design plan.

variables within the data are intercorrelated and the like. Second, the function of inferential statistics is to draw inferences about large populations by collecting data on relatively small samples. Correspondingly, inferential statistics involve using one or more small samples and then estimating the characteristics of the population (Leedy & Ormrod, 2001).

Descriptive Statistics

This statistical analysis design is used to describe the variables (question responses) in the data. Certain measures, such as the central tendency of the mean, mode, standard deviation and range, are forms of descriptive analysis. It is used to describe the sample data in such a way as to portray the "typical' respondent and reveal a general pattern of responses. Descriptive statistics utilizes parametric statistical tests such as percentages, mode, percentile and median. A frequency analysis and crosstab analysis are typically used with a statistical descriptive analysis (Burns & Bush, 2003).

Measures of Central Tendency

With descriptive statistics, there are three components of central tendency: the *mode*, the *median* and the *mean*. A point of central tendency is a point around which the data revolve, a middle number around which the data regarding a particular variable seem to hover. Statistics related to central tendency and variability help us summarize our data (Leedy & Ormand, 2001; Swanson & Holton, 2005).

The *mode* is the single number or score that occurs most frequently. As a measure of central tendency, the mode is of limited value, in part because it doesn't always appear near the middle of the distribution and in part because it isn't very stable from sample to sample (Burns & Bush, 2003). The *median* is the numerical center of a set of data; it is the measure of central tendency based on the exact midpoint of a distribution of data points related to a particular variable. The median is the number in the very middle of the scores, with exactly as many scores above it as below it (Swanson & Holton, 2005). Lastly, the *mean* is the arithmetic average of the scores within the data set. To find it, you must calculate the sum of all the scores (adding each score every time it occurs) and then divide by the total number of scores (Burns & Bush, 2003; Swanson & Holton, 2005).

Measures of Variability

The measures of variability are defined as an indication of the dispersion of a distribution. With descriptive statistics, there are four components of the measure of variability: interval or ratio data, range, variance and standard deviation (Byrne, 2002). The *range* measures the spread of the data, as it is simply the difference between the largest and smallest values in the sample. The *variance* is the mean squared deviation from the mean – that is, the average of the square of the deviations from the mean for all the values. The *standard deviation* is the square root of the variance. Thus, the standard deviation is expressed in the same units as the data, whereas the variance is expressed in squared units (Byrne, 2002; Kerlinger & Lee, 2007).

Primary Scales of Measurement

The primary scales of measurement are defined in the same way as variables are defined and categorized. With descriptive statistics, there are four components of the primary scales of measurement: (a) The *nominal scale* is a figurative labelling scheme in which the numbers serve only as labels or tags for identifying and classifying objects; (b) the *ordinal scale* is a ranking scale in which numbers are assigned to objects to indicate the relative extent to which the objects possess some characteristic; (c) the *interval scale* has numerically equal distances that represent equal values in the characteristic being measured; an interval scale contains all the information of an ordinal scale, but it also allows you to compare the differences between objects; and (d) the *ratio scale*, which allows the researcher to identify or classify objects, rank and order the objects and compare intervals or differences; it possesses all the properties of the nominal, ordinal and interval scales and, in addition, an absolute zero point (Burns & Bush, 2003; Kerlinger & Lee, 2007).

Inferential Statistics

Inferential statistics is a statistical analysis design that is used to generate conclusions about the population's characteristics based on the sample data. More particularly, inferential statistics have two main functions: (a) to estimate a population parameter from a random sample; and (b) to test statistically based hypotheses (Byrne, 2002). You could say that inferential statistics measure things that cannot be measured by descriptive statistics. This is a statistical procedure that is used by researchers to generalize the results of the sample to the population that it represents. Inferential statistics includes hypothesis testing and estimating the true population (Leedy & Ormrod, 2001; Kerlinger & Lee, 2007).

Many inferential statistical tests, especially those that allow a researcher to make comparisons among two or more groups; are based on the assumption that group membership is randomly determined and any pre-treatment differences between the groups result from chance alone (Malhotra, 2015). Inferential statistics utilizes parametric statistical tests such as the t-test, ANOVA, regression and factor analysis. Inferential statistics also provide a way of helping us make reasonable guesses about a large, unknown population by examining a small sample that is known (Kerlinger & Lee, 2007; Malhotra, 2015).

Selecting the Appropriate Statistical Test

There are two main things that statistical tests do: (1) investigate differences between groups; and (2) explore relationships between variables (known as an association or a correlation). There is also the issue of whether the same subjects are being measured several times or whether different subjects are being measured. Nevertheless, there are two main kinds of test, known as parametric and non-parametric (Shah & Peters, 2022) (see Figure 17.6).

Parametric Test

The parametric statistical test is based on hypothesis testing procedures that assume that the variables of interest are measured on at least an interval scale. Parametric tests typically provide inferences for making statements about the means of parent populations. Parametric tests use a *mean* compared to nonparametric tests that use an *average* in calculating the properties of the data.

Parametric analysis is the process of making inferences from the sample to the population's parameters. For example, for normally distributed variables,

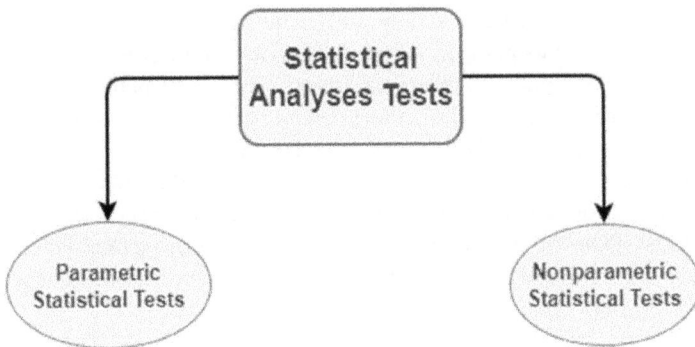

Figure 17.6 The statistical analysis design model.

the researcher assumes the normality and homogeneity of variances in the data. When a variable to be analyzed conforms to the assumptions of a given distribution, the distribution of the variable can be expressed in terms of its parameters (μ and ι). There are many parametric tests for both univariate and multivariate statistics. For univariate statistics, these include one group (t-test, z-test); two groups: (t-test; z-test); and paired samples (paired t-test) (Sheskin, 2000; Malhotra & Birks, 2007; Smith & Albaum, 2010; Corder & Foreman, 2014; Malhotra, 2015; Malhotra et al., 2017).

Concerning the issue of normality with parametric testing, the normality of variables is assessed by either statistical or graphical methods. There are two components of normality: *skewness* and *kurtosis*. Skewness has to do with the symmetry of the distribution; a skewed variable is a variable whose mean is not in the center of the distribution, while kurtosis has to do with the peakedness of a distribution. Furthermore, a distribution is either too peaked (with short, thick tails) or too flat (with long, thin tails) (Tabachnick & Fidell, 2007) (see Figure 17.7)

Nonparametric Test

Nonparametric tests are a distribution-free method in which inferences are based on a test statistic whose sampling distribution does not depend upon the specific distribution of the population from which the sample is drawn (Smith & Albaum, 2010). The variables are measured on a nominal or ordinal scale. Nonparametric tests use an *average* compared to parametric tests that use a *mean* in calculating the properties of the data. As a general rule, nonparametric tests are not as powerful as their parametric counterparts (Sheskin, 2000). However, parametric methods make inferences about the parameters of the population (μ and s), while nonparametric methods may be used to compare entire distributions that are based on nominal data.

There are other nonparametric methods that use an ordinal measurement scale test for the ordering of observations in the data set (Malhotra & Birks, 2007). Nonparametric tests based on observations are drawn from one sample. Some nonparametric tests include: *one sample* (Chi-square; K-S, Runs, Binomial); *independent samples* (Chi-square, Mann–Whitney, Median, K-S); and *paired samples* (Sign, Wilcoxon, McNemar, Chi-square) (Sheskin, 2000). For example, the Kruskal–Wallis one-way analysis of variance is the nonparametric test used when the dependent variable is on an ordinal scale and the independent variable is on a nominal scale. Three regularly used tests are the Wilcoxon Rank Sum (T), the Mann-Whitney U and the Kolmogorov-Smirnov test (Smith & Albaum, 2010). Notably, when the population distribution is normal, the asymptotic relative efficiency of most nonparametric tests will be less than 1. However, when the underlying population is not normal, it is not uncommon for a nonparametric test to have an asymptotic relative efficiency greater than one (Sheskin, 2000).

Nonparametric tests are also available for evaluating hypotheses relating to more than two samples. Many researchers use nonparametric tests with large samples, but this is not advisable. The result of this will be a false coefficient based on the

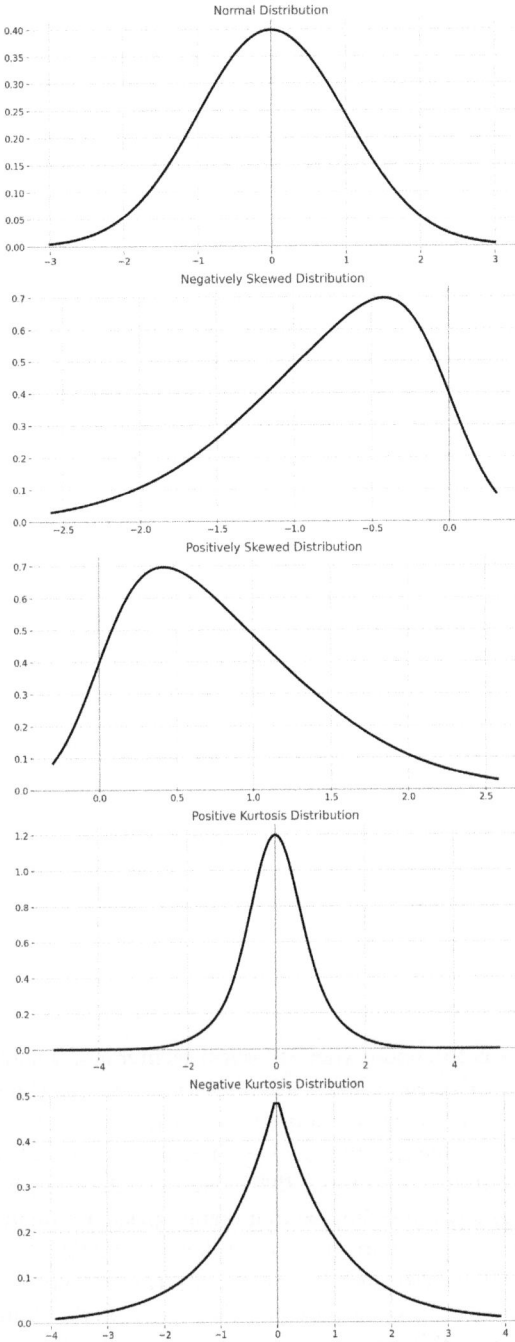

Figure 17.7 Normal, skewness and kurtosis distributions.

Source: Adapted from Tabachnick and Fidell (2007) and created using ChatGPT (OpenAI, 2023).

analysis of the data. Nonparametric tests should be used for small samples and to determine the normal distribution of the data. Parametric tests are far more appropriate for larger data sets (Malhotra & Birks, 2007; Smith & Albaum, 2010; Malhotra, 2015; Malhotra et al., 2017) (see Figure 17.7).

When do you use nonparametric statistics? The researcher must use non-parametric statistics when many of the parametric tests in traditional, introductory statistics do not follow certain assumptions. Furthermore, a nonparametric test does not depend on the assumption of normality of the population in the data. It depends on assumptions as to the form of the sample population parameters (Kerlinger & Lee, 2007). And notably, the parametric test does not violate the following assumptions: (a) the samples are randomly drawn from a normally distributed population; (b) the samples consist of independent observations, except for paired values; (c) the samples consist of values on an interval or ratio measurement scale; (d) the samples have respective populations of approximately equal variances; (e) the samples are adequately large; and (f) the samples approximately resemble a normal distribution (Corder & Foreman, 2014) (see Figure 17.7).

Conducting the Data Analysis

In order to conduct the data analysis, the researcher must use statistical software such as Excel or SPSS, which is often used to run statistical tests. The output from these tests requires interpretation. For example, the output from SPSS for a Chi-squared test shows whether there is an association between a cause of rioting and the police force using violence. The number to interpret is the asymptotic significance (2-sided) of the Pearson Chi-Square row (0.172). However, the Exact Sig. (2-sided) of the Fisher's exact test (0.214) can also be interpreted. As both these values are above the 0.05 threshold, we would conclude that there is insufficient evidence of an association (Shah & Peters, 2022).

Classification of Statistical Techniques

Univariate Statistical Techniques

The next step in the process is to choose your statistical techniques. There are two types, which can be classified as *univariate* or *multivariate*. Univariate techniques are appropriate when there is a single measurement of each element in the sample or when there are several measurements of each element, but each variable is analyzed in isolation (Malhotra & Birks, 2007; Smith & Albaum, 2010). Multivariate techniques are a statistical technique that is appropriate for analyzing data when there are two or more measurements on each element and the variables are analyzed simultaneously. Multivariate techniques are concerned with the simultaneous relationships among two or more phenomena (Anderson, 2003; Malhotra & Birks, 2007). For the purposes of this discussion, I will not use any nonparametric techniques; I will only discuss parametric statistical techniques. There are five basic

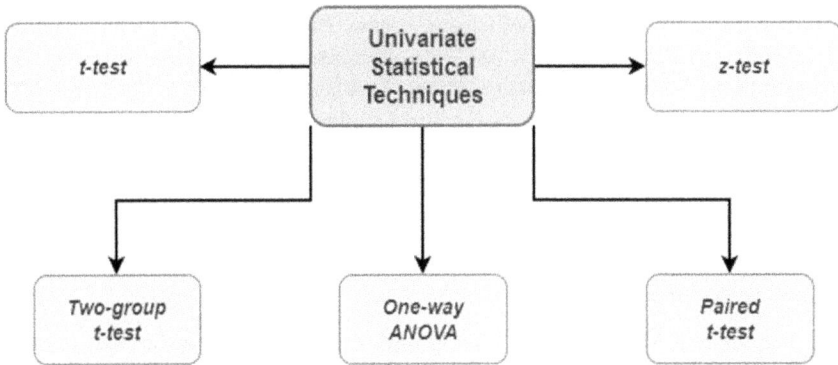

Figure 17.8 Univariate statistical techniques model.

statistical techniques: (a) *t-test*; (b) *z-test*; (c) *two-sample t-test*; (d) *one-way ANOVA*; and (e) *paired t-test* (see Figure 17.8).

T-TEST

A comparison of groups within the data. For example, if a sample of students takes a 10-point quiz and we wish to see whether women or men scored higher on the quiz, a t-test would be appropriate (Miles, 2013c).

Z-TEST

A z-test is a statistical test used to determine whether two population means are different when the variances are known and the sample size is large. The z-test is best used for greater-than-30 samples because, under the central limit theorem, as the number of samples gets larger, the samples are considered to be approximately normally distributed (Chen, 2021).

TWO-SAMPLE T-TEST

The two-sample t-test (also known as the independent samples t-test) is a method used to test whether the unknown population means of two groups are equal or not. It is used when your data values are independent and randomly sampled from two normal populations and the two independent groups have equal variances (*Two-Sample t-Test*, n.d.).

ONE-WAY ANOVA

The one-way analysis of variance (ANOVA) is used to determine whether there are any statistically significant differences between the means of three or more independent (unrelated) groups (Laerd Statistics, 2018).

PAIRED T-TEST

A paired t-test determines whether the mean change for these pairs is significantly different from zero. This test is an inferential statistics procedure because it uses samples to draw conclusions about populations. Common applications of the paired sample t-test include case-control studies or repeated-measures designs. An example of a common use of the paired t-test is a comparison of before and after situations. This would be like before and after a test or completing a training program (Frost, 2021b).

Bivariate Statistical Techniques

Bivariate analysis is defined as aiming to understand the relationship between two variables: x and y. Think of bivariate statistics as *measures of relationship*. When the two variables are measured on the same object, x is usually identified as the independent variable, whereas y is the dependent variable. Bivariate statistics is appropriate if the researcher wants to understand the relationship between two variables in the data to one another.

Conversely, if both variables were generated in an experiment, the variable manipulated by the experimenter is described as the independent variable. With bivariate analysis, the methods of statistics help describe the strength of the relationship between the two variables, either by a single parameter such as Pearson's correlation coefficient for linear relationships or by an equation obtained by regression analysis (Trauth, 2007). For every measurement of a variable, X, we have a corresponding value of a second variable, Y, and the resulting pairs of values are called a *bivariate population*. Also, we may have a corresponding value of the third variable, Z, or the fourth variable, W, and so on, and the resulting pairs of values are called a *multivariate population* (Kothari, 2004). There are three basic parametric statistical techniques: (a) *Pearson Correlation*; (b) *Simple Linear Regression,* and (c) *Scatterplot Diagram* (see Figure 17.9).

PEARSON CORRELATION

The most widely used statistic for determining correlation is the Pearson product moment correlation, which is sometimes called the Pearson r. This statistic, which is the square of the Pearson r, tells us how much of the variance is accounted for by the correlation. The Pearson correlation is a bivariate statistical test that is a measure of the strength of the linear relationship between two variables. Pearson's r ranges between -1 and $+1$, and the further away it is from 0, the stronger the relationship between the two variables. SPSS uses asterisks to show the strength of the relationship. Statistically significant relationships are marked with two asterisks. The researcher must keep in mind, however, that an independent variable's accuracy in predicting a correlated dependent variable does not necessarily indicate a cause-and-effect relationship. Thus, correlation does not mean causation (Leedy & Ormrod, 2001; Miles, 2013b).

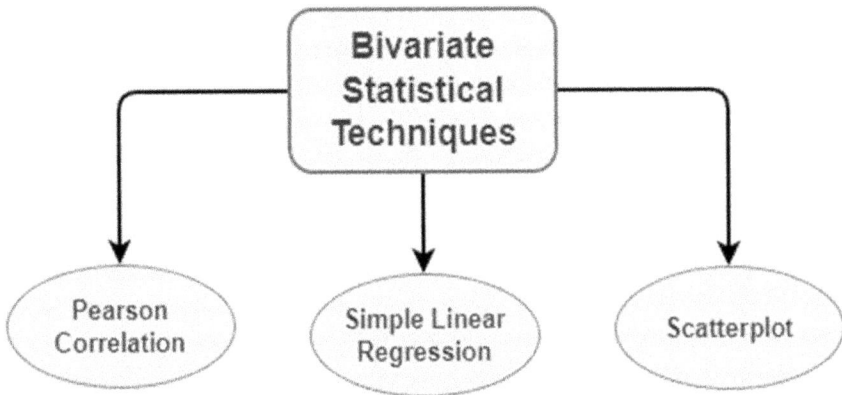

Figure 17.9 Bivariate statistical techniques model.

SIMPLE LINEAR REGRESSION

A simple linear regression is a bivariate statistical test that involves measuring the influence of a single independent (predictor) variable on the single dependent (criterion) variable. A simple linear regression generates an equation in which a single independent variable yields predictions for the dependent variable. A simple linear regression is used to predict the influence of the independent variable on the dependent variable. A simple linear regression approach is often chosen when the researcher wishes to control for the influence of other independent variables. It is especially useful when a relation between an observed dependent variable and a given observed independent variable is of interest (Leedy & Ormrod, 2001; Swanson & Holton, 2005; Trauth, 2007).

Regression analysis can perform simple, polynomial and multiple analysis. The output includes a linear regression equation, a table of coefficients, R^2, R^2 adjusted, an analysis of variance table and a table of fits and residuals that provide unusual observations (Smith & Albaum, 2010). In terms of the linearity test, when we do a linear regression, we assume that the relationship between the response variable and the predictors is linear. This is the assumption of *linearity*. If this assumption is violated, the linear regression will try to fit a straight line to data that does not follow a straight line. In SPSS, the regression output shows the model summary, which provides the value of R (Multiple Correlation), R^2 (Coefficient of Determination) and Adjusted R^2 (R^2 adjusted with Degrees of Freedom) (Sreejesh et al., 2014).

SCATTERPLOT

A scatterplot is used to explore the relationship between two quantitative (interval or ratio) variables. The horizontal axis (X) represents the values of one variable and the vertical axis (Y) represents the values of the other variable. This is simply a plot of the points (Xi, Yi) in the plane. A key feature of the scatterplot is the association, or trend, between X and Y (Miles, 2013b). The researcher uses scatterplots to show relationships between pairs of continuous variables. These graphs display symbols at the X, Y coordinates of the data points for the paired variables. Scatterplots are also known as *scattergrams* and *scatter charts*. The pattern of dots on a scatterplot allows the researcher to determine whether a relationship or correlation exists between two continuous variables. If a relationship exists, the scatterplot indicates its direction and whether it is a linear or curved relationship (Frost, 2021a).

Multivariate Statistical Techniques

Now, we will briefly describe the different types of multivariate techniques and the most commonly used for dissertation studies, such as the multivariate analysis of variance (MANOVA), discriminant analysis and canonical correlations. We will also describe, in brief, some of the other multivariate techniques, such as factor analysis, cluster analysis and structural equation modeling. Again, for the purposes of this discussion, I will not discuss any nonparametric techniques. I will only discuss parametric statistical techniques.

Multivariate statistics is defined as methods that examine the simultaneous effect of multiple variables. Based on the traditional classification of multivariate statistical methods, it is based on the concept of dependency between variables (Marinković, 2008; Samuels, 2020). An interesting aspect about the multivariate analysis of variance is that it is an extension of the bivariate analysis of variance. Conversely, multivariate analysis is focused on variables to which the ratio of among-groups variance to within-groups variance is calculated on a set of variables instead of a single variable (Kothari, 2004). There are nine basic multivariate statistical techniques: (a) *multiple linear regression*; (b) *logistic regression*; (c) *MANOVA*; (d) *MANCOVA*; (e) *discriminant analysis*; (f) *conjoint analysis*; (g) *cluster analysis*; (h) *factor analysis*; and (i) *structural equation modeling (SEM)* (see Figure 17.10).

Multiple Linear Regression

Multiple linear regression identifies the best combinations of predictors (independent variables) of the dependent variable. It is used when there are several independent quantitative variables and one dependent quantitative variable. To produce the best combination of predictors of the dependent variable, a sequential multiple regression selects independent variables, one at a time, by their ability to account for the most variance in the dependent variable (Miles, 2013b).

Logistic Regression

Logistic regression is used to predict a categorical (usually dichotomous) variable from a set of predictor variables. Logistic regression is often chosen if the predictor variables are a mix of continuous and categorical variables and/or if they are not

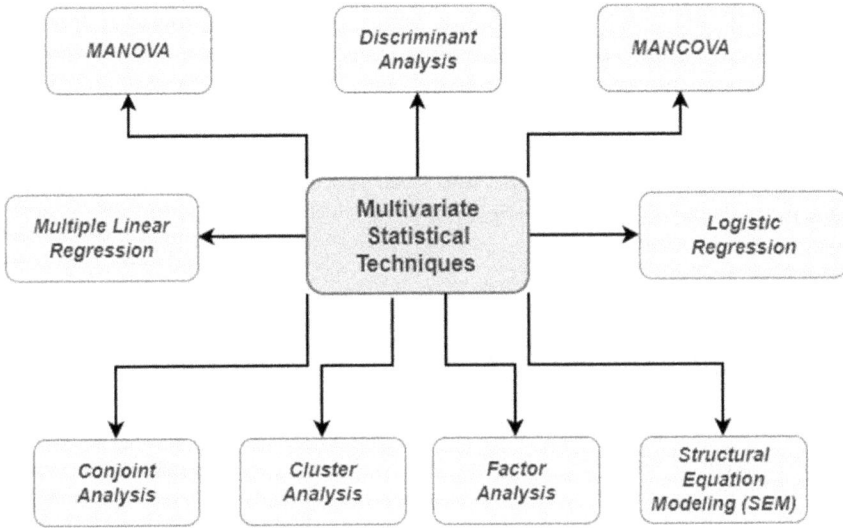

Figure 17.10 Multivariate statistical techniques model.

nicely distributed (logistic regression makes no assumptions about the distributions of the predictor variables) (Miles, 2013c).

Multiple Analysis of Variance (MANOVA)

The MANOVA tests the significance of group differences between two or more means, as it analyzes variation between and within each group. The MANOVA is an extension of the univariate analysis of variance (ANOVA). The MANOVA is a technique that determines the effects of independent categorical variables on multiple continuous dependent variables. It is typically used to compare several groups with respect to multiple continuous variables (*Multiple Analysis of Variance (MANOVA)*, n.d.; Miles, 2013b; Miles, 2013c).

Multiple Analysis of Covariance (MANCOVA)

MANCOVA is an extension of the ANCOVA. The MANCOVA investigates group differences among several dependent variables while also controlling for covariate(s) that may influence the dependent variables. For example, a research question would look like this, "Does ethnicity (independent variable) significantly affect reading achievement, math achievement, and overall achievement (dependent variable) among 6th grade students after adjusting for family income (covariate)?" (Miles, 2013b).

Discriminant Analysis

Discriminant analysis is used when you wish to predict group membership from a set of two or more continuous variables. The analysis creates a set of discriminant functions (weighted combinations of the predictors) that will enable you to predict into which group a case falls, based on scores on the predictor variables (usually continuous, but could include dichotomous variables and dummy coded categorical predictors). One might also determine how well a function separates each group from all the rest to help label the function (Miles, 2013b).

Conjoint Analysis

Conjoint analysis is a form of statistical analysis that firms use in market research to understand how customers value different components or features of a product or service. It's based on the principle that any product can be broken down into a set of attributes that ultimately impact users' perceived value of an item or service. Conjoint analysis is typically used with a specialized survey that asks consumers to rank the importance of the specific features in question (Stobierski, 2020; Miles, 2013b).

Cluster Analysis

Cluster analysis or clustering is the task of grouping a set of objects in such a way that objects in the same group (called a cluster) are more similar (in some sense or another) to each other than to those in other groups (clusters) (Miles, 2013b; Miles, 2013c).

Factor Analysis

Factor analysis allows the researcher to explore underlying structures of an instrument or data set and is often used to develop and test theory. Principal component analysis is generally used to reduce the number of independent variables, which is advantageous when conducting multivariate techniques in which the independent variables are highly correlated (Miles, 2013b; Miles, 2013c). A *principal component analysis* (PCA) (aka *exploratory factor analysis*) is used when the research purpose is data reduction (parsimony) or exploration. PCA is a variance-focused approach. Variance within the factor PCA is not used in causal modeling (e.g., not used with structural equation modeling). Factor analysis is primarily used for exploratory research and data reduction (Miles, 2013b; Miles, 2013c). A *principal axis factoring* (PAF) (aka *common factor analysis*) is used when the research purpose is theory confirmation and causal modeling. PAF is a correlation-focused approach and tends to be a shared variance. A type of PAF is built into structural equation modeling programs (e.g., AMOS and LISREL) (Miles, 2013b; Miles, 2013c).

Structural Equation Modeling (SEM)

This is a special form of hierarchical multiple regression analysis in which the researcher specifies a particular causal model in which each variable affects one or more of the other variables both directly and through its effects upon intervening variables. SEM can include latent variables (factors), constructs that are not directly measured but rather are inferred from measured variables (indicators). Confirmatory factor analysis can be considered a special case of SEM. In confirmatory factor analysis the focus is on testing an a priori model of the factor structure of a group of measured variables. It is used with special software such as AMOS (SPSS), LISREL, SmartPLS, OpenMx, Mplus and others (Miles, 2013b).

Types of Quantitative Data Analysis Used in Dissertation Research

There are different types of data analyses used for different dissertation research. Again, the data analysis strategy is based on the establishment of the research design. There are five statistical analysis designs: (a) *descriptive analysis*; (b) *inferential analysis*; (c) *differences analysis*; (d) *associative analysis*; and (e) *predictive analysis*. The types of statistical analysis can be properly performed and are based on the research design chosen for the study (Burns & Bush, 2003) (see Figure 17.11).

Descriptive Analysis

This statistical analysis design is used to describe the variable (question responses) in the data. Certain measures, such as the central tendency of the mean, mode, standard deviation and range, are forms of descriptive analysis. This is used to describe the sample data in such a way as to portray the "typical" respondent and reveal the general pattern of responses. A frequency analysis and crosstab analysis are typically used with the statistical descriptive analysis (Burns & Bush, 2003).

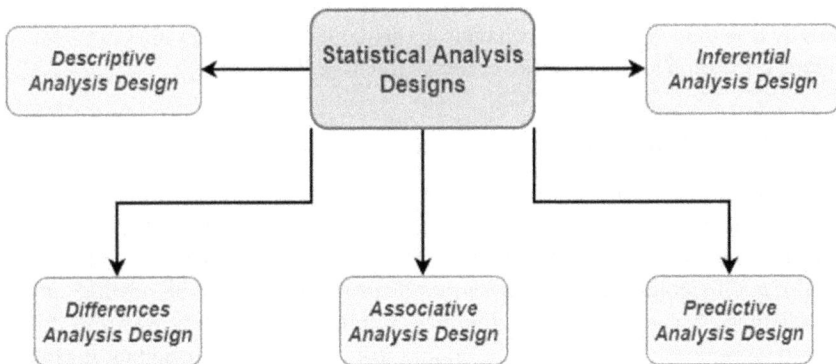

Figure 17.11 The statistical analysis design model.

Inferential Analysis

This statistical analysis design is used to generate conclusions about the population's characteristics based on the sample data. This is a statistical procedure that is used by researchers to generalize the results of the sample to the population that it represents. Inferential analysis includes hypothesis testing and estimating the true population (Burns & Bush, 2003).

Differences Analysis

This statistical analysis design is used to compare the mean of the responses of one group to that of another group. This is a statistical procedure that is used by researchers to determine whether two groups are different. The researcher statistically compares groups and uses differences analysis to determine the degree to which real and generalizable differences exist in the population. Statistical differences analysis includes the independent sample t-test and analysis of variance (ANOVA) (Burns & Bush, 2003).

Associative Analysis

This statistical analysis design is used to determine the strength and direction of relationships between two or more variables. This is a statistical procedure that is used by researchers to look for statistical relationships among variables. This technique examines if and how two variables are related. This statistical method is also used by researchers interested in determining complex patterns of association. It is a test of associations between two dependent variables. A Pearson correlation statistical test is typically used in this analysis (Burns & Bush, 2003).

Predictive Analysis

This statistical analysis design is used to make forecasts about future behavior or events. It is used by researchers to generalize the results of a sample to the population that it represents. A regression analysis or time series analysis is typically used by researchers to predict behavior in the data. This includes linear regression, logistic regression and time series analysis (Burns & Bush, 2003).

Reliability in Quantitative Data Analysis

Reliability is defined as the extent to which a measurement reproduces consistent results if the process of measurement were to be repeated. Approaches to assessing reliability include test–retest reliability, alternative-forms reliability and internal consistency reliability. Systematic sources of error do not have an adverse impact on reliability, because they affect the measurement in a constant way and do not lead to inconsistency. In contrast, random errors produce inconsistency, leading to lower reliability. Reliability can be defined as the extent to which measures are free from random error (Malhotra & Birks, 2007; Tabachnick & Fidell, 2007; Malhotra, 2015; Leedy & Ormrod, 2021). To measure reliability with an instrument or scale, a *coefficient alpha*, or *Cronbach's alpha*, is the average of all possible split-half coefficients resulting from different ways of measuring the reliability of the scale items. This coefficient varies from 0 to 1, and a value of 0.6 or less generally indicates unsatisfactory internal consistency reliability (Saunders et al., 2012; Malhotra, 2015).

Validity in Quantitative Data Analysis

Validity is defined as the extent to which a measurement represents characteristics that exist in the phenomenon under investigation. Validity can be assessed by examining three general types: (a) *content validity* (sometimes called *face validity*) is a subjective but systematic evaluation of how well the content of a scale represents the measurement task at hand; (b) *criterion validity* is a type of validity that examines whether the measurement scale performs as expected in relation to other selected variables as meaningful criteria; and (c) *construct validity* is a type of validity that addresses the question of what construct or characteristic the scale is measuring; it is an attempt to answer theoretical questions of why a scale works and what deductions can be made concerning the theory underlying the scale (Burns & Bush, 2003; Tabachnick & Fidell, 2007; Saunders et al., 2012; Malhotra, 2015).

Review the Results of the Data Analysis

Results need to be reported on after they are interpreted. This requires quoting relevant probability values, comparing them with the significance threshold in order to make a decision about a null hypothesis and referring this decision back to your research question. It is usually not appropriate to copy and paste software output into your findings, but this can be provided in an appendix. You may also need to compare your findings with other people's findings in the literature and discuss any differences or implications (Shah & Peters, 2022).

Qualitative Data Analysis

Qualitative analysis is about reviewing words, phrases and statements in a qualitative way and extracting descriptions and/or meanings to help address the research questions you have. Qualitative analysis can be seen as a systematic process of summarizing data, reducing it to concepts called codes and themes that can then be transformed into a model or theory when needed. It is an art, and it takes time and practice to perfect this art. The researcher analyzing qualitative data is viewed as an instrument subjectively transforming the data into meaningful outcomes to meet the purpose of the study. Due to the subjective nature of the data analysis process, the core strategy for ensuring the credibility of your findings is to be methodical in the data analysis process and transparent, making known the actions and decisions you make. Besides being systematic and transparent when analyzing data, you also engage in bracketing by reflecting on your beliefs, experience and preconceptions, suspending your judgment and thinking, deciding and acting based on your role as a qualitative researcher (Larsen & Adu, 2021).

Data Analysis Process

There are many ways of analyzing qualitative data. Before we discuss the most common types of qualitative analysis, let's look at a generic way of analyzing qualitative data. The point of showing these commonly followed steps is to give you a foundational knowledge of how qualitative data are generally analyzed. To learn more about the steps below, see *A Step-By-Step Guide to Qualitative Data Coding* by Philip Adu (2019).

- *Step 1: Review the transcripts.* The first step in conducting qualitative data is to review the content of the data you will be coding to familiarize yourself with it. As you go through the data, you will get a general understanding of what the participants were saying. It is also a great opportunity to write down or document what you see in the data and what you think. The former could be helpful when generating codes/themes, while the latter could assist in making sense of the codes, themes or findings.
- *Step 2: Label the research questions.* One of the main reasons why you are analyzing your data is to address the research questions. To make sure that the to-be-developed codes and themes adequately address the research questions, it is important to label the research questions and group the codes and themes generated under their respective labels.
- *Step 3: Determine an appropriate coding strategy.* A coding strategy is a technique used to extract relevant information from the data and transform them into codes and/or themes. There are many coding strategies you can choose from (see Saldaña, 2021). The two coding strategies that are mostly used are description-focused and interpretation-focused coding (Adu, 2019). You use description-focused coding if you plan to generate codes and/or themes that depict relevant information extracted from the data. In other words, with description-focused coding, you are telling us what the relevant information are in the form of phrases, which are then connected to codes or themes. However, with interpretation-focused coding, you first need to make sense of the relevant information extracted from the data before developing codes or themes. We normally use this type of coding strategy when the information needed to address the research questions is hidden in the data (Adu, 2019). To develop interpretation-focused codes, you first select the relevant information from the data, understand the excerpt, determine what it means considering the context, such as participant's demographics and background, and generate a code or theme. Nevertheless, description-focused coding is useful when what you are looking for in the data to address your research questions is explicit, meaning you can extract relevant information from the data and summarize them in the

form of codes and themes (Adu, 2019). Ultimately, the goal of utilizing a specific coding strategy is to develop codes that address the research questions and descriptively or interpretatively represent the extracts from the data.

- **Step 4: Code the data.** After determining the right coding strategy, your next step is to generate codes. Codes are generated based on the significant information selected from the data (Saldaña, 2021). Coding is the process of identifying relevant words, phrases, sentences or paragraphs in the data and generating labels (which are called codes) to represent the relevant excerpts (Adu, 2019). A code should be developed in such a way that it addresses its associated research question. Make sure you generate codes not to address the interview questions but to address your research questions.

- **Step 5: Categorize the codes.** At this stage, you may have a lot of codes under their respective research questions. The next step is to group them into clusters, transforming the codes into themes for each research question. The categorization process involves examining the characteristics of each code in terms of what they mean and any relevant information connected to them, exploring the relationships between the codes and grouping them based on their similarities (Adu, 2019). By the end, you may have come up with four to six groups of codes. You then label each group to reflect the codes under it. The labels become the themes that address the research question.

- **Step 6: Determine any relationships between the themes.** This final step is needed if your individual themes cannot independently address your research question(s) or if you plan to develop a model or theory that is supported by the data and address the research question(s). You determine if there are relationships between the themes by examining their features in terms of what they mean and represent. If relationships exist, you could explore the sequence of the relationship, finding out if they have a concurrent relationship (i.e., both happen at the same time) or a chronological relationship (i.e., one happens before the other). You could determine whether one theme can be embedded in a dominant theme or whether one theme affects another theme. Casagrande and Hale (1967) discuss types of relationship such as attributive ("X is defined with respect to one or more distinctive or characteristic attributes Y"), contingency ("X is defined with relation to a usual or necessary antecedent or concomitant Y"), synonymy ("X is defined as being equivalent to Y") and class inclusion ("X is defined with respect to its membership is a hierarchical class Y") (Casagrande & Hale, 1967, p. 168). Make sure the connections discovered are supported by your data (see Adu, 2019).

Types of Qualitative Analysis

There are many types of qualitative analysis, including variations under some of the types. The ones that are commonly used in dissertations focusing on qualitative research are thematic analysis, content analysis, grounded theory analysis and narrative analysis.

Thematic Analysis

Thematic analysis involves reviewing data, extracting relevant information based on the research question, assigning codes to them and examining the codes to help develop themes. This process is similar to the six steps provided above. Thematic analysis is appropriate if you want what you find in the data to dictate the development of your codes and themes.

- **Resources**
  - Adu, 2019; Braun & Clarke, 2006; Maguire & Delahunt, 2017; Strauss, 1989

Content Analysis

Content analysis involves generating codes and/or themes based on literature reviewed, theoretical or conceptual frameworks developed and/or initial data reviewed and using them to analyze the data. This group of codes and/or themes is called a coding frame. During data analysis, relevant information identified are connected to codes or themes belonging to the coding frame. Think of this process as going to a good market or grocery store with bags you plan to put your purchased food items into. When you go to the market, you buy cauliflower, leeks, kale and cabbage and put them into the "vegetable bag"; barley, millet, brown rice and oats, which go into the "grain bag"; and apples, pears, oranges and watermelons, which go into the "fruit bag." These bags represent codes or themes, and the food items bought represent the relevant information selected from the data. Lastly, all the food items in the grocery store are considered data. Normally, content analysis is appropriate if you want to use the concepts captured in your theoretical or conceptual framework or identified in the literature to directly inform the data coding process.

- **Resources**
  - Erlingsson & Brysiewicz, 2017; Schreier, 2012; Zhang & Wildemuth, 2009

Grounded Theory Analysis

Grounded theory analysis is the process of generating codes and themes based on evidence (i.e., significant portions of the data) and connecting these themes, leading to the development of a model or theory reflecting the data collected and addressing a research question. The main coding strategies you could use when conducting a grounded theory analysis are initial (open) coding, focused (axial) coding and theoretical coding (Charmaz, 2014). The data analysis process starts with conducting initial coding. This type of coding involves going through the data, extracting information that are relevant and assigning codes to them. An initial code is a phrase that usually starts with a gerund (e.g., "engaging in self-reflection") and is recommended to be between two and five words (Adu, 2019). The next step is to use focused coding to group codes, leading to the generation of themes. Next, relationships between the themes are examined and a potential model or theory is developed considering the evidence in the data. To refine and solidify the potential model or theory, you conduct a constant comparative analysis. This type of analysis focuses on comparing the initial theory developed to (usually) a new set of data. To get access to a new set of data, you sample participants who can provide rich data for further analysis. This kind of sampling technique is known as theoretical sampling, the process of constantly comparing the model or theory to a new set of data until saturation is reached. You reach saturation when the introduction of a new set of data does not lead to an adjustment of the theory. A theory contains concepts (i.e., themes) and their relationship. It also explains a process, an experience, an event and a situation.

- **Resources**
  - Charmaz, 2014; Sbaraini et al., 2011

Narrative Analysis

Narrative analysis involves extracting relevant information from data related to components of a story and using them to create a story that best represents the participants' stories. A good story should have the following components: orientation, abstract, complicating action and resolution (Richmond, 2002). Based on Richmond's (2002) description of these four story components, there are questions you could address when conducting a narrative analysis.

- *Orientation:*
  - What was the setting?
  - Who was/were the character(s)?
  - What were their roles?
- *Abstract:*
  - What were the incidences?
  - What was happening?
- *Complicating action:*
  - What was the conflict in the story?
  - What were the actions and reactions of the character(s)?
  - What were the thoughts and intensions of the character(s)?
- *Resolution:*
  - What were the consequences of the conflict?
  - What lessons can be learned from the story?

One of the ways of analyzing participant stories using a narrative analysis is to first familiarize yourself with the data. This helps you to get a big picture of participants' stories and think about how they will help you to address your research question. Secondly, with the research question in mind, you go through the data and extract codes addressing the question. In addition, you extract all the relevant components of their stories and generate phrases (codes) to represent the features captured. Thirdly, you then categorize the codes to develop themes that will be used to address the research question. Similarly, you also examine the codes generated under each of their story components and group them to generate concepts/themes. Fourthly, you connect these concepts (which depict the features of participants' stories) to the themes for the research questions. Fifthly, you write a story that has all the ingredients you have discovered in your analysis and best represents participants' stories.

- **Resources**
  - Mishler, 1999; Richmond, 2002; Saldaña, 2021; Stephens & Breheny, 2013

How to Determine the Right Type of Qualitative Analysis

When deciding on the right qualitative analysis technique for your study, you first need to consider the best practices by asking yourself, "What data analysis technique do researchers normally use when utilizing your research approach?" For instance, if you are planning to conduct a phenomenological study and want to describe participants' experience, leading to an attainment of the true nature of their experience, researchers are more likely to use a data analysis strategy informed by transcendental phenomenology (see Larsen & Adu, 2021).

Moreover, you can select the right data analysis strategy by looking for a technique that has been customized for your research approach. For example, narrative analysis is the right technique for a narrative approach, while grounded theory analysis is an appropriate data analysis strategy for a grounded theory approach (see Richmond, 2002; Saldaña, 2021).

Alternatively, you could use one of the generic qualitative data analysis techniques, such as thematic or content analysis. Considering your research purpose, questions and method, if you plan to extract relevant aspects of the data and generate codes and themes based on these extracts, then thematic analysis will help. However, if you want to use codes and/or themes generated from your conceptual/theoretical framework or literature to code relevant information from the data, then content analysis is the right data analysis strategy.

Ensuring the Credibility of Your Qualitative Findings

The credibility of findings is about the believability of what you have found. In other words, your findings are credible if people, including the research community, trust the results of your study. Because, in a qualitative study, researchers are instruments working with assumptions related to the acceptance of subjectivity and the acknowledgement of multiple realities, they must be transparent to ensure credibility. Being transparent at the data analysis stage involves making known your relevant history, which includes your experience related to the phenomenon of study, preconceptions and beliefs (Adu, 2019). All these background factors can influence how you make sense of what you are analyzing, but you could reduce their influence by setting them aside (i.e., by practicing bracketing) (Larsen & Adu,

2021; Tufford & Newman, 2012). To ensure credibility, you are expected to share how you engaged in bracketing or any related act of reflecting on your background, including expectations and judgment, and how you prevented them from influencing the data analysis process.

Another way of ensuring the credibility of your findings is to engage in member checking. One aspect of practicing member checking is to give participants their transcripts for them to review and provide feedback in terms of whether the data reflect what they shared (Birt et al., 2016; Candela, 2019). As part of member checking, you could also seek their feedback on how you made sense of their data. Another form of member checking is to ask another researcher to review your data analysis-related actions and outcomes and provide feedback.

You could also increase the credibility of your findings by giving a detailed description of your data analysis process. Adequately describing the data analysis process depends on your extensive documentation of the process. Therefore, it is important to always document how you selected relevant information from the data, generated codes and examined the codes to develop themes.

Lastly, presenting the findings in a way that makes sense to your audience increases the credibility of your findings (Adu, 2019). The common pattern of presenting qualitative results is to state and describe each theme, presenting what it means and represents, evidence in support of the theme and a statement showing how it addresses the research question.

Summary

The practice of data analysis is one of the most important aspects of research. There are several advantages and disadvantages of both quantitative and qualitative methods of data analysis. With data analysis, it is important to conduct the analysis with precision and reliability. The quantitative method of data analysis focuses on the measurement of variables and tendency that occur in the data, while the qualitative method of data analysis focuses on phenomena that occur in natural settings, and the data are typically analyzed from that approach.

In this chapter, we discussed six things: how to determine an appropriate data analysis technique for the study; how to develop data analysis for the study; the different types of quantitative data analysis used in dissertation research; reliability and credibility in the process of data analysis; validity in the process of data analysis; and, lastly, the distinct differences between the data analysis processes in quantitative and qualitative research. By the end of this chapter, the reader should be knowledgeable about these six core areas of data analysis.

References

Adu, P. (2019). *A step-by-step guide to qualitative data coding*. Routledge.

Anderson, T. W. (2003). *An introduction to multivariate statistical analysis* (3rd ed.). Wiley-Interscience.

Birt, L., Scott, S., Cavers, D., Campbell, C., & Walter, F. (2016). Member checking: A tool to enhance trustworthiness or merely a nod to validation? *Qualitative Health Research*, *26*(13), 1802–1811. https://doi.org/10.1177/1049732316654870

Braun, V., & Clarke, V. (2006). Using thematic analysis in psychology. *Qualitative Research in Psychology, 3*(2), 77–101. https://doi.org/10.1191/1478088706qp063oa

Burns, A. C., & Bush, R. F. (2003). *Marketing research: Online research applications* (4th ed.). Prentice Hall.

Byrne, D. (2002). *Interpreting quantitative data.* SAGE Publications Ltd.

Candela, A. G. (2019). Exploring the function of member checking. *The Qualitative Report, 24*(3), 619–628. Retrieved from https://nsuworks.nova.edu/tqr/vol24/iss3/14

Casagrande, J. B., & Hale, K. L. (1967). Semantic relationships in Papago folk-definitions. In D. H. Hymes & W. E. Bittle (Eds.), *Studies in southwestern ethnolinguistics: Meaning and history in the languages of the American Southwest* (pp. 165–193). Mouton & Co.

Charmaz, K. (2014). *Constructing grounded theory.* SAGE Publications.

Chen, J. (2021, November 7). *Z-Test.* Investopedia. www.investopedia.com/terms/z/z-test.asp

Corder, G. W., & Foreman, D. I. (2014). *Nonparametric statistics: a step-by-step approach.* Wiley Corporation.

Erlingsson, C., & Brysiewicz, P. (2017). A hands-on guide to doing content analysis. *African Journal of Emergency Medicine: Revue africaine de la medecine d'urgence, 7*(3), 93–99. https://doi.org/10.1016/j.afjem.2017.08.001

Frost, J. (2021a, October 24). *Paired t-test.* Statistics by Jim. https://statisticsbyjim.com/hypothesis-testing/paired-t-test/

Frost, J. (2021b, June 14). *Scatterplots: Using, examples, and interpreting.* Statistics by Jim. https://statisticsbyjim.com/graphs/scatterplots/

Jackson, S. L. (2009). *Research methods and statistics: A critical thinking approach* (3rd ed.). Wadsworth.

Kerlinger, F. N., & Lee, H. B. (2007). *Foundations of behavioral research.* Wadsworth.

Kothari, C. R. (2004). *Research methodology: Methods and techniques* (2nd ed.). New Age International Limited.

Laerd Statistics. (2018). *One-way ANOVA.* Laerd Statistics. https://statistics.laerd.com/statistical-guides/one-way-anova-statistical-guide.php

Larsen, H., & Adu, P. (2021). *The theoretical framework in phenomenological research: Development and application.* Routledge.

Leedy, P., & Ormrod, J. (2001). *Practical research: Planning and design.* Merrill Prentice Hall and SAGE Publications.

Leedy, P. D., Ormrod, J. E., & Johnson, L. R. (2019). *Practical research: Planning and design* (12th ed.). Pearson.

Maguire, M., & Delahunt, B. (2017). Doing a thematic analysis: A practical, step-by-step guide for learning and teaching scholars. *AISHE-J, 9*(3), 3351. https://ojs.aishe.org/index.php/aishe-j/article/view/335

Malhotra, N. K. (2015). *Essentials of marketing research: A hands-on approach.* Pearson.

Malhotra, N. K., & Birks, D. F. (2007). *Marketing research: An applied approach.* (3rd ed.). Pearson.

Malhotra, N. K., Nunan, D., & Birks, D. F. (2017). *Marketing research: An applied approach* (5th ed.). Pearson.

Marinković, J. (2008). Multivariate statistics. In W. Kirch (Ed.), *Encyclopedia of public health* (pp. 973–976). Springer. https://doi.org/10.1007/978-1-4020-5614-7_2264

McNiff, J. & Whitehead, J. (2010). *You and your action research project.* Routledge.

Miles, D. A. (2013a). *MBA workshops in marketing and statistics: Bivariate statistical methods map* [Workshop]. Business Research Methods Class, Our Lady of the Lake University, San

Antonio, Texas. www.researchgate.net/publication/278849676_WORKSHOP_MBA_ Workshops_in_Marketing_and_Statistics_Bivariate_Statistical_Methods_Map?enric hId=rgreq-b070ae550ebd96c24292ece8c3bee709-XXX&enrichSource=Y292ZXJQY WdlOzI3ODg0OTY3NjtBUzoyNDI5NDcyNzE3MjkxNTJAMTQzNDkzNDU1MTE 4Mw%3D%3D&el=1_x_3&_esc=publicationCoverPdf

Miles, D. A. (2013b). *MBA workshops in marketing and statistics: Multivariate statistical methods map* [Workshop]. Business Research Methods Class, Our Lady of the Lake University, San Antonio, Texas. www.researchgate.net/publication/278411412_WORKSHOP_ MBA_Workshops_in_Marketing_and_Statistics_Multivariate_Statistical_Meth ods_Map

Miles, D. A. (2013c). *MBA workshops in marketing and statistics: Univariate statistical methods map* [Workshop]. Business Research Methods Class, Our Lady of the Lake University, San Antonio, Texas. www.researchgate.net/publication/278411623_WORKSHOP_MBA_ Workshops_in_Marketing_and_Statistics_Univariate_Statistical_Methods_Map

Miles, D.A. & Scott, L. (2017, October 26–29). *Confessions of a dissertation chair, Part 1: The six mistakes doctoral students make with the dissertation* [Workshop]. 5th Annual 2017 Black Doctoral Network Conference, Atlanta, GA.

Mishler, E. (1999). *Storylines: Craftartists' narratives of identity.* Harvard University Press.

Multiple *analysis of variance* (MANOVA*).* (n.d.). Statistics.com. www.statistics.com/glossary/ multiple-analysis-of-variance-manova

OpenAI. (2023). ChatGPT (May 24 version) [GPT-4, Code Interpreter Model]. https:// chat.openai.com/chat

Richmond, H. J. (2002). Learners' lives: A narrative analysis. *The Qualitative Report, 7*(3), 1–14. https://doi.org/10.46743/2160-3715/2002.1973

Saldaña, J. (2021). *The coding manual for qualitative researchers.* SAGE.

Samuels, P. (2020). A really simple guide to quantitative data analysis. *Technical Report,* 2–6. https://doi.org/DOI: 10.13140/RG.2.2.25915.36645

Saunders, M., Lewis, P., & Thornhill, A. (2012). *Research methods for business students* (6th ed.). Pearson.

Sbaraini, A., Carter, S. M., Evans, R. W., & Blinkhorn, A. S. (2011). How to do a grounded theory study: A worked example of a study of dental practices. *BMC Medical Research Methodology, 11*, 128. https://doi.org/10.1186/1471-2288-11-128

Schreier, M. (2012). *Qualitative content analysis in practice.* Sage.

Sekaran, U. (2006). *Research methods for business: A skill building approach* (4th ed.). John Wiley & Sons.

Shah, R. D., & Peters, J. (2022). The hardness of conditional independence testing and the generalised covariance measure. The Annals of Statistics, 48(3). https://doi.org/ 10.1214/19-aos1857

Sheskin, D. J. (2000). *Handbook of parametric and nonparametric statistical procedures.* Chapman & Hall/CRC.

Smith, S. M., & Albaum, G. S. (2010). *An introduction to marketing research.* Qualtrics Survey University.

Sreejesh, S., Mohapatra, S., & Anusree, M. R. (2014). *Business research methods: An applied orientation.* Springer.

Stephens, C., & Breheny, M. (2013). Narrative analysis in psychological research: An integrated approach to interpreting stories. *Qualitative Research in Psychology, 10*(1), 14–27. https://doi.org/10.1080/14780887.2011.586103

Strauss, A. L. (1989). *Qualitative analysis for social scientists.* Cambridge University Press.

Stobierski, T. (2020, December 18). *Business insights: What is conjoint analysis, and how can it be used?* Harvard Business School Online. https://online.hbs.edu/blog/post/what-is-conjoint-analysis

Swanson, R. A., & Holton III, E. F. (2005). *Research in organizations: Foundations and methods of inquiry.* Berrett Koehler Publications.

Tabachnick, B. G., & Fidell, L. S. (2007). *Using multivariate statistics* (5th ed.). Pearson.

Trauth, M. H. (2007). Bivariate statistics. In *MATLAB® Recipes for earth sciences* (pp. 61–82). Springer. https://doi.org/10.1007/978-3-540-72749-1_4

Tufford, L., & Newman, P. (2012). Bracketing in qualitative research. *Qualitative Social Work, 11*(1), 80–96. https://doi.org/10.1177/1473325010368316

Two-sample t-test. (n.d.). JMP Statistical Discovery. www.jmp.com/en_us/statistics-knowledge-portal/t-test/two-sample-t-test.html

Zhang, Y., & Wildemuth, B. M. (2009). Qualitative analysis of content. In B. Wildemuth (Ed.), *Applications of social research methods to questions in information and library science* (pp. 308–319). Libraries Unlimited.

18 Ensuring Quality in the Study

Objectives

- Readers will be able to:
  1. Write about validity and reliability in a quantitative study
  2. Write about validity and reliability in a qualitative study
  3. Write about validity and reliability in a mixed methods study

Introduction

In the process of conducting research, there is the aspect of measurement. More specifically, reliability and validity. It is very important that the instruments we use to conduct the research are reliable and possess the characteristics of validity.

Inevitably, the task of research provides the much-needed information for their audience. Researchers will be interested in the problem identified as the basis for the line of inquiry, but it will also inspire them to be more interested in successfully dealing with problems. The concept of reliability and validity is integral to the practice of problem solving as a line of inquiry for research. Reliability and validity in the area of measurement is also the basis of sound research. Understanding the different characteristics of data, such as quantitative data and qualitative data, will really help in understanding the concept of reliability and validity.

Again, under the concept of measurement, data can be quantitative or qualitative. Each of the characteristics of scientific data can be explained in the context of research. We must consider the aspect of investigation having a foundation in measurement in terms of reliability and validity. We must examine the hallmarks of science and how it applies to this investigation and aligns with reliability and validity. Therefore, this chapter focuses on the importance of understanding reliability and validity.

Reliability and Validity in a Quantitative Study

In a quantitative study, the concept of reliability and validity is very crucial. That the task of measuring reliability is extremely complex is an understatement to say the least. The concept of reliability in relation to a research instrument has a

DOI: 10.4324/9781003268154-18

similar meaning. The research measurement tool for collecting data has to have some consistency. If a research tool is consistent and stable, therefore predictable and accurate, it is also said to be reliable. When measuring reliability, the mantra is that the greater the degree of consistency and stability in an instrument, the greater its reliability. Under the umbrella of reliability, a scale must be reliable. Therefore, "a scale or test is reliable to the extent that repeat measurements made by it under constant conditions will give the same result" (Kumar, 2011). In the area of quantitative methodology, the prevailing issues of validity and reliability are extremely important for quantitative data analysis.

The issue that afflicts the quantitative researchers' endeavor is showing their chosen methods and research design. This is so they can also show that their chosen methods succeed in measuring what they intend to measure. The researcher wants to make sure their instruments show a foundation of reliability and validity. They want to make sure that their measurements are stable and consistent and that there are no errors or bias present, either from the respondents or from the researcher (Dawson, 2002; Alasuutari et al., 2008).

Developing Reliability in a Quantitative Study

The task of developing reliability in a quantitative study is primarily based on measurement types. Reliability is defined as a statistical measure of how reproducible the survey instrument's data are. Reliability refers to the consistency with which the results are produced under the same conditions with the same or comparable populations (Litwin, 1995; Singh, 2020; Singh, 2007; Sreejesh et al., 2014). The practice of reliability inherently depends on three primary elements. The first is *stability*, which entails asking whether a measure is stable over time so that researchers can be confident that results relating to the measure for a sample of respondents will not fluctuate. The second issue is that of *interna reliability*, which seeks to assess whether the indicators that make up the scale are consistent. The last issue is *inter-observer consistency*, which may arise due to the involvement of more than one observer in activities such as the recording of observation or the translation of data into categories (Sreejesh et al., 2014).

In contrast, random error produces inconsistency, leading to lower reliability. Reliability can be defined as the extent to which measures are free from random error (Malhotra & Birks, 2007; Tabachnick & Fidell, 2007; Babbie, 2008; Bell & Waters, 2010; Malhotra, 2015; Leedy & Ormrod, 2021). To measure reliability with an instrument or scale, a *coefficient alpha*, or *Cronbach's alpha*, is used. There are minimal standards for the coefficient alpha. For example, a coefficient of 0.6 or more generally indicates a moderate satisfactory internal consistency reliability (Saunders et al., 2012; Leedy & Ormrod, 2021). The reliability coefficient is calculated to determine the extent of agreement between the two halves. As a general rule of thumb, the scale should have at least 16 to 20 items so that the halves have 8 to 10 items. The procedure also adjusts for the number of items in the scale, as a longer scale, in this case the full scale, is more reliable than a shorter one (Craig & Douglas, 2005).

Types of Reliability

When dealing with the task of reliability in quantitative research, the strategies designed to assess an instrument's reliability are based on four approaches. Again, the primary definition of reliability is the extent to which it is consistent and hence ensures consistent measurement across time and across the various items in the instrument. Nevertheless, the practice of reliability of a measure is an indication of the stability and consistency with which the instrument measures the concept and helps to assess the "goodness" of a measure (Zikmund & Babin, 2010). There are four good methods of measuring reliability in an instrument (see Figure 18.1).

TEST-RETEST TECHNIQUE

Test-retest is a technique generally used to administer the same research instrument/test/survey or measure to the same group of people twice under the same conditions but at different points in time. Reliability estimates are expressed in the form of a correlation coefficient, which is a measure of the correlation between two scores in the same group.

MULTIPLE FORMS

Multiple forms test the reliability of the research instrument by mixing up the questions in the research instrument and giving it to the same respondents again to assess whether it results in any different responses.

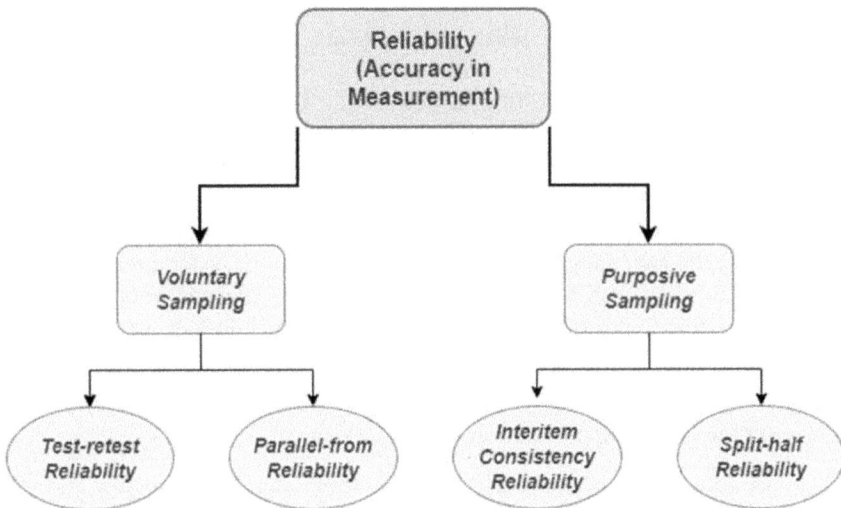

Figure 18.1 Testing goodness of measures: Forms of reliability model.

Source: Adapted from Sekaran (2003).

INTER-RATER RELIABILITY

Inter-rater reliability is used to assess the reliability of research tool instruments/ tests when more than one rater/interviewer is involved in interviewing or content analysis. It is calculated by reporting the percentage of agreement on the same subject between different raters or interviewers.

SPLIT-HALF RELIABILITY

In the case of the split-half reliability method, the results of this analysis are compared with the overall analysis to assess the reliability of the indicators, tests or instruments. Currently, many researchers use a Cronbach's alpha to test internal reliability, and it correlates performance on each item with an overall score. These techniques can be easily calculated by using statistical packages such as the Statistical Package for Social Sciences (SPSS) (Babbie, 2008; Singh, 2006; Singh, 2007; Singh, 2020; Little, 2014; Price et al., 2019; Mooi et al., 2018; Research Methods in Psychology, 2019).

INTERNAL RELIABILITY

This kind of reliability indicates how consistently all of the items in a scale measure the concept in question. If a scale is internally reliable, any set of items from the scale could be selected, and they will provide a measure that is more or less the same as any other group of items taken from that scale (Howitt & Cramer, 2011).

Three Principles of Reliability

There are three principles of reliability: (a) *stability* – in this form, reliability is a measure of consistency over time and over similar samples; a reliable instrument for a piece of research will yield similar data from similar respondents over time; (b) *equivalence* – in this form, reliability is achieved first through using equivalent forms of a test or data-gathering instrument; if an equivalent form of the test or instrument is devised and yields similar results, then the instrument can be said to demonstrate some form of reliability; and (c) *internal consistency* – in this form of reliability, the test/retest method and the equivalent-forms method require the tests or instruments to be done twice; demonstrating internal consistency demands that the instrument or tests be run once only through the split-half method (Cohen et al., 2007).

Internal Consistency of Measures of Reliability

There are some different approaches to measuring internal consistency and reliability. The goal of the internal consistency of measures is to show the homogeneity of the items in the measure. This can be done by examining if the items and the subsets of items in the measuring instrument are correlated or related in some way. Consistency can be examined through the inter-item consistency reliability and split-half reliability tests. To conduct the internal consistency of measuring reliability, the researcher has three strategies they can use: (a) *inter-item consistency reliability*; (b) *split-half reliability*; and (c) *coefficient alpha reliability*.

Inter-item Consistency Reliability

This is a test of the consistency of respondents' answers to all the items in a measure. To the degree that items are independent measures of the same concept, they will be correlated with one another (Price et al., 2019).

Split-Half Reliability

Split-half reliability, also called *split-half correlation*, reflects the correlations between two halves of an instrument. The estimates would vary depending on how the items in the measure are split into two halves. Split-half reliabilities could be higher than Cronbach's alpha only in the circumstance of there being more than one underlying response dimension tapped by the measure and when certain other conditions are met as well (Sekaran, 2003; Price et al., 2019; Research Methods in Psychology, 2019).

Coefficient alpha Reliability

The coefficient alpha reliability is a measure of internal consistency reliability that is the average of all possible split-half coefficients resulting from different splittings of the scale items. A coefficient of between 0 and 0.4 generally indicates an unsatisfactory internal consistency reliability. However, a value of 0.6 or more generally indicates a satisfactory internal consistency reliability. An interesting note is that a property of coefficient alpha is that its value tends to increase with an increase in the number of scale items. However, the coefficient alpha may be artificially, and inappropriately, inflated by including several redundant scale items. Another coefficient that can be employed in conjunction with the coefficient alpha is the coefficient beta. The coefficient beta assists in determining whether the averaging process used in calculating the coefficient alpha is masking any inconsistent items (Malhotra et al., 2017).

Other Measurements of Reliability

The use of measuring internal consistency and reliability has some different approaches. The goal of internal consistency of measures is used to show the indicative of the homogeneity of the items in the measure. This can be done by examining if the items and the subsets of items in the measuring instrument are correlated or related in some way. Consistency can be examined through the inter-item consistency reliability and split-half reliability tests. To conduct the internal consistency of measuring reliability, the researcher has about three strategies. They are; (a) *inter-item consistency reliability*; (b) *split-half reliability*; and (c) *coefficient alpha reliability*.

Inter-observer Reliability

Inter-observer reliability measures the degree to which two or more independent observers are in agreement. When observers disagree, we become uncertain about what is being measured and the behaviors and events that actually occurred. Low inter-observer reliability is likely to result when the event to be recorded is not clearly defined (Shaughnessy et al., 2012).

Item analysis

An item analysis is done to see if the items in the instrument belong there or not. Each item is examined for its ability to discriminate between those subjects whose total scores are high and those whose total scores are low. In an item analysis, the means between the high-score group and the low-score group are tested to detect significant differences through the t-values (Singh, 2006; Singh, 2007; Singh, 2020).

Alternative-forms Reliability

Alternative-forms reliability is an approach for assessing reliability that requires two equivalent forms of the scale to be constructed and then the same participants to be measured at two different times. In alternative-forms reliability, two equivalent forms of the scale are constructed. The same participants are measured at two different times, usually two to four weeks apart, with a different scale form being administered each time. The scores from the administrations of the alternative scale forms are correlated to assess reliability. The two forms should be equivalent with respect to content, i.e., each scale item should attempt to measure the same items. There are two major problems with this approach. First, it is time-consuming and expensive to construct an equivalent form of the scale. Second, it is difficult to construct two equivalent forms of a scale. In a strict sense, it is required that the alternative sets of scale items should have the same means, variances and intercorrelations. Even if these conditions are satisfied, the two forms may not be equivalent in content. Thus, a low correlation may reflect either an unreliable scale or non-equivalent forms (Malhotra et al., 2017; Jackson, 2009).

Measurement and Calculating Reliability

Reliability can be calculated statistically. Reliability may be calculated in a number of ways, but the most commonly accepted measure in field studies is internal consistency reliability using a Cronbach's alpha statistical test (Swanson & Holton, 2005). A Cronbach's alpha is a commonly used test of internal reliability. It calculates the average of all possible split-half reliability coefficients, and a computed alpha coefficient varies between 1, denoting perfect internal reliability, and 0, denoting no internal reliability. The basics of reliability in a marketing context are most commonly used in research (Peter, 1979; Finn, 2005; Smith & Albaum, 2010).

The practice of measuring reliability with an instrument or scale primarily uses a *coefficient alpha*, or *Cronbach's alpha*, which is the average of all possible split-half coefficients resulting from different ways of splitting the scale items. This coefficient varies from 0 to 1.00. A value of 0.6 or above generally indicates satisfactory internal consistency reliability, while a value of less than .05 generally indicates unsatisfactory internal consistency reliability (Saunders et al., 2012; Smith & Albaum, 2010).

Going further, the internal consistency reliabilities for each of the new scales is calculated. A large coefficient alpha (.70 for exploratory measures) provides an indication of strong item covariance and suggests that the sampling domain has adequately been captured (Swanson & Holton, 2005; Saunders et al., 2012). In general, a measurement of the reliability of a scale may be measured by one of three methods: test-retest, alternative forms or internal consistency. The figure of .75 or more is usually treated as a rule of thumb to denote an accepted level of reliability (Singh, 2020; Pedhazur & Pedhazur Schmelkin, 2006; Saunders et al., 2012).

Criteria for Good Measurement

It is critical that measurement has some sort of standard to evaluate reliability. When trying to attain good measurement, there are five approaches. The five major criteria for establishing good measurement are (a) *reliability*, which is assessed by the scale's stability (test-retest reliability) and internal consistency reliability (coefficient alpha); (b) *validity*, which means that we are measuring what we believe we are measuring, and the data must be unbiased and relevant to the characteristic being measured; (c) *sensitivity* – sensitivity or responsiveness to the treatment variable, or sensitivity in detecting small differences, because the larger the sample, the more sensitive the test is to detecting differences; (d) *generalizability*, which is the extent to which a study's findings can be applied to outside of its area, other people, situations or contexts; and (e) *relevance*, which is the extent to which all information collected addresses a research question that will help the decision maker address the current marketing problem (Zumbo & Rupp, 2004; Kaplan, 2004; Pedhazur & Pedhazur Schmelkin, 2006; Smith & Albaum, 2010).

Again, a good multi-item scale instrument is both *reliable* and *valid*. Reliability is assessed by the scale's stability (test-retest reliability) and internal consistency reliability (coefficient alpha). The achievement of scale reliability is highly dependent on how consistent the characteristic being measured is from individual to individual (homogeneity over individuals) and how stable the characteristic remains over time (Pedhazur & Pedhazur Schmelkin, 2006).

Measurement and Scaling

Measurement is defined as the assignment of scores to individuals so that the scores represent some characteristic of the individuals. This general definition is consistent with many kinds of measurement that everyone is familiar with, such as weight, temperature and others. The result of this procedure is a score that represents the object's potential energy (Price et al., 2019).

Scaling

The craft of scaling is considered an extension of measurement. The practice of scaling involves creating a continuum upon which measured objects are located. For example, each respondent is assigned a number indicating an unfavorable attitude (measured as 1), a neutral attitude (measured as 2) or a favorable attitude (measured as 3). However, measurement is the actual assignment of 1, 2 or 3 to each respondent. Scaling is the process of placing the respondents on a continuum with respect to their attitude. In this example, scaling is the process by which respondents would be classified as having an unfavorable, neutral or positive attitude (Malhotra & Birks, 2007).

Scaling has also been defined as a "procedure for the assignment of numbers (or other symbols) to a property of objects in order to impart some of the characteristics of numbers to the properties in question" (Malhotra & Birks, 2007). The researcher, having knowledge of the different scales and scaling techniques, helps people in business to administer short surveys by designing questions that use ranking or rating scales, as appropriate (Sekaran, 2003).

Scaling has the advantage of describing the procedure of assigning numbers to various degrees of opinion, attitude and other concepts. This can be done in two: (a) by making a judgment about some characteristic of an individual and then placing that individual directly on a scale that has been defined in terms of that characteristic; and (b) by constructing questionnaires in such a way that the score of an individual's responses assigns that individual a place on a scale (Sekaran, 2003).

In the practice of scaling, it must be remembered that a scale is a continuum, consisting of the highest point (in terms of some characteristic, e.g., preference, favorableness, etc.) and the lowest point, along with several intermediate points between these two extreme points. Numbers for measuring the distinctions of degree in the attitudes/opinions are, thus, assigned to individuals corresponding to their scale positions. Therefore, the term "scaling" is applied to the procedures for attempting to determine quantitative measures of subjective abstract concepts (Sekaran, 2003; Pedhazur & Pedhazur Schmelkin, 2006; Malhotra & Birks, 2007; Zikmund & Babin, 2010).

Rules of Measurement

Measurement is the foundation of reliability in research. Zikmund (2003) asserts that a *rule* is a guide that tells someone what to do. Consider this example of a measurement rule: "Assign the numerals, 1 through 7 to individuals, according to how brand loyal they are. The rule of measurement here is that values assigned in the measuring process can be manipulated according to mathematical rules. Under the rules of measurement, researchers to add, subtract, and multiply answers" (Zikmund, 2003).

The process of standardizing instruments also provides data on reliability and sometimes on the availability of the instrument. The availability of these three kinds of *data norms, estimate of reliability* and *estimate of validity* makes standardized instruments attractive to researchers, particularly to students doing research. The point here is that these attractions are quite real; using an instrument with norms and established reliability does have great advantages when these data have been obtained from samples from the same population, as we plan to study (Singh, 2006).

Scaling: Primary Scales of Measurement

The practice of measurement can be a complex endeavor. One of the prevailing issues that researchers face is the wide variety of measuring concepts at their disposal. Researchers can argue that the affective, cognitive and behavioral components of an attitude can be measured by different means. The measurement responses can be recorded using physiological measures to quantify affect. The design of a measurement scale is highly dependent on the objective of the research study and the mathematical or statistical calculations that a researcher expects to perform on the data collected using the scales (Pedhazur & Pedhazur Schmelkin, 2006; Saunders et al., 2012; Sreejesh et al., 2014; Leedy & Ormrod, 2015).

The objective of the research study may be as simple as classifying the population into various categories or as complex as ranking the units under study and comparing them to predict some trends. Most interestingly, all measures can be classified based on the way they represent scale differences between observations of the variable under examination. The level of scale measurement is seen as important for the reason that it determines the mathematical comparisons that are allowable. The four levels or types of scale measurement are nominal, ordinal, interval and ratio. The advantage of using four scale levels is that it offers the researcher more power in analyzing and testing the validity of a scale. The four different types of measurement scales can be seen in Figure 18.2.

Scales of Measurement

Scales of measurement are response options to questions that measure (or observe) variables in categorical or continuous units. Most importantly, scales of measurement need to be understood in order to assess the quality of an instrument and to determine the appropriate statistics to use in data analysis (Creswell, 2012). One of the easiest ways to understand the different scales of measurement is to remember that there are two basic types: (a) *categorical* and (b) *continuous*. Categorical scales have two types, nominal and ordinal scales, and continuous scales (often called scale scores in computer data analysis programs) also have two types, interval/ quasi-interval and ratio scales. These types of scales are shown in Figure 18.3 (Creswell, 2012).

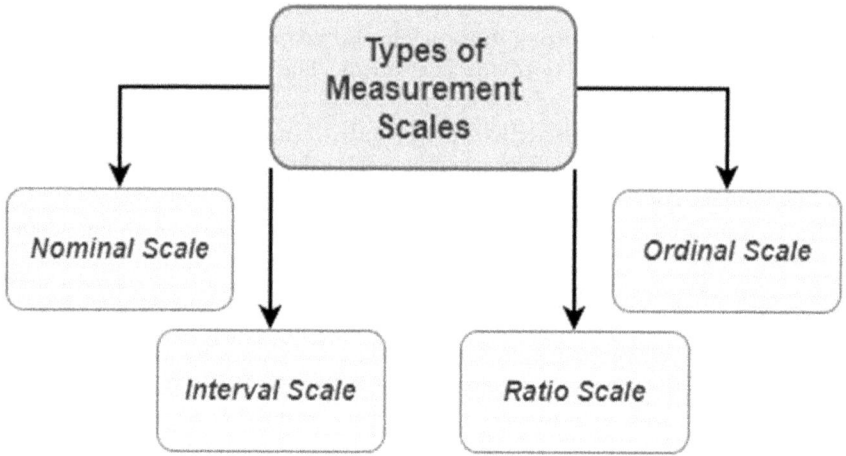

Figure 18.2 Descriptive statistics techniques model.

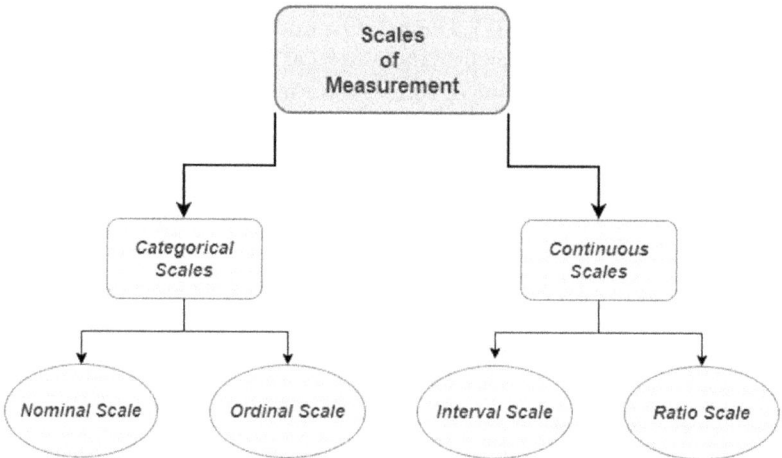

Figure 18.3 Scales of measurement model.

Nominal Scale

A nominal scale is a figurative labeling scale in which the numbers serve only as labels or tags for identifying and classifying objects. The numbers assigned to respondents in a study constitute a nominal scale. When a nominal scale is used for the purpose of identification, there is a strict one-to-one correspondence between the numbers and the objects. Each number is assigned to only one object, and each object has only one number assigned to it. Some common examples of nominal scales are social security numbers, the numbering of football players, brand numbers, store types and sex classification (Malhotra, 2015; Pedhazur & Pedhazur Schmelkin, 2006; Leedy & Ormrod, 2021).

Ordinal Scale

An ordinal scale is a ranking scale in which numbers are assigned to objects to indicate the relative extent to which the objects possess some characteristic. An ordinal scale allows you to determine whether an object has more or less of a characteristic than another object, but not how much more or less. Some common examples of ordinal scales are quality rankings, rankings of teams in a tournament, preference rankings, market position and social class (Malhotra, 2015; Pedhazur & Pedhazur Schmelkin, 2006; Leedy & Ormrod, 2021).

Interval Scale

In an interval scale, numerically equal distances on the scale represent equal values in the characteristic being measured. An interval scale contains all the information of an ordinal scale, but it also allows you to compare the differences between objects. The difference between any two adjacent scale values is identical to the difference between any other two adjacent values of an interval scale. Some common examples of interval scales are temperature (Fahrenheit/Celsius), attitudes, opinions and index numbers (Pedhazur & Pedhazur Schmelkin, 2006; Malhotra, 2015).

Ratio Scale

A ratio scale possesses all the properties of the nominal, ordinal and interval scales, plus an absolute 0 point. Thus, the ratio scale represents the highest level of measurement conveying the most information. In ratio scales, we can identify or classify objects, rank the objects and compare intervals or differences. Unlike the nominal, ordinal and interval scales, it is also meaningful to compute ratios of scale values. Some common examples are temperature, length, weight, age, income, costs, sales and market shares (Leedy & Ormrod, 2021; Malhotra, 2015).

Other Scaling Types and Rating Scales

There are many types of scales. However, we will only discuss a few of the most commonly used ones for studies: (a) *dichotomous scale*; (b) *itemized rating scale*; (c) *Likert scale*; (d) *numerical scale*; (e) *semantic differential scale*; and (f) *Stapel scale*.

Dichotomous Scale

This type of scale typically uses a two-item response. The dichotomous scale is used to elicit a "Yes" or "No" answer. This could also be used to describe gender: male or female. This is a nominal scale type of response (Sekaran, 2003; Malhotra & Birks, 2007).

Itemized Rating Scale

This type of scale typically uses a five-point or seven-point scale with anchors. This is provided for each item, and the respondent states the appropriate number on the side of each item or circles the relevant number against each item. The responses to the items are then summated using an interval scale (Sekaran, 2003; Zikmund, 2003; Zikmund & Babin, 2010).

Likert Scale

This popular scale is named after its creator, Rensis Likert. The Likert scale is one of the most widely used rating scales. It requires the respondents to indicate a degree of agreement or disagreement with each of a series of statements about the stimulus objects. Typically, each scale item has five to nine response categories, ranging from "strongly disagree" to "strongly agree" (Pedhazur & Pedhazur Schmelkin, 2006; Malhotra & Birks, 2007).

Numerical Scales

The numerical scales have numbers, rather than semantic space or verbal descriptions, as response options to identify categories. This scale is similar to the semantic differential scale, except that it uses numbers. This numerical scale uses bipolar adjectives in the same manner as the semantic differential scale (Kothari, 2004; Pedhazur & Pedhazur Schmelkin, 2006; Zikmund, 2003).

Semantic Differential Scale

The semantic differential scale is a seven-point rating scale with end points associated with bipolar labels that have semantic meaning. In a standard application, respondents rate objects on a number of itemized, seven-point rating scales bounded at each end by one of two bipolar adjectives (Zikmund & Babin, 2010).

Stapel Scale

The Stapel scale, named after its developer, Jan Stapel, is a unipolar rating scale with ten categories numbered from -5 to $+5$ and no neutral point (zero). This scale is usually presented vertically. Respondents are asked to indicate, by selecting an appropriate numerical response category, how accurately or inaccurately each term describes the object (Zikmund, 2003; Zikmund & Babin, 2010).

Threats to Reliability

Despite the many ways to establish reliability, there are also threats to reliability. Again, reliability is an indicator of a measure's internal consistency. The primary goal of reliability is consistency. Typically, different measures of reliability are used by different approaches. The threats to reliability need to be observed by the researcher and must be addressed. There are four key types of threats to reliability.

Participant Error

This refers to any factor that adversely alters the way in which a participant performs. For example, asking a participant to complete a questionnaire just before a lunch break may affect the way they respond compared to choosing a less sensitive time.

Participant Bias

This refers to any factor that induces a false response. For example, conducting an interview in an open space where participants fear they are being overheard rather than retaining their anonymity may lead them to provide falsely positive answers.

Researcher Error

This refers to any factor that alters the researcher's interpretation. For example, a researcher may be tired or not sufficiently prepared and misunderstand some of the more subtle meanings of his or her interviewees.

Researcher Bias

This refers to any factor that induces bias in the researchers' recording of responses. For example, a researcher may allow their own subjective view or disposition to get in the way of fairly recording and interpreting participants' responses (Saunders et al., 2012).

Developing Validity in a Quantitative Study

There is a history of how to properly define *validity*, which has been an issue with the research community for years. The major difficulty with defining validity is ascertaining what constitutes an appropriate definition, because you cannot measure validity, unlike its counterpart, reliability. Validity tends to be defined by the eye of the beholder. Whatever classification one chooses to adopt, it is important to bear in mind that validity is a "unitary concept." For organization purposes, it does not imply a set of mutually exclusive and exhaustive categories (Gorard, 2003; Pedhazur & Pedhazur Schmelkin, 2006; Corder & Foreman, 2014).

Currently, *validity* is defined as the extent to which a measurement represents characteristics that exist in the phenomenon under investigation. Validity can be assessed by examining three general types: (a) *content validity* (sometimes called *face validity*), which is a subjective but systematic evaluation of how well the content of a scale represents the measurement task at hand; (b) *criterion validity*, which is a type of validity that examines whether the measurement scale performs as expected in relation to other selected variables as meaningful criteria; and (c) *construct validity*, which is a type of validity that addresses the question of what construct or characteristic the scale is measuring; it is an attempt to answer theoretical questions of why a scale works and what deductions can be made concerning the theory underlying the scale (Sekaran, 2003; Pedhazur & Pedhazur Schmelkin, 2006; Malhotra & Birks, 2007; Zikmund, 2003; Saunders et al., 2012).

Unlike reliability coefficients, however, there is no established criterion for the strength of the validity coefficient. For example, coefficients as low as .20 or .30 may establish the validity of a measure. However, concerning validity coefficients, the important thing is that they are statistically significant at the .05 or .01 level. However, there is still the issue of how to properly measure validity (Kolb, 2008; Jackson, 2009). Furthermore, a behavioral measure is said to be valid if it measures what it is designed to measure. A measure of burnout should truly measure the phenomenon of burnout (Goodwin & Goodwin, 2013).

Validity vs. Reliability

The systematic and random error concepts are important because they relate to a measure's validity and reliability. Again, validity is harder to measure and tends to be what the researcher perceives it to be. *Validity* refers to whether we are measuring what we want to measure and, therefore, to a situation where the systematic error E_S is small. Conversely, *reliability* is the degree to which what we measure is free from random error and therefore relates to a situation where the error rate is zero (Mooi et al., 2018). Because there is no objective way of verifying what we are measuring, several forms of validity have been developed, which include face, content, predictive, criterion, discriminant and nomological validity (Mooi et al., 2018).

Types of Validity

As with reliability, there are different types of validity. In the context of experimental designs, there are two general types of validity: internal and external. With validity, we are concerned about the issue of the authenticity of the *cause-and-effect relationships* (internal validity) and their *generalizability* to the external environment (external validity).

The first thought that comes to mind is that researchers need to be aware of issues (e.g., develop a measuring instrument), with the hope that they are tapping the concept. The other thought is that researchers need to be certain that they are measuring the concept they set out to do and nothing else. This is why researchers need validity tests. Certain tests are determined by applying certain validity tests.

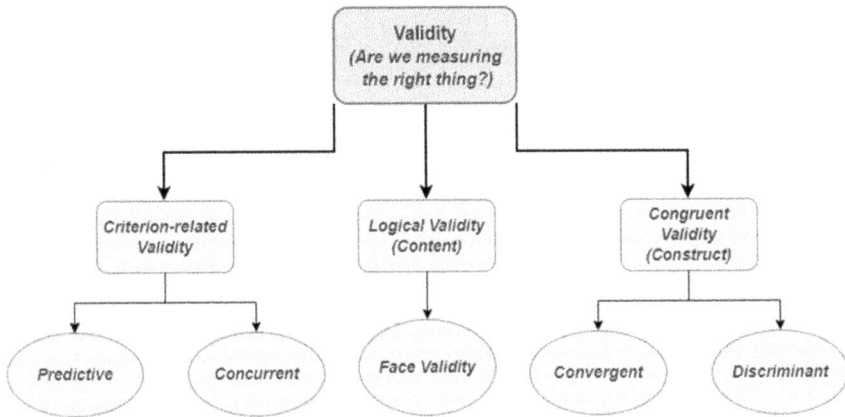

Figure 18.4 Testing goodness of measures: Forms of validity model.
Source: Adapted from Sekaran (2003).

Several types of validity tests are used to test the goodness of measures, and different writers use different terms to denote them. In order not to make the concept of validity too complicated, they are grouped together. Generally, validity tests fall under three broad headings: content validity, criterion-related validity and construct validity (Sekaran, 2003) (see Figure 18.4).

The practice of participant observation has a high *ecological validity* because it involves studying social actors and social phenomena (i.e., informants and their activities) in their natural settings. This is referred to as the *observer effect*. The implication of this effect is that informants will work harder or act more ethically when they know they are being observed (Saunders et al., 2012; Mooi et al., 2018).

Testing the Goodness of Measures

We want to call attention to the concept of internal and external validity as the goodness of measures. Campbell and Stanley (1963) describe two types of validity: *internal* and *external*. Their discussion describes internal validity as "the sine qua non," the essential validity, the essence of the experiment. Internal validity is examined when the researcher examines the research question. In contrast to internal validity, which is specific to the experiment, external validity asks the question of generalizability, or to what extent can the findings of an experiment be applied to different groups, settings or subjects, and under what conditions can this experiment be generalized (Miller & Yang, 2008).

Assessing Validity

Assessing validity can be a challenge, since it is not statistically measured like reliability. The question of assessing internal validity provides some strategies for the researcher. Again, *internal validity* in relation to questionnaires refers to the ability of your questionnaire to measure what you intend it to measure. It is sometimes termed measurement validity, as it refers to concerns that what you find with your questionnaire actually represents the reality of what you are measuring (Saunders et al., 2012; Mertens et al., 2017).

Researchers get around this problem by looking for other relevant evidence that supports the answers found using the questionnaire, the relevance being determined by the nature of their research question and their own judgment (Saunders et al., 2012; Mertens et al., 2017). Often, when addressing the validity of a questionnaire, researchers refer to three general types of *content validity, criterion-related validity* and *construct validity* to assess the internal validity.

Content Validity

This type of validity refers to the extent to which the measurement device, in our case the measurement questions in the questionnaire, provides adequate coverage of the investigative questions. Judgment of what is "adequate coverage" can be made in a number of ways. One is through a careful definition of the research, the literature reviewed and, where appropriate, prior discussion with others.

Criterion-related Validity

This type of validity, which is sometimes known as *predictive validity*, is concerned with the ability of the measures (questions) to make accurate predictions. This means that if you are using the measurement questions within your questionnaire to predict customers' future buying behaviors, then a test of these measurement questions' criterion-related validity will be the extent to which they actually predict these customers' buying behaviors.

Construct Validity

This type of validity refers to the extent to which your measurement questions actually measure the presence of those constructs you intended them to measure. This term is normally used when referring to constructs such as attitude scales, aptitude and personality tests. These are discussed in more detail in a range of texts (Blaxter et al., 2010; Saunders et al., 2012; Mertens et al., 2017; Sekaran, 2003).

Nomological Validity

This is a type of validity that assesses the relationship between theoretical constructs. It seeks to confirm significant correlations between the constructs as predicted by a theory (Malhotra et al., 2017).

Face validity is defined as the extent to which a measurement method appears "on its face" to measure the construct of interest. This can be esoteric to many people trying to understand what its purpose is. When the instrument or survey looks adequate, this would be said to have good face validity. Although face validity can be assessed quantitatively, by having a large sample of people rate a measure in terms of whether it appears to measure what it is intended to, it is usually assessed informally. Furthermore, face validity is really, at best, a very weak kind of evidence that a measurement method is measuring what it is supposed to. One reason is that it is based on people's intuitions about human behavior, which are frequently wrong. However, it is also the case that many established measures in psychology work quite well despite lacking face validity (Babbie, 2008; McNiff & Whitehead, 2010; Saunders et al., 2012; Price et al., 2019).

Threats to Validity

There are at least six possible threats to validity in terms of research: (a) *selection biases*; (b) *mortality*; (c) *history*; (d) *maturation*; (e) *instrumentation*; and (f) *testing*.

Selection Biases

This threat is when two groups are not matched or randomly assigned could contaminate the results. Also, the differential recruitment of the persons making up the two groups would confound the cause-and-effect relationship (Sekaran, 2003).

Mortality

This threat is when the dropout of individuals from groups can also confound the results and thus pose a threat to the internal validity (Sekaran, 2003).

History

This threat is when an unrelated event influences the outcomes. The participants are stressed on the date of the post-test, and performance may suffer (Bhandari, 2020).

Maturation

The outcomes of the study vary as a natural result of time. Most participants are new to the job at the time of the pre-test (Bhandari, 2020).

Instrumentation

Different measures are used in the pre-test and post-test phases. For example, in the pre-test, productivity was measured for 15 minutes, while the post-test was over 30 minutes long (Bhandari, 2020).

Testing

The pre-test influences the outcomes of the post-test. For example, due to famil-iarity or awareness of the study's purpose, many participants achieved high results (Babbie, 2008; Saunders et al., 2012).

Ensuring Trustworthiness in a Qualitative Study

Because qualitative research is informed by philosophical assumptions that are different from qualitative research, the process of ensuring research quality is also distinct. To recap, qualitative researchers believe that there are multiple realities due to our distinct view of the world and how our background and preconceptions influ-ence the way we make sense of the world. Also, in qualitative studies, researchers embrace subjectivity, including getting closer to relevant data sources to extract rich data and make meaning of them. Consequently, qualitative researchers are more likely to influence the research inquiry process, making both the qualitative research process and the findings unique. "[They] strive for the less explicit goal of trustworthiness, which means that when readers interpret the written work, they will have a sense of confidence in what the researcher has reported" (Stahl & King, 2020, p. 26). How do you ensure the quality of the study? How do you make sure that your audience/readers trust the findings? We will address these questions by discussing four kinds of trustworthiness in a qualitative study: credibility, transfer-ability, conformability and dependability.

Credibility

Credibility is about the level of trust we have in the data collected and the level of consistency between the data and the findings (Stahl & King, 2020). Credibility is related to the decisions and actions taken, making sure your audience believe that the data collected is a true reflection of what was gathered from the data source and the findings are a true representation of the data. There are a lot of strategies that researchers can implement to promote credibility, including promoting trans-parency, member checking and triangulation (Adu, 2019; Candela, 2019; Fereday & Muir-Cochrane, 2006; Stahl & King, 2020).

Transparency

Transparency involves being open about the decisions and actions taken in the study. As part of being transparent, you are expected to disclose your background, biases and beliefs relevant to your study and share how you plan to bracket them, which means preventing them from influencing the research process (Tufford & Newman, 2012). Further, if you are using a theorical lens, you need to provide details of the theory and its related assumptions and how you plan to use it in the study. Similarly, it is also important to clearly explain the role that your theoretical or conceptual framework will be playing in your study (Maxwell, 2013; Sinclair,

2007; Greckhamer & Cilesiz, 2014). Lastly, you need to be transparent by sharing how you collected and analyzed your data.

Member Checking

This process involves verifying the data gathered and/or its interpretation with participants. In this case, you send participants their transcripts for review and verification. Alternatively, you could have a session with each participant to review their transcript and seek clarifications by asking follow-up questions. However, Candela (2019) cautions utilizing member checking, especially when working with participants who have passed through a traumatic situation. She states, "Member checking could cause harm during research studies looking at experiences of marginalized populations or participants who have experienced trauma" (Candela, 2019, p. 620).

When feasible and appropriate, you can present the findings to participants and ask for their thoughts. Furthermore, if you collected data from a closed community, it is important that you share the research report with them before you publish it (Stahl & King, 2020). Another aspect of member checking is to give your documentation of the data analysis process and outcome to another researcher to review and provide feedback. The point of implementing any of the member checking strategies is to help improve the credibility of the findings.

Triangulation

This concept operates within the assumption that studying a phenomenon from a single perspective, and by one researcher utilizing a single research method with a data collection and analysis strategy, may not yield rich and credible research outcomes. Comparatively, when a study is conducted by multiple researchers who explore the phenomenon of study from multiple perspectives and use more than one research method, credibility is more likely to improve (Carter et al., 2014). Irrespective of the triangulation-related strategy you choose, your goal is to show the similarities of outcomes across multiple methods, perspectives, data sources, and data collection and analysis strategies. By doing so, your audience will trust what you found.

Transferability

Transferability is the ability to apply the findings of your study to similar contexts in terms of research location, participants' demographics and the situation participants find themselves in (Lincoln & Guba, 1985; Smith & McGannon, 2018; Stahl & King, 2020). So, how do you ensure that your findings are transferable? It is all about collecting information on the context of your research and providing a detailed description of the place where data was collected and the participants you collected the data from. According to Smith (2018):

The question then is ... "to what extent are these results transferable to other settings?" For example, a physical educator, sport community leader, or health policy-maker reading a qualitative report on how to promote active lifestyles might want to know: "Is this something I can apply to my physical education class, local community group, or country to encourage active lifestyles?" When readers feel as though this can be the case – when they believe that research overlaps with their own situation and/or they can intuitively transfer the findings to their own action – then the research can be said to generalise through transferability.

[Smith, 2018, pp. 140–141]

Another strategy for promoting transferability is to provide an extensive interpretation of your findings (Smith, 2018).

Confirmability

Confirmability is about whether the research outcomes can be achieved utilizing a research method different from what was initially used in the study, collecting data from other data sources or analyzing data by another researcher. Think about your findings when considering strategies to implement to ensure the confirmability of your results. Ask the question, "What can I do in the study to help confirm the results?" For instance, you can use a narrative method to confirm the findings of your phenomenological study. Also, you could ask another researcher to review your data analysis process to see whether it truly led to the results of the study.

Dependability

Dependability is the degree to which following a research procedure leads to similar results. The question is, can researchers follow your actions and decisions and arrive at findings similar to what you found in your study? To promote dependability, you first need to be systematic in carrying out your study, documenting every step you make. Another dependability-enhancing strategy is to provide detailed information (about the steps you took in your study) when writing a report about your study. In a dissertation, you are expected to share how you collected and analyzed the data, thus increasing the dependability of your findings.

Ensuring Quality in a Mixed Methods Study

As discussed earlier in this book, mixed methods research entails using quantitative and qualitative research methodology in a single study. This implies that, in general, you need to adhere to the research quality assurance principles under both quantitative and qualitative research. Because each of the research methods have distinctive phenomenological paradigms and/or assumptions, ensuring quality and rigor can be a challenge (Tashakkori & Teddlie, 2003). In response, Onwuegbuzie et al. (2011) suggested some criteria that researchers could use to assess the quality of a mixed methods study. They divided them into four domains: "philosophical assumptions and stances," "inquiry logics," "guidelines for research practice" and "sociopolitical commitments" (Onwuegbuzie et al., 2011, p. 1257). If you plan to do a mixed methods study, we suggest you review Onwuegbuzie et al.'s (2011) article, "Assessing Legitimation in Mixed Methods Research: A New Framework." There is other literature on promoting rigor in mixed methods research that you could read to take note of the best practices (see NIH Office of Behavioral and Social Sciences, 2018; Onwuegbuzie & Johnson, 2006).

To simplify the process of ensuring quality, you should implement validity-, reliability-, credibility-, confirmability-, dependability- and transferability-related strategies to improve the rigor of your research when conducting a mixed methods study. Besides this, you are expected to describe:

- The type of mixed methods design used in your study, including detailing the sequence of the methods' implementation
- The role each of the methods will be playing in your study, including whether they are playing an equal or unequal role
- Where and how you plan to integrate the two methodologies in the study

To learn more about mixed methods research best practices, see Table 18.1.

Summary

Researchers should be very familiar with the concept of reliability and validity. The core foundation of measurement in studies is based on reliability and validity. The task of dealing with reliability and validity will be a challenge for the researcher who does not understand it.

There are many types of reliability in the arena of quantitative research as well as qualitative research. There are many strategies for validity in both methodologies. This chapter discussed the different characteristics of quantitative reliability

Table 18.1 List of mixed methods research-related resources

Authors	Article/Book Title
Creswell & Clark (2017)	*Designing and Conducting Mixed Methods Research*
Creswell (2021)	*A Concise Introduction to Mixed Methods Research*
Hanson et al. (2005)	"Mixed Methods Research Designs in Counseling Psychology"
Castro et al. (2010)	"A Methodology for Conducting Integrative Mixed Methods Research and Data Analyses"
Dowding (2013)	"Best Practices for Mixed Methods Research in the Health Sciences"
Johnson & Onwuegbuzie (2004)	"Mixed Methods Research: A Research Paradigm Whose Time Has Come"

and validity and qualitative reliability and validity. It provided different conceptual models for understanding reliability and validity.

The purpose of this chapter was to provide some insight into reliability and validity in the study. It provided some valuable knowledge, including the importance of developing reliability and validity in the study. Thus, this chapter provided the researcher with guidance, understanding and strategies in this area. This chapter provided some practical strategies for researchers in terms of reliability and validity in the social sciences. We discussed three things: writing about reliability and validity in a quantitative study; writing about reliability and validity in a qualitative study; and, lastly, writing about reliability and validity in a mixed methods study. By the end of this chapter, the reader should be knowledgeable about these three core research methodologies and areas.

References

Adu, P. (2019). *A step-by-step guide to qualitative data coding*. Routledge.

Alasuutari, P., Bickman, L., & Brannen, J. (2008). *The SAGE handbook of social research methods*. SAGE.

Babbie, E. (2008). *The basics of social research* (4th ed.). Wadsworth Publishing Company.

Bell, J., & Waters, S. (2010). *Doing your research project: A guide for first-time researchers* (5th ed.). McGraw-Hill–Open University Press.

Bhandari, P. (2020, May 1). *Internal Validity | Definition, threats and examples*. Scribbr. www.scribbr.com/methodology/internal-validity/

Blaxter, L., Hughes, C., & Tight, M. (2010). *How to research* (4th ed.). Open University Press.

Campbell, D. T., & Stanley, J. C. (1963). *Experimental and quasi-experimental designs for research*. Ravenio Books.

Candela, A. G. (2019). Exploring the function of member checking. *The Qualitative Report, 24*(3), 619–628. Retrieved from https://nsuworks.nova.edu/tqr/vol24/iss3/14

Carter, N., Bryant-Lukosius, D., DiCenso, A., Blythe, J., & Neville, A. J. (2014). The use of triangulation in qualitative research. *Oncology Nursing Forum, 41*(5), 545–547. https://doi.org/10.1188/14.ONF.545-547

Castro, F. G., Kellison, J. G., Boyd, S. J., & Kopak, A. (2010). A methodology for conducting integrative mixed methods research and data analyses. *Journal of Mixed Methods Research, 4*(4), 342–360. https://doi.org/10.1177/1558689810382916

Cohen, L., Manion, L., & Morrison, K. R. B. (2007). *Research methods in education* (6th ed.). Routledge.

Corder, G. W., & Foreman, D. I. (2014). *Nonparametric statistics: A step-by-step approach*. Wiley.

Craig, C. S., & Douglas, S. P. (2005). *International marketing research* (3rd ed.). Wiley.

Creswell, J. W. (2012). *Educational research: Planning, conducting, and evaluating quantitative and qualitative research* (4th ed.). Pearson College Division.

Creswell, J.W. (2021) *A concise introduction to mixed methods research*. Sage Publications.

Creswell, J. W., & Clark, V. L. P. (2017). *Designing and conducting mixed methods research*. Sage Publications, Inc.

Dawson, C. (2002). *Practical research methods: A user-friendly guide to mastering research techniques and projects*. How To Books Ltd.

Dowding, D. (2013). Best practices for mixed methods research in the health sciences John W. Creswell, Ann Carroll Klassen, Vicki L. Plano Clark, Katherine Clegg Smith for the

Office of Behavioral and Social Sciences Research; Qualitative methods overview Jo Moriarty. *Qualitative Social Work, 12*(4), 541–545. https://doi.org/10.1177/1473325013 493540a

Fereday, J., & Muir-Cochrane, E. (2006). Demonstrating rigor using thematic analysis: A hybrid approach of inductive and deductive coding and theme development. *International Journal of Qualitative Methods*, 80–92. https://doi.org/10.1177/160940690600500107

Finn, J. A. (2005). *Getting a PhD: An action plan to help manage your research, your supervisor and your project*. Routledge.

Greckhamer, T., & Cilesiz, S. (2014). Rigor, transparency, evidence, and representation in discourse analysis: Challenges and recommendations. *International Journal of Qualitative Methods*, 422–443. https://doi.org/10.1177/160940691401300123

Goodwin, K. A., & Goodwin, C. J. (2013). *Research in psychology: Methods and design* (7th ed.). John Wiley & Sons, Inc.

Gorard, S. (2003). *Quantitative methods in social science research*. Continuum.

Hanson, W. E., Creswell, J. W., Clark, V. L. P., Petska, K. S., & Creswell, J. D. (2005). Mixed methods research designs in counseling psychology. *Journal of Counseling Psychology, 52*(2), 224–235. https://doi.org/10.1037/0022-0167.52.2.224

Howitt, D., & Cramer, D. (2011). *Introduction to research methods in psychology*. (3rd ed.). Prentice Hall.

Jackson, S. L. (2009). *Research methods and statistics: A critical thinking approach* (3rd ed.). Wadsworth.

Johnson, R. B., & Onwuegbuzie, A. J. (2004). Mixed methods research: A research paradigm whose time has come. *Educational Researcher, 33*(7), 14–26. https://doi.org/10.3102/0013189X033007014

Kaplan, D. (2004). *The Sage handbook of quantitative methodology for the social sciences*. SAGE.

Kolb, B. (2008). *Marketing research: A practical approach*. SAGE.

Kothari, R. (2004). *Research methodology: Methods and techniques*. New Age International.

Kumar, R. (2011). *Research methodology: A step-by-step guide for beginners*. Sage Publications Ltd.

Leedy, P. D., & Ormrod, J. E. (2015). *Practical research: Planning and design* (11th ed.). Pearson Education, Inc.

Leedy, P. D., & Ormrod, J. E. (2021). *Practical research: Planning and design* (12th ed.). Pearson Education, Inc.

Lincoln, Y. S., & Guba, E. G. (1985). *Naturalistic inquiry*. Sage.

Little, T. D. (2014). *The Oxford handbook of quantitative methods in psychology. Volume 2: Statistical analysis*. Oxford University Press.

Litwin, M. S. (1995). *How to measure survey reliability and validity*. Sage.

Malhotra, N. K. (2015). *Essentials of marketing research: A hands-on approach*. Pearson.

Malhotra, N. K., & Birks, D. F. (2007). *Marketing research: An applied approach* (3rd ed.). Pearson Education.

Malhotra, N. K., Nunan, D., & Birks, D. (2017). *Marketing research: An applied approach*. Pearson.

Maxwell, J. A. (2013). *Qualitative research design: An interactive approach*. Sage.

McNiff, J., & Whitehead, J. (2010). *You and your action research project*. Routledge.

Mertens, W., Pugliese, A., & Recker, J. (2017). *Quantitative data analysis: A companion for accounting and information systems research*. Springer International Publishing.

Miller, G. J., & Yang, K. (2008). *Handbook of research methods in public administration* (2nd ed.). CRC Press.

Mooi, E., Sarstedt, M., & Mooi-Reci, I. (2018). *Market research: The process, data, and methods using Stata*. Springer.

NIH Office of Behavioral and Social Sciences. (2018). *Best practices for mixed methods research in the health sciences* (2nd ed.). National Institutes of Health.

Onwuegbuzie, A. J., & Johnson, R. B. (2006). The validity issue in mixed research. *Research in the Schools, 13*, 48–63.

Onwuegbuzie, A. J., Johnson, R. B., & Collins, K. M. (2011). Assessing legitimation in mixed research: A new framework. *Quality & Quantity, 45*, 1253–1271.

Pedhazur, E. J., & Pedhazur Schmelkin, L. (2006). *Measurement, design, and analysis: An integrated approach.* Psychology Press, Taylor & Francis Group.

Peter, J. P. (1979). Reliability: A Review of psychometric basics and recent marketing practices. *Journal of Marketing Research, 16*(1), 6–17.

Price, P., Jhangiani, R., Chiang, I-C. A., Cuttler, C., & Leighton, D. C. (2019). *Research methods in psychology* (3rd ed.). Creative Commons Attribution NonCommercial ShareAlike.

Research Methods in Psychology. (2019). GitHub. https://saylordotorg.github.io/text_research-methods-in-psychology/

Saunders, M., Lewis, P., & Thornhill, A. (2012). *Research methods for business students* (6th ed.). Pearson Education Limited.

Sekaran, U. (2003). *Research methods for business: A skill-building approach* (4th ed.). John Wiley and Sons.

Shaughnessy, J. J., Zechmeister, E. B. & Zechmeister, J. S. (2012). *Research methods in psychology* (9th ed.). McGraw-Hill Humanities, Social Sciences & World Languages.

Sinclair, M. (2007). A guide to understanding theoretical and conceptual frameworks. *Evidence-Based Midwifery, 5*(2), 39.

Singh, K. Y. (2006). *Fundamental of research methodology and statistics.* New Age International.

Singh, K. Y. (2007). *Quantitative social research methods.* SAGE Publishing India.

Singh, S. (2020). *Methodological issues in management research: Advances, challenges and the way ahead.* Emerald Publishing Limited.

Smith, B. (2018). Generalizability in qualitative research: Misunderstandings, opportunities and recommendations for the sport and exercise sciences. *Qualitative Research in Sport, Exercise and Health, 10*(1), 137–149. https://doi.org/10.1080/21596 76X.2017.1393221

Smith, B., & McGannon, K. R. (2018). Developing rigor in qualitative research: Problems and opportunities within sport and exercise psychology. *International Review of Sport and Exercise Psychology, 11*(1), 101–121. https://doi.org/10.1080/1750984X.2017.1317357

Smith, S. M., & Albaum, G. S. (2010). *An introduction to marketing research.* Sage.

Sreejesh, S., Mohapatra, S., & Anusree, M. R. (2014). *Business research methods: An applied orientation.* Springer.

Stahl, N. A., & King, J. R. (2020). Expanding approaches for research: Understanding and using trustworthiness in qualitative research. *Journal of Developmental Education, 44*(1), 26–28.

Swanson, R. A., & Holton, E. F. (2005). *Research in organizations: Foundations and methods of inquiry.* Berrett-Koehler Publishers.

Tabachnick, B. G., & Fidell, L. S. (2007). *Using multivariate statistics* (5th ed.). Allyn and Bacon.

Tashakkori, A., Teddlie, C. (2003). The past and future of mixed methods research: From data triangulation to mixed model designs. In A. Tashakkori & C. Teddlie (Eds.), *Handbook of mixed methods in social and behavioral research* (pp. 671–701). Sage.

Tufford, L., & Newman, P. (2012). Bracketing in qualitative research. *Qualitative Social Work, 11*(1), 80–96. https://doi.org/10.1177/1473325010368316

Zikmund, W. G. (2003). *Essentials of marketing research*. South-Western Publication.

Zikmund, W. G., & Babin, B. J. (2010). *Exploring marketing research*. South-Western Cengage Learning.

Zumbo, B., &. Rupp, A., (2004). Responsible modeling of measurement data for appropriate inferences-important advances in reliability and validity theory. In D. Kaplan (Ed.), *The Sage handbook of quantitative methodology for the social sciences*. SAGE Publications.

19 Writing Your Dissertation

The Standard Format – Chapter 1 (Introduction)

Objective

- Readers will be able to:
  1. Write the introductory chapter of their dissertation

Introduction and Background of the Problem

The difficult endeavor that is writing the dissertation cannot be understated. With this chapter, we want to provide a clear roadmap on how to write each section of chapter one. There are some alternate versions of this chapter, so we want to provide a template to guide novice researchers and doctoral students. This chapter provides some practical strategies for researchers who are writing these core sections within the dissertation format. The chapter will start with the overview and the basics of how to write it.

When developing the background of the study, there are some items that need to be included. Many doctoral students have trouble writing this section. The problem they usually have is that they still do not really understand the basics of their study. When students begin to write this part, they are still confused about how they will start the beginning of the study. There is a solution to this problem. First, think of the background of the problem as the elevator pitch for the study. Second, think of someone who has never heard of your study. The researcher needs to think about how they will tell their story. Lastly, the researcher needs to state how and why the study is significant or of any interest to anyone.

This section can be defined as a brief sketch giving the background information necessary for readers' understanding of the proposal. The writing of this is most effective when it is (a) focused only on the background of the problem to be presented; (b) succinct and brief; and (c) supporting the section with enough documentation that justifies the need for the proposed study (Webster, 1998a).

DOI: 10.4324/9781003268154-19

Main Points and Directions

These are the main key points that doctoral researchers should consider when developing the "Introduction and Background of the Problem" section of chapter one:

- Provide a brief history of the problem
- Provide a summary of results from the prior empirical research on the topic
- Identify three to five research studies (primarily from the last three years) and identify the stated need or possible research "gap"
- Identify the need for the study or the defined gap that will lead to the research problem statement
- Build a justification for the current study by using a logical set of arguments supported by citations
- Discuss how the problem is applicable beyond the local setting and contributes to societal and/or professional needs
- Lastly, provide an overview of what will be discussed in the chapter
- Writing length: Minimum two to three paragraphs or approximately one page (Miles, 2022)

By following these key points, the researcher can fully develop the "Introduction and Background of the Problem" section of the chapter (see Example 19.1).

Example 19.1 Introduction and Background of the Problem

Field workers have a unique work environment that is different. The field workers in the agricultural industry face a set of different trials stemming from issues in the field. These issues with job stress for field workers is an unexplored topic (Miles et al., 2020; Miles et al., 2014; Adu et al., 2014; Adu, 2013). There is a need to address job stress levels in the agriculture industry and research institutional practices to better respond to job satisfaction (Miles, 2019; Miles et al., 2017). Adopting, integrating and successfully using job behavioral issues in the industry presents a challenge. Job satisfaction adds a difficulty for some field workers to manage and incorporate behavior modification practices successfully (Miles, 2015; Miles & Adu, 2017). As such, pursuing this study may involve difficulty experienced and may stimulate feelings of uncertainty and skepticism, which lead to job stress (Miles, 2017).

Job related stress is a term describing the anxiety, uncertainty and insecurity engendered by the utilization tasks of the job. This category of stress hinders individual field workers and productivity because it can result in resistance to performing job functions (Miles, 1982). At the job environment, the time it takes to learn new skills can perpetuate delays in job satisfaction. The field workers' job dissatisfaction continues piling up, prompting feelings of being unsatisfied with the organization (Miles, 1982; Miles et al., 2018). Job attrition rates can increase, while the job functions can be arduous, there is a steep learning curve and there is insecurity about job performance (Miles, 1982). Researchers have estimated that US agricultural organizations lose approximately $500 billion each year because of job stress and job dissatisfaction (Miles, 2018).

Prior researchers have explored the effects of job stress and job dissatisfaction on field workers and made connections between job stress and job outcomes such as job satisfaction and job performance (Miles, 2016; Adu & Robinson, 2019; Miles et al., 2019). Some studies, however, have focused on the forerunners of job stress, such as how personality types, demographic factors and job environment (e.g., length of time of employment) can affect technostress (Miles et al., 2017; Miles et al., 2016). Fewer studies have examined the effects of job stress within the context of the job satisfaction demographic phenomenon in the US agricultural industry (Miles et al., 2016). These researchers called for further examination of job stress and field workers in more diverse populations (Miles & Adu, 2014). The examination of job stress within the population of the US agricultural industry remains an untapped opportunity to be researched (Miles et al., 2017; Miles et al., 2016).

[Note: In-text citations included for illustrative purposes only]

Overview of Chapter

This chapter will discuss the background of the study and the problem statement sections of the study. The chapter will also discuss the purpose of the study, the research questions and hypotheses sections, and it will introduce the research methodology, design, target population and four research questions for examining job stress in the US agricultural industry with field worker employees. Lastly, the chapter will discuss the study's significance, methodology rationale and research design, introduce study-specific terms and highlight the assumptions, limitations and delimitations of the study.

The Research Problem and the Problem Statement

After the background and introduction of the study has been written, now the problem statement must be developed. There is a certain template when writing up the problem statement. This section can be defined as a specific statement of what the research will accomplish (Webster, 1998a). The research problem should be broken down into sub-issues as discussed in Chapter 6 by using the *Statement Grid* (Miles & Scott, 2017).

- **Directions:** *First,* write the overall problem statement. *Second,* divide the problem to be investigated into two or three parts (or subproblems) that are compelling. Please note, use the word *issue* when writing about the subproblem so that it is not misinterpreted as three to four separate problem statements.

Main Points and Directions

After using the *Statement Grid* to develop the problem statement, the researcher should put it in paragraph form and add more content. These are the main key points that the doctoral researcher should consider when developing the "Problem Statement" section of chapter one:

- State the specific problem proposed for the research with a clear declarative statement ("The central problem to be researched by the proposed study is …")
- Break down the central problem into subproblems (issues) (use the Statement Grid)
- Discuss the problem statement in relation to the gap or need in the world if possible.
- Describe the <u>general population affected by the problem</u>. The general population refers to all individuals that could be affected by the study problem
- Describe the <u>unit of analysis,</u> which is the phenomenon, individuals, group or organization under study
- Discuss the importance, scope or opportunity for the problem and the importance of addressing the problem
- Writing length: Minimum of three to four paragraphs or approximately one page (Miles, 2022)

By following these key points, the researcher can fully develop a cogent "Problem Statement" section (see Table 19.1).

Example 19.2 Problem Statement

The central problem to be researched by the proposed study is the lack of literacy skills and content knowledge of 6th-grade students in middle school. As a basis for this study, the researcher identified the problem to be threefold. First, the prevailing issue is that many adolescent students entering middle school lack the literacy skills that are foundational for reading comprehension (Miles, 2013; Adu et al., 2018). According to Miles et al. (2015), secondary students demonstrate insufficient "comprehension skills to be successful learners in the classroom (p. 258)."

Secondly, the prevailing issue is that CCSS have increased the need for students to interact with expository non-fiction text (Miles & Adu, 2015; Adu et al., 2013). Social studies as a field is an area of interest due to the challenges that social studies texts impose on students and the increased demands of literacy instruction in secondary content-area classes (Adu & Miles, 2012; Miles, 2014). Many times, social studies textbooks are often written with high complexity, which impacts students' text comprehension (Miles et al., 2014). Because of this, social

---

studies teachers must employ instructional strategies that will increase students' ability to comprehend content.

Lastly, the prevailing issue is that 6th-grade adolescents in a large urban school district in the southeast are under-represented in previous social studies research (Adu et al., 2012; Miles, 2012). Much of the prior research has shown that students transitioning to 6th-grade often experience gaps in learning that often perpetuates once they enter middle school (Miles et al., 2015). Standardized assessments have shown that there is a decline in 6th-grade students' test scores (Miles, 2015).

[Note: In-text citations included for illustrative purposes only]

The Purpose Statement

The purpose statement is defined as a declarative statement that defines the goal and objective of the study. The purpose statement is a type of go-between for the problem statement and the research statement with research questions. The

Table 19.1 Example: The Statement Grid for problem statement development

Problem Statement:
The central problem to be researched by the proposed study is the shortage in the nursing field. This has a lot to do with the current nursing shortage and the need for more nurses in the field. There is a huge problem with this shortage and the availability of nurses. As a basis for this study, the researcher identified the problem to be threefold.

Issue (subproblem) 1:	Issue (subproblem) 2:	Issue (subproblem) 3:
First, the prevailing issue is that the education of new nurses is the responsibility of institutions of higher education, but there is a national shortage of nursing faculty (McSherry et al., 2012; Rosseter, 2015) , which is limiting the enrollment, education and graduation of new nurses from institutions of higher learning.	Second, the prevailing issue in the United States is that 75% of the nursing faculty will reach retirement age in 2017 (Brett et al., 2014). This is alongside the existing problem that 6.9% of nursing faculty positions remain unfilled due to a lack of qualified nursing educators (Rosseter, 2015).	Last, the prevailing issue is that the current nursing faculty express low job satisfaction (Bittner & O'Connor, 2012) due to complexities of the nursing educator role making the retention and recruitment of qualified faculty difficult (Byme & Martine, 2014). The current problems include a shortage of qualified nursing faculty to educate new nurses, the complexity of nursing education and current faculty complaints of poor job satisfaction (Cook, 2017).

Note: In-text citations included for illustrative purposes only.

research purpose statement should be stated objectively or in a way that does not reflect particular biases or values of the researcher (Long et al., 1985; Calabrese, 2006; Jacobs, 2011; Terrell, 2015; Abbas, 2020).

Again, the purpose statement should be broken down into subobjectives as discussed in Chapter 7 by using the *Statement Grid* (Miles & Scott, 2017), and they should align with the sub-issues in the problem statement (see Chapter 9 on research alignment).

- **Directions:** *First,* write the overall purpose statement. *Second,* divide the purpose to be investigated into two or three objectives (or subpurposes) that align with the issues (subproblems) of the problem statement (see Table 19.2). Please note, use the word *objective* when writing about the subpurpose so that it is not misinterpreted as four separate purpose statements.

Main Key Points and Directions

After using the Statement Grid to develop the purpose statement, the researcher should put it in paragraph form and add more content. These are the main key points that the doctoral researcher should consider when developing the "Purpose Statement" section of chapter one:

- Present a declarative statement: ("The purpose of this study is to …")
- Break down the purpose statement from the central problem into subpurposes (objectives) (use the Statement Grid)
- Write and align the purpose statement (and objectives) with the problem statement (and sub-issues)
- Describe the target population and geographic location
- Quantitative studies: Define the variables and the relationship of the variables
- Qualitative studies: Describe the nature of the phenomena to be explored
- ALIGNMENT: Make sure the purpose statement (and objectives) aligns with the problem statement (and sub-issues)
- Writing length: Minimum of two to three paragraphs (Miles, 2022)

By following these key points, the researcher can fully develop the "Purpose Statement" section of the study (see Table 19.2).

Example 19.3 *Purpose Statement*

The purpose of this study is to investigate the lived experiences of parental involvement and how it contributes to the lives of their deaf children in their classrooms and education in a Title 1 school in Houston, Texas. This is a qualitative research study using a descriptive approach that will utilize structured interviews with open-ended questions to investigate the lived experiences of participants on parental involvement in the lives of their deaf students.

The sample is derived from a population of parents of deaf children studying in Title 1 schools that offer education programs in Houston, Texas. The study employs a sample size of 25 parents who are committed or involved with the educational activities of their deaf children. The participants share their lived experiences through interviews that will focus on questions centered specifically on the six categories outlined by Monica Weinstein.

Thus, the purpose of this study is to illustrate how the lived experiences of parental involvement contribute to the academic achievement of deaf children in classrooms in Houston, Texas. As a basis for the study, the researchers identified two primary objectives of the study. The first objective is to examine the parents' lived experiences with deaf children in classrooms. Based on this objective, the researchers seek to know how the parents' experiences influence the academic performance of their deaf children. Moreover, the objective is derived from categories of the Epstein Parental Involvement Model, whereby various involvement approaches are proposed and proven to influence the academic achievement of deaf children (Weinstein, 1989).

Last, the second objective is to investigate the experiences of parental involvement and its importance for the development of the deaf child. The development of deaf children is determined by parental care and overall parental involvement in every other aspect of the child's life. This objective seeks to know how using the six categories of the Weinstein Parental Involvement Model impacts on the overall development of deaf children (Weinstein, 1987; Weinstein, 1989).

[Note: In-text citations included for illustrative purposes only]

Research Statement and Research Questions

The research statement is a somewhat new concept with dissertations. It is just a statement in which the researcher describes the research and aligns it with the problem statement and purpose statement. It does not have to be anything long and

Table 19.2 Example: The Statement Grid for purpose statement development

---

The Purpose Statement:

The purpose of this study is to investigate the issues affecting job satisfaction by nursing faculty members in metropolitan New York. Interviewing and questioning nursing faculty living in metropolitan New York provides insight into their personal experiences of job satisfaction while working in the nurse educator role. The researcher has identified three primary objectives as a basis for this study.

Objective 1:	**Objective 2:**	**Objective 3:**
First, the objective of this study is to examine the issue of job satisfaction among nursing faculty.	Second, the objective of this study is to investigate the impact of low wages on the nursing faculty,	Lastly, the objective of this study is to examine the complexities of the nursing faculty role (Cook, 2017).

---

elaborate. The research statement is the statement before the research questions. This is an example of a research statement: "The central problem to be researched is the shortage in the nursing field. There are three research questions that will guide this research (Cook, 2017)." This research statement aligns with the problem statement and purpose statement.

Research Questions

Again, the research question is usually the first step in any research project. The research question is the primary interrogation point of your research, and it sets the pace of your work. The research question focuses on the research, determines the methodology and hypothesis and guides all stages of inquiry, analysis and reporting. The research question is defined as the questions asked to address the problem raised in the problem statement (Calabrese, 2009;). Furthermore, the research question orients everything the researcher does with the study. The research question (a) is precise, (b) covers exactly the issue you wish to address, and (c) indicates how you will create your answer (Bryant, 2004).

The research questions should align with the problem statement (sub-issues) and the purpose statement (subobjectives) (see Chapter 9 on research alignment). Developing the research questions is one of the hardest parts of starting the dissertation for doctoral students. It is important to make sure your research questions address these characteristics: (a) they must be precise; (b) they must cover the problem you want to address; and (c) they must indicate how you will create the answer (Creswell, 2009; Rudestam & Newton, 2007; Creswell, 2013; Singh, 2020).

- **Directions: *First,*** write the research statement. ***Second,*** divide the research questions to be investigated into two or three questions that align with the issues (subproblems) of the problem statement and the purpose statement objectives (see Table 19.3).

Table 19.3 Example: The Statement Grid for research statement development

The Research Statement:
The central problem to be researched involves how principals manage job stress. There are three research questions that will guide this research.

Research Question 1:	**Research Question 2:**	**Research Question 3:**
RQ1: How do K–12 principals and administrators describe their experiences of job stress in an urban Central Texas school district environment?	RQ2: How do K–12 principals and administrators describe their experiences of using coping skills for job stress in an urban Central Texas school district environment?	RQ3: How do K–12 principals and administrators describe their experiences of coping with work-life balance and job stress in an urban Central Texas school district environment (Beltran, 2020)?

Again, when developing the research questions, we will use the *Statement Grid*. The *Statement Grid* is a helpful tool that aids students visually with the research statement. See Table 19.3 for an example of the development of the research statement and research questions using the *Statement Grid*.

Main Key Points and Directions

After using the *Statement Grid* to develop the research statement and research questions, the researcher should put it in paragraph form and add more content. These are the main key points that the doctoral researcher should consider when developing the "Research Questions" section of chapter one:

- Prepare a declarative statement: ("The central problem to be researched involves …")
- Develop the research questions
- Write and align the research questions with the purpose statement (and objectives) and with the problem statement (and sub-issues)
- For qualitative studies: State the research question(s) the study will answer and describe the phenomenon to be studied. Note: The research questions provide guidance for the data that will be collected to answer the research questions; they do not identify the instruments
- For quantitative studies: State the research questions the study will answer, identify and describe the variables and state the hypotheses (predictive statements) using the appropriate format for the specific design and statistical analysis
- This section includes a <u>discussion of the research questions, relating them to the problem statement</u>. If quantitative, the research questions need to be connected to the theory(s) or model(s) from the theoretical foundation section as well
- ALIGNMENT: Make sure the purpose statement (and objectives) aligns with the problem statement (and sub-issues)
- Writing length: Minimum of two to three paragraphs or one page (Miles, 2022)

By following these key points, the researcher can fully develop the "Research Statement and Research Questions" section of the study. Again, by making sure to follow these main points, the researcher will be able to fully develop the research questions to address the problem statement.

Example 19.4 *Research Questions*

The central problem to be researched involves how principals manage job stress. There are three research questions that will guide this research. This qualitative, descriptive study examines how principals experience job satisfaction. There is a need for research examining the job satisfaction of principals (Adu, 2015; Miles & Adu, 2015; Miles, 2017). It is critical to learn what factors affect the job satisfaction of principals in metropolitan Colorado. Factors affecting job satisfaction potentially provide positive or negative personal experiences related to work and the workplace environment. Listed below are the guiding research questions for this research study.

Research Questions:

- RQ1: How do the principals in K–12 schools describe their experience of job satisfaction working in a college or university?
- RQ2: How do the principals in K–12 schools describe their experience of factors that cause positive job satisfaction?
- RQ3: How do the principals in K–12 schools describe their experience of factors that cause negative job satisfaction?

This study uses a qualitative methodology and a descriptive research design. This study asks principals in K–12 schools to describe their experience of job satisfaction. The literature review presents multiple theories and causations for poor job satisfaction and methodologies for improving job satisfaction. The problem statement reflects that it is not known how principals working in Colorado experience job satisfaction. The guiding research questions for this study ask principals to describe their experience of job satisfaction.

Furthermore, the research questions probe nursing faculty members to clarify factors causing positive or negative job satisfaction. Weinberg's Motivation-Hygiene Theory describes hygiene factors affecting job satisfaction (Weinberg, 1985). Using Weinberg's Motivation-Hygiene Theory as the organizing theoretical framework for this study, the research questions are narrowed to examine factors that enhance job satisfaction or cause job dissatisfaction for principals in K–12 schools.

[Note: In-text citations included for illustrative purposes only]

Theoretical/Conceptual Framework

The theoretical/conceptual framework is defined as the practice of describing the theory used by the researcher to guide the study. The researcher's choice of a well-developed theoretical perspective is grounded in the researcher's theory of the focus of inquiry. In describing the theoretical frameworks, the researcher attempts to provide the theoretical and empirical antecedents to some theoretical perspectives (Calabrese, 2009).

The theoretical framework is also called a *theoretical base*. However, not all dissertation committees require a separate section on theoretical frameworks in chapter one. Every school is different, and every school has a different policy regarding this first chapter. The theoretical framework provides the foundation for the study based on theory and the prior research (Long et al., 1985; Bryant, 2004; Calabrese, 2009) (see Example 19.5).

Main Key Points and Directions

These are the main key points that the doctoral researcher should consider when developing the "Theoretical Foundations" section of chapter one:

- Find a theory or theoretical model as a basis for the study
- Cite the appropriate pivotal sources for each theory or conceptual model
- Discuss the basic framework of the theory or concept
- Justify the theoretical foundation and framework as relevant to the study
- Connect the study directly to the theory and provide a narrative of the connection
- Describe how the study will add or extend the theory or model
- For quantitative studies: Have one theory for each variable. For example, use the model the survey is based on or use the theory or model upon which the instrument is based
- Distinguish between the model or theories being used for the research questions and data collection vs. the background models and theories generically relevant to the study
- Build a logical argument for how the research questions are developed based on the theoretical foundation for the study
- Writing length: Minimum of two to three pages (Miles, 2022)

Again, by following these key points, the researcher can fully develop this section of the study (see Example 19.5).

Example 19.5 *Theoretical / Conceptual Framework*

The job stress-demographic model (Miles & Adu, 2014) is the theoretical framework for the proposed study. The aim of the proposed study is understanding the effects of demographic factors on job stress among US agricultural field workers. The job stress-demographic model provided a framework for this investigation. Miles and Adu (2014) looked at relationships between demographic factors (gender, age, tenure, technological awareness and marital status) and job stress among field workers working in the agriculture industry in Wyoming. Specifically, the researchers designed the job stress-demographic model for postulating the existence of relationships between demographic factors such as those included in Miles and Adu's (2014) study and those included in the current study. Figure 19.1 provides a graphical representation of the job stress conceptual model used by Miles and Adu (2015).

Miles and Adu (2014) created and used the job stress-demographic model when examining job stress in academicians working in universities in India ($N = 216$). The job stress-demographic model was helpful in determining that male field workers experienced more job stress than female workers ($t = -3.51, p < 0.01$). In addition, the job stress-demographic model was helpful in determining

---

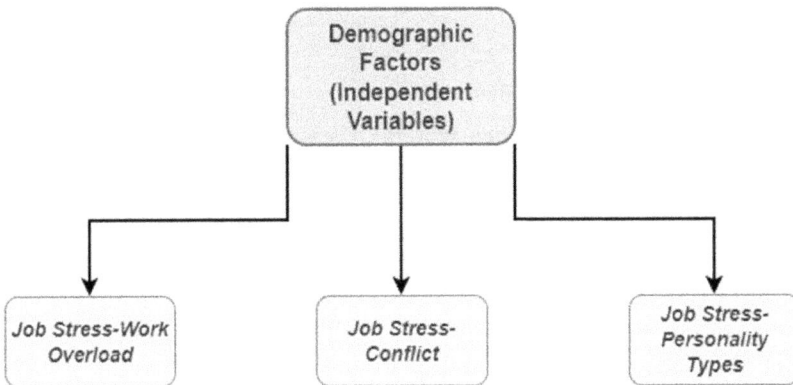

Figure 19.1 Job stress-demographic model.

that faculty members with more job dissatisfaction experienced less job stress than those with less job stress awareness ($t = -3.51$, $p < 0.01$), and field workers above 35 years of age felt more job stress than field workers below 35 years of age ($t = 3.12$, $p < 0.05$).

Finally, the job stress-demographic model was helpful in determining that marital status did not affect levels of job stress among field workers working in factories in Wyoming. The proposed study answers the call for future job stress research to include more diverse samples within the agriculture sector and additional demographic variables (Miles & Adu, 2014). The job stress-demographic model was useful when examining relationships between demographic factors and job stress among field workers in factories in Wyoming. The job stress-demographic model, revised to include the current study's demographic variables, will, therefore, provide a suitable framework for examining demographic factors (job stress awareness, gender and position status) and their effects on job satisfaction in US agricultural field workers.

[Note: In-text citations included for illustrative purposes only]

Assumptions, Limitations and Delimitations

The assumptions, limitations and delimitations section sets the conditions for the study. For example, the assumptions are what the researcher assumes about the study, the limitations are the constraints of the study based on the methodology, and the delimitations are the constraints of the study based on the population scope. In my experience, novice researchers and doctoral students still have trouble understanding these three terms and their meanings. Establishing these three terms will set the standard for the study (Long et al., 1985; Bryant, 2004; Miles & Scott, 2017) (see Example 19.6).

Main Key Points and Directions

These are the main key points that the doctoral researcher should consider when developing the "Assumptions, Limitations and Delimitations" section of chapter one:

- Provide a definition of the terms *assumption, limitation* and *delimitation* at the beginning of each section
- State the assumptions being made in the study (methodological, theoretical and topic-specific)
- Provide a rationale for each assumption
- Identify the limitations of the research method, design sampling strategy, data collection approach, instruments and data analysis
- Provide a rationale for each limitation
- Discuss any associated consequences for the generalizability and applicability of the findings
- Identify the delimitations of the research design and any associated consequences for the generalizability and applicability of the findings
- Provide a rationale for each delimitation
- Writing length: Minimum of two to three paragraphs or one page (Miles, 2022)

Again, by following these key points, the researcher can fully develop the "Assumptions, Limitations and Delimitations" section of the study (see Examples 19.6, 19.7 and 19.8).

Limitations

In my many years of work with doctoral students, I have found that there is still a prevailing confusion between the terms *limitation* and *delimitation*. I have seen this to be the case with both experienced researchers and novice researchers. Limitations are defined as constraints on the study based on the research methodology and research design (Miles & Scott, 2017). Limitations are things the researcher cannot control because they are constraints inherent in the research methodology (see Table 19.4 and Example 19.6).

Example 19.6 Limitations of the Study

Limitations are comprised of the restrictions implemented by the researcher's choice of methodology. These are factors in the study that cannot be controlled by the researcher. As a basis for the study, the limitations were threefold.

---

1. The first limitation in this study is the instrumentation. This study used an instrument that was closed and did not have open-ended questions.
2. The second limitation is the data collection. This study used aggregated data that was collected from the state in a publicly accessible medium. This is limited in descriptive statistics.
3. The last limitation was the course. Teen Leadership is one of several different character education opportunities offered throughout the state. Further investigation into other programs may offer different insights (Zeig, 2019).

Table 19.4 Examples of limitations

Common Quantitative Limitations	Common Qualitative Limitations
• Research methodology • Research design (type) • Use of self-reported data (survey) • Time constraints (time to collect data) • Length of survey instrument • Design of survey instrument • Sampling design (random, stratified or clustering, systematic, convenience); probability sampling-based • Sampling bias • Target population constraints • Data collection modality type • Survey question types (closed-ended) • Survey bias • Researcher misinterpretation of participant data from surveys	• Research methodology • Research design (type) • Use of self-reported data (interviews) • Time constraints (time to interview subjects) • Length of study's interview time with participants • Design of interview questions • Sampling design (purposive, quota and snowball); non-probability sampling-based • Target population constraints • Data collection modality type • Interview question types (open-ended) • Researcher bias • Researcher misinterpretation of participant data from interviews

Delimitations/Scope of the Study

Delimitations are defined as constraints on your study based on the *population scope* (Miles & Scott, 2017). Think of delimitations as the boundaries of your study. Delimitations are defined as chiefly concerned with the *scope of the study*. Again, another recurring problem that doctoral students have is misunderstanding the true meaning of a delimitation. This is confusing to them because of the generic definition of a delimitation: The characteristics of a study in which the researcher can control the delimitations.

When you write about the delimitations, the sentence should always begin as follows: *This study was delimited to ....* You have to set the parameters of your study so that you cannot say your results are generalizable to other areas of the country or other studies with dissimilar results. You want to start off with four categories, from the unit of analysis to the state of the data collection (see Table 19.5 and Example 19.7).

Table 19.5 The Statement Grid for delimitations

Overall Statement:
This study had some delimitations that restricted the study. The researcher identified four delimitations concerning the scope of this study. The study was delimited by certain conditions that were identified for this research inquiry.

Delimitation 1:	**Delimitation 2:**	**Delimitation 3:**	**Delimitation 4:**
First, the study was delimited to domestic violence victims (DVV). (unit of analysis)	Second, the study was delimited to the metropolitan city of Los Angeles. (metropolitan city)	Third, the study was delimited to the surrounding counties of the Los Angeles area. (surrounding counties and non-city areas)	Lastly, the study was delimited to the state of California. (state)

Example 19.7 Delimitations of the Study

The delimitations of a study are those characteristics that arise from limitations in the scope of the study (defining boundaries) and by the conscious exclusionary and inclusionary decisions made during the development of the study plan (Simon & Goes, 2013). The delimitations are those characteristics that limit the scope and define the boundaries of your study (Miles & Scott, 2017). The following delimitations will be present at the time this study is conducted:

1. The study is delimited to air transportation organization employees and will not assess other types of organizations in the geographical location of Puerto Rico. To mitigate the delimitation of the organizations where the study will be conducted, the researcher will collect data from the most possible air transportation companies.
2. The study is delimited to organizations in Puerto Rico. To minimize the delimitation of the employees, the study will collect data from employees in all positions within the organization.
3. The study is delimited to floor employees, office employees and managers at the air transportation organization site. No employees at the high leadership level (CEO, vice presidents of operations, etc.) will be assessed in this study (Morales, 2017).

Assumptions

Assumptions can be defined as things that are somewhat out of your control, but if they disappeared your study would become irrelevant (Hubbard, 1973; Simon, 2011; Simon & Goes, 2013). Another definition of an assumption is an unexamined belief that the researcher brings to the study and that is accepted as being valid (Bryant, 2004).

General Types of Assumptions

When considering the assumptions, the researcher should list the major assumptions underlying the study. Here are some general types of assumptions:

* Behavior is characterized by some degree of consistency
* The behavior of interest is observable and properly measured
* All individuals in a group benefit equally from a group treatment
* Subjects have the ability to report their perceptions accurately
* The time allotted for the treatment is adequate to produce the desired effects
* All the important variables influencing the dependent variable have been controlled or explicitly included in the design
* Student achievement is a function of both in-school and out-of-school factors (Long et al., 1985) (see Example 19.8)

Example 19.8 Assumptions of the Study

The school district that is the foundation of this study has a variety of races, which is represented in the teaching pool. Though there are more non-performing arts teachers than performing arts teachers in the school district, there should be a good representation as far as the data is concerned. The following assumptions are present in this study:

1. It is assumed that the participants in this study will answer the survey as honestly as possible.
2. It is assumed that the participants will be mentally capable of answering and completing the survey.
3. It is assumed that the participants have the background and experience to answer and complete the survey.
4. It is assumed that the participants are employed as teachers in the K–12 school system in the area where the study is being conducted (Jefferson, 2021).

Significance of the Study

Significance is an explanation of why the proposed study is important and why it represents a potential contribution to the field. Its emphasis should be on why the study is worthwhile (Webster, 1998b). The significance of the study is your argument as to why the study makes a significant and original contribution to the profession, the scholarly literature and your discipline. The significance of a study answers questions related to why the topic is worth studying (Calabrese, 2006).

The significance of a study describes why the study is important. There are three types of significance of a study: (a) *theoretical significance*, (b) *practical significance*, and (c) *research significance*. Of the three types of significance, the researcher provides arguments for the theoretical contributions that should be developed from the literature (Long et al., 1985; Miles & Scott, 2017).

Main Key Points and Directions

These are the main key points that the doctoral researcher should consider when developing the "Significance of the Study" section of chapter one:

- Describe how the research fits with and will contribute to or advance the current literature, body of research or body of knowledge
- Describe the significance of the study (theoretical, practical or research)
- Describe the contributions of the study (theoretical/conceptual, empirical or methodological) (see Chapter 12 for more on this)
- Describe the potential practical applications of the research
- Identify the theory(ies) or model(s) that provide the theoretical foundations or conceptual frameworks for the study
- Connect the study directly to the theory and describe how the study will add or extend the theory or model
- Describe how addressing the problem will add value to the population, community or society
- Writing length: Minimum of one to two pages (Miles, 2022)

Again, by following these key points, the researcher can fully develop the "Significance of the Study" section. This will meet the standards of the university's dissertation committee (see Example 19.9).

Example 19.9 *Significance of the Study*

As a basis for this study, the researcher identified two major reasons why this study is significant. First, this study is important because it provides practical significance. This study is important because of its application of the study's results to limited research on 6th-grade mathematics literacy strategies that improve mathematics comprehension and increase mathematics content. Not only does this study contribute to the field of K–12 education, but it also provides valuable insight and perspective to support the literacy needs of rural communities. In a study that examined the disproportionate use of referrals and out-of-school suspensions by mathematics teachers, the researchers found a correlation between 6th-grade students who experienced one or more suspensions and those who experienced suspensions in 7th grade (Miles & Adu, 2012). Additionally, it was found that the same 6th-grade students who experienced one or more suspensions scored below the 50th percentile on a standardized mathematics assessment (Miles & Adu, 2012). Therefore, insufficient literacy skills can impact student behavior, absenteeism partially due to referrals and suspensions, disengagement and overall school success (Adu & Miles, 2015).

Second, this study is important because it provides research significance. This study is an extension of prior research on the use of Type X assessments in 6th-grade mathematics classrooms. This study will help rural communities to improve because of the implementation of instructional practices that meet the needs of disproportionate youth. When students in rural areas increase their reading abilities by taking an active role in their learning process, student discipline concerns will decrease. Students may be more engaged and less bored, which will decrease the possibility of them acting out in class. Type X implemented with content area instruction aids students in active engagement and increased motivation. This research study will analyze the pre- and post-assessment results of students who have received mathematics instruction using a Type X assessment compared to students who have received traditional lecture and note-taking instruction (Miles & Gleason, 2003; Adu et al., 2015; Miles et al., 2017). The present study extends the study of the impact of Type X assessments on increasing 6th-grade students' mathematics content knowledge. The study will present instructional strategies that will help secondary educators to understand how the current literacy practices for 6th-grade mathematics teachers might be improved.

Contributions of the Study

As a basis for this study, the researcher identified a key contribution. This study offers an empirical contribution. This study offers two key empirical contributions to the body of knowledge. First, this study makes an empirical contribution because of its evaluation of the study's results to limited research on 7th-grade mathematics literacy strategies. These are strategies that improve mathematics comprehension and increase mathematics content. Not only does this study contribute to the field of K–12 education, but it also provides valuable insight and perspective to support the literacy needs of rural communities. In a study that examined the disproportionate use of referrals and out-of-school suspensions by mathematics teachers, the researchers found a correlation between 6th-grade students who experienced one or more suspensions and those who experienced suspensions in 7th grade (Miles & Adu, 2012). Additionally, it was found that the same 7th-grade students who experienced one or more suspensions scored below the 50th percentile on a standardized mathematics assessment (Miles & Adu, 2012). Therefore, insufficient literacy skills can impact student behavior, absenteeism partially due to referrals and suspensions, disengagement and overall school success (Adu & Miles, 2015).

Second, this study makes another empirical contribution because it will help rural communities to evaluate and improve the implementation of mathematics instructional practices for the disproportionate youth. When students in rural areas increase their mathematics abilities by taking an active role in their learning process, student discipline concerns will decrease. Students may be more engaged and less bored, which will decrease the possibility of acting out in class. Type X implemented with content area instruction aids students in active engagement and increased motivation. This research study will analyze the pre- and post-assessment results of students who have received mathematics instruction using a Type X assessment compared to students who have received traditional lecture and note-taking instruction (Miles & Gleason, 2003; Adu et al., 2015; Miles et al., 2017). The present study extends the study of the impact of Type X assessments on increasing 7th-grade students' mathematics content knowledge. The study will present instructional strategies that will help secondary educators to understand how the current literacy practices for 7th-grade mathematics teachers might be improved.

[Note: In-text citations included for illustrative purposes only]

Summary

This chapter discussed the writing of chapter one of your dissertation. It provided a conceptual model for developing the sections of the chapter and a conceptual model and tool to help doctoral students and researchers develop the chapter. To begin writing a chapter is the first step in the dissertation journey. This is an enormous task. In this chapter we provided a basis for the researcher to develop their dissertation. This chapter provided researchers with some valuable knowledge on and insight into the correct dissertation format.

This chapter provided some practical strategies for researchers who are writing these core sections within the dissertation format. In this chapter, we discussed five things: first, how to write the introduction and background of the study; second, how to write the problem statement, purpose statement and research statement of the study; third, how to write about the significance of the study; fourth, how to write about the assumptions, limitations and delimitations of the study; and, lastly, how to write the main points and directions for the sections in the study. By the end of this chapter, the reader should be knowledgeable about these five core areas of the dissertation's first, introductory chapter.

References

Abbas, W. (2020). *The Research Purpose*. PDF4PRO. Retrieved from https://pdf4pro.com/view/the-research-purpose-3-dr-wafa-a-k-abbas-definition-6307e5.html

Beltran, V. (2020). *A descriptive study of central Texas urban school principals' experience of influences contributing to job stress*. ProQuest Dissertations and Theses.

Bryant, M. T. (2004). *The Portable Dissertation Advisor*. Corwin Press, Inc.

Calabrese, R. (2006). *The Elements of An Effective Dissertation And Thesis: A Step-By-Step Guide To Getting It Right The First Time*. Rowman & Littlefield Education, Inc.

Calabrese, R. (2009). *The Dissertation Desk Reference: The Doctoral Student's Manual To Writing The Dissertation*. Rowman & Littlefield Education, Inc.

Cook, L. (2017). *The Current Issues Affecting Job Satisfaction By Nursing Faculty As A Lived Experience* [Unpublished dissertation].

Creswell, J. W. (2009). *Research design: Qualitative, quantitative, and mixed methods approaches* (3rd ed.). Sage. www.ucg.ac.me/skladiste/blog_609332/objava_105202/fajlovi/Creswell.pdf

Creswell, J. W. (2013). *Qualitative inquiry and research design choosing among five approaches*. Sage.

Hubbard, A. (1973). *Research methods in health, physical education and recreation*. American Association for Health, Physical Education, and Recreation.

Jacobs, R. L. (2011). Developing a research purpose and purpose statement. In T. S. Rocco and T. Hatcher (Eds.), *The handbook of scholarly writing and publishing* (pp. 125–141). Jossey-Bass.

Jefferson, R. (2021). *A quantitative study on the opinions of K–12 administrators towards music education* [Unpublished dissertation].

Long, T., Convey, J., & Chwalek, A. (1985). *Completing dissertations in the behavioral sciences and education: A systematic guide for graduate students*. Jossey-Bass.

Miles, D. (2022). 360 review tool for auditing dissertation chapters. From *Confessions of a dissertation chair: Dissertation chapter auditing* [Virtual workshop for doctoral students].

Miles, D. A., & Scott, L. (2017, October 26–29). *Confessions of a dissertation chair, Part 1: The six mistakes doctoral students make with the dissertation*. 5th Annual 2017 Black Doctoral Network Conference, Atlanta, GA.

Morales, L. (2017). *A Baldrige assessment of an organization: An empirical study of Baldrige criteria and organizational performance in air transportation organizations* [Unpublished dissertation]. ProQuest Dissertations and Theses.

Rudestam, K. E., & Newton, R. R. (2007). *Surviving your dissertation: A comprehensive guide to content and process*. Sage Publications Inc.

Simon, M. K. (2011). *Dissertation and scholarly research: Recipes for success*. Dissertation Success, LLC.

Simon, M. K., & Goes, J. (2013). *Dissertation and scholarly research: Recipes for success*. Dissertation Success, LLC.

Singh, S. (2020). *Methodological issues in management research: Advances, challenges and the way ahead*. Emerald Publishing Limited.

Webster, W. G. (1998a). *Developing and writing your thesis, dissertation or project*. Academic Scholarwrite.

Webster, W. G. (1998b). *21 models for developing and writing theses, dissertations, and projects*. Academic Scholarwrite.

Zeig, M. (2019). *Effects of a character education course on standardized testing in Texas high schools* [UMI No. 5458799]. ProQuest Dissertations and Theses.

20 Writing Your Dissertation

The Standard Format – Chapter 2 (Literature Review)

Objective

- Readers will be able to:
  1. Write the literature review chapter of their dissertation

Introduction and Overview

In this section, you first remind your readers about the problem and the purpose of the study. Then, you share what should be expected in this literature review chapter, highlighting the main sections and/or topics you will be writing about.

Main Points and Directions

These are the main key points that the doctoral researcher should consider when developing the "Overview" section of chapter two:

- State the research problem or gap
- State the purpose of the study
- Provide an overview of what you plan to discuss in this chapter

---

Example 20.1 *Overview*

Although there have been conservations within the academic community about the use of ChatGPT (an artificial intelligence chatbot), there was limited empirical evidence in support of how university faculty and graduate students view the utilization of this AI tool and the concerns they have about it (D'Agostino, 2023). The purpose of the study was to examine how ChatGPT can be used in the academic world and explore concerns associated with adopting this AI chatbot. In this chapter, I review relevant literature in relation to the topic of ChatGPT adaptation, use and concerns within the academic field. I started this

---

DOI: 10.4324/9781003268154-20

review by describing where and how the literature was accessed. After describing the literature search strategies, detailed information about the conceptual framework and concepts related to ChatGPT adoption and utilization literature were reviewed.

Notes about ChatGPT

ChatGPT is an artificial-intelligence-powered chat system that is capable of responding to questions you ask or command/prompt you give (Atlas, 2023). This chatbot, developed by OpenAI (https://openai.com/), has been trained on a huge amount of information gathered from the Internet. If an appropriate prompt is given, ChatGPT (https://chat.openai.com/) can provide useful information, dramatically cutting the amount of time spent in getting similar information from conventional means. As Alshater (2022) puts it, "It is trained on a large dataset of human-human conversations and can generate appropriate responses to questions and prompts given by users. It can also generate complete conversations on its own, making it a powerful tool for NLP research" (p. 2).

Literature Search and Selection

The literature search strategies section is where you present how and where you searched for literature related to your topic and selected relevant ones for review. There are three main reasons why this section is very important. Firstly, as part of promoting the transparency of the study, you are expected to share the strategies you used to search for appropriate literature for review. Secondly, it is a way of educating your readers in the techniques used to search and select the right literature for your study. Lastly, sharing how you got the literature you reviewed helps future researchers to replicate what you did if need be.

Main Points and Directions

These are the main key points that the doctoral researcher should consider when writing the "Literature Search and Selection" section in chapter two:

- Describe the databases you used to search for literature related to your topic
- State the search terms you used to search for the literature
- Share the criteria you used to selected relevant literature for review

---

Example 20.2 Literature Search and Selection

At the time that I was searching for literature to review, ChatGPT had been released for public use for about three months. Due to this there were a few databases that had literature relevant to my topic. I used the Sage Journal and

ERIC databases to get access to ChatGPT-related literature. Besides, the Google Scholar search engine was used to search for literature, including their sources. The following terms were used to access articles: "ChatGPT impact on education," "ChatGPT and Research" and "ChatGPT and education." To be selected as a part of the review, the literature should touch on one of the following areas:

- Role of ChatGPT in promoting academic work
- Functions of ChatGPT
- Meaning of ChatGPT
- Limitations of ChatGPT
- Benefits of ChatGPT
- Ethical issues related to ChatGPT

In addition, I searched for literature that focused on studying or discussing the diffusion of innovation theory. The diffusion of innovations was the theory I used to develop the conceptual/theoretical framework for this study. The terms I used to search for literature related to this theory were "Rogers' diffusion of innovations," "diffusion of innovations and technology" and "diffusion of technology." Utilizing these search strategies helped in getting access to relevant literature to review.

Conceptual/Theoretical Framework

The conceptual/theoretical framework reflects a description of the theory, model or concepts that inform your study. The framework for your study can be written in chapter one. However, some institutions or dissertation chairs/supervisors may ask you to expand what was written in chapter one by sharing and synthesizing academic authors' and researchers' views on the features, components, strengths, weaknesses and/or assumptions about the theory, model or concepts you have selected for your study. In addition, you are expected to review how the selected theory, models or concepts have been used by researchers if studies related to your framework have been done.

Main Points and Directions

These are the main key points that the doctoral researcher should consider when writing the "Conceptual/Theoretical Framework" section in chapter two:

- State the theory, model or concepts used in the development of the framework
- Describe the originator(s) of the theory, model or concepts
- Describe the characteristics of the theory, model or concepts
- Present the components of the theory or model

- Describe the views and assertions of scholars and researchers in relation to the theory, model or concepts
- Describe the studies done (if any) that utilize the theory, model or concepts

---

Example 20.3 Conceptual/Theoretical Framework

The theory selected to inform this study was the diffusion of innovations (Dearing & Cox, 2018). This theory was developed by Rogers (2003). The diffusion of innovation theory explains how innovations are adopted and used by people over time. In other words, the theory evolves around how new technologies are accepted and utilized over time (Sahin, 2006). "Rogers' diffusion of innovations theory is the most appropriate for investigating the adoption of technology in higher education and educational environments" (Sahin, 2006, p. 14). Similarly, the theory best informed this study because it focused on exploring the diffusion process of ChatGPT within the academic world, examining the use of this AI chatbot among the university faculty and graduate students. Diffusion is how the information about, and utilization of, an innovation moves from the innovators of a technology to the end users (Wejnert, 2002).

Diffusion

Informed by Rogers' (2003) diffusion of innovation theory, Dearing and Cox (2018) asserted that the factors impacting diffusion are characteristics of innovation, characteristics of innovators (or adopters) and environmental context. According to Rogers (2003), there are five stages of the innovation-decision process (which is also known as communication or diffusion channels). These are the *knowledge stage* (where adopters have information about the innovation), *persuasion stage* (where adopters' affect, feelings or emotions towards the innovation is ignited), *decision stage* (where adopters make a choice to use or not use the innovation), *implementation stage* (where adopters use the innovation) and *confirmation stage* (where adopters seek support for their decision to utilize the innovation) (Sahin, 2006).

Innovation

Based on the diffusion of innovations, features of the innovation could impact the diffusion of new technology such as ChatGPT (Çakıroğlu et al., 2022). Five main factors related to innovation characteristics that could affect diffusion are adopters' perceived "relative advantage, compatibility, complexity, trialability, and observability" of the innovation (Çakıroğlu et al., 2022, p. 89). These factors help address questions like: Will the new technology efficiently and effectively help the adopters accomplish a task better than the old one (i.e., *relative advantage*)? How consistent is the innovation to the adopters' "values, culture and needs" (i.e., compatibility)? How much easier can the innovation be used (i.e., *complexity*)? Can the innovation be experimented with less or no risk (i.e., *trialability*)? Can the outcome of utilizing the innovation be easily noticed (i.e., *observability*) (Goh & Sigala, 2020; pp. 5–6). Empirically, the relationship between the diffusion of innovations and the above-mentioned factors has been explored in studies. One of these was a study conducted by Lee and Worthy (2021) to determine whether relative advantage, compatibility, complexity and trialability are related to the adoption of fad diets. Based on the results, there was a statistically significant relationship between complexity, trialability and fad diet adoption, but not between relative advantage, compatibility and fad diet adoption.

Characteristics of Innovators (or Adopters)

When looking at a community of users of innovations, according to Rogers (2003), there are five different kinds of adopters. These include innovators, early adopters, early majority, late majority and laggards (Sahin, 2006). Innovators are adopters who are ready to explore and use new technologies, while early adopters adopt innovations and show people how to use them (Çakıroğlu et al., 2022). The early majority adopt new technologies as they interact with people utilizing them, while the late majority "wait until most of their peers adopt the innovation" (Sahin, 2006, p. 20). Finally, the laggers have limited interactions with the initial users of the innovations, such as the innovators and early adopters. They normally use new technologies after observing a successful outcome of the adoption by other members of the society (Sahin, 2006). The early and late majority form two-thirds of a community of users of innovations (Rogers, 2003). However, the distribution for the groups of adopters observed by Rogers (2003) does not apply to all studies. In Çakıroğlu et al.'s (2022) study about the adoption of online instruction, 40% of academics were considered part of the early and late majority compared to Rogers' study, which reported 68% (see Table 20.1).

Table 20.1 Adopter groups and their distribution under Rogers' (2003) and Çakıroğlu et al.'s (2022) study

Adopter Group	Rogers' (2003) Study	Çakıroğlu et al.'s (2022) Study
Innovators	2.5%	11%
Early adopters	13.5%	23%
Early majority	34%	18%
Late majority	34%	22%
Laggard	16%	26%

Environmental Context

Environmental context is one of the contributing factors in the diffusion of innovations. To Wejnert (2002), environmental context plays a crucial role in the innovation diffusion process, since the adopters are living in "geographic sittings," within "societal culture" and amidst certain "political conditions" (p. 310). Moreover, Dearing and Cox (2018) indicated that the context does not only influence the diffusion of innovations but also how the inventers create and introduce the new technology to the public. In addition, Dearing and Cox (2018) highlighted the reciprocal effect of innovation by stating that innovation can change the society and vice versa. Also, continuous innovations with their associated sustained diffusion can lead to changes in institutions and communities (Dearing & Cox, 2018). Similarly, as the inventors are shaping an AI tool such as ChatGPT, the invention is also changing the society, hence, the need to explore the views of the potential users of this AI Chatbot.

Review of the Literature

Before writing the "Review of the Literature" section, you should decide on a list of topics or concepts you want to write about. The topics should be consistent with what you are studying while at the same time reflecting what you have learned or observed in the relevant literature you have reviewed. When writing your literature review, you are expected to report on what you have found in the literature. However, the report should not just be a summary of the literature but a synthesis of your commentary on the literature. As a rule of thumb, a synthesized paragraph should have the following minimum features: two or more intext citations; transitional words such as "in addition," "moreover," "on the contrary" and "however"; and a topic sentence and concluding statement.

Main Points and Directions

These are the main key points that the doctoral researcher should consider when writing the 'Review of the Literature' section in chapter two:

- State the topics you want to include in your literature review
- Under each topic, write a synthesis of what you have reviewed
- For each paragraph:
    - State a topic sentence that will help readers to know what the paragraph is about
    - Present your observations, patterns identified and themes emerged, comparing and contrasting researchers' studies, assertions, views, interpretations and conclusions
    - State a concluding statement(s)

Example 20.4 *Review of the Literature*

Because ChatGPT was released for public use in November 2022, not a lot of empirical research has been done (Alshater, 2022). However, there are positional papers or articles written about the adoption and impact of this AI tool in the academic world. Some of these articles were reviewed, which included synthesizing scholars' observations, perspectives, arguments and assertions. The review was organized under the following topics: roles and functions, benefits, limitations and adoption of ChatGPT. Equally important, a review on ethical issues related to ChatGPT was also presented.

Roles and Functions of ChatGPT

Exploring the unique functions of ChatGPT, researchers and scholars are in agreement that it has a role to play in education and research. Evidently, Alshater (2022) asserted that the ability for ChatGPT to make sense of language and give responses similar to what humans do makes it a great tool for assisting researchers. Specifically, Alshater (2022) further indicated that the AI tool could help researchers generate potential research questions for proposed studies and make sense of the data collected. In addition, Zhai (2022), who was an aspiring researcher, shared that ChatGPT is seen as a useful research tool that can assist novice researchers to easily learn about research terms and best practices. Similarly, when highlighting the characteristics of ChatGPT, Zhang (2023) emphasized its efficiency, stating that it saves time when using the AI tool to brainstorm ideas and make sense of concepts. On the whole, ChatGPT can help promote research, teaching and learning, and it can be a useful tool for researchers, teachers and students (Kasneci et al., 2023). Although the AI chatbot has a huge role to play in education, it will not, however, replace the jobs of educators (Alshater, 2022).

[Paragraph #2]
[Paragraph #3]

Limitations of ChatGPT

Researchers have acknowledged the weaknesses of ChatGPT one of which was the possibility of obtaining a biased outcome. According to Alshater (2022), the mechanisms powering ChatGPT are based on natural language processing models, which were originally built on data generated by humans. Therefore, because the data used to train the models may have biased elements, the results that ChatGPT produces could also be biased (Alshater, 2022). As Kasneci et al. (2023) put it, if trained data is gathered from a society that is biased, it will lead to a biased outcome. Correspondingly, Atlas (2023) also shared another factor that may contribute to a biased outcome. He indicated that a user could ask ChatGPT biased questions or provide prejudiced prompts that could lead to biased responses. This problem of inputting biased questions could be attributed to users' (including researchers, practitioners, educators and students) lack of skills in developing appropriate prompts as they interact with ChatGPT (Kasneci et al., 2023).

Another concern raised by researchers was the dependence of researchers, educators, practitioners and students on ChatGPT (Alshater, 2022). To Alshater (2022), the continuous use of ChatGPT could lead to users' over reliance on it. In the same way, Kasneci et al. (2023) noted that overdependence on the AI chatbot could adversely affect learners' critical thinking and creativity. Further, Zhang (2023) reviewed that ChatGPT, like other AI chatbots, lacks self-awareness in terms of how limited its expertise is. Therefore, wholly relying on ChatGPT outcomes without critically reviewing experts (if possible) or cross-checking with other sources could lead to their misuse or misapplication.

[Paragraph #3]

Benefits of ChatGPT

[Paragraph #1]
[Paragraph #2]
[Paragraph #3]
[Paragraph #4]

Adoption of ChatGPT

[Paragraph #1]
[Paragraph #2]
[Paragraph #3]

Ethical Issues Related to ChatGPT

[Paragraph #1]
[Paragraph #2]
[Paragraph #3]
[Paragraph #4]

Summary

Writing the literature review chapter can be challenging. However, having a clear understanding of what is expected of you in this chapter will make the process less daunting. You start this chapter by providing a chapter overview, giving a brief description of the problem and purpose of the study. You then share what readers should expect in this chapter. Also, before you write about what you found in the literature, you need to show where and how you got access to and selected relevant literature for the review, hence the need to complete the "Literature Search and Selection" section. The next section is "Conceptual/ Theoretical Framework," which contains a description of the theory, model and/ or concepts informing your study. It also includes a review of research done and researchers' and scholars' conversations surrounding aspects of the framework. Next, you work on the main section, which is "Review of Literature," focusing on synthesizing the literature under its respective topics. Lastly, you write a summary of the chapter, touching on the main points/ideas/topics described in the chapter. We hope the examples provided will help you to successfully complete this chapter.

References

Alshater, M. (2022). Exploring the role of artificial intelligence in enhancing academic performance: A case study of ChatGPT. SSRN. https://ssrn.com/abstract=4312358 or http://dx.doi.org/10.2139/ssrn.4312358

Atlas, S. (2023). ChatGPT for higher education and professional development: A guide to conversational AI. College of Business Faculty Publications. https://digitalcommons.uri.edu/cba_facpubs/548

Çakıroğlu, Ü., Saylan, E., Çevik, İ., Mollamehmetoğlu, M. Z., & Timuçin, E. (2022). Faculty adoption of online teaching during the Covid-19 pandemic: A lens of diffusion of innovation theory. *Australasian Journal of Educational Technology*, *38*(3), 87–103. https://doi.org/10.14742/ajet.7307

D'Agostino, S. (2023, January 11). *Academic experts offer advice on CHATGPT*. Inside Higher Ed. Retrieved February 14, 2023, from www.insidehighered.com/news/2023/01/12/academic-experts-offer-advice-chatgpt#.Y8GDBx0SMxR.linkedin

Dearing, J. W., & Cox, J. G. (2018). Diffusion of innovations theory, principles, and practice. *Health Affairs (Project Hope)*, *37*(2), 183–190. https://doi.org/10.1377/hlthaff.2017.1104

Goh, E., & Sigala, M. (2020). Integrating information & communication technologies (ICT) into classroom instruction: Teaching tips for hospitality educators from a diffusion of innovation approach. *Journal of Teaching in Travel & Tourism*, *20*(2), 156–165. https://doi.org/10.1080/15313220.2020.1740636

Kasneci, E., Seßler, K., Küchemann, S., Bannert, M., Dementieva, D., Fischer, F., Gasser, U., Groh, G., Günnermann, S., Hüllermeier, E., Krusche, S., Kutyniok, G., Michaeli, T., Nerdel, C., Pfeffer, J., Poquet, O., Sailer, M., Schmidt, A., Seidel, T., … Kasneci, G. (2023, January 30). ChatGPT for good? On opportunities and challenges of large language models for education. https://doi.org/10.35542/osf.io/5er8f

Lee, H., & Worthy, S. (2021). Adoption of fad diets through the lens of the diffusion of innovations. *Family & Consumer Sciences Research Journal*, *50*(2), 135–149. https://doi.org/10.1111/fcsr.12419

Rogers, E. M. (2003). *Diffusion of innovations* (5th ed.). Free Press.

Sahin, I. (2006). Detailed review of Rogers' diffusion of innovations theory and educational technology-related studies based on Rogers' theory. *The Turkish Online Journal of Educational Technology*, *5*, 14–23.

Wejnert, B. (2002). Integrating models of diffusion of innovations: A conceptual framework. *Review of Sociology, 28,* 297–326.

Zhai, X. (2022). ChatGPT user experience: Implications for education. SSRN. https://doi.org/10.2139/ssrn.4312418

Zhang, B. (2023). Preparing educators and students for ChatGPT and AI technology in higher education: Benefits, limitations, strategies, and implications of ChatGPT & AI technologies. https://doi.org/10.13140/RG.2.2.32105.98404

21 Writing Your Dissertation

The Standard Format – Chapter 3
(Research Methodology)

Objective

- Readers will be able to:
  1. Write the research methodology chapter of their dissertation

Introduction and Overview

In this chapter of their dissertation, the researcher reintroduces the topic and reiterates the research problem as the basis for the study. The chapter also provides another introduction and overview of the research topic. This section mirrors chapter one, so the content should be exactly the same as the content in chapter one. There should not be any difference between them. So, the researcher does not have to reinvent the wheel. This section of the chapter should be easy to develop.

Main Points and Directions

These are the main key points that the doctoral researcher should consider when developing the "Introduction and Overview" section of chapter three:

- Reintroduce the dissertation topic
- Provide an <u>overview</u> of what is contained in the chapter
- Writing length: Minimum of three to four paragraphs or approximately one page (Miles, 2022)

By following these key points, the researcher can fully develop the "Introduction and Overview" section of the chapter (see Example 21.1).

DOI: 10.4324/9781003268154-21

Example 21.1 Introduction and Overview

The purpose of this study is to investigate how field workers in agricultural industries in a rural area in Wyoming feel about their working conditions. The participants describe their experiences and reflect on the challenges of field work, the challenges of professional mentoring and the challenges of access to agricultural resources for their jobs. Wong & Lee's (2015) study examined field workers from 20 companies in Texas. Some of these studies have indicated that networking for field workers plays a direct role in empowering those within the network to achieve job success.

Although previous researchers have established a relationship between agricultural work and job satisfaction, this relationship is also noted to improve field-worker morale (Jermain & Derkowitz, 2014); yet, Docker et al. (2013) explained that social interaction is a critical factor in a field worker's needs and job satisfaction. According to Ingol and Marshall (2014), social networking and job satisfaction provide field workers with resources to further their careers and strengthen themselves professionally. Therefore, a qualitative descriptive design will lead the researcher to investigate their experiences.

Overview of the Chapter

This chapter presents the problem statement and delineates the research questions under investigation. This chapter discusses the research methodology, the research design of the study and the participants. This chapter also presents details regarding the sample selection and the sources of data for the study. Next, the chapter outlines how the study will address the trustworthiness of the data collected, in addition to how the data will be analyzed. Ethical considerations will then be discussed. These considerations will ensure the protection of the participants and support the integrity of the research. Lastly, the limitations and delimitations of the study will be reviewed, followed by a summarization of the main points of the chapter.

[Note: In-text citations included for illustrative purposes only]

Problem Statement

In this chapter, the researcher reiterates the research problem as the basis for the study. This section should be exactly the same as the content in chapter one. There should not be any difference between them. So, the researcher does not have to reinvent the wheel. This section of the chapter should be easy to develop.

Main Points and Directions

These are the main key points that the doctoral researcher should consider when developing this section of chapter three:

- Restate the research problem for the convenience of the reader
- Align the problem statement with the related section in chapter three
- Writing length: Minimum of one to two paragraphs (Miles, 2022)

By following these key points, the researcher can fully develop the "Problem Statement" section of the chapter (see Example 21.2).

Purpose Statement

After the problem statement is done, the purpose statement must be developed. Again, this section should be exactly the same as the content in chapter one. There should not be any difference between them. This section of the chapter should be easy to develop.

Main Points and Directions

These are the main key points that the doctoral researcher should consider when developing the purpose statement in this section of chapter three:

- Restate the purpose statement for the convenience of the reader
- Align the purpose statement with the related section in chapter one
- Writing length: Minimum of one to two paragraphs (Miles, 2022)

By following these key points, the researcher can fully develop the "Purpose Statement" section of the chapter (see Example 21.3).

Research Statement and Research Questions

After the problem statement and purpose statement are done, the research statement and research questions must be developed. Once again, this section should be exactly the same as the content in chapter one. There should not be any difference between them. Again, this section of the chapter should be easy to develop.

Main Points and Directions

These are the main key points that the doctoral researcher should consider when developing the "Research Questions" section of chapter three:

- **For quantitative studies**: Describe the variables at the conceptual, operational and measurement levels, then restate the research questions from chapter one and present the matching hypotheses
- **For qualitative studies**: Restate the research questions and the phenomena for the study from chapter one
- Describe the nature and sources of the necessary data to answer the research questions (primary vs. secondary data, specific people, institutional archives, Internet open sources, etc.)

- **For quantitative studies**: <u>Describe the data collection method(s), instrument(s) or data source(s)</u> used to collect the data for each variable
- **For qualitative studies**: <u>Describe the data collection method(s), instrument(s) and/or data source(s)</u> used to collect the data to answer each research question
- Restate the purpose statement for the convenience of the reader
- Align the purpose statement with the related section in chapter one
- Writing length: Minimum of one to two pages (Miles, 2022)

By following these key points, the researcher can fully develop the "Purpose Statement" section of the chapter (see Example 21.4).

Research Alignment: Definition and Meaning

Alignment is defined as the logical progression of ideas between the structural elements of your dissertation proposal (Booton, 2014). One of the most important factors to keep in mind is that alignment between your problem statement, purpose statement and research questions is critical. The *Research Alignment Tool* is used to help align these three items (the problem statement, purpose statement and research questions) (see Table 21.1).

Table 21.1 Example: The research alignment model

Problem Statement:		
Issu e (subproblem) 1:	**Issue (subproblem) 2:**	**Issue (subproblem) 3:**
Purpose Statement:		
Objective 1:	**Objective 2:**	**Objective 3:**
Research Statement:		
Research Question 1:	**Research Question 2:**	**Research Question 3:**

Example 21.2 Problem Statement

The central problem to be researched by the proposed study is the shortage in the basketweaving field. This has a lot to do with the current crop shortage and the need for more basketweaving in the field. There is a huge problem with this shortage and the availability of wheat and crops. As a basis for this study, the researcher identified the problem to be threefold.

First, a prevailing issue is that the education of new agricultural workers is the responsibility of the corporations in the industry, but there is a national shortage of field workers (Harris & Miles, 2012; Robbins, 2015), which is limiting the education and graduation of field workers from the corporations. There is a need to incorporate technology into agricultural institutional practices to better respond to labor pressures, provide flexible learning options for field workers and remain competitive in the agricultural industry (Abbas, 2019; Rokanta, 2017).

Second, a prevailing issue in the United States is that 75% of field workers will reach retirement age in 2018 (Morris, 2023; Harris, 2015). This is alongside the existing problem that 6.9% of field positions remain unfilled due to a lack of qualified field workers (Roberts, 2005). There is a need to incorporate technology into agricultural practices to better respond to financial pressures, provide flexible learning options for workers and remain competitive (Abbas, 2019; Rokanta, 2017).

Last, a prevailing issue is that the current field workers express low job satisfaction (Michaels, 2012) due to the complexities of the field workers' role, making the retention and recruitment of qualified workers difficult (Burns & Miles, 2014). The current problems include a shortage of qualified field workers to educate new field workers, the complexity of job education and current faculty complaints of poor job satisfaction (Donald, 2017).

[Note: In-text citations included for illustrative purposes only]

Example 21.3 Purpose Statement

The purpose of this study is to investigate the issues affecting job satisfaction among field workers in rural Wyoming. Interviewing and questioning field workers living in rural Wyoming provides insight into their personal experiences of job satisfaction while working in the field worker role. The researcher has identified three primary objectives as a basis for this study.

First, the objective of this study is to examine the issue of job satisfaction among field workers. There is a need to incorporate technology into agricultural institutional practices to better respond to labor pressures, provide flexible learning options for field workers and remain competitive in the agricultural industry (Abbas, 2019; Rokanta, 2017).

Second, the objective of this study is to investigate the impact of low wages on field workers. Professionals working in the agricultural industry face a set of new trials stemming from advances in technology and a new breed of technically capable field workers. There is a need to incorporate technology into agricultural practices to better respond to financial pressures, provide flexible learning options for field workers and remain competitive (Abbas, 2019; Rokanta, 2017).

Lastly, the objective of this study is to examine the complexities of field work-related stress. Field work-related stress, also known as field stress, is a term describing the anxiety, uncertainty and insecurity engendered by the utilization or perceived ease of use of field work. This facet of stress hinders field workers' and organizational productivity because it can result in a resistance to utilizing mandated field work and technology (Williams, 2005).

[Note: In-text citations included for illustrative purposes only]

Example 21.4 Research Questions

The central problem to be researched involves how principals manage job stress. There are three research questions that will guide this research:

- RQ1: How do field workers and managers describe their experience of job stress in a rural Central Wyoming environment?
- RQ2: How do field workers and managers describe their experience of using coping skills for job stress in a rural Central Wyoming environment?
- RQ3: How do field workers and managers describe their experiences of coping with work-life balance and job stress in a rural Central Wyoming environment (Miles, 2020)?

These three questions guide the direction of this study. Researchers have explored the effects of field stress and made connections between field stress and job outcomes such as job satisfaction and job productivity/performance (Darren, 2016; Corbett, 2019; Florkowski, 2019).

[Note: In-text citations included for illustrative purposes only]

Research Methodology

After the research questions are done, the research methodology must be developed. The research methodology describes the research method undertaken by the study. This section provides a strong basis for using a particular methodology in the study. This is really important in chapter three. This section may be challenging because novice researchers are not familiar with the advantages and capabilities of their methodology.

Main Points and Directions

These are the main key points that the doctoral researcher should consider when developing the "Research Methodology" section of chapter three:

- Provide a rationale for the research methodology used in the study (quantitative, qualitative or mixed methods) based on research books and articles
- Provide three major reasons why the selected methodology is the optimal choice for the study (quantitative, qualitative or mixed methods) based on research methods materials
- Provide a rationale for the selected methodology based on empirical studies on the topic
- Use an authoritative source(s) to justify the selected methodology
- Writing length: Minimum of one to two pages (Miles, 2022)

By following these key points, the researcher can fully develop the "Research Methodology" section of the chapter (Example 21.5).

Example 21.5 *Research Methodology*

The researcher made the decision to use a qualitative methodology as a research approach for the study. The researcher identified three key reasons for choosing a qualitative approach as the optimal choice for the study. First, a qualitative methodology is the best for this study because it is needed for a smaller sample size (20 participants). As the sample size is not large enough for a quantitative methodology, a quantitative methodology will not be adequate for this study. Second, according to Ashcroft et al. (2017), a qualitative methodology is the most appropriate way to understand personal meaning. A qualitative methodology allows the researcher to draw conclusions based on how we should understand the nature of the individual's experience (Firm & Patton, 2011). The researcher decided on a qualitative approach for the study as the optimal choice because it allows the researcher to explore and understand individual experiences.

Last, the researcher chose a qualitative methodology as the optimal choice for the study because it is concerned with an in-depth understanding of how

---

participants perceive experiences, and it is used to study participants' lived experiences (Tucker & Black, 2015). Furthermore, Martinez (2018) proposed that a qualitative research methodology is the best choice for understanding local knowledge and individuals' experiences, meanings, relationships, social processes and contextual factors that marginalize a group of people.

[Note: In-text citations included for illustrative purposes only]

Research Design

After the research methodology is written, the next step is to develop the research design. The research methodology describes the specific research technique undertaken by the study. This section provides a strong basis for using this particular research design for the study. Again, this section may be challenging because novice researchers are not familiar with the advantages and capabilities of their research design, much less the methodology.

Main Points and Directions

These are the main key points that the doctoral researcher should consider when developing the "Research Design" section of chapter three:

- Provide a rationale for the research design of the study (quantitative, qualitative or mixed methods) based on research books and articles
- Provide three major reasons why the selected research design is the optimal choice for the study (quantitative, qualitative or mixed methods) based on research methods materials
- Provide a rationale for the selected methodology based on empirical studies on the topic
- Describe how the specific selected research design will be used to collect the type of data needed to answer the research questions and the specific instruments or data sources that will be used to collect this data
- **For quantitative studies**: Provide the variable structure and state the <u>unit of analysis and unit of observation</u>. If multiple data sources have different units of observation, specify the key variable for matching cases
- **For quantitative studies**: An a priori and/or post hoc <u>G-Power analysis is required to justify the minimum study sample size</u> based on the anticipated effect size and selected design. Describe the general population (e.g., students with disabilities), target population (e.g., gifted students in one specific district/ geographic location) and study sample (student gifted with cognitive abilities in the district that participated in the study/actual study sample)
- Align the research design with the research methodology in the study
- Writing length: Minimum of one to two pages (Miles, 2022)

By following these key points, the researcher can fully develop the "Research Design" section of the chapter (see Example 21.6).

Example 21.6 *Research Design*

The optimal choice for the research design is a causal-comparative design. The researcher will utilize a causal-comparative research design to answer research questions that determine a causal relationship within the study. It measures differences in predictive abilities in the quantitative data. The researcher utilized the causal-comparative design. It is the optimal choice for the study for three reasons.

First, the researcher chose this design as the study used a random assignment because conditions that make up the demographic groups under investigation can be controlled. The advantage of a random assignment is a trait of a true experimental design, and causal-comparative designs use a random assignment (Koran, 2013; Schneider, 2004). Researchers commonly use causal-comparative designs when random assignment is not possible or when naturally occurring group assignments are most practical (Kirk, 2013; Schenker & Jr, 2004).

Second, the researcher chose a causal-comparative design because it allows the independent variables under investigation to act as predictor variables, which are demographic data such as gender and ethnicity, and cannot be manipulated, as would otherwise occur in an experimental study (Killmonger, 2018). Examining the extent of the differences germane to linear regression among such demographical groups is a common characteristic of causal-comparative research designs (Killmonger et al., 2015; Moncrief, 2008).

Lastly, the researcher chose the causal-comparative research design because there are predictive advantages of measuring the data. The current study employs examinations of relationship differences between the independent variable and the dependent variable. The utilizing of the causal-comparative design allows the research to measure for mean difference comparisons when there is a manipulation of variables, and, as such, this is the optimal research design for the current study (Shubert, 2008).

[Note: In-text citations included for illustrative purposes only]

Population, Sample and Sampling Technique

The next section is to develop the population, sample and sampling technique. After the research methodology and design section is written, the items in the research population section must be developed. This section describes the population, sample and sampling technique, and the areas related to this section.

This section describes the specific research sampling technique undertaken by the study. It provides a strong basis for the study's sampling techniques and sampling design. Again, this section may be a really big challenge if the researcher is not well versed in their sampling techniques and sampling methods.

Main Points and Directions

These are the main key points that the doctoral researcher should consider when developing the "Population, Sample and Sampling Technique" section of chapter three:

- Describe the population of interest for the study
- Describe the target population from which the sample is selected
- Describe the unit of analysis
- Describe the process for securing site authorization (if necessary) to access the target population
- Describe the site authorization process (what needs to be included in the request), confidentiality measures, study participation requirements and geographic specifics
- Describe the sampling strategy and process for recruiting individuals to comprise the sample
- Describe the study sample size. Provide evidence (based on the empirical research literature) that the sample size is adequate for the research design and meets the minimal sample size requirement
- Writing length: Minimum of two to three paragraphs or approximately one page (Miles, 2022)

By following these key points, the researcher can fully develop the "Population, Sample and Sampling Technique" section of the chapter (see Example 21.7).

Example 21.7 Population, Sample and Sampling Technique

The population for the proposed study is agricultural field workers. According to the Wyoming Bureau of Labor Statistics (2015), there is a shortage of field workers. Studying the field worker population is imperative because these individuals often utilize noncomplex tasks when performing daily agricultural work-related functions. In addition, field workers also utilize farm equipment, including but not limited to farm devices, farm supplies and agricultural services (Shorter, 2019; Marcy, 2013).

Target Population. The target population of the study is field workers in two plants located in West Wyoming, in the cities of Hotter and Colder. Both farms are private and not-for-profit entities offering a variety of agricultural products. Farm workers in the target population working in these agricultural plants are in job roles that provide training, farm training and support roles. The target

---

population is comprised of full-time and part-time farm workers yielding approximately 5,075 farm workers on a variety of job functions. The target population size was derived by conducting a search using each farm plant's employee directories and from an authorized dealer contact at each farm plant.

Site Authorization. The preliminary site authorization for the farm plant was obtained by contacting the IRBs and authorized personnel of each plant. Each farm plant received a brief description of the study, noting the population under question and the need for examining field worker stress and job satisfaction. Each farm plant granted the researcher site authorization contingent upon the researcher's own institution's IRB approval.

Sample Selection Method. The researcher surveyed the entire population of field worker employees at the various plants, therefore utilizing a sample representative of the population (Warner & Essenes, 2016). The sampling categories were available when conducting research using probability sampling. Random sampling, a probability sampling strategy (Miles, 2015), is the chosen sampling method for this proposed study. Most researchers like probability sampling because it allows for minimizing bias in the sample due to each respondent having an equal chance of being selected. However, this strategy is costly and requires having access to respondents' contact information (Coatania et al., 2014). The research posted a link to the survey in an LMS and relied on voluntary participation from students ($N = 530$). Field workers who saw the link and wanted to participate in the study clicked on the survey link. The researchers found that utilizing the random sampling method by posting the survey link in a website portal was a suitable method for obtaining study respondents.

Sample Size. The minimum sample size needed for the proposed study is ($N = 200$) respondents. The minimum sample size was calculated using the G*Power analysis application. Calculating an a priori sample size by using a medium effect size coefficient of 0.25, an alpha level coefficient of .05 and a minimum power level coefficient of 0.80 yielded the minimum sample size calculated. The researcher aims to collect more than 300 data points to ensure that there will be a sufficient sample remaining if any data collected are invalid or incomplete. The factor analysis helps evaluate differences in the various dependent variables based on the groups in the independent variable (Kramer et al., 2015). The factor analysis is, therefore, helpful for determining group mean differences in technostress levels based on study variables. Utilizing the G*Power calculator is a common approach when determining the minimum sample size needed for conducting a study. Howard (2012) used the G*Power calculator, which resulted in the sample size ($N = 650$) for performing a multivariate analysis, a factor analysis with four groups when examining the effects of technostress and technology interruptions on an aging workforce. The researchers utilized a medium effect size, an alpha level of .05 and a minimum power level coefficient of 0.50. For the researcher to ensure a sufficient sample size is reached, the researcher aims to reach the minimum target sample size ($N = 200$). The researcher will provide incentives for the field workers to complete the survey. Also, the researcher will provide a link to the survey in authorized online site locations that the target population can access. The researcher will keep the survey open until after reaching at least the minimum number of completed responses needed.

[Note: In-text citations included for illustrative purposes only]

Instrumentation

Instrumentation is defined as the device the researcher uses to collect data for the study. In this section, the researcher will describe the structure of the data collection instrument. Furthermore, the researcher will discuss the instrumentation and the appropriate materials for data collection. The researcher needs to also mention the reliability and validity of the data collection instrument. The researcher wants to provide a rigorous background and writing of the data collection instrument. The characteristics of the instrument should be discussed in the section as well.

Main Points and Directions

These are the main key points that the doctoral researcher should consider when developing the "Instrumentation" section of chapter three:

- Provide a detailed discussion of the <u>instrumentation and materials</u> for data collection, which includes the validity and reliability of the data, collection instrument or experiment
- Describe the <u>structure of each data collection instrument</u> and data sources (tests, questionnaires, interviews, observations databases, media, etc.; create a table)
- Specify the type and level of data collected with each instrument. When using materials for an experiment, describe the structure of the experiment and the materials used for it
- Cite the original publications by instrument developers (and subsequent users as appropriate) or related studies
- Writing length: Minimum of one to three pages (Miles, 2022)

By following these key points, the researcher can fully develop the "Instrumentation" section of the chapter (see Examples 21.8 and 21.9).

Example 21.8 *Instrumentation (Quantitative)*

The research will be conducted using a validated instrument. The proposed study will use a multi-scale instrument called the *Field Worker Job Stress Instrument*. The instrument includes validated subscales adopted for measuring attitudes on three field worker job stress creators (Saradar et al., 2007): (a) *Job Stress-Work Overload Scale* ($\alpha = 0.89$); (b) *Job Stress-Conflict Scale* ($\alpha = 0.88$); and (c) *Job Stress-Personality Type Scale* ($\alpha = 0.90$). Permission was obtained for using the Field Worker Job Stress Instrument as illustrated in Appendix E. The instrument field worker job stress creators are factors contributing to perceived job stress in the workplace for the field worker when working in the field environment (Saradar et al., 2015). The instrument creators identified three sub-dimensions of field worker job stress creators that include *Job Stress-Work Overload Scale, Job Stress-Conflict Scale* and *Job Stress-Personality Type Scale* (ibid). The job stress creators are measured on a discrete and continuous scale that requires using a seven-point Likert scale ranging from 1 to 7, where a one indicates the lowest level of agreement and a seven indicates the highest level of agreement (see Table 21.2).

Subscales in the Instrument

Job Stress-Work Overload Scale. This scale is for measuring perceived job stress because of field employees' attitudes towards the required use of work-related resources and tools on personal time outside of the workplace. These resources include using job related things like equipment, farming equipment, animal care, gardening tools and related. Toure and Nasheed (2012) used the Job Stress-Work Overload Scale for examining the effects of job stress on work-family conflict among field workers in the US ($N = 589$). Using this scale was useful for showing a relationship between the job stress caused by overload and work-family conflict ($r = 0.89$, $p < 0.03$). The results indicated that techno-invasion contributed 31% of the variance in work-family conflict.

Job Stress-Conflict Scale. The Job Stress-Conflict Scale is used for measuring perceived stress caused by conflicts and difficulties in using work equipment and resources in the workplace. Ferris and Monclaire (2014) used the scale for investigating the effects of self-inflicted job stress on job satisfaction when using

Table 21.2 Field Worker Job Stress Instrument and subscales

Scale Type	Number of Questions
Scale 1: Job Stress-Work Overload Scale	10
Scale 2: Job Stress-Conflict Scale	10
Scale 3: Job Stress-Personality Type Scale	10

workplace equipment among field employees (N = 568). Miles et al. (2022) found that using workplace equipment significantly contributed to overall job stress, and that overall stress from using workplace equipment was responsible for 65% of the variance in job dissatisfaction.

Job Stress-Personality Type Scale. The Job Stress-Personality Type Scale is for measuring perceived stress based on personality type. These fears of job loss often exist because of having poor technology skills. Wetherhold and Krier (2012) utilized the scale for examining the effects of personality types and their influence on job stress (N = 501). These researchers divided the sample into two groups: field workers (n = 340) and field managers (n = 161). Kryssler et al. used predictive analytics to find a significant predictive relationship between personality type and field managers who experience significant job stress and who rated themselves (r = 0.50, p <0.01). The findings in the data also revealed similar sentiments from field workers, indicating that personality type is a good predictor of job stress in the agricultural environment (r = 0.35, p <0.04).

Demographics. Demographic independent variables are not part of the Field Worker Job Stress Instrument. However, the researcher needed to collect independent variables for the robustness of the study. The demographic variables included as study variables are gender, age, ethnicity, marital status, education level, work experience/length of time of employment and gross income. The gender demographic variables will be used for assessing differences in levels of perceived job stress between men and women working in the US agricultural sector.

Age will be used for evaluating differences in levels of perceived job stress among age groups of US field worker employees. Length of time of employment will be used for assessing differences in levels of perceived job stress related to field worker participants' years of service in their current occupation. Ethnicity will be used for determining differences in levels of perceived job stress between field workers of different ethnic and racial backgrounds. The respondents will be able to choose the "other ethnicity" category if not appropriate for them (see Table 21.3).

Table 21.3 Demographic variables

Demographic Scale	Number of Variables
Gender	2
Age	5
Ethnicity	6
Marital status	6
Education	6
Work experience/Length of time in job	6
Gross income	6

[Note: In-text citations included for illustrative purposes only]

Example 21.9 Instrumentation (Qualitative)

This study will be using two types of data. The first type of data for this study is an in-depth, open-ended structured interview. This will be the instrumentation for this qualitative study. This qualitative research is best served by utilizing interviews as opposed to surveys. This approach is more appropriate for exploring the feelings and descriptions of the experiences of the participants regarding their job stress, ability to use coping skills and work-life balance. The second type of data is demographic data or participant profiles. For collecting this type of day, a closed-ended survey questionnaire based on Likert scale-type responses will be used. The researcher will build a demographic profile of each of the participants in the study. The participant profile questionnaires will provide demographic background information on the participants of this study.

Interviews. This study will use interviews as an instrument for collecting data. The interviews will be semi-structured and consist of a series of open-ended questions based on the topic areas the researcher wants to cover. The respondents in a semi-structured, in-depth interview will answer structured, open-ended questions. Structured, in-depth interviews are used extensively as an interviewing format with an individual or sometimes with a group (Jamison, 2018). Interviews have five key advantages for collecting data.

First, semi-structured interviews include a sequence of broad questions that may be followed by some probing questions to assist the interviewee. Second, the open-ended nature of the questions describes the subject under investigation in more depth and offers opportunities for the interviewer and interviewee to discuss some topics in more detail. Third, semi-structured interviews allow the researcher to facilitate an intimate discussion with the interviewee. Fourth, the semi-structured interview gives the researcher the freedom to probe a subject in more depth with the interviewee and have them elaborate more on it. Lastly, the use of semi-structured interviews has expanded into various forms of data to evaluate, approve, authorize, disprove or expand on present knowledge or generate new knowledge. It is for these five key reasons that the researcher will use the semi-structured interview format as the data collection method for this study.

Demographic Profile of Participant and Demographics. The second type of data is the demographic profile of the participants. This data collection approach collects demographic data and build a demographic profile of the participants in the study. The researcher can develop and illustrate descriptive statistics of the sample of participants for the study. The most common type of demographic profile data collection technique is the use of a Likert scale. This

Table 21.4 Demographic profile of participant survey questions

Demographic Scale	Number of Variables
Gender	2
Age	5
Ethnicity	6
Marital status	6
Education	6
Work experience/Length of time in job	6
Gross income	6

is a closed-ended type question with no open-ended responses. Resendic (2018) explained that survey questionnaire research uses a variety of data collection methods, with the most conventional being questionnaires.

The questionnaire data gained from the study describes the participants' demographics. The survey questionnaire asks the participants the following closed-ended (scaled) questions: highest level of education, marital status, years of experience as principal, years in education, how many hours worked in a week and others. A common rule of thumb was used for this type of data collection. To build the demographic profile, it is best to ask a maximum of 10 to 12 demographic, scaled, closed-ended questions. I recommend not using any open-ended questions when building the participants' demographic profile. If open-ended questions need to be asked, then ask them in the semi-structured interview period (Miles & Adu, 2022).

Again, the demographic profile can be highly useful in assisting with the descriptive statistics on the participants based on the demographic data collected. The questionnaire information can also help to accurately describe the participants and their coping skills (Harold et al., 2019). There is a second benefit to building the demographic profile, which is that the data can be collected with ease, and it is less time consuming and less cost prohibitive. The demographic profile was built from 25 participants that were field workers in Southern Wyoming in the United States rural area. The interviews consisted of closed-ended questions regarding demographic information such as age, ethnicity, marital status and so on (see Table 21.4).

[Note: In-text citations included for illustrative purposes only]

Data Collection (Procedure)

Once more, the task of data collection is a very technical process. The key to writing up the data collection process is to make sure it aligns with every point discussed in chapter one. Again, problems researched with the use of appropriate methods will greatly enhance the value of the research. Nevertheless, there are two primary data collection methods: quantitative and qualitative.

In this section, the researcher will describe the data collection process. Furthermore, the researcher will discuss the data collection and the materials used for the data collection. The researcher needs to also mention the protocols and processes used for the data collection. The researcher wants to provide a thorough background when writing about the data collection process.

Main Points and Directions for Quantitative Data Collection

These are the main key points that the doctoral researcher should consider when discussing the "Quantitative Data Collection" section of chapter three:

- Describe the <u>procedure for the actual data collection</u>. This includes how each instrument or data type was used and how and where the data were collected and recorded
- Include a <u>linear sequence of actions</u> or the <u>step-by-step procedure</u> used to carry out all the major steps of data collection. This could be a workflow and corresponding timeline presenting a logical, sequential and transparent protocol for data collection
- Describe how the raw data are <u>prepared for analysis</u> (e.g., downloading from SPSS and checking for missing data)
- <u>Data management and security</u> will describe how the researcher will secure the data and information collected
- Writing length: Minimum of two to three paragraphs (Miles, 2022)

By following these key points, the researcher can fully develop the "Quantitative Data Collection" section of the chapter (see Example 21.10).

Example 21.10 Data Collection (Quantitative)

The data collection section will describe how the researcher will collect, analyze and manage the data of the study. The section will also discuss the step-by-step procedure for using the survey, which consists of the *Field Worker Job Stress Instrument*, to collect data, including the processes for obtaining informed consent. In addition, this section will include the procedure for storing and securing the data collected for the study.

Data Collection Procedures. The data collection will take place starting with SurveyMonkey. This will consist of two parts after the informed consent has been obtained. Also, the researcher will prescreen

---

the respondents by issuing a qualifying question. Then the data collection will take place in SurveyMonkey. The data collection will be entirely collected from SurveyMonkey. The respondents must answer the prescreening question. The survey will cease for any individuals who do not answer the prescreening question. Then if the prescreening question is passed, respondents will advance forward to the rest of the survey. Then the online survey will begin with the *Field Worker Job Stress Instrument* (30 questions). This will begin with demographic questions (independent variables) such as gender, age, length of time of employment, ethnicity and so on. Then the researcher will extract the raw data from SurveyMonkey. Lastly, the responses from the survey will be coded as numbers in SurveyMonkey.

Informed Consent Process. The process for obtaining informed consent is as follows: (a) respondents will be invited to participate in the study via a link posted to the chosen institution's online locations; (b) when individuals click on the link to the survey, they will be redirected to a brief explanatory statement of the research and study purpose, eligibility, risks and benefits; (c) the respondents will be told that the survey responses are confidential and anonymous and that participation is completely voluntary; (d) the respondents will be given contact information to use for any questions they may have before, during or after survey completion; and, lastly, (e) the *informed consent form* (TBD) will be attached to the survey starting on page one; the respondents must indicate their agreement to participating in the study before being allowed to move forward with the survey.

Data Security Protocols. The researcher will take every precaution to secure the data for this study. Every effort will be taken to secure the data. By using the online survey approach, the only identifying information is the IP addresses, which do not have any names or any other identifying information. The online survey will not capture names or any other personally identifiable information. Surveys are considered one of the most secure forms of data. The online survey will capture computer metadata to track, eliminate and reduce duplicate survey responses. Furthermore, the researcher will be the only person to have access to the password-secured Excel data file and SPSS data file. The researcher will store all the data files on the researcher's password-protected desktop computer. The researcher will also back up all files on a second portable hard drive in case of a fire or accident that will cause the data to be destroyed or lost. The final protocol of data security will be to permanently delete the data files after six years.

Data Management Protocols. Data management protocols will be in place to maintain the highest management standards with the data. At the close of the survey data collection period, the respondents who click on the survey link will receive a message thanking them and letting them know that the survey has now closed. Next, the online data will be downloaded from SurveyMonkey into an Excel file for clean-up and coding, then uploaded into SPSS version 23.0 for data analysis. The preparation for the downloaded data for analysis will include checking for missing data, accuracy and duplicate entries and removing records with missing data from skipped questions. If there are missing responses, the researcher will code the data with a middle variable response (4 = neutral). If the missing data responses cannot be salvaged, then the data will be deleted. All scales in the Field Worker Job Stress Instrument use a seven-point Likert scale, ranging from "7–Strongly agree," the highest score, to "1–Strongly disagree," the lowest score. Specific statistical tests and analyses to be used in the proposed study will be discussed in the Data Analysis section.

Main Points and Directions for Qualitative Data Collection

These are the main key points that the doctoral researcher should consider when developing the "Qualitative Data Collection" section of chapter three:

- Provide a detailed description of the data collection process, including all types of data (e.g., interviews and demographic profiles) and methods used, such as interviews, member checking, observations and expert panel review
- Describe how the raw data are prepared for analysis (e.g., transcribing interviews, conducting member checking)
- Describe the data management procedures adopted (for both paper-based and electronic data) to maintain data securely. This includes the length of time data will be kept, where it will be kept and how it will be destroyed
- Describe the procedures for obtaining participants' informed consent and for protecting the rights and wellbeing of the study's sample participants
- Include the site authorization letter(s) and participants' informed consent in the appendices
- Writing length: Minimum of two to three paragraphs (Miles, 2022)

By following these key points, the researcher can fully develop the "Qualitative Data Collection" section of the chapter (see Example 21.11).

Example 21.11 Data Collection (Qualitative)

The data collection section will discuss the data collection protocols and strategies. The researcher collected data from interviews with field workers in a farming corporation. This study will produce a comprehensive investigation and relevant conclusions regarding the field workers' experiences with job stress, coping ability and work-life balance. The researcher also collected data from semi-structured interviews with the participants of the study and demographic profile questionnaires. With the data collection, the researcher obtained the approval of the Harvard University's Institutional Review Board (IRB). Also, the researcher obtained site authorization using the university's letterhead.

IRB Approval and Protocols. The researcher filled out and completed all the required forms for the farming corporation, explaining the study and the implications of the study's findings. The chief executive officer and vice president of the company's research review board granted approval and permission to conduct the research. After the researcher obtained the IRB's approval, a recruitment email letter was sent out to the field worker participants. The field workers who decided to participate were contacted via email or telephone. They provided their availability for the interviews and demographic profile. As a friendly reminder, the researcher sent a courtesy email to the participants. The researcher primarily used the field workers' company email addresses. They were notified entirely by email. The researcher arranged an interview appointment with the participants.

Interviews and Protocols. The interviews with the field worker participants took place at their employer's corporate site. With all the interviews, the field worker participants were asked to read and sign an informed consent form prior to the start of the interview. Then two interview procedures took place. First, the participants were asked to complete the demographic profile survey questionnaire. Second, the researcher began the interview with the field workers on their job site. With the administering of the demographic participant profile and the semi-structured interviews, each interview lasted roughly 60–90 minutes. This was the data collection protocol. Each of the interviews was digitally recorded for accuracy, thoroughness and analysis. The researcher sent the interview questions prior to the interview so that the participants could give more solid and robust interviews. The researcher aligned each interview question with the research questions they used to guide this study. At the end of each demographic profile questionnaire and interview, the researcher thanked each of the participants for being part of the study. Lastly, the researcher went through the coding and transcribing process. The researcher transcribed the interviews and paper questionnaires using NVivo and labelled them with identifiers.

Member Checking. To evaluate the data, the researcher conducted the member checking procedure with the participants. Next, the researcher transcribed the interviews of all 25 participants. Member checking is a data validation method that is primarily used in research to check for accuracy, credibility, validity and transferability (Harris & Coleman, 2015). Member checking commonly occurs when researchers collect data from participants and check with participants to ensure that their interpretation was accurate. The researcher also used member checking (also called participant or respondent validation) to establish both reliability and validity. The researcher focused on three things: (a) confirmation,

(b) modification, and (c) verification. While the participants answered the interview questions, the researcher asked questions for verification, modification or confirmation. This was done by restating or summarizing some of the questions and responses. This was to ensure that the researcher understood while digitally recording the responses correctly.

University Institutional Review Board. Additionally, along with approval from the Harvard University Institutional Review Board (IRB), the researcher received documentation for written site approval from the farming corporation's research review board. This gave the researcher the approval to conduct research on their premises. The IRB application included a request letter and the university's Confidentiality Statement and Conflict of Interest documents. In the written request to the farming corporation, the researcher expressed how the data and information will be collected and how it will benefit the institution. The researcher also described the study's protocols and purpose, how the participants' informed consent will be collected and how field worker confidentiality will be guaranteed.

Data Security. For data security, the researcher will engage in activities to ensure that both the data and the participants are protected. The researcher composed a written request. The purpose of the written request is to define the methods of documentation storage. Schenker and Tanareno (2016) explained that data collection and protection is crucial to any research. This includes storing downloaded audio recordings and other related confidential materials from the study. In addition, the data will be stored in a password-protected personal desktop computer and a secured file cabinet. Concerning the security of the raw data, this will be kept secured and stored for seven years. After this time, the data will be destroyed and shredded.

[Note: In-text citations included for illustrative purposes only]

Data Analysis (Quantitative)

In this section, the researcher discusses the data analyses and statistical tests. The researcher provides the basis for the research problem as the basis for the data analysis. Furthermore, the researcher will discuss the instrumentation and the appropriate statistical tests for the data analyses. The researcher needs to also mention the reliability and validity of the data collection instrument. The characteristics of the instrument/scale should be discussed in the section as well. The researcher wants to provide a rigorous background when writing about the data analyses.

Main Points and Directions for Quantitative Data Analysis Procedures

These are the main key points that the doctoral researcher should consider when developing the "Data Analysis" section of chapter three:

- Relist the problem statement or purpose statement along with the research question(s). Also includes the null and alternative hypotheses for quantitative studies
- Provide evidence that the quantity and quality of data is sufficient to answer the research questions
- Provide details on the instrument and scale (and subscales) and the type of data for each variable of interest
- Describe in detail the <u>data management practice, including how the raw data were organized and prepared for analysis</u>
- Describe the software packages used for analyzing the data and analyses (Miles, 2022)

Quantitative Analysis Steps

- Describe data file preparation (descriptive statistics used to check completeness and accuracy)
- Describe descriptive statistics analyses (univariate statistics; demographics, frequencies, and crosstabs)
- Describe inferential statistics analyses (bivariate statistics and multivariate statistics)
- Provide and describe reliability analysis for all scales and subscales
- Provide and describe validity analysis for all scales and subscales
- Describe and justify all statistical tests needed to generate the information to answer all research questions
- Discuss the assumptions for each of the statistical tests (if necessary)
- State the <u>level of statistical significance for each statistical test</u>
- Writing length: Minimum of one to two pages (Miles, 2022)

By following these key points, the researcher can fully develop the "Data Analysis" section of the chapter (see Example 21.12).

Example 21.12 Data Analysis (Quantitative)

The central problem to be researched in the proposed study is the examination of the three components of field worker job stress in a farming environment. The following research questions guide the study:

- **RQ1:** Is there a statistically significant difference in levels of Job Stress-Work Overload between demographic factors (genders, age groups, length of time of employment, etc.) among US field workers as measured by the Field Worker Job Stress Instrument?

- **RQ2:** Is there a statistically significant difference in levels of Job Stress-Conflict between demographic factors (genders, age groups, length of time of employment, etc.) among US field workers as measured by the Field Worker Job Stress Instrument?
- **RQ3:** Is there a statistically significant difference in levels of Job Stress-Personality Type between demographic factors (genders, age groups, length of time of employment, etc.) among US field workers as measured by the Field Worker Job Stress Instrument?

These three questions guide the direction of this study. Researchers have explored the effects of field worker stress and made connections between field stress and job outcomes such as job satisfaction and job productivity (Marshall, 2015; Cary, 2016; Flores, 2016).

Dependent Variable Details. The Field Worker Job Stress Instrument is used for collecting data on field workers' perception of using new and changing complex technology for completing work-related tasks, causing anxiety, stress and strain (Tabott et al., 2009). The Field Worker Job Stress Instrument includes a four-item scale for measuring Job Stress-Work Overload, a four-item scale for measuring job stress, a five-item scale for measuring Job Stress-Conflict, a five-item scale for measuring job stress and a four-item scale for measuring Job Stress-Personality Type. Job stress is a continuous variable. Calculating a final mean score for job stress is by measuring each dimension and sub-dimension of job stress for each participant and dividing the total score by the number of items. A mean score that is less than the median value of the results indicates a low level of job stress, and a mean score that is above the median value or includes the median value indicates a high level of job stress (Miles et al., 2015; Adu, 2016).

This method of scoring is the method used by the creators of the instrument and other researchers who have utilized the instrument for assessing job stress in different populations (Khan, 2016; Jarrett & Morgan, 2015; Tabott et al., 2010). Miles and Adu (2014) utilized this method of scoring when assessing relationships between demographic variables and job stress among academicians working in universities in London. Khan (2013) employed the same scoring method as Tabott et al. (2009) when validating the job stress instrument using a sample of Chinese knowledge workers. All scales in the Field Worker Job Stress Instrument are five-point Likert scales, ranging from "strongly agree" to "strongly disagree."

Independent Variable Details. The independent variables include gender, age, length of time of employment, ethnicity, employment status and position type. All independent variables are measured as nominal data. See Figure 1 for groupings and other details concerning categorical demographic variables. See Figure 4 for groupings and details concerning job characteristics categorical variables.

Data Management. The raw data downloaded from SurveyMonkey (an online survey platform) will undergo necessary data preparations. The researcher will download data from SurveyMonkey.com periodically during the open period and review data for missing information and duplicates to ensure the sample size ($N = 586$) is reached with complete information and usable data. The researcher will remove data with missing relevant information and duplicates, which can occur if a respondent completes the survey more than once, and possible outliers.

Data Analysis. Data analysis will be performed using SPSS version 26.0. First, the data will be summarized using descriptive statistics, which include measures of central tendency and dispersion for continuous variables and frequency tables for displaying demographics. The mean and standard deviation will be reported for continuous variables and frequencies for categorical variables. Second, the results will be summarized using inferential statistics. Multiple regression analysis will be used for responding to all three research questions to determine the differences in means between groups. The researcher will conduct multiple linear regression analysis ($\alpha = .01$).

The results of prior job stress studies revealed that age and gender are significantly positively related to job stress among various populations (Miles, 2016; Adu, 2016; Miles & Adu, 2017). Placing these independent variables in the regression model will control for the credit these variables may receive, allowing for observed independent effects of length of time of employment and ethnicity. Utilizing SPSS, the researcher will test for all assumptions and make appropriate adjustments, such as removing outliers, transforming data, dropping variables or using other comparable statistical methods such as time-series methods. Utilizing a large sample size will lessen the effects of assumption violations of the independent t-test (Miles & Adu, 2015).

The other tests the researcher will conduct include the independent sample t-test with categorical demographic variables having two groups, such as gender. The researchers utilized the independent sample t-test when examining differences in means between two groups (Miles, 2016). The one-way ANOVA will be used to examine differences in three or more groups in the data. The researchers will utilize the ANOVA to avoid alpha inflation, which occurs when conducting too many two-group t-tests resulting in increased chances of making a Type I error (Miles & Adu, 2014).

The null hypothesis, when utilizing the one-way ANOVA for examining group mean differences, states that the means between each group are equal. The F and df statistics are used for calculating the significance using $\alpha = 0.05$ as the alpha level (Miles & Adu, 2013). The researcher rejecting the null hypothesis means that there are significant differences in means between any of the groups (Miles & Adu, 2016). The results from the one-way ANOVA will highlight if group mean differences exist. However, they do not indicate which group means differ. Therefore, the researcher will run post hoc tests for determining specific group mean differences (Miles & Adu, 2015). When determining the appropriate post hoc tests, it depends on the outcome of meeting assumptions for running the one-way ANOVA.

Sample Size. For the study, the sample calculations were performed using G*Power 4.0 and assuming a .01 Type I error and 80% power. A minimum number of ($N = 589$) participants will be required to detect an effect size of .15. The effect size of .15 is considered a medium effect size in the multiple regression model with ten predictors.

[Note: In-text citations included for illustrative purposes only]

Data Analysis (Qualitative)

In this section, the researcher discusses the data analyses and statistical tests. The researcher provides the basis for the research problem as the basis for the data analysis. Furthermore, the researcher will discuss the instrumentation and the appropriate statistical tests for the data analyses. The researcher needs to also mention the reliability and validity of the data collection instrument. The characteristics of the instrument/scale should be discussed in this section as well. The researcher wants to provide a rigorous background when writing about the data analyses.

Main Points and Directions for Qualitative Data Analysis Procedures

These are the main key points that the doctoral researcher should consider when developing the "Data Analysis" section of chapter three:

- Relist the problem statement or purpose statement along with the research question(s)
- Provide evidence that the quantity and quality of data is sufficient to answer the research questions
- Provide details on the instrument (interview questions) and demographic profile of participants (gender, age, ethnicity, education, marital status, etc.). Provide a minimum of 10 to 12 demographic, closed-ended questions (scaled, Likert type)
- Describe in detail the <u>data management practice, including how the interviews and raw demographic data were organized and prepared for analysis</u>
- Describe the software packages used for analyzing the data and analyses (Miles, 2022)

Qualitative Analysis Steps

- Describe the transcription process for interviews, focus groups and so on
- Describe the descriptive statistics (mean scores, percentages) calculated from the demographic profile data of the participants
- **WHAT**: Describe in detail the non-statistical analysis used and the procedures used to conduct the data analysis
- **WHY**: Provide the justification for each of the (non-statistical) data analysis procedures used in the study
- **HOW**: Demonstrate how the non-statistical data analysis techniques align with the research questions and research design
- Identify and discuss the specific analysis approach or strategy (thematic analysis, narrative analysis, phenomenological analysis or grounded theory analysis)
- Discuss and describe the coding procedures and theming process used in the data analysis
- Provide evidence of how codes moved to themes must be presented
- Writing length: Minimum of two to three paragraphs (Miles, 2022)

By following these key points, the researcher can fully develop the "Data Analysis" section of the chapter (see Example 21.13).

Example 21.13 *Data Analysis (Qualitative)*

The central problem to be researched by the proposed study is the challenges of access to resources experienced by women field workers that affect the growth of their businesses. This descriptive design will assist the researcher in investigating the experiences of participants. The following research questions will examine the phenomena:

- **RQ1:** How do women field workers in the agricultural industry describe their experiences with the challenges of professional social networks?
- **RQ2:** How do women field workers in the agricultural industry describe their experiences with the challenges of professional mentoring?
- **RQ3:** How do women field workers in the agricultural industry describe their experiences with the challenges of access to resources?

The sources for the data collection will be based on semi-structured interviews through in-person administration.

Data Preparation. First, each interview will be recorded and then downloaded to a computer. The researcher will use audio recording devices for the interview. In addition, the researcher will have a journal available for note taking. The data from the interviews will be recorded. Second, the data preparation includes collecting data and transcribing interviews. Next, the coding process will be accomplished through identifying similar words and related themes. The researcher will minimize the risk of the identity being revealed if anonymity is applied (Miles, 2015). As explained by Adu (2012), "The purpose and outcome of data analysis are to reveal to others through fresh insights what we've observed" (p. 109). The researcher will allow the participants the opportunity to review their transcripts for accuracy, member checking before the analysis of the data.

Data Collection and Sample. The study will be based on the collection of data from 25 participants: women field workers who are also small business owners in agricultural industries. The data collection will consist of open-ended questions, which will be transcribed using NVivo. The interview sessions will last a minimum of 60 minutes. Thematic analysis allows the researcher to identify patterns and themes (Adu & Miles, 2018). Adu et al.'s (2015) guiding principles discuss a four-step process that researchers will adhere to in the data analysis process (Adu et al, 2011; Miles, 2020). Adu (2012) proposed extensively reviewing the data, generating codes based on the relevant information extracted from the data, organizing the codes under each of the research questions and categorizing the codes, leading to the development of themes. Miles and Adu (2012) defined coding as the process that allows collected data to be gathered, categorized and thematically sorted while discovering meanings and themes. The coding process in qualitative data analysis is integral to the development of themes, while Adu and Miles (2012) add that the researcher can "factor cluster items that were related" (p. 254).

Data Analysis Procedures. In step one, the researcher will summarize the passages of the data using themes. In the case of interviews, the collected data will be analyzed using NVivo. The researcher will assign labels and descriptive codes to passages of data. The themes in NVivo will be displayed in the margins of coded passages of text. The researcher will code the transcripts generated through interviews first. After the transcripts from the interviews have been coded, the transcripts will be coded. The researcher will review the data and highlight relevant phrases and descriptions that are pertinent to the ideas and concepts of the research questions. In step two, the researcher will code the data. This will involve the researcher distinguishing commonalities between codes then grouping these codes into categories. In step three, the researcher will review the high-level categories and search for themes. The researcher will conceptualize on the relationships identified between high level categories; analytic mining will be used.

Data Analysis Strategy. Data collected throughout the interviews will be transcribed using automated AI-powered transcription software. Additionally, the researcher will use a content analysis method approach to explore diverse patterns or themes developed though the data collection. Adu (2005) noted that "content analysis is a technique that provides new insights [and] increases a researcher's understanding of a particular phenomenon" (p. 18). While analyzing the interviews after data collection, the researcher will eliminate potential sample bias in the analysis by being objective. To ensure the integrity of the study, the researcher will follow strict data collection protocols. After completing the study, the researcher will destroy the data after seven years.

Data Management. Data management procedures for this study will be strictly adopted to maintain data securely for both paper-based and electronic data. The researcher will secure paper-based and or electronic data in a home office safe box for seven years per the university's requirements. However, the researcher will upload any paper files to a password-protected portable hard drive by scanning them. There will not be any paper-based data. If there is, it will be destroyed and shredded after seven years. The researcher will destroy the portable hard drive files after seven years with a hammer. Again, the purpose of this study will be to gain an understanding of how women field worker business owners describe and reflect on their experiences with challenges of job stress and agricultural resources. The underlying goal of using the thematic analysis approach in this study is to develop themes that originate from the qualitative data collected in this study. The qualitative data collected from semi-structured interviews and focus groups will be analyzed to answer the research questions in this study.

[Note: In-text citations included for illustrative purposes only]

Reliability

In this section, the researcher discusses reliability within the instrumentation section of the chapter. The researcher will provide evidence of the instruments' reliability. Furthermore, the researcher will discuss the instruments' reliability, consistency and internal consistency. The researcher basically provides evidence of the instruments' characteristics of reliability. The characteristics of the instrument (scale) should be discussed in the section as well. The researcher wants to provide a rigorous background of the instrument used in the study.

Main Points and Directions for Quantitative Reliability

These are the main key points that the doctoral researcher should consider when developing the "Reliability" section of chapter three:

- Provide specific reliability statistics for the instrument; discuss how the statistics were developed

- Explain the specific approaches for how reliability was proven for the study and the data collection approaches
- **Instrument reliability**: Provide evidence of the instrument's reliability. Provide evidence of the instrument's consistency in terms of its ability to consistently measure what it is intended to measure
- **Inter-rater/Observer reliability**: Provide evidence concerning the degree to which different raters/observers give consistent answers or estimates
- **Test-retest reliability**: Provide evidence concerning the consistency of a measure evaluated over time
- **Parallel-forms reliability**: Provide evidence concerning the reliability of two tests constructed the same way from the same content
- **Internal consistency reliability**: Provide evidence concerning the consistency of results across items; measure with Cronbach's Alpha statistical test
- Writing length: Minimum of one to two pages (Miles, 2022)

By following these key points, the researcher can fully develop the "Reliability" section of the chapter (see Example 21.14).

Example 21.14 *Reliability of the Instrument in the Study*

Prior researchers have tested the reliability of the Field Workers Stress Instrument. Miles et al. (2007) performed reliability testing of the Field Workers Stress Instrument after identifying the sub-factors of job stress (e.g., job stress creators) resulting from validity testing. In their study, Miles et al. (2007) also investigated relationships between job stress creators (Job Stress-Work Overload, Job Stress-Conflict and Job Stress-Personality Type) in two private companies in the US ($N = 533$). These researchers calculated the reliability of each sub-factor using Cronbach's alpha. Results indicated that all sub-factors met or exceeded recommended Cronbach's alpha values of 0.70 or greater (Miles et al., 2015; Adu & Miles, 2016; Miles et al., 2007; Tarafdar et al., 2007). Cronbach's alpha results for technostress creators were as follows: Job Stress-Work Overload, $\alpha = 0.85$, Job Stress-Conflict, $\alpha = 0.82$, and Job Stress-Personality Type, $\alpha = 0.88$. In addition, Miles et al. found significant relationships between job stress creators and productivity ($r = -0.275, p < 0.01$) and Job Stress-Conflict ($r = -0.650, p < 0.01$).

Reliability Scores. Miles (2016) confirmed reliability scores ≥ 0.70 of three technostress scales when investigating relationships between the three technostress creators (Job Stress-Work Overload, $\alpha = 0.88$; Job Stress-Conflict, $\alpha = 0.82$; and Job Stress-Personality Type, $\alpha = 0.83$) and productivity among business professionals ($N = 455$). Miles (2016) found significant correlations between productivity and Job Stress-Work Overload ($r = -.630$, p<0.01); Job Stress-Conflict ($r = -.641$, p<0.01); and Job Stress-Personality Type ($r = -.585$, p <0.01). Results of the study indicate that, as these factors of technostress increased, aviation crew productivity decreased. Miles et al. (2013) also utilized the Field Workers

Stress Instrument and confirmed reliability scores $\geq .70$ of three job stress scales (Job Stress-Work Overload, $\alpha = 0.81$, Job Stress-Conflict, $\alpha = 0.796$, and Job Stress-Personality Type, $\alpha = 0.801$) when investigating the relationship between the three technostress creators (Job Stress-Work Overload, Job Stress-Conflict and Job Stress-Personality Type) and the job stress of basketball referees in India ($N = 216$). Adu et al. (2013) found significant relationships between job stress and job satisfaction. The result of the multiple regression analysis revealed that together, the job stress creators accounted for 28.3% of the variance in job satisfaction among this population.

Miles and Adu (2014) utilized the Field Workers Stress Instrument when examining the relationship between demographic factors and all five job stress creators among Indian field workers ($N = 116$) and confirmed Miles et al.'s (2007) reliability findings of the following: Job Stress-Work Overload, $\alpha = 0.83$, Job Stress-Conflict, $\alpha = 0.87$, and Job Stress-Personality Type $\alpha = 0.82$. In addition, Miles and Adu (2015) found significant relationships between the following demographic factors and job stress: male managers had higher levels of job stress than female managers ($t = -3.54$, $p < 0.05$), older managers (≥ 35) experienced more job stress than younger managers ($t = 3.10$, $p < 0.05$), and those managers with a longer length of time of employment experienced less job stress than those with less organizational tenure ($F = 2.32$, $p < 0.05$). These arguments confirm that the Field Workers Stress Instrument has acceptable reliability for use in the proposed study.

[Note: In-text citations included for illustrative purposes only]

Main Points and Directions for Qualitative Reliability

These are the main key points that the doctoral researcher should consider when developing the "Reliability" section of chapter three:

- Qualitative studies: Establish the consistency and repeatability of the data collection through in-depth documented methodology, detailed interview/observation/data collection protocols and guides, the creation of a research database or the use of triangulation
- **Dependability**: Define and discuss how the study documents research procedures
- **Confirmability**: Define and discuss how the study could be confirmed or findings corroborated by others
- Describe the threats to the dependability and confirmability of the study inherent in the study design, sampling strategy, data collection method instruments and data analysis
- Address how these threats will be minimized

- Appendices must include copies of instruments, materials, qualitative data collection protocols, codebook(s) and permission letters from instrument authors (for validated instruments, surveys, interview guides, etc.)
- Define the concepts of credibility and transferability
- **Credibility**: Define and discuss how the study represents the participants' experiences
- **Transferability**: Define and discuss how the study represents the participants' experiences
- Writing length: Minimum of two to four paragraphs or approximately one page (Miles, 2022)

By following these key points, the researcher can fully develop the "Reliability" section of the chapter (see Example 21.15).

Example 21.15 *Reliability for the Instrument in the Study*

The researcher must address the reliability of the instrument in the study. There are five key concepts of reliability in a qualitative study: (a) Dependability and (b) Confirmability. In qualitative research, the two areas of reliability need to be addressed. The objective of reliability in qualitative research is to establish consistency and repeatability of data collection. This is through an in-depth documented methodology.

Dependability. The concept of dependability is an important concept in a qualitative study because it is seen to establish trustworthiness and reliability. To secure dependability, the researcher needs to ensure that the analysis process is aligned with the accepted standards for the design (Miles & Adu, 2018). Miles (2019) asserts dependability refers to the constancy of data over time and is an evaluation of data collection quality and theory generation that has been undertaken in a study. Reliability will be established through the researcher adhering to consistent and repeated data collection, documented methodology, detailed interviews, and use of triangulation. The interview questions will be validated by a three-member expert panel who each hold terminal degrees. Lastly, Miles (2020) argues the researcher might adjust the data collection method contingent on the information the researcher obtains during the data collection process; during this process, any changes must be documented.

Confirmability. The researcher will take some steps to address reliability for the study. The researcher will use a panel of three experts to review the interview questions associated with the proposed research questions in this study. They will also review the demographic profile questionnaire of the participants for the study. Miles (2019), determined in research the audit trail confirms how data is collected and interpretations were made. According to Miles, Adu, and Robinson (2019), asserts confirmability describes the degree of neutrality or the extent to which findings of the study reflect the participants experiences and opinions rather than the researchers' personal biases and interests. In this case the researcher, needs to ensure objectivity because they are a small business owner. To assist with confirmability, in addition triangulation will be used to reduce researcher bias throughout the study. Nevertheless, the auditing trail is essential for qualitative research and proper documentation is important for the researcher.

The original quotes and other data that form the researcher's interpretations are defined as conformability (Miles, 2018). The scope of this qualitative study will use two types of data: semi structured interview and a demographic profile questionnaire for the participants. The demographic profile questionnaire will consist of closed-ended, Likert type questions. So, the researcher will prepare interview questions with open ended so the participants can give details and elaborate on their answers where no follow up questions are needed. The data collection method will be appropriate to answer the research questions. A possible threat to confirmability and dependability would be misrepresenting quotes or answers from the participants. The researcher must give detailed descriptions of observations including which documents and how they were included (Miles, 2021).

[Note: In-text citations included for illustrative purposes only]

Validity

In this section, the researcher discusses the validity for the instrument section in the chapter. The researcher provides the discussion the validity for the instrument and provides some evidence of the instrument's validity. Furthermore, the researcher, will discuss the instrumentation's validity. The researcher basically provides the evidence of the instrument's characteristics of validity. The researcher wants to provide a rigorous background of the instrument used in the study.

Main Points and Directions for Quantitative Validity

These are the main key points that doctoral research wants to consider when developing this validity section of Chapter 3:

- Provide evidence the instrument has validity. Validity is the extent to which an instrument measures what it is supposed to measure and performs as it is designed to perform.
- Provide evidence the study has external validity. External validity is the extent to which the results of a study can be generalized from a sample to a population.
- Provide evidence the instrument has content validity. Content validity refers to the appropriateness of the instrument accurately assess what you want to know.

- Provide evidence the instrument has <u>discriminant validity</u>. This validity is concerned with the extent to which the instrument can measure different constructs.
- Provide evidence the instrument has <u>convergent validity</u>. This validity is concerned with to the extent to which the instrument can measure the same or similar constructs.
- Provide evidence the instrument has <u>criterion-related validity</u>. This validity is concerned with the ability of the measures (questions) to make accurate predictions.
- Provide evidence the instrument has <u>construct validity</u>. This validity is concerned with the extent to which your measurement questions actually measure the presence of those constructs you intended them to measure.
- Provide evidence the instrument has <u>face validity</u>. This validity is concerned the extent to which a measurement method appears "on its face" to measure the construct of interest.
- Provide evidence the instrument has <u>nomological validity</u>. This validity is concerned with assesses the relationship between theoretical constructs.
- Writing length: Minimum of two to three paragraphs (Miles, 2022)

By following these key points, the researcher can fully develop the "Validity" section of the chapter (see Example 21.16).

Example 21.16 Validity of the Instrument in the Study

The researcher must address the validity of the instrument in the study. Validity is defined as the extent to which an instrument measures what it is supposed to measure and performs as it is designed to perform. The research must be able to provide evidence of the validity of the instrument used for the study. An interesting note is that validity is more difficult to prove compared to reliability. While validity is difficult to measure, there are many approaches to address that.

Validity. The task of conducting social science research requires utilizing validated instruments to accurately measure intended variables, test theories through hypotheses and answer research questions (Miles & Adu, 2016). The Field Worker Job Stress Instrument has been previously validated for content validity, discriminant and convergent validity and reliability (Miles et al., 2007). The instrument is comprised of three scales for measuring job stress creators. Utilizing a previously validated instrument is recommended because it eliminates the need for testing the reliability and validity of the instrument. This is certainly valuable if the manner of administering the instrument is similar to the original instrument (Adu & Miles, 2012). Researchers consider an instrument valid if it measures what it is intended to measure. In other words, validity refers to measuring the true meaning of the concept under investigation (Miles et al., 2014).

Validity – Field Worker Job Stress Instrument. Miles et al. (2007) established and confirmed the validity of the Field Worker Job Stress Instrument in three ways. First, these researchers used subject matter experts to provide content validation on job stress for the instrument. Within the context of job stress and organizational response, four experts from business organizations and six experts from the agricultural industry provided instrument feedback germane to item relevance and clarity, based on their expertise and professional experiences. Second, Miles et al. (2016) performed a factor analysis and kept items having EFA factor loadings ≥ 0.4. Third, in addition, Miles et al. (2016) conducted discriminant and convergent validity testing on the job stress-satisfaction model. Results of the validity testing confirmed that all five indexes met or exceeded acceptable values (GFI = 0.945, AGFI = 0.925, NFI = 0.965, CFI = 0.965, and RMR = 0.051), indicating acceptable validity of the Field Worker Job Stress Instrument. Miles et al. (2014) utilized the Field Worker Job Stress Instrument when developing an instrument for measuring job stress among online students ($N = 210$) and conducted validity testing. Results indicated that the ratio of the chi-square first order to second order model exceeded the recommended value of 85%, thus also confirming the validity reported by Miles et al. (2007). These arguments support the validity of the Field Worker Job Stress Instrument.

[Note: In-text citations included for illustrative purposes only]

Main Points and Directions for Qualitative Validity

These are the main key points that the doctoral researcher wants to consider when developing the "Validity" section of chapter three:

• Define the concepts of credibility and transferability
• **Credibility**: Discuss how the study represents the participants' experiences
• **Transferability**: Discuss how the study's findings may be applicable to policy, practice and future research.
• Describe the threats to the credibility and transferability of the study that are inherent in the study's design, sampling strategy, data collection method/ instruments and data analysis
• Address how these threats to credibility and transferability will be minimized
• Writing length: Minimum of two to three paragraphs (Miles, 2022)

By following these key points, the researcher can fully develop the "Validity" section of the chapter (see Example 21.17).

Example 21.17 Validity of the Instrument in the Study

The researcher must address the validity of the instrument in the study. There are two key concepts of validity in a qualitative study: (a) credibility, and (b) transferability. In qualitative research, these two key areas of validity need to be addressed. Credibility is a method of defining and discussing how the study represents the participants' experiences. Transferability is a method for how the study represents the participants' experiences. These are the two strategies used to establish the validity of an instrument (interviews) in a qualitative study.

Credibility. According to Miles (2014), credibility is supported in qualitative studies when the researcher demonstrates engagement methods of observation and evidence of auditing. Miles et al. (2020) stated that negotiating credibility came forth at the end of the analytic process as a method of reflecting the level of active engagement of participants. The researchers further added that there were reviewers who questioned the generalizability of the study results, which ensured alignment of the study's methodology. However, the concept of member checking will also be used to establish credibility. Miles and Adu (2018) assert that transcripts of the interviews should be sent to participants for feedback and the findings should be presented to participants to confirm any theories. After the interviews, member checking will be conducted so that participants can review the accuracy of their answers. As such, the researcher must also constantly read and reread data, analyze them, theorize them and revise concepts accordingly (Miles & Adu, 2018). Lastly, the researcher will use thematic analysis to analyze the data from the interviews.

Transferability. As Miles et al. (2019) explained, transferability refers to the external validity of a study: Can the results of the study be applied to a similar study. Furthermore, transferability is similar to generalizability, where the researcher provides sufficient information about the researcher as an "instrument and the research context, processes, participants, and researcher-participant relationships to enable the reader to decide how the findings may transfer" (Miles et al., 2019, p. 358). Open-ended questions will be used for validity purposes. The researcher will conduct interviews throughout in conjunction with journaling for data collection. Additionally, validity must also be considered. In the process of ensuring validity while collecting data, the researcher must put aside personal biases and be diligent in remaining objective by providing accurate recordings and transcriptions of participants' own words. According to Miles & Adu (2018), the researcher will design the study then determine which strategies will be appropriate for the study. Another method to ensure credibility is through triangulation. The researcher will verify the participants' responses in the transcript by member checking (Miles, 2010).

[Note: In-text citations included for illustrative purposes only]

Ethical Issues and Research Process

In this section, the researcher discusses the ethical issues in the study. The researcher discusses any potential risks for harm in the study. The IRB process is discussed, as are key ethical issues related to anonymity, confidentiality, privacy, strategies to prevent coercion and any potential conflict of interest. Lastly, the researcher discusses the data management procedures and data security. The section primarily deals with ethical issues and security. This section should perfectly match the section in chapter one. This section should be aligned with chapter one.

Main Points and Directions

These are the main key points that the doctoral researcher should consider when developing the "Ethical Issues and Research Process" section of chapter three:

- Provide a discussion of the ethical issues. This might include the Belmont Report and any IRB guidelines relating to the study and the population of interest
- Explain which principles and issues are relevant to the study
- Identify the <u>potential risks for harm</u> that are inherent in the study
- Describe the <u>procedures for obtaining informed consent</u> and for protecting the rights, wellbeing and privacy of the study's participants
- Address the key <u>ethical criteria</u> of anonymity, confidentiality, privacy, strategies to prevent coercion and any potential conflict of interest
- Describe the <u>data management procedures</u> used to store and securely maintain paper and electronic data. This includes the length of time data will be kept, where it will be kept and how it will be destroyed
- Describe how the researcher plans to implement each of the items that are relevant to the study's data management, data analysis and publication of findings
- Writing length: Minimum of two to three paragraphs (Miles, 2022)

By following these key points, the researcher can fully develop the "Ethical Issues and Research Process" section of the chapter (see Example 21.18).

Example 21.18 Ethical Issues and Research Process

The study has some considerations for ethical issues and the research process. For the study, the researcher will work with the participants by getting informed consent prior to collecting data. Since the study will be based on a farming company, an agricultural organization, the entity will need to approve the research before it takes place. A formal letter, on the university's letterhead, will be sent to all participants (and management) to invite them to take part in the study. In addition, a consent form will be sent to participants for their approval to participate in the study. The form will include an explanation of the purpose and benefits of the study and the role and time commitment of the participants. The researcher has considered certain basics and obligations when it comes to conducting research involving human participants. Miles & Adu (2013) added that the basics concepts will be "tenet primum non nocere" (first do no harm), "which posits that the risk of harm to the research participants should normally never outweigh that which they would be expected to encounter during the course of their everyday lives" (p. 23).

Belmont Report. Based on the Belmont Report, which focuses on the ethical implications of a study, the researcher will use the three principles (respect for persons, beneficence and justice). Miles et al. (2015) illustrated that "the expanding scope of research ethics has sensitized the society, which has become conscious of the necessity of getting involved in decision-making on issues or procedures which ultimately affect their health, wellbeing and liberty" (p. 253). The first step in this process will be to receive approval from the institutional review board at Stanford University (SU) to conduct research with human subjects. Since the interviews will be coded, the identity of the participants will be concealed. In addition, the participants will be aware of the study's content, such as its purpose, benefits and any risks that could be associated with it. The researcher will need to acknowledge all requirements of Stanford University (SU) procedures through their doctoral process. Therefore, it is important and even critical that the researcher adhere to all the rules established in Stanford University's policy and following IRB requirements. Therefore, it would be unethical for the researcher to collect any data without first getting the IRB approval letter (Stanford University, 2017b).

Ethical Considerations. Further, ethical considerations in a research study will cover more than informed consent forms (Miles & Adu, 2014). The researcher must plan their time for a more manageable research design while considering the reviewers' approval. This would be critical in conducting the study. As required by any research to be undertaken, the Institutional Review Board (IRB) will receive all appropriate forms to be submitted to the participants before the study takes place, in accordance with the research guidelines and regulations for approval.

Data Management Procedures. It is also critical for the researcher to keep the data secure and in a confidential location that only they know about. The data can then be destroyed after a period of seven years. The participants will receive a letter explaining the reason for the study as well as its purpose and benefits. The participants will receive information about their right to either participate or withdraw from the interview. Furthermore, confidentiality is also a critical factor in this study. Assumed names or pseudonyms will be given to each participant to ensure their privacy. All information will be collected according to the Institutional Review Board (IRB) and Stanford University (SU) guidelines to ensure that participants are protected from any harm.

Participant Confidentiality. All the participants of the study will need to be treated with respect because they will be giving up their free time to be interviewed by the researcher. The researcher will ensure that none of the participants can be matched to the interview responses provided. Also, the researcher will ensure that none of the participants' names are disclosed in the study. No personal information about the participants will be made public. So, it is the researcher's responsibility to ensure and maintain participant anonymity, as well as the confidentiality of the participants and the organization in this study. Another ethical concern for the researcher is to advise participants that all information will be kept secure and not shared in any way with anyone in the organization outside of the dissertation committee. The data from the study will be secured for seven years, which will be discussed with the participants. Also, the researcher will allow the participants some consideration for their decision, either accepting the invitation for the interview process or withdrawing from participating. No costs will be applied to their decisions.

[Note: In-text citations included for illustrative purposes only]

Assumptions, Limitations and Delimitations

In this section, the researcher discusses the limitations and delimitations in the study. First, with the limitations, the researcher provides the constraints of the study based on the research methodology and research design. In this regard, the researcher has no control over the limitations. Second, the researcher discusses the delimitations, which are the constraints of the study based on the population scope for collecting the data. In this regard, the researcher has control over the delimitations (Miles & Scott, 2017). Lastly, assumptions are statements that are considered true, though they have not been scientifically tested. Assumptions provide a basis for the development of theories and research instruments and, therefore, influence the development and implementation of the research process (Happen, 2008; Patidar 2010; Sampson, 2010). This section should perfectly match the section in chapter one. This section should be aligned with chapter one.

Main Points and Directions

These are the main key points that the doctoral researcher should consider when developing the "Assumptions, Limitations and Delimitations" section of chapter three:

- Describe the assumptions related to statements that are scientifically unproven but need to exist for your study to be valid or trustworthy
- Describe the limitations in terms of the research methodology and design of the study

- Describe the delimitations in terms of the population scope of the study
- Present strategies to minimize and mitigate the negative consequences of both the limitations and delimitations
- Align the "Assumptions, Limitations and Delimitations" section with the section in chapter one
- Writing length: Minimum of two to three paragraphs (Miles, 2022)

By following these key points, the researcher can fully develop the "Assumptions, Limitations and Delimitations" section of the chapter (see Example 21.19).

Example 21.19 Assumptions, Limitations and Delimitations

There are assumptions, limitations and delimitations to be addressed for this study. All are addressed in this section.

Assumptions. Assumptions are an opportunity for the researcher to establish the value of research regarding experimentation (Miles, 2004; Miles & Adu, 2014). The researcher identified three major assumptions in this study. First, it is assumed that respondents in this study did not manipulate their ASVAB test scores in any way. It is assumed the answers on the test were answered completed honestly and to the best of their ability. This is assumed because the ASVAB testing procedures are implemented to protect the testing security. Second, it is assumed that the respondents in the study did not manipulate their student academic records in any way and that the documentation was completed accurately. It is assumed that these documents are reported accurately to the Wyoming state agencies for legal purposes. Lastly, it is assumed that this study is an accurate representation of the conditions at the time of the implementation of a psychological profiling program in the state of Wyoming. Documentation to the Wyoming state reporting agency has been used to ensure the authenticity of these conditions.

Limitations. Limitations are defined as the constraints of the study based on the methodology and design (Miles, 2016; Adu & Miles, 2014). Limitations are related to the research approach and methodologies resulting from the parameters of the study, over which the researcher has no control. Limitations consist of the constraints related to the researcher's choice of methodology. As a basis for the study, the limitations were threefold as identified by the researcher. The first constraint of this study is that the instrument was closed and did not have open-ended questions. The second constraint of this study is based on the use of aggregated data that was collected from the state in a publicly accessible medium. The last constraint of this study is related to the use of a comparative design based on other limitations and restricted data. However, these limitations are mitigated by the fact that these procedures were implemented to increase the security of the testing instrument.

Delimitations. Delimitations are defined as constraints of the study based on the population scope (Miles & Adu, 2009; Miles, 2016). Delimitations are things over which the researcher has control, such as the place of the study (Adu, 2011). In some cases, these delimitations may prevent an exact replication in other situations (Miles, 2004). Furthermore, the study gathered data from a specific assessment given at a specific time, which may not be applicable to other situations. As a basis for the study, the delimitations were threefold as identified by the researcher. The following delimitations confined the study. Firstly, this study was delimited to the state of Wyoming. As such, the results of the study may not be applicable to entities outside of this state. Secondly, this study was delimited to traditional public high schools. The study did not look at alternative, charter or private school campuses. Lastly, this study is delimited to gifted and talented students in public schools. The study did not look at other specific groups. The study did not look at other groups such as special education student groups, and gender-based delineations or ethnicity-based delineations were not considered. The study was delimited to the investigation of overall testing groups only. The task for a future researcher may have some 30 conditions. The exact replication of this study may be difficult; however, this study may have wider parameters that may provide more nuanced results.

[Note: In-text citations included for illustrative purposes only]

Summary

The methodology chapter is one of the most rigorous parts of the dissertation. In this chapter we provided the basis for the researcher to develop their dissertation from the methodology plan. This chapter provides some practical strategies and templates for the researcher when writing these core sections within the dissertation format.

In this chapter, we discussed how to write the following nine sections: introduction; problem statement, purpose statement and research questions; research method and design; population, sample and sampling technique; instrumentation; data collection; validity; reliability; and, lastly, ethical issues and research process. By the end of this chapter, the reader should be knowledgeable about these nine core areas of the dissertation.

References

Booton, C. (2014). *How to align the elements of your dissertation proposal.* Love Your Dissertation. Retrieved November 26, 2019, from https://loveyourdissertation.com/wp-content/uplo ads/2015/01/how-to-align-the-elements-of-your-diss-proposal.pdf

Miles, D. A. & Scott, L. (2017, October 26–29). *Confessions of a dissertation chair, Part 1: The six mistakes doctoral students make with the dissertation* [Workshop]. 5th Annual 2017 Black Doctoral Network Conference, Atlanta, GA.

Miles, D. (2022). 360 review tool for auditing dissertation chapters. From *Confessions of a dissertation chair: Dissertation chapter auditing* [Virtual workshop for doctoral students].

22 Writing Your Dissertation

The Standard Format – Chapter 4 (Data Analysis and Findings)

Objectives

- Readers will be able to:
  1. Determine the structure for communicating their results
  2. Present their findings

Presenting Results in Quantitative Research

Introduction

We have spent an enormous amount of time discussing the importance of data collection and data analysis in the previous chapters. Collecting data is a difficult task with research. However, presenting the results and discussing them is quite an enormous task. Not everyone is qualified to discuss or explain the results from the study. Presenting the results of the study is an art form. The researcher has to take into consideration the audience and the reader. Many statisticians are great at dazzling an audience with sophisticated statistical charts and matrices. However, it is an art form to take something sophisticated and make it simple for the audience.

Many researchers make this mistake. As researchers, we ourselves have certainly made this mistake. A considerable number of novice researchers and doctoral students have difficulty presenting and discussing the results. There are many reasons for this. One, the researcher is not comfortable with presenting and discussing statistics. Some are not confident presenting information in front of an audience. Lastly, some are not good at presenting information in front of an audience. It is imperative that the readers and novice researchers who have this book understand the concepts in this chapter.

It is our objective to help novice researchers and doctoral students master this task. It is imperative. In this section, we discuss the time-honored rules of presenting quantitative results. We will provide readers with a roadmap for discussing quantitative results. Again, presenting and discussing results is an art form. In this section we will provide examples of how to both present results and discuss them.

DOI: 10.4324/9781003268154-22

How to Present Results in Quantitative Research

The task of presenting quantitative research is difficult yet manageable. The difficult part of presenting and discussing results is understanding what to present and what not to present. First of all, the researcher should review the results. Second, they should present and discuss the descriptive results. Third, they should present and discuss the inferential results. Lastly, they should summarize and discuss the significance of the results (Figure 22.1).

The use of tables and figures is a standard way of illustrating the results of the study. Notably, the researcher should summarize the significant results of the study. Using unnecessary tables and figures is ill advised when presenting the results. Lastly, in a presentation of the results, the researcher should only explain the detailed information that they can explain and not the detailed information that they cannot explain in terms of statistics.

The next step in the process is to choose your statistical analysis design strategy for presenting the results. The data analysis strategy is based on the establishment of the research design. There are generally two statistical analysis designs used when presenting quantitative results: (a) *descriptive analysis*, which is used to describe what the data look like, where their center or midpoint is, how broadly they are spread, how closely two or more variables within the data are intercorrelated and the like; and (b) *inferential analysis*, which is used to draw inferences about large populations by collecting data on relatively small samples (Leedy & Ormrod, 2019; Burns & Bush, 2003; Field, 2017; Harrison et al., 2020).

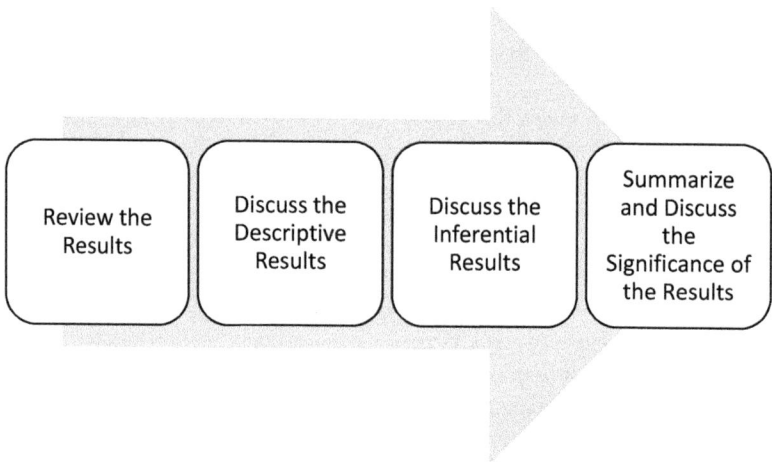

| Review the Results | Discuss the Descriptive Results | Discuss the Inferential Results | Summarize and Discuss the Significance of the Results |

Figure 22.1 Flow diagram of the results presentation process.

Descriptive Statistics: Univariate Statistics – Presenting Results

Descriptive Statistics Results

The first step in presenting the results is to show the descriptive statistics of the study. The objective is to present the descriptive and frequency results of the study. It is my preference that novice researchers and doctoral students use parametric tests such as: (a) *central tendency* (mean, mode and median) and other forms of descriptives such as crosstabulation; and (b) *dispersion of distribution*, which is a parametric statistical test that measures the data (percent distribution, minimum and maximum, percentile) (Burns & Bush, 2003; Harrison et al., 2020). The most commonly used statistical techniques for presenting descriptive techniques are shown in Figure 22.2. SPPS 26.0 was used for displaying the results in Figures 22.3 and 22.4.

Presenting and Writing Up Descriptive Results

There is a method that researchers should follow to present the results of a quantitative study. With presenting and describing the results in a descriptive table, there are two objectives. The first objective is to be succinct. When presenting the data from the analysis, let the table describe the results. Let the data in the table tell the story. As the saying goes, "A picture is worth a thousand words." This statement is true when it comes to describing the results in quantitative research.

The second objective is to describe the data properly. When writing about the results of the data in a table, give the highest number and the lowest number in the table. It is not necessary to give a full narrative of the descriptive table. You will take the visual effect away from the table, and it conflicts the reader. By describing the highest and lowest numbers, you let the reader see the data in between the two. That way, the reader can see for themselves. For example, "In describing

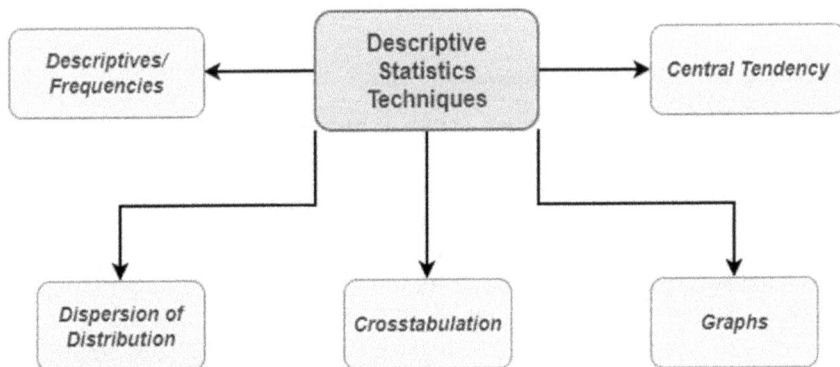

Figure 22.2 Descriptive statistics techniques model.

V2D-Age				
				Cumulative
		Frequency	Percent	Valid Percent	Percent
Valid	19 to 24	36	12.9	12.9	12.9
	25 to 29	57	20.5	20.5	33.5
	30 to 35	73	26.3	26.3	59.7
	36 to 39	30	10.8	10.8	70.5
	40 to 45	30	10.8	10.8	81.3
	46 to 49	12	4.3	4.3	85.6
	50 to 55	18	6.5	6.5	92.1
	56 to 59	9	3.2	3.2	95.3
	60 and older	13	4.7	4.7	100.0
	Total	278	100.0	100.0	

Figure 22.3 Descriptive results of age in the data.

Source: Excerpt from a presentation at the *Fall 2020 Academy of Business Research Conference* (Miles et al., 2020).

Figure 22.3, the highest age group is 26.3% in the 30 to 35 age group. The lowest age group is 3.2% in the 56–59 age group."

Again, the second objective is to describe the data properly. By describing the highest and lowest numbers, you let the reader see the data in between the two. For example, "In describing Figure 22.4, the highest number in the ethnic group is 57% in the Caucasian/European category. The lowest number in the ethnic group is 1.1% for both the Middle Eastern (Arab) and Native American (American Indian) category."

Presenting and Writing Up Crosstab Results

Writing about the results of the data in a crosstabulation table is a different animal compared to the typical descriptive table. When writing the narrative for the crosstab table, again the researcher wants to give the highest number and the lowest number in the table. Again, it is not necessary to give a full narrative of the crosstabulation descriptive table. By describing the highest and lowest numbers, you let the reader see the data in the middle of the two frequencies. For example, "In describing Figure 22.5, the highest number that 'Strongly Agreed' with Question 7 was 23 respondents in the 25 to 29 age group. The lowest number that 'Strongly Agreed' with Question 7 was 3 respondents in the 55 to 59 age group." Because the crosstabulation table is so concentrated with information, the researcher has to provide a minimal narrative of the data in the table.

V3D-Ethnicity				
			Valid	Cumulative
	Frequency	Percent	Percent	Percent
Valid African/ African American (Black)	25	9.0	9.0	9.0
Asian (Paciific Islander)	34	12.2	12.2	21.2
Caucasian/European (White)	158	56.8	56.8	78.1
Hispanic/Latino	33	11.9	11.9	89.9
Middle Eastern (Arab)	1	.4	.4	90.3
Native American (American Indian)	3	1.1	1.1	91.4
Native American (Indian)	16	5.8	5.8	97.1
Native American (American Indian)	1	.4	.4	97.5
Other Ethnicity	7	2.5	2.5	100.0
Total	278	100.0	100.0	

Figure 22.4 Descriptive results of ethnicity in the data.

Source: Excerpt from a presentation at the *Fall 2020 Academy of Business Research Conference* (Miles et al., 2020).

V2D-Age * *V7-Most often when I purchase products from an online retailer, I read the past online reviews Crosstabulation								
Count								
	*V7-Most often when I purchase products from an online retailer, I read the past online reviews							
	Strongly Agree	Agree	Somewhat Agree	Neither Agree nor Disagree	Somewhat Disagree	Disagree	Strongly Disagree	Total
V2D 19 to 24	21	13	2	0	0	0	0	36
Age 25 to 29	23	20	9	2	2	1	0	57
30 to 35	19	38	9	6	0	1	0	73
36 to 39	10	13	6	0	0	1	0	30
40 to 45	14	10	4	1	1	0	0	30
46 to 49	4	4	4	0	0	0	0	12
50 to 55	6	9	3	0	0	0	0	18
56 to 59	3	4	0	0	0	1	1	9
60 and older	4	6	1	1	1	0	0	13
Total	104	117	38	10	4	4	1	278

Figure 22.5 Crosstab results of age and online retail purchases in the data.

Source: Excerpt from a presentation at the *Fall 2020 Academy of Business Research Conference* (Miles et al., 2020).

Presenting and Writing Up Histogram Results

Writing about the results of the data in a histogram graph is another different animal compared to the typical descriptive table. When writing a narrative of the histogram, again the researcher wants to give the highest number and the lowest number in the table. Because of the crosstab properties of the histogram graph, the researcher must be prudent and let the graph do the talking. To write a narrative of the results, the researcher must follow the high/low formula: only briefly describe the two frequencies.

For example, "In Figure 22.6, the highest number among the respondents 'Agreed' with Question 7 (Most often when I purchase products from an online retailer, I read the past online reviews). The lowest number among the male respondents 'Strongly disagreed'." Normally, the information in a histogram table is straightforward. Because of this, the researcher can provide a standard narrative of the data in the table that is most significant to the reader and audience (see Figure 22.6).

Figure 22.7 shows another example of a histogram with more variables to present and discuss. Again, following the high/low formula, when writing a narrative of the histogram, the researcher wants to give the highest number and the lowest number in the table. Because of this histogram graph, the researcher can present the high/low results and let the graph do the talking. Again, to write a narrative of the results, the researcher follows the high/low formula: only briefly describe the two frequencies.

For example, "In Figure 22.7, on a 7-point Likert scale, the highest number among the male respondents 'Agreed' with Question 7 (Most often when I purchase products from an online retailer, I read the past online reviews). The lowest number among the male respondents 'Disagreed.' For the female respondents, the highest number 'Strongly agreed' with Question 7. The lowest number among the female respondents was 'Neutral'." Because this histogram table is so concentrated with information, the researcher has to provide a minimal narrative of the data in the table that is most significant to the reader and audience (see Figure 22.7).

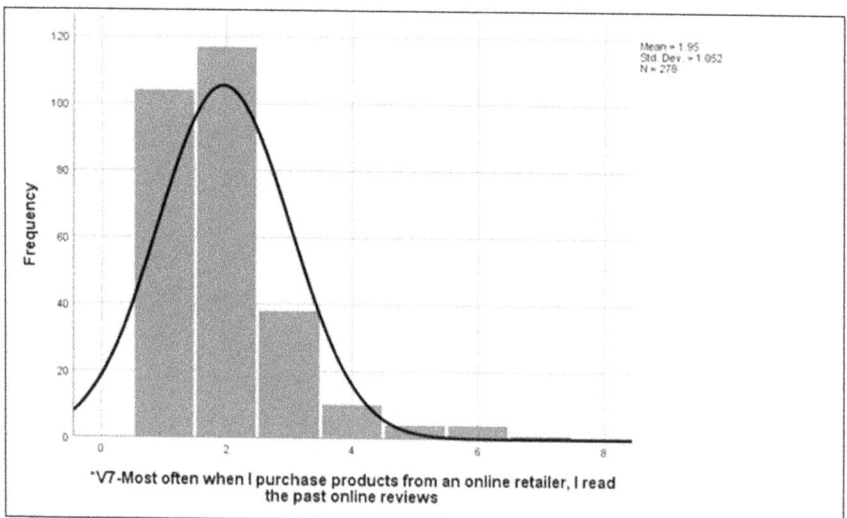

Figure 22.6 Histogram results of gender, age and online retail purchases in the data.

Source: Excerpt from a presentation at the *Fall 2020 Academy of Business Research Conference* (Miles et al., 2020).

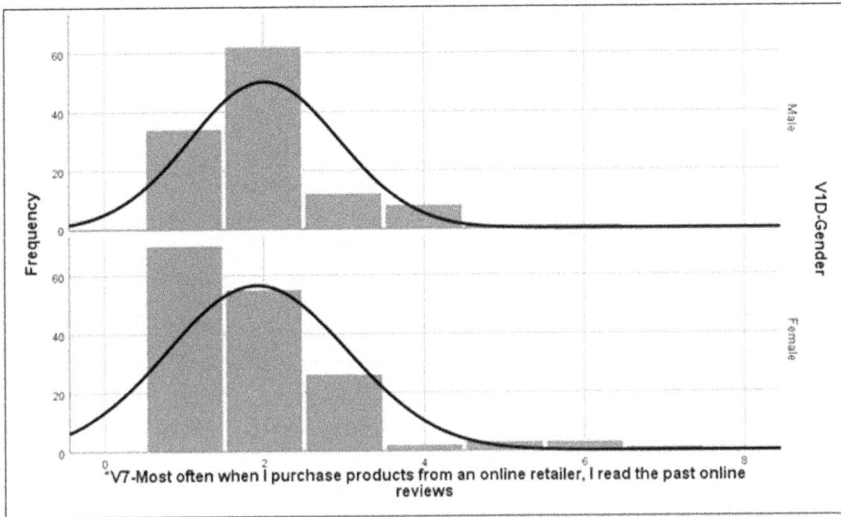

Figure 22.7 Histogram results (two charts) of gender, age and online retail purchases in the data.

Source: Excerpt from a presentation at the *Fall 2020 Academy of Business Research Conference* (Miles et al., 2020).

Presenting and Writing Up Mean and Standard Deviation Results

Writing about the results of data in a table with standard deviation and mean can be an overwhelming task. This is a bit more difficult compared to the previous tables. Because the table is only dealing with gender, which has two values, the narrative has to focus on the high/low formula. Also, since there are two items of description, the mean and standard deviation, the researcher has to be succinct in their narrative.

In writing the narrative of the mean and standard deviation, again the researcher wants to give the highest number and the lowest number in the table. To write a narrative of the results, the researcher must follow the highest/lowest formula, only briefly describing the two frequencies. For example, "In Figure 22.8, the male respondents had a slightly higher mean and standard deviation (M = 2.01, SD = .938) compared to the female respondents (M =1.91, SD = 1.129) with Question 7. However, the female respondents had a higher standard deviation." Again, because the mean and standard deviation table is so concentrated with information, the researcher has to be careful and provide a minimal narrative of the data in the table that is most significant to the reader and audience (see Figure 22.8).

Bivariate Statistical Techniques

The next phase in the descriptive statistics process is the use of bivariate statistics to present the results. This part of the descriptive statistics process is optional and

V1D-Gender		*V7-Most often when I purchase products from an online retailer, I read the past online reviews	*V8-Most often when I purchase products from an online retailer, I rely on word-of-mouth from	*V9-Most often I purchase products from a retailer (brick & mortar), I read the past online reviews	*V10-Most often I purchase products from a retailer (brick & mortar), I rely on word-of-mouth from people
Male	Mean	2.01	2.99	2.64	2.82
	N	118	118	118	118
	Std. Deviation	.938	1.349	1.381	1.388
Female	Mean	1.91	3.07	3.10	2.86
	N	160	160	160	160
	Std. Deviation	1.129	1.463	1.698	1.376
Total	Mean	1.95	3.04	2.91	2.85
	N	278	278	278	278
	Std. Deviation	1.052	1.414	1.585	1.378

Figure 22.8 Results of gender mean and standard deviation of consumer behavior purchases online and offline in the data.

Source: Excerpt from a presentation at the *Fall 2020 Academy of Business Research Conference* (Miles et al., 2020).

depends on the research questions and the research objectives. Using bivariate statistics is not as essential as univariate statistics in descriptive statistics. The primary objective of bivariate statistics is the *measure of relationships*. Bivariate analysis is defined as aiming to understand the relationship between two variables, *x* and *y*. The measure of relationships can be studied through (a) *Pearson correlation*; (b) *simple linear regression*, where the cause-and-effect relationship can be studied through simple regression equations; and (c) *scatterplots* (Figure 22.9).

The first most common bivariate statistical technique is *correlation*. More specifically, it is called the *Pearson correlation*. When the researcher uses bivariate statistics, one of the primary approaches to this analysis is correlation. Correlation is defined as the measurement of the relationship between two variables (usually dependent variables). This bivariate statistical technique was invented by Karl Pearson. Karl Pearson's coefficient of correlation is also known as the *product moment correlation coefficient*. The value of *r* lies between ± 1. A positive value of *r* indicates a positive correlation between the two variables, while a negative value of *r* indicates an inverse relationship or *negative correlation*. This occurs when two measured variables take place in the opposite direction. A zero value of *r* indicates that there is no association between the two variables (Kothari, 2009; Field, 2017; Morgan et al., 2017).

Another bivariate statistical technique is a *simple linear regression*. A simple linear regression is defined as the determination of a statistical relationship between two

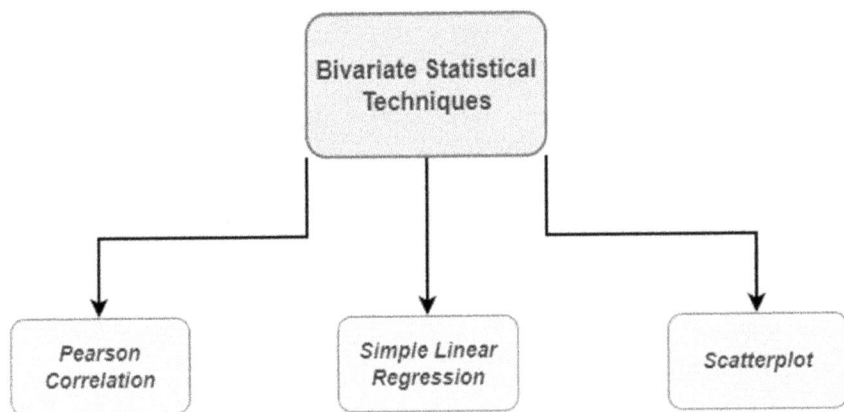

Figure 22.9 Bivariate statistical techniques model.

or more variables. In a simple regression, we have only two variables, one variable (defined as independent) is the cause of the behavior of the other (defined as dependent) (Kothari, 2009). This is primarily a measure of the relationship between the independent variable's influence (*cause*) on the dependent variable (*effect*) (Kothari, 2009; Tabachnick & Fidell, 2007). Lastly, the final bivariate statistical technique is the *scatterplot*. A scatterplot is defined as a figure showing the relationship between two variables; it is a graphical representation of a correlation coefficient. In a scatterplot, two measurements are represented for each participant by the placement of a marker such as the horizontal x-axis and the vertical y-axis. A scatterplot may show four basic patterns: a positive relationship, a negative relationship, no relationship or a curvilinear relationship (Jackson, 2009; Field, 2017).

Presenting and Writing Up Pearson Correlation Results

Again, the primary objective is to describe the data properly. When writing about the results of data in a table for a Pearson correlation, give the highest significant coefficient relationship in the table. It is not necessary to give a full narrative of the Pearson correlation table. There were very few correlations in the data.

For example, "The researcher conducted a Pearson correlation statistical test for the data. The researcher wanted to measure the relationship between Questions 13 to 17. When we measured the relationship between 'Question 17 (Most often when I seek to stay at a hotel for travel, I read the prior online customer reviews) and 'V15 (Most often when I seek to buy a consumer electronic device (headphones, iPod, & etc.) from an online retailer, I read the past customer reviews), we found a significant relationship between the two variables with an ($r = .506$) coefficient. The Pearson correlation indicated that there is a strong relationship between the two variables" (see Figure 22.10).

		*V13-Most often when I seek to buy a new car from a dealer, I read the reviews of about the dealer online	*V14-Most often when I seek to buy a new car from a dealer, I rely on word-of-mouth from people I trust	*V15-Most often when I seek to buy a consumer electronic device (headphones, iPod, & etc) from an online retailer, I read the past customer reviews	*V16-Most often when I seek to buy a consumer electronic device (headphones, iPod, & etc) from an online retailer, I rely on word-of-mouth from people	*V17-Most often when I seek to stay at a hotel for travel, I read the prior online customer reviews
*V13-Most often when I seek to buy a new car from a dealer, I read the reviews of about the dealer online	Pearson Correlation	1	.200**	.368**	.302**	.468**
	Sig. (2-tailed)		.001	.000	.000	.000
	N	278	278	278	278	278
*V14-Most often when I seek to buy a new car from a dealer, I rely on word-of-mouth from people I trust	Pearson Correlation	.200**	1	.173**	.414**	.249**
	Sig. (2-tailed)	.001		.004	.000	.000
	N	278	278	278	278	278
*V15-Most often when I seek to buy a consumer electronic device (headphones, iPod, & etc) from an online retailer, I read the past customer reviews	Pearson Correlation	.368**	.173**	1	.118*	.506**
	Sig. (2-tailed)	.000	.004		.050	.000
	N	278	278	278	278	278
*V16-Most often when I seek to buy a consumer electronic device (headphones, iPod, & etc) from an online retailer, I rely on word-of-mouth from people	Pearson Correlation	.302**	.414**	.118*	1	.140*
	Sig. (2-tailed)	.000	.000	.050		.019
	N	278	278	278	278	278
*V17-Most often when I seek to stay at a hotel for travel, I read the prior online customer reviews	Pearson Correlation	.468**	.249**	.506**	.140*	1
	Sig. (2-tailed)	.000	.000	.000	.019	
	N	278	278	278	278	278

**. Correlation is significant at the 0.01 level (2-tailed).
*. Correlation is significant at the 0.05 level (2-tailed).

Figure 22.10 Pearson correlation.

Source: Excerpt from a presentation at the *Fall 2020 Academy of Business Research Conference* (Miles et al., 2020).

Presenting and Writing Up Simple Linear Regression Results

When presenting and writing up the results of a simple linear regression in a table, the researcher should give only the most significant predictor variables (independent variables) on the dependent variable. Again, if possible, it is not necessary to give a full narrative of the simple linear regression results.

For example, "In the results, we found that the independent variable 'V6D-Children' has a strong significant influence on the dependent variable 'V8-Most often when I purchase products from an online retailer, I rely on word-of-mouth)'" (see Figure 22.11).

Here is another example. Again, when writing up the results of a simple linear regression in a table, the researcher should give only the most significant predictor variables (independent variables) on the dependent variable. If possible, it is not necessary to give a full narrative of the simple linear regression results.

| | | | Standardized | | |
| | Unstandardized Coefficients | | Coefficients | | |
Model	B	Std. Error	Beta	t	Sig.
1 (Constant)	1.822	.611		2.981	.003
V1D-Gender	-.101	.166	-.035	-.605	.546
V2D-Age	.156	.039	.240	3.959	.000
V3D-Ethnicity	.029	.051	.033	.576	.565
V4D-Education	-.126	.073	-.101	-1.733	.084
V5D-Marital Status	.064	.094	.041	.680	.497
V6D-Children	.701	.177	.247	3.974	.000

a. Dependent Variable: *V8-Most often when I purchase products from an online retailer, I rely on word-of-mouth from

Figure 22.11 Simple linear regression example 1.

Source: Excerpt from a presentation at the *Fall 2020 Academy of Business Research Conference* (Miles et al., 2020).

| | | | Standardized | | |
| | Unstandardized Coefficients | | Coefficients | | |
Model	B	Std. Error	Beta	t	Sig.
1 (Constant)	2.181	.678		3.216	.001
V1D-Gender	.313	.185	.098	1.697	.091
V2D-Age	.209	.044	.287	4.786	.000
V3D-Ethnicity	-.016	.057	-.016	-.287	.774
V4D-Education	-.205	.081	-.146	-2.534	.012
V5D-Marital Status	.086	.104	.050	.829	.408
V6D-Children	.073	.196	.023	.373	.710

a. Dependent Variable: *V9-Most often I purchase products from a retailer (brick & mortar), I read the past online reviews

Figure 22.12 Simple linear regression example 2.

Source: Excerpt from a presentation at the *Fall 2020 Academy of Business Research Conference* (Miles et al., 2020).

For example, "In the results, we found that the independent variable 'V2D-Age' is a significant ($p = .001$) influence on the dependent variable 'V9-Most often I purchase products from a retailer (brick & mortar), I read the past reviews.' In addition, we found that the independent variable V3D had a moderately significant influence ($p = .012$) on the dependent variable V9" (see Figure 22.12).

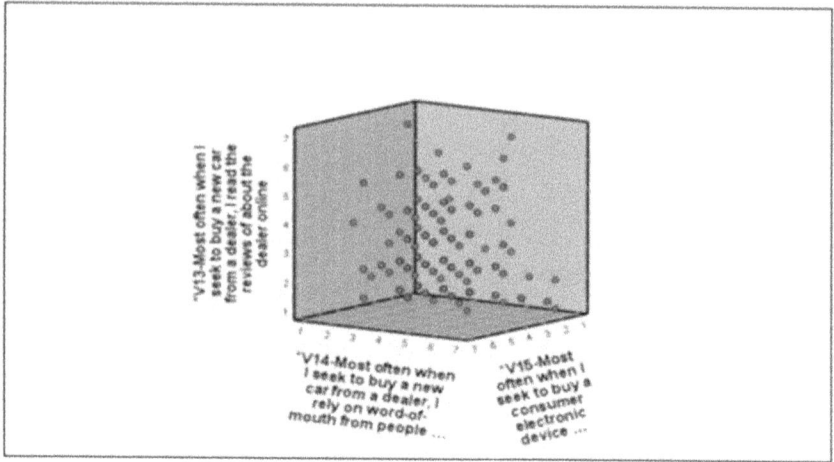

Figure 22.13 Scatterplot example.

Source: Excerpt from a presentation at the *Fall 2020 Academy of Business Research Conference* (Miles et al., 2020).

Presenting and Writing Up Scatterplot Results

Here is an example of a scatterplot. When writing up the results of a scatterplot, the researcher should review the scatterplot configuration and discuss what is significant. There is not a considerable narrative here.

For example, "In conducting a scatterplot analysis, the results show there was a significantly weak relationship between the three variables V13, V14 and V15. We found no significant relationship between the three variables" (see Figure 22.13).

Inferential Statistics: Multivariate Statistics

Inferential Statistics Results

The first step in statistical analyses usually involves the researcher conducting a descriptive analysis of the data, with a focus on measures of frequencies, central tendency and variation. The second step in statistical analyses is to conduct an inferential analysis of the data, which is a more sophisticated measurement that is used to test hypotheses and examine confidence intervals and effect sizes. Inferential statistics measure things that cannot be measured by descriptive statistics. The practice of using inferential statistical tests tends to measure relationships between variables that cannot be done with descriptive statistics. For example, this allows the researcher to make comparisons among two or more groups.

Inferential statistics makes it possible for the researcher to draw inferences about large populations from relatively small samples. Inferential statistics have two primary functions: (a) to estimate a population parameter from a random sample;

and (b) to test statistically based hypotheses (Jackson, 2009; Kothari, 2009; Leedy & Ormrod, 2019). Under inferential statistics, it utilizes statistical elements such as the alpha levels, the actual *p* values, the critical region of rejection, test statistic results, the degrees of freedom, effect size and confidence intervals (Creswell, 2012). The use of inferential statistics involves hypothesis testing. There are two types of hypotheses: (a) *alternative hypothesis*, which is a type of hypothesis that the researcher wants to support, predicting that a significant difference exists between the groups being compared; and (b) *null hypothesis*, which is the hypothesis predicting that no difference exists between the groups being compared (Creswell, 2012).

There are two types of error involved in inferential statistics: (a) *Type I error*, which is an error in hypothesis testing where the null hypothesis is rejected when we should have failed to reject it; and (b) *Type II error*, which is an error in hypothesis testing when there is a failure to reject the null hypothesis when we should have rejected it (Creswell, 2012).

Inferential statistics primarily utilizes parametric statistical tests. Some of the most utilized inferential statistical techniques and their purpose are listed here: (a) *t-test*, which is used to determine whether a statistically significant difference exists between two groups; (b) *analysis of variance* (ANOVA), which is used to examine differences among three or more groups by comparing the variances within and across groups; (c) *multiple analysis of variance* (MANOVA), which is used to examine differences among groups for two or more dependent variables rather than for the single dependent variable; (d) *analysis of covariance* (ANCOVA), which is used to look for differences among groups while controlling for the effects of a variable that is correlated with the dependent variable (and a covariate); (e) *multiple linear regression*, which examines how accurately one or more variables enable predictions regarding the values of another (dependent) variable; (f) *factor analysis*, which is used to examine the correlations among a number of variables and identify clusters of highly interrelated variables that reflect general underlying categories within the data; and (g) *structural equation modeling* (SEM), which is used to examine the correlations among a number of variables. It is typically used to test a previously hypothesized model of how variables are causally interrelated; SEM uses two approaches such as path analysis and confirmatory analysis (Creswell, 2012).

Multivariate Statistical Techniques

We will now briefly describe the different types of multivariate techniques. We will discuss the most commonly used multivariate statistical techniques for dissertation studies. We will also describe, in brief, some of the other multivariate techniques, such as factor analysis, cluster analysis and structural equation modeling. Again, for the purposes of this discussion, nonparametric techniques will not be discussed. In this book, only parametric statistical techniques will be discussed.

Multivariate statistics is defined as methods that examine the simultaneous effect of multiple variables. The traditional classification of multivariate statistical methods is based on the concept of dependency between variables (Marinković, 2008). An interesting aspect of the multivariate analysis of variance is that it is an extension of the bivariate analysis of variance. Conversely, multivariate analysis is focused on variables to which the ratio of among-groups variance to within-groups variance is calculated on a set of variables instead of a single variable (Kothari, 2009).

Presenting and Writing Up Exploratory Factory Analysis Results

Writing about the multivariate statistical results of data in a table or figure is somewhat more complex compared to univariate statistical results. This is a bit more of a challenge compared to the previous tables. Also, since there are numerous items in the factor analysis graph, the researcher wants to just give a basic description of the results. When writing a narrative of the factor analysis, this also means providing a narrative on the most significant coefficients. The narrative does not have to include all the coefficients, only the most significant ones. Example 22.1 shows how to write up the results of an exploratory factor analysis (see Table 22.1).

Table 22.1 Exploratory factory analysis

	1	2	3
*V16	.731		
*V8	.723		
*V10	.717		
*V30	.703		
*V18	.703		
*V32	.666		
*V14	.630		
*V28	.627		
*V22	.599		
*V12	.599		
*V20	.550		
*V34	.474		
*V17		.772	
*V31		.760	
*V15		.753	
*V7		.689	
*V27		.687	
*V29		.600	
*V11		.574	
*V23		.561	
*V24		.551	
*V26		.509	
*V13		.473	
*V35			.805
*V21			.671
*V25			.596

Source: Excerpt from a presentation at the *Fall 2020 Academy of Business Research Conference* (Miles et al., 2020).

Example 22.1

The researchers conducted the initial exploratory factor analysis (EFA). The researchers used SPSS 23.0. A principal component analysis (PCA) with a varimax rotation was used for extraction. The rationale for using the PCA was for when the research purpose is data reduction or exploration and when the research is a variance-focused approach (Garson, 1998; Brown, 2006; Hair et al., 1998). For establishing the criteria for the EFA, we set a benchmark of a minimum coefficient of .3 or higher for the factors. This indicates that some of the scale factor loadings measured for this PCA (29 items) met and surpassed the minimum standard for the benchmark coefficient score of greater than .3.

Thus, the factor loadings were considered a reasonable measure in the factor (Rummel, 1970; Mulaik, 1972). For the pilot study, the observed screen test in the EFA suggested an optimal solution of four factors. In order for the researchers to properly assess the validity of the factor solutions, coefficient patterns for each factor and the theoretical four-factor solution were tested using the statistical properties. To establish the factor names, we conducted a subsequent factor analysis.

In the PCA, the Kaiser-Meyer-Olkin Measure (KMO) of sampling adequacy resulted in a .883, thus above the commonly recommended value of .3; the Barlett's test of sphericity was significant $\chi 2$, $df(171) = 1758$, $p < .000$. In terms of PCA, a finding that indicators have high loadings on the predicted factors indicates convergent validity conceptually. Interestingly, a few items loaded into more than one factor, which indicates good discriminant validity. Eigenvalues (λ) are a statistic used in the factor analysis to show how much variation in the group of variables is accounted for by a particular factor (Mulaik, 1972; Rummel, 1970; Tabachnick & Fidell, 2007). The researcher made the decision that the standard for an eigenvalue score is greater than 1.0 (Vogt, 1993) (see Table 22.1) (Miles et al., 2019).

Presenting and Writing Up Confirmatory Factor Analysis Results

Writing about the confirmatory factor analysis results of data in a figure is a more complex task compared to univariate statistical results. Again, this is a bit more of a challenge compared to the previous tables. Also, since there are numerous items in the confirmatory factor analysis graph, the researcher wants to just give a basic description of the results. In terms of writing a narrative of the confirmatory factor analysis, this means just providing a narrative on the most significant coefficients. The narrative does not have to include all the coefficients, only the most significant ones. Example 22.2 shows how to write up the results of an exploratory factor analysis.

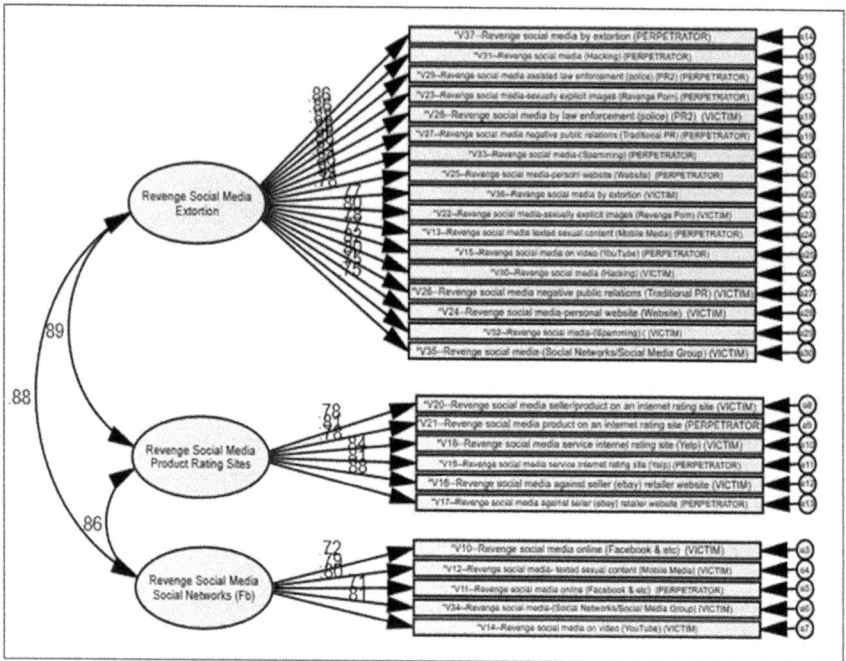

Figure 22.14 Confirmatory factor analysis.

Source: Excerpt from a presentation at the *Fall 2020 Academy of Business Research Conference* (Miles et al., 2020).

Example 22.2

A confirmatory factor analysis (CFA) was conducted to assess the construct validity of the model. The researchers wanted to assess the convergent validity and determine confirmation of the existence of a construct model. To assess the convergent validity, the loading estimates and construct reliability were investigated. To assess the convergent validity, we used **SPSS AMOS 23** to analyze the data. It was used to assess and test using the measurement model by determining the significant t-value of each item's estimated pattern coefficient in the construct factor (see Figure 22.14).

A structural equation model (SEM) was conducted to examine the predictability of the moviegoer's reaction to the influence of advertising models for seeing the movie *Black Panther*. The CFA was also performed to measure the unidimensionality, convergent and discriminant validity in the RMS instrument. The CFA results provide overall fit indices ($\chi 2 = 971.11$). The $\chi 2$ test in the table also clearly shows compelling results that the sample was not drawn from the hypothesized population. Based on the GIF results, the statistical test supports the rejection of the hypothesized model. The RMSEA coefficients was close to meeting the benchmark of the desired confidence intervals (.04–.11 and .06–.08, respectively). RMSEA (root mean square error of approximation) = 0.122, GFI (goodness-of-fit) = 0.78, AGFI (adjusted goodness-of-fit) = 0.72, CFI (comparative fit index) = 0.87, RMR (root mean square residual) = 0.39 and NFI (normed fit index) = 0.82. Figure 22.14 presents the results of the CFA analysis and the fit statistics results (Miles et al., 2019, p. 1099)

Presenting and Writing Up Path Analysis Model Results

Writing about the results of a path analysis in a figure is, again, a more complex task. Also, since there are numerous items in a path analysis graph, the researcher wants to just give a basic description of the results. In terms of writing a narrative of the path analysis, this means just providing a narrative of the most significant elements of the path and coefficients. The narrative does not have to include all the elements and coefficients, only the most significant ones. Example 22.3 shows how to write up the results of a path analysis. The authors reference Tabachnick & Fidell (2007) for an example of how to write a narrative of the results. Also see the advanced path analysis in Figure 22.15 (Khan & Miles, 2020).

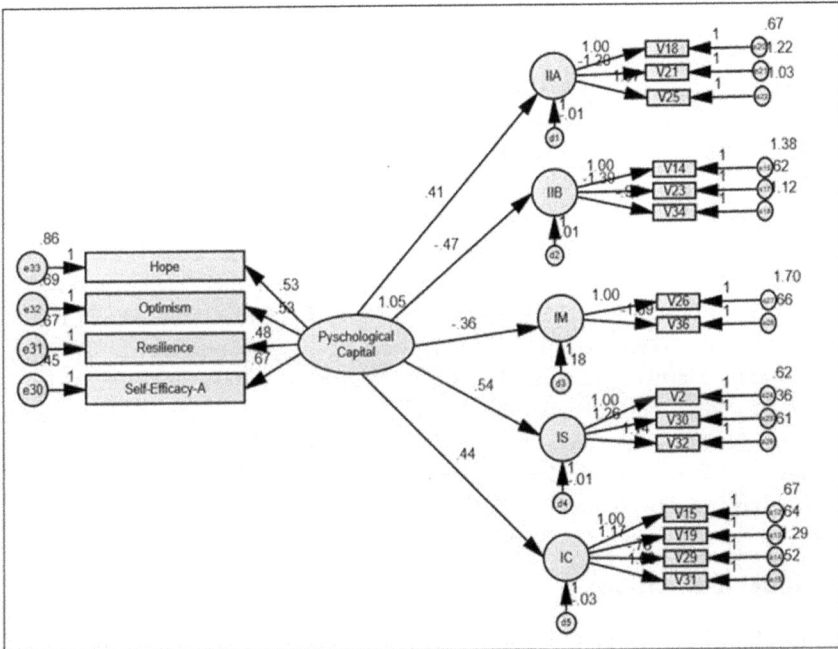

Figure 22.15 Path analysis.

Source: Excerpt from a presentation at the *Fall 2020 Academy of Business Research Conference* (Miles et al., 2020).

Example 22.3

The hypothesized model is in Figure 22.15. Circles represent latent variables, and rectangles represent measured variables. Absence of a line connecting variables implies lack of a hypothesized direct effect. The hypothesized model examined the predictors of health care utilization. Health care utilization was a latent variable with 2 indicators (number of visits to health professionals and frequency of drug use).

It was hypothesized that perceived ill health (a latent variable with 2 indicators – number of mental health problems and number of physical health problems), age and number of life stress units directly predicted increased health care utilization. Additionally, it was hypothesized that perceived ill health is directly predicted by poorer sense of self, greater number of life change units and increasing age. Perceived ill health served as an intervening variable between age, life change units, poor sense of self and health care utilization. Additionally, it was hypothesized that perceived ill health is directly predicted by poorer sense of self, greater number of life change units and increasing age. Perceived ill health served as an intervening variable between age, life change units, poor sense of self and health care utilization.

Assumptions

The assumptions were evaluated through IBM SPSS and EQS. The dataset contains responses from 459 women. There were complete data for 443 participants on the nine variables of interest. Five participants (1.1%) were missing data on attitudes toward marriage (ATTMAR), 4 participants (.9%) were missing age (AGE), and 7 (1.5%) are missing the stress measure (STRESS). This analysis used only complete cases (N = 443).

There were no univariate or multivariate outliers. There was evidence that both univariate and multivariate normality were violated. Eight of the measured variables (TIMEDRS, PHYHEAL, MENHEAL, DRUGUSE, ESTEEM, CONTROL, STRESS and ATTMAR) were significantly univariately skewed, $p < .001$. Mardia's normalized coefficient = 6.42, $p < .001$, indicating violation of multivariate normality. Therefore, the models were estimated with maximum likelihood estimation and tested with the Satorra–Bentler scaled chi square (Satorra & Bentler, 1988). The standard errors also were adjusted to the extent of the nonnormality (Bentler & Dijkstra, 1985; Mack et al., 2018).

Model Estimation

Only marginal support was found for the hypothesized model Satorra–Bentler x2 (20, N = 443) = 86.91, p < .05, Robust CFI = .88, RMSEA = .08. Post hoc model modifications were performed in an attempt to develop a better fitting model.

On the basis of the Lagrange multiplier test and theoretical relevance, two residual covariances were estimated (residual covariance between the number of physical health problems and number of visits, and the residual covariance between frequency of drug use and number of visits to health professionals). The model was significantly improved with the addition of these paths, Satorra– Bentler x2 difference (2, N = 443) = 37.33, $p < .05$. The final model fit the data well, Satorra– Bentler x2 (18, N = 443) = 40.17, p < .05, Robust CFI = .96, RMSEA = .05. Because post hoc model modifications were performed, a correlation was calculated between the hypothesized model estimates and the estimates from the final model, r(20) = .97, $p < .01$. This high correlation indicates that the parameter estimates from the first and last models are highly related to each other. The final model with standardized and unstandardized coefficients is in Figure 22.16 (Tabachnick & Fidell, 2007; Moore & Rudd, 2006).

Presenting Results in Qualitative Research

Introduction

After collecting the data, you next step is to make sense of it and present what you found to your audience. At this point, your goal is not to *draw conclusions* from what you found but *to present* what you found (Sreejesh et al., 2014). Whether conducting quantitative, qualitative or mixed methods research, there are standards set by the research community that need to be followed when conducting data reduction to attain valid, credible and meaningful results. In a qualitative study, the data reduction process begins with generating phrases based on the significant information extracted from the data, clustering the codes with the goal of creating themes. These themes are then presented in a way that addresses the research question for the study and makes sense to the audience. For a mixed methods study, quantitative and qualitative data are analyzed concurrently or sequentially to arrive at findings that are then used to address the research questions. The presentation of the findings report can be grouped into six main sections: overview, research setting, participants' demographics, data analysis process, findings and summary (see Adu, 2021). The information being presented in this chapter was based on the presentation on 'Writing your results' by Adu (2021).

Overview

In this section, you are expected to present some brief background information about your study, reminding your readers about the research gap you will be filling (i.e., research problem) and what you did in the study (i.e., purpose of the study). In addition, you could highlight the main topics you will be discussing in the chapter (for a dissertation). A common list of contents that are normally presented in the findings chapter of a dissertation is as follows: research setting, participants' demographics (features of the data sources), data analysis process and presentation of

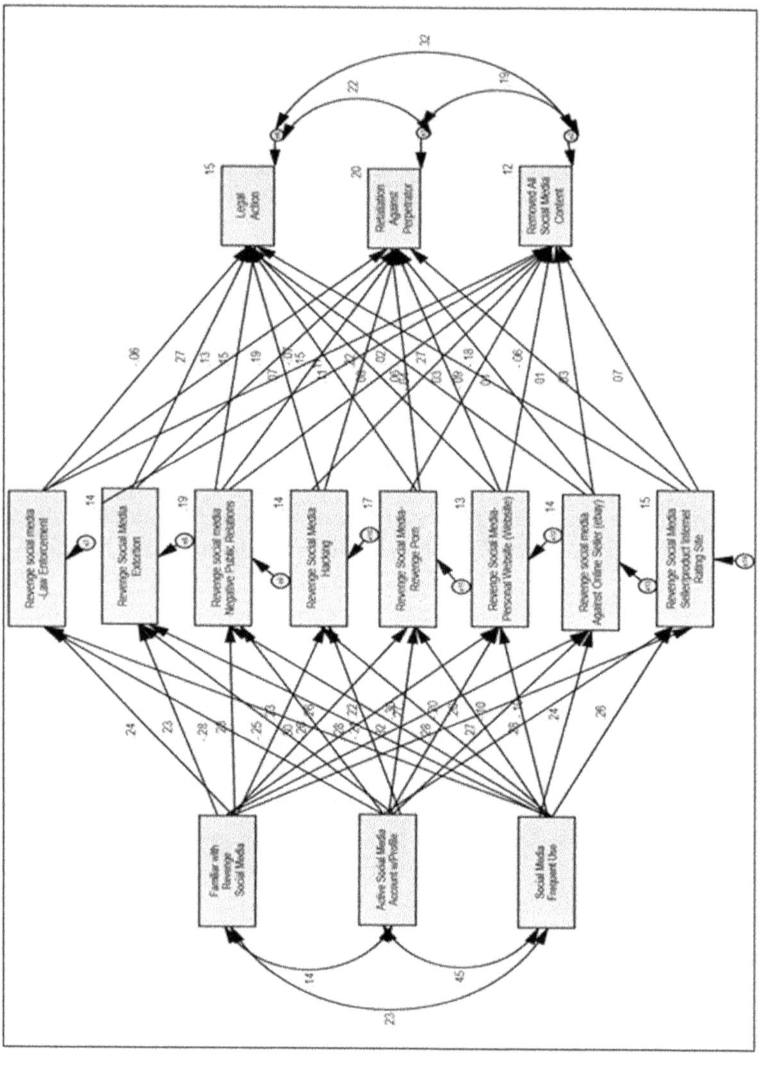

Figure 22.16 Advanced path analysis.

Source: Excerpt from a presentation at the *Fall 2020 Academy of Business Research Conference* (Miles et al., 2020).

the findings. The essence of this section is to introduce the findings chapter to your readers so that, after reading the content of this section, they know what both the study and the content of the chapter are about. Here are questions that need to be addressed in this section:

- What was the problem that led to the design and implementation of the study?
- What was the purpose of the study?
- What is the findings chapter about?
- What are the main topics you will be addressing in this chapter?

Research Setting

In this section, you focus on brief information about where, how and when the data was collected and what your experience was at the data collection stage. This section should not be a repetition of the "Procedure/Data Collection" section in the "Research Methodology" chapter but succinct information on how, where and when the data was retrieved, portraying the context and conditions surrounding the data collection process, experience and outcomes. It is not required to have a "Research Setting" section, but sharing such information reminds readers of how and where the data was collected. It also helps readers to have an understanding of your experience when collecting the data. Lastly, based on the information shared, readers can learn from any challenges faced and recognize best practices that can be useful in their research.

Participants' Demographics

This section houses the presentation of results related to the features of your data source. If your source of data was people, then you are expected to present the participants' demographics. The way demographics are presented in a quantitative study can be different from how they are presented in a qualitative study. The next paragraph explains how you should describe your participants when conducting a quantitative or qualitative study.

When reporting participants' demographics in a qualitative study, you could present in an individualized or a collective way or even present a mixture of both (Adu, 2019). With the individualized way of presenting participants' background information, each participant with unique demographic characteristics is highlighted. This approach is consistent with the assertion that participants' background, beliefs and preconceptions influence how they experience a phenomenon and make sense of or share their experience. It is therefore appropriate to share their background and its uniqueness when presenting what you found. However, if there are commonalities between participants' demographics that are worth highlighting, you can present them in a collective fashion.

An Example of an Individualized Presentation of Participants' Demographics

Participant P5 was one of five females in the study (see Table 22.2). She was an artist. Participant P5 had been in this profession for about 20 years. She became fascinated with art works when she was a child. She remembered at the age of eight years old her parents took her to the Guggenheim Museum in New York. That was the place her interest in art began. At the time of the data collection, she was 48 years old and was doing artwork, including organizing workshops for young people who were interested in art.

An Example of a Collective Presentation of Participants' Demographics

In all 10 participants were interviewed for this study of which half of them were females. Majority of them were in between 24 and 35 years old (n=6, 60%). Also, half of the participants were married. They have diverse profession ranging from artist through to teacher.

As stated above, you could present participants' demographics in both individual and collective form if you plan to showcase the commonalities among them and, at the same time, highlight the unique characteristics that each person has. Also, as shown in Table 22.2, the demographic features of each participant have

Table 22.2 Participants' demographics

Participant	Gender	Age	Profession	Marital Status
P1	Male	55	Physician	Married
P2	Female	23	Content creator	Single
P3	Female	32	Teacher	Married
P4	Male	31	Dentist	Married
P5	Female	48	Artist	Single
P6	Female	52	Nurse	Single
P7	Female	44	Farmer	Single
P8	Male	35	Police officer	Married
P9	Male	24	Construction worker	Married
P10	Male	25	Plumber	Single

been displayed. The point of having this kind of table is to help readers to quickly know who your participants were, especially when one of them is quoted to support a theme or an assertion (Adu, 2019). Besides this individualized demographic table, you could also have a collective table, especially if you have a lot of participants and want to show the number of participants under each category of a demographic variable (see Adu, 2019). Lastly, if you are doing a mixed methods study, you could present participants' demographics in both an individualized and a collective manner.

Data Analysis Process

This section focuses on addressing the question, "How did you arrive at your finding?" By addressing this question, researchers can follow your data analysis steps and get the same or similar results, promoting the reliability or dependability of your study (Creswell, 2012; Moon et al., 2016;). Also, sharing how you analyzed your data increases the credibility of the finding. In order words, readers will believe what you found if you show them how you conducted your data analysis.

Presenting the Data Analysis Process in Qualitative Research

You start describing your data analysis process by stating the specific type of analysis you used. There are many qualitative data analysis techniques you could choose from (see Onwuegbuzie et al., 2012). The three main types of data analysis mostly used by researchers are thematic analysis, content analysis and grounded theory analysis (constant comparative analysis) (Adu, 2019; Onwuegbuzie et al., 2012; Saldaña, 2021). With thematic analysis, you generate codes as you go through the data to identify relevant information (Adu, 2019). You then categorize these codes, leading to the development of themes at the end of the analysis (see Figure 22.17) (Adu, 2019; Maguire & Delahunt, 2017). However, with content analysis, codes/themes are first generated based on the literature reviewed and/or conceptual/theoretical framework developed (Zhang & Wildemuth, 2009; Moustakas, 1994). The codes/themes are used to label relevant information extracted from the data (see Figure 22.18). Lastly, the constant comparative method is a data analysis strategy used mostly in grounded theory studies to examine how the themes and model/theory generated align with a new set of data (Charmaz, 2014; Kolb, 2012; Strauss, 1989) (see Figure 22.19).

Figure 22.17 Thematic analysis process.

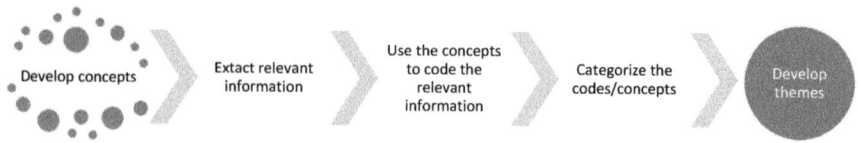

Figure 22.18 Content analysis process.

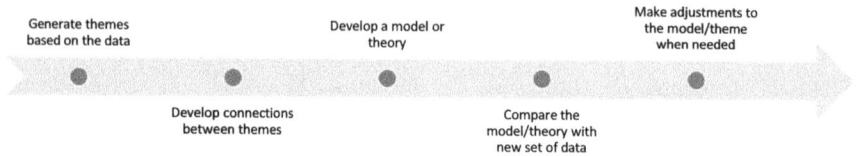

Figure 22.19 Grounded theory (constant comparative) process.

After writing about the type of qualitative data analysis used and explaining what it involved, you then provide, in detail, the steps you took to analyze the data. Also, you are expected to present what the outcomes are after each major step. For example, after the following step, "Relevant information selected from the data were assigned codes," you would state, "At the end, 25 and 58 codes were generated under research questions one and two." You could also provide examples of the codes generated to help your readers to have an idea about the kind of codes developed. In summary, your goal in this section is to provide clear steps on how you analyzed your data.

Presentation of the Findings

Here is where you present the outcomes of the data analysis that address your research questions or test your hypotheses. There are different ways of presenting the findings, but the most important thing is to make sure you present them in the format accepted by your research community or discipline. You could follow the format suggested by the American Psychological Association (see American Psychological Association, 2019; Appelbaum et al., 2018; Levitt et al., 2018).

Presenting the Findings in Qualitative Research

There are many ways of presenting your qualitative findings. The most important thing is to make sure you are presenting them in such a way that the results are directly addressing your research questions. That way, your reader will more likely understand what you found (Adu, 2019). The common presentation strategy is to state the research question you addressed and describe the themes addressing the question. For each theme, you are expected to:

- Provide a description in terms of what the theme represents
- Explain what the theme means
- Support the theme with evidence
- Make a concluding statement showing how it addresses the research question

In Example 22.4, you can see how the theme is presented to address the research question, "What were the factors contributing to public concerns about GM (genetically modified) research and foods in the UK?" (Adu, 2019, p. 348).

Example 22.4 (Theme:) GM Risks Uncertainties

Similar to any technological innovation such as the production of self-driving vehicles, GM research and products have potential risks. The findings show that the public wanted an assurance from GM scientists that there were no side effects associated with GM technology and crops. To them, the scientists should be certain about the risks involved before making them available for consumption. However, according to one GM scientist ("S16"), not many studies have been conducted about GM side effects, making it challenging to completely promise safe GM technology outcomes. Moreover, due to the nature of scientific inquiry, they could not guarantee that GM foods are totally safe, although there has not been any evidence proving otherwise. As a student/staff ("NS2") asserted, GM scientists could not assure the public that there was no risk due to the nature of scientific studies. In effect, this lack of assurance from GM scientists about GM safety and related uncertainties influenced the public negative attitude towards GM research and crops (Adu, 2019, pp. 354–355).

Example 22.4 is just one way of presenting themes (see Table 22.3). In this case, based on the data, you have established relationships among the themes generated, you can also present the connections between the themes as you address the research question. Adu (2019) calls this structure of presentation a "synthesized theme-driven format" (p. 360).

Creating visual representations such as tables, mind maps, charts, tables, word clouds and word trees could add to the understanding of your findings. One of the visual aids you could create is a summary table (see Adu, 2019; Saldaña, 2021). A summary table normally contains all the themes presented, the number of participants connected to the theme (if available), the number of excerpts extracted from the data connected to the theme (if available), a brief description of the themes in terms of their meaning or what they present and evidence from the data supporting each theme.

Table 22.3 Excerpts from the description of the themes and their respective features

Excerpts from the Description of the Themes	Labels for the Theme Description Excerpts
• "Due to the nature of scientific inquiry, they could not guarantee that GM foods and totally safe although there has not been any evidence proving otherwise" (Adu, 2019, p. 355).	What the theme represents
• "Similar to any technological innovation such as the production of self-driving vehicles, GM research and products have potential risks" (Adu, 2019, p. 354).	Explanation of the theme
• "The findings show that the public wanted an assurance from GM scientists that there were no side effects associated with GM technology and crops. To them, the scientists should be certain about the risks involved before making them available for consumption" (Adu, 2019, p. 354).	
• "According to one GM scientist ("S16"), not many studies have been conducted about GM side effects, making it challenging to completely promise safe GM technology outcomes" (Adu, 2019, p. 355).	Supporting evidence
• "As a student/staff ("NS2") asserted, GM scientists could not assure the public that there was no risk due to the nature of scientific studies" (Adu, 2019, p. 355).	
• "In effect, this lack of assurance from GM scientists about GM safety and related uncertainties influenced the public negative attitude towards GM research and crops" (Adu, 2019, 355).	Concluding statement

"Summary" Section

The summary section could include an overview briefly describing the research problem and purpose. It could also contain highlights of participants' demographics and the data analysis procedure. In addition, you are also expected to briefly share the key findings. Lastly, you end this section with a concluding statement (Adu, 2021). The easiest way of getting this section done is to first write a sentence for each of the below components:

- Research problem
- Research purpose
- Demographics
- Statistical tests or data analysis process
- Main findings
- Concluding statement

After that, you can arrange them in such a way that there is a logical flow of information presented in the summary section.

Summary

The credibility of a study could depend on how the findings are presented. For a quantitative study, you are expected to present the collective characteristics of the participants, sharing the counts, percentages, mean and standard deviations for the demographic variables. In addition, you are expected to present the results from conducting descriptive and inferential statistics. However, with a qualitative study, you are more likely to present participants' demographics in an individual format, helping your audience to know the characteristics of each participant. Further, the main findings are normally presented in themes and organized under their respective research questions. This chapter focused on demonstrating the best way of structuring the presentation of your qualitative, quantitative or mixed methods study. By the end of the chapter, you should be able to communicate your results in a meaningful way and show how you arrived at the research outcomes.

References

Adu, P. (2019). *A step-by-step guide to qualitative data coding*. Routledge.

Adu, P. (2021, March). *Writing your results*. ResearchGate. https://doi.org/10.13140/RG.2.2.14640.12800

American Psychological Association. (2019). *Publication manual of the American Psychological Association* (7th ed.). American Psychological Association.

Appelbaum, M., Cooper, H., Kline, R. B., Mayo-Wilson, E., Nezu, A. M., & Rao, S. M. (2018). Journal article reporting standards for quantitative research in psychology: The APA Publications and Communications Board task force report. *American Psychologist, 73*(1), 3–25. https://doi.org/10.1037/amp0000191

Bentler, P. M., & Dijkstra, T. K. (1985). On the implications of Bartholomew's approach to factor analysis. *British Journal of Mathematical and Statistical Psychology, 38*(2), 129–131. https://doi.org/10.1111/j.2044-8317.1985.tb00825.x

Brown, T. A. (2006). *Confirmatory factor analysis for applied research*. The Guilford Press.

Burns, A. C., & Bush, R. F. (2003). *Marketing research: Online research applications.* (4th ed.). Prentice Hall.

Charmaz, K. (2014). *Constructing grounded theory*. SAGE Publications.

Creswell, J. W. (2012). *Educational research: Planning, conducting, and evaluating quantitative and qualitative research* (4th ed.). Sage Publishers.

Field, A. (2017). *Discovering statistics using IBM SPSS statistics.* (5th ed.). Sage Publishers.

Garson, D. G. (1998). *Factor analysis*. Retrieved from http://faculty.chass.ncsu.edu/garson/PA765/factor.htm#factoring

Hair, J. F., Anderson, R. E., Tatum, R. L., & Black, W. C. (1998). *Multivariate data analysis*. Prentice Hall.

Harrison, V., Kemp, R., Brace, N., Snelgar, R. (2020). *SPSS for psychologists* (7th ed.). Bloomsbury Publication.

Jackson, S. L. (2009). *Research methods and statistics: A critical thinking approach* (3rd ed.). Wadsworth.

Khan, H. & Miles, D. A. (2020). Statistics research: Predictor models in management and leadership: An empirical study on naturalistic behavioral outcomes of superior leadership performance and effectiveness in organizations. 2020 Spring Academy of Business Research Conference (ABR).

Kolb, S. M. (2012). Grounded theory and the constant comparative method: Valid research strategies for educators. *Journal of Emerging Trends in Educational Research and Policy Studies, 3*, 83–86.

Kothari, C. R. (2009). *Research methodology: Methods and techniques* (2nd ed.). New Age International Limited.

Leedy, P. E., & Ormrod, J. E. (2019). *Practical research: Planning and design* (12th ed.). Pearson.

Levitt, H. M., Bamberg, M., Creswell, J. W., Frost, D. M., Josselson, R., & Suárez-Orozco, C. (2018). Journal article reporting standards for qualitative primary, qualitative meta-analytic, and mixed methods research in psychology: The APA Publications and Communications Board task force report. *American Psychologist, 73*(1), 26–46. https://doi.org/10.1037/amp0000151

Mack, C., Su, Z., & Westreich, D. (2018). *Managing missing data in patient registries: Addendum to registries for evaluating patient outcomes: A user's guide* (3rd ed.). Agency for Healthcare Research and Quality (US).

Maguire, M., & Delahunt, B. (2017). Doing a thematic analysis: A practical, step-by-step guide for learning and teaching scholars. *AISHE-J, 9*, 3351. http://ojs.aishe.org/index.php/aishe-j/article/view/3354

Marinković, J. (2008). Multivariate statistics. In W. Kirch (Ed.), *Encyclopedia of public health* (pp. 973–976). Springer. https://doi.org/10.1007/978-1-4020-5614-7_2264

Miles, D. A., Garcia, J., Gerald, R., Goodnough, W., Mendez, L., ogilvie, dt, Olagundoye, E., Robinson, S., & Seay, E. L. (2019). Ethnic consumer markets and movie marketing: An empirical study on Marvel's "Black Panther" and predictive analytics of ethnic consumer behavior of moviegoers. *Journal of Economics and Business, 2*(4). https://doi.org/10.31014/aior.1992.02.04.153

Miles, D. A., Garcia, J., Gerald, R., Goodnough, W., Mendez, L., ogilvie, dt, Olagundoye, E., Robinson, S., & Seay, E. L. (2020). STATISTICS RESEARCH: The social media weaponization and revenge social media: An empirical study on the social media weaponization and black marketing on consumer behavior. *Fall 2020 Academy of Business Research Conference (ABR)*. https://doi.org/10.13140/RG.2.2.12674.50885

Moon, K., Brewer, T. D., Januchowski-Hartley, S. R., Adams, V. M., & Blackman, D. A. (2016). A guideline to improve qualitative social science publishing in ecology and conservation journals. *Ecology and Society, 21*(3), 17. http://dx.doi.org/10.5751/ES-08663-210317

Moore, L. L., & Rudd, R. D. (2006). Leadership styles of current extension leaders. *Journal of Agricultural Education, 47*(1), 6–16. https://doi.org10.5032/jae.2006.01006

Morgan, S., Reichert, T., & Harrison, T. R. (2017). *From numbers to words: Reporting statistical results for the social sciences* (1st ed.). Routledge. https://doi.org/10.4324/9781315638010

Moustakas, C. (1994). *Phenomenological research methods*. Sage.

Mulaik, S. A. (1972). *Foundations of factor analysis*. McGraw-Hill.

Onwuegbuzie, A. J., Leech, N. L., & Collins, K. M. (2012). Qualitative analysis techniques for the review of the literature. *The Qualitative Report, 17*, 1–28.

Rummel, R. J. (1970). *Applied factor analysis*. Northwestern University Press.

Saldaña, J. (2021). *The coding manual for qualitative researchers* (3rd ed.). Sage.

Satorra, A., & Bentler, P. (1988). *Scaling corrections for statistics in covariance structure analysis*. eScholarship. https://escholarship.org/uc/item/3141h70c

Sreejesh, S., Mohapatra, S., Anusree, M. R. (2014). *Business research methods.* Springer.

Strauss, A. L. (1989). *Qualitative analysis for social scientists.* Cambridge University Press.

Tabachnick, B. G., & Fidell, L. S. (2007). *Using multivariate statistics* (5th ed.). Pearson.

Vogt, P. W. (1993). *Dictionary of statistics and methodology: A nontechnical guide for the social sciences.* Sage Publications.

Zhang, Y., & Wildemuth, B. M. (2009). Qualitative analysis of content. In B. M. Wildemuth (Ed.), *Applications of social research methods to questions in information and library science* (pp. 308–319). Libraries Unlimited.

23 Writing Your Dissertation

The Standard Format – Chapter 5 (Discussion and Conclusions)

Objective

- Readers will be able to:
  1. Write the discussion and conclusions chapter of their dissertation

Introduction and Overview

In this chapter, the researcher reintroduces the topic again and reiterates the research problem as the basis for the study. This chapter provides another introduction and overview of the study and the topic. In this section, the researcher discusses the findings of the study. The researcher provides a discussion of the findings for the instrument and provides some evidence in support of the study's findings. Furthermore, the researcher will provide an overview of why the study is important and how the study was designed to contribute to our understanding of the topic. The researcher basically provides a transition, explains what will be covered in the chapter and reminds the reader of how the study was conducted. The chapter provides a discussion and overview of what is contained in the chapter.

Main Points and Directions

These are the main key points that the doctoral researcher should consider when developing the "Introduction and Overview" section of chapter five:

- Provide a summary of the study framework, including a recap of the research problem and purpose statement
- Remind the reader of the research questions and how the reported data analysis (not findings) align with answering the research questions
- Provide an overview as to why the study is important and how the study was designed to contribute to our understanding of the topic
- Provide a transition, explain what will be covered in the chapter and remind the reader how the study was developed

DOI: 10.4324/9781003268154-23

- Provide an overview of what is contained in the chapter
- Writing length: Minimum of two to four paragraphs or approximately one page (Miles, 2022)

By following these key points, the researcher can fully develop the "Introduction and Overview" section of the chapter (see Example 23.1).

Example 23.1 Introduction and Overview

The purpose of this study was to determine if statistically significant differences existed between two groups, employees that participated in leadership education program and employees that did not, and the performance on a company-mandated assessment for employees throughout the company. The researcher identified three key research objectives in this study. The first objective of the study was to determine whether a statistically significant difference existed between a group taking the leadership education program and a group that did not, and if it had an influence on Leadership Intelligence Quotient (LIQ) scores for the management competence part of the assessment. The second objective of the study was to determine whether a statistically significant difference existed between a group taking the leadership education program and a group that did not, and if it had an influence on LIQ scores for the leadership trust worthiness part of the assessment. The last objective of the study was to determine whether a statistically significant difference existed between a group taking the leadership education program and a group that did not, and if it had an influence on LIQ scores for the leadership commitment part of the assessment.

This study was developed because of the need to gain insights regarding the extent to which a specified leadership education program impacts employees or future managers based on their success on the company's LIQ test. The results of the study should contribute to the literature addressing the needs of companies with increasing incidents of office politics, workplace politics, nepotism, workplace bullying and other bad organizational behaviors identified by the Employee Leadership Behavior and similar behavioral assessment tools.

Finally, it should also contribute to the body of knowledge and prior research addressing the relevance of zero-tolerance policies in private and public organizations and their settings. The study examined whether the personal character development curriculum influenced overall company assessment scores. The data was analyzed in company departments with a leadership education program and compared to the same data in departments without a leadership education program.

Overview of Chapter

This chapter will discuss the primary objectives for this study. The sections included in this chapter will review the research questions, summarize the study, summarize the findings and conclusions, discuss the research questions and accompanying hypotheses, review the conclusions and implications of the study and suggest recommendations regarding the study. This quantitative study examined whether leadership education has any influence on employee weighted percentage of change year-over-year on company standardized testing in departments throughout the company. Based on the results of the analysis, this study indicated considerable significance between the implementation of a leadership education program and weighted percentage of change year-over-year on the LIQ.

Summary of Findings and Conclusions

In this section, the researcher summarizes the findings and conclusions of the study. The researcher provides a convincing discussion on how the study is aligned with and advances the research on the topic. Furthermore, the researcher will discuss the significance of the findings. The researcher basically provides a conclusion to the findings in the study. The researcher wants to provide a rigorous discussion of the findings and conclusions in the study.

Main Points and Directions

These are the main key points that the doctoral researcher should consider when developing the "Summary of Findings and Conclusions" section of chapter five:

- Summarize the study's findings. Compare, contrast and synthesize the study's findings in the context of prior research on the topic
- Provide a convincing discussion on how the study is aligned with and advances the research on the topic
- Illustrate that the findings are aligned with the research study design described in the previous chapters (chapters one, two and three)
- Illustrates how the findings are supported by the data and theory and how the findings directly align with and answer the research question(s)
- Discuss the significance (or non-significance) of the findings
- Directly relate each of the findings to the Significance of the Study section of chapter one
- Abstain from including unrelated or speculative information in this section
- Provide a conclusion to summarize the key findings
- Relate the key findings back to chapter one and link the study to it
- Writing length: Minimum of three to five pages (Miles, 2022)

By following these key points, the researcher can fully develop the "Summary of Findings and Conclusions" section of the chapter (see Example 23.2).

Example 23.2 Summary of Findings and Conclusions

The demand for employee improvement and corporate achievement in the organization's departments, as well as the rest of the company, has increased since the passage of equity and inclusion policy and practices. The ensuing pressure caused by this legislation has caused the company's gender bias-based environment to change over time (Miles, 2015). According to the literature, there has been an increase in inappropriate workplace behaviors and productivity disruptions, as well as increased efforts in employee inclusion practices. This has influenced an increase in the number of employee complaints about upward mobility and employee attrition.

This company-based study began by identifying an opportunity to investigate the impact of a leadership character education course on employee training achievement as described in Chapter 1. This section provides a summary of key findings that were uncovered from data analysis on the leadership training program as offered in Chapter 4. The findings from the weighted percentage of change between the organization's departments are organized based on the research questions and hypotheses that are specific to this study. After examining the findings for each question, conclusions will be drawn based on the analysis of the results. Furthermore, the findings will be discussed as they pertain to current research on leadership education.

In conclusion, the results of the data indicated that there may be a significant gain in testing scores as a result of a character education program in the company. There was a similar result in the analysis for overall scores, management competence scores, leadership trust worthiness scores and leadership commitment scores. However, more information may be determined from looking at the score distributions themselves.

[Note: In-text citations included for illustrative purposes only]

Discussion: Research Question and Hypothesis One, RQ1: *Is there a statistically significant difference between a group taking the leadership education program and a group not taking it, as measured by the Leadership Intelligence Quotient (LIQ) instrument?*

The first research question investigated the relationship between taking a character education class and overall passing success on the LIQ instrument. It was hypothesized that there would be positive, statistically significant relationships between leadership education and the overall test passing percentages. The set of data was collected using the Management Excellence Indicator System (MEIS),

---

which is a publicly accessible record through the IRS and other government agencies (IRS, 2018). The researcher collected data regarding demographics such as gender, while management experiences and education achievement results were not included because they were not part of the original instruments' questions.

The percentage for each department was calculated by using the population of the school and the number of employees for that department who achieved a passing rate on the LIQ assessment. The information was then subjected to an independent sample t-Test that was used to determine the significance of the findings. A t-Test was conducted to determine if there were differences in populated weighed percent of the change between the two groups for LIQ overall scores. The 215 participants who received the leadership program training ($M = 480$, $SD = 34.5$) compared to the 28 participants in the non-participating group who did not take the leadership program course ($M = 425$, $SD = 31$) demonstrated significantly better peak flow scores, $t(51) = 2.1$, $p = .04$. There was a significant effect for sex, $t(38) = 1.7$, $p = .004$, despite women ($M = 55$, SD = 8) attaining higher scores than men ($M = 53$, $SD = 7.8$). These were similar, as assessed by a visual inspection. The null hypothesis was rejected ($M = 445$, z = 1.272, $p = .003$), using an exact sampling distribution (Miles & Adu, 2014). The key finding from the results indicate there was a significant difference between the two groups with the implementation of the leadership program.

Discussion: Research Question and Hypothesis Two, RQ2: *Is there a statistically significant difference between a group taking the leadership trust worthiness test and a group not taking it, as measured by the Leadership Intelligence Quotient (LIQ) instrument?*

The second research question was content-based and focused on the leadership trust worthiness test. It investigated the relationship between taking a leadership education class and passing percentage rates for employees taking the Leadership Intelligence Quotient (LIQ) instrument. It was hypothesized that there would be a positive, statistically significant relationship between leadership education and percentage of passing scores on the LIQ instrument.

Again, an independent sample t-Test was conducted to determine if there were differences in populated weighed percent of the change between groups for LIQ scores. These were similar, as assessed by a visual inspection. The null hypothesis was rejected ($M = 344$, $p = .003$), using an exact sampling distribution for the mean (Miles & Adu, 2003). The participants who received the leadership program training ($M = 480$, $SD = 34.5$) compared to the 28 participants in the non-participating group who did not take the leadership program course ($M = 425$, $SD = 18$) demonstrated significantly better peak flow scores, $t(51) = 2.1$, $p = .04$. There was a significant effect for sex, $t(38) = 1.7$, $p = .004$, despite women (M = 55, SD = 8) attaining higher scores than men (M = 53, SD = 7.8). These were similar, as assessed by a visual inspection. The null hypothesis was rejected (M = 445, z = 1.272, p = .003), using an exact sampling distribution (Miles & Adu, 2014). Based on the statistical test, the results found that there was a statistical significance for leadership trust worthiness test scores. The key finding from the results indicates there was a significant difference between the two groups with the implementation of the leadership education program in a private company.

Discussion: Research Question and Hypothesis Three, RQ3: *Is there a statistically significant difference between a group taking the leadership education program and a group not taking it, as measured by the Leadership Intelligence Quotient (LIQ) instrument?*

The last research question was content-based and focused on the leadership education program LIQ test. It investigated the relationship between taking a character education class and passing percentage rates for students taking the Leadership Intelligence Quotient (LIQ) instrument and Skills. It was hypothesized that there would be a positive, statistically significant relationship between character education and percentage of passing scores on the LIQ administration. Again, an independent sample t-test was used to determine if there were no differences in populated weighed percent of the change between groups for LIQ scores. These were similar, as assessed by a visual inspection (Adu & Miles, 2004). The null hypothesis was rejected (M = 344, p =.003), using an exact sampling distribution for the mean (Miles & Adu, 2003). The participants who received the leadership program training (M = 480, SD = 34.5) compared to the 28 participants in the non-participating group who did not take the leadership program course (M = 425, SD = 18) demonstrated significantly better peak flow scores, t(51) = 2.1, p = .04. There was a significant effect for sex, t(38) = 1.7, p = .004, despite women (M = 55, SD = 8) attaining higher scores than men (M = 53, SD = 7.8). These were similar, as assessed by a visual inspection. The null hypothesis was rejected (M = 445, p = .003), using an exact sampling distribution (Miles & Adu, 2014). Based on the statistical test, the results found that there was no statistical significance for leadership trust worthiness test scores. The key finding from the results indicates there was a significant difference between the two groups with the implementation of the leadership education program in a private company. Based on the statistical test, the results found that there were not any statistical significance differences for LIQ test scores. The key finding from the results indicates there was no significant difference between the two groups with the implementation of the leadership education program.

Conclusions of the Study

The research found three key conclusions from this study. This study investigated the potential role of participation in a leadership education program in employee success on company-mandated standardized assessments. First, based on the first key finding of the study, the conclusion is that there is a strong nexus between the leadership education program and change in a year over-year test score performance. The key finding from the results indicates there was a significant difference between the two groups with the implementation of the leadership education program in the department and company. In fact, the implementation of leadership programs in departments was found to be significant in its relationship with the test scores in both departments of the company. This finding is consistent with other studies investigating potential relationships between character leadership program participation and attendance (Miles, 2016; Miles et al., 2018; Adu et al., 2019; Miles et al., 2016).

Second, based on the second finding of the study, the conclusion is that there is strong nexus between the character education program and leadership trust worthiness test score performance. The key findings from the research indicate there was no difference between the two groups with the implementation of the leadership program. The implementation of the leadership program in the company departments was found to be significant in its relationship with the test scores in the departments and the company.

Lastly, based on the third key finding of the study, it is concluded that there is no nexus between the character education program and leadership commitment year-over-year test score performance. The key finding from the results indicate there was no significance between the two groups with the implementation of the leadership education program. Implementation of the employee leadership program in schools was found to be insignificant in its relationship with the year-over-year test scores in the department and the company. The overall conclusion of the study is that participation in a leadership program did have a noticeable impact on employee year-over-year performance on company-mandated assessments. This may have been attributed to a couple factors. First, many of the previous studies were qualitative in nature, giving a direct record of the participants' perceived impact of employee participation in the course. Lastly, the use of primary data may have impacted the results.

[Note: In-text citations included for illustrative purposes only]

Interpretation of the Findings

In this chapter, the researcher discusses the interpretation of the findings. In this section, the researcher discusses the findings of the study section in the chapter. The researcher provides a discussion of the findings in regard to the instrument and provides some evidence in support of the study findings. The researcher basically provides a transition to the findings section in the chapter. The chapter explains the interpretation of the findings and how the study was conducted. The chapter also provides a discussion of the interpretation of the findings in the chapter.

Main Points and Directions

These are the main key points that the doctoral researcher should consider when developing the "Interpretation of the Findings" section of chapter five:

- Reiterate the research problem, purpose statement and research questions (if necessary)
- Describe the key interpretations and make sure they are relevant to the research problem, purpose statement and research questions
- Describe the key findings from the study that are significant and relevant
- Describe and discuss the content that advances the findings to interpretations
- Describe and discuss the content that does not generalize beyond the evidence of the findings
- Discuss and directly relate the interpretation to the research problem that guided the study
- Describe and provide logical interpretations of the findings from the research
- Describe and discuss the topic of the interpretation. Do not stray into other areas that are not relevant; remain on the key topic
- Describe and discuss content that states whether your interpretations align with those of previous researchers
- Describe and provide content as to whether the interpretations have some adherence to previous research findings or whether they are a departure from previous research findings
- Describe and provide content regarding the reasons for the adherence or departure (such as different patient populations, different procedures or different level of data quality)
- Writing length: Minimum of two to four paragraphs or approximately one page (Miles, 2022)

By following these key points, the researcher can fully develop the "Interpretation of the Findings" section of the chapter (see Example 23.3).

The task of interpreting the findings is the most critical part of chapter five. The researcher should take this process very seriously. The task of developing the findings can also be a difficult endeavor for the novice researcher or the doctoral student. This part of the process can be very difficult for them. One way to address this is to follow this process. The basic task of interpreting your findings is a three-step process (see Figure 23.1).

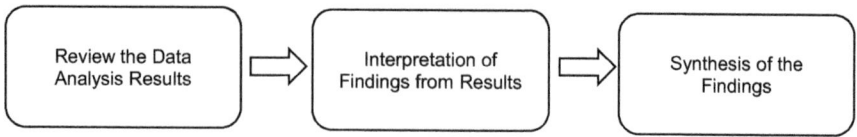

Figure 23.1 The interpretation of the findings process.

Review the Data Analysis Results

The first step in the interpretation of findings is to review the data analysis results. The researcher wants to review the results to see what the data is telling them. As a researcher, you want to see the story the data and results are telling you. All data tells a story. You want to see the story the data is telling you. Next is to look for patterns in the data analysis. The researcher wants to look for emergent patterns among their results that can be considered a first round of analysis. When you find patterns, you can tell what is consistent in the data analysis. Also, you want to look for inconsistencies in the data results. Again, what is the story that the data results are telling you. That is what you want to do in this step (Kliewer, 2007; Bloomberg & Volpe, 2008).

Interpretation of Findings from Results

The task of interpreting the findings from the data is a critical part of the process. A critical part of the interpretive reading of your data analysis results involves constructing a version of what you infer from it. First, the task of interpretation essentially involves reading through or beyond the data analysis results and interpreting the findings (e.g., making sense of the findings). This is focused on answering the "why?" and "why not?" questions around the results (Kliewer, 2007). Interpretation involves identifying the important understanding from the detail and complexity of the findings. We know there are differences between interpreting findings in quantitative and qualitative results. So, the researcher must learn the characteristics of each methodology and look for the significance in the results and deduce the findings from those results.

Second, when composing the findings, the researcher must understand that the findings of the study will either confirm what is already known about the subject area surrounding their research problem or diverge from it (Bloomberg & Volpe, 2008). You as the researcher must put forward your interpretations concerning the patterns and idiosyncrasies in the results. Lastly, the researcher needs to make the audience understand that they looked at different angles to conclude their findings. This involves giving the audience the confidence that the researcher did their due diligence to develop convincing findings. The researcher must be diligent in performing this. The reader should get the sense that you have looked at your findings from different angles, that you have taken into account all the information relevant to the analysis, that you have identified and discussed the most important themes, and that your argument is systematically constructed (Long et al., 1985; Miles & Scott, 2017).

Synthesis of the Findings

The last step in the process is the task of synthesizing the findings. Synthesis involves the task of pulling everything together from the different parts of the data analysis results. These turn into your findings. The incredible advantage of synthesis is that it puts everything together in one place. Furthermore, the task of synthesis involves combining the individual units of analysis into a more integrated whole. Synthesis can also allow the researcher to see how the interpretation of the individual findings conflate or contrast with each other (Webster, 1998a, 1998b; Kliewer, 2007). (see Example 23.3).

Example 23.3 Interpretation of the Findings

For the purpose of the analysis and interpretation, the researcher used Adu's (2008) seminal work and how he perceived leadership in corporations and the need for such leaders in the business world today. Adu's (2008) framework served as a lens to filter the data. A persistent theme in the literature was consistent with Adu's (2008) perception of crisis leadership. The literature suggested that, as employment demographics change in the United States, the demographics of the corporations do not mirror this change. The research also revealed a consistent theme regarding an area that will contribute to the much-needed studies on crisis leadership. This concept of leadership is based on the attitudes, beliefs and life experiences of managers in corporations today and how they are meeting the needs of a growing multicultural population. This type of literature resonated with Adu's (2008) concept of crisis leadership. The following are the key findings that were significant in the data. There were three key findings from the data analysis results.

Key Finding #1: Inconsistent Crisis Approaches to Problems

The first key finding based on the data analysis is the issue of inconsistent crisis approaches to problems. The participants were dedicated in their efforts to provide a coherent environment conducive to team building. A secondary theme and aspect of the research was that of formerly marginalized female managers who now serve as business leaders. How are these female leaders meeting the needs of a growing culturally diverse population? It was on this premise that the female leaders connected with their staff and students in such a way that the notion of crisis leadership could not be ignored. The notion of crisis leadership was a salient aspect of how the leaders connected to their employees. The participants had very similar backgrounds to the employees, which provided a level of insight

---

that prepared the leaders to meet their employee's needs. These leaders enacted agendas that were similar and brought action to what Adu's (2007) model defined as crisis leadership. Furthermore, the managers focused on meeting the needs of all employees. This was integral to keeping the issues of the marginalized at the center of all decisions made in each department of the corporation. According to Adu (2007), how these leaders utilize crisis leadership in their decision making in the manager role gives them a unique perspective on the resistance they feel as they work to move their vision of crisis.

Key Finding #2: Transition Crisis Leadership Behavior Characteristics

The second key finding is the issue of transition crisis leadership characteristics. The participants exemplified the characteristics of transition crisis leadership. They all agreed that crisis leadership is an arduous and unfulfilling task that must be embraced. This mindset puts it into perspective for these managers and their crisis leadership approaches to problems. Their vision of handling the crisis for each department was equally as important. This vision established at the outset of each fiscal year must be articulated in such a way that all employees, shareholders and stakeholders know how to share it. These managers are aware that this requires a transition crisis approach from the organization, not only in the physical sense but also in the subliminal sense, to the employees. According to Miles and Adu (2005), transition crisis leadership is the ability to articulate a vision in a crisis situation and an uncertain environment. Transition crisis leadership creates a sense of empowerment and calm throughout the crisis for employees and staff. The vision of the managers becomes an infectious attitude during a crisis that can empower employees and the department. In turn, crisis leadership yields an environment of uncertainty and calamity among employees. Managers need to practice crisis leadership during a crisis and when there is no crisis.

Key Finding #3: Societal Perceptions of African American Principals

The third key finding is the issue of transition crisis leadership characteristics. Managers are exposed to a certain level of scrutiny as leaders in a crisis. The managers expressed the same sentiment in regard to the actions of their employees and how they affect the leadership role. Adu (2005) asserts that "sometimes, crisis leadership is not automatic in the way that you would speak around your manager peers and how you speak to employees. It may be different than how you would speak during a crisis setting; sometimes leaderships are tested during a crisis." Female managers have been marginalized for quite some time. A stimulating aspect of this research to me was how female managers viewed themselves during a crisis leadership situation. How do marginalized female managers who ascend to the leadership position address a crisis leadership situation in their department or organization? The participants do not dwell on these bad circumstances; instead, they focused on what they could have done better in a crisis and learn from it and use it to their advantage in the next crisis. Being vigilant toward these crisis situations can promote a level of careful decision making in that environment. This can yield positive or negative results in a crisis. These were the key findings of this study.

[Note: In-text citations included for illustrative purposes only]

Implications and Applications of the Findings

In this chapter, the researcher reintroduces the implications and applications of the findings in the chapter. This chapter provides insight into what those implications are for the study. The chapter lays down the foundation and also provides an introduction and overview of the study. Next, the chapter discusses the theoretical implications of the study. In this section, the researcher discusses the theory and its implications on the findings of the study. Next, the chapter discusses the practical implications of the study. In this section, the researcher discusses the study's practical nature and how the research is applicable to the workplace.

Furthermore, the researcher will discuss the strengths and weaknesses of the study. This involves the assumptions, limitations and delimitations. Lastly, the researcher basically provides a transition and explains what will be covered in the chapter to remind the reader how the study was conducted. The chapter provides a discussion and a special overview of what is contained in the chapter.

Main Points and Directions

These are the main key points that the doctoral researcher should consider when developing the "Implications and Applications of the Findings" section of chapter five.

Theoretical Implications

- Provide and discuss a retrospective examination of the theoretical framework presented in chapter two in light of the dissertation's findings
- Discuss and connect the findings of the study back to the theoretical framework or conceptual framework
- Discuss and connect the study results in context to how the results advance practitioners' knowledge of that theory, model or concept

Practical Implications

- Discuss and connect the study's findings back to the prior research discussed in chapter two
- Discuss and develop the practical implications of the study based on how the results advance practitioners' knowledge of the topic and influence future practice

Future Implications

- Develop and discuss the future implications of the study based on new insights derived from the research and how it may influence future research
- Develop and discuss possible underserved populations that could be pursued as a line of inquiry for future research.
- Develop and discuss possible diverse research methodology and designs that could open up new and diverse lines of inquiry for future research.

Strengths and Weaknesses

- Indicate and discuss all the limitations of the study and critically evaluate the study's strengths and weaknesses
- Indicate and discuss the degree to which the conclusions are credible given the methodology, research design and data analysis and results
- Writing length: Minimum of one to four pages (Miles, 2022)

By following these key points, the researcher can fully develop the "Implications and Applications of the Findings" section of the chapter (see Example 23.4).

Example 23.4 Implications and Applications of the Findings

Implications for Theory and Research

The findings of this study will be discussed in the context of the leadership theory and the concept of "followership," along with some other traditional leadership theories. According to the principles of leadership theory, certain persons usually become leaders only when they are perceived as leaders because of their visual qualities, skills or attributes (Miles, 2014). The result of this study aligns with the leadership/followership theory because field workers reported that they were not promoted to leadership positions because their managers and supervisors did not observe the qualities of leadership in these employees. In the context of the leadership theory, the researchers also focused on the role of followership in influencing managers' promotion decisions.

According to the researchers, some field workers were more often viewed as potential leaders than followership-oriented field workers because of associations between leadership and followership in people's perceptions (Miles et al., 2015; Adu et al., 2015). This study provided evidence from the field worker participants' narratives to support the idea that leadership-oriented field workers were often selected to be promoted to higher positions because of their leadership qualities, even if they did not have enough experience.

Implications for Practice

The current study has many implications for practitioners and professionals in the field of management. First, the results of this study can be effectively applied by managers and supervisors in US agricultural organizations to over-come obstacles with field workers in the situation of their promotion. The field worker participants revealed that they were not perceived as leaders by their colleagues because of followership qualities; the field workers needed to prove their skills and qualifications. Furthermore, they were not discriminated against in the process of promotion because of their ethnicity or gender but because of the high-level of followership traits they displayed. Managers working with followership-oriented field workers need to take these challenges into account to improve their support and socialization. Their leadership traits need to be trained as well to demonstrate leadership credibility and leadership account-ability (Miles et al., 2017; Adu, 2018). The associated reason for using the implications of this study in practice is that the researcher discovered no pre-vious studies related to the lived experiences of field workers belonging to the age group of 35–45 years, and this research provided information for leaders in US agricultural organizations.

The second reason is that the findings of this research can be successfully used in order to modify and enhance the field worker policies and practices adopted in predominately US agricultural organizations. Furthermore, while following the concept of providing equal opportunities for all employees, it could also pre-vent interdepartmental dissonance and conflict. This study examined the lived experiences of field workers related to their career development to determine cer-tain negative aspects in practices that were used in U.S. agricultural organizations. This was conducted at all stages of hiring, retaining and promoting leadership-oriented qualified field workers for the study.

Lastly, managers can apply the results of the study to focus only on leader-ship qualification or on followership qualifications. This study can help man-agers to understand and improve their hiring practices. The results of this study provided more significant implications for recruiting new employees. The results help to support the key principles of leadership practices, with a focus on the potential of leadership-oriented field workers for advancement in US agri-cultural organizations. The study supported the views of management in US agricultural organizations that followership-oriented employees (field workers) are not viewed as effective leaders, and they are rarely promoted because of an assumed lack of leadership qualities. The study also supported the conclusions made by the students. This was also supported by management among the

US agricultural personnel. According to the field worker participants, multiple barriers to promotion do not allow them to overcome the "experience ceiling." Lastly, this study could contribute to an expansion of knowledge through the lived experiences of women of ethnicity in the area of their professional development with reference to the existing theories. The field worker participants' expressions of their experiences added to the understanding of how the "experience ceiling" can affect them, and workplace discrimination is still used in corporations.

[Note: In-text citations included for illustrative purposes only]

Limitations

In this section, the researcher discusses the limitations of the study. The researcher discusses the limitations concerning the methodology. The researcher discusses the limitations concerning the research design. The researcher provides a discussion of the data collection. The researcher should provide a rigorous narrative of the limitations concerning the study and the instrument used in the study.

Main Points and Directions

These are the main key points that the doctoral researcher should consider when developing the "Limitations" section of chapter five:

- Discuss the limitations concerning the research methodology
- Discuss the limitations concerning the research design
- Discuss the limitations concerning the design sampling strategy
- Discuss the limitations concerning the data collection approach
- Identify and discuss the instruments and data analysis
- Provide a rationale for each limitation
- Identify the limitations of the research design and associated consequences for the study's generalizability
- Discuss the limitations concerning the applicability of the findings
- Writing length: Minimum of two to three paragraphs (Miles, 2022)

By following these key points, the researcher can fully develop the "Limitations" section of the chapter (see Example 23.5).

Example 23.5 Limitations

In this study, the data were collected from a sample including 20 field worker participants. Non-probability purposive sampling was used to recruit the participants. The researcher found three key limitations related to and influencing this study. The first limitation is that the study used a purposive sampling technique, which can limit study results in terms of their generalizability, but this limitation is typical of qualitative studies, and they are considered by the researcher. Furthermore, while reflecting on the experience of conducting a qualitative phenomenological study, it is possible to state that one of the key difficulties was the application of a bracketing technique. It was used to avoid the problem and impact of the researcher's bias on the description or interpretation of the findings. It has been problematic to identify codes and themes that reflected the participants' unique lived experiences associated with their career paths and perceptions rather than issues associated with the literature reviewed by the researcher because the focus was on data-driven coding (Miles, 2015).

The second limitation is associated with the research methodology and design. The methodology was a limitation due to the obstacles experienced by the researcher when collecting data from the field workers. The research design is related to the specifics of phenomenological studies where the number of participants is always limited. The use of the research design, which is a descriptive study, was a limitation in terms of the ability of the researcher to collect data expediently. This was an obstacle for the researcher and presented a limitation as well. Furthermore, the collected data were subjective in their nature, not allowing for making generalized conclusions. However, this limitation was addressed with reference to the research methodology, which was aimed at an in-depth understanding of field worker participants' lived experiences and the barriers they faced in the workplace.

The last limitation of this study was associated with the affected validity or credibility of the results because of the reliance on self-reported data. It was important to note that, during interviews, the participants could possibly conceal data, provide inaccurate details or change facts (Miles et al., 2013). In contrast to the interpretive phenomenology, the researcher described a meaningful structure of the participants' lived experiences without misinterpreting them or conceptualizing through the researcher's own perspective. Furthermore, when conducting coding and identifying themes, it was difficult to avoid the impact of the researcher's biases on the data analysis process and guarantee the trustworthiness of the described results. There were issues of credibility and trustworthiness. There were issues of self-selection bias by the researcher when choosing the participants, which presented a limitation.

The possible personal biases that could influence data analysis were associated with the researcher's interest in discovering data related to barriers or obstacles faced by the field worker participants in the US agricultural organizations. However, it is worth noting that it is important to apply the bracketing technique and concentrate on the actual data presented in the narratives. This should be done without the impact of the researcher's biases and assumptions. The research tried fervently to avoid the influence of researcher bias. Therefore, the researcher contributed to developing conversations without expressing her own ideas and views regarding the topic.

As a result, the study's integrity was ensured and accurate descriptions of the field worker participants' lived experiences and meanings ascribed to them were presented as the findings. These findings were discussed with a focus on the existing literature. Based on this study, the researcher was able to concentrate on the techniques of working with the self-reported data of the field worker participants. The influence of researcher bias on the study's results was strictly addressed. Lastly, the researcher made note of the fact that the field worker participants could provide inaccurate information or data or change the facts related to their experiences. Furthermore, the researcher's own assumptions could minimally influence the results of the data. The aforementioned items in the study were considered during the data analysis process.

[Note: In-text citations included for illustrative purposes only]

Recommendations for Future Research

In this section, the researcher discusses future recommendations for further research. The researcher also provides recommendations for future practices in the study. Furthermore, the researcher will discuss the significance of the findings and more possible recommendations.

The researcher basically provides the rationale for future research recommendations. The researcher wants to provide a rigorous study in terms of data collection and participant diversity in the research.

Main Points and Directions

These are the main key points that the doctoral researcher should consider when developing the "Recommendations" section of chapter five:

- Develop a list of at least four to six recommendations for practitioners and future research
- Identify and discuss the areas that need further examination or that will address any gaps or needs the study found
- Provide recommendations that relate back to the study significance and knowledge sections in chapter one

- Provide recommendations that relate back to the theoretical foundation section in chapter two
- Writing length: Minimum of one to two pages (Miles, 2022)

By following these key points, the researcher can fully address the required items in the "Recommendations" section of the chapter (see Example 23.6).

Example 23.6 Recommendations for Future Research

The researcher has identified four major recommendations for future research in this subject area. First, as suggested in Chapter 4 of the study, those companies that use leadership programs may be achieving a higher passing percentage of met standard scores on the LIQ. This also suggests that similar findings may be attained with the other assessment systems. The LIQ has been used as a more vigorous assessment tool by companies. Thus, future research could be conducted with a gender study. This could be used to measure differences between males and females in leadership programs. This type of study could determine the impact of gender on leadership education program courses. This would be an interesting line of inquiry.

Second, another future line of inquiry would be to examine ethnicity and its impact on leadership education programs. This line of inquiry would provide another interesting study that focuses on examining ethnicity. Adu (2010) suggested a possible connection between ethnicity and leadership education and possible decreased incidents of negative behaviors in the workplace. Future researchers should consider exploring this line of inquiry and replicate this study to examine the impact of ethnicity on leadership education. This type of research could bear some interesting fruit.

Third, another future line of inquiry would be to examine the impact of age on leadership education. Different age levels could have a significant result on this as a study. With most of the leadership education programs investigated, age has not been taken into consideration for future research. This would provide not only an interesting line of inquiry but also a possible unique focus that has not been captured in the prior research. This would be a fruitful and interesting line of inquiry. Therefore, a study examining the impact of age on leadership program assessment would be relevant for further study as an empirical line of inquiry.

Lastly, another future line of inquiry would be to use a qualitative methodology approach. This type of further research could explore previous limitations of the current research methodology. A qualitative approach to this type of research could get more in-depth information that would not be possible with an empirical type of research. This could definitely add a body of knowledge on leadership programs at private companies. Qualitative research would be a welcome approach that has not been captured in the prior research. Future researchers may consider utilizing publicly accessible quali-tative software to analyze data and bring new findings that could add to the body of knowledge. Using a qualitative approach to analyze leadership educa-tion programs would indeed be very interesting. While prior investigation has determined the impact on employees with preexisting conditions or behavioral concerns, this area of future study should explore the influence of leadership education programs with a focus on current managers at the workplace (Miles et al., 2008). Since this population of employees is in the private sector, this typ-ically would be of interest in measuring current management leadership skills to help researchers understand if they perform better on company-mandated standardized tests. This also could use a combination of qualitative and quan-titative methodologies.

[Note: In-text citations included for illustrative purposes only]

Summary

The development of the results chapter is at the heart of the research endeavor. Understanding and writing up the findings of the study can be a challenging endeavor. The foundation of research is based on providing meaningful and sig-nificant finds, and this is imperative. This chapter discussed writing up the sections in the final chapter for novice and burgeoning researchers. The chapter provided models and tools to help doctoral students and researchers develop the results chapter in their dissertation.

This chapter discussed how to write the following six sections: introduction; sum-mary of the findings; interpretation of the findings; implications and applications of the findings; limitations; and, lastly, recommendations. We hope that our proposed models and frameworks have provided students and researchers with a template for developing a solid chapter five in their dissertation.

References

Bloomberg, L. D., & Volpe, M. (2008). *Completing your qualitative dissertation: A roadmap from beginning to end*. Sage.

Kliewer, M. A. (2007). Writing it up: A step-by-step guide to publication for beginning investigators. *Canadian Journal of Medical Radiation Technology, 38*(3), 27–33. https://doi.org/10.1016/s0820-5930(09)60208-5

Long, T., Convey, J., & Chwalek, A. (1985). *Completing dissertations in the behavioral sciences and education: A systematic guide for graduate students*. Jossey-Bass.

Miles, D. A. & Scott, L. (2017, October 26–29). *Confessions of a dissertation chair, Part 1: The six mistakes doctoral students make with the dissertation* [Workshop]. 5th Annual 2017 Black Doctoral Network Conference, Atlanta, GA.

Miles, D. (2022). 360 review tool for auditing dissertation chapters. From *Confessions of a dissertation chair: Dissertation chapter auditing* [Virtual workshop for doctoral students].

Webster, W. G. (1998a). *Developing and writing your thesis, dissertation or project.* Academic Scholarwrite.

Webster, W. G. (1998b). *21 models for developing and writing theses, dissertations, and projects.* Academic Scholarwrite.

Index

For Product Safety Concerns and Information please contact our EU
representative GPSR@taylorandfrancis.com
Taylor & Francis Verlag GmbH, Kaufingerstraße 24, 80331 München, Germany